The Trickle-Down Delusion

How Republican Upward Redistribution of Economic and Political Power Undermines Our Economy, Democracy, Institutions, and Health —and a Liberal Response

John Seip
Dee Wood Harper

University Press of America,® Inc.
Lanham • Boulder • New York • Toronto • Plymouth, UK

4501 Forbes Boulevard, Suite 200, Lanham, Maryland 20706
UPA Acquisitions Department (301) 459-3366

Unit A, Whitacre Mews, 26-34 Stannary Street,
London SE11 4AB, United Kingdom

Printed in the United States of America
British Library Cataloguing in Publication Information Available

Library of Congress Control Number: 2016931376
ISBN: 978-0-7618-6697-8 (pbk : alk. paper)—ISBN: 978-0-7618-6744-9 (electronic)

∞™ The paper used in this publication meets the minimum requirements of American National Standard for Information Sciences Permanence of Paper for Printed Library Materials, ANSI/NISO Z39.48-1992.

To my conservative Republican parents,
who taught me my liberal values.

—John Seip

Contents

Preface

A Call to Action

Trickle-down economics—or, if one prefers it, "supply-side" economics or "Reaganomics"—is undermining the United States economy, creating a bubble-bust depressionary feedback loop with accompanying slow growth, wage stagnation and impeded social mobility, and is undermining our democracy, institutions and health. However, we, the American people, have the power to begin to rescue our nation if only we vote against the Republicans who promote trickle-down and vote for Democrats in the election of 2016 and thereafter, *including* in midterm elections and elections for state and local office.

Although the Republicans have lost the popular vote in five of the last six presidential elections, the Republican Party nonetheless is "winning" with its trickle-down ideology—holding a majority in the Senate, a majority in the House, a majority of governorships, and a majority of seats in a majority of houses in a majority of state legislatures. An aspect of this trickle-down conservative Republican ideology critical to its tremendous electoral success is excessive partisanship, especially as promoted by the "Tea Party" therein.[1] For but one illustration of this excessive partisanship, in late 2015, after Speaker of the House John Boehner (R-OH) announced his resignation, a race was on among House Republicans to be his successor, with candidates touting *not* their ability to run the House of Representatives and ensure its operation in accordance with the Constitution but, rather, their ability to promote the agenda of the Republican Party and especially its Tea Party faction at the expense of the Democrats in the 2016 election.[2]

As will be shown, those who succumb to the ideology of trickle-down conservative Republican theory must, for the good of America and the world, be confronted, and their philosophy must be defeated with the truths that support liberalism, in an ideological battle waged on a national basis,[3] for trickle-down theory is contradicted by the facts, by the theory that its adherents claim for inspiration, and by public opinion regarding the extreme policies it promotes.

The good news is that despite liberal reluctance over much of the past three and a half decades of trickle-down's existence to wage such an ideological confrontation with trickle-down conservatism, that battle has begun. Winners of the Nobel Prize in economics Paul Krugman and Joseph Stiglitz, and politicians including President Barack Obama, former President Bill Clinton, former Secretary of Labor Robert Reich, Senator Elizabeth Warren (D-MA), and all the candidates for the 2016 Democratic nomination for the presidency remaining in the race one year from the election—former Secretary of State and New York Senator Hillary Rodham Clinton, Senator Bernie Sanders (I-VT) and former Governor Martin O'Malley (D-MD)—have criticized trickle-down economics, and the intensity of that criticism will increase dramatically with the approach of the 2016 presidential election and thereafter.[4]

In the final months of 2015, two films were released, each dealing with fraud at the highest levels. The first, *Spotlight*, addressed the courageous efforts of reporters at *The Boston Globe* in exposing fraud at the highest levels of the Roman Catholic Church, which had hid for years numerous cases of sexual abuse conducted by priests and seminarians. The second, *The Big Short*, exposed fraud at the highest levels of the financial markets, as bankers for years profited fabulously off of a rigged, fraudulent system that financed the nation's real estate industry. *The Trickle-Down Delusion* is about the fraudulent ideas of the Republican Party that united fundamentalist Christianity with a fundamentalist free market philosophy, and wrapped it all up in star-spangled patriotism, securing electoral successes that led to implementation of policies detrimental to the nation and the world. In opposition, it presents a liberal response to stop and reverse the damage this fraudulent philosophy has wrought.

We must act now not only because of the immediacy of the 2016 election but also because, as slow as the recovery from the Great Recession has been, it was helped by the growth of the "BRICS"—Brazil, Russia, India, China and South Africa—but with their economic slowdown—especially the slowdown in China—and the slowdown in the rest of the world economy, we must now rely more upon ourselves.[5] And, to complicate our situation, to paraphrase W. B. Yeats, the informed lack all conviction, while those devoted to the delusion of trickle-down economics, austerity and the Republican Party are full of passionate intensity.

This bubble-bust depressionary feedback loop in which we find ourselves, marked by oversupply and aggregate demand suppressed by upward redistribution of income and wealth,[6] has been created by trickle-down ideology, and has been perpetuated by that ideology's rejection of fiscal policy, while being exacerbated by the loose monetary policy trickle-down's proponents have allowed to fight the resultant economic stagnation. It explains the deep recessions experienced in the past 15 years[7] and explains the current bubble we are in[8] —one perhaps beginning to burst—as the stock market ended 2015 with the S&P 500 Index having lost 0.7 percent for the year[9] and began 2016 with the worst start in the history of the index, which was started in 1928.[10]

Because these conditions of chronic oversupply and starvation of demand are caused *not* by economics but, rather, by government policies implemented pursuant to misguided trickle-down ideology,[11] the election of a Republican president in 2016 would be a tragic disaster for economies of the US and the world, practically ensuring the continuing of the very same policies that created and maintain these conditions.

When Americans do reject trickle-down economics and return to the center-left of the ideological spectrum, where the United States was immediately after World War II and through the 1970s, they will force Republicans to rejoin reality, and the Republican Party, the nation and the world will be better for it. The ideas that will shape that ideological battle follow.

COVER: Depicted is a "star spangled dollar cross" representing trickle-down, a political philosophy masquerading as an economic theory, synonymous with supply-side economics and Reaganomics. It represents the three constituencies described herein as composing the "trickle-down conservatism" of the Republican Party: the Religious Right, the plutocracy and neoconservatism, which match up with three powerful faiths: faith in God, faith in the free market, and faith in country. Artwork by Ana E. Seip and Amanda Koffskey.

NOTES

1. The importance of the ideology behind the Democratic and Republican parties—regardless of candidate chosen for the 2016 election—was addressed by Paul Krugman in his columns titled "It Takes a Party," *The New York Times*, April 13, 2015, and "Ideology and Integrity," *The New York Times*, May 1, 2015. Krugman won the Nobel Prize in economics in 2008, is a distinguished professor of economics at the Graduate Center of the City University of New York, and writes an op-ed column for *The New York Times*.

2. See Steven Dennis, "Kevin McCarthy Gives Boehner B-, Credits Benghazi Committee for Hurting Hillary Clinton's Poll Numbers," *Roll Call*, September 30, 2015. See also E.J. Dionne Jr., "Kevin McCarthy's Truthful Gaffe on Benghazi," *The Washington Post*, September 30, 2015 and Kathleen Parker, "It's Up to Voters to Break Up the GOP Brat Pack," *The Washington Post*, September 30, 2015.

3. See Thomas Frank, "We Are Such Losers," *Salon.com*, October 26, 2014.

4. A good overall critique of trickle-down, addressing many ideas appearing herein, is *23 Things They Don't Tell You About Capitalism* (2010) by Cambridge University economist Ha-

Joon Chang. Similarly, see Paul Krugman, "Republican Elite's Reign of Disdain," *The New York Times*, March 18, 2016, and see David Brooks, "The Post-Trump Era," *The New York Times*, March 25, 2016.

5. The term was originally "BRICs"—including Brazil, Russia, India and China—coined in 2001 by then-chairman of Goldman Sachs Asset Management, Jim O'Neill. South Africa was added in 2010, and the term changed to "BRICS."

6. The term "aggregate demand" means the total demand in the economy (because there is no discussion herein of demand other than aggregate demand, for shorthand, the term "demand" is used). As will be explained herein, while productivity has been growing, the revenues attributable to increased productivity have been upwardly redistributed, resulting in a productivity/wage disconnect and in upward redistribution of income and wealth. Fiscal policies could have been used to reconnect productivity and wages, but they have been rejected due to trickle-down ideology. The stagnation in wages was attempted to be compensated for with debt, encouraged by low interest rates and loose monetary policy, but starvation of demand has nonetheless resulted, resulting in oversupply. See David Stockman, "The End of the Bubble Finance Era," The Daily Reckoning blog, December 13, 2016. See also Raúl Ilargi Meijer, "2016 Is an Easy Year to Predict," The Automatic Earth blog, December 28, 2015. This essay is repeated in printer-friendly form at the Naked Capitalism website, December 29, 2015. Meijer and his colleague Nicole Foss formerly worked at the website The Oil Drum, where they were quite familiar with the phenomenon of oversupply.

7. The National Bureau of Economic Research (NBER) defines recessions starting at the peak of a business cycle and ending at the trough. It defined the first recession of the twenty-first century as beginning in March 2001 and ending in November 2001 and the second, popularly called the "Great Recession," as beginning in December 2007 and ending in June 2009 (per the NBER website, "US Business Cycle Expansions and Contractions," Monday, April 23, 2012).

8. Henry Blodget, "A Stock-Market Crash of 50%+ Would Not Be a Surprise—or a Worst-Case Scenario," Business Insider UK, January 4, 2016.

9. Anna-Louise Jackson, "Final-Day Selloff Sends S&P 500 to First Yearly Drop Since 2011," *Bloomberg*, December 31, 2015.

10. The S&P 500 Index began 2016 with the worst first five days in its history. Rodrigo Campos, "Global Stocks Crater in Worst Week in Four Years; Oil Crumbles," *Reuters*, January 8, 2016. The Standard & Poor's 500, typically abbreviated as the S&P 500, is an American stock market index based on the market capitalizations of 500 large companies listed on the New York Stock Exchange and the NASDAQ (National Association of Securities Dealers Automated Quotations) Exchange.

11. Joseph E. Stiglitz, "The Great Malaise Continues," Project Syndicate, January 3, 2016.

Acknowledgments

The authors would like to thank the owners of the copyrights to numerous quotes that appear herein for their permission to use them herein, beginning with Kalle Lasn, editor of *Adbusters* magazine, for his promptly granted permission to use the quotes that appeared July 13, 2011 on the blog that appears at its website and that launched the Occupy Wall Street movement. Thanks also to the editors of *Mother Jones* for their promptly granted permission to reprint several quotes that appear therein.

Thanks also to Beacon Press, for permission to use the quote from Barrington Moore's *The Social Origins of Dictatorship and Democracy: Lord and Peasant in the Making of the Modern World* (Boston: Beacon Press, 1966). And, thanks to Democracy Corps for permission to use an informative quote from a conservative focus group responder that appeared in Stan Greenberg, James Carville, and Erica Seifert, "Inside the GOP: Report on Focus Groups with Evangelical, Tea Party, and Moderate Republicans," Democracy Corps, October 3, 2013. A special thanks goes to *Dissent* magazine, for permission to quote from Tom Kahn's important article "Problems of the Negro Movement," *Dissent*, Vol. 11, January 1964, No. 1, pp. 108–138.

Thanks also to the editors of *Fordham International Law Review* and *Fordham Law Review* for permission to use quotes from articles that appeared in their publications.

Thanks to Harper Collins, University of Chicago Press and MIT Press for providing broad fair use guidelines at their respective websites, of which the authors availed themselves herein for numerous quotes from their publications.

Thanks also to Harvest/Harcourt Brace for permission to use a quote from Daniel Patrick Moynihan in *Family and Nation* (Orlando, FL: Harvest/Harcourt Brace Jovanovich, 1986, 1987).

Thanks to several publishers of works in the public domain due to their age, but which were made by them user-friendly in book form: Liberty Fund press of Indianapolis, IN, for Alexis de Tocqueville's *Democracy in America* and translation; to Prometheus Books, for Adam Smith's *The Theory of Moral Sentiments*, Random House, publisher of Adam Smith's *An Inquiry into the Nature and Causes of the Wealth of Nations*, Simon & Schuster, publisher of *The Communist Manifesto* by Karl Marx and Friedrich Engels and Rutgers University Press for Friedrich Ratzel, *Sketches of Urban and Cultural Life in North America* [1876], trans. and ed. Stewart A Sehlin (New Brunswick, NJ: Rutgers University Press, 1988).

Much appreciation to Random House for permission to use quotes from James Carville's *We're Right, They're Wrong*, Daron Acemoglu and James Robinson's *Why Nations Fail*, Charles Murray's *Coming Apart* and Kevin Phillips' *Post-Conservative America.*

And, thanks to the editors of the New Press for permission to reprint a quote from Peter B. Edelman, *So Rich, So Poor: Why It's So Hard to End Poverty in America* (New York: The New Press; 2012).

Thanks to the editors of *National Review* for their permission to reprint quotes from the November 1955 Publisher's Statement by William F. Buckley, Jr. and several quotes from more recent editions of the magazine. And thanks to Oxford University Press, for permission to quote from an interview conducted with Senator John Breaux (D-LA), July 25, 1990, quoted in Nicol C. Rae's *Southern Democrats* (Oxford, New York: Oxford University Press, 1994).

And thanks especially to those publishers whose works are either in the public domain or readily approved for quoting subject to attribution, including especially the federal government, National Bureau of Economic Research and the Organization for Economic Cooperation and Development.

Among publishers for whom we are grateful for permission to reprint quotes from their works, thanks to our publishers, Rowman and Littlefield, for permission to quote from Lawrence E. Harrison's *Underdevelopment Is a State of Mind: The Latin American Case.*

On behalf of John Seip, special thanks to William W. Falk, Professor Emeritus of Sociology at the University of Maryland; F. Andrew Deseran, Professor Emeritus, Departments of Sociology and Criminology & Criminal Justice Studies at Sonoma State University; and Paul R. Baier, Professor of Law at the Paul M. Hebert Law Center at Louisiana State University; all of whom provided the instruction and encouragement to the author that made this work possible.

Finally, a debt of gratitude is owed to the amazing Internet, and the wonderful leap forward in sharing of knowledge it has created, especially due to the emergence of web logs such as Business Insider, edited by Henry Blodget; Huffington Post, edited by Arianna Huffington, Jesse's Café Américain; Zero Hedge, edited by "Tyler Durden," and Naked Capitalism, edited by Yves Smith. And, thanks to all the participants in the email group LA-WATT, for their invaluable insights, as well as to Susan, Adam, Elly and Daniele for your wisdom and patience.

Introduction

Triumph of the Delusion That to Help the Middle Class and Poor Policies Must Help the Rich

Government is not the solution to the problem; government *is* the problem.
—President Ronald Reagan, First Inaugural Address, January 20, 1981

Since 1980, the economy has been growing, and productivity has been growing, but trickle-down values—*that we, the American people promote pursuant to the Republican Party's conservative ideology*—have rigged the economy to continuously upwardly redistribute those revenues attributable to our increased productivity, yielding a productivity/wage[1] disconnect, resulting in increased concentration of income and wealth at the top, in corporations and among older Americans (beneficiaries of income from Social Security, pensions and investments and continuing income due to delaying retirement),[2] and the lowest percentage of GDP attributable to wages and highest attributable to profits since World War II.[3] But trickle-down has not only distorted our economic thought; it has also distorted our political thought, our sociology and our concept of the rule of law. The result has been that the trickle-down policies promoted by the Republican Party are undermining our economy, democracy, institutions and health.

A seriously bad idea that rules a society truly triumphs only when most of that society's members, including those suffering most because of it, take it as fact, not even realizing it is only a seriously bad idea, perhaps even tried before and discarded when it failed a previous generation. Trickle-down is such a seriously bad idea.[4]

Trickle-down economics, also called "supply-side economics"[5] and "Reaganomics"—appropriately derided as "voodoo economics"[6] —has guided government economic policy off and on for the past three and a half decades in this country and much of the world, resulting in implementation of government policies that—figuratively and literally—kill. The evidence shows that under trickle-down policies the economy grows more slowly and creates fewer jobs, our democracy is open to fewer people, and more Americans will suffer needlessly and die earlier. The theory, when we elected Ronald Reagan president in 1980 and accepted trickle-down economics as our economic program, was that we had developed an unhealthy dependency on government. Now, instead, we have developed an unhealthy dependency on the richest 1%, with the result that inequality is back up to the level just before the Great Depression, real middle class incomes are falling, poverty is rising, minorities' right to vote is being denied, our institutions are being undermined, we are being fooled into wars on false pretenses and life spans are shorter. And, due to trickle-down's rapid spread abroad, trickle-down undermines the economies, democracies and health of the people of the UK,[7] Europe, Japan and elsewhere.[8] Due to Republican Party discipline, a vote for a Republican today is, as it has been for the past three and a half decades, a vote in favor of trickle-down and a vote against wage increases, job growth, unions, the middle class and the poor.

The arc of trickle-down's initial triumph at the ballot box and failure in practice was launched by the quote above, starting in 1981, the first year of trickle-down's implementation as policy (although an early version of trickle-down economics was practiced during the Gilded Age and the Roaring Twenties). President Ronald Reagan, in his first Inaugural Address stated the simple idea that became a mantra for conservatives: Government (except for the military) is the enemy and can't do anything right.[9] David Stockman, President Reagan's Director of the Office of Management and Budget, in his famous interview with the journalist William Greider, confessed that his boss's "supply-side" economics theory was really trickle-down economics, and that the tax cuts for all Americans provided in the comprehensive Kemp-Roth tax cut bill were but a Trojan Horse to bring down the top tax rate.[10] In other words, supply-side economic theory was not economic theory at all but, rather, political theory, the end of which was never to grow the economy faster but, rather, to simply upwardly redistribute income and wealth. Thus, not only was it political theory rather than economic theory—it was also a fraud.

And, George Gilder, in "the Bible of the Reagan Revolution," *Wealth and Poverty*, along with others helped establish the wrongheaded idea that direct governmental benefits to the middle class and poor are a waste because all they do is impede the productivity of the rich.[11] (The term "rich" throughout here has the same imprecise and elastic meaning as when used by conservatives, interchangeable with "job creators.")

In contrast, the *zeitgeist*—the "spirit of the age"—of the period commencing with the end of World War II and running through the 1970s was the middle class as hero. Commencing in 1980, and running through the present, the *zeitgeist* became the rich, the capitalists, the investors and the businessmen as heroes. Even the day traditionally set aside to honor the ordinary Americans who labor—Labor Day—was misconstrued by the formerly second most powerful Republican in the House of Representatives, House Majority Leader Eric Cantor (R-VA)—who would lose his seat in a primary election two years later because he was not conservative *enough* (despite a lifetime rating of *95 percent* from the American Conservative Union!). On Labor Day 2012, Cantor sent out a Twitter post glorifying trickle-down values and misconstruing Labor Day itself as a celebration of the business owner[12] —in trickle-down Republican world, Labor Day is for celebrating American entrepreneurs, *not* for celebrating American workers.

Not surprisingly, trickle-down does not work and has never worked. It *is* voodoo economics. As Nobel Prize winning economist Joseph Stiglitz observed,[13] and he is joined in his opinion by fellow Nobel Prize winning economist Paul Krugman,[14] the economic policies that we have chosen—driven as they have been off and on for more than three decades by a misguided trickle-down vision—have delivered colossal failure. As Stiglitz observes, *we created the inequality we are suffering from; we chose failure*. Job growth is anemic, real wages are falling, and the economy is starving for demand. When the policy recommendations of trickle-down are tested against the facts of their performance in practice over the past three decades, their support in the classical liberal theory they claim for inspiration,[15] and their support in public opinion, trickle-down is revealed as a delusion. We are living in an unnecessary mass human tragedy of our own making—a crisis unnecessary because it is brought on by a delusional trickle-down worldview supported by Republicans and not confronted and defeated by Democrats.

All that will be asked herein is to make the United States, and the world, better by abandoning the failed, radical delusion of trickle-down and returning to the use of the liberal policies that were in place for most of the post-World War II period that preceded the past three and a half decades of trickle-down. Of course, to get Americans to abandon the trickle-down delusion, it is important to get them to understand that it, in fact, demands policies favoring the wealthy—and, fortunately, a poll taken on the eve of the 2014 midterm elections indicates most Americans understand that already, finding that a majority of adult Americans (71 percent) agree that the US economic system generally favors the wealthy (this includes liberals, 84 percent; moderates, 74 percent; and even conservatives, 59 percent[16]).

REBIRTH OF THE DELUSION THAT TO HELP THE MIDDLE CLASS AND POOR POLICIES MUST HELP THE RICH

Buckley, Goldwater, Reagan, Thatcher, George W. Bush, the Tea Party's War on "Losers," Romney-Ryan, the International Monetary Fund and the World Bank

As will be seen, the Great Depression resulted from an early version of trickle-down economics practiced during the Gilded Age and the Roaring Twenties that upwardly redistributed revenues attributable to increased productivity. The New Deal reforms in response to the Great Depression confronted and reversed this upward redistribution of income and wealth and thereby helped create the great American middle class. "Modern Republicanism" of Republican President Dwight Eisenhower made peace with the New Deal in the 1950s. In response, in staunch opposition to the New Deal and modern Republicanism, William F. Buckley, Jr. and his fellow editors and staff founded *National Review* magazine in 1955 to promote a "New Right."

As is recounted by George H. Nash in *The Conservative Intellectual Movement in America Since 1945* (1976), Frank S. Meyer, an editor at *National Review*, conceived of the New Right as a combination of traditionalism[17] and libertarianism (addressed below), combining the traditionalists' struggle for virtue with the libertarians' struggle for freedom. Traditionalist conservative L. Brent Bozell, Jr. (Buckley's brother-in-law) dubbed the concept "fusionism." As Nash observed, these two elements were often at odds with each other, creating a constant friction, however, the two philosophies would later combine with anti-communism, which served to hold the two fractious elements together because communism was the hated opponent of each. Fusionism was exemplified in Buckley's own libertarian philosophy tempered by his Roman Catholic faith and staunch opposition to communism, which he combined with a charismatic and erudite plutocratic personal style.[18]

Buckley's "Publisher's Statement" that accompanied the first issue of *National Review*, November 19, 1955, established the mission of the new magazine as to confront the liberal direction of the nation since the beginning of the New Deal: "It stands athwart history, yelling Stop, at a time when no one is inclined to do so, or to have much patience with those who so urge it."[19]

The New Right itself (also sometimes referred to as the "new conservatism") later came to be called "movement conservatism."[20] The three ideologies that composed movement conservatism in its infancy—traditionalism, libertarianism and anti-communism—continue today to match up with the key Republican issues of culture, the economy and national defense.[21]

The first movement conservative presidential candidate was Senator Barry Goldwater of Arizona, who lost in a landslide in 1964 to Democrat incumbent Lyndon Johnson. However, his philosophy, captured in the book *The Conscience of a Conservative* (1960) published under his name (and ghost-written by Bozell) provided a popular introduction to this new version of conservatism. The first successful movement conservative presidential candidate was former California Governor Ronald Reagan who, in 1980, benefitted greatly from conservative support of trickle-down economics as the antidote to severe back-to-back recessions, the latter of which was still raging at the time of the election. On a parallel track the UK came under the influence of trickle-down due to Prime Minister Margaret Thatcher's embrace of it starting in 1979 (also in response to a prolonged and deep recession).

Two important leaders of the supply-side or trickle-down economics movement were Jude Wanniski, a former associate editor of *The Wall Street Journal*, in his book *The Way the World Works* (1978) and George Gilder in his book *Wealth and Poverty* (1981), which in its time peaked at number four on *The New York Times* bestseller list. Gilder argued that it was government waste to attempt to directly help the middle class and poor—that the only efficient way to help them was to help the rich. He also linked capitalist success with God's will. Thus, Gilder's work (as well as that of other conservatives) hints at the dream of Buckley and his colleagues to make "the Holy Rollers lie down with the high rollers"[22] —to unite the Religious Right[23] and the plutocrats. (This project will be addressed in detail in Chapter 3, while Chapter 2 and elsewhere will address the result of realization of this dream: The Republican base, composed of dedicated voters who imagine they are getting the truth by watching Fox News, listening to Rush Limbaugh and reading Drudge Report—embodied in the Tea Party and the House Freedom Caucus—have taken over the direction of the Republican Party, leaving a party that governs only for Christian fundamentalists broadly [conservative Roman Catholics and conservative evangelical Protestants], multimillionaires and billionaires.)

The next movement conservative presidential candidate after Reagan was former Texas Governor George W. Bush, who promoted trickle-down with, among other measures, two tax cuts tilted toward upper incomes and an attempt to privatize Social Security. His two tax cuts failed to prevent economic suffering from two recessions during his tenure, and, combined with slow economic growth, they converted federal budget surpluses into budget deficits. And, guided by his blustery trickle-down-inspired advisors and their neoconservative allies, he led the nation into a costly and unnecessary war in Iraq.

Movement conservatism came to be dominated by trickle-down economics to such a degree that it essentially evolved into what is called here "trickle-down conservatism" as trickle-down's philosophy overtook conservatism and the Republican Party. And, less than a month after the first inauguration of President Barack Obama, a Democrat who had campaigned in opposition to the trickle-down vision, trickle-down economics was re-invigorated by the emergence of the Tea Party.

The Tea Party arose on February 19, 2009, when CNBC financial reporter Rick Santelli called from the floor of the Chicago Mercantile Exchange for a "Chicago Tea Party in July" to protest the federal government's taxpayer-funded bailout of homeowners who were in danger of defaulting on their mortgages (the Homeowners Affordability and Stability Plan, announced the day earlier by the new administration). Santelli was not incensed that money was being forced by the federal government onto banks that *caused* the financial crisis, thereby ensuring that multimillionaire investment bankers would continue to reap their lavish bonuses—he was upset that his *neighbors* who might have been wiped out in the housing crash might get their loans modified.[24] Santelli's rant succinctly summarized the trickle-down philosophy of the Tea Party he inspired: Government attempts to directly aid "losers"—those of the middle class and poor who have fallen on hard times and need help—are government waste; the appropriate way for government to aid the middle class and poor is to ensure the comfort of the rich.[25]

The Tea Party provided the popular support to energize trickle-down conservatism and keep it going as a popular movement even in the face of nonexistent factual and weak public support for its proposals—including weak public support even among Tea Partiers *themselves*, who supported the "repeal the New Deal" dream *rhetorically*, but who, when individually polled, expressed an incoherent philosophy supporting maintenance of Social Security, Medicare and Medicaid—combined with cutting of taxes (especially on the rich), cutting of regulations, and cutting of spending on programs upon which the middle class and poor rely, spending more on defense, and promotion of more expensive and intrusive social regulation.

The trickle-down view that what is good for wealthy investors is good for all spread globally with the support of the International Monetary Fund (IMF) and World Bank via what has been alternatively termed "globalization,"[26] the "Washington Consensus"[27] and "neoliberalism,"[28] all based on "neoclassical" economics,[29] resulting in a race-to-the-bottom in which all the countries of the world work to suppress labor costs—perhaps none more successfully than China.[30] And, as observed by Joseph Stiglitz, Columbia University professor who won the Nobel Prize in economics in 2001, the IMF seems to extend the trickle-down view globally: that what is good for the financial community is good for the global economy.[31]

Until President Obama confronted it, the trickle-down delusion had survived largely unchallenged for most of the past three decades. This work will pick up that challenge and confront trickle-down, and propose a liberal alternative in its place.

It's Even Worse Than It Looks . . .

The enormity of the challenge facing liberals was addressed by Thomas E. Mann of the centrist Brookings Institution and Norman J. Ornstein of the conservative American Enterprise Institute in their book published in the months leading up to the fall 2012 election: *It's Even Worse Than It Looks: How The American Constitutional System Collided with the New Politics of Extremism.*[32] The authors observed that there are two aspects to this challenge: (1) The ideological extremism divorced from facts exhibited by the Republican Party and (2) The abandonment by the media of its historical role to challenge based on facts.

Angie Drobnic Holan, editor of *PolitiFact,* a political fact-checking website, put numbers to the observations of Mann and Ornstein in an op-ed in which she published rankings made by *PolitiFact* of statements since 2007 by presidential candidates (and some current and former candidates and presidents) from most dishonest to least dishonest. Ben Carson was most dishonest at 84 percent false, followed by Donald Trump at 76 percent and Ted Cruz at 66 percent; further down the rankings was Marco Rubio at 40 percent. The most honest was Bill Clinton at 24 percent false, followed by Martin O'Malley at 25 percent, Barack Obama at 26 percent, and Hillary Clinton and Bernie Sanders at 28 percent.[33]

Mann and Ornstein are rightly concerned about the future of American democracy, as Krugman and Stiglitz are rightly concerned about the future of the American and world economies. The potential for politics to work for good was observed by the great liberal[34] Daniel Patrick Moynihan, who observed that conservatives have it right when they observe that culture determines economic success, but liberals have it right when they observe that politics can change culture and thereby deliver economic success: "The central conservative truth is that it is culture, not politics, that determines the success of a society. The central liberal truth is that politics can change a culture and save it from itself."[35] However, as observed by Barack Obama, when he paraphrased Moynihan's lesson in *The Audacity of Hope* (2006), politics also holds the potential to result in government policies that shape culture in ways that harm society.[36] To the observations of Moynihan and Obama it can be added that economic circumstances themselves can change culture and, even if they do not change culture, change behavior, for better or worse. Thus, economics cannot be studied in a vacuum but, rather, must be studied along with sociology and political science, and economic success or failure is determined via the interaction of government, the market and civil society. In the case of trickle-down, government has played a dominant role, through the promotion of bad ideas in a setting of deteriorating economic circumstances for the poor and middle class, in directly undermining, and shaping culture in ways that are undermining, our economy, democracy, institutions and health.

IDEOLOGY AND TERMINOLOGY

The Importance of a Vision: Define Your Values, or Your Opponents Will Do It for You—and You Won't Like It!

A "vision" is a way of describing the world and how it works, and the government policies that are appropriate pursuant to that vision. Other names for this are "worldview" and, in German, *Weltanschauung*. A vision is essentially an operating system for a society, and visions, thus, guide policy. A vision, in turn, is shaped by ideology and ideas.

Theorists as disparate as the traditionalist conservative Richard Weaver, the liberal economist John Maynard Keynes and the "godfather of neoconservatism" Irving Kristol all have addressed the importance of ideology. In the late 1940s Weaver wrote a book on the subject, titled *Ideas Have Consequences*. Keynes weighed the importance of ideas versus that of vested interests in a famous passage at the end of *The General Theory of Employment, Interest and Money*, and concluded that ideas are more important.[37] Irving Kristol's observation regarding ideas is extremely important for the purposes of this work—he observed of ideas that they rule the world because they shape the way we perceive reality.[38]

Conservatism, from its beginning, has harbored a fatal flaw in its vision. That flaw, which will be elaborated on in detail, is the inability to see that, even in a society that practices democracy, capitalism and governmental fiscal responsibility, liberal values are necessary to ameliorate the potentially negative effects of capitalism and democracy because what is good for the rich and powerful is *not* necessarily good for the middle class and poor.[39] This oversight—combined with the inability to see the importance of *institutions* to support these liberal values and protect the weak from the powerful—renders conservatism incapable of providing the best society achievable. And these institutions cannot evolve absent the values that demand their creation.[40]

Liberalism, Conservatism, Neoconservatism, Libertarianism and Trickle-Down—and the Plutocracy's Purchase of Libertarianism and Conservatism

The greatest conflict in social, political and economic thought now is not between capitalism and socialism, nor is it between capitalism and the now thoroughly discredited cradle-to-grave welfare state; capitalism has won those battles. The greatest battle now is that between the trickle-down vision of conservatism versus the vision of liberalism.

Conservatism, liberalism, libertarianism and neoconservatism all spring from classical liberalism, and continue to hold to classical liberal values in varying degrees. The point of departure for this work from what has preceded it is that it takes at their word the classical liberal philosophers when they argued in favor of their liberal vision of *sharing* economic profits and *dispersing* political power—*the exact opposite* of the conservative trickle-down economics vision of "winner-take-all"[41] and upwardly redistributing economic and political power in the vain hopes that benefits will trickle-down upon the middle class and poor. While the classical liberal Adam Smith urged that as a matter of "equity" "they who feed, cloath and lodge the whole body of the people, should have such a share of their own labour as to be themselves tolerably well fed, cloathed and lodged,"[42] modern liberal John Maynard Keynes later complemented Smith and carried forward his idea of sharing the revenues attributable to increased productivity through high wages but provided the rationale for them in terms liberal economists stress today: as necessary for the preservation and growth of *demand*, which, in turn, is necessary for economic growth.

As will be seen, a large role for government is found even in *The Road to Serfdom* (1944) by Friedrich Hayek, winner of the 1974 Nobel Prize in economics, champion of classical liberalism (at least in his early writings), hero to conservatives and Keynes's chief protagonist. And, it is no surprise that Keynes wrote a note to Hayek saying, in what appears as a jacket endorsement of paperback versions of that book: "Morally and philosophically I find myself in agreement with virtually the whole of it." (Keynes, presumably, read the book as a *warning—not* a prediction—that Western democracies, by increasing government intervention in the market and thereby eroding economic freedom, risk going down a road to a serfdom in which citizens sacrifice economic *and* social freedom.) And, upon Keynes's death, Hayek wrote admiringly of him.[43]

The conservatism of Presidents Dwight Eisenhower, Richard Nixon and George H. W. Bush contains within it a substantial measure of the same modern liberal values championed herein, which came from classical liberalism. As will be seen, however, with the rise of movement conservatism, these values have been replaced by the values of the Religious Right—replacing liberal, tolerant Protestant values[44] with the values of fundamentalist Catholicism and evangelical Protestantism imposed with intolerance—in combination with libertarian economic policy and neoconservative foreign policy.

Under movement conservatism, the right[45] has taken classical liberalism and distorted its messages and the left has quietly acquiesced, leaving a nation intellectually incapable of defending itself in the face of twin economic and political crises—an economic depression[46] and political gridlock—both of which we, the American voters, created pursuant to our delusional trickle-down vision.

Liberalism

The term "liberalism" is used herein to refer to the political philosophy that defends liberal democracy which, as used here, means a capitalist economy and democracy of one-person-one-vote elections, along with such freedoms as freedom of speech, press, religion, assembly and petition, accompanied by classical liberal values—here these are presented as checks and balances, respect for knowledge, tolerance, equality, peace and the rule of law. In accordance with classical liberal theory, the institutions of liberal democratic *government* are envisioned as combining with capitalism (the institutions of the *market*) and the institutions of *civil society* (the family and voluntary associations) to create the institutional framework for our actions (termed herein a system of "societal checks and balances" to distinguish the concept from governmental checks and balances). Thus, "liberalism" as used herein is intended to mean modern American liberalism, although modern liberalism that traces its roots to classical liberalism.

"Liberalism," so defined, is distinguished from "liberalism" and "market liberalism," as used outside of the US and from "libertarianism," as addressed in detail below. "Liberalism" as used herein is also distinguished from "neoliberalism." In this sense, then, the "liberalism" here is "old liberalism"—perhaps it can be called "paleoliberalism," describing a modern liberalism that draws inspiration from the liberalism that was popular in the US from the end of World War II through the mid-1960s (failing when the New Left arose in the early 1960s and, in 1968, the liberal government of President Lyndon Johnson overreached, waging a War on Poverty simultaneously with the unwise and arguably unconstitutional Vietnam War) and again, later, in the 1970s, when liberal economists failed to promote the raising of interest rates to combat rising inflation.[47]

Liberalism believes in the existence of "society" and the "social contract." That social contract elsewhere has been defended out of *fear* (the Hobbesian bargain) and *social justice* (for example, by John Rawls in *A Theory of Justice*). Here, however, its defense is motivated by classical liberalism's *enlightened self-interest*[48] and the facts—the defense of liberalism here is a utilitarian defense based on economic data more overwhelmingly supportive than ever before in history. Politically, liberalism is associated herein with the Democratic Party, and conservatism is associated with the Republican Party.

Conservatism

"Conservatism" is defined herein as the modern successor to the New Right or movement conservatism that arose in 1955 with the founding of *National Review* and evolved after 1980, with the advent of "supply-side" economics, "trickle-down" economics or "Reaganomics" (all synonymous) into "trickle-down conservatism." Although not every conservative today is a movement conservative, nearly all conservatives embrace the trickle-down philosophy promoted by their hero, Ronald Reagan. Regardless of this consensus, conservatives are divided among the "establishment"[49] conservatives who supported the bailouts of Wall Street and General Motors versus the right wing populists[50] represented by the illiberal Tea Party conservatives who embrace a populist version of trickle-down, and who generally opposed the bailouts and generally support breakup of big banks. Establishment conservatives supported most strongly former Florida Governor Jeb Bush in the race to determine the 2016 Republican presidential candidate, and to a somewhat lesser degree Senator Marco Rubio (also of Florida), and Governor John Kasich of Ohio. The Tea Partiers most strongly supported multibillionaire Donald Trump, former neurosurgeon Dr. Ben Carson and former Hewlett-Packard CEO Carly Fiorina—none of whom had any previous governmental experience. They also supported maverick Senator Ted Cruz (R-TX).

Neoconservatism

"Neoconservatism" is a term used to describe a movement of former liberals who in the 1950s and 1960s were alienated by the rise of the New Left and became concerned about the failure of the welfare state, however, rather than end it they wanted to mend it, using social science statistical analysis as a guide (many of these early neoconservatives were distinguished social scientists themselves, among them Daniel Patrick Moynihan, Daniel Bell, Nathan Glazer, Seymour Martin Lipset and others). Later, in the 1970s, they became concerned about the decline of American military authority. These concerns led them to join with conservatives. Prominent neoconservative Irving Kristol famously defined a neoconservative as a "liberal mugged by reality."[51] Later neoconservatives, influenced by their hero Leo Strauss, believe that too much liberalism leads to nihilism and totalitarianism, thus, to save liberalism, they argue in favor of applying illiberal policies. With the decline of communism, they replaced the anticommunists in the conservative fusionism trinity. They wrote profusely in the 1990s promoting, especially, their foreign policy views, and they played a prominent role in the administration of President George W. Bush.

Libertarianism

It should be observed that there is no consensus regarding whether libertarianism is: (1) The modern term for classical liberalism; (2) The governing philosophy that the state's sole functions are to "protect our freedom both from enemies outside our gates and from our fellow-citizens: to preserve law and order, enforce private contracts, to foster competitive markets"[52] (the definition of one of libertarianism's and conservatism's heroes, Milton Friedman); or (3) A philosophy that only endorses a free market and its only value is that violence may not be used to achieve ends.

There is, thus, a debate among libertarians who favor abolition of the state ("radical libertarians;" "anarcho-capitalists" or "anarchists") versus those who favor a minimal state ("minarchists")—but even the libertarian minimal state accords far too much authority to the market for libertarianism to be confused with classical liberalism for, as will be seen herein, many of the heroes of the libertarians—including the classical liberals Adam Smith and Alexis de Tocqueville, and modern interpreters of classical liberalism (both of whom called themselves classical liberals) Friedrich Hayek and Milton Friedman—all favored greater government intervention in the economy than do libertarians (even the "minarchists").

Although many conservatives continue to view libertarianism as essentially the modern version of classical liberalism, that view is rejected here. As will be elaborated on below, libertarianism, in its rejection of a role for the state in promotion of liberal values (more on those below), is not a classical liberal philosophy at all but is in fact illiberal.[53]

The libertarian philosophy is promoted by the Reason Foundation and *Reason* magazine, however, by far the greater influence on libertarianism is provided by the Cato Institute, the leading libertarian think tank. The Cato Institute was founded originally as the Charles Koch Foundation in 1974 by Charles Koch, multibillionaire Chairman and Chief Executive Officer of Koch Industries, the second-largest privately-owned corporation in the US. Charles Koch's brother David was the Libertarian Party vice presidential candidate in the 1980 election, and their father, Fred Koch, was a co-founder of the far right John Birch Society.[54] Charles Koch provided the funding for the Cato Institute and was joined in its management by libertarian and "Austrian School" economist Murray Rothbard and Ed Crane. In 1976, the name of the foundation was changed to the Cato Institute.

The Cato Institute is among several think tanks that were founded in the 1970s and early 1980s by wealthy families inspired in great part by a memo written in 1971 by Lewis Powell, Jr., for the US Chamber of Commerce (Powell, a Richmond, Virginia lawyer and former American Bar Association President, would go on to be appointed to the US Supreme Court by President Nixon).[55] Powell, in his memo, urged business to organize to respond to what it characterized in its title as an attack on the American free enterprise system by liberals supported by foundations funded by some of America's most successful businesses.[56]

The Cato Institute is distinguished from the rest of the conservative think tanks in that, with its motto of "Individual Liberty, Free Markets, and Peace" Cato claims to promote libertarianism—although, in reality, it has always defined its fight for "freedom" as consisting of fighting for low taxes, abolition of business regulations designed to protect workers and consumers (especially among the middle class and poor), and abolition and privatization of social services on which the middle class and poor rely. "Peace" it has come to define as neoconservative foreign policy. And it has steadily supplied Republican administrations with conservative economic and neoconservative foreign policy staff.[57]

Libertarianism's early promoters did not envision their philosophy as servant to a plutocracy bent on concentrating wealth and political power through policies promoted by the Cato Institute and other think tanks. Karl Hess, a libertarian and speechwriter for Senator Barry Goldwater (R-AZ) in his 1964 presidential campaign, observed in his 1975 book, *Dear America*, that the left has historically been associated with opposition to concentration of economic and political power, therefore, he associated libertarianism with the left.

Similarly, Cato Institute co-founder Murray Rothbard in his essay "Left and Right: The Prospects for Liberty," which appeared in the first issue of *Left and Right: A Journal of Libertarian Thought*" (Spring 1965), situated libertarianism on the left and situated conservatism on the right as the modern version of the pre-industrial *ancien régime* and, accordingly, claimed conservatism had no future.[58] Carl Oglesby, an admirer of Rothbard and from 1965 to 1966 President of the liberal Students for a Democratic Society (SDS)—the main organization of the "New Left"—in essays approvingly cited libertarians and linked the "Old Right" and the "New Left."[59]

Yet, as the Cato Institute illustrates, conservatism, guided by the modern successors to the *ancien régime*, captured libertarianism—many of those who call themselves libertarians espousing libertarianism also call themselves conservatives and espouse conservatism (among them the former radio host Neal Boortz).[60] And, *contra* Rothbard and Hess, conservatism has gone on to play a prominent role in American politics for more than four decades thereafter, providing a social philosophy that endorses the rise of concentrated wealth and political power in business and the rich, and allies with neoconservatives to support an interventionist foreign policy.

In a variation on Irving Kristol's observation regarding neoconservatives, many modern liberals[61] might be properly described as libertarians who were mugged by the reality that the libertarian movement mainly exists to promote the interests of multimillionaires and multibillionaires, as is illustrated each summer when thousands of libertarians gather at "FreedomFest" in Las Vegas, which the advertisements for the event describe as "the world's most libertarian city." Of the four keynote speakers for FreedomFest 2011, two were multibillionaires: Peter Thiel (co-founder of Pay Pal and early investor in Facebook) and John Mackey (founder and CEO of Whole Foods Market) and a third, Steve Forbes, a multimillionaire—they were joined by former Fox News commentator Judge Andrew Napolitano. For its libertarianism, Las Vegas in 2010 led the nation in foreclosures, and real estate prices were down more than 50 percent from their high in August 2006. The unemployment rate for Las Vegas-Paradise, Nevada at the beginning of 2011 was the second-highest among the 49 metropolitan areas with populations over 1 million—13.7 percent.[62] Yet, the convention's promotional literature gave no evidence the libertarians were aware of the irony that the facts of life in Las Vegas, city of their dreams, illustrated so unmistakably the harshness and the failure of their philosophy—and the Libertarian Party National Convention was held there in 2012.

Libertarians will object to the term "trickle-down" and instead argue that they are not favoring the rich but, rather, only favoring allowing the market to operate in a setting of "freedom." They are deluding themselves, as is revealed by reference to economic data over the past three decades—especially over the past decade and a half. The trickle-down reforms implemented to achieve more of a "free market" delivered inequality and massive income and wealth redistribution upward, and recurrent bubbles that have grown and then burst, destroying trillions of dollars in wealth (concentrated among the middle class and poor) each time they did. And, it is suspected, these bubbles continue to exist now in varying degrees (in, e.g., real estate, the stock market and emerging markets) and continue to pose the risk they will again burst and destroy trillions of dollars in wealth—and even if they do not burst, their existence will continue to hinder economic growth.

The result, then, is that the libertarian argument in favor of the "free market" is, in reality, the argument for trickle-down and continued upward redistribution of income and wealth to those at the top. Libertarian economic policy—notwithstanding its appeals to "freedom"—is thus in effect synonymous with trickle-down, and it should be no surprise that Libertarian Party links to the Republican Party are extensive. In 1972, the first presidential election in which it participated, the Libertarian Party received its first and only electoral vote in history when a Republican elector pledged to Richard Nixon gave his electoral vote to the Libertarian candidates. In the 1976 election, that elector, Roger Lea MacBride, was the Libertarian Party candidate for president, and his campaign book's title *A New Dawn for America* (1976) bore a striking resemblance to the 1984 Reagan re-election campaign's series of "It's Morning Again in America" commercials. The 1980 Libertarian Party ticket was composed of presidential candidate Ed Clark and vice presidential candidate David Koch, who, with his brother Charles, would go on to fund Republican candidates and causes. Ed Clark's campaign book, published in August of 1980, was titled *A New Beginning*—Ronald Reagan's theme in his acceptance speech at the Republican convention in July 1980 was "A New Beginning," and the Osmonds launched his campaign at the convention singing the convention's theme song, "Together a New Beginning." Ron Paul, who later went on to become a Republican congressman from Texas and Republican presidential candidate in 2012, was the Libertarian Party's presidential candidate in 1988; Republican former congressman from Georgia, Bob Barr, was the Libertarian Party's presidential candidate in 2008; and Republican former Governor of New Mexico and, briefly, Republican presidential candidate in 2012, Gary Johnson, was the Libertarian Party's presidential candidate that year. And, Ron Paul's son, Senator Rand Paul (R-KY), who defined his philosophy as libertarian, was an early leader in the race for the 2016 Republican presidential nomination.[63] The Libertarian Party, which has run presidential and vice presidential candidates in every election since 1972, has only once—in *1980*—gotten even slightly over 1 percent of the popular vote, as philosophical libertarians have mainly voted Republican.[64]

As will be addressed below, with the spread of trickle-down and libertarian conservatism, the very concept of freedom has changed. The US Supreme Court case of *Buckley v. Valeo* (1976) is cited for having established that money equals speech, however, the trickle-down libertarian conservative vision is broader than that—it is that *money equals freedom*, so that we are spreading freedom when we cut taxes and regulation, and that, obviously, we get the biggest return on this effort—we get the most freedom—when we cut taxes and regulations on the rich whose wealth itself, because it symbolizes freedom, is a measure of their civic virtue.

Trickle-down has also infected foreign policy—in the form of its ally neoconservatism's simplistic formulation that what is good for wealthy Americans is good for the world. And, it has infected social policy, as members of the Religious Right—certain that they have glimpsed ultimate truth and must impose their morality on America—ally with multibillionaires and multimillionaires who will abandon their own "libertarian" concerns about social freedom in exchange for Republican votes by those of the Religious Right.

Led by the libertarians and their focus on helping the rich, in 2012 Republicans opposed raising marginal income tax rates even on the less than *1 percent* of American individuals making over $400,000 per year and couples making over $450,000 per year—while remaining silent as the payroll tax holiday expired, resulting in a 48 percent increase in payroll taxes from 4.2 percent to 6.2 percent, raising taxes on *77 percent* of taxpayers.[65]

And the Nordic Model, Socialism and Communism

Senator Bernie Sanders (I-VT), candidate for the Democratic Party's nominee for president in 2016, has referred to himself as a "socialist" and a "democratic socialist."[66] In contrast to capitalism's private ownership of property, socialism envisions state ownership of the means of production—in the words of *The Communist Manifesto* (1848) by Karl Marx and Friedrich Engels, in which the "proletariat" consists of the workers: "The proletariat will use its political supremacy to wrest, by degrees, all capital from the bourgeoisie, to centralize all the instruments of production in the hands of the state, *i.e.,* of the proletariat organized as the ruling class; and to increase the total of productive forces as rapidly as possible."[67] In the Preface to the German Edition, 1890, Engels, in notes from London dated May 1, 1890, explained "why we could not have called it a *socialist* manifesto": "Socialism in 1847 signified a bourgeois movement, communism a working-class movement."[68] Thus, while both socialism and communism desire state ownership of the means of production, Marx and Engels envisioned a workers' revolution to bring about this state ownership and, thus, named their manifesto calling for a workers' revolution to implement a system of state ownership of the means of production a communist manifesto.

"Democratic socialism" is an ambiguous term, referring to either a system of socialism—an economy in which the state owns the means of production—combined with a democratic political system, or, alternatively, to the system of the Scandinavian countries that provides for a capitalist economy and a strong safety net with liberal democracy—more accurately called the "Nordic Model."[69] Pursuant to the Nordic Model, Scandinavian countries have maintained the highest levels of prosperity and living standards in the world. Senator Sanders, in an interview after he announced his candidacy, clarified that he intends the latter definition, expressing admiration for the Scandinavian countries as he did,[70] and he again expressed admiration for the policies of Denmark in the first Democratic presidential nomination debate October 13, 2015.[71] A somewhat less ambiguous term, "social democracy," has been used as synonymous with a system following the Nordic Model by Lane Kenworthy, Professor of Sociology and Yankelovich Chair in Social Thought, University of California-San Diego, in his 2014 book *Social Democratic America.*[72]

However, the liberalism proposed herein, drawing its inspiration from, among others, Adam Smith, Alexis de Tocqueville, Friedrich Hayek (in his early writings) and John Maynard Keynes, proposing a capitalist system and liberal democracy combined with an extensive system of social insurance, while sharing with Senator Sanders and Professor Kenworthy desire to apply a Nordic Model to the United States, endorses the Nordic Model and understands the Nordic Model not as a rejection of classical liberalism but, rather, *as* classical liberalism, correctly understood and applied. And, because the liberalism proposed herein stands firmly in opposition to socialism and communism, the terms "socialism," "democratic socialism" and "social democracy" are rejected as descriptors for this liberalism.[73]

In a Word: Philosophies of "Power": Liberalism and "Connectedness" versus Trickle-Down and "Freedom"

In a word, this book is about the profoundly sociological phenomenon of power and, in particular, it is a study of the power of ideology to determine the distribution of economic and political power—whether economic and political power are concentrated upward among a small group of the already economically and politically powerful, or diffused downward among the less economically and politically powerful—and the resultant effects on society.[74]

Conservatives still recall the efforts of liberals, especially in the 1960s, on behalf of their favored special interests (e.g., the poor, minorities, unions and women) to grow the size of government, and even to profess an affinity for socialism, the goal of which is to concentrate ultimate economic power in government. Thus, they will assign to liberals the effort to concentrate power. Liberalism, however, commencing with the presidency of Jimmy Carter and continuing through the presidencies of Bill Clinton and Barack Obama, has sought to strike a balance of power among government, the market and civil society (evidenced by restraint on inflation and relative restraint on government deficits and government growth) and to diffuse downward economic and political power. And, as can be seen from the conservative effort beginning in the 1950s to forge a Holy Roller-high roller movement, while conservatives *talked of* diffusing power among, for example, Nixon's "silent majority," in reality the effort of the New Right—today's movement conservatives—was always since that time to concentrate economic and political power upward to deliver to conservatism's own favored special interests, delivering to the rich concentrated economic and political power in favor of trickle-down policies, and delivering to the New Right Christian fundamentalists at least the hope of concentrated political power to secure greater government interference in social matters (although the fruition of this effort has been in great part foiled by the Supreme Court).

Whereas the classic work of the sociologist C. Wright Mills, *The Power Elite* (1956), addressed the intersection of military, corporate and political power in society and the groups composing the "power elite," the present work addresses the ideology that enables one party, the Republican Party, to fool enough of the people enough of the time to maintain political power and economic influence—convincing them to vote for policies that can be shown factually to be against their own personal interest; against the theory that

Republicans themselves claim for inspiration of their ideology; and against public opinion—while also undermining our national economy, democracy, institutions and health. At issue is whether, for the good of society, we should continue to promote, as conservatives urge, governmental policies that distribute upward economic and political power or, instead, as liberals urge, governmental policies that tend to diffuse downward economic and political power.

Supporting the ideological arguments of liberals and conservatives regarding distribution of power are two themes of the 2008 and 2012 elections: the liberal theme of "connectedness" and the conservative theme of "freedom." On the liberal side, Senator Obama observed on the campaign trail in 2007 and, later, President Obama observed on the campaign trail in 2011 that we are all "connected."[75] In contrast, while the term "trickle-down" captures the economic vision of conservatism since its ascendancy in 1980, "trickle-down" also evokes the alluring ideal of allowing "freedom" of the market and of political campaign spending to work magic.

Millions of Americans first heard Barack Obama's philosophy of connectedness at the 2004 Democratic National Convention[76]:

> Yet even as we speak, there are those who are preparing to divide us, the spin masters and negative ad peddlers who embrace the politics of anything goes. Well, I say to them tonight, there's not a liberal America and a conservative America, there's a United States of America. There's not a black America and white America and Latino America and Asian America; there's the United States of America. The pundits like to slice-and-dice our country into Red States and Blue States; Red States for Republicans, Blue States for Democrats. But I've got news for them, too. We worship an awesome God in the Blue States, and we don't like federal agents poking around our libraries in the Red States. We coach Little League in the Blue States and have gay friends in the Red States. There are patriots who opposed the war in Iraq and patriots who supported it. We are one people, all of us pledging allegiance to the stars and stripes, all of us defending the United States of America.

The worldview of a society based on a liberal vision is that every individual life has value, and we all are connected; and through these connections the whole is strengthened—a whole that functions best at delivering freedom and prosperity when it is recognized that there is an ever-shifting necessary balance between the institutions that compose the governing elements of society: civil society, the market and government.[77]

This is not to say that liberalism envisions a Lake Wobegon world in which "all our children are above average." Rather, liberalism seeks to provide the greatest opportunity to all so that those who are above average may excel, and those who are not may, nonetheless, live lives of dignity in a setting of peace and prosperity.

The one word, thus, to describe the liberal vision is "connectedness." The concept that all individuals are connected carries with it a sense that although freedom is cherished, the exercise of that freedom is subject to *restraint* on the part of the powerful—subject, in other words, to what appears to be, in the short-term, *sacrifice* by the powerful, withholding their ability to block opportunity for, and a better quality of life on the part of, the powerless. This concept of sacrifice has been expressed repeatedly, as will be seen herein, in classical liberal philosophy, especially by Adam Smith and Alexis de Tocqueville and in the context of "enlightened self-interest" and *noblesse oblige* (that with wealth and power comes responsibility), as well as in religion and morality. Of course, this sacrifice is, in reality, as is revealed in the concept of enlightened self-interest, actually not a sacrifice at all but, rather, an investment made in their fellow citizens for the benefit of not only the futures of their fellow citizens but also their own future—an investment in their own self-interest rightly understood.

This concept of connectedness was also present in President John F. Kennedy's famous speech at the American University commencement, June 10, 1963, wherein he observed, "For in the final analysis, our most basic common link is that we all inhabit this small planet. We all breathe the same air. We all cherish our children's futures. And we are all mortal." And that concept of connectedness was present in the mantra from the Clinton-Gore campaign of 1992, borrowing it from the Democratic Leadership Council: "opportunity, responsibility and community."[78]

The sense of connectedness liberals feel extends not only to their fellow humans, but to all life itself, and drives the environmental and animal rights movements. As the great naturalist John Muir observed, "When we try to pick out anything by itself, we find it hitched to everything else in the Universe."[79] As stated by Dr. Martin Luther King, Jr., in his Nobel Prize Lecture: "All life is interrelated, and all men are interdependent. The agony of the poor diminishes the rich, and the salvation of the poor enlarges the rich. We are inevitably our brother's keeper because of the interrelated structure of reality."[80]

In that statement, Dr. King harkened to President Theodore Roosevelt, who observed, "The welfare of each of us is dependent fundamentally upon the welfare of all of us."[81] Both harkened to the words of the poet, lawyer and clergyman in the Church of England, John Donne (1572-1631), in *Meditation XVII* from *Devotions upon Emergent Occasions* (1624), typically referred to as the poem "No Man Is an Island" (following is the modernized version): "No man is an island, entire of itself; every man is a piece of the continent, a part of the main; if a clod be washed away by the sea, Europe is the less, as well as if a promontory were, as well as if a manor of thy friends or of thine own were; any man's death diminishes me, because I am involved in mankind; and therefore never send to know for whom the bell tolls; it tolls for thee."

And, when President Obama announced that his post-presidency will concentrate on helping youth, returning to his life's love of the work he did as a young community organizer and politician, through his My Brother's Keeper Alliance, he was announcing he will be concentrating on returning to the liberal pursuit of where the connectedness of Donne, Roosevelt, Kennedy, King and others leads him.[82]

This focus on connectedness leads liberals to tend to view society as an organism, best studied by a combination focused on sociology, political science, economics, psychology and law all together—the term for this discipline, though it has fallen out of use, is "organic sociology."[83] This work may be viewed as an attempt to resurrect this discipline, especially relevant at a time when free markets, free elections and technology—all the supposed miracle-producing faiths of our time—are failing us, and we are coming to recognize the critical importance of *how* individuals can most efficiently for mutual good work together, not only in the realm of politics, the economy and civil society, but also in foreign policy (as evidenced by military victory in Iraq in contrast with continuing political failure there).[84]

"Freedom"—the value stressed by conservatives—while shared as a liberal value, is recognized by liberals as a necessary but insufficient guiding vision that must be subject to restraint and sacrifice on the part of the powerful in the best interest of all. The liberal critique of conservatism is that it stresses freedom without the restraint and sacrifice applied to it under liberal democracy, converting appeals to "freedom" into support for an authoritarian hierarchical vision of Darwinian survival of the fittest as ordained by God, governed by the privileged, and cushioned only by private charity. Liberals, in contrast, also recognize the importance of private charity, but realize that private charity will simply not be sufficient—therefore liberals recognize the necessity of some degree of government compulsion of giving and government provision of benefits. Liberals also recognize that it is in the best interest of society—so it is also in the best interest of the powerful, themselves—that economic and political power be shared.

As will be shown herein the term "freedom" is manipulated by the trinity of elements that compose trickle-down conservatism, and all of the bad ideas of conservatism—in social, political, economic and foreign policy—complement and reinforce each other. The traditionalists have yielded to the more extreme Religious Right, focused on the "values voter" divisive issues of opposition to contraception, abortion and equal rights for gays, driving the Republican Party socially rightward, as revealed in a 2014 poll by the Public Religion Research Institute: When white evangelicals are removed, Republicans are nearly evenly split on legalization of gay marriage (opposed 47% to 45%) and legalization of abortion in all or most cases (opposed 49% to

48%).[85] With the demise of communism, the anticommunists yielded to the neoconservatives opposed to a new global threat—that of Islamist terrorism. And, the libertarians have yielded to the multibillionaires and multimillionaires who organized in special interest groups and think tanks supporting the trickle-down-supply-side and crony capitalist visions driven by the delusional self-serving happy coincidence that what's good for the wealthy (them) is good for the world.

The term "crony capitalism," like the term "trickle-down," is pejorative. While one might proudly call oneself a libertarian or a supply-sider, seldom are there proud self-professed proponents of trickle-down or crony capitalism. As observed by George Packer, crony capitalism is less a philosophy than an outlook on the world that assumes that the "right" men—businessmen presumably—should be in charge of government, and liberal institutions are not seen as important.[86] An example of this crony capitalist outlook was expressed by Representative Spencer Bachus (R-AL) who, in an interview after receiving his appointment as Chairman of the House Financial Services Committee, observed that he was there to serve the banks.[87]

Liberals, in contrast to conservatives, see trickle-down conservatism's unholy trinity of multibillionaires and multimillionaires directing libertarianism for their benefit, neoconservatives yearning to conquer new lands and Religious Right adherents demanding government support their evangelism and tolerate their intolerance as exercise of their religion[88] *not* as evocative of freedom but, rather, as coercive power exercised as an existential threat to freedom—of all Americans—and in opposition to it, liberalism reclaims its traditional, rightful place as the defender of freedom. Liberalism also reclaims its traditional, rightful place as defender of scientific analysis based in fact in opposition to conservatism's faith based in mysticism.

As Democratic political strategist James Carville observed regarding the liberal vision of appropriate policy[89]:

> Let me say in very clear terms that bringing down the rich is not the answer. Some of my best friends are rich people. Hell, I'm pretty well off myself. The problem is not that we have too many rich people or that the rich have too much money. It's that the rest of the country is standing still or getting poorer.

That observation was made in 1996, and the facts are no more favorable for trickle-down now: Trickle-down has failed miserably, demanding too much of the market—and thereby forcing the failure of the market.

THE METRIC AND THE ARGUMENT

The metric for judging the economy of the United States, as it should be for all economies, is its ability to generate prosperity; to generate a rising standard of living for all members of society, including those at the bottom. And by that metric, trickle-down is proven a failure and a delusion.

Thus, the argument that unfolds herein at its simplest is that the truth is ironic: *Not only are trickle-down's policies designed to benefit the rich, investors and business not in the best interest of everyone—they are not even in the long-run best interest of the rich, investors and business.*[90] For, if this book had been written in 2000, the warning would have been that income and wealth are being unhealthily concentrated in the top 20 percent of households[91]; in 2005, the top 10 percent; and in 2010 the top 5 percent. As it is written in 2016, the warning is that income and wealth are being unhealthily concentrated in the top 1 percent. And the trend clearly indicates that, in the future, if we do not rebut trickle-down and substitute for it liberal policies, the only income group seeing real income growth will be the top 0.1 percent; then the 0.01 percent; etc. And although corporate profits are at a record high now, it is unimaginable that this upward redistribution, thereby starving demand, can be sustained without negatively affecting investors, businesses and the rich generally in the long-run.

Trickle-down, in historical context, is simply another rationale for exploiting labor economically and suppressing its political power by upwardly redistributing economic and political power, in the tradition of similar bad ideas from slavery to Jim Crow to discrimination against minorities and women. In contrast to these examples of exploitation, however, trickle-down is self-imposed exploitation—imposed mainly through the legitimate democratic process upon themselves by the deluded middle class and poor.

The argument that unfolds herein more broadly is summarized below, addressing failings of trickle-down versus liberalism in four respective areas—political thought, economics, sociology and the rule of law.

Political Thought

Trickle-down has been, off and on for the past three and a half decades, the prevailing economic philosophy, implemented through the political process, in this country and much of the world, however, liberals will defeat the nonsense of trickle-down if they engage in a debate with conservatives regarding ideas, rather than engaging in *ad hominem* abusive personal attacks on conservatives. When liberals do decide to engage with conservatives on ideas, they will find that trickle-down is not supported by facts; classical liberal theory conservatives claim for inspiration; or public opinion, as evidenced by numerous polls.

Movement conservatism began as a combination of libertarianism, traditionalism and anticommunism; under the influence of trickle-down it has evolved rightward into a combination of plutocracy, the Religious Right and neoconservatism—of which plutocracy is the main driving element, under the influence of a small group of multibillionaire and multimillionaire right-wing extremist families with influential ties to media through News Corp and Fox News Channel.

There are two distinct—liberal and conservative—understandings of classical liberalism. The modern liberal vision understands the essence of classical liberalism as enlightened self-interest, supporting liberal democracy (democracy with liberal values) combined with capitalism, but guided by the concept of "connectedness" and the philosophy that "we all do better when we *all* do better"; thus it sees the true nature of classical liberalism as requiring sacrifice on the part of the wealthy and powerful, in the concept of enlightened self-interest, in which such sacrifice is actually investment in the futures of themselves and their fellow citizens, and, thus, modern liberalism is the sole defender of classical liberalism against increasingly extremist and illiberal trickle-down conservatism.

The trickle-down conservative vision is erroneous in its oversimplification of the classical liberal vision as simply meaning "freedom" in a setting of unfettered capitalism combined with crude one-person-one-vote democracy void of critical liberal values ("illiberal democracy"), with the result that conservatism embraces an ideal of "what's good for the rich and corporations is good for all" that creates a "culture of dependency" upon the rich and business comfortable with crony capitalism, and, accordingly, rejects enlightened self-interest of classical liberalism and substitutes therefor simple self-interest, especially of the rich and business, perhaps supplemented by private charity.

As a corollary to these two distinct—liberal and conservative—understandings of classical liberalism, the modern liberal vision understands the critical importance of the middle class in promoting economic growth and stability and political stability. The recognition of the importance of a large and growing and happy middle class comes in the recognition of the vision of Adam Smith regarding, as a moral value, the importance of liberally compensating workers, as complemented by the utilitarian vision of John Maynard Keynes that economic growth is driven by *demand*. The political importance of a large and growing and happy middle class to political stability and creation of liberal democracy is recognized due to the statements of, among others, Aristotle, Karl Polanyi, Friedrich Hayek, Barrington Moore and Daniel Bell, complemented by confirming research.

The trickle-down conservative vision devotes lip service to promoting a large and growing middle class, but it believes that economic growth, in the vision of the conservative economists (supply-siders, monetarists and Austrians, among them) is driven by *supply*. Thus, economic policy is directed toward cutting taxes for those at the top, cutting government regulation, and cutting spending on social safety net programs upon which the middle class and poor rely. Similarly, this vision is oblivious to how the loss of political power by the middle class and poor promotes political instability.

Conservatives, driven by their trickle-down delusion, thus repeat the mistake for which Alexis de Tocqueville chided his fellow Europeans in 1835: Conservatives endorse "self-interest" (perhaps tempered by private charity) as an organizing basis for society, while liberals, as did the Americans so admired by Tocqueville, endorse "*enlightened* self-interest" (self-interest tempered by charity, but also by a willingness to give to the state for the benefit of all, recognizing this as an investment in their fellow citizens).

Trickle-down conservatism has also, throughout the West, with the discontent it sewed among the middle class, prompted a reaction in the form of illiberal right wing populism exemplified most prominently in the US by the Tea Party.

The crisis trickle-down conservative theory presents in political thought is three-fold. It is incompatible with classical liberalism because it has evolved into a *faith*, impervious to facts. As such, it promotes the idea that there are certain people—conservatives—who have grasped ultimate truth and in accordance with that truth should govern the world. It also promotes the idea that the end of politics should be to interfere with the "free market" to the least extent possible, with the result that classical liberalism's concept of enlightened self-interest has been corrupted into an illiberal use of politics to promote the raw self-interest of the rich and corporations. And, finally, it promotes the related idea that "politics is a marketplace," whereby, despite holding the above vision that there is ultimate truth which should guide governing, conservatives simultaneously hold the contradictory vision that spreading falsehoods is all part of the "permanent campaign;" and "money is speech," so that votes and influence over lawmakers are to be bought with dollars invested in yielding a return to the investor—"investments" that, if made wisely, will pay off much more lucratively than would investments in capital to enhance competitiveness and increase productivity—thus also tolerating the outright suppression of votes for the opposing candidates.

This suppression of the right to vote undermines democracy directly by suppressing the rights of fellow citizens to exercise their constitutionally guaranteed right to vote. Democracy is indirectly undermined by having triumphed in the Supreme Court with the view of democracy as a marketplace, with the result that the richest Americans have the loudest political voices, resulting in disproportionate weight being given to their opinions and, also, by creation of a system of "virtual reality" based on falsehoods maintained by the Republican propaganda machine of Fox News Channel and other conservative news outlets, conservative commentators and irresponsible extremist Republican politicians.

Finally, the political philosophy of trickle-down undermines not only our democracy but also our economy. Trickle-down was always a political theory that we would all be better off if we upwardly redistributed economic and political power. Its economic masquerade was as utopian economic thought, combining the ideology of trickle-down economics—supply-side economics—Reaganomics with the understandings of crony capitalism, implemented politically by the alliance of the plutocracy and the Religious Right, which has succeeded in gaining control over, first, the Republican Party, followed by the nation and, finally, the world, pursuant to an argument justified only by resort to faith and not facts.

Economics

There are two types of recession. An inventory recession is the type of recession experienced from the end of World War II through the back-to-back recessions of the early 1980s, marked by high consumer price inflation, rising wages and relatively low inequality. Such recessions are cured by defeating inflationary expectations by raising interest rates, which worsens the recession, but which, when interest rates are lowered later after inflationary expectations are wrung out of the economy, yields to a relatively rapid recovery. The other type of recession, a balance sheet recession, is the type of recession experienced since the early 1980s, marked by low consumer price inflation and stagnant or declining real wages, rising income and wealth inequality, and high asset price inflation that results in bubbles that burst, in a depressionary feedback loop resembling conditions prior to and during the Great Depression; recovery is slow and protracted, and interest rate policy is of only partial help and must be accompanied by fiscal stimulus due to the combination of oversupply and chronically sluggish demand. In the housing bubble of 2008, these elements were illustrated by an oversupply of housing encouraged by low interest rates promoted to overcome the limited buying power of consumers due to years of stagnant wages. In the current period of a commodities bubble and bust (with the example of oil, at $110 a barrel in mid-2014 versus less than $30 per barrel in early 2016), again oversupply, due to massive capital expenditures (CAPEX) to increase production, encouraged by low interest rates, has outpaced demand—which, again, has been suppressed by stagnant wages the world over.

Because of the differences between inventory recessions and balance sheet recessions both as to causes and, even more importantly, cures (in the case of inventory recessions, combatting their inflation with raised interest rates; and in the case of balance sheet recessions, combatting their stagnant demand with fiscal policy), even though they are similar in exhibiting shortfalls in demand, it is entirely inappropriate to compare, as Republicans do, recoveries following an inventory recession—such as during the Reagan administration in the early 1980s—versus the recovery following the most recent balance sheet recession inherited by President Obama.

The proposed Republican trickle-down policy responses have already been tried and found wanting: taxes have been cut (2001, 2003 and 2009), deregulation was implemented (under every president commencing with Carter), services have been privatized and austerity has been imposed at the federal, state and local levels—and state and local governments have implemented layoffs of employees and reduction in services—yet all these measures have failed to put the economy back on the path of steady rapid economic, job and income growth.

Trickle-down economics evolved from a political effort on behalf of conservatism to reverse and undo the policies of President Franklin Roosevelt's New Deal and President Lyndon Johnson's Great Society, and in the course of this effort re-wrote history to distort the lessons of the great economist John Maynard Keynes that it is appropriate to use not only monetary policy (with which conservative economists agree) but also fiscal policy to promote growth and equality and thereby increase demand.

The crisis trickle-down conservative theory presents in economics is that, pursuant to a political theory masquerading as economics, over much of the past three and a half decades, the economy has been growing, and productivity has been growing, but trickle-down values—*that we, the American people promote, pursuant to the Republican Party's conservative ideology*—have rigged the economy to continuously upwardly redistribute those revenues attributable to our increased productivity, yielding a productivity/wage disconnect, resulting in increased concentration of income and wealth at the top, in corporations and among older Americans (beneficiaries of income from Social Security, pensions and investments and continuing income due to delaying retirement), and the lowest percentage of GDP attributable to wages and highest attributable to profits since World War II. This, in turn, has resulted in slower economic growth, rising inequality, falling social mobility, declining public health, rising political dysfunction and rising economic instability illustrated by recurring bubble-bust episodes and balance sheet recessions, in turn creating low demand and reinforcing low wages in a depressionary feedback loop of our own creation. The federal government has countered these conditions with low interest rates and reduced regulation of the extending of credit, but for America to grow it must begin rebuilding its middle class and reversing this upward redistribution by, among other things, implementing fiscal policies such as spending more to promote job creation, promoting wage increases and returning to more progressive taxation.

Sociology

There are two distinct conservative and liberal versions of a "culture of poverty"—and, hence, of how economic development happens. The conservative model ignores the influence of economic circumstances on culture and begins its culture of poverty explanation with factors related to culture, such as weak work ethic; weak intellect; and the failure of elites to defend values supportive of development, leading to a weak work ethic on the part of non-elites. The liberal model is of a theory of culture of poverty extended by the concept of "social isolation," by which is meant that economic circumstances can influence culture and, even if they do not influence culture they may, nonetheless influence behavior—thus the liberal model begins with economic circumstances and proceeds to address how those influence culture and behavior positively or negatively and, where those influences are negative, addresses how politics, through influencing culture and behavior directly by promotion of values and indirectly by support of income-and wealth-redistributing institutions, can promote prosperity and happiness.

Classical liberal theory provides the liberal values of checks and balances, respect for knowledge, tolerance, equality, peace and the rule of law, all of which must be applied to a one-person-one vote democracy with capitalism to convert that democracy into a liberal democracy. And, as the value of checks and balances guided the authors of the Constitution to provide for three branches of government—legislative, executive and judicial—so there are three branches of society in which there are institutions that defend an individual from abuse of power and leverage that individual's efficacy in a system of "societal checks and balances": the market, government and civil society.

The crisis trickle-down conservative theory presents in sociology is two-fold. First, it directly promotes the dismantling of the essential government institutions that spread income and wealth downward, resulting in greater concentration of income and wealth at the top and greater numbers of people dependent upon disappearing government institutions among the lower 99 percent, resulting in increased social isolation among the lower 99 percent undermining the economy, democracy, institutions more broadly and public health; and it indirectly promotes the undermining of civil society institutions such as marriage and religious institutions by undermining self-esteem economically, promoting withdrawal from society. Second, with its ally, neoconservatism, it ignores the importance of all liberal values—especially tolerance—and in the Islamic world, which more than anything else needs the spreading of liberal values, trickle-down and neoconservatism are only capable of further destruction and further undermining of American foreign policy.

The Rule of Law

There are two distinct—conservative and liberal—understandings of the rule of law. The conservative version is inspired by an illiberal trickle-down vision which requires that the "freedom" of the rich and powerful not be overly burdened by attempts through law to enhance opportunity and quality of life for the middle class and poor. In contrast, the liberal version is inspired by the classical liberal value of checks and balances which, in turn, includes the idea that the powerful must share power with the powerless, for the good of all.

The crisis trickle-down conservative theory presents the rule of law is that the conservatives, so concerned that government not get too big and powerful so that it becomes the source of privilege in violation of the rule of law, have, instead, accorded to the propertied—the wealthy and corporations—so much power that they can now bend government to their will and direct to themselves privileges in violation of the rule of law. Commencing with the case of *Bush v. Gore*—although the opinion was famously "limited to the present circumstances"—the Supreme Court has begun to undo the equal protection component of the rule of law by weighing proposed remedies on behalf of the less powerful against their effect on the rich and powerful—first, by providing a "second bite" equal protection review to protect the ability of the rich and powerful to preferentially exercise their wealth and power, and second, by using the freedoms of the First Amendment as a bludgeon on behalf of the privileged, striking down laws that help the less powerful. The reality is that classical liberal theory decrees, pursuant to the value of checks and balances and in accord with enlightened self-interest, the rich and powerful must sometimes sacrifice for the benefit of the rest of society, and to thwart this value is to undermine the rule of law.

Conclusion: The Republican Party Is Not the Solution to the Problem. It *Is* the Problem.

The Republican Party—driven by the trickle-down delusion—is not the solution to the problem; it *is* the problem. As established by more than three and half decades of evidence, the Republican Party is undermining the American economy (promoting inequality, ignoring unemployment, impeding economic growth and growing the deficit), undermining our democracy, undermining our institutions and undermining the health of our fellow Americans (measurable in terms of increasing mortality and morbidity rates for white Americans without a college degree). Due to continuing failure of the Republican Party to make the lives of its middle class and poor constituents better, the party is torn by their anger. But, as will be seen in following pages, its adherence to its trickle-down conservative philosophy renders the party incapable of improving their lives. It is the responsibility of liberals to free the nation and the world from the trickle-down delusion, recognizing the stark contrast between the core of their philosophy and the conservatism of the Republican Party: "The conservative Republican believes we all do better when the rich do better. The liberal Democrat knows we all do better when we *all* do better."

NOTES

1. A "wage" is compensation paid on a regular basis (e.g., hourly, daily, weekly, biweekly or monthly) for work done. In contrast, a person's "income" consists of money received, especially on a regular basis, and also money received from investments including income from sale of investments, dividends, and interest. Thus, as will be observed herein, income inequality is rising because of an upward redistribution of the revenues attributable to increased productivity, away from wages and into the other sources of income mainly, and, to a lesser extent, because of large increases going to the very highest wage earners but smaller or no increases to all other wage earners.

2. See especially Dionne Searcey and Robert Gebeloff, "U.S. Seniors Prosper, Finding 'Sweet Spot' in Middle Class," *The New York Times*, June 15, 2015.

3. Source: FRED St. Louis Fed Reserve data series WASCUR (wages), CP (corporate profits) and GDP, 1947-present.

4. See, for example, Paul Krugman, "Charlatans, Cranks and Kansas," *The New York Times*, June 30, 2014 and "Seriously Bad Ideas," *The New York Times*, June 12, 2015.

5. See Paul Krugman, "Cranking Up for 2016," *The New York Times*, February 20, 2015.

6. The term was actually "voodoo economic policy" as used by George H. W. Bush, in the Republican Primary Debate, Carnegie Mellon University, Pittsburgh, PA April 10, 1980. *NBC Nightly News*, John Chancellor and Ken Bode, February 10, 1982.

7. See e.g., Paul Krugman, "Economics and Elections," *The New York Times*, April 6, 2015 and "That Old-Time Economics," *The New York Times*, April 17, 2015.

8. Numerous studies link income equality of the sort exacerbated by trickle-down with shorter life spans, lower birth weight and higher infant mortality, and many will be addressed in Chapter 11. More than 170 such studies have been reviewed in the journal *Social Science and Medicine*; for detail see the website of the Equality Trust in the UK. See also, e.g., David A. Kindig and Erika R. Cheng, "Even As Mortality Fell in Most US Counties, Female Mortality Nonetheless Rose in 42.8 Percent of Counties from 1992 to 2006," *Health Affairs*, Vol. 32, Issue 3, March 2013.

9. See Paul Krugman, "Hating Good Government," *The New York Times*, January 19, 2015.

10. The Kemp-Roth Bill, when signed into law by President Reagan, put into effect his tax cuts of 1981. Stockman was quoted by William Greider in Greider's article, "The Education of David Stockman," *The Atlantic Monthly*, December 1981.

11. George Gilder, *Wealth and Poverty* (New York: Basic Books, 1981), p. 224.

12. Paul Krugman, "Love for Labor Lost," *The New York Times*, September 2, 2013.

13. See for example Joseph Stiglitz, "America Is No Longer a Land of Opportunity," *Financial Times*, June 25, 2012; the interview conducted by Alexander Jung and Thomas Schultz with Joseph Stiglitz, "The American Dream Has Become a Myth," *Spiegel Online*, October 2, 2012; Joseph Stiglitz, address to the AFL-CIO Convention in Los Angeles, September 8, 2013, quoted in "Joe Stiglitz: The People Who Break the Rules Have Raked in Huge Profits and Wealth and It's Sickening Our Politics," *AlterNet.com*, September 11, 2013. And see Jonathan Fisher, "Nobel Laureate Joseph Stiglitz: 'There Is No Magic Bullet' to Fix Income Inequality," *Business Insider*, May 6, 2015. The article is derived from an interview conducted with Stiglitz before he addressed the Commonwealth Club in Palo Alto, after the release of his book the *Great Divide*. See also Joseph Stiglitz, *Rewriting the Rules of the American Economy: An Agenda for Growth and Shared Prosperity* (2015).

14. See, for example, Paul Krugman, "The Big Fail," *The New York Times*, January 7, 2013. The op-ed was an attack on austerity, an element of trickle-down economics.

15. This same observation was made by Ralph Nader in *Unstoppable: The Emerging Left-Right Alliance to Dismantle the Corporate State* (2014), where he refers to the classical liberalism that formerly inspired conservatives like those here (among them, Adam Smith, Ludwig von Mises, Friedrich Hayek, Wilhelm Röpke and Milton Friedman), however, so much of this has been forgotten that it will explored in depth herein.

16. *Washington Post*-ABC News Poll October 23–26, 2014—Midterm Elections.

17. See Russell Kirk, in the most important exposition on traditionalism, *The Conservative Mind: From Burke to Eliot* (Washington, D.C.: Regnery Publishing, Inc.; 1953, 1972, 1985, 2001), p. 8; see also pp. 7–11 and p. 460. Nash's book remains by far the best source for the origins of the ideology of conservatism. It was updated with a 1996 version which was republished with a new preface in 2006 and in these later editions Nash added treatments of neoconservatism and the Religious Right as in addition to, rather than viewed as here overwhelming and substituting for anticommunism and traditionalism. Also, Sidney Blumenthal's *The Rise of the Counter-Establishment* (1986) is useful as a supplement and for its elaboration on trickle-down, which it terms "supply-side."

18. This charismatic, erudite plutocratic style was on display for 33 years on the PBS show he hosted, *Firing Line*, in which he engaged with and debated guests—an important recurring guest was the liberal economist John Kenneth Galbraith. Buckley's father was from Texas and mother from New Orleans, so that, although he spent much of his life in Connecticut (after spending early years in Mexico and then later the UK and Europe), he was not raised with the Eastern establishment liberal Republican vision.

19. William F. Buckley, Jr., "Publisher's Statement," *National Review*, November 19, 1955. ©2015 *National Review*. Used with permission.

20. Paul Krugman, in *The Conscience of a Liberal* (New York: W. W. Norton; 2007), especially pp. 9–10, describes the precursor of "movement conservatism" as "new conservatism." Consistent with this characterization see, by the conservative R. Emmett Tyrell, founder and editor-in-chief of the conservative magazine *The American Spectator*, *After the Hangover: The Conservatives' Road to Recovery* (2010). However, the term "New Conservatism" also applied to a strain of conservatism led by the conservative Peter Viereck and admiring of liberal Democrats like Adlai Stevenson. See Richard Brookhiser, "Bill Buckley and the Future of Conservatism," *The Wall Street Journal*, June 2, 2009. Brookhiser was a close associate of Buckley and is a senior editor at *National Review* and author of *Right Time, Right Place: Coming of Age with William F. Buckley, Jr. and the Conservative Movement* (2009). Thus, the term "New Right" is used for the conservatism of Buckley and his allies, and the New Right of the 1950s is viewed herein as the precursor to movement conservatism.

21. See Mary Matalin, *NBC News Meet the Press*, September 2, 2007. This conservative focus is so consistent that *National Review* magazine observed, in its endorsement of presidential primary candidate Governor Mitt Romney (R-MA) for president in 2008, "His moral positions, and his instincts on taxes and foreign policy, are the same" as President Bush. "Romney for President," *National Review*, December 31, 2007. ©2015 *National Review*. Used with permission.

22. This quote comes from Buckley colleague Neal B. Freeman, as a panelist on the program "Buckley's Legacy: How Would the Patron Saint Turbo-Charge Conservatism?" C-SPAN, Yale University, New Haven, Connecticut, November 4, 2011. According to Freeman, it is a phrase that appeared in a memo circulated in the offices of *National Review*. See also Neal B. Freeman, "Goodbye to Most of That," *American Spectator*, November 2008. The reference is to a popular misquote from the Bible, that the lion shall lie down the lamb. The actual quote, from the English Standard Version of *Isaiah* 11:6, is: "The wolf shall dwell with the lamb, and the leopard shall lie down with the young goat, and the calf and the lion and the fattened calf together; and a little child shall lead them." David Stockman, mentioned earlier as Director of the Office of Management and Budget under President Reagan and a supply-side disciple early on, embodied this change, having attended Harvard Divinity School after his graduation from Michigan State University.

23. The term Religious Right refers to the politicization of Christianity by, among others, the Moral Majority, the Christian Coalition and the Family Research Council. Members of the Religious Right are referred to as Christian fundamentalists, a group including not only evangelical protestants (included in this group: Southern Baptists, Seventh-Day Adventists and the newer nondenominational Christian fundamentalists) but also conservative Roman Catholics. These two groups share, importantly, a view that life begins not at birth but at conception, which drives zero tolerance for abortion. And, they are staunchly anti-gay rights.

24. See Steven Perlberg, "Rick Santelli Started The Tea Party With A Rant Exactly 5 Years Ago Today—Here's How He Feels About It Now," *Business Insider*, February 19, 2014. See

also Thomas Frank, *Pity the Billionaire: The Hard-Times Swindle and the Unlikely Comeback of the Right* (New York: Metropolitan Books, Henry Holt and Company, LLC; 2012), p. 45. See also "Santelli's Tea Party Moment," February 19, 2009, *CNBC Video* (cnbc.com). Some Tea Party leaders themselves have credited Keli Carender as being the first Tea Partier. She held a rally in Seattle to protest the $787 billion stimulus bill three days before Santelli's rant, and afterwards was given the "tea party" label. However, it was Santelli who gave the movement its name and its national exposure. See Kate Zernike, "Unlikely Activist Who Got to the Tea Party Early," *The New York Times*, February 28, 2010.

25. See Stan Greenberg, James Carville and Erica Seifert, "Inside the GOP: Report on Focus Groups with Evangelical, Tea Party and Moderate Republicans," Democracy Corps, October 3, 2013, especially pp. 19–20.

26. See Joseph Stiglitz, *Globalization and Its Discontents* (2002) and Noreena Hertz, *The Silent Takeover: Global Capitalism and the Death of Democracy* (2002), especially p. 3.

27. See William Finnegan, "The Economics of Empire: Notes on the Washington Consensus," *Harper's*, May 2003, p. 41.

28. "Neoliberalism" is used both as synonymous with libertarianism and to refer to the liberalism practiced by the Democratic administration of Bill Clinton in the US and the New Labour administration of Tony Blair, which pursued a "Third Way" of deregulation and loose monetary policy but in the context of protecting social insurance. Additionally, the term "neoliberalism" carries a wholly different (albeit nearly forgotten) definition—that of the philosophy of Charles Peters, long-time editor of *The Washington Monthly*, who expounded on his version of neoliberalism (a version much closer to modern liberalism) in his book *Tilting at Windmills: An Autobiography* (1988).

29. Neoclassical economics, as defined by E. Roy Weintraub, economics professor at Duke University and associate editor of History of Political Economy in his essay, "Neoclassical Economics," consists of three assumptions: People rationalize preferences, maximize preferences (as do firms) and act based on full and relevant information.

30. In this regard, see Hung Ho-Fung, "America's Head Servant? The PRC's Dilemma in the Global Debt Crisis," *The New Left Review*, November-December 2009. That said, China has at least invested in its poor, more so than India, and that is to China's benefit and to the detriment of India. See Amartya Sen, "Why India Trails China," *The New York Times*, June 20, 2013.

31. Joseph E. Stiglitz, in *Globalization and Its Discontents*, (W. W. Norton & Company, New York; 2002), p. 195.

32. Thomas E. Mann and Norman J. Ornstein, *It's Even Worse Than It Looks: How The American Constitutional System Collided with the New Politics of Extremism* (New York: Basic Books; 2012) .

33. Angie Drobnic Holan, "All Politicians Lie. Some Lie More Than Others." *The New York Times*, December 13, 2015.

34. Moynihan broke with the neoconservatives in the 1980s. See Michael Lind, "A Tragedy of Errors," *The Nation*, February 23, 2004.

35. Daniel Patrick Moynihan, *Family and Nation* (Orlando, FL: Harvest/Harcourt Brace Jovanovich, 1986, 1987), pp. 190 and 214. So struck by the wisdom of this quote was Moynihan's colleague and fellow Harvard University professor, Lawrence Harrison, that he titled a book, addressed later herein, *The Central Liberal Truth* (2006).

36. Barack Obama, *The Audacity of Hope* (New York: Three Rivers Press, an imprint of Crown Publishing Group division of Random House, Inc.; 2006), p. 63.

37. John Maynard Keynes, *The General Theory of Employment, Interest and Money* (1936, Macmillan, 2007) pp. 383 and 384.

38. Irving Kristol, *Neoconservatism, The Autobiography of an Idea* (New York: Free Press, 1995), p. 233. See also Irving Kristol's *Reflections of a Neoconservative*, originally published in 1983 (Basic Books, Inc., New York).

39. While it may seem obvious that what is good for the rich is not necessarily good for everyone else, as recently as early 2014 Paul Krugman felt obligated to stress the point in several editorials: "Liberty, Equality, Efficiency," *The New York Times*, March 10, 2014;

"Wealth Over Work," *The New York Times*, March 24, 2014 and "Oligarchs and Money," *The New York Times*, April 27, 2014.

40. See Lawrence E. Harrison, *The Central Liberal Truth: How Politics Can Change Culture and Save It From Itself* (Oxford: Oxford University; 2006), pp. 36–37. Harrison addressed Latin America, but the same observations apply to the Islamic world, as will be seen.

41. In this regard, see *Winner-Take-All Politics: How Washington Made the Rich Richer—and Turned Its Back on the Middle Class* (2010) by political scientists Jacob S. Hacker and Paul Pierson.

42. Adam Smith, *An Inquiry into the Nature and Causes of the Wealth of Nations* , abbreviated *The Wealth of Nations* (New York: The Modern Library, Random House, Inc.; 1937; originally published 1776), pp. 78 and 79.

43. Nicholas Wapshott, *Keynes Hayek: The Clash That Defined Modern Economics* (New York: W. W. Norton & Company, Inc.; 2011), p. 206.

44. Eisenhower was Presbyterian; Nixon, Quaker; Reagan, Presbyterian; and George H. W. Bush, Episcopal.

45. The terms "left" and "right" in politics originated in 1789 in the National Assembly during the French Revolution. Those who sat on the right side supported concentrated power in the dethroned monarchy, the aristocracy and the Church—the *Ancien Régime* ("old order")—and were the conservatives. Those who sat on the left side supported the republic, secularism, civil liberties and dispersal of power, and included the classical liberals. The left today in the US consists of modern liberals; the right, conservatives.

46. The economic depression was diagnosed by Paul Krugman, in his 2012 book, *End This Depression Now!*, based on the definition of depression from John Maynard Keynes. This will be addressed in detail in Chapter 7. Krugman returned in his opinion pieces to the concept of depression—see especially "The Story of Our Time," *The New York Times*, April 29, 2013, wherein he linked austerity to depression.

47. Hillary Clinton's philosophy has been described as "new paleoliberalism" and "neo-paleoliberalism"—see Matthew Yglesias, Hillary Clinton's New Paleoliberalism," July 13, 2015, Vox.com, and David Brooks, "The New Old Liberalism," *The New York Times*, July 18, 2015.

48. The term "enlightened self-interest" is a translation of Alexis de Tocqueville's "la doctrine de l'intérêt bien entendu" from his *Democracy in America* (1835)—also translated as the doctrine of "self-interest rightly understood" or "interest well understood" (addressed later herein).

49. The establishment is represented most prominently by the US Chamber of Commerce, which recognized in 2014 that it may be in the best interests of business to back Senator Mary Landrieu (R-LA) against Republican challengers possibly beholden to the populist Tea Party. See Joe Nocera, "Chamber Lost Its Way in Right Turn," *The New York Times*, July 26, 2014.

50. "Right wing populism" combines a faith in an extensive safety net and a regulated free market with a deep distrust of elites and of government, which adherents believe does not work for them but, rather, liberal elites who make government work for those seen as getting a free ride from the system: the poor, minorities and immigrants—in return for votes. In addition to rejecting government, they reject liberal values—they promote illiberalism, as will be explored in detail herein—as they reject immigration reform, same sex marriage, and, historically, civil rights. Thus, while libertarians initially claimed the Tea Party as libertarian, polls have consistently shown self-described Tea Partiers divide roughly evenly between libertarians and social conservatives. See the following chapter for the distinction between right wing or conservative populism and liberal populism.

51. See David Brooks, "The Neocon Revival," *The New York Times*, August 2, 2013.

52. Milton Friedman, *Capitalism and Freedom* (Chicago: University of Chicago Press; 1962), p. 2. Elsewhere, libertarianism is defined as favoring "private property, individual liberty and limited government," and as a philosophy of free minds, free markets, fiscal responsibility and a non-interventionist foreign policy. "Free minds, free markets" is the slogan of the libertarian magazine *Reason*.

53. For different reasons, this opinion is joined by both a critic of libertarianism and a libertarian: See Samuel Freeman, "Illiberal Libertarians: Why Libertarianism Is Not a Liberal

View," *Philosophy and Public Affairs*, vol. 30 no. 2, pp. 105–151 and Walter Block, "Illiberal Libertarians: Why Libertarianism Is Not a Liberal View, and a Good Thing, Too; Reply to Samuel Freeman," *Journal of Libertarian Studies*, vol. 22 (2011), pp. 537–580.

54. For background on the John Birch Society, see Sean Wilentz, "Confounding Fathers: The Tea Party's Cold War Roots," *The New Yorker*, October 18, 2010. Wilentz is a professor of history at Princeton University.

55. See Lewis F. Powell, Jr., "Attack on American Free Enterprise System," a confidential memorandum to Eugene B. Sydnor, Jr., Chairman, Education Committee, U.S. Chamber of Commerce, August 23, 1971. A link to the memo appears with the blog post by Charlie Cray titled "The Lewis Powell Memo—Corporate Blueprint to Dominate Democracy," August 23, 2011, at the Greenpeace website.

56. The effect of Powell's memo and the think tanks, funding of conservative books and other publications and the growth of conservative mass media distribution that followed it are addressed by the former editor of *Harper's* magazine, Lewis H. Lapham, in his essay titled "Tentacles of Rage," *Harper's*, September 2004. It is also addressed in book form by former conservative and later founder of Media Matters for America, David Brock, in *The Republican Noise Machine* (2004). Powell's memo struck a responsive chord as businessmen in the 1970s had begun to express frustration that foundations such as the Ford Foundation, Rockefeller Foundation, Carnegie Foundation and Kellogg Foundation were taking corporate profits and channeling them into support of liberal institutions. The desire to re-channel corporate profits into conservative causes, with the goal of redistributing economic and political power in America upward, as before the New Deal, and repealing the New Deal, Great Society and their progeny, drove the founding of conservative think tanks modeled after the Brookings Institution (which had been intended as a nonpartisan think tank to conduct research into social policy, but which came to be seen by conservatives as liberal). Charles and David Koch also founded Citizens for a Sound Economy in 1984; in 2004 it split into Americans for Prosperity Foundation and FreedomWorks, entities that fund the Tea Party. Among other families involved in funding of conservative causes, the Coors family funded the Heritage Foundation from its founding in 1973 by Joseph Coors, Edward Feulner and Paul Weyrich. The Heritage Foundation, in 2012, spurred by the passage of the Affordable Care Act, created Heritage Action, a 501(c)(4) advocacy group which, incomprehensively, under IRS rules is a tax-exempt "social welfare" organization deemed "operated exclusively for the promotion of social welfare" because its funds are spent on "educational" efforts to influence elections so that *less* money is spent by the government on the promotion of social welfare (more on such organizations follows in Chapter 6). Heritage also received funding from the John M. Olin Foundation, founded in 1953 by the heir to the Olin chemical business (and disbanded in 2005). The Bradley Foundation, founded by Harry Bradley (along with Fred Koch and Robert Welch, a charter member of the John Birch Society founded in 1958) since 1985 has donated millions of dollars to the Heritage Foundation, the American Enterprise Institute and Americans for Tax Reform (a 501(c)(4) entity founded in 1985 by Grover Norquist). The American Enterprise Institute (founded in 1938 as the American Enterprise Association, it changed its name to the American Enterprise Institute in 1962) supported Goldwater in the 1964 election, received a big funding boost after Powell's memo and helped supply ideas to the Reagan campaigns and administration. Other conservative think tanks of note (and the years they were founded) are the Manhattan Institute (1978), the Claremont Institute (1979) and the Competitive Enterprise Institute (1984). Other influential conservative groups are the American Legislative Exchange Council (ALEC; founded 1973); the Federalist Society (founded in 1982) the Club for Growth (1999), the Senate Conservatives Action Fund (founded by former South Carolina Senator Jim DeMint in 2008) and American Crossroads/Crossroads GPS, founded by Karl Rove in 2010. Another major funder of conservative causes is the Scaife Foundation, established by the heir to the fortune of Andrew Mellon, Richard Mellon Scaife.

Businesses themselves organized to advocate for lower taxes and less regulation as far back as 1912, when the US Chamber of Commerce was founded, however, the Business Roundtable, founded by business groups in 1972, one year after the Powell memo, was founded to push this agenda harder, resulting in an increasingly conservative agenda for both groups.

57. Mark Ames, "Independent and Principled? Behind the Cato Myth," *The Nation*, April 20, 2012.

58. The journal and the essay appear at the website Mises.org. Rothbard was echoing sentiments expressed by Friedrich Hayek in his 1960 essay "Why I am Not a Conservative," addressed later.

59. Carl Oglesby, "The Vietnamese Crucible," from Oglesby's and Richard Shaull's *Containment and Change* (1967) and Carl Oglesby, *The Yankee and Cowboy War* (1977). See also Bill Kauffman, "Writer on the Storm," *Reason*, March 26, 2008 and "When the Left Was Right," *The American Conservative*, May 19, 2008.

60. See, for example, the text of a proposed commencement speech widely thought among conservatives to have been given by Neal Boortz at the 2012 commencement at his alma mater Texas A&M. In reality, although Boortz authored it, it was never given, but the text can be found at the website RedState.com. There Boortz champions conservatism and counts himself as one.

61. These liberals' views would be consistent with the views based on polling and described by Mark Warren in "The New American Center," *Esquire*, November 2013.

62. The highest was Riverside-San Bernardino-Ontario, California, with 14.2 percent; per the "Metropolitan Area Employment and Unemployment Summary," Bureau of Labor Statistics, March 18, 2011.

63. See Robert Draper, "Has the 'Libertarian Moment' Finally Arrived?" *The New York Times Magazine*, August 10, 2014; and see Paul Krugman, "Phosphorous and Freedom: The Libertarian Fantasy," *The New York Times*, August 11, 2014.

64. Although the Libertarian Party in the 2012 election recorded the most votes since it first ran a presidential and vice presidential ticket in 1972, that number was still a lower percentage of total votes cast than it received in the election of 1980 (in 2012 the party received 1,275,804 votes, or 0.99 percent of total votes cast, while in 1980 the party received 921,299 votes, which was 1.06 percent of total votes cast).

65. The cap on the level of wages so taxed also rose, to $113,700. See Stephen Ohlemacher, "Fiscal Cliff Deal Will Raise Taxes On 77 Percent of Americans: Tax Policy Center Analysis," *Huffington Post*, January 2, 2013.

66. Philip Bump, "Bernie Sanders Is an Avowed Socialist. 52 Percent of Democrats Are OK with That" The Fix Blog, *The Washington Post*, April 29, 2015.

67. Karl Marx and Friedrich Engels, *The Communist Manifesto* (New York: Washington Square Press Pocket Books; 1964; 13th Printing 1974), p. 93. Emphasis original. The version quoted was edited by Joseph Katz; introduction was by Francis B. Randall of Sarah Lawrence College; and the translation was by Samuel Moore. *The Communist Manifesto* was first published in 1848.

68. Ibid, pp. 134–135. Emphasis original.

69. The Nordic countries are Finland, Sweden, Norway, Denmark and Iceland.

70. See Bernie Sanders in an interview on ABC News' *This Week* with George Stephanopoulos, May 3, 2015.

71. Paul Krugman found much to recommend these policies in "Something Not Rotten in Denmark," *The New York Times*, October 19, 2015.

72. See also, Lane Kenworthy, "America's Social Democratic Future," *Foreign Affairs*, January-February 2014.

73. To his credit, the MSNBC commentator and host of MSNBC's "Hardball," Chris Matthews repeatedly raised the question of whether a declared socialist can be a Democrat—with, among others, Debbie Wasserman Schultz, Representative (D-FL) and Chair of the Democratic National Committee, Howard Dean, former Governor of Vermont and former Chair of the Democratic National Committee, and former Governor Michigan, Jennifer Granholm, also a Democrat.

74. A book which analyzes the ideology of conservatism historically through the present and concludes that it has always been about upwardly concentrating economic and political power is Corey Robin's *The Reactionary Mind: Conservatism from Edmund Burke to Sarah Palin* (2011). Robin is an associate professor of political science at Brooklyn College and the Graduate Center of the City University of New York.

75. From an interview, "Special Edition: Sojourners Presidential Forum," *The Situation Room*, CNN, June 4, 2007. And, in a speech at George Washington University widely recognized as a signal of a return to campaign mode for 2012, he returned to the theme that "we're all connected." George Packer, "Deepest Cuts," *The New Yorker*, April 25, 2011.

76. 2004 Obama Keynote Speech Transcript from the second day of the Democratic National Convention in Boston, Massachusetts. Barack Obama gave the keynote speech, C-SPAN, July 27, 2004.

77. A similar vision of balance appears in the book by Robert Reich, *Supercapitalism: The Transformation of Business, Democracy and Everyday Life* (2007).

78. See Al From, *The New Democrats and the Return to Power* (2013).

79. John Muir, *My First Summer in the Sierra* (1911).

80. Martin Luther King, "The Quest for Peace and Justice," Nobel Prize Lecture (December 11, 1964) from Nobel Lectures, Peace 1951–1970, Editor Frederick W. Haberman, Elsevier Publishing Company, Amsterdam, 1972, found at http://nobelprize.org/peace/laureates/1964/king-lecture.html.

81. This quote comes from one of President Roosevelt's speeches addressing the "Square Deal," delivered at the New York State Fair, September 7, 1903.

82. See Peter Baker, "Obama Finds a Bolder Voice on Race Issues," *The New York Times*, May 5, 2015.

83. The term "organic sociology" is used in Ludwig von Mises, *Socialism: An Economic and Sociological Analysis* (New Haven: Yale University Press, 1951), Chapter 18 ("The Society"), pp. 289–314.

84. See, for example, Kenneth M. Pollack, "ISIS is Losing in Iraq. But What Happens Next?" *The New York Times*, February 4, 2015. Pollack is a senior fellow at the Brookings Institution. Although the field of medicine is not addressed herein, improving communication in the medical profession and thereby saving lives is addressed by the physician Atul Gawande in several prominent books and articles—see especially *The Checklist Manifesto: How to Get Things Right* (2009).

85. Frank Bruni, "The G.O.P.'s Assertive God Squad," *The New York Times*, February 25, 2015.

86. George Packer in "A Confederacy of Cronies," *Mother Jones*, November/December 2002, p. 22; p. 24. George Packer is now a staff writer with *The New Yorker*, and authored, among other books, *The Assassins' Gate: America in Iraq* (2005) and *The Unwinding: An Inner History of the New America* (2013). He also authored an essay, "The Broken Contract. Inequality and American Decline," which appeared in the November/December 2011 issue of *Foreign Affairs*, and which expressed many of the same themes herein. Returning to crony capitalism, see also Jonathan Chait, *The Big Con: The True Story of How Washington Got Hoodwinked and Hijacked by Crackpot Economics* (New York: Houghton Mifflin; 2007). Chait is a senior editor at the *New Republic*. And, see "The Wrecking Crew: How a Gang of Right-Wing Con Men Destroyed Washington and Made a Killing," *Harper's*, August 2008, wherein Thomas Frank details how the crony capitalists came to power in an essay adapted from his book of the same name. Crony capitalism will be addressed in greater detail later herein.

87. Quoted by Mary Orndorff Troyan, in *The Birmingham News*, December 9, 2010.

88. See, for example, Bobby Jindal, "Holding Firm Against Gay Marriage," *The New York Times*, April 23, 2015.

89. James Carville, *We're Right, They're Wrong: A Handbook for Spirited Progressives* (New York: Random House; 1996), p. 87.

90. See Harold Meyerson, "For Retailers, Low Wages Aren't Working Out," *The Washington Post*, August 20, 2013.

91. This was, in fact, the concern raised by New York University economics professor Edward N. Wolff in *Top Heavy: The Increasing Inequality of Wealth in America and What Can be Done About It* (New York: The New Press; 2002), p. 67.

I

The Delusional Trickle-Down Conservative Republican Virtual Reality Bubble and Liberal Refusal to Confront It

Chapter One

The Delusional Trickle-Down Conservative Republican Virtual Reality Bubble and the 2012, 2014, and 2016 Elections and Beyond

In August of 2012, at the Republican National Convention in Tampa, Republican presidential nominee Mitt Romney was being criticized for not telling the truth, and two of his colleagues came forward in his defense. His campaign pollster Neil Newhouse bristled, saying the Romney campaign would not be run by fact checkers.[1] And former New York City Mayor Rudy Giuliani provided a non sequitur observation that in political speeches not all the facts are accurate.[2] In sum, the response of these Republican leaders showed a disturbing trait that would be repeated over and over again during the 2012 campaign and thereafter—that Republican leaders do not feel a responsibility to defend the truth because they don't really value truth—they value winning and acquiring power.

More broadly, the conservative political philosophy drives these Republican leaders to delude themselves that they are exempt from truthfulness, with various means that will be addressed herein. One of those means is the promotion of the cynical belief that everyone in politics and the media plays the same way, and that politics and the media constitute a market itself that will sort out truth. Another means is that it is imperative that they triumph, for they are the sole force for good in a world of much evil, thus they are exempt from having to be truthful, including regarding the truth that trickle-down has been tried in the past before and failed.[3] They engage in politics in a way that makes it seem easy, validating the uninformed opinions of their base of conservatives who get their "news" by watching Fox News Channel, listening to Rush Limbaugh, and reading Drudge Report and thereby imagine themselves to be informed of the facts. It is easy to win by such deception but campaigning on such deception undermines our democracy, and policymaking based on delusion undermines our economy, democracy, institutions and health.

Trickle-down conservatism long ago abandoned fact-based arguments for "the sell," in which it has become unhinged from reality and factual analysis. In this strategy, facts—which have always before been commonly understood as accurate although some additional facts may be appropriate to provide context lest they be misinterpreted—now are nothing other than words used by Republicans in selling their brand. And, that conservative—Republican—brand is increasingly based on stoking the anger, fear and unfounded suspicions of ill-informed voters that America is in decline, threatened by social and economic collapse, with Islamic radicalism threatening its very existence (the definition of an "existential" threat).[4] After Republicans had claimed President Obama was not born in the United States, was not qualified to be president, was a socialist tool of a global Marxist-Muslim conspiracy bent on implementing the anti-colonial, anti-white, anti-American socialist ideology of his Kenyan father—*in 2015, in President Obama's seventh year in the presidency*—Rudy Giuliani added that he did not believe President Obama loves America. The event at which he said this was a private group dinner in New York for Wisconsin Governor Scott Walker. Asked for comment, Walker said he, himself, had never asked the president about it. The real shock, however, came when a poll was released showing *only 11% of Republicans disagreed* with Rudy Giuliani.[5]

Statements like those above and others by Romney-Ryan 2012 campaign supporters and conservative commentators (many of whom predicted Republican victory in 2012[6]) illustrate that many influential Republicans and their base live in a virtual reality apart from the reality of their fellow Americans. Bruce Bartlett, who held senior policy roles in the administrations of Ronald Reagan and George H. W. Bush and served on the staff of Representatives Jack Kemp and Ron Paul, in an article written after the 2012 election, accused conservatives of living in their own virtual reality bubbles.[7] Coincidentally, the comedian Bill Maher had, on his HBO show in 2011 instituted an occasional segment in which he placed a "typical Republican voter" on the stage in a giant clear "fact-proof" plastic bubble and from the outside debunked conservative nonsense with facts, while the person inside the bubble remained oblivious to the critiques. And, in late 2015, economist Paul Krugman joined in, accusing conservatives of living in a bubble impervious to inconvenient facts.[8]

Thomas E. Mann of the Brookings Institution and Norman Ornstein of the American Enterprise Institute (whose book, *It's Even Worse Than It Looks*, was addressed in the Introduction) wrote an op-ed in early 2012 for *The*

Washington Post, the title of which summarized their conclusion: "Let's Just Say It: The Republicans Are the Problem."[9] Looking back on the elections afterwards Ornstein commented on the massive asymmetry of the misrepresentation of facts on the part of the Republicans and deemed it the great unreported story of the campaign.[10]

Conservatives who got their "news" by watching Fox News Channel, listening to Rush Limbaugh, and reading Drudge Report were shocked by Mitt Romney's defeat. In contrast, liberals were not surprised if they followed two websites whose authors did not conduct polls themselves, but applied statistical analysis to polls taken by others—both accurately predicted days before the election a most likely outcome of an Obama win with over 300 electoral votes.[11]

As will be shown herein, the Republican Party has become the party for those who *think* they think about politics. Republicans live in a delusional bubble in which they are wrong about the facts, wrong about the origins of their own conservative political philosophy, and wrong about public opinion. Their political opinions are far too often based on misrepresentations and half-truths fed into their conservative bubble, presented by their "intellectual leaders": entertainers, Republican propagandists playing journalists on television and charismatic politicians with only a superficial understanding of the Constitution, American history and facts generally. Magic is the art of deception, and conservatism is the art of deception in politics,[12] surviving because of the disregard of knowledge and promotion of ignorance that is the litmus test demanded of their followers by conservative leaders.

THE ROMNEY-RYAN CAMPAIGN: "WE BUILT IT" ON DECEPTION

Congressman Paul Ryan's acceptance speech of the 2012 vice presidential nomination was widely criticized for its inaccuracies, even by a commentator with the conservative Fox News Channel.[13] By far the best example of Republican deception, however, was the success of Mitt Romney in the first presidential debate of the 2012 election campaign, and that success serves as a warning to Democratic presidential candidates in 2016 and beyond.

The Critical Importance of the First 2012 Presidential Debate

On the last round of Sunday talk shows (September 30, 2012) before the first presidential debate, conservatives led with a full court press of deception: Congressman Paul Ryan on *Fox News with Chris Wallace*, Ralph Reed on NBC's *Meet the Press* and New Jersey Governor Chris Christie on ABC News' *This Week with George Stephanopoulos* all made abundantly clear that the Republican pre-debate strategy would be to double down on their virtual reality of untruths about the Obama administration's record and untruths and vagueness about their own policy proposals. This would be complemented by Mitt Romney launching a barrage of deception in the debate. Not only would this hobble the president by forcing him to use valuable time to correct the record rather than talk about his own ideas, but it also led him into his habit of pedantic lecturing, forcing him to lose touch with the audience. As is recounted by Mark Halperin and John Heilemann in their account of the 2012 election, *Double Down* (2013), the president and his advisors were clearly rattled after the debate.

One exchange in particular on one talk show the Sunday before the debate especially tipped the Republicans' hand. George Stephanopoulos on ABC News' *This Week* confronted Governor Christie with a quote from President Obama, in which the president accurately diagnosed Governor's Romney's scheme as more trickle-down nonsense. When Stephanopoulos asked how Governor Christie, if he were on stage in the debate the following Wednesday night, would respond to that, the Governor replied that he would tell the president to stop lying. An incredulous Stephanopoulos asked the Governor where the lie was, to which Governor Christie responded that Governor Romney was not talking about tax cuts for the wealthy. Stephanopoulos pointed out that Governor Romney proposed to lower the wealthy's marginal tax rates into a percentage range in the 20s. Governor Christie then agreed that Governor Romney would cut rates but that due to loss of *unspecified* deductions and *unspecified* loopholes the wealthy would not see their taxes lowered. Stephanopoulos incredulously persisted regarding details, and Christie persisted in refusing to elaborate—also failing to give assurance that the top tax rates would not be cut absent the abolition of offsetting deductions and loopholes, or that taxes on the middle class and poor would not be raised to offset these cuts in the top rates.

Like the big buddy of the kid running for kindergarten class president who promised candy for everyone at lunch, Governor Christie had dutifully fended off the question of *how* his friend would accomplish this—the problem was, however, what his friend had proposed was to cut tax rates to a level that would reduce revenues by $5 trillion over ten years, and to offset this reduction by eliminating deductions worth $5 trillion over that same period—without offering a single example of such a deduction; or pledging to not cut tax rates absent such deductions; or pledging to not cut deductions that would raise taxes for the middle class to make up for the cut in tax rates skewed toward the rich.

The first debate was famous for its dismal performance by President Obama. Governor Romney lectured the president that, as he had told his boys when they were growing up, repeating something that was untrue will not ultimately render it truthful. The topic was, as it was with Governor Christie, the $5 trillion in cuts in tax rates balanced by undisclosed eliminations of deductions. Romney, by stressing that he did not promise a $5 trillion tax cut, deflated the president's attempt to focus on the ridiculous request for trust in Congress regarding the deductions to be eliminated. Romney also chastised the president for going too easy on the financial industry in Dodd-Frank—while a Republican talking point was that Dodd-Frank had been a totally unnecessary intrusion in the free market in the first place. He repeated his claim that his own health care program in Massachusetts had been unlike the Affordable Care Act—although he had declared in a 2009 op-ed in *USA Today* that his program was based on the individual mandate to purchase private health insurance, enforced with a "tax penalty"—as is the Affordable Care Act—proudly observing that this discourages abuse of the system by "free riders."[14] He also repeated the claims that his proposed substitute for the Affordable Care Act covered pre-existing conditions, which it did not, and that the Congressional Budget Office (CBO) reported the Affordable Care Act would force 20 million people to lose their insurance coverage, which it did not. And, he repeated the claim that President Obama was cutting Medicare by $716 billion, when in fact, through the Affordable Care Act, reimbursements to hospitals were reduced by $716 billion over the next ten years, resulting in a savings to Medicare. He repeated his claim that under President Obama drilling permits on federal lands had decreased by half. However, according to Bureau of Land Management (BLM) statistics, the number of Applications for Permits to Drill (APDs) on onshore federal lands issued annually during the Obama administration had averaged only about 20 percent fewer than under the preceding Bush administration, and the number had steadily risen during the previous three years. As for APDs issued for offshore wells, this number was skewed negatively due to a moratorium instituted to re-evaluate safety standards and compliance in the wake of the *Deepwater Horizon* blowout in April 2010 resulting in 11 deaths and the worst oil spill in history (debate continues regarding ultimate size, but government estimates placed it about 16 times as large as the *Exxon Valdez* spill).

The critical turning point in the debates, when the president regained his footing, came in the second debate, before CNN's Candy Crowley as moderator, when President Obama asserted to Governor Romney, regarding the attack on Benghazi, Libya, that the day after the attack he had stood in the Rose Garden and condemned this "act of terror". Governor Romney replied with what had become a conservative talking point, alleging that the president had not called it "an act of terror" at the time—prompting an exchange between the two that led to the president urging referral to the transcript, and moderator Candy Crowley clarifying that the president was correct.

And, in fact, a review of the transcript of the Rose Garden speech of September 12, 2012 revealed that President Obama said regarding the Benghazi attack[15]:

> No acts of terror will ever shake the resolve of this great nation, alter that character, or eclipse the light of the values that we stand for. Today we mourn four Americans who represent the very best of the United States of America. We will not waiver in our commitment to see that justice is done for this terrible act. And make no mistake, justice will be done.

Thus, in the delusional trickle-down bubble, it was reported that Candy Crowley and CNN had just revealed their favoritism toward the president—the president had not condemned the Benghazi attack by using the precise words "an act of terror" but rather condemned "acts of terror" such as that in Benghazi.[16] Crowley was criticized not only from the right but also from the mainstream for failing to play the role of enabler of the Republicans' deception—demonstrating the dual threat to democracy observed by Mann and Ornstein in their book published only months before. (Research by *The New York Times* later revealed, as administration intelligence had indicated, al Qaeda had not been behind the attack; instead the attack had been fueled in large part, as alleged by the administration, by reaction toward an insulting video titled "Innocence of Muslims" that began in neighboring Egypt and spread to Libya.[17]) Ominously, however, the Republicans had validated their strategy of airing on weekend talk shows and in the following presidential debates misleading and false talking points more appropriate for the friendly confines of Fox News Channel, putting Democrats on notice for 2016.

An Aside: The Uncomfortable (for Conservatives) Truth of Obamacare: It's Based on a Conservative Idea

Ironically, for all the conservative opposition to it, prominent conservatives had conceived of and implemented the main ideas that formed the model for the Patient Protection and Affordable Care Act (alternatively the "Affordable Care Act;" "PPACA;" "ACA;" and "Obamacare"): An individual mandate to purchase private health insurance and enforcement of that mandate via a tax penalty. Their proposal would use the marketplace to provide affordable health care, enforce personal responsibility and bring down health care costs. It was originally the idea of Stuart Butler, who, while working at the conservative Heritage Foundation, proposed it in 1989. The idea was later advocated by the Nobel Prize-winning libertarian conservative economist Milton Friedman in a November 12, 1991 article in *The Wall Street Journal.*[18] Robert E. Moffitt of the Heritage Foundation defended the individual mandate as a constitutional, nonpartisan health care solution in "Choice and Consequences: Transparent Alternatives to the Individual Insurance Mandate" in the *Harvard Health Policy Review*, Spring 2008. The 2012 Republican presidential candidate Mitt Romney, as Governor of Massachusetts from 2003 through 2007, instituted a health care system in his state using the individual mandate enforced via a tax penalty, and he endorsed his state's approach as a model for President Obama in the 2009 *USA Today* op-ed cited earlier.[19] And, an April 2010 Congressional Research Service memo titled "The PPACA Penalty Provision and the Internal Revenue Service" observed that the Affordable Care Act incorporated *every element of the original Heritage proposal.*

Yet, in 2012, Stuart Butler, in a misleading op-ed in *USA Today* disavowed responsibility for the individual mandate,[20] for which he was called out in *The Wall Street Journal* online blog.[21] And, famously, Governor Romney vowed to rescind the Affordable Care Act if elected president. Conservatives, most stridently 2012 vice presidential candidate Representative Paul Ryan (R-WI), Speaker John Boehner (R-OH), and Senator Mitch McConnell (R-KY), joined by former individual mandate supporters Governor Romney and former House Speaker and presidential candidate Newt Gingrich, stepped up their misleading criticism of "government takeover of health care."

Amidst the fear expressed by Tea Party favorite Senator Ted Cruz (R-TX) that Americans will *like* Obamacare,[22] Republicans fought more tenaciously than ever pursuant to their trickle-down delusion, attempting to repeal Obamacare, aided by the botched rollout of the Affordable Care Act website. Ironically, funded by plutocrats and supported on the ground by a disproportionately large and growing percentage of elderly white retirees dependent on Social Security and Medicare *provided by the federal government* to cover their retirements and healthcare, the Tea Party led opposition to Obamacare pursuant to the faith that the federal government—again, except the military—is incapable of doing anything right. However, even after more than 50 votes in the House of Representatives to repeal it, the Republicans continued to be thwarted either in the Senate or with a presidential veto.

The Deception of the "We Built It" Theme

An especially memorable distortion of the facts is recalled in the title to this section. At a campaign stop in July 2012, President Obama returned to a theme he often stressed, as observed in the Introduction: connectedness. He observed that, notwithstanding our sense of rugged individualism, if we build a successful business, we should recognize that the hardworking people who came before us built the schools that educated us, built the roads and bridges we may be sending our goods over, and invented the Internet we use for accepting our company's orders. In short, he observed, "If you've got a business—you didn't build that. Somebody else made that happen. The Internet didn't get invented on its own. Government research created the Internet so that all the companies could make money off the Internet. The point is, is that when we succeed, we succeed because of our individual initiative, but also because we do things together."[23]

The theme was reiterated days later—but this time by Governor Romney, who indicated he full well understood what the president meant as he acknowledged that everyone in business benefits from help—from banks, investors, their parents, teachers, those who provide public services.[24] Nonetheless, the Romney campaign launched a commercial based on the misrepresentation that the president had said that if you owned a business, you hadn't built it. Ironically, the star of the commercial, business owner Jack Gilchrist, appeared on Fox News Channel with Neil Cavuto and, in answer to prompting by Cavuto, offered a story about a teacher who was instrumental in his own life, and agreed that the government building of the Interstate highway system and the Internet were important to his success and the building of his business as well.[25]

Regardless, "We Built It" signs were distributed at the 2012 Republican National Convention, and Ann Romney, in her speech to humanize her husband, said of the son of George Romney, the former Chairman of American Motors, Governor of Michigan and Republican presidential candidate that he was not handed his success but built it himself. Delegates dutifully began chanting "We built it!"—the official theme for the convention on its opening day.[26] Another irony of the theme, beyond its application to a candidate already born at the top was that the convention was held in an arena which was built with public funds. The Romney-Ryan campaign produced numerous other factual distortions as well.[27]

The Romney-Ryan Campaign's Aloofness from Ordinary Americans

Among the candidates in the 2012 Republican presidential primary, former Massachusetts Governor Mitt Romney, Minnesota Congresswoman Michele Bachmann and Texas Governor Rick Perry all expressed concern that 47 percent of Americans do not pay federal income tax. Yet, according to the Tax Policy Center of the Urban Institute and Brookings Institution, while 46.4 percent of households paid no federal income tax for 2011, 61 percent of them paid payroll taxes. Of the remaining 18.1 percent of households that paid neither income nor payroll taxes, more than half were elderly (10.3 percent of total households); over one-third nonelderly with income under $20,000 (6.9 percent of total households); and about one in twenty nonelderly with income over $20,000 (*thus, 0.9 percent—less than 1 percent of total households—was nonelderly with income over $20,000 and paid neither income nor payroll taxes*).[28] Additionally, the Tax Policy Center observed that this relatively high number of households that paid no income tax was an aberration due to the down economy. It predicted that in 2013 43 percent of tax units would pay no federal income taxes and, due to rising real incomes and fixed-dollar tax guidelines the percentage would be further reduced over time to an estimated 34 percent by 2024.[29]

Regardless, in marked contrast to the complaints of the trickle-down conservative Republicans that 47 percent of households didn't pay income tax, President Reagan, hero to conservatives and Republicans, passed an expansion of the earned-income tax credit (EITC) as part of the 1986 Tax Reform Act[30] proudly declaring it pro-family, anti-poverty and job-creating.[31] Similarly, a previous generation of Republicans often observed that when the income tax first went into effect in 1913, it was intended that it would only be paid by a minority of taxpayers. It provided for a $3,000 exemption for single filers—in 2014 dollars, $72,225—and a $4,000 exemption—in 2014 dollars, $96,300—for married couples.[32] These levels of exemption applied today would exempt somewhere around 70 percent of income earners—much more than today.

Governor Romney was the early presumptive favorite for the Republican nomination. In his acceptance speech after his victory in the New Hampshire primary, he attributed to those who criticized his campaign "the bitter politics of envy," and elaborated on his convictions in an interview with Matt Lauer on *The Today Show* the next morning, attributing it to class warfare and accusing President Obama of encouraging this in his campaign.[33]

During the Republican presidential debates Governor Romney challenged Texas Governor Perry to a $10,000 bet—which Perry wisely refused to take, and another time joined with all the other Republican presidential candidates in rejecting a moderator's proposal to cut the deficit consisting of a 10:1 ratio of spending cuts to tax increases.

In response to questions, Romney estimated his effective tax rate was about 15 percent (the capital gains tax rate at the time)—except, that is, for the income from his speaking fees, which he said was "not very much." *The New York Times* observed he made in excess of $374,000 in speaking fees over the previous year—an amount that, *alone*, would nearly put him in the top 1 percent of American households in income.[34] On the campaign trail, he volunteered that he was not concerned about the very poor because of government's safety net.[35]

When, after much pressure, he released his tax return for 2010, he revealed his effective tax rate that year was 13.9 percent on his $21.7 million income (mostly from income held in a blind trust, with as much as $8 million in accounts in the Cayman Islands and Bermuda, and a Swiss bank account that was closed in 2010). By comparison, the average effective tax rate paid by a family that made $70,000—whose income was ordinary income from wages—was 20 percent.[36] His effective tax rate was so low because the bulk of his income was from capital gains—although he could honestly tell a group of unemployed Floridians in Tampa in June 2011 that he also was unemployed[37] —while he was making more income *in one day* (about

$58,000) from blind trusts which by law he could not "work" *than the average American family made in a year*. Thus, by his own admission Governor Romney revealed the function of the (then) 15 percent capital gains tax rate for himself and similarly situated fellow Americans: To subsidize the lifestyles of the idle rich. Under Congressman Paul Ryan's tax proposal, Governor Romney would have paid an effective tax rate of just *0.82 percent* in federal income taxes in 2010.[38]

Tellingly, Governor Romney had a pre-election exchange with George Stephanopoulos, who asked the Governor if $100,000 was middle income—to which the Governor responded that it is not—$200,000 to $250,000 is.[39] In reality, according to the Census Bureau's then-current 2012 report, middle income—defined as the 60 percent of American households whose incomes fell between the 20th percentile and 80th percentile—was between $20,262 and $101,582 (median was $50,054). The top 2 to 3 percent of household incomes were in the range of $200,000 to $250,000 and less—Governor Romney's definition of "middle income."

Despite its proposed policy similarities with the administration of President George W. Bush, the Romney-Ryan campaign disabused anyone of supposed similarities with President Bush's sentimental "compassionate conservatism" and "ownership society," proposing trickle-down on steroids (with a gift to defense contractors):

1. Cut federal revenue over the next 10 years by nearly $5 trillion[40]:

a. Personal income taxes: Make permanent the Bush federal income tax cuts, then cut those rates by 20 percent across the board and repeal the taxes enacted by the Affordable Care Act;
b. Interest, dividends and capital gains taxes: Maintain current tax rates;
c. Estate taxes: Abolish;
d. Alternative Minimum Tax: Abolish;
e. Corporate taxes: Cut the corporate income tax rate from 35 percent to 25 percent and make permanent the research and experimentation tax credit.

2. Repeal the financial reforms of Dodd-Frank;

3. Oppose the DREAM Act, which would allow those children of illegal immigrants who came to this country before age 16 to earn citizenship by service in the military or securing a college education (during the Republican presidential primary debates, he even opposed the practice of providing in-state college tuition to the children of illegal immigrants, defended by Texas Governor Rick Perry—in lieu of these measures, Governor Romney expressed support for "self-deportation"[41]);

4. Raise "core" defense spending (i.e., not including many additional war expenses) to 4 percent of GDP—a 61 percent increase at the end of a decade-long cycle over the Obama administration spending plans of about 3.2 percent GDP.[42]

5. Convert Medicaid into block grants to the states, cut spending on Medicaid and other programs (such as Pell Grants and student loans), and cap federal spending at below 20 percent of GDP (for recent years it was slightly above 22 percent).

6. Make it more difficult for unions to organize.

7. Convert Medicare to a voucher program for Americans under age 55.

8. Repeal the Affordable Care Act.

According to a study conducted by the Tax Policy Center, under Governor Romney's proposed tax policies, the top 0.1 percent would see after-tax incomes rise by 4.4 percent, while the bottom 95 percent would see after-tax incomes fall by about 1.2 percent—with their taxes rising by about $500 on average. The study also found that, contra a Romney campaign pledge, it was not mathematically possible to design a revenue-neutral plan preserving existing incentives for savings and investment and that would not result in a net tax cut for high-income taxpayers and a net tax increase for lower- and/or middle-income taxpayers under Governor Romney's tax plan.[43]

Additionally, Governor Romney had expressed admiration for the budget plan of his vice presidential running mate, Chairman of the House Budget Committee Congressman Paul Ryan—Chairman Ryan's proposal, like Governor Romney's, also proposed to repeal the Affordable Care Act, cut federal spending on Medicaid and convert it into block grants to the states and convert Medicare into a voucher program for those under age 55. A study by the Congressional Budget Office calculated that institution of these changes would take away health insurance for 48 million Americans (32 million due to repeal of the Affordable Care Act, 15 million from Medicaid cuts as Medicaid is converted to a block grant system, and 1 million from conversion of Medicare to a voucher system).[44]

Congressman Ryan, however, additionally proposed to resurrect President George W. Bush's efforts to privatize Social Security. In the interim since President Bush left office however, a report by the Congressional Research Service found that the combination of bubbles bursting in housing and the stock market had, by 2010, resulted in a decline in the average American family's household net worth to $77,300—*below the level of 1989.*[45] Americans already have 401(k) plans for investments. They need social insurance, which Social Security provides.

CONSERVATISM'S MORAL UNIVERSE OF "MAKERS" VERSUS "TAKERS"

> There are 47 percent of the people who will vote for the president no matter what. All right, there are 47 percent who are with him, who are dependent upon government, who believe that they are victims, who believe the government has a responsibility to care for them, who believe that they are entitled to health care, to food, to housing, to you-name-it. That's an entitlement. And the government should give it to them. And they will vote for this president no matter what . . . These are people who pay no income tax . . . [M]y job is not to worry about those people. I'll never convince them they should take personal responsibility and care for their lives.—*Governor Mitt Romney, May 17, 2012, Boca Raton, Florida*[46]

> Right now about 60 percent of the American people get more in benefits in dollar value from the federal government than they pay back in taxes. So we're going to a majority of takers versus makers.—*Congressman Paul Ryan, June 2010 edition of* Washington Watch, *quoted in* Mother Jones.[47]

The plutocrats who fund the Republican Party have skillfully fanned the flames of resentment from the birth of the Tea Party movement[48] through the narrative that the Republican Party and its "Makers" lost the 2012 election because of President Obama's "gifts" to "Takers" like African Americans, Hispanics and younger voters (especially young women) and on through the 2016 campaign. An especially good example of this narrative was presented on election night 2012 by conservative commentator and Fox News Channel personality Bill O'Reilly, who explained that Mitt Romney was going to lose because the white establishment was in the minority. O'Reilly elaborated on the essential difference between the white establishment and those other voters now in the majority, in terms reminiscent of Governor Romney's "47 percent" comment, saying that half the country wants government to give them "stuff," and President Obama ran on obliging them.[49] In a phone call with supporters the week after the election, Governor Romney echoed O'Reilly's analysis, observing that President Obama had given "gifts" to those outside of the older white male establishment—specifically African Americans, Hispanics and young people—to buy their votes.[50]

Ezra Klein, writer for *The Washington Post* and commentator for MSNBC, summarized Mitt Romney's "political cosmology"[51] as one in which the Democrats bribe the moochers while Republicans try to free the makers with tax cuts and deregulation. Surveys have revealed that this is a widely held view among Republicans: That Democratic support for policies aimed at helping the middle class and poor directly, as well as helping illegal aliens, is viewed as simply buying votes of moochers with promises of government benefits.[52] Thus, Republicans are hobbled in their attempts to help the middle class and poor not only because it goes against their trickle-down philosophy but also because they see it as helping the enemy Democrats win, leading Republicans to oppose government policies to save the American economy, American democracy, and the health of their fellow Americans.

Insight into the mindset of Mitt Romney's richest backers was provided in a fascinating post-election interview by Ezra Klein with Chrystia Freeland, Liberal Member of the Canadian Parliament for Toronto Centre, former editor of Thomson Reuters Digital, a frequent guest political commentator and former US managing editor of the *Financial Times*, and author of *Plutocrats: The Rise of the New Global Super-Rich and the Fall of Everyone Else* (2012). In the interview, she recounted in vivid detail the attitudes of the super-rich backers who had flown into Logan Airport in Boston for the Romney victory party on election night, fully confident of victory—and she expressed her own astonishment at their stunned disbelief when their candidate lost to the hated President Obama.[53] (Freeland was joined in her astonishment regarding the disconnect of the super-rich with election reality by James Carville, in a post-election interview in *Rolling Stone.*[54] And Republicans in the runup to the 2016 election are displaying a similar degree of disconnect from reality regarding Hillary Clinton in 2016 as they did toward Barack Obama in 2012.[55])

Freeland found that the sentiments behind Governor Romney's pre-election "47 percent" and post-election "gift" comments were shared by the super-rich. She elaborated on the change in values that is the main subject of this work—the mistaken, self-serving and comfortable idea that what is good for the rich and business is good for everyone, and that when businessmen are successful they are serving the collective good. She added that with the context of the consensus among the super-rich that what is good for them is good for everyone, it is easier to understand how radical President Obama appears to them—for he is the most prominent person in politics to question this attitude since the advent of trickle-down three decades ago, and they know it.

Ezra Klein then added his own insights, foretelling dissatisfaction on the part of the rich that they, themselves would verbalize later, observing regarding their perceptions of President Obama that they did not care for the lack of admiration he showed toward them. Similarly, two prominent examples of the rich's feelings of persecution were observed by Paul Krugman in a 2013 op-ed.[56] The first was a statement by Robert Benmosche, CEO of American International Group (AIG), which played a famously prominent role in the global financial crisis of 2008 by issuing debt guarantees far beyond its ability to honor. He criticized the uproar by the federal government—which bailed out AIG—over the massive bonuses granted by AIG while recovering with the government's help. In an interview chronicled in *The Wall Street*

Journal, Benmosche said the uproar over bonuses was intended to stir up people's anger and get people out with their pitchforks and hangmen's nooses like in the Deep South.[57] The second, from Stephen Schwarzman, chairman of the large private equity firm the Blackstone Group, addressed attempts to close the carried-interest loophole that enabled hedge fund and private equity managers like him to pay only 15 percent tax (raised to 20 percent under President Obama) on much of their income, and analogized it to Hitler's invasion of Poland in 1939.

Krugman, in a later op-ed, observed a similar theme in a letter to the editor of *The Wall Street Journal* published in early 2014, in which Tom Perkins, billionaire co-founder of venture capital firm Kleiner Perkins Caulfield & Byers, analogized Nazi Germany's war on the Jews to a progressive war on the rich and warned of a potential progressive *Kristallnacht.*[58] A later editorial in *The Wall Street Journal* supported Perkins and warned that liberals were abusing power to punish rich opponents[59] —this just weeks after several aides of Republican Governor Chris Christie of New Jersey had to resign for using government power to shut down a busy bridge to punish Christie's Democratic political opponents.

The moral views of the super-rich create an interesting parallel with a criticism of liberalism in the 1960s: Sixties liberalism established a "culture of dependency" on top-down control of the government, and instilled a "sense of entitlement" on the part of the beneficiaries of the welfare programs that destroyed their will to work and imperiled the capitalist system. An equally valid criticism of conservatism under the influence of its trickle-down vision, however, based on the above is that over the past three decades a *new* culture of dependency has been created—a culture of dependency on top-down control of the wealthy and business—accompanied by a sense of entitlement on their part as "job creators"—yet, policies supporting this constituency result in ever more income and wealth redistributed upward while real wages fall among the rest of the population, also imperiling the capitalist system—the very system they profess to support.

Critically, however, what is plaguing our political system is worse than simply the rich putting their self-interest above the interests of other people. The key problem plaguing our economic system is that the trickle-down delusion—that we will all be better off as a nation if we *all* put the interests of the rich above the interests of other people, ensuring that they do better—is held by a substantial percentage of Americans, the vast majority of whom are not rich. This leads them to support trickle-down policies of the Republican Party that upwardly distribute economic and political power and to believe that Democrats secretly also acknowledge that the rich are the economy's heroes, so that Democratic attempts to use government to directly help the poor and middle class are simply cynical attempts to buy them off, with no potential to actually help them.

A quote from a focus group member in Raleigh, North Carolina, identified with the Tea Party, appearing in a 2013 report by James Carville and Stanley Greenberg on the attitudes of evangelicals, Tea Partiers and moderate Republicans summarized this attitude toward the Democrats and President Obama[60]:

> The whole middle-class-up economy format is completely ridiculous. Because who's going to give the middle class their money? The upper class. The middle class isn't going to make money coming out of nowhere. They've got to get a job. And who gives the jobs? The rich people. So if you take all the rich people's money, they're not going to be able to give anybody a job. Just it's so backwards. He keeps talking about a strong middle class. I don't want a strong middle class. I want to make all the middle class rich people, because then you've got even more rich people who can give more jobs. It's like a—it's just ridiculous.

This is the attitude that must be overcome by Democrats if they are to defeat trickle-down: That Democrats are cynically manipulating the weaknesses of the middle class and recklessly daring the rich to withdraw their hard-earned fortunes from the American economy, thereby risking the destruction of millions of jobs. Reflecting on the sad delusion of members of the middle class that their fate is tied more closely to government unburdening the rich than their own initiative supported by America's institutions—and the *fear* underlying this attitude—one cannot help but wonder how we got here. That is the subject of Chapters 2 through 9; but first, developments since the 2012 election are addressed below.

2013: Hostage-Ransoming of Debt Default to Provoke Obamacare Repeal

Senate Minority Leader Mitch McConnell (R-KY), at the end of the debt crisis in August 2011, declared he and other Republicans had learned that the debt default could be used as a hostage to ransom in exchange for favored conservative policies.[61] This lesson had not been lost on former Reagan administration Attorney General Ed Meese and the numerous well-funded conservative groups who hit upon shutting down the federal government in October of 2013 and later threatening default on the federal debt in an attempt to repeal, then defund, and finally delay implementation of Obamacare.[62]

Going against them were the facts that the Affordable Care Act had been passed and signed into law a full three years before. Democrats held not only a majority in the Senate but also the Executive Office—President Obama having just become the first president since President Eisenhower (in 1952 and 1956) to win two terms with more than 50 percent of the vote. And numerous polls showed consistent majorities opposing shutting down the government to force action on Obamacare, and supporting either keeping Obamacare unchanged or strengthening it.[63] The "hostage-taking" failed miserably.

The 2014 Election's Lesson: The Facts Are in the Democrats' Favor But Won't Help Them If They Run from Them

Polls taken in October 2014, on the eve of the 2014 midterm elections, revealed that for voters who leaned Republican they did so mainly because they wanted, specifically, more job creation and, generally, a more vibrant economy. When President Obama took office, the economy was losing 700,000 jobs per month; by October 2014 it was averaging adding over 200,000. The economy after six years in office under President Obama had added 6.7 million jobs, while at this point under President George W. Bush the economy had added just 3.1 million—and under President Bush over that same period government employment was up 1.2 million while under President Obama government employment was down by 600,000.[64] Through June 2015, the private sector had 64 straight months of private sector job growth, the longest streak on record. And, as revealed by the Labor Department's monthly report issued in February 2015, since November 1, 2014 employers had hired more than a million workers—the most job growth in three months in 17 years, *and more workers were hired in 2014 than in any year since 1999.*[65]

When President Obama took office, the Great Recession was underway and the unemployment rate was 7.8%, and it deepened to 10% by October of 2009; by October 2014 it was 5.9% and by December it fell to 5.6%. Memorably, Governor Romney had promised during the 2012 campaign to get the unemployment rate down to 6 percent by 2016—President Obama beat that by two years.

The S&P 500 passed its pre-recession high. The Dow Jones and S&P 500 both more than doubled from Inaugural Day, January 20, 2009, to December 31, 2014.[66] Further, in October 2014, the Conference Board's consumer confidence index rose to its highest level since October 2007—before the recession. The GDP growth rate for the Third Quarter of 2014 was announced as a healthy 3.5%—following a healthy 4.6% growth rate for the Second Quarter of 2014. The Treasury Department released its federal budget deficit results, and, for every year of the Obama administration the federal deficit, as a percentage of GDP, had declined—the preliminary estimate for FY 2014, of 2.8%, was below the level of President George W. Bush's administration in FY 2008.[67] And, gasoline prices—for which presidents are irrationally blamed or credited with—averaged below $3 per gallon nationally, a four-year low. Additionally, approximately 10 million Americans who did not previously have health insurance now did. GM and Chrysler were still with us; Osama Bin Laden was not.

President Obama had amassed an admirable record of management of the government and of economic growth and rising economic productivity, but revenues attributable to that increased productivity continued to be upwardly redistributed to the rich, corporations and older Americans, with the result captured well in the title of an op-ed in *The New York Times* by Steven Rattner that appeared less than two weeks after the election: "Inequality, Unbelievably, Gets Worse."[68] Voters had overwhelmingly elected Republicans, dedicated to maintaining the trickle-down economics policies that promised to continue the upward redistribution of revenues attributable to increased productivity to the rich, corporations and older Americans.

Former Governor of Vermont and former Democratic National Committee Chairman Howard Dean, on NBC News' *Meet the Press*, November 9, 2014, observed that Democrats had inexplicably run away from President Obama and his record.[69] (This reluctance of liberals and Democrats to champion the facts in their favor will be addressed in the next chapter.)

The "Message" Voters Are Sending: Incoherence

Numerous Democratic Party candidates ran away from President Obama and his accomplishments in the 2014 midterm campaign.[70] Losing Senate candidate Alison Lundergan Grimes of Kentucky, in her campaign against Senator Mitch McConnell, (R-KY), refused to admit she voted for him—and this in Kentucky, where the KYNECT state response to Obamacare had been broadly popular.[71]

Former Senate Majority Leader Harry Reid and President Obama, in response to the question, "What message did the voters send?," replied the same as did new Senate Majority Leader Mitch McConnell: They want us to work together—although, presumably, President Obama and Senator Reid were not agreeing with Senator McConnell that the first order of business for this new bipartisanship was for Democrats to join with Republicans in repeal of Obamacare.

In reality, of course, the "message" from voters was the same as it has been in most elections since 1980: a message of *incoherence*. Going behind that message, what voters were saying was they were admitting that they were struggling, that they did not know why, nor did they know what to do. They were suffering from stagnant wages and wanted continued maintenance of the social safety net upon which they rely, yet they voted for Republicans pledged to oppose increasing wages and to undo that very social safety net.[72] In the 2014 midterms, voters in the states of Arkansas, Nebraska, South Dakota and Alaska joined with other states in voting overwhelmingly for Republicans for statewide offices and the House of Representatives—yet they also voted heavily in favor of state minimum wage laws above the national minimum wage—a measure condemned by Republicans as killing jobs and economic growth.

In the weeks following the election, the Republicans took two actions that seemed to be designed to test their ability to abuse voters' intelligence. House Speaker Boehner issued a press release in July which criticized President Obama for *not taking executive action on his own*, "to secure our borders" and to address the problem of illegal aliens. Taking a cue from Republican Presidents Reagan and George H. W. Bush, who issued Executive Orders exercising the prosecutorial discretion of the presidency—in both cases declaring that certain groups of aliens in the US illegally would not be deported—President Obama announced he would take executive action to not deport about 5 million illegal aliens who are the parents of children who are US citizens. This would be combined with enhanced border security. Regardless of the precedent, Speaker Boehner criticized the president, calling him "Emperor Obama;" Representative Steve King (R-IA) mischaracterized the president's action as "amnesty" (giving a path to citizenship to illegal aliens, which it did not); and Representative Mo Brooks (R-TX) threatened impeachment and prison time.[73] And, as observed above, the day after the president's announcement—even though he had presided over numerous votes to repeal, defund or delay all or parts of Obamacare—House Speaker Boehner filed a lawsuit challenging the Obama administration's *delay* of certain of the law's provisions and the provision in the law providing that government cover some of the costs to insurers for out-of-pocket expenses incurred in insuring low-income customers.[74]

How did conservatism and the Republican Party devolve to such depths, and how did politics become so incoherent? An attempt at an explanation begins in the next chapter—but first, one more observation will be made regarding the absolute imperative to defeat trickle-down. It was encapsulated in the title of an Associated Press article appearing in *The New York Times* of January 11, 2015: "Markets Slide on Weak Wage Growth." The article appeared below the jump from a page 1 article[75] on the absurd claim by Senate Majority Leader Mitch McConnell (R-KY) that the upbeat December economic data was due to the public's anticipation of the Republicans taking the Senate in the November 2014 midterm election.[76] November 2014 was the 57th straight month of private-sector job growth (a streak that continued thereafter) and, as observed above, under President Obama the stock market had doubled—Senate McConnell's claim that the public had anticipated by nearly five years this moment of Republican triumph seriously strained credibility.

Regardless, the Republicans in November 2014 took back control of the Senate and again won control of the House. With their victory, the Republicans assumed a mandate from the public to continue their trickle-down-inspired war on wages. With their House and Senate majorities, the GOP responded by passing budgets based on the fraud of repealing the Affordable Care Act and its taxes that pay for its insurance subsidies—*but including the $1 trillion in revenue created by those taxes in revenue calculations.*[77]

The 2016 Republican Messages to the Poor and Working Class: Trust Us: The Real "Takers" Are Illegal Immigrants and Their Children

In 2014 a group of conservatives calling themselves the YG Network, and popularly referred to as "reform conservatives," issued a report titled "Room to Grow: Conservative Reforms for Limited Government and a Thriving Middle Class." The report consisted of policy essays that were the subject of a conference that took place in Middleburg, Virginia in March of that year. The "YG" refers to the "Young Guns" movement that began in the House of Representatives with former House Majority Leader Eric Cantor (R-VA), then-House Majority Whip and successor to Cantor as House Majority Leader Kevin McCarthy (R-CA) and House Budget Chairman and former Vice Presidential candidate Paul Ryan (R-WI). The editors of the report are Yuval Levin and Ramesh Ponnuru, who also each authored an essay in the report.[78]

To their credit, the report marked a break from trickle-down dogma, proposing policies to directly benefit the middle class, rather than benefitting the rich and imagining the benefits will trickle down to the middle class. However, these policies were mainly an extension to the middle class and poor of those proposed to benefit the rich: tax cuts and deregulation. Examples of the tax cuts proposed are expansion of the Earned Income Tax Credit and implementation of a new child credit (both of which President Obama has supported). Borrowing the report's definitions of "lower class" as consisting of 12 percent of the population and of "lower middle class" as consisting of 26 percent,[79] with around 43 percent of households not paying income tax, this means that *the poor and working class are not helped by these proposals*.

Several articles written about the time of the release of the report provided more insight into the reform conservatives. Among them was one by Ramesh Ponnuru in *National Review*, in which he assured the reader that "my opposition to almost all of Obama's policies is quite sincere."[80] Similarly, Yuval Levin was quoted by Sam Tanenhaus in *The New York Times Magazine*[81] as admiring the Tea Party but observing that it is missing policy, which, presumably, the YG Network aimed to provide. Additionally, as observed by Tanenhaus, these reformers—especially Levin and Ponnuru—share the Tea Partiers' social conservatism, strongly opposing both abortion and same-sex marriage (no insight was provided regarding foreign policy).

The inability of conservatives generally, and Republicans in particular, to actually help the poor and working class was underscored in an op-ed by conservative Ross Douthat in March 2015 in which he framed the social policy argument between left and right as a problem of economics or culture.[82] As will be seen later herein, the framing of the argument as such sets up a false dichotomy and lets conservatives too easily off the hook for providing actual government solutions to address the social crisis among America's poor and working class by attributing the crisis to their own culture.

In reality, the social crisis among America's poor and working class is best understood as a problem of economics, culture and government, because economic circumstances are not only influenced by culture but also influence culture, and economic circumstances are also influenced by government policy—thus, government policy can counteract the market's built-in tendency to upwardly redistribute revenues attributable to increased productivity and raise relative incomes for the working class and poor, thereby making it easier for them to buy into prevailing culture (the liberal vision). Alternatively, government policy can encourage the market's upwardly redistribution of revenues attributable to increased productivity and hold relatively stagnant incomes for the working class and poor (the trickle-down conservative vision), thereby making it more difficult for them to buy into prevailing culture. And, as will be seen, numerous social commentators in the 1950s and 1960s foresaw and warned against the upwardly redistributive aspects of the oncoming Information Revolution and globalization—but in response government policy, commencing with Reagan's inauguration in January 1981, aided this upward redistribution.

Returning to Douthat's op-ed, he observed that, during the period between 1979 and 2010, the inflation-adjusted after-tax incomes for the poorest quintile of American households rose from $14,800 to $19,200; and for the second-poorest quintile, from $29,900 to 39,100—respectively, growth of 30 percent and 31 percent.[83] However, this growth took place over the course of 32 years, amounting to annual growth of a barely perceptible 1.3 percent. In contrast, the income of the top 1 percent over this same period *tripled* from $335,700 to $1,012,700, growing by *202 percent*, with a respectable annual growth of 3.6 percent. In fact, the working poor were joined by their fellow members of the lower 90 percent who also endured over that period declining shares of after-tax income. In contrast, the share of after-tax income of the top 1 percent rose from 7.5 percent to *13.12 percent* of overall after-tax income (more detailed presentation of this analysis follows in Chapter 7). Thus, in shares of after-tax income, the rich are getting much, much, richer, and the middle class and poor are getting poorer, as trickle-down upwardly redistributes income and wealth. And, as will also be seen (in Chapter 11) numerous studies now show that a decline in relative status has a detrimental effect on individuals' self-worth and, thus, relative economic circumstances themselves change behavior and culture and even health outcomes.

That same month as Douthat's op-ed, House Budget Committee Chairman Tom Price (R-GA) released the Republicans' proposed Fiscal Year 2016 budget, which proposed to weaken the social safety net upon which millions of middle class and poor Americans depend, proposing repeal of Obamacare and major cuts to Social Security, Medicare, Medicaid and food stamps, while maintaining high defense spending. Additionally, the budget plan proposed to convert Medicare into a voucher program consisting of "premium support" and proposed to convert Medicaid into a block grant system with grants to states to administer as they see fit (both measures that would decrease aid to the poor and middle class and further upwardly redistribute shares of national income and wealth).

Meanwhile, potential Republican 2016 presidential candidates, in books published in advance of the 2016 campaign, confirmed the timidity of Republican leaders about straying from the trickle-down fold, and all avoided discussing potential government solutions to wage stagnation, as observed by Michael Tomasky in a March 2015 article in *The New York Review of Books*.[84] At a presidential forum in January 2015 in Palm Springs, California, sponsored by the Freedom Partners Chamber of Commerce (funded by conservative multibillionaires Charles and David Koch), Senators Ted Cruz (R-TX), Rand Paul (R-KY) and Marco Rubio (R-FL) all observed that growing inequality was a problem, but Senators Cruz and Paul rejected government intervention and Senator Rubio appeared in agreement.[85]

Former Florida Governor Jeb Bush was running as the Republican moderate—although he was a staunch supporter of trickle-down, supporting lower taxes for those at the top, privatization of Social Security as proposed by his brother and raising the retirement age (in which he was joined by other Republican candidates[86]), reliance upon states to raise minimum wages but holding flat or abolishing entirely the federal minimum wage[87] and supporting Paul Ryan's budget proposals including conversion of Medicare to a voucher program (or outright "phase out" of Medicare for those not yet receiving benefits[88]) and Medicaid to a block grant system,[89] as well as staffing his foreign policy team with his brother's advisors during his presidency, and stating that for foreign policy expertise he trusts his brother (who invaded Iraq in March 2003—a mid-2015 poll showed a majority of Americans opposed to having sent troops to Iraq[90]).

The 2016 Republican Presidential Candidates Revolt against the Reality-Based Community

Reporter Ron Suskind stunned and disturbed the political world when he recounted that in a summer of 2002 meeting with a senior advisor to President George W. Bush he was told that he and people like him lived in "the reality-based community"[91] as opposed to those in the Bush administration who would make their own reality. But, as will be seen herein, the Republican Party's departure from reality even predates the Bush administration. The conservatism of the Republican Party departed from reality when its economic policy became trickle-down economics, foreign policy became neoconservatism, and traditionalism was overtaken by religious fundamentalism; and in the campaign leading up to the 2016 election this departure from reality became more prominent than ever before.

As the Republican Party struggled through the process of selecting its candidate for the presidency, the importance of reality itself to the Republican Party came to be questioned by numerous commentators, among them conservative commentator David Brooks on NBC News' *Meet the Press*, September 27, 2015, when he observed that he was not quite sure reality matters to the electorate in the upcoming election. That was probably an overstatement in that reality did still appear to matter to most of the electorate, but reality did not appear to matter for more than half of Republican voters who, as reflected by polls at the time, supported Donald Trump, Dr. Ben Carson and Carly Fiorina—none of whom had any experience governing,[92] and all of whom displayed a level of ignorance in the Constitution they proposed to take the oath to "preserve, protect and defend" that should have disqualified them from any support from the electorate as they sought the presidency.

As was observed by Nicholas Kristof, no president has ever served that office without first having held elective office, served in the military, or held a cabinet post, as none of these have.[93] Chapter 3 observes that trickle-down economics enabled the conservatives to realize their dream to "make the Holy Rollers lie down with the high rollers," but that dream was never more fully realized—or, more accurately for members of the Republican establishment, that dream had never more fully backfired—than in the 2016 presidential race when whites without college degrees kept atop polls two candidates in particular who had never held elective office, served in the military, or held a cabinet post. Polls showed that those whites without college degrees who were evangelicals flocked to the Seventh-Day Adventist Dr. Ben Carson; those whites without college degrees who were secular, and for whom social issues did not matter, flocked to the billionaire Donald Trump.

Donald Trump proposed to send back to Mexico, with their parents, those children born in this country, apparently ignorant of the 14th Amendment's grant of citizenship to anyone born in this country and the constitutional problems such a policy would present. Ben Carson, on NBC News' *Meet the Press* (September 20, 2015), stated that he would not agree with having a Muslim president, although his opinion might be different regarding a Muslim in Congress—seemingly oblivious to the provisions of Article VI of the

Constitution, that "no religious test shall ever be required as a qualification to any office or public trust under the United States"—and seemingly oblivious to the fact there was already a Muslim in Congress, Representative Keith Ellison (D-MN), who took his oath of office on Thomas Jefferson's copy of the Koran.[94]

Polls supported the assertion that reality did not matter to more than half of Republicans. Donald Trump had announced his candidacy for the 2016 presidential nomination with a speech often mocked for its lack of factual basis,[95] and a Public Policy Polling national poll released September 1, 2015 found among Trump supporters: 66 percent believed that President Obama is a Muslim to just 12 percent that believed he is a Christian; 61 percent thought President Obama was not born in the United States to only 21 percent who accepted that he was; and 63 percent wanted to amend the Constitution to eliminate birthright citizenship, to only 20 percent who wanted to leave the Constitution alone. And Trump's supporters' beliefs represented the majority opinion among the Republican electorate: 54 percent of them thought President Obama is a Muslim; only 29 percent believed that President Obama was born in the United States (44 percent believed he was not; 26 percent were not sure); and, in contrast, 40 percent of them thought Canadian born Ted Cruz was born in the United States. And 51 percent of them wanted to eliminate birthright citizenship.[96]

During the 2016 presidential campaign, much was made of the populism on display by candidates from both the major parties: The liberal populism on display by Senator Bernie Sanders in his campaign for the Democratic nomination and the conservative populism on display by Donald Trump in his campaign for the Republican nomination. Populism is almost always about blaming an enemy for economic misery. Liberal populists, like Bernie Sanders, tend to blame the elites—the rich and powerful—for rigging the system in their favor and against the rest of us. Conservative populists, like Donald Trump, tend to blame somebody who's getting a free ride from the system (see Introduction). Thus, the conservative populism—the "Trump card"—Trump was displaying was just an updated version of the blame game that Romney and Ryan tried in 2012. Romney-Ryan blamed the "takers"—the 47 percent who didn't pay income taxes—who mooched off the "makers". Trump blamed the millions of illegal immigrants and their children and, to a lesser degree, the hedge fund managers who take advantage of carried interest capital gains treatment of their income.[97]

Ironically, too, the neurosurgeon Dr. Ben Carson had a populist blame-game of his own in late 2015, claiming there are 10 times more people on welfare in 2015 than in the mid-1960s.[98] In reality, the term "welfare" has been understood, since it began under the New Deal in the 1930s, to mean Aid to Families with Dependent Children (AFDC), a program intended to provide financial aid to families with children and little or no income. Under the Personal Responsibility and Work Opportunity Act (popularly, the Welfare Reform Act of 1996), signed by President Clinton, AFDC was changed to Temporary Assistance for Needy Families (TANF), and a lifetime benefit of 60 months was imposed along with a 24-month period to find a job. The result has been to reduce the number of welfare recipients: In 1965, there were 4.4 million recipients of AFDC (just over 1 million families); in 2015 the number of TANF recipients was down to about 3.0 million. According to the Census Bureau, the population of the US in 2015 was about 320 million, about 70 percent greater than the 1965 population of about 194 million. Thus, in reality, *we do not have 10 times more people on welfare in 2015 than in 1965—we have nearly one-third fewer people on welfare now than in 1965*, and *we have cut by nearly 59 percent the percentage of the population on welfare since 1965.*[99] Carson also displayed a disturbing ignorance of history, claiming that gun laws in Nazi Germany were responsible for the Holocaust[100] and comparing the United States under a liberal president to Nazi Germany under Hitler and the Affordable Care Act to slavery.[101]

At a campaign rally in Rochester, New Hampshire, two nights after the September debate, Donald Trump was confronted by a questioner who acknowledged Trump's having been a leader of the challenge to the legitimacy of Barack Obama's birth certificate and who characterized President Obama as a Muslim and unqualified to be president. Rather than confront the questioner as Senator John McCain had confronted a similar questioner in the 2008 campaign, Trump promised to look into the questioner's concerns about radical Muslim training camps in the United States.[102]

Later that month, in an interview with Sean Hannity on Fox News Channel that aired September 29, 2015, the at-that-time expected successor to John Boehner (R-OH) as Speaker of the House, Kevin McCarthy (R-CA), committed a huge "gaffe" (defined by numerous commentators, crediting liberal commentator Michael Kinsley as the originator of the definition, as occurring when someone in politics inadvertently tells an obvious truth). McCarthy proudly claimed credit for securing the Benghazi select committee—the eighth congressional investigation into Benghazi and the longest-running congressional special select investigative committee in recent history (longer than Watergate, Iran-Contra and the Warren Committee). And, he proudly gave the reason: Not to get at the truth regarding the loss of four American lives at the diplomatic mission Benghazi, Libya in September 2012 but, rather, to make the public question Hillary Clinton's trustworthiness, thereby bringing down her poll numbers in advance of the November 2016 election—and he proudly cited success in this regard and impliedly promised more such partisan abuses of power after he became Speaker of the House.[103] McCarthy's account of the rationale for the committee was later given credit by a fellow Republican Congressman, Representative Richard Hanna (R-NY),[104] as well as a former investigator for the Republicans on the staff of the commission[105] although these accounts were denied by the chairman of the commission, Representative Trey Gowdy (R-SC), who told his colleagues to "shut up" about it.[106]

In the runup to the 2016 election, polls made clear that the majority of Republicans, including all the Republican presidential candidates, consistent with Republican trickle-down conservatism since its beginning three and a half decades ago, had no respect for the facts—no respect for reality.[107] The irony, thus, of the abuse of congressional power to make Hillary Clinton seem untrustworthy was that rigid embrace of trickle-down conservatism, a philosophy that demands no respect for truth, renders *all* Republican candidates untrustworthy. And, as will be seen in Chapter 8, not only do Republicans undermine our democracy by wasting our tax dollars on partisan abuse of congressional power (at the time of Kevin McCarthy's statement, an estimated $4.5 million had been wasted on the Benghazi special committee), but they also undermine democracy by partisan abuse of their power in state legislatures by preventing voters who might be expected to vote Democratic from exercising their constitutionally guaranteed right to vote.

The concerns expressed by Norman Ornstein and Thomas Mann regarding the 2012 election and the Republican Party's disregard for truth and facts became widely vocalized during the campaign runup to the 2016 election as the Republican candidates for the presidency continued promoting their reality-free philosophy, pandering to the ignorance of their ill-informed base and undermining our fragile democracy, while the media continued to avoid challenging them on it. In an outstanding interview with Ornstein and Mann conducted in October 2015 by Francis Wilkinson,[108] the two again traced how we had gotten to this point and acknowledged the situation had not gotten any better. Paul Krugman joined them in their analysis of the twin dysfunctions of the Republican Party and the media,[109] and even David Brooks faulted his party,[110] although Krugman found his colleague's critique lacking[111] and the Editorial Board for *The New York Times*, Brooks' employer, issued an editorial after the first Democratic debate titled "The Grown-Ups Take the Stage at the Democratic Debate."[112]

Later that month, however, came the Republican presidential candidates' debate on CNBC, which ultimately led the Republican Party to suspend the next planned debate on NBC and NBC affiliate Telemundo, originally set for February 26, 2016. The official reason given was that CNBC had been unfair to the candidates. Yet, Carly Fiorina resolutely held to her account of having seen a horrifying scene in a Planned Parenthood video that never happened and resumed the Mitt Romney 2012 claim of job losses for women under Barack Obama, which even Romney had abandoned after having been proved inaccurate. Donald Trump denied criticizing Facebook founder and CEO Mark Zuckerberg, although the criticism appeared at his own campaign website on the Internet. And, when confronted by the facts that his tax plan did not work as claimed (to be fair, none of the candidates' tax plans did), and his appearance in promotional videos on behalf of a questionable nutritional supplement company that directed its marketing to Christians, Ben Carson simply denied the truth.[113] In a November 4, 2015 Facebook post, Carson made the absurd claim that none of the signers to Declaration of Independence had any elected office experience. (Of course, all of the 56 signers of the Declaration had been elected to represent their respective colonies at the convention, and more than half of them had some elected office experience,[114] with many having already served with distinction in their respective colonial assemblies—after being confronted with the facts, the Facebook entry was changed to having held no "federal" elected office—of course, the federal government only came into existence 13 years later, in 1789, after the Constitution was ratified and went into effect). Ultimately, the real reason for the attack on CNBC in particular and on the media generally was that the Republican candidates joined in revolt against reality itself, and this revolution would continue.

Donald Trump, not surprisingly, provided the exclamation mark on trickle-down Republican policy roughly one year before the election. While Democratic candidates united in their diagnosis that the economy was suffering from wages having declined in real value since the 1970s, and they provided various prescriptions to raise wages, including all giving proposals for a higher minimum wage, all the Republican candidates united in opposing the minimum wage. Donald Trump went further, however, declaring in the November 12, 2015 debate that wages in America were too high.[115] Recall, too, that Donald Trump also made famous, on his "reality" television show, the phrase, "You're fired!"—and that 2012 Republican presidential nominee, Mitt Romney, said he liked being able to fire people. Working poor and middle class Americans were not yet suffering enough. Why liberal Democrats have been so limited in their ability to help them will be addressed in the next chapter.

NOTES

1. Rosalind S. Helderman, "Bitter Campaign and Its Rhetoric Bring Fact Checkers to the Center of Debate," *The Washington Post*, August 30, 2012.
2. Neil Brown, "You Can Handle the Truth," *Tampa Bay Times*, September 8, 2012.
3. See, for example, Paul Krugman, "This Republican Economy," *The New York Times*, June 4, 2012.
4. See, e.g., Jeremy Peters, "Gloomy G.O.P. Leaves Behind Reagan Cheer," *The New York Times*, September 13, 2015; especially the observations therein by David Gergen, longtime political commentator and former advisor to Presidents Ford, Reagan and Clinton, and Matthew Dowd, conservative commentator and former advisor to President George W. Bush.
5. Darren Samuelsohn, "Rudy Giuliani: President Obama Doesn't Love America," *Politico*, February 18, 2015. And, Nick Gass, "Poll: Obama May Not Love America," *Politico*, February 25, 2015.

6. Among them: Michael Barone, Peggy Noonan, Dick Morris, Glenn Beck and George Will—see Hendrik Hertzberg, "Comment: Mandate with Destiny," *The New Yorker*, December 3, 2012. They were joined by Rush Limbaugh, who predicted a Romney victory on his radio show, and Karl Rove, who predicted a Romney victory in an opinion piece in *The Wall Street Journal* ("Rove: Sifting the Numbers for a Winner," October 31, 2012).

7. Bruce Bartlett, "Revenge of the Reality-Based Community," *The American Conservative*, December 2012. The context of the term "reality-based community" is an article by the reporter Ron Suskind, "Faith, Certainty, and the Presidency of George W. Bush," *The New York Times Magazine*, October 17, 2004, which is addressed in greater detail later in this chapter.

8. Paul Krugman, "Partisan Growth Gaps," *The New York Times*, November 2, 2015.

9. Thomas E. Mann and Norman J. Ornstein, "Let's Just Say It: The Republicans Are the Problem," *The Washington Post*, April 27, 2012.

10. Dan Froomkin, "How the Mainstream Press Bungled the Single Biggest Story of the 2012 Campaign," *Huffington Post*, December 7, 2012. Froomkin is the Senior Washington Correspondent for the *Huffington Post*.

11. The two analysts are Nate Silver of fivethirtyeight.com and Sam Wang of Princeton Election Consortium.

12. This is captured well by *The New Republic's* Jonathan Chait in the title of his book on conservative economics: *The Big Con: Crackpot Economics and the Fleecing of America* (2007).

13. Sally Kohn, "Paul Ryan's Speech in 3 Words," *FoxNews.com*, August 30, 2012.

14. Mitt Romney, "Mr. President, What's the Rush?" *USA Today*, July 30, 2009.

15. "Remarks by the President on the Deaths of U.S. Embassy Staff in Libya," *The White House Office of the Press Secretary*, September 12, 2012.

16. Bryan Monroe, "The Truth About What Candy Crowley Said," *CNN.com*, October 20, 2012. As observed therein, an editorial criticizing Crowley, "Candy's Not Dandy," appeared in the Rupert Murdoch-owned *New York Post*, October 18, 2012, repeating therein criticisms leveled by Romney campaign supporter John Sununu.

17. David D. Kirkpatrick, "Deadly Mix in Benghazi: False Allies, Crude Video," *The New York Times*, December 29, 2013. The research did, however, reveal that there had been no political demonstration preceding the attack, as the administration had alleged. Additionally, numerous government investigations found no wrongdoing; among them were investigations conducted by: (1) the House Armed Services Committee; (2) the Senate Select Committee on Intelligence; (3) the State Department's independent Accountability Review Board (ARB) and (4) the House Intelligence Committee. Nonetheless, more investigations followed, including the investigation led by Representative Trey Gowdy (R-SC), acknowledged by Representative Kevin McCarthy (R-CA) as being politically motivated to bring down Hillary Clinton's poll numbers in advance of the 2016 presidential election.

18. Friedman saw himself as a classical liberal, and the National Health System he proposed is a good example of a classical liberal limited government response to provide a basic quality of life for all—similar to Friedrich Hayek's thought in *The Road to Serfdom* (addressed later herein).

19. Mitt Romney, "Mr. President, What's the Rush?" *USA Today*, July 30, 2009.

20. Stuart Butler, "Don't Blame Heritage for ObamaCare Mandate," *USA Today*, posted February 2, 2012, updated February 6, 2012.

21. James Taranto, "Heritage Rewrites History," *The Wall Street Journal* Best of the Web Today blog, February 8, 2012.

22. Interview, Sean Hannity with Senator Ted Cruz (R-TX), July 25, 2013.

23. "Remarks by the President at a Campaign Event in Roanoke, Virginia," *The White House Office of the Press Secretary*, July 13, 2012.

24. Rebekah Metzler, "Mitt Romney Ramps Up Right-leaning Rhetoric," *USNews.com*. July 19, 2012.

25. "[VIDEO] Business Man in Romney's Attack Ad Agrees with Obama 100% on Fox News," *Daily Kos*, July 19, 2012. See also, Glenn Kessler, "An Unoriginal Obama Quote,

Taken Out of Context," *The Fact Checker, The Washington Post*, July 23, 2012. "'You Didn't Build That,' Uncut and Unedited," *Factheck.org*, July 23, 2012, updated July 24, 2012.

26. See Glenn Kessler, "Fact Checking the GOP Convention's Opening Night," *The Fact Checker Blog, The Washington Post*, August 29, 2012.

27. Ten more examples of Romney-Ryan campaign deception:

1. *"If we keep talking about the economy, we're going to lose"*: Governor Romney's initial television commercial when he launched his campaign against President Obama showed President Obama saying, "If we keep talking about the economy, we're going to lose." The Romney campaign had clipped the quote—it had appeared in Candidate Obama's 2008 presidential campaign against John McCain, and in the full quote Obama clearly said, "Senator McCain's campaign actually said, and I quote, if we keep talking about the economy, we're going to lose." When questioned, Governor Romney's nonsensical, widely quoted response was, "what's sauce for the goose is now sauce for the gander." See, for example, Seema Mehta and Michael A. Memoli, "Mitt Romney Defends Use of Obama Quote in Campaign Ad," *Los Angeles Times*, November 23, 2011.
2. *President Obama's "World Apology Tour"*: Governor Romney on the campaign trail promoted variations on this misrepresentation about President Obama—from September 22, 2011: "He went around the world and apologized for America." Romney was so enamored of the concept that he titled his campaign book *No Apology*. However, the *Fact Checker* blog tracked down every statement alleged to be an apology and found all to have been misquoted or quoted out of context. Glenn Kessler, "Romney's Claim That Obama Apologizes for U.S. Is Based on Distortions," *The Fact Checker, The Washington Post*, December 10, 2011.
3. *"We tried our plan—and it worked"*: The Romney campaign again clipped a quote from President Obama, this time regarding the policies of President Clinton, implying the falsehood that the Obama administration was claiming victory in the economy with unemployment remaining over 8 percent. Oliver Willis, "We've Tried Our Plan": Fox, Limbaugh & Co. Truncate and Distort Yet Another Obama Quote," Media Matters blog, July 26, 2012. See also Glenn Kessler, "An Obama Quote Taken Out of Context, Yet Again," *The Fact Checker, The Washington Post*, July 30, 2012.
4. *"Contracts were steered to 'friends and family'"*: Near the end of a Romney campaign ad in mid-2012 appeared the line regarding the green energy company Solyndra: "The Inspector General said contracts were steered to 'friends and family." Michael Grunwald of *Time* magazine's *Swampland* blog asked the Romney campaign for documentation, and they steered him to a *Newsweek* article that was an excerpt from the book *Throw Them All Out*, a book by Peter Schweizer, former adviser to Sarah Palin's PAC and editor of one of Andrew Breitbart's websites. Research by Grunwald revealed the Inspector General had never so testified. Michael Grunwald, "Mitt Romney's Ads: Still Wrong on the Stimulus," *Time Swampland* blog, May 31, 2012.
5. *"Obama guts welfare reform"*: In August 2012, the Romney campaign released a 30-second television commercial titled "Right Choice" which said, "Obama guts welfare reform." The basis for that claim lay in the announcement by the Department of Health and Human Services on July 12, 2012, that it would consider requests for waivers from states seeking more leeway in administering Temporary Assistance for Needy Families (TANF), created as part of the Welfare Reform Act of 1996 under President Clinton and establishing work requirements for recipients. To secure a waiver, however, under the law states must show that their welfare programs will *increase* job placements by at least 20 percent—and, as Governor of Massachusetts in 2005, Governor Romney was one of *28 Republican governors* who signed a petition filed with Congress *requesting state welfare waivers that were more expansive* than those his campaign attacked. Phillip Rucker and Bill Turque, "Mitt Romney Attacks President Obama over Welfare Reform," *The*

Washington Post, August 7, 2012. Glenn Kessler, "Spin and Counterspin in the Welfare Debate," *The Fact Checker, The Washington Post*, August 8, 2012.

6. *"As President, Barack Obama has never visited Israel."* Also in August, the Romney campaign ran a commercial observing that, as president, Barack Obama had not visited Israel, and implying he had snubbed Israel in favor of Middle Eastern countries—omitting that he had visited Israel *before*, in 2008, as Senator Obama, while campaigning for president. Glenn Kessler, "Obama Knocked for Not Visiting Israel," *The Fact Checker, The Washington Post*, August 6, 2012.

7. *"This president stole—he didn't cut Medicare—he stole $700 billion from Medicare to fund Obamacare."* According to Reince Priebus, Republican National Committee Chairman, President Obama "stole" from Medicare when he signed the Affordable Care Act that reduced reimbursements under Medicare to providers (hospitals, drug companies and supplemental private insurance plans) by $716 billion while leaving benefits untouched. As David Axelrod observed on *Meet the Press*, "We extended the life of Medicare by eight years, according to the Congressional Budget Office." (Sahil Kapur, "Republicans Defend Paul Ryan: Obama Cut Medicare Too!" *Talking Points Memo*, August 12, 2012. See also Bill Press, "Who's Telling the Truth about Medicare?" *Chicago Tribune*, August 23, 2012. And, as was observed by numerous commentators, Congressman and Republican Vice Presidential Candidate Paul Ryan proposed the same cuts.

8. *President Obama failed to keep General Motors' Janesville, Wisconsin plant open.* Candidate Obama, on the campaign trail in 2008, stressed the importance of the auto bailout to keeping open plants such as General Motors' plant in Congressman Ryan's hometown of Janesville, Wisconsin. As a senator, he had voted for the auto bailout, however, the plant nonetheless closed later in 2008. Congressman Ryan, in his speech before the Republican National Convention, nonetheless blamed President Obama for failing to keep the plant open—even though the plant closed in 2008, before he took office—*and even though Congressman Ryan, himself, voted against the bailout.*

9. *The president failed to attempt to implement the recommendations of his debt-reduction commission, the Simpson-Bowles Commission.* The president was prevented from implementing the recommendations of the Simpson-Bowles Commission because, as the Republican ranking member on the House Budget Committee, *Congressman Ryan led a bloc of three House Republicans who denied the additional votes needed to send the plan to Congress for a vote.* Heidi Przybyla, "Ryan Helped Derail Simpson-Bowles Plan Romney Now Sees as Model," *Bloomberg Businessweek*, August 13, 2012.

10. *The president failed to deliver on his promises once in office.* As was often noted by political commentators, this charge resembled the case of a lad accused of killing his parents throwing himself on the mercy of the judge for sympathy as an orphan. Republicans in the Senate and the House opposed President Obama on almost all of his legislative efforts (more on this in Chapter 3).

28. "Who Doesn't Pay Federal Taxes," Chart of the Tax Policy Center of the Urban Institute and Brookings Institution, 2012.

29. Roberton Williams, "Who Pays No Income Tax? A 2013 Update," The Tax Policy Center, Tax Notes, September 30, 2013, p. 1615.

30. The EITC, originally signed into law by Republican President Gerald Ford as part of the Tax Reduction Act of 1975, acts to provide a minimum level of income, especially for working families with children.

31. David Welna, "Why Some Are Exempt from Federal Income Taxes," *NPR Morning Edition*, September 19, 2012.

32. Paul Solman, "The Income Tax in 1913: A Way to 'Soak the Rich'," PBS News Hour, April 15, 2013. CPI Inflation Calculator, Bureau of Labor Statistics.

33. Interview, Matt Lauer with Mitt Romney, NBC's *The Today Show*, January 11, 2012.

34. Nicholas Confessore, David Kocieniewski and Ashley Parker, "Romney Shares Some Tax Data; Critics Pounce," *The New York Times*, January 17, 2012.

35. Z. Byron Wolf, Emily Friedman, "Romney: Campaign Not Concerned About the Very Poor," ABC News The Note, February 1, 2012.

36. Steve Holland and Kim Dixon, "Mitt Romney Tax Returns Released: Paid Just 13.9% Rate in 2010, Had a Swiss Bank Account," *Reuters*, January 24, 2012.

37. Jeff Zeleny, "Romney: I'm Also Unemployed," *The Caucus* blog, *The New York Times*, June 16, 2011.

38. Matthew O'Brien, "Mitt Romney Would Pay 0.82 Percent in Taxes under Paul Ryan's Plan," *The Atlantic*, August 11, 2012. As the article notes, the vast majority of Romney's income came from capital gains, interest and dividend income—which would have been *exempt from taxation* under the Ryan plan.

39. Interview between George Stephanopoulos and Mitt Romney, *Good Morning America*, September 13, 2012.

40. "The Romney Tax Plan," Urban-Brookings Tax Policy Center, March 1, 2012.

41. In the Republican presidential debate of January 23, 2012, Governor Romney expressed support for "self-deportation" of illegal immigrants, apparently unaware that the concept was invented in 1994 by two Mexican-American satirists, Lalo Alcaraz and Esteban Zul, who became "sickened" by the Proposition 187 ballot initiative in California that sought to prohibit illegal immigrants from using state-run hospitals and schools in California. The two men issued a fake news release promoting the benefits of "self-deportation centers" and invited reporters seeking more information to consult a Latino Republican and "militant self-deportationist" named Daniel D. Portado, played by Alcaraz in interviews with reporters. See Robert Mackey, "The Deep Comic Roots of 'Self-Deportation,'" *The Lede* blog of *The New York Times*, February 1, 2012.

42. Michael Kranish, "Mitt Romney's Defense Budget Target Is Lofty," March 19, 2012.

43. Samuel Brown, William Gale and Adam Looney, "On the Distributional Effects of Base-Broadening Income Tax Reform," The Urban-Brookings Tax Policy Center, August 1, 2012.

44. Igor Volsky, "Estimate: At Least 48 Million Could Become Uninsured Under Paul Ryan's Budget," *ThinkProgress*, March 20, 2012, based on "The Long Term Budgetary Impact and Paths for Federal Revenues and Spending Specified by Chairman Ryan," March 2012, Congressional Budget Office.

45. Linda Levine, "An Analysis of the Distribution of Wealth Across Households, 1989–2010," Congressional Research Service, July 17, 2012.

46. David Corn, "SECRET VIDEO: Romney Tells Millionaire Voters What He REALLY Thinks of Obama Voters," Politics blog, *Mother Jones* September 17, 2012 and Scott A. Hodge, "States Vary Widely in Number of Tax Filers with No Income Tax Liability," Tax Foundation, May 24, 2010.

47. Brett Brownell and Nick Baumann, "VIDEO: Paul Ryan's Version of '47 Percent'—the 'Takers' vs. the 'Makers'," *Mother Jones* October 5, 2012. To his credit, Representative Paul Ryan in August 2014 recanted his "makers versus takers" characterization. See Nick Baumann, "Paul Ryan Changes His Story on 'Makers and Takers'," *Mother Jones*, Jan. 22, 2013 and "Rep. Ryan Calls for 'Culture of Inclusion' to Tackle Poverty," *NPR Morning Edition*, August 29, 2014, interview with host Steve Inskeep.

48. See Matt Taibbi, "The Truth About the Tea Party," *Rolling Stone*, October 14, 2010. Taibbi marks the inception of the Tea Party movement with the presidential campaign of former Congressman Ron Paul (R-TX) in 2008.

49. Editorial Board, "Mitt Romney's Parting 'Gifts'," *The Washington Post*, November 15, 2012.

50. For elaboration on the contents of the phone call, see Ashley Parker, "Romney Blames Loss on Obama's 'Gifts' to Minorities and Young Voters," The Caucus Blog of *The New York Times*, November 14, 2012.

51. Ezra Klein, "From the 47% to 'Gifts': Mitt Romney's Ugly Vision of Politics," Wonkblog, *The Washington Post*, November 15, 2012.

52. See Stan Greenberg, James Carville and Erica Seifert, "Inside the GOP: Report on Focus Groups with Evangelical, Tea Party and Moderate Republicans," Democracy Corps, October 3, 2013.

53. Ezra Klein, "Romney Is Wall Street's Worst Bet Since the Bet on the Subprime," Wonkblog, *The Washington Post*, November 28, 2012.

54. James Carville, interviewed by Tim Dickinson, in "How President Obama Won a Second Term," *Rolling Stone*, December 6, 2012.

55. See, for example, Greg Sargent, "Morning Plum: Republicans Are 'in Denial' about Hillary Clinton," The Plum Line blog, *The Washington Post*, October 26, 2015 and Mark Halperin, "The Most Likely President Is Hillary Clinton: And the Republicans Are in Denial About It," *Bloomberg*, October 26, 2015.

56. Paul Krugman, "Plutocrats Feeling Persecuted," *The New York Times*, September 27, 2013.

57. See also Leslie Scism, "AIG's Benmosche and Miller on Villains, Turnarounds and Those Bonuses," *The Wall Street Journal* blog, September 23, 2013.

58. See Paul Krugman, "Paranoia of the Plutocrats," *The New York Times*, January 27, 2014. See also Tom Perkins, Letter to the Editor, *The Wall Street Journal*, January 24, 2014. And see James Surowiecki, "Moaning Moguls," *The New Yorker*, July 7, 2014.

59. "Perkinsnacht: Liberal Vituperation Makes Our Letter Writer's Point," *The Wall Street Journal*, January 24, 2014.

60. Stan Greenberg, James Carville, and Erica Seifert, "Inside the GOP: Report on Focus Groups with Evangelical, Tea Party, and Moderate Republicans," Democracy Corps, October 3, 2013.

61. See for example, David A. Fahrenthold, Lori Montgomery and Paul Kane, "In Debt Deal, the Triumph of Old Washington," *The Washington Post*, August 2, 2011.

62. Sheryl Gay Stolberg and Mike McIntyre, "A Federal Budget Crisis Months in the Planning," *The New York Times*, October 6, 2013. See also Paul Krugman, "The Boehner Bunglers," *The New York Times*, October 7, 2013.

63. CNN/ORC Poll taken on September 27–29, 2013, released Monday, September 30, 2013.

64. Paul Krugman, "The Obama Recovery," *The New York Times*, December 29, 2014.

65. Nelson D. Schwartz, "Job Count Finds Best 3 Months Since 1990s," *The New York Times*, February 7, 2015.

66. The Dow went from 7,949 to 17,823; the S&P 500 from 805 to 2,059.

67. John Cassidy, "Obama's Well-Earned Victory Lap on the Economy," *The New Yorker*, March 19, 2015.

68. Steven Rattner, "Inequality, Unbelievably, Gets Worse," *The New York Times*, November 17, 2014. Rattner is a Wall Street executive, contributing opinion writer and commentator for MSNBC.

69. See also Jonathan Martin and Julie Hirschfeld Davis, "On Campaign Road, Uneasy Democrats Show Obama Their Tail Lights," *The New York Times*, October 26, 2014. Therein they recount their conversation with Senator John Breaux (D-LA), recalling a conversation he had with a Republican official back home regarding the Republican Party's anti-Obama campaign message deployed against Senator Mary Landrieu in the 2014 midterm election campaign.

70. Jonathan Martin and Julie Hirschfeld Davis, "On Campaign Road, Uneasy Democrats Show Obama Their Tail Lights," *The New York Times*, October 26, 2014.

71. Philip Bump, "40 Painful Seconds of Alison Lundergan Grimes Refusing to Say Whether She Voted for President Obama," *The Fix* blog, *The Washington Post*, October 9, 2014.

72. See Paul Krugman, "Triumph of the Wrong," *The New York Times*, November 7, 2014 and David Firestone, "The Tornado Election," The Taking Note Blog, *The New York Times*, November 5, 2014.

73. Chris Moody, "On the Border with Obama's Immigration Foes," *CNN News*, November 25, 2014.

74. The Editorial Board of the Los Angeles Times, "Editorial: The GOP's Shameful Lawsuit against Obamacare," *The Los Angeles Times*, November 24, 2014.

75. Jonathan Weisman, "Economy Up, G.O.P. Wants a Little Credit," *The New York Times*, January 10, 2015.

76. James Carville, on the January 11, 2015 *Meet the Press*, observed this claim sounded like a headline in the satirical paper *The Onion*.

77. Paul Krugman, "Trillion Dollar Fraudsters," *The New York Times*, March 20, 2015.

78. Other participants in the project: John Murray, Senior Strategist; Stacey Johnson, Chief of Staff; April Ponnuru, Policy Director; advisor, Kate O'Beirne; and other essay authors: Peter Wehner, James C. Capretta, Robert Stein, Frederick M. Hess, Andrew P. Kelly, Scott Winship, Michael R. Strain, Adam J. White, James Pethokoukis, Carrie Lukas and W. Bradford Wilcox.

79. Oddly, the report repeatedly refers to the middle class as consisting of 85 percent of the population so self-identified, although the numbers provided in the report, which come from the *Allstate/National Journal* Heartland Monitor Poll XVI, conducted April 5–9, 2013, are identified as 26 percent lower middle class; 46 percent middle class; and 12 percent upper middle class—adding up to just 84 percent (the lower class, 12 percent; and the upper class, 2 percent; 1 percent didn't know or refused to say).

80. Ramesh Ponnuru, "Right Reforms," *National Review*, June 23, 2014. ©2015 *National Review*. Used with permission.

81. Sam Tanenhaus, "The Spirit of '14," *The New York Times Magazine*, July 6, 2014.

82. Ross Douthat, "For Poorer and Richer," *The New York Times*, March 15, 2015.

83. These income figures come from Table 13 of *The Distribution of Household Income and Federal Taxes, 2010*, published by the Congressional Budget Office, December 2013, as do the figures quoted herein for share of after-tax income (percent).

84. Michael Tomasky, "2016: The Republicans Write," *The New York Review of Books*, March 19, 2015. The six books reviewed: Marco Rubio, *American Dreams: Restoring Economic Opportunity for Everyone*; Rick Santorum, *Blue Collar Conservatives: Recommitting to an America That Works*; Paul Ryan, *The Way Forward: Renewing the American Idea*; Ben Carson with Candy Carson, *One Nation: What We Can All Do to Save America's Future*; Mike Huckabee, *God, Guns, Grits, and Gravy*; and Scott Walker with Marc Thiessen, *Unintimidated: A Governor's Story and a Nation's Challenge*. Jeb Bush later published an e-book that also avoided addressing government solutions to wage stagnation.

85. Noam Scheiber, "2016 Hopefuls and Wealthy Are Aligned on Inequality," *The New York Times*, March 30, 2015.

86. Not included in this list of other candidates was Donald Trump (who, alone among the 17 early Republican presidential primary candidates, supported leaving Social Security alone), but the list did include Scott Walker, Marco Rubio, Rand Paul and Ted Cruz—who also favored privatization. Paul Krugman, "Republicans Against Retirement," *The New York Times*, August 17, 2015.

87. See Ben Kamisar, "Jeb Bush Signals Opposition to Minimum Wage Increase," *The Hill*, May 17, 2015. Jeb Bush stated at a March 17, 2015 rally in South Carolina, "I think state minimum wages are fine; the federal government shouldn't be doing this." *The Hill* requested clarification from Bush's representatives to clarify whether he meant the federal government should not be raising the wage or the federal minimum wage should be abolished, but received no clarification.

88. Jeb Bush, quoted by Steve Benen in "Jeb Bush Pushes to Phase-Out Medicare," MSNBC The Rachel Maddow Show / TheMaddowBlog, July 23, 2015. See also Paul Krugman, "Zombies Against Medicare," *The New York Times*, July 27, 2015.

89. See, for example, Eric Alterman, "A Great Newspaper's Shame," *The Nation*, January 12/19, 2015 and Paul Krugman, "Voodoo, Jeb! Style," *The New York Times*, June 19, 2015.

90. The Economist/YouGov Poll, May 16–18, 2015: "Decision to send troops to Iraq: Do you think the United States made a mistake sending troops to fight in Iraq back in 2003?" 55 percent of respondents replied "Yes."

91. Ron Suskind, "Faith, Certainty, and the Presidency of George W. Bush," *The New York Times Magazine*, October 17, 2004.

92. This fact was widely observed, and its meaning for the Republican Party was reflected upon by conservative commentator Peter Wehner in "Seeking President, No Experience Neces-

sary," *The New York Times*, October 4, 2015. Wehner is a senior fellow at the Ethics and Public Policy Center and served in the three previous Republican administrations.

93. Nicholas Kristof, "3 Peerless Republicans for President," *The New York Times*, October 8, 2015.

94. The book was published in London in 1764. See Frederic J. Frommer, "Ellison Uses Thomas Jefferson's Quran," *The Associated Press*, January 5, 2007. See also Charles M. Blow, "Ben Carson and the Truth," *The New York Times*, November 9, 2015.

95. See, for example, Philip Bump, "Donald Trump's Spectacular, Unending, Utterly Baffling, Often-Wrong Campaign Launch," *The Washington Post*, The Fix blog, June 16, 2015. See also Dana Blanton, "Fox News Poll: Reshuffling of GOP Field, Many Agree with Trump on Immigration," FoxNews.com, July 17, 2015. Trump advocated mass deportation, removal of the 14th Amendment's birthright citizenship and, unlike other Republican candidates, leaving Social Security alone, raising personal taxes on hedge fund managers, and raising tariffs. Alan Rappeport, "Increase Taxes? Talk by Donald Trump Alarms G.O.P.," *The New York Times*, September 1, 2015. Trump's candidacy announcement was followed by that of Governor Chris Christie of New Jersey—which, in turn, was followed by an editorial by editor Tom Moran in the Newark *Star-Ledger* titled "After 14 Years of Watching Christie, A Warning: He Lies," June 27, 2015. Governor Christie got no better treatment from his neighbors—see "Gov. Christie's Phony Truth-Telling," The Editorial Board, *The New York Times*, July 1, 2015.

96. "Trump Supporters Think Obama Is a Muslim Born in Another Country," Public Policy Polling, September 1, 2015.

97. A somewhat similar analysis was presented on NPR's *Morning Edition* September 4, 2015, wherein Mara Liasson quoted the liberal Michael Lind and the conservative Steve Schmidt regarding the populism on display in the 2016 election campaign. Schmidt was continuing a theme that he had observed as a guest on *NBC News Meet the Press*, June 15, 2014—that an opportunity existed for someone to run in 2016 on the populist right. He observed, also, this populism of the right was already a global phenomenon driven by people dissatisfied with what they perceive as elite and out-of-touch leaders—in all of the Western democracies (citing the rise of UKIP in England, the National Front in France, the Netherlands, Sweden and Australia). It can be observed in retrospect that his prescience regarding populism on the right was seen soon afterward in the US with the candidacies of Trump, Carson and Fiorina, but more recently populism on the left has arisen as well in the US with Sanders and globally.

98. Ben Carson, interview on CNN, August 26, 2015.

99. See Glenn Kessler, "Ben Carson's Claim that "We Have 10 Times More People on Welfare" Since the 1960s," *The Washington Post* Fact Checker, September 8, 2015. Kessler allowed Carson's spokesman, Doug Watts, to after-the-fact amend Carson's statement to include all means-tested programs and not just welfare—an obviously much larger number—which Kessler still could not square with the 10 times claim or another claim Carson made, that $19 trillion had gone into fighting poverty since the mid-1960s. To check the calculations herein: 4.4—3.0 = 1.4, and 1.4 / 4.4 equals a 32 percent reduction in welfare recipients. And, 4.4 / 194 = 2.27 percent; 3.0 / 320 = 0.94 percent; 2.27 x 0.585 = 1.33; 2.27—1.33 = 0.94. Thus, there has been a 58.5 percent reduction in the percentage of the population on welfare since 1965.

100. See Alan E. Steinweis, "Ben Carson's Bad History," *The New York Times*, October 15, 2015. Steinweis is a professor of history and Holocaust studies at the University of Vermont. As observed by Steinweis, Jews constituted less than 1 percent of Germany's population (about 500,000 out of a total German population of about 67 million, according to the United States Holocaust Memorial Museum website).

101. See Peter Wehner, "Why Ben Carson's Nazi Analogies Matter," *The New York Times*, October 20, 2015. Wehner is senior fellow at the Ethics and Public Policy Center, served in the last three Republican administrations and is a contributing opinion writer.

102. See, e.g., Theodore Schleifer, "Trump Doesn't Challenge Anti-Muslim Questioner at Event," *CNN.com*, September 18, 2015. The 2008 campaign incident is addressed in Chapter 3.

103. See Steven Dennis, "Kevin McCarthy Gives Boehner B-, Credits Benghazi Committee for Hurting Hillary Clinton's Poll Numbers," *Roll Call*, September 30, 2015. See also E.J. Dionne Jr., "Kevin McCarthy's Truthful Gaffe on Benghazi," *The Washington Post*, September

30, 2015, Kathleen Parker, "It's Up to Voters to Break Up the GOP Brat Pack," *The Washington Post*, September 30, 2015 and this opinion piece coincidentally published the day before Kevin McCarthy made his statement, Richard Cohen, "The Benghazi Panel Is a Scandal of a Committee," *The Washington Post*, September 28, 2015.

104. Maggie Haberman, "Another Republican Lawmaker Suggests Benghazi Inquiry Is Going After Hillary Clinton," First Draft blog, *The New York Times*, October 15, 2015.

105. The name of the former investigator was Bradley F. Podliska, a major in the Air Force Reserve. Noam Scheiber, Eric Lipton and Michael C. Schmidt, "Suit Over Firing Exposes Strife Within Benghazi Panel," *The New York Times*, October 11, 2015.

106. See Michael S. Schmidt, "Flare-Up on Benghazi Committee As Hillary Clinton Testimony Nears," *The New York Times*, October 19, 2015.

107. Similar observations were made in an editorial titled "Crazy Talk" in *The New York Times* after the debate and an op-ed by Paul Krugman, "Fantasies and Fictions," that appeared in the same edition of *The New York Times* of September 18, 2015. See also Chauncey DeVega, "The GOP Debate's Terrifying Alternate Reality: Inside the Political Delusions of a Party on the Edge," *Salon.com*, September 18, 2015.

108. Francis Wilkinson, "Republicans Gone Wild: Q&A with Mann and Ornstein," Bloombergview.com October 14, 2015. See also Eric Alterman, "St. Paul Returns," *The Nation*, November 16, 2015.

109. Paul Krugman joined in criticizing the combination of conservative and Republican dysfunction and the media's complicity in the spectacle in "It's All Benghazi," *The New York Times*, October 9, 2015.

110. David Brooks, "The Republicans' Incompetence Caucus," *The New York Times*, October 13, 2015.

111. Paul Krugman, "Everett Dirksen Doesn't Live Here Anymore," Paul Krugman, The Conscience of a Liberal Blog, *The New York Times*, October 13, 2015.

112. The Editorial Board, "The Grown-Ups Take the Stage at the Democratic Debate," *The New York Times*, October 14, 2015.

113. See, for example, Catherine Rampell, "The Republicans are Right. We in the Media Do Suck." *The Washington Post*, October 29, 2015. Her analysis was that the media had failed by failing to confront the Republican candidates when they did not tell the truth, thereby encouraging them to not tell the truth in the future. See also Charles M. Blow, "Gotcha, G.O.P.," *The New York Times*, November 2, 2015. The name of the Dallas-based company, Mannatech, evokes reference to manna (a sort of food of debated characteristics) from heaven referred to in *Exodus* 16:1–36 and in *Numbers* 11:1–9. Carson was a speaker for the company in a video and speaker at company functions four times, and referred to its "glyconutrient" product in a PBS special. See Jim Geraghty, "Ben Carson's Troubling Connection," *National Review*, January 12, 2015 and Jim Geraghty, "What Ben Carson's Mannatech Answer Tells Us," *National Review*, October 29, 2015.

114. Glenn Kessler, "Ben Carson's Absurd Notion That the Founding Fathers Had 'No Elected Office Experience'," Fact Checker blog, *The Washington Post*, November 5, 2015.

115. Jeremy Diamond, "Trump Digs in on 'Wages Too High' Comment," CNN.com, November 12, 2015. And see Bryce Covert and Mike Konczal, "Trump vs. Immigrants," *The Nation*, April 11/18, 2016. This article addresses the ineffectuality of Trump's proposed immigration policies regarding raising of wages.

Chapter Two

Democrats Must Elaborate On and Sustain an Anti-Trickle-Down Narrative to Defeat Republicans

Liberals—Democrats—have in the past failed to confront conservatism and the Republican Party. Possible explanations for this failure are, first, liberals and Democrats have engaged in ad hominem personal attacks on conservatives and Republicans, as though to believe what conservatives and Republicans believe would require that one have a personality flaw. Second, when liberals and Democrats have resisted such ad hominem attacks and have, instead, engaged in a fact-based criticism of at least one element of conservatism of the Republican Party—trickle-down—as President Obama did both as a candidate for the presidency and president—Democrats have not extended that attack to observe that trickle-down is an integral part of the conservative philosophy and the Republican Party. Additionally, this criticism of trickle-down did not extend to a full narrative critique. That will be remedied in this work. Finally, though, unless Democrats vote in not only presidential elections but also off-year elections, we will continue to have trickle-down's upward redistribution of economic and political power far into the future. Next, however, below is a review of the criticisms liberals have made of trickle-down and conservatism—criticisms that have not turned the electoral tide in favor of Democrats.

BARACK OBAMA VERSUS TRICKLE-DOWN

Trickle-down has been the dominant economic philosophy in the nation off and on for the past three and a half decades and, as Nobel Prize laureates

Paul Krugman and Joseph Stiglitz have observed, we have been able to study Republican trickle-down policies in effect during that time and, accordingly, have been able to observe their failure. The competing philosophy to trickle-down conservatism, liberalism, drives the Democratic Party. Liberalism holds that, even in a capitalist system, it is appropriate for government to provide both social insurance to cushion the middle class and poor from the harshness of the market and to provide public institutions to expand opportunity for the middle class and poor, the sum of which stimulates the economy generally.

The trickle-down conservatism of the Republican Party is a direct attack on the liberal institutions—historically established and maintained by Democrats *and* Republicans—that help the poor move up into the middle class, the middle class to move up into the rich, and cushion the middle class against falling into poverty. Trickle-down has converted conservatism into a radical ideology and the Republican Party into a radical party, and the economic and political history since 1980 of the United States and the world cannot be understood without reference to trickle-down's ideological triumph.[1] The failure to successfully confront trickle-down theory, expose it as delusion, and defeat it with a liberalism based in the truths of classical liberalism threatens the future of America's middle class, economy and democracy by undermining necessary institutions, and by ever-further concentrating economic and political power in the hands of a few—a prescription for self-destruction, as illustrated by study of the histories of our own and other nations.[2]

President Obama is among those to confront trickle-down, most strongly as Senator Obama on the campaign trail early in 2008[3] and in the 2012 presidential election, in critiques that will be addressed below. In his first State of the Union Address, he described the decade bookending the Bush administration as a "Lost Decade." Even after two large tax cuts in 2001 and 2003, the economy ended those eight years with fewer jobs than with which it began. Although President Obama did not argue that trickle-down economics is the critical element of conservatism, rendering conservatism, as a philosophy, and the Republican Party, as a party, incapable of governing, he has been an outspoken and continuing critic of trickle-down. In November of 2009 he critiqued trickle-down and observed that one of the nation's challenges is to develop a "post-bubble growth model, one that is sustainable."[4]

Trickle-down economics, as President Obama observed in a 2011 speech in Osawatomie, Kansas "doesn't work. It's never worked."[5] Trickle-down has never worked because, as he also observed, "In this country, prosperity has never trickled down from the wealthy few. Prosperity has always come from the bottom up, from a strong and growing middle class."[6] In October of 2014, in a speech at Northwestern University in Evanston, Illinois, he returned to this critique, observing: "American economic greatness has never trickled down from the top. It grows from a rising, thriving middle class and opportunity for working people. That's what makes us different."[7] Returning to his October 2014 speech, he referred to his record for support of his assertion:

> Here are the facts: When I took office, businesses were laying off 800,000 Americans a month. Today, our businesses are hiring 200,000 Americans a month. (Applause.) The unemployment rate has come down from a high of 10 percent in 2009, to 6.1 percent today. (Applause.) [The next day, October 3, 2014, it was announced as 5.9 percent.] Over the past four and a half years, our businesses have created 10 million new jobs; this is the longest uninterrupted stretch of private sector job creation in our history. Think about that. And you don't have to applaud at—because I'm going to be giving you a lot of good statistics. (Laughter.) Right now, there are more job openings than at any time since 2001. All told, the United States has put more people back to work than Europe, Japan, and every other advanced economy combined. I want you to think about that. We have put more people back to work, here in America, than Europe, Japan, and every other advanced economy combined.

It was, as observed earlier, an excellent record, against which Republicans defended their trickle-down faith with anecdotal biographies of fellow Republicans who triumphed against the odds. Among the prominent conservatives who delivered the official Republican State of the Union responses over the past several years are Representative Cathy McMorris Rodgers (R-WA), who grew up on a small family farm in eastern Washington; Senator Marco Rubio (R-FL), whose parents emigrated from Cuba; and Governor Bobby Jindal (R-LA) whose parents emigrated from India.

These biographies all anecdotally reinforce the conservative narrative that anyone can still make it in America if they work hard enough. Their stories are compelling, and liberals share admiration for their striving. Liberals counter, however, that there are many millions of other Americans who are also entitled to the American Dream, even though they do not have an MBA from the University of Washington, a Law Degree from the University of Miami, or a Bachelor of Science in biology and public policy from Brown University and graduate degree from Oxford University courtesy of a Rhodes scholarship. Evidence is overwhelming that trickle-down is failing that latter group of Americans, and that evidence will be reviewed herein.

Trickle-Down Will End Only When the Middle Class Sees It's in Their Interest to End It

Notwithstanding President Obama's critiques of trickle-down, when Grover Norquist of the Americans for Tax Reform says of government, "I want to reduce it to the size where I can drag it into the bathroom and drown it in the bathtub,"[8] he is also saying that he wants to shrink or abolish the government programs upon which millions in the middle class and poor rely for their very survival. And yet, millions of middle class and poor Americans continue to vote for Republican proponents of trickle-down. In a section titled "Is There Hope?" appearing near the end of his book, *The Price of Inequality*, Joseph Stiglitz observed that, even with democracy tilted toward the interests of the 1 percent, the 99 percent could yet come to realize that they have been dupes for the 1 percent[9] or, alternatively, the 1 percent could realize that it is in their enlightened self-interest to support liberal programs.[10]

Similarly, Georgetown University law professor Peter Edelman observed in his 2012 book, *So Rich, So Poor: Why It's So Hard to End Poverty in America*[11]:

> As long as middle-income voters think they have more in common with the people at the top than the people at the bottom, we are cooked . . . .The challenge is to get people in the middle to understand which side of the line they are on. If they continue to believe that social mobility is realistically available for themselves and their children the way things are playing out, they will be much less likely to do what they have to do to protect themselves, let alone sympathize with people down the line. The people have the power if they will use it, but they have to see that it is in their interest to do so.

And, similarly, Francis Fukuyama, sociologist, former neoconservative and author of *The End of History*, in a 2012 essay in *Foreign Affairs* appropriately wondered at the fact that despite the anger toward the Wall Street bailouts compounded on over three decades of income and wealth stagnation and growing inequality, it is right-wing populism that has arisen in response, as exemplified by the Tea Party, rather than populism of the left. He concluded, consistent with the case made herein, that the left has failed because of a failure of ideas—a failure to overcome the narrative of the right that the interests of the middle class and working poor are better served by free markets and small government.[12]

Finally, as observed by Kevin Drum, political blogger for *Mother Jones*, in his 2011 essay, "Plutocracy Now," *Mother Jones* March/April 2011, " . . . 30 years of free-market evangelism have convinced nearly everyone—even middle class voters who keep getting the short end of the economic stick—that policy preferences of the business community are good for everyone . . . .It's not clear how this will get turned around." Nonetheless, he concluded: "If the left ever wants to regain the vigor that powered earlier eras of liberal reform, it needs to rebuild the infrastructure of economic populism that we've ignored for too long. Figuring out how to do that is the central task of the new decade."[13] This work is a response to the calls of Stiglitz, Edelman, Fukuyama and Drum. But first, we try to explain why liberals have not so responded before.

THE LIBERAL PREFERENCE TO PSYCHOANALYZE

How Conservative Intellectual History Was Met by Liberal Psychoanalysis

The Introduction touched upon Friedrich Hayek's 1944 book, *The Road to Serfdom*, and how it inspired Prime Minister Thatcher in the UK and President Reagan in the US, as well as others in the late 1970s and 1980s, and facilitated the conservative victories in their respective countries. In his book, Hayek issued a warning to the people of Great Britain and the Continent that the welfare state and socialism were along the road to totalitarian dictatorship. With the advantage of hindsight, we can see he was wrong, as no nation that adopted a welfare state suffered that fate.

In contrast, regarding Germany, it is clear that John Maynard Keynes was correct in warning, in *The Economic Consequences of the Peace* (1919), of the danger of placing excessively burdensome war reparations on it after World War I. While Germany could grow even with this burden prior to the Great Depression, once the Great Depression arrived, servicing the debt became impossible, prompting inflation of the currency that led to hyperinflation, and preparing the way for Hitler and his Nazi Party. Regarding the former Soviet Union, the other totalitarian nation of his day, it is clear that totalitarianism followed not a gradual growth of the welfare state but, rather, a revolution against the Czar that was captured by Lenin and fellow communist revolutionaries. Similarly, the totalitarianism of Communist China followed not a gradual growth of the welfare state but, rather, a revolution that was led and captured by Mao Tse Tung and fellow communist revolutionaries.

At the time, however, Hayek's book was very popular with conservatives, and that popularity continues through the present—although, as will be seen, Hayek was also a harsh critic of conservatism. Nonetheless, Hayek's vision and the similar vision of other heroes of conservatism inspired victory over the prevailing thought of the day, Keynesianism, named after Hayek's rival, and inspired in great part by Keynes's influential book, *The General Theory of Employment, Interest and Money* (1936).[14]

Keynes and his followers favored government intervention in the economy to encourage economic growth and prosperity—such interventions as fiscal stimulus (increases in government spending), monetary stimulus (low interest rates) and spreading of income and wealth via highly progressive tax rates. For most of the post-World War II period growth and prosperity resulted. However, beginning in the 1970s, economic stagnation and rising unemployment began to take hold in the UK and in the US—where it combined with rising consumer price inflation (generally rising prices due, in great part, to the twin oil supply crises of the Arab oil embargo of 1973 and the Iranian Revolution in 1979-1980) in what came to be called "stagflation."

In response, Thatcher, as Prime Minister, and Reagan, as presidential candidate, both promoted "free market" reforms in 1979 and 1980 in their respective countries. Coinciding with Reagan's run for the presidency were several movements with similar goals. In Orange County, California, property owners, enraged because inflation was pushing up their annual property tax assessments, staged a property tax revolt, securing in 1978 the passage of Proposition 13, limiting property tax assessments. About the same time, several pro-free market movements were underway among academic economists: monetarism at the University of Chicago ("the Chicago School"—leader of which was Milton Friedman, who had been influenced by Hayek), "supply-side" economics (led by Robert Mundell of Columbia University and Art Laffer of the University of Southern California), and "Austrian School" economics (like that of Friedrich Hayek).[15] Simultaneously, questions were being raised by academicians regarding the effectiveness of growing welfare expenditures, and these academicians were aided by the emergence and growth of conservative think tanks created to promote tax cuts for the rich and repeal of the social insurance programs and regulation that arose during and after the New Deal.

Of the three schools of influence, "supply-side" came to dominate the public imagination. The triumph of the trickle-down-supply-side vision was due to the influence of several books—not only *The Road to Serfdom*, but others including Jude Wanniski's *The Way the World Works* (1978) and George Gilder's *Wealth and Poverty* (1981) previously mentioned; and Milton Friedman's *Capitalism and Freedom* (1962) and *Free to Choose* (1980; sponsored by the Scaife Foundation and Olin Foundation); and Charles Murray's *Losing Ground* (1984; sponsored by the Olin Foundation and the Smith Richardson Foundation); as well as works of numerous other authors and columnists both conservative and libertarian.

In contrast, no book critical of trickle-down has similarly captured the attention of the public. Liberals have confronted conservatism more broadly, but even then they typically have done so not by directly confronting conservative ideas but, instead—other than with Barack Obama's critiques—by waging personal attacks on conservatives. These attacks have attributed to conservatives an "authoritarian personality," anti-intellectualism, paranoia, racism, "demographic panic," bitterness about economic decline and succumbing out of ignorance to social arguments that made them abandon their economic self-interest. Liberals have also blamed the success of trickle-down on the work of multimillionaires and multibillionaires and other rich supporters of trickle-down who waged class warfare against the middle class and poor and staged a *coup d'état*, taking over the highest levels of government.

All of these explanations will be reviewed below and rejected as inadequate explanations for conservative success. The American people deserve better—they deserve a fact-based liberal critique of trickle-down. A prominent example of the liberal tendency to psychoanalyze conservatives rather than confront conservative trickle-down theory with the facts occurred on the campaign trail in 2008, when then Senator Obama made an offhand remark on the campaign trail in San Francisco which he regretted, observing that in small towns in Pennsylvania and the Midwest people have fallen on hard times and defensively they tend to cling to guns or religion and harbor anti-immigrant or anti-trade sentiment.[16]

It should be observed that liberals have not been alone in criticizing conservative personality traits. Friedrich Hayek remarked upon conservatives' "fondness for authority" in his classic *The Constitution of Liberty* (1961).[17] Similarly struck by this adoration of authority was former Nixon advisor John Dean in *Conservatives Without Conscience* (2006). The study of the "authoritarian personality" occupies much of Dean's book, continuing a line of critique begun by Theodor Adorno in *The Authoritarian Personality* (1950).[18]

The most famous dismissal of conservative intellect by a liberal was that by the literary critic and author Lionel Trilling, who famously observed in the Preface to his 1950 book *The Liberal Imagination* that in the United States the only intellectual tradition is liberalism and denied that conservatism even had ideas.[19] A few observations about that quote are appropriate. First, it illustrates a liberal prejudice that may have been somewhat accurate in its time but is no longer so. Second, it illustrates the tremendous progress conservatism has made in generating ideas over the space of the mere half century since the beginnings of the post-World War II conservative movement. In fact, as will be seen here, the reality of the vast volume of intellectual work by conservatives in support of the trickle-down vision facilitates the task of confronting trickle-down and exposing it as a delusion. Finally, the triumph of trickle-down from beginnings so devoid of respect for intellectual underpinnings is but one illustration of a point that will be stressed throughout: As one acknowledges the vast expansion of influence of conservatism since Trilling's time, one observes that culture is malleable and subject to sometimes rapid, tremendous change. As conservatives were able, through effort, to challenge and ultimately dominate liberals in the world of ideas, similarly, liberals, through effort, will be able to challenge and dominate conservatives in the world of ideas. For liberals, the time is long overdue for re-engaging in the world of ideas, which over the past three and a half decades has been dominated by conservatives.[20]

The liberal critique of conservative anti-intellectualism continued from the 1950s into the 1960s with Richard Hofstadter's *Anti-intellectualism in American Life* (1963) followed by *The Paranoid Style in American Politics*

(1965). A similar theme has emerged recently, that of blaming conservative rage on what Michael Lind calls "demographic panic" due to demographic decline[21] —the same phenomenon is referred to as "white minority politics" by John Avlon, who based his observations in part on Hofstadter's works and attributed the term to conservative David Frum.[22] As columnist Frank Rich of *The New York Times* explained the concept, whites are anxious over the declining percentage of population constituted by white non-Hispanics—in 2012, white non-Hispanic births were projected to be in the minority.[23] A corollary to the observation of the facts regarding projected demographics is liberal smugness regarding the "inevitability" of a more liberal, Democratic America in the future because of a white minority future. But nothing in politics in inevitable, and such a future is neither imminently nor even ultimately inevitable unless Democrats give these minorities compelling arguments for why they should vote Democrat.

In a column that preceded the publication of *The Conscience of a Liberal* (2007), Paul Krugman characterized movement conservatism as a corrupt political machine combining business and religious interests that may once have been based on ideas but no longer is.[24] Movement conservatism is, indeed, a corrupt political machine combining business and religious interests (as will be addressed in detail in the next chapter), but *it has always been, and remains, intensely ideological, and never more so than after the rise of trickle-down ideology in the late 1970s and early 1980s.* In fact, it is precisely movement conservatism's intensely ideological nature that made it succumb to the ideology of trickle-down. Movement conservatism, having taken over the Republican Party, has, itself, been taken over by the trickle-down delusion, converting movement conservatism into what is called herein trickle-down conservatism—an evolution apparently lamented by William F. Buckley, Jr. himself in his last years.[25]

In *The Conscience of a Liberal*, Krugman attributed Republicans' ability to win presidential elections and gain control of Congress to movement conservatives pushing the Republican Party to the right and the party's resultant exercising of its ability "to exploit the race issue to win political dominance in the South. End of story."[26]

Race is certainly part of the story, but it is actually only part of a larger issue of class, and, while somewhat relevant to campaigning, it is irrelevant regarding most of policymaking. It is true, as observed by Dan T. Carter, former professor of history at the University of South Carolina, that there is abundant evidence in Richard Nixon's electoral success of the adoption of a "Southern Strategy"—of a racial theme first exploited by George Wallace.[27] And, for many white conservatives not only in the South but across the country, the Republican Party continues to appeal because of lingering racial resentments. Ronald Reagan, of course, followed similarly well-trod ground, with his launching of his 1980 presidential campaign by declaring his support for states' rights in his speech to the Neshoba County Fair in Philadelphia, Mississippi (where three civil rights workers had been murdered just 16 years before), and his continuing references to the mysterious rich "welfare queen" in Chicago.[28]

However, Reagan's appeal went beyond that, as he stressed supply-side economics and rebuilding military might. And, Republican success at exploiting racial resentment in the South does not explain the popularity of major policy issues of the conservative administration of President George W. Bush, nor does it guarantee political success. Appeals to racism—coded or direct—had nothing to do with the popularity of policies of continued implementation of trickle-down economics via tax cuts tilted toward the rich and continued financial and business deregulation and privatization of government services and the social safety net, or going to war in Iraq, use of torture, or the major social issues of abortion and same-sex marriage. And, importantly, the 2008 election, featuring the first African American major party presidential candidate, refueled racist appeals by the opposition, however, victories by Candidate Obama in the Old Confederacy states of Virginia, North Carolina and Florida rebut the argument that race determines elections in the South (and, of course, before that President Bill Clinton won numerous Southern states twice by appeals across racial lines).

Trickle-down economics does not build on racial resentment, however, it does build on a "Southernization" of the Republican Party, which consists of policy preferences that go beyond race, as will be addressed in detail in Chapter 3.[29] Thus, what a race-based explanation for Republican electoral success fails to observe is that the Republican Party since Reagan's election in 1980 has presented a vision of the way the world works that resonates with conservative Southerners and includes an explanation of the importance of race but places it in the context of class. The economic theme is that hard-scrapping whites must make sure their rich betters are happy, for it is upon them that they count for jobs and income (refer to the representative quote in the previous chapter from the Raleigh, North Carolina Tea Partier). And, they believe, the threat to their own wellbeing is not from the greed of their betters but, rather, the attempts of their inferiors in this class system—distinguished by color and lack of citizenship—to get their own piece of the economic pie. To this worldview add receptivity to the illiberal values above and a deep distrust of the federal government, governmental process and unions.

Similar fault is found in the argument made by Thomas Frank, in his influential book, *What's the Matter with Kansas?*, that poor and middle class Americans are supporting economic policies that hurt them because they are so enamored with conservative social policy.

Frank's argument was seriously called into question by a study conducted at the University of Arizona examining voting behavior of the 45 percent of white Americans who describe themselves as working class, using data from the General Social Survey. The findings of the study were addressed by George Packer in an article in *The New Yorker* magazine published weeks before the 2008 election.[30] The study set out to explain the decline in white working class support for Democrats and, as Packer observed, concluded that social issues had little to do with the shift. Instead, it was based on a judgment that the Democratic Party no longer was relevant to these voters. As Packer observed, the Democrats lost the white working class vote because the Democratic Party failed to make the case that the Democrats' solution—government—could help provide economic security.

Having lost faith in the inclination or ability of the Democratic Party to use government to restore economic security to them, working class whites migrated to the beguiling Republican idea that trickle-down's policies will ultimately work for their economic benefit—will result in economic growth that will expand the number of jobs and raise their incomes. And, they stay with Republicans today because they have seen nothing from Democrats to rebut that assumption, nor have they seen anything proposed by the Democrats in its place.

A related line of attack liberals have used is to accuse the rich of waging "class warfare"—famously, multibillionaire investor Warren Buffet, in an interview with conservative Ben Stein in 2006, agreed that there was class warfare and that his class was winning.[31] Liberals picked up this attack in 2011—one prominent example was from liberal Senator Bernie Sanders (I-VT), in response to an interview question in February of that year regarding how to mobilize workers not just in Wisconsin, in response to Governor Scott Walker's attacks on public unions, but on a national scale. Senator Sanders urged recognition that this was part of a concerted class warfare attack on the middle class and working families by the Koch brothers and other wealthy Americans.[32]

Prominent liberals have also accused the financial elite of committing a financial *coup d'état*, among them, Representative Marcy Kaptur (D-OH), former IMF chief economist Simon Johnson and *Rolling Stone* reporter Matt Taibbi.[33]

However, as Thomas Frank observed in his 2012 book *Pity the Billionaire,* conservatism made a comeback because it converted Americans to the idea that greater reliance on the free market is the appropriate response to economic stagnation.[34] Thus, Frank corrected his earlier error that attributed conservative success to fooling poor and middle class Americans into supporting economic policies that hurt them by luring them into supporting conservative social policy—in reality, he concluded, these poor and middle class voters had been fooled into support for trickle-down theory itself, as it is argued herein.

But Frank theorized that conversion happened with the bailouts that led to the rise of the Tea Party. In reality, that conversion has been going on for more than three and a half decades, and the groundwork for it was laid by the New Right of Buckley and others in the mid-1950s, ultimately winning over a substantial portion of the middle class with trickle-down beginning in the late 1970s, strengthened by Reagan in the 1980s, and continuing through today.

There is no "class war" going on any more than there is a "generational war." Instead, millions of Americans, regardless of class or age, have become deluded into thinking that a "free market" that upwardly redistributes the revenues attributable to their increased productivity to the wealthy, older Americans and corporations is in their best interest. And, this represents not only a triumph of conservatives but also an unconscionable failure on the part of liberals—a failure that must be confronted and reversed to avoid continued needless suffering. Conversely, this work does not urge that liberals wage class war on the wealthy and business. To the contrary, it urges policymaking based on liberal enlightened self-interest, reason and fact.

THE LIBERAL INABILITY TO COMMUNICATE WITH MIDDLE AMERICA

A perhaps inconvenient truth for liberals is that it might not be the personal failings of those who succumb to conservative ideology that render them unmoved by liberalism but, rather, the inability of liberals to articulate their ideas that should be so immediately recognizable as compelling. It is critical that liberals confront the trickle-down vision and develop a competing liberal vision, and present both in a form that wins over Middle America—the Middle America consisting of millions of families who have been victimized by trickle-down. Yet, the most visible proponent of a liberal vision, President Obama, is also widely acknowledged as failing to speak to and for Middle America. This failure created the opening for Republican victories in 2010 and 2014.

That the conservatives would bounce back from defeat in 2008 should never have been in doubt. The McCain-Palin ticket garnered more than 58 million votes in 2008 (*nearly 8 million more than Bush-Cheney won in 2000*).[35] And, poll results as recently as 2011 consistently showed *nearly twice as many Americans describing themselves as conservative versus liberal*—39 percent to 21 percent (36 percent described themselves as moderate)[36] —although in 2015 a shift was observed in a prominent poll as the percentage of Americans identifying as conservative declined to 33 percent while the percentage describing themselves as liberal rose to 26 percent.[37]

Middle America deserves a fact-based debate over trickle-down. As E.J. Dionne, Jr. observed in a year-end 2005 opinion piece in *The Washington Post*[38], even then it appeared that the nation had sufficient facts to rebut the supply-side ideas promoted over the previous 30 years, especially by Jude Wanniski in 1978 with his book, *The Way the World Works* (more on this later). And three years later, Dionne predicted in his election-eve 2008 column in *The Washington Post* that if Senator Obama won the election, it would be a clear repudiation of trickle-down.[39]

To the contrary, however, a theme among commentators emerged early in the Obama presidency. John Heilemann and Mark Halperin observed in the Afterword to the paperback edition of *Game Change* (2010), their acclaimed account of the historical 2008 election, after having made a compelling case for change on the campaign trail, once in office the president failed to continue making that case for activist government.[40] Liberals agreed. David Corn, in a year-end 2010 article in *Mother Jones* magazine,[41] observed that, notwithstanding the president's health care reform victory, during his first two years in office, the president failed at "telling the nation's story." He quoted Democratic consultant Paul Begala, who said that when the country was in recession and Ronald Reagan was facing the 1982 midterm, Reagan "didn't blame President Carter or the Democrats. He indicted liberalism: too much government, too much taxation. To fix this mess, he said, we have to stay the course. That was his narrative. It was ideological; it was philosophical. It had sides. It had a story." Similarly, Ari Berman, in a 2011 article in *The Nation* agreed that Reagan won the philosophical battle because he had a narrative. Berman quoted pollster and Democratic political consultant Stanley Greenberg who observed that the Obama narrative is obviously that Democrats have the economic philosophy to make the middle class richer while the Republicans have trickle-down.[42]

Yet, despite all the critiques above, as observed in the beginning of this chapter, Senator Obama, on the campaign trail early in 2008 and in the 2012 campaign observed that trickle-down economics creates a bubble-dependent growth model, and that the failure of conservative trickle-down economics created the ongoing economic crisis.

And, once in office, President Obama continued to deliver that narrative as observed above, returning to critiques of trickle-down on the re-election campaign trail in his December 6, 2011, speech at Osawatomie, Kansas, echoing the speech given a century before in that same venue by President Theodore Roosevelt. And, he again returned to his critique of trickle-down in an April 3, 2012 speech to the Associated Press, in an after re-election speech on economic mobility December 4, 2013 and in an October 2, 2014 address at Northwestern University.

What President Reagan had that President Obama lacked, thus, was not the narrative itself. Rather, he lacked two things regarding that narrative.

First, he lacked an exposition of his basic narrative. The books that propelled Reaganomics were not written by Reagan but by his conservative supporters, so that his references to his vision elicited an understanding of a fully developed critique of liberalism and a conservative vision to take its place. President Obama, in contrast, in his critique of trickle-down has received support from numerous liberals and commentators, but no thorough critique of conservatism and detailed exposition of that narrative has yet been written.

Second, as observed by MSNBC commentator Rachel Maddow,[43] President Obama repeatedly criticized trickle-down as a philosophy but did not criticize either conservatism or the Republican Party for embracing it—a mistake that, as she also observed, has *not* been made by Hillary Clinton as, for example, she took the opportunity during the first debate among candidates for the 2016 Democratic presidential nomination (October 13, 2015) to muse that among enemies she has made she should probably include Republicans. In contrast, when Vice President Joseph Biden announced the following week, October 21, 2015, that he was not running for president, he took the opportunity to distinguish Republicans not as enemies but as the opposition with whom Democrats must work together with for the good of the country. But the original question in the debate was for her to say who viewed *her* as an enemy and, while a positive outlook on politics is commendable, as Vice President Biden himself often observed, "This is not your father's Republican Party"—and this is also not your father's political environment. Republicans say they view liberals and Democrats as the enemy; Republicans in the House of Representatives held more than 50 votes to repeal the Affordable Care Act, the centerpiece legislation of the Obama administration and legislation for which a majority of Americans have, as reflected in numerous polls, expressed support for either maintaining as it is or even strengthening it (see Chapter 6). It is wrong and naïve to believe that Republican politicians and commentators are not telling the truth when they say they view Democrats like Hillary Clinton and Barack Obama as their enemy, and President Obama potentially impaired his effectiveness when he failed to account for the degree of animosity Republicans felt toward him—this animosity and its accompanying obstructionism successfully waged against any proposed use of government to help the American people is an integral part of the new trickle-down conservative Republican extremism addressed herein.[44]

In fact, President Obama persisted in criticizing trickle-down but not linking trickle-down with conservatism and the Republican Party. After having expressed surprise after his 2008 election at the resistance of Republicans to work with him, after his re-election in 2012 he again expressed surprise that Republicans continued to oppose him—overlooking, to his detriment, the extent of Republican animosity toward him.

It is critical, not just to the future of liberalism and the Democratic Party, but also to the future of conservatism and the Republican Party, and the future of the American middle class, economy and democracy, that liberals confront the ideology of trickle-down with an elaborate narrative that illustrates its failings, links trickle-down and its failings squarely with the conservative philosophy and the Republican Party, sustains this confrontation, and refutes trickle-down, conservatism and the Republican Party and provides the alternative liberal vision and policies to take trickle-down's place. This work is intended as part of this effort.

We know how to undo this upward redistribution: *Undo the policies that we, the American people, have implemented pursuant to the trickle-down delusion promoted by conservatives and the Republican Party.* As a guide, we should keep in mind that the policies we are implementing going forward should not only be undoing the upward redistribution of the past three decades, but we should also be increasing *demand*—and it is lack of demand that is inhibiting investment right now, not some conservative nonsense about "uncertainty" on the part of businesses regarding taxes or health care policy.

These are themes in an outstanding column written by liberal commentator Harold Meyerson in *The Washington Post* and published less than 45 days before the 2012 election.[45] There, Meyerson was among the first commentators to expose the lie of trickle-down: that revenues attributable to productivity gains are shared with the workers. In detail Myerson recounted the reality of the productivity/wage disconnect that has occurred in the United States, contrasting the period that immediately followed World War II and ran through the 1970s, when government intervened on behalf of workers, versus our current period since 1980 when government stepped back to let the "free market" operate (more on this in Chapter 7).

Continuing, Meyerson observed that the costs of this upward redistribution are seen not just in economic but also social indexes, most apparently among poorly educated whites. Meyerson cited the decline in marriage rates and family stability among the white working class as observed by conservative commentator Charles Murray in his 2012 book *Coming Apart: The State of White America 1960-2010* (addressed later herein) and the decline in longevity as reported by Sabrina Tavernise of *The New York Times*, summarizing a recent study's conclusion that although other Americans' life expectancy has advanced, since 1990 the life expectancy of whites without high school diplomas has declined by three years for men and five years for women.[46]

Stagnant economic growth, stagnant and falling wages, declining marriage rates, declining attendance at religious services, declining family stability, and declining life expectancy—these are all the results of trickle-down policies. And these will not be reversed by insulting conservatives but, rather, by, as observed above, directly confronting the ideology of trickle-down with an elaborate narrative that illustrates its failings, linking trickle-down and its failings squarely with the conservative philosophy and the Republican Party, sustaining this confrontation, and refuting trickle-down, conservatism and the Republican Party and providing the alternative liberal vision and policies to take trickle-down's place.

NOTES

1. As was observed by columnist for *The New York Times* , Thomas Friedman, on *Meet the Press* April 1, 2012. See also E. J. Dionne, Jr., "The Right's Stealthy Coup," *The Washington Post* , April 1, 2012.
2. See Daron Acemoglu and James A. Robinson, *Why Nations Fail: The Origins of Power, Prosperity and Poverty* (2012), addressed later herein. See also Chrystia Freeland, "The Self-Destruction of the 1 Percent," *The New York Times*, October 14, 2012, and Chrystia Freeland, *Plutocrats: The Rise of the New Global Super-Rich and the Fall of Everyone Else* (2012), from which her opinion essay is adapted.
3. See, for example, David Leonhardt, "Closing Income Gap Tops Obama's Agenda for Economic Change," *The New York Times*, February 2, 2008. See also "Statement from Senator Barack Obama on Today's Decline in our GDP," Chicago, IL October 30, 2008, *Organizing for America* website, barackobama.com. Quoted in E. J. Dionne, Jr., "Referendum on Trickle-Down," *The Washington Post*, October 31, 2008.
4. President Barack Obama, Presidential Remarks on the Economy, C-SPAN, November 2, 2009. See also Neil Irwin, "Aughts Were a Lost Decade for U.S. Economy, Workers," *The Washington Post*, January 2, 2010.
5. President Barack Obama, in Osawatomie, Kansas, December 6, 2011. Osawatomie, Kansas, is where Theodore Roosevelt launched his "new nationalism" program in a speech August 31, 1910.
6. President Barack Obama, "Remarks by the President on the Economy," Florida Atlantic University, April 10, 2012. For the applicability of this idea internationally, see Lawrence Summers, "Time US Leadership Woke Up to a New Economic Era," *Financial Times*, April 5, 2015. Summers is Charles W. Eliot university professor at Harvard and former US Treasury secretary.
7. President Barack Obama, Northwestern University, Evanston, Illinois, October 2, 2014.
8. Interview, Grover Norquist with Mara Liasson, on "Morning Edition," National Public Radio, May 25, 2001.
9. Joseph Stiglitz, *The Price of Inequality: How Today's Divided Society Endangers Our Future* (New York: W. W. Norton & Company, Inc.; 2012), p. 287.
10. Joseph Stiglitz, *The Price of Inequality: How Today's Divided Society Endangers Our Future* (New York: W. W. Norton & Company; 2012), p. 288.
11. Peter B. Edelman, *So Rich, So Poor: Why It's So Hard to End Poverty in America* (New York: The New Press; 2012), p. 160. Similar ideas were expressed in Peter Edelman, "Poverty in America: Why Can't We End It?" *The New York Times*, July 28, 2012.
12. Francis Fukuyama, "The Future of History," *Foreign Affairs*, January/February 2012.
13. Kevin Drum, "Plutocracy Now," *Mother Jones* March/April 2011.
14. The rivalry between Friedrich Hayek and John Maynard Keynes is documented by Daniel Yergin and Joseph Stanislaw in their book *The Commanding Heights* (1998), and in their PBS series of the same name, addressed in the following chapter. As their analysis concluded in 1998, they declared Hayek the victor. With the benefit of further hindsight, however, we can see that as Hayek won we all lost. See also Nicholas Wapshott, *Keynes Hayek: The Clash That Defined Modern Economics* (New York: W.W. Norton & Company, Inc.; 2011).

15. Inspired by the work of Austrians Friedrich Hayek, Ludwig von Mises, Carl Menger, Eugen von Böhm-Bawerk and Friedrich von Wieser, prominent members of the "Austrian School" were Murray Rothbard at Columbia University, Israel Kirzner at New York University and Gottfried Haberler at Harvard University.

16. Katharine Q. Seelye and Jeff Zeleny, "On the Defensive, Obama Calls His Words Ill-Chosen," *The New York Times*, April 13, 2008.

17. Friedrich Hayek, *The Constitution of Liberty* (Chicago: The University of Chicago Press; 1960), p. 400. Other characteristics of conservatism observed by Hayek and relevant today are "hostility to internationalism" and "strident nationalism" (observed by Hayek in *The Constitution of Liberty*, in his Postscript tilted "Why I am Not a Conservative;" p. 405).

18. The present work resists the temptation to ascribe to conservatives a variety of psychosis—be it an authoritarian personality or "anti-intellectualism" or "paranoia"—from previous critiques of conservatism.

19. Lionel Trilling, *The Liberal Imagination: Essays on Literature and Society* (New York: Charles Scribner's Sons; 1950 and 1976), p. ix. Lionel Trilling (1905–1975) was an American literary critic, author and professor of English at Columbia University. He was also a member of "the New York Intellectuals" and a member of the staff of the *Partisan Review*. Among the other members of the New York Intellectuals were Paul Goodman, Irving Howe, Saul Bellow, Daniel Bell, Hannah Arendt, Susan Sontag, Norman Podhoretz and Hilton Kramer.

20. See Jonathan Darman, "Here They Go Again," *Newsweek*, September 29, 2008.

21. Michael Lind, "Why Republicans Want Gridlock, *Salon.com*, March 1, 2010. Lind, as a young man, was mentored by William F. Buckley, Jr., in which he was joined by a young Fareed Zakaria, whose ideas also will be extensively addressed herein.

22. John Avlon, *Wingnuts: How the Lunatic Fringe Hijacked America* (2010). Avlon writes from the perspective of a centrist.

23. Frank Rich "The Rage Is Not About Health Care," *The New York Times*, March 28, 2010.

24. Paul Krugman, "The Great Revulsion," *The New York Times*, November 10, 2006.

25. For an appreciation of the disappointment on the part of William F. Buckley, Jr. regarding the evolution of movement conservatism toward what is called herein trickle-down conservatism, see Johann Hari's "Titanic," *The New Republic*, July 2, 2007 (a version of the article was repeated under the title "Ship of Fools: Johann Hari Sets Sail with America's Swashbuckling Neocons" in *The Independent*, July 13, 2007). In the article Hari, a young British writer, recounted his adventures on the annual *National Review* ship cruise. He ably captured the fault lines in the movement and the eccentricities of some of its well-heeled patrons, as well as the bittersweet reflections of William F. Buckley, Jr., on the movement he led, on what would be his last cruise.

26. Paul Krugman, *The Conscience of a Liberal* (New York, London: W. W. Norton & Company, Inc.; 2007), p. 182.

27. Dan T. Carter, *From George Wallace to Newt Gingrich: Race in the Conservative Counterrevolution, 1963–1994* (1996).

28. Reagan's speech was delivered August 3, 1980. An extensively researched article on the woman who inspired the "welfare queen" label, Linda Taylor, was written by Josh Levin—see "The Welfare Queen," *Slate*, December 19, 2013. Disturbingly, it appears that public outrage over the $8,000 in welfare fraud for which she was convicted diverted attention from allegations against her of murder, kidnapping and baby trafficking.

29. For a brief discussion of the Southernization of the nation, see Nicholas Lemann, "The Price of Union: The Undefeatable South," *The New Yorker*, November 2, 2015.

30. George Packer, "The Hardest Vote," *The New Yorker*, October 13, 2008.

31. Warren Buffett to Ben Stein, quoted in Ben Stein, "In Class Warfare, Guess Which Class Is Winning," *The New York Times*, November 26, 2006.

32. Senator Bernie Sanders in "A Concerted Attack on the Middle Class," MSNBC interview with Cenk Uygur, February 22, 2011.

33. Representative Kaptur agreed with Michael Moore's characterization of a "financial *coup d'état*" in Moore's film, "Capitalism: A Love Story." See also Bill Moyers' interview with Representative Kaptur and Simon Johnson on *Bill Moyers' Journal*, interview transcript

posted at the *AlterNet website* October 12, 2009. See also Matt Taibbi, "The Big Takeover," *Rolling Stone*, March 19, 2009, and Simon Johnson, "The Quiet Coup," *The Atlantic*, May 2009.

34. Thomas Frank, *Pity the Billionaire: The Hard-Times Swindle and the Unlikely Comeback of the Right* (New York: Metropolitan Books, Henry Holt and Company, LLC; 2012); p. 3.

35. McCain-Palin in 2008 got 58,343,671 votes versus Bush-Cheney in 2000 with 50,406,002—and, it should be remembered, that Gore-Lieberman lost the election but won the popular vote with 50,999,897.

36. "Beyond Red vs. Blue: Political Typology," Pew Research Center for the People & the Press; May 4, 2011. Self-described ideology was based on polls conducted from January through March 2011 with 5,917 respondents. Results were similar to those of the *Washington Post*-ABC News Poll conducted of American adults by telephone April 14-17, 2011 quoted above, as well as earlier versions of these polls, and Gallup polls, conducted over the previous decade. Roughly consistent results have been observed over the past decade and in various polls as well regarding party identification, although party identification breaks out as follows: 38 percent Democrat 25 percent Republican and 33 percent identify themselves as independent. "Party Identification and Election Polls," Pew Research Center, August 3, 2012.

37. The poll was an NBC News/Wall Street Journal poll—see Dana Milbank, "Americans Reclaim the Liberal Label," *The Washington Post*. June 19, 2015.

38. E. J. Dionne, Jr., "The New Worn-Out Ideas," *The Washington Post*, December 16, 2005.

39. E. J. Dionne, Jr., "Referendum on Trickle-Down," *The Washington Post*, October 31, 2008.

40. John Heilemann and Mark Halperin, *Game Change: Obama and the Clintons, McCain and Palin, and the Race of a Lifetime* (New York: Harper Perennial, 2010), p. 443.

41. David Corn, "How Obama Lost the Narrative, *Mother Jones*, November/December 2010.

42. Ari Berman, "Obama: Triangulation 2.0?" *The Nation*, February 7, 2011.

43. On MSNBC's *The Rachel Maddow Show*, October 14, 2015.

44. See, for example, James Vega, "A Democratic Strategist Strategy Memo," *The Democratic Strategist*, November 2014 and Marc Armbinder, "Why Democrats Should Treat Republicans Like Their Mortal Enemy," *The Week*, December 3, 2014.

45. Harold Meyerson, "Redistributing Wealth Upward," *The Washington Post*, September 25, 2012.

46. See: Sabrina Tavernise, "Life Spans Shrink for Least-Educated Whites in the U.S.," *The New York Times*, September 20, 2012, and "Life Spans of the Rich Leave the Poor Behind," *The New York Times*, February 13, 2016.

II

The Trickle-Down Delusions

Chapter Three

Trickle-Down

Enabling Realization of the Dream to Make the "Holy Rollers Lie Down with the High Rollers"

As observed in the Introduction, movement conservatism was created out of the combination of traditionalism, libertarianism and anti-communism. Movement conservatism, with the advent of the trickle-down ideology, evolved in a more extremist direction[1] as traditionalism was overtaken by the Religious Right; anti-communism was replaced by neoconservatism; and libertarianism was captured and redefined by a cadre of wealthy plutocrats who forged an easy alliance of supply-siders and crony capitalists.

Key to understanding the critique that follows is the recognition that movement conservatism, a philosophy that originally rallied around a "leave us alone" small government vision, evolved under the influence of trickle-down ideology—a political philosophy masquerading as an economic theory, synonymous with supply-side economics and Reaganomics. The broad acceptance of trickle-down enabled the realization of the conservative Republican dream to "make the Holy Rollers lie down with the high rollers" and the political union of the plutocrats, the Religious Right and neoconservatives. Plutocrats poured money into libertarian and conservative think tanks and lobbying organizations, achieving a near-consensus nationally around lower taxes, abolition of business regulations and shrinking of government services and benefits upon which the middle class and poor rely. The result of trickle-down is that these plutocrats, in undermining the public institutions upon which the middle class and poor rely, leave them ever more exposed to the harshness of the market and the power of the plutocrats over it—power evidenced by more than three decades of stagnating or even shrinking real wages. Support for these policies is combined with support of a larger military and more interventionist foreign policy which requires large standing armies the plutocrats are content to staff with these same economically squeezed middle class and poor.

It has not always been this way. Historically, wealthy elites, among them Carnegie, Rockefeller, Ford and others, notwithstanding their personal conservative values, funded foundations that supported liberal institutions. This practice, however, as addressed previously, was roundly criticized in the 1970s and, in response, wealthy elites began to direct their contributions to conservative causes. It is difficult to imagine that there was not a substantial amount of cynicism coupled with raw self-interest associated with doing so, and, as will be observed by conservatives themselves in Chapter 5, they turned conservative political philosophy itself into a self-serving near-religion organized around the unshakable faith in the upward redistribution of income and wealth.

And, again, President Obama captured the essence of this change[2]:

> The congressional Republican budget is something different altogether. It is a Trojan Horse. Disguised as deficit reduction plans, it is really an attempt to impose a radical vision on our country. It is thinly veiled social Darwinism. It is antithetical to our entire history as a land of opportunity and upward mobility for everybody who's willing to work for it; a place where prosperity doesn't trickle down from the top, but grows outward from the heart of the middle class. And, by gutting the very things we need to grow an economy that's built to last—education and training, research and development, our infrastructure—it is a prescription for decline.

THE SHARED AUTHORITARIAN HIERARCHICAL VISION OF TRICKLE-DOWN CONSERVATISM'S ELEMENTS

As observed in the Introduction there was friction among the philosophies originally composing movement conservatism. Traditionalism's distrust of capitalism and critique of greed as the motivating force for society provided a healthy restraint on libertarianism's excess. And, conversely, libertarianism's embrace of classical liberalism's emphasis on freedom was a healthy restraint on traditionalism's attempts to legislate morality. Later, as neoconservatism began to exert influence with the waning of anticommunism, neoconservative support of capitalism was not the unabashed support of libertarians but, instead, was always tentative.[3] Also, while neoconservatives wanted to reform the welfare state, libertarians wanted to abolish it, and while neoconservatives urged military adventures abroad, libertarians urged restraint, and traditionalists were divided.

With the emergence of trickle-down, the tension within conservatism disappeared as all three elements were united by their support of policies to benefit the wealthy. The libertarian vision evolved to a supply-sider-crony capitalist vision. Libertarians joined with neoconservatives to become hawkish on defense. And traditionalism was replaced by the Religious Right, comfortable with capitalism. The result was a conservatism that supports a vision of business and the wealthy serving God's will, and a more interventionist foreign policy urged on in part by the most extreme among the Religious Right demanding intervention in the Middle East to make way for the Rapture. There emerged a quiet consensus that, as with Christian salvation, in which everyone must work hard, lead a good life and suffer patiently on Earth awaiting spiritual reward in heaven by God, trickle-down economics means that the middle class and poor must work hard, lead a good life and suffer patiently on Earth awaiting their material award later in life as benefits trickle-down to them from the rich. This lack of friction propelled the movement in a radical direction based more on faith than fact, moving it ever further from classical liberalism and toward illiberalism, and uniting it under a mission to "recover" for America her position as number one economic and military superpower, guided by Christian values, pursuant to an authoritarian hierarchical vision of Darwinian survival of the fittest as ordained by God.

To the question of "What do conservatives conserve?" the answer has always been something to the effect that they conserve order, based on existing hierarchy and privilege, and the trickle-down vision unites all three elements of movement conservatism around a shared understanding of order, hierarchy and privilege. And, those who challenge that order provoke outlandish, untrue, hyperbolic extremist rhetoric that goes beyond attacking Democrats to attacking Republican moderates who don't share that vision, dubbing them "RINOs" ("Republicans in Name Only") and making them the objects of Internet pages of "RINO-hunting clubs."[4]

In the 2012 Republican primary in Indiana, Republican voters rejected Senator Richard Lugar (R-IN), who had served with distinction since 1977. Lugar was described during the course of the campaign as a "moderate"—yet, he had earned a lifetime rating of 77 percent from the American Conservative Union. This is but one example of the rightward drift in politics conservatives have secured, so that being "only" 77 percent conservative *is* moderate.[5] Two years later, however, the standard had, arguably, shifted further rightward for, as observed in the Introduction, former House Majority Leader Eric Cantor (R-VA), holder of a lifetime rating of *95* percent from the American Conservative Union, lost in a primary.

A quick look at some of the titles of recent books written by conservatives illustrates how the increasingly radical and delusional rightward evolution of conservatism has led influential conservative writers to coarsen American discourse.[6] Another uncivil (albeit juvenile) tactic popularized among conservatives has been for all true believers to refer to the opposition party as the "Democrat" Party.

The Mainstreaming of the Far Right

Christopher Buckley observed in a 2008 essay that he, the son of movement conservatism founder William F. Buckley, Jr. was endorsing Democrat Barack Obama for president because, as he described it, the extremism in the Republican Party had driven a good man (John McCain) rightward into becoming snarly (whereas before he was statesmanlike), selecting Sarah Palin as a running mate (despite her lack of qualifications) and making outlandish promises (like to balance the budget in his first term).[7]

In the 2008 presidential campaign, right wing extremists interrupted vice presidential candidate Sarah Palin on the stump in Clearwater, Florida with a call from the crowd to kill Barack Obama and a racial epithet shouted at an African American cameraman.[8] In Waukesha, Wisconsin, when Senator McCain mentioned Barack Obama's name the crowd denounced the Democratic nominee as a socialist, and one man seized the microphone and referred to Senator Obama and House Speaker Representative Nancy Pelosi as "hooligans".[9]

Elsewhere, Senator Obama was called a "terrorist" and a "traitor".[10] On the evening of October 9, 2008, the conservative political commentator David Gergen appeared on CNN's *Anderson Cooper 360*, urging the candidates to calm people down. Similar criticisms of the campaigns were levied by John Weaver, John McCain's former top strategist.[11] The next day, at a speech in Lakeville, Minnesota, Senator McCain reassured a man who told him he was "scared' of an Obama presidency. The crowd booed. Later, a woman told Senator McCain she could not trust Senator Obama because he was an "Arab." Senator McCain, admirably, calmly corrected the woman's misconception, and assured her that Senator Obama was a good man with whom he happened to disagree on the issues.[12] Nonetheless, sporadic hateful calls continued from crowds on the campaign trail.

The radicalism of trickle-down conservatism only intensified after the election of President Obama. After the 2010 midterm elections, in an interview with Major Garrett of the *National Journal*, incoming Senate Majority Leader Mitch McConnell declared that for him and his fellow Republicans the most important thing they could do was make Barack Obama a one-term president.[13]

The Senate, however, was the epitome of decorum in comparison to the House of Representatives as the Tea Party brought its radical trickle-down agenda to that body. In President Obama's address before Congress laying out his health care proposal, he observed (correctly) that illegal aliens were prohibited under the proposal from receiving federal aid. In response, Representative Joe Wilson (R-SC), loudly accused him of being a liar.

Not only in Congress, but throughout the country, incivility, intimidation and ignorance re-emerged as favored tools of conservatism. When President

Obama announced a proposed back-to-school address to schoolchildren, similar to one in 1991 delivered by President George H. W. Bush, conservative parents demanded their children be excused from school.

The theory of a global Marxist-Muslim conspiracy of which the "Kenyan-born" Barack Hussein Obama is the main tool for realization of the dream of the conspirators, as he attempts to implement the anti-colonial, anti-white, anti-American socialist ideology of his father, along the way to which there will be global economic collapse, World War III, and the development of a "United States of Islam" in the Middle East was neatly wrapped up in the film *2016: Obama's America* by conservative Dinesh D'Souza, released months before the 2012 election. The success of the film, combined with the success of Tea Partiers in unseating "establishment" Republican politicians, revealed that the ideology of extremist right wing populist hate-filled conspiracy theorists was driving a significant share of the Tea Party, the Republican Party and conservatism, with the support of the Internet.[14]

CONSERVATISM'S MELDING OF GODLINESS AND SELFISHNESS

The Virtue of Selfishness: The Gospel of Ayn Rand and the Incoherent Philosophy of the Intellectual Leader of the Republican Party

Russell Kirk, famous traditionalist conservative, observed of conservatism that it has the vice of selfishness.[15] Conservatives appropriately criticized the self-absorption and selfishness of the Baby Boomer generation in the Sixties, yet, when that generation aged and many of its members became conservatives themselves, selfishness was converted into a virtue—credit for which is due in great part to the writings of Russian émigré Ayn Rand (her chosen name; she was born Alisa Zinov'yevna Rosenbaum), whose book, *The Virtue of Selfishness*, elaborating on her philosophy of "Objectivism," happened to be published the same year (1966) as Harvard University Professor Timothy Leary exhorted President George W. Bush's generation of youth to "turn on, tune in, drop out."

Rand promoted acceptance of the shared hierarchical authoritarian vision addressed previously (absent God)—especially in her books *The Fountainhead* (1943; also made into a movie of the same name) and *Atlas Shrugged* (1957). *Atlas Shrugged*, in particular, became a favorite among libertarians and conservatives.

Ironically, not only was Rand staunchly atheist, but she repeatedly condemned empathy and all forms of charity—not just from the government, but also private charity, thus ignoring the famous passage familiar to Christians from Paul's letters to the Corinthians (from *1 Corinthians* 13:13; from the King James Bible): "And now abideth faith, hope, charity, these three; but the greatest of these is charity." Her opposition to charity, public or private, nonetheless did not prevent her from accepting Social Security and Medicare when she got the chance.[16] Rand used her novels to promote her values, staunchly opposing empathy itself, which she expressed through the hero of her novel *The Fountainhead*, Howard Roark.[17]

Pursuant to the philosophy of Ayn Rand, conservatives could believe that they *are* promoting the common good when they promote polices that are good for themselves and the wealthy because they believe what is good for conservatism and the wealthy is good for America and the world. An appropriate warning regarding such a self-serving ideology was issued by that hero to conservatives, Friedrich Hayek: "A movement whose main promise is the relief from responsibility [citation omitted] cannot but be antimoral in its effect, however lofty the ideals to which it owes its birth."[18] Similarly, William F. Buckley Jr. rejected Rand's philosophy.[19]

The man deemed the modern "intellectual leader of the Republican Party" in 2012 in the pages of William Kristol's *The Weekly Standard*, however, Paul Ryan, embraced the philosophy of Rand, at least before he was challenged on it.[20] The most basic elements of his philosophy were probed in an interview with *National Review Online* on the day before he delivered an address to Georgetown University in April 2012. In the interview he called it an "urban legend" that he admired Ayn Rand, and elaborated that he rejected her philosophy as atheist (which it is).[21] And, the next day, he made no reference to Ayn Rand in his speech at Georgetown University. However, it is simply untrue to term his admiration an "urban legend." In 2005, in an address before the Atlas Society (an organization under Ayn Rand's Objectivist Movement, taking its name from *Atlas Shrugged*), he said both that his admiration for Ayn Rand inspired him to public service and led him to require his staff to read two of her books: *Atlas Shrugged* and *The Fountainhead*, and recommended Ayn Rand's works as the best place to start to find a moral basis for individualism and capitalism.[22]

Conservatives melded their admiration for Rand and their Christian faith without a conscious reconciliation of their mutual exclusivity. Former vice presidential candidate and Representative Paul Ryan is unique among conservatives only in the ease with which evidence of this lack of self-examination is found.[23] And, as evidence of the extremism of trickle-down conservatism, after House Speaker John Boehner announced he was retiring in late 2015, conservatives took to the Internet to make clear that Paul Ryan—who credited his admiration for Ayn Rand for having gotten him into politics, and who made required reading for his staff *Atlas Shrugged* and *The Fountainhead*—was too liberal for their tastes as a replacement.[24]

Trickle-Down: God's Plan That to Help the Middle Class and Poor, Policies Must Help the Rich

George Gilder, in *Wealth and Poverty* (1981) addressed in the Introduction, expounded upon what could be called "trickle-down theology," as he linked the origins of capitalism with the altruism observable in the rituals of South Sea Island tribes and the "potlatch" tradition of North American tribes.[25] As will be seen later, of course the origin of capitalism is not altruism but, rather, as Adam Smith observed more than two centuries prior, self-interest.

Gilder wrote, in his concluding chapter, "The Necessity for Faith," of an intertwining of faith in God, capitalism and the leadership of superior men. Gilder was clear in the anticipated source of his God-fearing men who would save humanity, and he concluded, as observed in the Introduction, that to help the poor and middle class, *tax policy must first help the rich.*[26]

Gilder's philosophy that to help the middle class and poor we must help the rich was complemented by the theory of fellow conservative Charles Murray, who argued, in his 1984 book, *Losing Ground*, that aiding the poor "underclass" through welfare simply contributed to the corrupted values that mired the poor in the underclass in the first place. Income redistribution upward that had begun in the inflationary mid-1970s accelerated with globalization and the Information Revolution supported by upwardly redistributionist government policies implemented by the Reagan administration and supported by Republicans then and since.

Echoes of Rand and Gilder also resonated in *Unintended Consequences: Why Everything You've Been Told About the Economy Is Wrong* (2012), the book by Edward Conard, former managing director of the Romney-founded Bain Capital—and the mystery donor behind the formation of a sham corporation in Massachusetts founded in 2011 with the sole purpose of donating $1 million to the Romney-friendly PAC Restore Our Future.[27]

Conard, in his book, in terms evocative of Rand, lamented that talent to bring to fruition investment opportunities is in short supply because young people are wasting their time in the arts. He concluded on a moralistic and altruistic tone strikingly similar to that of George Gilder, with the hope that perhaps morality will persuade them to help their fellow less fortunate by devoting their lives to finance.[28]

Yet, Conard and his former colleague Romney both failed Rand and Gilder. Governor Romney famously observed on the campaign trail he was unemployed—thereby also admitting that the quarter of a billion dollars he had banked was not enough to entice him to keep providing his business talents to a nation Conard believed was so desperately in need of their talents that they needed to be coaxed forth with lower taxes. Conard retired even earlier—at age 51—five years before his book was published—so morality and his millions were not enough to keep him working either. Of course, the reality is that both men retired because they *could*—so, even they did not buy into the Randian idea that by enslaving themselves to the market for life they would free themselves. Even worse, however, is Governor Romney's admission that not only did he not continue using his business talents to create jobs—he didn't even use his money to create jobs. Instead, it was in blind trusts and bank accounts in the Cayman Islands, Switzerland and Bermuda. Thus, the very lives of Governor Romney and his business partner Edward Conard, while both admirable, bear witness to the false promise of their shared philosophy. And, given that their fortunes were made in the moving of money—in Conard's opinion the highest possible calling—it is worth recalling that Jesus of Nazareth famously cast the moneychangers from the temple in *Matthew* 21: 12-13. This characterization of finance—of the conduct of business generally—as essentially a religious experience (recall Chrystia Freeland's observations in Chapter One) was accomplished by conscious effort, as will be seen below.

Making the "Holy Rollers Lie Down with the High Rollers"

The selfishness promoted by Ayn Rand and other heroes of conservatism would facilitate the transformation, in trickle-down conservatism, of the creation of wealth into worship of God. This was ironic, for not only was Ayn Rand a staunch atheist, but Jesus of Nazareth, hero to Christians, condemned the worship of money numerous times in the Bible, among them the statement in *Matthew* 6:24: "You cannot serve both God and money."

Kevin Phillips, in *Post-Conservative America: People, Politics and Ideology in a Time of Crisis* (1982) predicted that the wealthy and big business would forge an alliance with the Religious Right, thereby marginalizing those libertarians who remained in the Republican Party.[29] Phillips was led to this prediction by his observation of the emerging of two key alliances: First, the Protestant evangelical movement combined with the Catholics, strengthening the Religious Right. Second, this newly powerful Religious Right combined with the supply-side-crony capitalists.[30] Thus was complete the conservative mission, as described by Neal Freeman, a colleague of William F. Buckley, Jr. and Frank Meyer at *National Review*, quoting a *National Review* office memo, to make the "Holy Rollers lie down with the high rollers."[31] Phillips also acknowledged having invented the concepts of "Frost Belt" and "Sun Belt,"[32] and of the latter observed in 1982, "Today's Sun Belt represents a confluence of Social Darwinism, entrepreneurialism, high technology, nationalism, nostalgia and fundamentalist religion, and any Sun Belt hegemony over our politics has a unique potential—not present in the Jackson-to-Bryan frontier or the Adams-to-Taft Eastern establishment—to accommodate a drift toward apple-pie authoritarianism."[33] Phillips later addressed how the supply-side economic theory applied to upwardly redistribute economic power and wealth during the Reagan era in his *The Politics of Rich and Poor: Wealth and the American Electorate in the Reagan Aftermath* (1990).[34]

This reactionary evolution continued to evolve, so that the Southwestern aspect of the Republican Party evolved to Southern, based on culture, as observed in the Introduction, and it stoked Republican intransigence on immigration. This was politically deadly for Republicans in presidential elections because, as observed in 2014 by Republican strategist Steve Schmidt, Republicans need about 40 percent of the Hispanic vote to have a chance of winning.[35]

Others commented upon the intertwining of neoconservatism and the religious fundamentalism of the Religious Right. Claes Ryn, in an article adapted from a chapter in his book *America the Virtuous: The Crisis of Democracy and the Quest for Empire* (2003) reflected on the "neo-Jacobinism"[36] of neoconservatives and their influence on aspects of American foreign policy and observed that the ideology of the American empire identifies the United States of America with God's will.[37] Similarly, social philosopher John Gray, in his book *Black Mass: Apocalyptic Religion and the Death of Utopia* (2007), linked the illiberal ideas of the Jacobins with conservatives who have succumbed to an illiberal utopian vision based on religious fundamentalism.[38]

One organization in particular demonstrates the degree to which the Holy Rollers have lain down with the high rollers—or, even more accurately, how neoconservatism, market fundamentalism and religious fundamentalism have intertwined and united: the super-secret Council for National Policy (CNP), chronicled by Kevin Phillips in *American Theocracy* (2006) and by reporter David D. Kirkpatrick in an article in *The New York Times* which recounted a meeting of the group in February 2007 at the Ritz-Carlton on Amelia Island, Georgia.[39] Founded in 1981 by Tim LaHaye, author of the *Left Behind Series*, leaders include Richard Viguerie, Paul Weyrich, Howard Phillips, Phyllis Schlafly, Morton C. Blackwell, former Representative Woody Jenkins (R-LA) and Family Research Council President and former Representative Tony Perkins (R-LA). The CNP was founded as a conservative counterpart to what was seen by these conservatives as a liberal Council on Foreign Relations. According the CNP's website, speakers at the Spring 2008 meeting in New Orleans included Louisiana Governor Bobby Jindal and Senator John McCain. Council for National Policy members were in attendance at the 2008 Republican National Convention in Minneapolis-St. Paul and were quoted anonymously by David Kirkpatrick in a news story published during the convention.[40] At the Conservative Political Action Conference held in February 2012 (CPAC 2012), Bob Reccord, Executive Director of the Council for National Policy, delivered the Invocation. And, in August 2012 the CNP convention was held alongside the Republican National Convention in

Tampa, and members heard from Representative Michele Bachmann (R-MN) and Senator Rand Paul (R-KY) and urged support for Representative Todd Akin (R-MO).[41]

Was trickle-down conservatism the product of divine inspiration, or profane cynicism, or something else? Facts are no help in answering that. What facts can tell us, though, is that trickle-down conservatism has been tremendously successful at controlling the Republican Party and securing the Republicans the power to, if not control, at least influence both US domestic policy and foreign policy. George W. Bush was a plutocrat (although neither a fundamentalist evangelical or a Roman Catholic—he left the Episcopal Church for the United Methodist Church). Mitt Romney was a plutocrat with a net worth of roughly a quarter billion dollars, and a Mormon. The 17 major candidates at the peak of the 2016 Republican presidential primary were a mix of plutocrats, fundamentalists and Roman Catholics: Donald Trump, the multibillionaire plutocrat (Presbyterian)[42]; Jeb Bush, a plutocrat who converted from being an Episcopal to being a Roman Catholic, backed by wealthy donors to his super PAC; Rand Paul, a plutocrat (Presbyterian); Mike Huckabee, a fundamentalist evangelical Southern Baptist minister; Ted Cruz, fundamentalist evangelical Southern Baptist son of a fundamentalist evangelical minister with the backing of wealthy donors to his super PAC; Scott Walker, a fundamentalist nondenominational evangelical and the son of a fundamentalist nondenominational evangelical minister with the backing of wealthy donors to his super PAC; Rick Santorum, a Roman Catholic; Chris Christie, a Roman Catholic; Marco Rubio, a Roman Catholic and Southern Baptist backed by Florida billionaire Norman Braman; Bobby Jindal, a Roman Catholic backed by wealthy contributors to his PACs and super PACS; Rick Perry, who attended a fundamentalist nondenominational megachurch; Carly Fiorina, a multimillionaire former CEO of Hewlett-Packard who combined a business background with a staunch anti-abortion stand; Ben Carson, a member of the fundamentalist evangelical Seventh Day Adventist Church; John Kasich, a Roman Catholic; George Pataki, a Roman Catholic; and Lindsey Graham, a fundamentalist Southern Baptist (the 17th candidate, former Virginia Governor Jim Gilmore, was a relatively moderate Methodist—neither a fundamentalist nor a plutocrat, this may help explain his failure to move up beyond the bottom of the pack). The fact is the Republican Party is now the realization of the dream of Buckley and his colleagues—the party in which the conservative Roman Catholics have united with the conservative evangelicals—together, the Holy Rollers—who have, in turn, united with the high rollers—around the philosophy of trickle-down conservatism.

The Establishment Republican Yankees versus Republican Confederates

Attendees at a rally held in October 2013 led by Tea Party favorites Senator Ted Cruz (R-TX) and former Governor Sarah Palin of Alaska were observed standing in front of the White House while one waved a Confederate Battle Flag—the battle flag of the side that had withdrawn from the Union and taken up arms against American soldiers in battle a century and a half ago—as a patriotic symbol, and demanded President Obama be impeached.[43] The rally was in support of the government shutdown in opposition to the Affordable Care Act. As observed in the Introduction, liberal critiques of the Southernized Republican Party tend to concentrate on racial resentment, but race is only part of an overall class structure envisioned by this illiberal philosophy, in which class is based not only on race but also citizenship and ownership of property, and "freedom" is the freedom to use one's property as one sees fit. The philosophy also supports trickle-down's and neoconservatism's recommendations to make tax policy less progressive, shrink the federal government, deregulate business and employ an aggressive foreign policy abroad.

This trickle-down philosophy of the Southernized Republican Party is a winner-take-all philosophy in which all support is lent to ensuring the propertied atop society are maintained in comfort. Concern for checks and balances in government is less of a concern than ensuring the "right" people are in charge. Knowledge, at least for the masses, is not prized, for that is the currency of the famously characterized "pointy-headed intellectuals."[44] Tolerance has never been a value for, along with concerns for equality, it conflicts with the preordained class system. Peace is not a value, either, for the Southernized Republican Party is romantic and finds opportunities for heroism in war. And, the rule of law is bent to the will of the plutocracy.

The Tea Party's trickle-down argument resonates well with this Southernized Republican Party worldview that the good fortune of everyone else depends on the good fortune of the rich as illustrated by the fact that after thc November 2012 election, the eleven former states of the Confederacy had less than 1/3 of the US population but roughly 2/3 of House and Senate Tea Party members. And ten of the eleven former Confederate states refused to participate in the Affordable Care Act's expansion of Medicaid.[45]

As observed by Michael Lind in his outstanding book illustrating how illiberalism and liberalism can coexist in the same state, *Made in Texas: George W. Bush and the Southern Takeover of American Politics* (2003), the South was historically colonial in nature, behaving as a colonial outpost trading agricultural goods with industrial countries.

This was the case, of course, regarding the antebellum South, as observed by the young French aristocrat Alexis de Tocqueville on his travels through the United States in 1831, during the era of slavery in the South[46]:

> The American of the South loves grandeur, luxury, glory, fame, pleasures, idleness above all; nothing forces him to make efforts in order to live, and as he has no necessary work, he falls asleep and does not undertake even useful work.
>
> Because equality of fortunes reigns in the North, and slavery no longer exists there, man there is absorbed, as it were, by these very material concerns that the white scorns in the South. From his birth he is busy fighting poverty, and he learns to place material comfort above all the enjoyments of mind and heart.

However, even after the Civil War the differences between North and South were obvious to European visitors, as was observed during his travels from 1873 through 1874 by another European visitor, Friedrich Ratzel[47]:

> [T]he general character of Southern cities [is] . . . very different from their Northern and Western counterparts . . . [T]he commerce of this area is still not connected to any industrial activity to speak of. For that reason, besides the big merchants here there are no big industrialists, no skilled workers, nor a vigorous white working class of any size worth mentioning. The shopkeepers and handworkers cannot make up for the lack of these hearty classes that create civilization and wealth. Therefore . . . this society has an incomplete, half-developed profile like that which one tends to associate with the industry-less large cities of predominantly agricultural countries. In this regard, New Orleans, Mobile, Savannah, and Charleston look more like Havana and Veracruz than, say, Boston or Portland.

The South was shaped not by a bourgeois ethic as was the North, but by an aristocratic ethic that disdained labor and general education[48] and, instead, championed "chivalry" and "honor." This ethic was reinforced by, as Lind described it, a pre-modern ruling class system based on power derived from heredity and land ownership, and dominating politics and the military.[49]

Lind's observations were echoed in the observations of former Senate Majority Leader Trent Lott (R-MS), when he was a Mississippi congressman, quoted in an interview after addressing the Convention of the Sons of Confederate Veterans: "I think that a lot of the fundamental principles that Jefferson Davis believed in are very important today to people all across the country, and they apply to the Republican Party," adding: "The platform we had in Dallas, the 1984 Republican platform, all the ideas we supported there—from tax policy to foreign policy, from individual rights to neighborhood security—are things that Jefferson Davis and his people believed in."[50]

The Tea Party's trickle-down conservatism also resonated well with America's plutocrats and Wall Street, thus uniting the trickle-down era Republican Party of plutocratic elements[51] of "Wall Street" and "Southerners" (and, it is mainly the South and not the Sun Belt more broadly that is affected). This merger was invigorated with the birth of the Tea Party movement and it, in turn, reinvigorated illiberal elements in American politics.

This switch from the business-oriented more liberal establishment Republicanism to a Southern variety of Republicanism is epitomized by both the families of William F. Buckley Jr. and George W. Bush.[52] Other wealthy Republican families addressed in the Introduction also joined under the banner of a Republican Party guided by trickle-down conservatism, funding with hundreds of millions of dollars conservative and libertarian interest groups in Washington, DC. The result has been a stronger and more united plutocracy than has been seen any time in this country since the Roaring Twenties, and loss of classical liberal values of previous generations of Yankees to the illiberalism of the Republican Party of the South and Wall Street (we turn to the latter below).

The High Rollers: Supply-Siders and Crony Capitalists

Again, the supply-side-crony capitalist vision actually combines two distinct visions sharing a trickle-down "what's good for the wealthy is good for the world" attitude. The supply-side vision arose in support of Ronald Reagan in the late 1970s and early 1980s and was initially profoundly libertarian.[53] This supply-side libertarian vision evolved to focusing not on the various issues of freedom addressed by libertarianism but, rather, on the narrow interests of reduction of taxes, especially for the wealthy and business, and reduction in regulation of business and shrinkage of government support for programs for the middle class and poor. This group gave intellectual support to trickle-down and supply-side economic theory. Among the major figures here were authors George Gilder and Jude Wanniski and economists Art Laffer and Robert Mundell. The main publication supporting this vision, besides books written by Gilder and Wanniski, was the opinion page of *The Wall Street Journal*, under opinion page editor Robert Bartley.

The other vision is that of the "crony capitalist" vision embodied by Karl Rove, Dick Cheney, Newt Gingrich, Tom DeLay, Grover Norquist, Jack Abramoff, and the influence-peddling rent-delivery machine[54] Norquist and DeLay launched in 1995 known as the "K Street Project." This vision too, shares the attitude that taxes should be low on the wealthy, business and regulation should be cut and spending for the middle class and poor reduced, but also has the attitude that government is for sale to the highest bidder—that businesses and people supporting conservatism and the Republican Party should be rewarded with government patronage—of the kind like no-bid contracts for Kellogg Brown and Root and Halliburton in Iraq during the Bush administration.

James K. Galbraith's *The Predator State* (2008) provides insight into the crony capitalist vision. Galbraith, a professor of economics at the University of Texas, identified the predator state as composed of the Washington lobbyists and influential bureaucrats who collude with favored corporations to direct public funding to those corporations for the purpose of deriving private benefits from ostensibly public projects.[55]

The deregulation efforts of the supply-siders and crony capitalists combined to create the circumstances that led to the Crash of 2008. To his credit, Galbraith is unsparing in his criticism of liberals who fell under the spell of conservative "free market" theory, and among the most damaging acts of deregulation was that committed by President Bill Clinton in the waning days of his presidency in 2000, when he signed the Commodity Futures Modernization Act of 2000, making it no longer illegal to engage in the buying of derivatives (essentially, bets that a debt would or would not be paid). That change in the law led to the creation of the $62 trillion credit default swap market. The law repealed to render these purchases legal had been put in place in response to the excesses of "bucket shops" that had been selling such opportunities and led to the Panic of 1907.[56]

The two separate visions, despite their great similarities, split on the issue of the "Wall Street bailout" in the final months of 2008 and on continuing bank bailout efforts. The supply-siders were far more inclined to let the market sort out winners and losers, while the crony capitalists expected government to absorb the losses of the suffering financial entities and fund the recovery of the financial markets.

The Holy Rollers: The Religious Right's Voice of the Loud Minority

The Religious Right can be identified with individuals, their government lobbying organizations and their other institutions—e.g., the deceased Reverend Jerry Falwell (the Moral Majority and Liberty University), Pat Robertson and Ralph Reed (the Christian Coalition, Christian Broadcasting Network, the *700 Club* and Regent University), James Dobson (Focus on the Family), Gary Bauer (Family Values), Tony Perkins (the Family Research Council), Paul Weyrich, Richard Viguerie, Alan Keyes and Bob Jones University (founded in 1927).

The Religious Right is composed of those conservative Christian fundamentalists and evangelicals, combined with conservative Roman Catholics, who believe that their vision, though it is in the minority, because it is "the truth," should be the law of the land. The Religious Right rose to prominence with the founding of the Moral Majority in 1979 and about that time the launching of direct-mail campaigns by Viguerie and Weyrich. It has imbued its followers with the conviction that their vision alone is of the truth, and government policies should be designed in accordance with their vision, thus rejecting liberal democracy. While the Religious Right gave ground beginning in 2012 on the issue of same-sex unions, commentary heralding its decline was premature, as the Democrats' goal of making abortion "safe, legal and rare" was successfully undermined by efforts in numerous statehouses across the country in 2013 to make it nearly impossible for abortion providers to operate.[57]

The Grand Old Plutocracy Blindly Undermines Its Own Support System

Trickle-down is not a movement that looks forward but, rather, one that looks back—urging policies that have succeeded in returning us to the level of inequality of 1928, on the eve of the Great Depression, when America was ruled by a plutocracy oblivious to the dangers that they had created with their self-serving economic system. Yet, Republicans who urge trickle-down delude themselves into believing, as described by Nicholas Lemann in an article on Karl Rove in *The New Yorker*, that the Republican Party is anti-elitist, engaged in a battle against government which represents elitism.[58] However, as observed by Barbara Ehrenreich in her aptly-titled *Fear of Falling: The Inner Life of the Middle Class* (1989), the middle class and poor share a distinction from those atop the economy: They do not have the luxury to stop working. Absent government benefits, should they lose their jobs they face the real danger of falling into poverty because they do not have substantial additional income from dividends, interest and capital gains, nor can they count on a big inheritance. Thus, from the liberal view, in attacking democracy and government, Rove's fellow Republicans are fighting on the side of the real elites against the vast majority of Americans who do not have the luxury of imagining themselves to never need government help.

Some light was shown on this confusion over the plutocratic takeover of the modern Republican Party and the loss of values that accompanied it in the July 12, 2012, issue of *The New York Times*, in opinion columns by two of that newspaper's outstanding columnists—the conservative David Brooks and the liberal Paul Krugman. In "Why Our Elites Stink," Brooks addressed a recently published book by Christopher Hayes of *The Nation* and MSNBC, titled *Twilight of the Elites*, in which Hayes argued that meritocracy has a tendency to lead to oligarchy—which it does, absent values held by elites that prevent it. Brooks elaborated on the nature of those values, essentially defining the concept of *noblesse oblige,* observing that among elites there previously had been a mentality of stewardship of the establishment institutions, but that this had given way to everyone imagining themselves counterculture rebels against the establishment.

A more convincing explanation for the loss of these values among Republican plutocrats, and their blindness toward their party's plutocratic foundation, was offered in Krugman's column, titled "Who's Very Important?" The column opened with a quote from a donor waiting to get into one of Mitt

Romney's fundraisers in the Hamptons, asking for the VIP entrance because they were VIP. Krugman observed that such plutocrats had captured the Republican Party and with that capture abandoned sense of responsibility for others.

This capture of conservatism and the Republican Party by the plutocrats is lamented and recent—contrast this focus on selfishness with the "compassionate conservatism" of President George W. Bush and his speechwriter and later *Washington Post* columnist Michael Gerson—President Bush's efforts to combat AIDS in Africa through, especially, his Presidential Emergency Plan for AIDS Relief (PEPFAR), are emblematic of this compassionate conservatism and the best in America[59] —but such talk is gone from the Republican Party now.

And, as the plutocrats captured the Republican Party, the idea that what is good for them is good for everyone has strengthened its hold in American politics. While David Brooks was right that elites were, previously, caretakers of institutions, he does not go so far as to observe the uncomfortable truth—for elites—about those institutions: they were designed to spread opportunity and, thereby, income and wealth and political power downward from themselves to the middle class and poor. Elites supported them because they recognized it was in their enlightened self-interest to do so. Blindness on the part of Republicans to their culpability in undermining these institutions leaves them impediments to needed reform.

Drinking the Tea: The Political Ignorance and Incoherence of the Tea Party

Supporters of the Tea Party tend, as do most Americans, to be more concerned about the economy and jobs than about tax and budget concerns.[60] And, as observed in the Introduction, Tea Partiers *themselves*, when individually polled, expressed support for maintenance of Social Security, Medicare and Medicaid (while also, incomprehensively, supporting cutting of taxes necessary to support these programs, spending more on defense, and promotion of more intrusive social regulation).[61] And, while Tea Partiers criticized the debt of the Obama administration, before the Tea Party came into being the people who would become Tea Partiers were silent when the federal debt under President Reagan nearly tripled and under President George W. Bush roughly doubled.[62]

The Tea Party has been seen by commentators on the left[63] and the right[64] as the successors to the John Birch Society, which, as observed above, William F. Buckley Jr. had famously opposed. Buckley's passing has been lamented by some for having left conservatism without a similar personality to confront the Tea Party, however, it has long been forgotten just how radical Buckley and his New Right allies were and, in that context, the Tea

Party is but a modern extension of the conservatism of Buckley and his New Right allies. A major distinction between the two, however, is that while the New Right was led by intellectuals, the Tea Party is led and funded by Americans for Prosperity, in turn funded by the billionaire Koch family, and FreedomWorks, a corporate-funded organization formerly run by former Republican House Majority Leader Dick Armey, a consummate corporate-political insider.

In contrast to the intellectualism of the New Right, Bruce Bartlett, the former Reagan administration economist and author cited in Chapter 1, observed in a 2010 essay that Tea Partiers' level of misinformation regarding taxes (their main complaint) was appalling.[65] He reported on the results of an informal survey the conservative commentator and former Bush speechwriter David Frum had conducted of Tea Partiers. Frum found that only 4 percent knew that the Obama administration had actually lowered their taxes, and they were woefully misinformed regarding the amount of taxes paid by the average American, the percentage of income that the average American pays in taxes and the percentage of GDP that taxes represent. Frum's finding that 4 percent of Tea Partiers knew that the Obama administration had actually lowered their taxes was similar to the number found in a February 2010 CBS News/New York Times Poll of Tea Partiers: 2 percent.[66]

Tea Partiers' lack of intellectual integrity was on display as well in their continuing belief, evidenced by polls, that President Obama was born in Kenya and ineligible for the presidency because he was not a "natural born citizen" as the Constitution requires. Yet, many supported Senator Ted Cruz (R-TX), for president in 2016. Senator Cruz was born in Canada, and, like Obama, his mother was American. If being born abroad, as a substantial percentage of Tea Partiers mistakenly alleged President Obama was, even of a mother who was an American citizen, disqualified him from being eligible for the presidency, then Senator Cruz was also ineligible—an uncomfortable fact Tea Partiers ignored.

Finally, the Tea Partiers' most important delusion is that their movement—which takes its name from one of the legendary incidents leading up to the American Revolution—is, like the American Revolution, a revolt against taxation. The American Revolution was not a revolt against taxation—it was a revolt in favor of self-government—which the Tea Party is dedicated to destroying in favor of government run by and for billionaire plutocrats.[67] Fortunately, polls indicate shrinking Tea Party support. After enjoying its highest level of support in April 2010 when 24 percent of American voters said they were members of the Tea Party, a Rasmussen poll in early January 2013 found only 8 percent of Americans claimed they were Tea Party members.[68]

Plutocracy-Imposed Abandonment by Republicans of Using Government to Help the Middle Class and Poor

As disturbing as is the emergence of the Tea Party indicating the spread of ignorance, more disturbing is the rightward swing of conservatism, indicating purchase of the libertarian movement, the conservative movement and the Republican Party by a plutocracy. One such example of this purchase is the sudden switch of prominent respected conservatives from support to opposition of conservative ideas such as the "individual mandate" requiring Americans to purchase health insurance from private health insurance providers, enforced by a tax penalty, thereby using the free market to provide health insurance rather than direct government payment, and encouraging personal responsibility rather than freeloading. As observed previously, this idea originated with the conservative Heritage Foundation, was championed by the libertarian conservative Milton Friedman, and was implemented in his state by conservative Republican Governor Mitt Romney of Massachusetts—the Republican candidate for president in 2012.

There are numerous historical examples of Republicans having led attempts to provide government measures to help the middle class and poor. Chief Justice Earl Warren, who secured a bipartisan 9 to 0 vote in *Brown v. Board of Education* (1954) striking down the "separate but equal" doctrine was a Republican former Governor of California, appointed by Republican President Dwight Eisenhower. Pursuant to the *Brown v. Board of Education* opinion, President Eisenhower famously sent the National Guard into Little Rock, Arkansas, to integrate public schools. Eisenhower also launched the Interstate highway system, the most ambitious federal public works project in history.

As observed in Chapter 1, Republican President Gerald Ford signed into law the Earned Income Tax Credit, which was extended with great fanfare by Republican President Reagan. This provides a minimum level of income, especially for working families with children. The idea for such a program also originated with the libertarian conservative economist Milton Friedman, who proposed a "negative income tax" that would consist of a set of graduated rates of subsidy enabling the federal government "to set a floor below which no man's net income (defined now to include the subsidy) could fall."[69] The original attempt to implement such a program, which would provide for a minimal stipend for all families with children, was the Family Assistance Plan (FAP) announced by Republican President Richard Nixon in 1969. FAP was promoted by Nixon's Assistant for Urban Affairs, liberal Democrat Daniel Patrick Moynihan (Moynihan recounted the politics behind the failure of FAP to get through Congress in his 1973 book, *The Politics of a Guaranteed Income: The Nixon Administration and the Family Assistance Plan*[70]).

In an effort to use the free market rather than direct government control to reduce industrial pollution, conservatives proposed a "cap and trade" system to cap emissions of carbon dioxide and trade emission credits. Such a system had been signed into law by Republican President George H. W. Bush in the Clean Air Act Amendments of 1990, which passed the Senate 89 to 10 and the House 401 to 25. That law established three cap and trade programs—the Clean Air Interstate Rule (CAIR), the Acid Rain Program (ARP) and the NO_x Budget Trading Program (NBP) which have substantially reduced emissions of sulfur dioxide and nitrogen oxides, significantly benefitting human health and welfare.[71] Expansion of cap and trade programs was supported by both Governor Romney and former House Speaker Gingrich. Yet, when liberals adopted this conservative proposal and urged its implementation regarding carbon dioxide, they were accused of wanting to stifle industry with "cap and tax."

Finally, among President Obama's proposals in his February 12, 2013 State of the Union Address was expansion of access to pre-kindergarten, a policy supported by Republican governors in Alabama, Michigan, Tennessee and elsewhere—yet roundly criticized by conservative pundits as a waste of money.[72]

The Invisible Hand of the Market as the Divine Hand of God

Ronald Reagan delivered what came to be known as the "Time for Choosing"[73] speech October 27, 1964 when he was campaigning for Barry Goldwater for president. The conflict between freedom and government was a main theme in a passage that gave the speech its name: "The Founding Fathers knew a government can't control the economy without controlling people. And they knew when a government sets out to do that, it must use force and coercion to achieve its purpose. So we have come to a time for choosing." On progressive taxation, Reagan put the issue in moral terms: "Have we the courage and the will to face up to the immorality and discrimination of the progressive tax and demand a return to traditional proportionate taxation? . . . Today in our country the tax collector's share is 37 cents of every dollar earned. Freedom has never been so fragile, so close to slipping from our grasp."

The University of California-Davis sociologist Fred Block observed that the conservative intellectuals who overcame the deep distrust between the traditionalist conservatives and libertarians—who made the Holy Rollers lie down with the high rollers—treated the market as a divine force and moral arbiter[74] punishing the poor because of their lack of self-discipline and rewarding the rich who responded to its signals—in opposition to godless liberalism and socialism.

George Gilder's *Wealth and Poverty* was crucial in forging a link between Church and Wall Street at the beginning of the Reagan era, and Gilder's vision remains relevant. His sentiments were echoed in a November 2009 interview Goldman Sachs Chairman Lloyd Blankfein gave to the London *Sunday Times*, essence of which was captured in the title of the article: "I'm Doing God's Work. Meet Mr Goldman Sachs."[75]

Robert Bartley, former editor of the editorial page of the *Wall Street Journal*, predicted in 1995 that the twenty-first century would bring a new dawn of moralism.[76] Writing in *The Wall Street Journal*, echoing Gilder and Charles Murray, Irving Kristol attributed economic inequality to spiritual failing.[77]

Thus, we arrived at today's unspoken vision of a Divine Order imposed on society wherein the invisible hand of the market is but the Divine Hand of God, and the self-interest that makes the market work is but God's work, through humanity. Wealth is next to godliness. Progressive taxation and regulation are immoral confiscation of property in violation of God's will, as is welfare—immoral confiscation of the spirit—in violation of God's will. Welfare for the well-to-do,[78] through government favors to the politically well-connected (supply-side-crony capitalism), is seen as carrying out God's will to those chosen. And, it is America's duty, as God's chosen "exceptional" representative on Earth, to spread freedom and democracy around the world (and, to the most extreme Christian fundamentalists, hasten the "end days" and the Rapture).

Actually, much of this ground had been plowed before. The conservative Edmund Burke, inspiration to traditionalist conservatives, saw *virtue* as the greatest value.[79] Virtue was critical for, to Burke, the laws of commerce were God's law[80] and Burke saw the hand of God guiding the self-interest of men to serve the general good.[81] And, Burke viewed all efforts to fight poverty as the proper sphere solely of Christian charity rather than government. The Republican Party has, thus, in a sense returned to its conservative roots when it linked wealth with Godliness, and made charity the province solely of voluntary organizations in civil society.

And *The Wall Street Journal*, since 2007 owned by Rupert Murdoch, has continued to polish its theological chops. In 2013 Ohio Republican Governor John Kasich signed up his state for the Affordable Care Act's Medicaid expansion, explaining, when the day came, he did not expect St. Peter to quiz him regarding whether he held down the growth of government but, rather, what he did for the poor—to which the editorial staff replied with a perfect trickle-down version of a St. Peter concerned about whether Medicaid reimbursed doctors sufficiently that they will continue to treat the poor.[82]

TRICKLE-DOWN CONSERVATISM MIRRORS SIXTIES LIBERALISM

As observed in the Introduction, and from the above, it can be seen that trickle-down conservatism is a radical ideology, radicalized in part by its response to Sixties liberal extremism both regarding social welfare and freedom. The views of the Republicans who support trickle-down economics create an interesting parallel with liberalism of the 1960s: Sixties liberalism failed because it placed excessive faith in *government*; trickle-down fails because it places excessive faith in the *market*. Below are other parallels:

The Politics of Dependency. As observed previously, as Sixties liberalism created a "politics of dependency" on government, so trickle-down conservatism creates a "politics of dependency" on the wealthy and corporations. Ironically, it is the politics of dependency that conservatives like Mitt Romney and Bill O'Reilly accused the Democrats of practicing in the 2012 election, acquiring votes in return for "gifts"—while they demanded a return to the Gilded Age and Roaring Twenties politics of dependency on the wealthy and corporations.

Counterrevolution. Thomas Frank, in *The Wrecking Crew: How Conservatives Rule* (2008) observed conservatism's similarities with Sixties liberalism as well, elaborating on the revolution conservatives envision themselves as waging: Conservatives see their revolution as waged by "insurgents,"[83] although these insurgents are infused with cynicism towards the government they claim to seek to reform.[84] In this revolution to spread trickle-down conservatism, the conservative revolutionaries never compromise, for compromise is weakness, never look for balance, and, in good times and bad, they relentlessly push to cut taxes, cut regulation, cut government spending (except on the military) and cut and privatize government services.

Obvious examples of conservatism's revolutionary mentality are conservative references to the "Reagan Revolution," the "Reagan-Thatcher Revolution"[85] and the "Republican Revolution of '94" led by Newt Gingrich (the 1994 midterm elections were the first since 1952 to deliver the Republican Party majority status in the House and Senate). What conservatives labeled the "mainstream media" ("MSM") has been interpreted as talking euphemistically, but the statements of trickle-down conservatives—especially Tea Partiers—clarify that they do not use such terms as euphemisms.

Perhaps the best statement of this revolutionary attitude came from Paul Weyrich, who, along with Edwin Feulner, co-founded the Heritage Foundation in 1973 with financial backing from the Coors and Scaife families. Weyrich defiantly described the conservative movement he led as being a movement of "radicals" bent on revolutionary overturn of the country's power structure.[86] All Americans lost in this revolution for, in reality, it was not a revolution in the sense of returning power to the people, as it promised, but, rather, it was counterrevolution against liberalism and with the true intent to upwardly redistribute economic and political power.

Hubris in Domestic Social, Economic and Foreign Policy—U.S. as "World's Policeman." Movement conservatism bears a striking resemblance to Sixties liberalism in a foreign policy vision dominated by hubris and best summed up as the United States as the "world's policeman."

Calamitous Fiscal Irresponsibility. Fiscal irresponsibility was taken to a new level by conservatives, first, by the Reagan administration, and later by the administration of George W. Bush, as was reported by journalist Ron Suskind in his book written with former Treasury Secretary Paul O'Neill, and as was confirmed by O'Neill in his interview with Leslie Stahl on the March 22, 2004, CBS News show *60 Minutes.* As Stahl recounted, at a meeting soon after the mid-term elections in 2002, and after the budget deficit was rising due to response to 9/11 and the war in Afghanistan, O'Neill expressed concern about yet another round of tax cuts. O'Neill famously quoted Vice President Dick Cheney's response that Reagan proved deficits don't matter.

Messianic, Utopian and Confrontational Visions. Sixties liberalism shares with movement conservatism messianic, utopian and confrontational qualities attached to its ideas, and anyone who dares to question those conservative ideas is "the enemy." Both movements focused on tearing down perceived impediments to their Utopia—for Sixties liberalism it was "the establishment;" for trickle-down, government—*excluding* the military.

Excessive Partisanship, Corruption and the Violation of the Rule of Law. Sixties liberalism confused winning and governing, however, even in the 1960s there was more of an atmosphere of bipartisanship than there is today in Washington and the nation, as observed previously regarding the atmosphere of the 2008 and 2010 elections. Movement conservatism, with its famous "K Street Project" to force replacement of Democratic lobbyists with Republicans, took partisanship to a new low. "Bipartisanship is another name for date rape," famously declared former House Republican Majority Leader Dick Armey (R-TX). In only a slightly less offensive description of compromise, Richard Mourdock, after his defeat of six-time incumbent Richard Lugar in Indiana's Republican senatorial primary in May 2012, said it was his hope to change bipartisanship to mean Democrats joining with Republicans in implementing trickle-down policies.[87] And, as observed previously, then-newly-installed Senate Majority Leader Mitch McConnell described his reason for being in office as to limit the president, from the other party, to one term (a mission which he failed).

Economic Abandonment of the Middle Class. A criticism of Sixties liberalism was that it abandoned economic concerns of the middle class, favoring policies to help the preferred liberal special interest group—the poor—at the expense of middle class Americans. The economic evidence, however, does not support that criticism. Real (inflation-adjusted) wages for the average American male worker continued to grow through the Sixties and peaked in 1973.[88] On the other hand, there is ample evidence to support the assertion that conservatives have ignored the economic plight of the middle class in their eagerness to support policies to help the preferred conservative special interest group—the rich—as over the past thirty-five years, the share of national income going to the richest 1 percent of Americans has grown, while the share going to everyone else has shrunk.

A New Class Structure Based on Redefinition of Work. Related to the above is the institution of a new class structure in which the very value of work is redefined. Sixties liberalism condemned work for its bourgeois capitalist materialist striving. Trickle-down conservatism commends work—but reserves for the rich the option to retire from working early. As observed previously, Mitt Romney retired early, as did his colleague at Bain Capital, Edward Conard—yet no one criticized either for availing himself of the opportunity to spend more time with children and grandchildren, write books, run for political office, or engage in other pursuits besides work. This was a marked contrast with the response from conservatives that greeted a report released by the Congressional Budget Office (CBO) in February 2014 that observed because the Affordable Care Act has removed the necessity of remaining working until age 65 so as to qualify for Medicare (so that they know they will have affordable health insurance), perhaps more than 2 million Americans will retire early from working—will have the option to do what Mitt Romney, Edward Conard, and other rich Americans have done. In fact, they might even leave their job to become entrepreneurs, not only freeing up a slot for someone else to fill but also creating more job openings. However, conservatives misconstrued that "Obamacare" was reducing the need for work and instead condemned it for "killing 2 million jobs"—a similar condemnation could be made against Social Security, Medicare and Medicaid for enticing workers to leave their jobs. The episode begged the question of just what is the Republican version of the American Dream. "Vote Republican—Die at Your Desk!"?[89]

Creating the Opening for Its Response to Replace It. The opening for conservatism's great success was created by the extremism of Sixties liberalism, and conservatism has returned the favor, creating an opening for liberalism with its own extremism. Liberals, now, have only to articulate a sustained critique of trickle-down, conservatism and the Republican Party, and propose a convincing liberalism in its place.

NOTES

1. The observation that conservatism has been evolving into an ever more extreme version of itself was made over a quarter century ago by Thomas Byrne Edsall in *The New Politics of*

Inequality (New York: W. W. Norton; 1984), p. 73. Thomas B. Edsall is the political editor of the *Huffington Post* and author of an opinion column for *The New York Times*, and was previously an award-winning political reporter for *The Washington Post*.

2. President Barack Obama, at the Associated Press Luncheon, the Marriott Wardman Park Hotel, Washington, DC April 3, 2012. The term "social Darwinism" refers to a philosophy of governance addressed at length by the historian Richard Hofstadter in his 1944 book, *Social Darwinism in American Thought*, and used by historian Kenneth M. Stampp in his book *The Era of Reconstruction, 1865–1877* (1965). Envisioned is a society in which rugged individualism is championed and maximum productivity and efficiency are achieved, and those who cannot compete die off and the human species is thereby strengthened.

3. See, e.g., Irving Kristol's *Two Cheers for Capitalism* (1978) and Daniel Bell's *The Cultural Contradictions of Capitalism* (1976, 1996).

4. During the 2004 campaign a "RINO Hunters Club" was maintained on the Internet, and an effort to weed out RINOs was led by The Club for Growth.

5. See E. J. Dionne, Jr., "Mourdock Republicans, Embracing Dangerous Austerity," *The Washington Post*, May 9, 2012.

6. Examples of excessively partisan book titles: Michael Savage: *The Enemy Within: Saving America from the Liberal Assault on Our Churches, Schools, and Military* (2004) and *Liberalism Is a Mental Disorder* (2005); Ann Coulter: *How to Talk to a Liberal (If You Must) : The World According to Ann Coulter* (2004); *Godless: The Church of Liberalism* (2006) and *If Democrats Had Any Brains They'd Be Republicans* (2007); David Limbaugh: *Persecution: How Liberals Are Waging War Against Christians* (2003) and *Bankrupt: The Intellectual and Moral Bankruptcy of the Democratic Party* (2006); Sean Hannity: *Deliver Us from Evil: Winning the War Against Terrorism, Despotism and Liberalism* (2004); Ramesh Ponnuru: *The Party of Death: The Democrats, the Media, the Courts and Disregard for Human Life* (2006); Dinesh D'Souza: *The Enemy at Home: The Cultural Left and Its Responsibility for 9/11* (2007) and *The Roots of Obama's Rage* (2010), as well as serving as executive producer, co-director, co-writer, and star in the film *2016: Obama's America* (2012); and Jonah Goldberg: *Liberal Fascism: The Secret History of the American Left from Mussolini to the Politics of Meaning* (2008).

7. Christopher Buckley, "Sorry Dad, I'm Voting for Obama," *The Daily Beast*, October 10, 2008. The essay led to his resignation from the magazine his father founded. See Jason Linkins, "Christopher Buckley Resigns from *National Review* after Obama Endorsement," *Huffington Post*, October 14, 2008.

8. Dana Milbank, "Unleashed, Palin Makes a Pit Bull Look Tame," *The Washington Post*, October 7, 2008.

9. Michael D. Shear and Perry Bacon, Jr., "Anger Is Crowd's Overarching Emotion at McCain Rally," *The Washington Post*, October 10, 2008.

10. See, for example, Russell Goldman, "Is Negative Rhetoric a License to Taunt?" *ABC News*, October 8, 2008.

11. Rachel Weiner, "Former McCain Strategist Warns Against 'Angry Mob'," *Huffington Post*, October 10, 2008.

12. Elisabeth Bumiller, "McCain Draws Line on Attacks as Crowds Cry 'Fight Back,'" *The New York Times*, October 11, 2008.

13. Major Garrett, "After the Wave," *The National Journal*, October 23, 2010.

14. See David Barstow, "Tea Party Lights Fuse for Rebellion on Right," *The New York Times*, February 16, 2010; Arthur Goldwag, "McCarthy, Beck and the New Hate," *The Atlantic*, February 2012; and Arthur Goldwag, *The New Hate: A History of Fear and Loathing on the Populist Right* (Pantheon, 2012).

15. Russell Kirk, *The Portable Conservative Reader* (New York: Viking Press, 1982), p. xxiii.

16. Joshua Holland, "Ayn Rand Railed Against Government Benefits, But Grabbed Social Security and Medicare When She Needed Them," *AlterNet*, January 28, 2011.

17. See especially Ayn Rand, *The Fountainhead*, p. 94. And, even more disturbingly, Rand expressed admiration for an American serial killer named William Edward Hickman, who strangled to death and dismembered the body of a twelve-year-old girl he had kidnapped for

ransom in 1927. See Jennifer Burns' biography of Rand, *Goddess of the Market*, and the blog page article about Rand at Mark Ames, "Paul Ryan's Guru Ayn Rand Worshipped a Serial Killer Who Kidnapped and Dismembered Little Girls, *Naked Capitalism* blog, August 12, 2012.

18. Friedrich A. Hayek, *The Road to Serfdom* (Chicago: The University of Chicago Press, 1944, 1976), p. 212.

19. Michael Lind, "Conservatives Once Ridiculed Ayn Rand," *Salon.com*, August 8, 2013.

20. Stephen F. Hayes, "Man with a Plan: How Paul Ryan Became the Intellectual Leader of the Republican Party," *The Weekly Standard*, July 23, 2012. See also Alec MacGillis, "The Philosopher Prince: How Paul Ryan Convinced Washington of His Genius," *The New Republic*, October 4, 2012.

21. Robert Costa, "Ryan Shrugged," *National Review Online*, April 26, 2012. The text of the speech can be found at the conservative website *The Daily Caller*.

22. "Paul Ryan and Ayn Rand's Ideas: In the Hot Seat Again," *The Atlas Society*, April 30, 2012. See also Paul Krugman, "The Crazies and the Con Man," *The New York Times*, October 12, 2015. The "con man" is Paul Ryan, and Krugman criticizes the media for their unwillingness to expose his lack of depth and seriousness.

23. MSNBC's Lawrence O'Donnell exposed and reviewed this hypocrisy brilliantly—see "Paul Ryan rewrites himself over Ayn Rand," *The Last Word*, April 30, 2012.

24. Jennifer Steinhauer, "Latest Unease on Right: Ryan Is Too Far Left," *The New York Times*, October 13, 2015. See also Eric Alterman, "St. Paul Returns," *The Nation*, November 16, 2015.

25. George Gilder, *Wealth and Poverty* (New York: Basic Books, 1981), p. 23.

26. Ibid, pp. 304, 313, 315 .

27. Maggie Haberman, "Mystery Mitt Romney Donor Comes Forward," *Politico*, August 8, 2011.

28. Edward Conard, *Unintended Consequences: Why Everything You've Been Told About the Economy Is Wrong* (New York: Portfolio; 2012), pp. 276–277.

29. In this regard, see Ryan Sager's *The Elephant in the Room: Evangelicals, Libertarians and the Battle to Control the Republican Party* (2006) and Victor Gold's *The Invasion of the Party-Snatchers: How the Holy-Rollers and the Neo-Cons Destroyed the GOP* (2007).

30. Kevin P. Phillips, *Post-Conservative America: People, Politics and Ideology in a Time of Crisis* (New York: Random House, 1982) pp. 190-191. This was due, in great part, to the efforts of the Reverend Billy Graham. Those efforts were later extended, into the political sphere, by the Reverend Jerry Falwell, whose influence continued long after the "Moral Majority" organization he founded in 1979 folded in 1989, and by Pat Robertson, with his televised *700 Club*. Cynthia Tucker, "Values Promoted by Falwell Are Dangerous to Democracy," *Atlanta Journal-Constitution*, May 20, 2007.

31. As observed in the Introduction, this quote comes from Buckley colleague Neal B. Freeman, as a panelist on the program "Buckley's Legacy: How Would the Patron Saint Turbo-Charge Conservatism?" C-SPAN, Yale University, New Haven, Connecticut, November 4, 2011. It is a phrase that appeared in a memo circulated in the offices of *National Review*. See also Neal B. Freeman, "Goodbye to Most of That," *American Spectator*, November 2008.

32. Phillips invented these terms in *The Emerging Republican Majority* (1969), which was reissued in paperback in 2015 by Princeton University Press (Princeton and Oxford) as part of the James Madison Library in American Politics, Sean Wilentz, General Editor. The term "Sun Belt" is addressed in detail beginning on p. 507. For the summary of his theory of an emerging Republican majority, see especially pp. 228–272 and 554–556. Phillips also noted in *Post-Conservative America* that he was often erroneously credited with providing Richard Nixon his "Southern strategy," inspired by George Wallace's 1968 presidential campaign.

33. Kevin P. Phillips, *Post-Conservative America* (New York: Random House, 1982), p. 239. All of the quotes from *Post-Conservative America* are taken from pages 239–241.

34. See especially the Introduction to *The Politics of Rich and Poor*, pp. xix-xx.

35. Steve Schmidt, *NBC News Meet the Press*, June 15, 2014.

36. "Neo-Jacobinism" is a concept introduced by Claes G. Ryn, professor of politics at the Catholic University of America, chairman of the National Humanities Institute and editor of the

journal *Humanitas*. The concept, applied to neoconservatism, has been embraced by Paul Craig Roberts and Pat Buchanan, among others. Ryn addressed the concept in his book, *America the Virtuous: The Crisis of Democracy and the Quest for Empire* (New Brunswick, NJ: Transaction Publishers; 2003), and he discussed concepts from the book in an article titled "Jacobin in Chief," *The American Conservative*, April 11, 2005, pp. 11–13. Ryn's critique of neoconservatism is strikingly similar to that herein, but with critical differences. Ryn traces neoconservatism's excesses to similarities with the Jacobins of the French Revolution, a leftist movement, while herein the excesses are critiqued as putting the nation on a road to right-wing excess—illiberalism resembling fascism. And, Ryn's interpretation of neoconservatism and its roots from Allan Bloom is as anti-elitist and excessively egalitarian, while herein Leo Strauss, his neoconservative student Bloom and neoconservatism generally are critiqued as elitist and anti-egalitarian. Notwithstanding these differences, more important are the similarities between Ryn's critique of neoconservatism and the one herein. As in the current work, the two main neoconservative philosophical influences analyzed are those of Leo Strauss and Allan Bloom. Recurring themes in both are critiques of the messianic (pp. 134-138) and Manichean (pp. 1, 7 and 8) qualities of neoconservatism, and that philosophy's dearth of humility (pp. 29 and 39) and tolerance (p. 35). Also Ryn critiques the concept of "American exceptionalism" based on "universal values" (pp. 8, 11 and 83–89) that the United States has embraced as inspiration to spread in a military crusade around the world, in an effort that represents a recipe for perpetual war (pp. 9 and 12) driven by push for empire (p. 11). And, thus, those who oppose them oppose God (pp. 7–8 and 126).

37. Claes Ryn, "The Ideology of American Empire," *Orbis*, Summer 2003, p. 396.

38. John Gray, *Black Mass: Apocalyptic Religion and the Death of Utopia* (New York: Farrar, Straus and Giroux; 2007), pp. 168–169.

39. David D. Kirkpatrick, "Christian Right Labors to Find '08 Candidate, *The New York Time*, February 25, 2007.

40. David D. Kirkpatrick, "Wooing Conservatives Pays Off," *The New York Times*, September 3, 2008.

41. Akin, again, as the Republican candidate running for Senator against incumbent Claire McCaskill (D-MO) infamously said, in response to a reporter's question regarding his view on whether rape is an exception to a ban on abortion that he thought in cases of "legitimate rape" it was rare for a woman to become pregnant because a woman's body "has ways to try to shut that thing down." See Sarah Wheaton and Andrew Siddons, "Conservative Forecasts, Meteorological and Political, *The Caucus Blog, The New York Times*, August 24, 2012.

42. The Holy Rollers and high rollers lay down together in support of the candidacy of Donald Trump, giving him a wide early lead in the polls for the 2016 Republican presidential nomination—see Frank Bruni, "Trump-ward Christian Soldiers," *The New York Times*, August 26, 2015.

43. Jonathan Weisman, "Spending Dispute Leaves a Senate Deal Elusive," *The New York Times*, October 14, 2013. See also Colbert I. King, "The Rise of the New Confederacy," *The Washington Post*, October 4, 2013; Stephan Richter, "Shutdown Shows the Civil War Never Ended," Salon.com, October 7, 2013; Garry Wills, "Back Door Secession," *The New York Review of Books*, October 9, 2013; Harold Myerson, "A Tea Party Purge Among the GOP," *The Washington Post*, October 15, 2013; and Michael Lind, "Tea Party Radicalism Is Misunderstood: Meet the 'Newest Right'," Salon.com., October 6, 2013. See also Michael Lind, *Made in Texas: George W. Bush and the Southern Takeover of American Politics* (2002). An insightful essay was written by author Sara Robinson, "Conservative Southern Values Revived: How a Brutal Strain of American Aristocrats Have Come to Rule America," AlterNet.org., June 28, 2012.

44. A term popularized by conservative Alabama Governor George Wallace—see Howell Raines, "George Wallace, Segregation Symbol, Dies at 79," *The New York Times*, September 14, 1978.

45. Of the eleven states of the former Confederacy, only Arkansas had agreed to participate in the Affordable Care Act's expansion of Medicaid at the time of the federal government shutdown, October 2013. The others: Alabama, Florida, Georgia, Louisiana, Mississippi, North Carolina, South Carolina, Tennessee, Texas and Virginia.

46. Alexis de Tocqueville's *Democracy in America, De La Démocratie en Amérique*, Bilingual Edition, edited by Eduardo Nolla, translated by James T. Schleifer (Indianapolis, IN: Liberty Fund; 2010), vol. II, part II, Chapter 10, p. 602.

47. Friedrich Ratzel, *Sketches of Urban and Cultural Life in North America* [1876]. Translated by Stewart A Sehlin. Copyright © 1988 by Rutgers, the State University. Reprinted by permission of Rutgers University Press, pp. 147–148. Cited in D. W. Meinig, *The Shaping of America*, vol. 3, *Transcontinental America, 1850–1915* (New Haven: Yale University Press, 1998), p. 225; and cited in Michael Lind, *Made in Texas: George W. Bush and the Southern Takeover of American Politics* (New York: Basic Books; 2003), pp. 41–42.

48. Ratzel was also struck by the relative poverty of intellectual life in Southern cities, the shortage of public libraries there in comparison to the North and West, and the vastly greater spending on primary and secondary education in the North and West as opposed to the South. Yet, as he also observed, after slavery the people of the South had been made more aware of the necessity for knowledge than ever would have been the case during the age of slavery. Friedrich Ratzel, *Sketches of Urban and Cultural Life in North America* [1876]. Translated by Stewart A Sehlin. Copyright © 1988 by Rutgers, the State University. Reprinted by permission of Rutgers University Press, pp. 148–149.

49. Michael Lind, *Made in Texas: George W. Bush and the Southern Takeover of American Politics* (New York: Basic Books; 2003), pp. 45–46.

50. Deroy Murdock, "Disqualified!" *National Review Online*, December 18, 2002, referring to an interview given to *Southern Partisan* magazine. ©2015 *National Review*. Used with permission. See also Peter Applebome, *Dixie Rising: How the South Is Shaping American Values, Politics and Culture* (New York: Times Books, a Division of Random House, Inc.; 1996) and Euan Hague, Heidi Beirich and Edward H. Sebesta, editors, *Neo-Confederacy: A Critical Introduction* (Austin: University of Texas Press; 2008).

51. See, for example, Carroll Quigley, *Tragedy and Hope: A History of the World in Our Time* (1975), Carl Oglesby, *The Yankee and Cowboy War* (1977) and C. Wright Mills, *The Power Elite* (1956).

52. See Charles Babington, "Republican Party Continues to Struggle One Year after Mitt Romney Loss," Associated Press, October 28, 2013. William Frank Buckley, Sr. was a lawyer from Texas who had an extremely successful career in the oil business there and in Mexico, and married Alois Steiner from New Orleans (she was also, like him, Catholic; while his family came from Ireland by way of Canada and then Texas, her heritage was German Swiss). The family settled in Connecticut, and William F. Buckley, Jr. was educated at Yale. Buckley's brother, James, also found the Republican Party too moderate, and was elected US Senator from New York as a member of the Conservative Party serving from 1971 to 1977 (he switched to the Republican Party in 1976). Prescott Bush, George H. W. Bush's father, was a successful Wall Street investment banker and Senator from Connecticut. George H. W. Bush came to Texas after serving in the Navy in World War II and graduating from Yale, and he built a successful career in the oil business before becoming a congressman from Houston, CIA Director, vice president and president.

53. Manuel Klausner, "Inside Ronald Reagan" *Reason*, July 1975.

54. The concept of "rent" will be addressed later herein.

55. James K. Galbraith, *The Predator State* (New York: Free Press, a Division of Simon & Schuster, Inc.; 2008), p. 131.

56. An excellent story on this was done by CBS News reporter Steve Kroft in a *60 Minutes* segment that aired October 26, 2008.

57. Examples of the premature death knell for the Religious Right: Frank Rich, "Rudy, The Values Slayer," *The New York Times*, October 28, 2007. David D. Kirkpatrick, "The Evangelical Crackup, *The New York Times Magazine,* October 28, 2007. Frances Fitzgerald, "The New Evangelicals," *The New Yorker* June 30, 2008. Fitzgerald has published several books, including *Cities on a Hill* and *Way Out There in the Blue*.

58. Nicholas Lemann, "The Controller," *The New Yorker*, May 12, 2003.

59. See especially Eugene Robinson, "George W. Bush's Greatest Legacy," *The Washington Post*, July 26, 2012.

60. See Dana Milbank, "A Census Sign That the Tea Party Is Less Than It Seems," *The Washington Post*, April 11, 2010.

61. See Chapter 6 ("Trickle-Down Conservatism versus Public Opinion").

62. During the fiscal years covered by Ronald Reagan's budgets (October 1981-September 1989) the debt rose from $1.0 trillion to $2.9 trillion; and during the fiscal years covered by George W. Bush's budgets (October 2001-September 2009), the debt rose from $5.9 trillion to $12.0 trillion. *Historical Tables, Budget of the United States Government, Fiscal Year 2008*, U.S. Government Printing Office, Washington, 2007.

63. See, for example, E. J. Dionne, Jr., "The Gilded Age vs. the 21st Century," *The Washington Post*, November 4, 2012.

64. See, e.g., David Welch, "Where Have You Gone, Bill Buckley?" *The New York Times*, December 4, 2012. Welch is a former research director for the Republican National Committee. As observed herein and as observed by Jacob Heilbrunn in a blog post at *The National Interest*, December 4, 2012, titled "Does the GOP Need a New William F. Buckley, Jr.?" Buckley launched his campaign in 1955 *against* the Republican establishment, and his victory established today's extremist version of conservatism. Additionally, as observed herein, the views of Tea Partiers are less radical regarding middle class social insurance ("entitlements") than were Buckley's.

65. Bruce Bartlett, "The Misinformed Tea Party Movement," *Forbes*, March 19, 2010. The survey was of 57 Tea Partiers.

66. "The Tea Party Movement, February 5-10, 2010," *CBS News/New York Times Poll*, February 11, 2010.

67. A similar version of this idea appears in E. J. Dionne's *Our Divided Political Heart: The Battle for the American Idea in the Age of Discontent* (2012).

68. "Just 8% Now Say They Are Tea Party Members," *Rasmussen Reports.com*, January 7, 2013. Rasmussen is a highly respected conservative-leaning polling organization.

69. Milton Friedman, *Capitalism and Freedom* (Chicago: University of Chicago Press; 1962), addressed in pp. 191–192. He elaborated on the idea of a negative income tax in Milton Friedman and Rose Friedman, *Free to Choose* (University of Chicago Press; 1979), pp. 120–123.

70. See Peter Passell and Leonard Ross, "Daniel Moynihan and President-Elect Nixon: How Charity Did Not Begin at Home," *The New York Times*, January 14, 1973.

71. See the EPA's website on the Clean Air Markets 2012 Progress Report. See also Chris Arnold, "GOP Demonizes Once Favored Cap-and-Trade Policy," NPR, June 3, 2014.

72. See E. J. Dionne, "When Republicans Were Problem-Solvers," *The Washington Post*, February 17, 2013. Among the critics of the proposal as wasteful was conservative commentator George Will, on *This Week with George Stephanopoulos*, February 17, 2013.

73. The speech was delivered while on the campaign trail, not when Barry Goldwater's name was placed in nomination at the Republican National Convention of 1964—that nominating speech was delivered by Richard Nixon. The speech is quoted from the website of the Ronald Reagan Presidential Foundation and Library.

74. Fred Block, "The Right's Moral Trouble," *The Nation*, September 30, 2002, pp. 20–22.

75. John Arlidge, "I'm Doing God's Work. Meet Mr Goldman Sachs," *Sunday Times*, November 8, 2009.

76. Robert L. Bartley, "A Time for Moralism," *Wall Street Journal*, May 26, 1995. Quoted in Robert H. Nelson, *Economics as Religion: From Samuelson to Chicago and Beyond* (University Park, Pennsylvania: The Pennsylvania State University Press; 2001), p. 333 (footnote).

77. Quoted in Nelson, pp. 305–306.

78. This concept comes from Gordon Tullock, *Welfare for the Well-to-Do* (Dallas, TX: Fisher Institute; 1983).

79. Edmund Burke, *Reflections on the Revolution in France*, ed. J. G. A. Pocock (Indianapolis: Hackett Publishing Company, 1987), p. 181.

80. *Thoughts and Details on Scarcity*, in *The Works of the Right Honourable Edmund Burke*, Volume VI (London: Oxford University Press, 1907), p. 22.

81. Ibid, p. 9.

82. "Medicaid and the Apostle Kasich," *The Wall Street Journal*, October 22, 2013.

83. Thomas Frank, *The Wrecking Crew: How Conservatives Rule* (New York: Metropolitan Books; Henry Holt and Company, LLC: 2008), pp. 48 and 68. In this context, Frank cites conservative commentator Fred Barnes' book, *Rebel-in-Chief: Inside the Bold and Controversial Presidency of George W. Bush* (2006).

84. Ibid, see pp. 32–46.

85. From Francis Fukuyama, "The Fall of America, Inc." *Newsweek*, October 13, 2008.

86. Victor Gold, *The Invasion of the Party-Snatchers: How the Holy-Rollers and the Neo-Cons Destroyed the GOP* (2007). p. 24.

87. Jonathan Miller, "Mourdock: Compromise Is Democrats Agreeing with Republicans," *National Journal*, May 9, 2012.

88. Carmen DeNavas-Walt and Bernadette D. Proctor, U.S. Census Bureau, Current Population Report, P60-252, *Income and Poverty in the United States: 2014*, U.S. Government Printing Office, Washington, D.C., September 2015. Figure 2 and Table A-4 "Number and Real Median Earnings of Total Workers and Full-Time, Year-Round Workers by Sex and Female-to-Male Earnings Ratio: 1960 to 2014."

89. See "The Budget and Economic Outlook: 2014 to 2024," the Congressional Budget Office of the United States, February 2014. See also Dana Milbank, "From Obamacare to the IRS Scandal, Republicans Are Ignoring the Facts," *The Washington Post*, February 5, 2014 and Paul Krugman, "Health, Work, Lies" *The New York Times*, February 7, 2014.

Chapter Four

Trickle-Down Conservatism Versus the Facts

Returning to the narrative he developed in his December 6, 2011, speech at Osawatomie, Kansas, President Obama appropriately linked trickle-down to its antecedent in history, the Gilded Age, and observed of trickle-down:

> Now, just as there was in Teddy Roosevelt's time, there is a certain crowd in Washington who, for the last few decades, have said, let's respond to this economic challenge with the same old tune. "The market will take care of everything," they tell us. If we just cut more regulations and cut more taxes—especially for the wealthy—our economy will grow stronger. Sure, they say, there will be winners and losers. But if the winners do really well, then jobs and prosperity will eventually trickle down to everybody else. And, they argue, even if prosperity doesn't trickle down, well, that's the price of liberty.
>
> Now, it's a simple theory. And we have to admit, it's one that speaks to our rugged individualism and our healthy skepticism of too much government. That's in America's DNA. And that theory fits well on a bumper sticker. But here's the problem: It doesn't work. It has never worked. It didn't work when it was tried in the decade before the Great Depression. It's not what led to the incredible postwar booms of the '50s and '60s. And it didn't work when we tried it during the last decade. I mean, understand, it's not as if we haven't tried this theory.

The president elaborated on that theme:

> We simply cannot return to this brand of "you're on your own" economics if we're serious about rebuilding the middle class in this country. We know that it doesn't result in a strong economy. It results in an economy that invests too little in its people and in its future. We know it doesn't result in a prosper-

> ity that trickles down. It results in a prosperity that's enjoyed by fewer and fewer of our citizens.

We know trickle-down doesn't work and has never worked because we have the evidence of history: All that happens is that the revenues from increased productivity are redistributed upward, with the result that income and wealth keep being redistributed upward. It's not as if we have never tried this before. It was tried before and failed, miserably, resulting in the Great Depression. After being tried again it has resulted in the current trickle-down depression.

The president continued: "This isn't about class warfare. This is about the nation's welfare." He observed of America's inequality that "this kind of inequality—a level that we haven't seen since the Great Depression—hurts us all . . . ," adding:

> [It] also distorts our democracy. It gives an outsized voice to the few who can afford high-priced lobbyists and unlimited campaign contributions, and it runs the risk of selling out our democracy to the highest bidder. It leaves everyone else rightly suspicious that the system in Washington is rigged against them; that our representatives aren't looking out for the interests of most Americans.

Of course Americans are rightly suspicious that the system in Washington is rigged against the middle class and poor because, lured by the delusion of trickle-down economics, *the middle class and poor and their fellow Americans themselves have rigged the system in Washington that way.* And they have done so because they believe the numerous delusions supporting the trickle-down delusion—delusions that can be refuted by reference to easily obtainable facts, as shown below.

FACTS CONFRONTING THE DELUSIONS SUPPORTING THE TRICKLE-DOWN DELUSION

A calibration: For income earned in 2015, the highest income tax bracket applied to dual incomes over $464,850 and single incomes over $413,200 (less than 1% of households) was 39.6%. The employee's share of the Social Security portion of the payroll (FICA) tax was 6.2% of gross compensation up to a limit of $118,500 (employers match with 6.2%; maximum social Security tax of $7,347). The long-term capital gains tax rate was 0% for taxpayers in the 10% and 15% ordinary income tax brackets; 15% for all other taxpayers below the 39.6% bracket; and 20% for taxpayers in the 39.6% bracket. The American Taxpayer Relief Act of 2012 (ATRA) established that "qualified" dividends (as defined therein[1]) are taxed at long-term capital gains rates, while "ordinary" dividends are taxed at ordinary income rates. And, under ATRA, for decedents dying in 2015, all individual estates below $5,430,000 were exempt from any tax at all, and on amounts in excess of that the tax was 40% (although the effective estate tax rates were much smaller).[2] Finally, conservatives continue to obsess over "welfare." The Welfare Reform Act of 1996 (officially, the Personal Responsibility and Work Opportunity Reconciliation Act of 1996 or PRWORA), replaced the Aid to Families with Dependent Children (AFDC) program with the more restrictive Temporary Assistance for Needy Families (TANF), which limits lifetime receipt of welfare benefits to five years and requires recipients to find a job within two years of entering the program—shrinking the number of welfare recipients from 12.3 million in 1996 to 4.4 million by 2010.[3]

Additional Truths to Counter the Delusions that Support Trickle-Down[4]

If we cut government spending—impose austerity and balance the federal budget with cuts in spending—we also will cut GDP and jobs. GDP = C + I + G + NE. In this simple formula for Gross Domestic Product, GDP equals consumption (consumption spending by businesses and consumers) plus investment plus government spending plus net exports (exports—imports). Thus, by definition, because government spending is an element of GDP, when we cut government spending—when we implement "austerity"[5] —we are cutting GDP (all other inputs remaining constant). Similarly, when government spending cuts result in cuts in government jobs, those cuts decrease jobs in the overall economy and increase unemployment.

Thus, as Paul Krugman has observed, if cuts in government spending and jobs—austerity—spurred economic growth, the economy would already have begun growing more rapidly. In reality, GDP has been growing more slowly than desired—and economists blame this slow growth in part on slowdown in government job creation at all levels.[6] Although during the first three years of the Obama administration, the number of private sector jobs increased by more than 4 million, due to austerity-inspired state and local spending cuts resulting in massive job cuts, overall jobs growth, while positive, was less robust than it would have been without austerity—misguided austerity resulted in *2.2 million fewer* jobs in early 2013 relative to policy responses typical of the five preceding recessions according to a study by the Hamilton Project.[7]

According to another analysis, by Paul Krugman in a chart presented at his blog site, the rate of change of real government spending per capita (federal, state, and local) *is already declining* due to trickle-down faster than any other period since the demobilization that followed the Korean War in the 1950s,[8] and annualized growth in real per capita government spending under President Obama was actually *negative*—and, thus, lower than any previous president since Nixon.[9] Public investment—spending by government on infrastructure, science and education—has fallen to its lowest level as a percentage of GDP since the demobilization that followed World War II, according to the Bureau of Economic Analysis, as reported in a *Financial Times* article in late 2013,[10] and that failure to invest is due to the misguided ideology of trickle-down, as observed by Krugman.[11]

In August 1966, the federal government had 2,721,000 employees—4.3 percent of the people with jobs in the country; 47 years later, in September 2013, the federal government had 2,723,000 employees—2 percent of the people with jobs.[12] Public construction spending has collapsed unlike ever before in history, dropping more than 16 percent since the peak soon after President Obama took office,[13] and the public sector, through September 2013 had *lost* 752,000 jobs since President Obama took office, impeding overall job and economic growth—by comparison, the public sector *grew* by 1.4 million jobs under Reagan; 1.9 million under Clinton; 1.1 million under George H. W. Bush; and 1.7 million under George W. Bush.[14]

As observed by Krugman, the effect of this reduction in state and local spending is that if state and local government spending had continued to grow since 2008 at the same rate of increase as population growth (as it did during the Bush administration) there would be about 1.3 million additional workers. A similar analysis applied to spending would result in additional $300 billion in spending. Accounting for indirect effects of the additional jobs would result in a total addition of about 3 million jobs[15] and an unemployment rate reduction of at least 1.5 percent.[16]

Thus, concludes Krugman, while Republicans argue for austerity under the misconception that government spending cuts encourage private sector growth, we have, in fact, *been implementing austerity for the past several years*, and economic growth has been sluggish. (And, by an alternative measure of austerity, about 7% of Americans work for federal, state and local government—about the same percentage of Americans who were working for the government 35 years ago, in the late 1970s.)[17]

As observed by Deutsche Bank's economist Joe LaVorgna in 2012, sharp cuts in government spending have been hurting the economy and impeding economic recovery.[18] Fortunately, with the documented failure of austerity during the Great Depression in the UK, Germany, France and Japan, and the modern failures of austerity in the UK, Latvia and Greece, austerity finally, mercifully, appears in retreat.

Of course, government spending must be paid for, so it cannot continue to grow indefinitely, but as long as GDP growth is weak, it is appropriate to stimulate GDP and job growth with government spending—especially of the variety that builds infrastructure and creates jobs. Further, the size of the deficit at any given time is mostly a function of *economic growth*—not spending or taxes—which is why *deficits as a percentage of GDP trend along with the unemployment rate* and, accordingly, as Nomura economist Richard Koo observed regarding Japan, premature reduction of fiscal stimulation in 1997 and 2001 weakened the economy, *reducing* revenue and *increasing* the deficit.

Building on that latter observation, as Joe Weisenthal illustrated at the blog *Business Insider,*[19] deficits are primarily due to lack of economic growth. And, if unemployment drops, the deficit as a percentage of GDP tends to drop. Economic growth drives deficit reduction, not the reverse—but prominent Republicans under the trickle-down delusion continue to propose a balanced budget amendment and cuts to government spending in a sluggish economy.[20]

It is often assumed by Republicans that spending on social programs—such as the Supplemental Nutritional Assistance Program (SNAP), formerly called Food Stamps—is wasted on freeloaders and should, therefore, be cut. Yet, a study by *Bloomberg* found that in 2012 Romney Country was Food Stamp Country: Among the 254 counties where food stamp recipients doubled between 2007 and 2011, Republican presidential candidate Mitt Romney won 213 of them in the 2012 presidential election, according to U.S. Department of Agriculture data compiled by *Bloomberg*. Owsley County, Kentucky, which backed Romney with 81 percent of its vote, had the largest proportion of food stamp recipients among those counties he carried.[21] Food Stamps disproportionately feed Republican voters.

We are not in an age of scarcity, and we do not have to cut spending. The delusion of scarcity represents the triumph of the trickle-down strategy of "starve the beast": cut tax revenues to such an extent that deficits rise, forcing cuts in government spending on behalf of the middle class and poor. This is another argument offered in favor of austerity, pointing to the growing federal debt as evidence that spending is out of control, and government must be cut. As observed above, however, spending increases under President Obama are at the lowest levels since the 1950s. And, it should be observed, that Republicans only raise concerns about deficits and debt when Democratic administrations are in power. For reference, the federal debt *nearly tripled* under President Reagan (increasing to 2.88 times its size) and *nearly doubled* under George W. Bush (increasing to 1.86 times its size)—and, by comparison, even with the Great Recession to fight his administration's way out of, after nearly seven years in office, President Obama had grown the federal debt by a factor of roughly 1.71; President Clinton grew the federal debt by a factor of roughly 1.50; based on a fairly conservative assumption, we can project that the federal debt will grow by about a factor of 1.76 under President Obama—still less than under Presidents Reagan and George W. Bush.[22] The fact is, if you are concerned about deficits and the debt, you should vote Democrat.

Regardless, the Republicans' delusion of scarcity and its accompanying alleged need for austerity are so successful, in fact, that even liberals are joining with conservatives in acknowledging the dawn of an age of austerity. Liberals should reject this characterization not only because it does not fit reality *but also because it reflects an attitude of defeatism that is uncharacteristically un-American and implies that our best days are behind us*—emphatically, our best days are ahead of us, if we just reject the defeatist delusion of Republican trickle-down conservatism.[23]

Lack of demand is the main suppressant of economic growth, not budget deficits and uncertainty over regulatory and tax policy. According to numerous surveys taken of businessmen and economists, the main impediment to economic growth is lack of *demand,* and, accordingly, lack of business confidence in demand.[24] And that lack of demand is usually attributed to consumers attempting to reduce debt. The truth is, thus, as observed in an editorial written by Nick Hanauer, venture capitalist and author, which appeared in *Bloomberg* in December 2011, it is actually middle class consumers who create jobs, which is why it is appropriate to ensure that the middle class thrives and also to provide for progressive tax rates.[25]

A fascinating comparison illustrating the fact of the primacy of demand appeared at the website *StreetTalkLive*, wherein the percentage of small businesses reporting "poor sales" as a main concern on the National Federation of Independent Businesses (NFIB) small business survey was graphed against the unemployment rate. The correlation between the two was striking and unmistakable, as was the lesson that to improve unemployment, convince businesses that higher sales growth is imminent.[26] Support for this conclusion was lent by the Federal Reserve Bank of New York's *Empire State Manufacturing Survey* for January 2012: "High expected sales growth was widely deemed to be the most important factor among those who planned to add workers." Not expectations of removal of uncertainty regarding taxes and regulations. Not lower personal income and capital gains tax rates. Not expectations of less regulation. Not lower federal deficits. Not balanced budgets. Hiring increases are based on expectations of higher sales growth—of higher demand. And, sluggish demand in the US and around the world—due at least partly to the spread of the delusion of trickle-down globally, has been driving down prices of numerous commodities, among them oil, natural gas, iron ore, copper, gold and cotton.

Regarding federal budget deficits, however, for an overall observation regarding performance of Republican versus Democratic administrations: Going back to the Kennedy administration, every Democratic administration left office with a smaller deficit as a percentage of GDP than they inherited, and every Republican administration left office with a larger deficit as a percentage of GDP than they inherited.

Specifically, as to the Obama administration's performance regarding federal deficits[27]: Federal budgets run on a fiscal year basis from October 1st through September 30th, and the highest deficit on record was for the budget shared by President George W. Bush and President Obama, for Fiscal Year (FY) 2009 (October 1, 2008 through September 30, 2009, and included Bush administration expenditures for the financial and auto industry bailouts, and the Obama administration stimulus in response to the financial crisis). This budget amounted to 24.4 percent of GDP. President Obama's first two budgets all his own (FY 2010 and FY 2011) each provided for spending in the amount of 23.4 percent of GDP—for comparison purposes, only slightly higher as a percentage of GDP than Ronald Reagan's FY 1982 and 1983 budgets when he also was trying to pull the nation out of recession (22.5 and 22.8 percent, respectively). And, Obama administration deficit spending as a percentage of GDP has declined every year.

The relatively high deficits under the Obama administration are due to federal revenue as a percent of GDP in FY 2009, FY 2010, FYI 2011 and FY 2012 having shrunk to just 14.6, 14.6, 15.0 and 15.3 percent, respectively—the last time there were four years in a row of revenues below 16% of GDP, as President Obama faced in FY 2009-2012: *FY 1948-1951*. By comparison, revenue as a percent of GDP in FY 2000 (the last full FY budget under Clinton) was 20.0 percent—roughly 1/3 higher. And those federal revenues are so low because, under President Bush, tax cuts rendered *average* tax rates (as distinguished from highest marginal tax rates) so low on higher income earners that, as observed in a report by the Congressional Budget Office, *Americans in 2009—under President Obama—paid the lowest average tax rate since 1979—17.4 percent.*[28] Further, as observed by Citizens for Tax Justice, US average tax levels for the year 2010 (the most recent year analyzed) placed the US 32nd lowest out of 34 members of the Organization for Economic Cooperation and Development (OECD)—ahead of only Chile and Mexico.[29]

Cutting taxes, especially upper bracket income taxes and capital gains taxes, to encourage investment, because those in the top brackets are the "job creators," will not make the economy grow faster, and benefits will not trickle-down to everyone else in the form of more jobs and rising incomes, and revenues to the government will not grow. The truth is that even after having cut taxes in 2001, 2003 and 2009, the economy is growing more slowly than in the past. We have not seen trickle-down work its "magic". Instead, we have seen income and wealth redistributed upward to the wealthy and older Americans[30] and corporations.

Grover Norquist, of the Americans for Tax Reform, in a July 13, 2011, interview on CNN with Wolf Blitzer, got away unchallenged with the false statement that the economy grew when capital gains taxes were cut and shrank when they were raised.[31] Ordinary income tax rates were cut under

President George W. Bush in 2001, ordinary income and capital gains tax rates were cut (from 20 percent to 15 percent, the lowest level since the Great Depression) under President Bush in 2003, and $288 billion in tax cuts in 2009 were part of President Obama's stimulus. Yet, as President Obama observed in his first State of the Union address, the decade of 1999-2008 was a "lost decade" in which the stock market, as measured by the S&P 500 index, lost more than a quarter of its value (in nominal terms—more in real terms), GDP growth was actually *slower* than during any previous decade since World War II, and both the number of private sector jobs and incomes shrank.

Updating income observations through 2014, according to the Census Bureau, real (inflation-adjusted) median family incomes were lower than in *1997*, and real median earnings, as observed earlier, for male full-time workers were lower than in *1973*![32] The national average wage index (AWI), which is based on compensation (wages, tips, etc.) subject to federal income taxes, as reported by employers on Form W-2, released by the Social Security Administration October 23, 2015, revealed that the median wage for American workers—that is, the wage level that half of American workers make less than or equal to—was just $28,851.21.[33]

As observed by the Congressional Research Service, in a report reviewing the effects of the Bush tax cuts of 2001 and 2003[34]:

> By almost any economic indicator, the economy performed better in the period before the tax cuts than after the tax cuts were enacted, regardless of whether recession years are omitted from the comparison. GDP growth, median real household income growth, weekly hours worked, the employment-population ratio, personal saving, and business investment growth were all lower in the period after the tax cuts were enacted.

A later Congressional Research Service report (issued in 2012, hence the out-of-date tax rates) elaborated on this conclusion, not only rebutting the misplaced faith that tax cuts spur growth, but also linking tax cuts with upward redistribution of income, concluding[35]:

> The top income tax rates have changed considerably since the end of World War II. Throughout the late-1940s and 1950s, the top marginal tax rate was typically above 90%; today it is 35%. Additionally, the top capital gains tax rate was 25% in the 1950s and 1960s, 35% in the 1970s; today it is 15%. The average tax rate faced by the top 0.01% of taxpayers was above 40% until the mid-1980s; today it is below 25%. Tax rates affecting taxpayers at the top of the income distribution are currently at their lowest levels since the end of the second World War.
>
> The results of the analysis suggest that changes over the past 65 years in the top marginal tax rate and the top capital gains tax rate do not appear correlated with economic growth. The reduction in the top tax rates appears to

be uncorrelated with saving, investment, and productivity growth. The top tax rates appear to have little or no relation to the size of the economic pie.

However, the top tax rate reductions appear to be associated with the increasing concentration of income at the top of the income distribution. As measured by IRS data, the share of income accruing to the top 0.1% of U.S. families increased from 4.2% in 1945 to 12.3% by 2007 before falling to 9.2% due to the 2007-2009 recession. At the same time, the average tax rate paid by the top 0.1% fell from over 50% in 1945 to about 25% in 2009. Tax policy could have a relation to how the economic pie is sliced—lower top tax rates may be associated with greater income disparities.

Alternatively, as Bruce Bartlett observed in a July 2011 essay, regarding the 2001 and 2003 Bush tax cuts, federal revenue fell for the first three years of the Bush presidency and federal revenue as a share of GDP was lower every year of the Bush presidency than it was in 2000, the year before Bush took office.[36] And, as observed by Paul Krugman, taxes on the very rich in 2012 were the lowest they had been in *80 years*.[37]

It is also a misconception that all, or even a majority, of the rich oppose raising taxes on themselves. *The Wall Street Journal* reported in October 2011 that a survey by the Spectrem Group found that 68 percent of millionaires (those with investments of $1 million or more) join with Warren Buffett in support of raising taxes on those earning $1 million or more.[38] Similarly, the 2012 Survey of Affluence and Wealth in America, conducted by American Express Publishing and Harrison Group found 62 percent of One Percenters favored an income tax increase.[39]

Regarding tax increases: President Reagan, in 1982, signed into law what was at the time the largest tax increase in history—that was one of *eleven tax increases*[40] he signed—and he finished his eight years in office having overseen the creation of nearly 17 million jobs. Similarly, President Clinton, in 1993, signed into law what was at that time the largest tax increase in history, and during his eight years in office oversaw creation of 22.5 million jobs. Additionally, President Obama signed into law an increase in the capital gains tax rate on the highest incomes from 15% to 20%—and the economy proceeded to grow at the fastest rate of his presidency. Thus, evidence over the past three-plus decades refutes the twin gospel verses of trickle-down theology: Tax cuts have not accelerated job creation and economic growth, nor have tax increases hindered job creation and economic growth.

A low-wage policy is crony capitalism in practice, with private profits being underwritten by public spending. According to a study by researchers with the University of California, Berkeley, 73 percent of enrollees in public support programs such as food stamps are members of working families (defined in the study as families with at least one member working 27 or more weeks per year and 10 hours or more per week). Researchers attributed this to low wages, observing that, in comparing 2013 versus 1979, real hourly wages of the median American worker were only 5 percent higher, and for the bottom 10 percent of workers were 5 percent lower. The researchers also found that 56 percent of federal and state-level assistance went to working families—amounting to $127.8 billion in federal spending and $25.0 billion in state spending, for a federal and state total of $152.8 billion. They concluded that higher wages and employer-provided health insurance would result in significant savings in federal and state government spending on social safety net programs.[41] In effect, the high profits and high compensation for those atop the economy enabled by payment of low wages are being subsidized by the American public in a crony capitalist system.[42] And, as observed in the Introduction, the economy has been experiencing the lowest percentage of GDP attributable to wages and highest attributable to profits since World War II. Similarly, in 2015, the share of corporate income going to workers was at its lowest level since 1951.[43]

We will not destroy the incentive to invest if we modestly raise tax rates on capital gains, dividends and interest. Jonathan Alter, writing in 1998 in *Newsweek*, observed that numerous Republicans warned in apocalyptic terms that President Clinton's 1993 tax increases (which fell most heavily on the rich) would increase unemployment and lead to recession. Instead, unemployment remained at a 28-year low and Clinton finished his eight years in office having overseen the creation of 22.5 million new jobs—40 percent more jobs than the 16 million jobs created under President Reagan. Concluded Alter, the Republicans were wrong, and trickle-down was repudiated.[44]

In contrast, about 5 million jobs were created during the eight years President George W. Bush was in office—less than one quarter of those under Clinton—despite tax cuts in 2001 and 2003 (and, in just the first six years under President Obama, 6.7 million jobs were created—more than under President Bush).

Tax rates on long-term capital gains and qualified dividends on income exceeding $450,000 for filers of joint returns (and $400,000 for filers of individual returns) were raised by the Obama administration from 15 percent to 20 percent, however, the fear that these increases will destroy the incentive to invest is, based in the above evidence, almost certainly unfounded. Similarly almost certainly unfounded are concerns regarding raising the tax rates on capital gains, dividends and interest to the same level as ordinary income tax rates, as long favored by a majority of voters[45] and as they were after the second round of tax cuts by the Reagan administration.[46]

Work—resulting in ordinary income—has been taxed at rates as high as 91 percent during the 1950s and up to the Kennedy tax cuts when the top rate was reduced to 70 percent; under the first round of Reagan tax cuts the top rate was reduced to 50 percent—and yet, still, Republicans can point to no evidence indicating people were discouraged from working. Further, 71 percent of all capital gains in 2012 were projected to be attributable to just the top 1 percent of households, resulting in, from 1996 to 2006, changes in capital gains and dividends being the largest contributor to overall income inequality.[47]

What we know about the incomes of the top 1 percent is that much of it is, as was that of the Romney family, held in blind trusts which by law they could not "work" with by directing investments—as Mitt Romney observed, while he made roughly $20 million dollars each year (2010 and 2011), he was "unemployed," paying people to manage his assets for him out of the income from those assets. It strains credibility to argue that an increase in the tax rates on capital gains, dividends and interest will convince multimillionaires and multibillionaires to mope around, too discouraged to invest.

We do not need to simplify the tax code with a flat tax—we already essentially have one, when we account for all taxes paid. Conservatives, since the beginning of trickle-down, have promoted "simplification of the tax code" by implementation of a "flat tax," which, they argue, is the fairest form of tax. And they appear to have a good argument that the current income tax laws unfairly burden those at the top when it is observed that the top 1% of income earners pay roughly 34.3% of all the individual income taxes paid.[48] However, *when we look at not just the federal income tax but all taxes paid,* we essentially already have a flat tax.

First of all, as Table 4.1 following illustrates, if we take into account *all* taxes paid, *the effective tax rate* for the top 40 percent of income earners falls in the very narrow range of 30 percent to 33.3 percent; and, secondly, *the share of total taxes paid by each income group is strikingly similar to each group's share of income*—for example, in 2014, the top 1% of income earners paid about 23.7% of total taxes paid, a share only slightly larger than their share of total income earned (21.6%), as shown in Table 4.1.[49]

In contrast to the near-flat tax policy of the US, a study of 54 nations found that those with more progressive tax rates had happier citizens, on average.[50]

We do not need, in order to promote economic growth and job growth, to cut the regulations designed to cushion the middle class and poor from the harshness of the market and to protect the environment. Over the past three and a half decades we have abolished various regulations in the financial industry designed to protect the middle class and poor, with the result that we created bubbles and crashes in the housing market and the stock market, with continuing repercussions in the nation's banks.[51] Supposedly the deregulation resulted in financial innovation that spurred economic growth, however, former Federal Reserve Chairman Paul Volcker told attendees at a *Wall Street Journal* conference in December 2009 that he had not seen any evidence of such innovation having led to economic growth.[52]

Table 4.1. Shares of Taxes Paid by Income Group

Income Bracket	Total Income	Total Taxes	Share of Federal, State and Local Taxes Paid as a Percentage of Income
Lowest 20%	3.3%	2.1%	19.1%
Second 20%	6.8%	5.1%	22.9%
Middle 20%	11.2%	9.9%	26.9%
Fourth 20%	18.6%	18.3%	30.0%
Next 10%	14.2%	14.7%	31.5%
Next 5%	10.1%	10.7%	32.3%
Next 4%	14.2%	15.2%	32.6%
Top 1%	21.6%	23.7%	33.3%
Bottom 99%			29.5%

As for the benefits of deregulation, the verdict from Alan Greenspan, Volcker's successor as Federal Reserve Chairman and libertarian conservative Republican, on October 23, 2008, in response to questions as he testified before the House Committee on Oversight and Government Reform, was that he had "found a flaw" in his free market philosophy.[53]

As for alleged benefits of cuts in regulations to protect the environment, Richard Morgenstern, a senior fellow at the nonpartisan think tank Resources for the Future, in a landmark study looked at the effect of regulations on four heavily polluting industries: pulp and paper mills, plastic manufacturers, petroleum refiners, and iron and steel mills, between 1979 and 1991. The study concluded that higher spending for compliance with environmental rules does not cause a "significant change" in industry employment, and that when jobs were lost, they were often made up elsewhere in the same industry.[54]

The US is among the most unequal nations not only in the developed world but in the entire world. The income gap between rich and poor Americans has grown to the widest in more than 40 years, and the poverty rate has stubbornly remained at an almost two-decade high.[55] The fact is that the US has among the highest levels of inequality in the entire world—according to the CIA World Factbook,[56] the United States ranks 98th in the world in equality—*more unequal than any other OECD (i.e., developed) nation*—and more unequal than Iran, Uganda, Nigeria and Russia (other measures of inequality will be addressed in Chapter 11).

For its inequality, the US has suffered slower economic growth and less income mobility than that of numerous other developed nations. Thus, as will be seen later herein, contrary to popular delusion, *the United States is sacri-*

ficing long-term economic growth and upward mobility as it supports increasing income and wealth inequality.

If we modestly raise taxes, there will not be a mass exodus of the rich to where taxes are lower. Research indicates that people generally move for jobs, cost of housing, family ties or a warmer climate—not lower taxes. There are anecdotal examples of famous people moving for tax reasons, but, as observed by Cristobal Young, an assistant professor of sociology at Stanford who studied the effects of tax increases in New Jersey and California, neither modest tax increases on the rich nor modest tax decreases have affected migration rates of the rich.[57] From another perspective, if high tax rates forced the rich to flee their home countries, then countries like Norway, Sweden, Denmark and France, with substantially higher tax rates than the US, would be losing their rich. In fact, each of these countries is represented by residents on the Forbes 400 list of the world's richest people.[58] Finally, as revealed in a 2012 survey by KPMG International, in 2012 the US ranked 55th in the world based on taxes levied on $100,000 income and 53rd in the world based on taxes on $300,000 income.[59]

There is no economic consensus regarding job loss attributable to a minimum wage hike, but there is consensus that a higher minimum wage will raise wages for millions of workers. Conservatives seized upon a Congressional Budget Office report published in February 2014[60] for evidence that raising the minimum wage to $10.10 per hour, as proposed by the Harkin-Miller Fair Minimum Wage Act of 2013, supported by President Obama, would cost the economy 500,000 jobs—perhaps a million jobs. The report actually stated, regarding job loss, "in CBO's assessment, there is about a two-thirds chance that the direct effect would be in the range between a very slight reduction in employment and a reduction in employment of 1.0 million workers (see Table 1)"—reference to Table 1 clarified this estimate was the "likely range" while the "central estimate" was 500,000 workers. The report also observed that by the second half of 2016, when the law was fully implemented, about 16.5 million workers would see higher wages directly—including approximately 900,000 pulled out of poverty, and "a few higher-wage workers would owe their jobs and increased earnings to the heightened demand for goods and services that would result from the minimum-wage increase"—thus implying that job increases due to the minimum wage increase would be seen in the intermediate to longer term.

The report was issued just weeks after delivery of an open letter signed by over 600 PhD economists to President Obama in support of the bill,[61] thus illustrating the opinion in the economics community. Additionally, many economists cite a 2010 study comparing state minimum wage policies as a rebuttal to the job loss argument.[62] Of course, regarding the lure of low wages to attracting business, if low wages were all it took to attract jobs, then the countries and states with the lowest wages would always have the fastest job growth—but we know that is not the case.

And, due to three and a half decades of relative wage stagnation, as observed in an editorial in *The New York Times*, an estimated 27.8 million people would more broadly benefit with a higher minimum wage, and these are not, as in the past, teenagers with part-time summer jobs but, rather, most of these workers are adults working full time, they are in their mid-thirties, more than a quarter are parents and they are earning half their families' income.[63]

American families cannot forever substitute debt for falling real income. A key unstated assumption underlying trickle-down is that we can forever avoid using government policies to support real wage growth and compensate for the resultant falling real value of wages with limitless debt. In truth, no economy can maintain prosperity and long-term growth without broad, robust and sustained real wage growth.

The American government cannot go broke as it helps the middle class and poor. Households can go broke. Even countries whose currency is the euro (e.g., Portugal, Italy, Greece, or Spain) can go broke. Neither households nor countries that are members of a currency union can print their own money. In contrast, the US can, essentially, print its own money because the US government is the issuer of the reserve currency of the world: the US dollar. However, there is a valid fear that if the US runs too high of a debt, those who purchase our government debt instruments will demand higher interest rates to compensate for the increased risk they are undertaking by loaning to the US government. But, we have a relatively recent incident by which we can measure the degree of concern on the part of the world regarding US government debt levels: the crisis generated in summer 2011 by Republicans in the House of Representatives regarding the raising of the debt ceiling (a "ceiling" that in reality is merely a confirmation to pay off debt already incurred). What did interest rates do then? They fell. Additionally, as observed previously in this chapter, in every year of the Obama administration the deficit has been shrinking as a percentage of GDP. The "debt crisis" is a figment of the trickle-down conservative Republican imagination.[64]

"Free trade" is not the answer to raise Americans' incomes and add jobs. A 2013 study by the Brookings Institution concluded that sending offshore the labor intensive part of the US production process was the leading explanation for decline in the labor share of national income.[65] "Free trade" is not the answer. Measures to increase jobs and raise wages are.

By reporting "per capita" income, "per capita" wealth, "real wages per worker" and "real hourly wage rate" trickle-down's acolytes mislead by use of aggregates. Some proponents of trickle-down play a superficially clever game: They look at overall income, overall wealth, overall wages or overall hourly wages and divide them by the number of workers and conclude that we are all getting richer. They also imagine that, in their virtual reality, it does not matter who gets this money anyway. They reason, even the 1 percent spend on consumer goods and if they do not, they will save the money or invest it, thereby benefitting the economy. Of course, in actual reality, there is only so much in consumer goods the rich will buy, and the balance will be saved, perhaps in offshore accounts, or it may be invested, perhaps even in the US as opposed to abroad, but with demand falling due to upward redistribution of income and wealth that is less likely. They allege that those who criticize trickle-down are Marxists. It is they, however, who are using Marxist analysis, imagining that all the income and all the wealth belongs to all of us, and that we are all benefitting when it grows—they are the true believers in the mantra "a rising tide lifts all boats." Of course, it does not, because, in actual reality, trickle-down upwardly redistributes the gains in income and wealth to those at the very top.

Obamacare has not cost the economy jobs. According to the Department of Labor, in the first year of the Affordable Care Act, the US economy added 3.3 million jobs—the most since the presidency of Bill Clinton in the 1990s.[66] The unemployment rate was 9.9 percent in March 2010, when President Obama signed the Affordable Care Act, and by June 2015, the unemployment rate had fallen to 5.3 percent, and the economy had added more than 12 million jobs since the depths of the Great Recession.

The housing bubble that led to the financial crisis was not due to the Community Reinvestment Act and irresponsible borrowing by minorities. A popular conservative misconception is that the housing bubble that led to the financial crisis of 2008 was due in great part to President Bush and Republican congressmen having been victimized by political pressure from liberals, especially Democratic Representative Barney Frank of Massachusetts who used the Community Reinvestment Act of 1977 (CRA) to force banks to engage—with the facilitation of Fannie Mae (the Federal National Mortgage Association) and Freddie Mac (Federal Home Loan Mortgage Corporation; also the FHLMC)—in irresponsible lending to the poor and minorities.

Explanations for the housing bubble based on the CRA and Fannie and Freddie fail for reasons they share, and for reasons unique to them.[67] First of the reasons shared is the fact that, as observed above, trickle-down was not limited to the US—it went global, and housing bubbles were also created in the UK, Australia, Canada, and much of Europe (especially Spain), as in these and other developed countries people willingly substituted for nonexistent income irresponsibly high levels of debt.

Second, President George W. Bush—many then said to his credit—in 2002, pursuant to his "Ownership Society" vision announced his goal of increasing the number of minority homeowners by 5.5 million by the end of the decade, and he reiterated this pledge on the campaign trail in 2004. Bush, a Republican president who enjoyed a Republican-majority House for six years of his presidency (2001-2007) pressed for increased lending, and the congress delivered. It is a myth that a Republican president and Republican-majority congress were rolled by one lone minority-party Democratic Representative from Massachusetts named Barney Frank. In reality, the conservative Republican push to extend the ability to get into indebtedness further down the economic ladder is part and parcel of trickle-down's overall approach of substituting debt for non-existent income growth.

Third, sadly, the indebtedness of the African Americans who availed themselves of these programs is so small relative to the economy as a whole that the effect of all of them going under would barely have registered in the economy.

Four points also, regarding the CRA: (1) The CRA went into effect in *1977*; no explanation is offered by conservatives for why its effect lay dormant for a quarter century—and, of course, there is none. (2) The CRA *does not apply to the financial institutions that issued the vast majority of subprime loans*. The CRA applies only to banks that handle checking accounts and savings deposits. The biggest lenders in the subprime market were mortgage banks like Countrywide and AmeriQuest, which got their money from Wall Street and did not take checking and savings deposits. (3) The CRA *did not apply to the homes that were bought with the vast majority of subprime loans*. The CRA applies to inner-city properties; the subprime loans were issued mainly for suburban and exurban homes—hence, the collapse of housing markets was most acutely felt in markets with an unusually high percentage—not of urban homes—but of suburban and exurban homes: Nevada, Arizona, Florida and California. (4) As a corollary to that last observation, *foreclosure filings increased at a faster pace in middle- and higher-income areas* than in lower-income areas that are the focus of the CRA.[68]

Regarding Fannie and Freddie specifically, two points: (1) Fannie and Freddie got their mandate to encourage home ownership *in 1992*. Again, no explanation is offered by conservatives for why their impact lay dormant for more than a decade and, again, there is none. (2) Fannie and Freddie *were extensively criticized precisely for losing share in the housing market because they had not gotten into* the subprime loan market, in great part due to appropriate restrictions on their activities. These criticisms were issued as late as *December 2006* by Moody's, and *McClatchy News* noted that, according to Federal Reserve Board Data, in 2006 private lending institutions made more than 84 percent of all subprime mortgages and nearly 83 percent of the subprime mortgages to low-and moderate-income borrowers.[69] It was not until late 2006, after subprime lending and the housing prices had already peaked, that the restrictions on Fannie and Freddie were lifted and they got into the subprime, adjustable-rate and hybrid mortgage markets in a significant way.

Blame for the housing bubble and resultant crash lays squarely with Republican proponents of trickle-down conservatism who championed blind faith in the "free market" and loosened financial regulations to facilitate irresponsible substitution of credit for nonexistent wage growth—credit secured by the homes of millions of unsuspecting Americans.

Housing prices over the past two years nationwide have outpaced wage growth by a 13:1 ratio and have outpaced wage growth in 76 percent of US housing markets. This is perhaps the most disturbing—most ominous—fact of all, especially for what it says regarding the future of America and the American Dream, and the dominance of the rich and super rich. RealtyTrac released in March 2015 the results of an analysis of wage growth and home price appreciation occurring over the previous two years of the housing recovery.[70] The study found that during the two years of the housing recovery housing prices nationwide have outpaced wage growth by a 13:1 ratio and have outpaced wage growth in 76 percent of US housing markets. While the decline in the percentage of owner-occupied housing has been taken in stride as a healthy, appropriate reduction in risk by reducing exposure to another housing price decline, what these figures show is the other side of that observation—that during the recovery, going all the way back to 2009, the percentage of owner-occupied housing has been in decline while the percentage of renting households has been increasing dramatically, thus accounting for the entire growth in households created.[71] Of course, this means that the rich and super rich are increasing shares of ownership of the housing market while the share attributable to the rest of Americans is shrinking. And, not surprisingly, renting has become less affordable than ever before.[72]

If trickle-down economics were right, you would have a raise by now. The link between falling unemployment rates and rising wages long ago became unhinged because the application of the policies of trickle-down economics made it become unhinged.[73] And, this disconnect continues. The facts regarding the decline in incomes before taxes for the period July 2013 through June 2014 were released by the Bureau of Labor Statistics in April 2015, and they are disturbing: For the lowest 20th percentile real incomes declined by 3.5 percent; for the second 20th percentile they declined by 2.7 percent; for the third 20th percentile they declined by 2.8 percent; for the fourth 20th percentile, they declined by 2.1 percent—but for the highest 20th percentile, they rose by 0.9 percent.[74] And, contrary to the idea promoted among conservatives, a shift to greater benefits does not explain stagnant wage growth. As observed by the Center for Economic and Policy Research, based on Bureau of Economic Analysis, wages accounted for 83.2 percent of labor compensation in the corporate sector on 2007; in the 3rd Quarter 2015, 83.8 percent—thus, wages are accounting for a *greater*, not lesser, share of compensation.[75] Making matters worse, as discovered by Tom Porcelli at RBC Capital Markets LLC using Labor and Commerce Department data, the link between spending and earnings is greater now than in any previous expansion period over the past 50 years (presumably due to reluctance of consumers to incur debt after the last recession).[76] Falling unemployment and rising economic growth, before the application of trickle-down economics, resulted in rising wages because liberal economic polices promoted by Democrats forced the sharing of revenues attributable to increased productivity among all workers. The trickle-down consensus resulted in a productivity/wage disconnect, meaning that under trickle-down rising productivity for most workers does not raise their wages.

If you want the economy to grow and the number of jobs to grow, vote Democrat. So strong is the trickle-down consensus and so powerful is the trickle-down conservatism of the Republican Party that the effects of trickle-down policies continue to undermine our economy (and, as will be shown, our democracy, our institutions and our health as well) even given the facts above and even with a Democratic administration in the presidency. Yet, to put an exclamation point on these facts, *as illustrated by six studies described below, the economic performance of Democratic administrations is remarkably better than the economic performance of Republican administrations.*

In 2008, Michael Kinsley reported at *Slate.com* that a review of the annual report titled "Economic Report of the President" revealed Democratic administrations were better for the economy than Republican ones.[77]

Richard Carroll, an economist at the World Bank, updated this analysis in 2012 in *The President as Economist: Scoring Economic Performance from Harry Truman to Barack Obama* and reached similar conclusions, which he summarized in a June 2012 article for *Bloomberg*.[78]

In August 2012, Lew Goldfarb and Bob Deitrick reported in their book *Bulls, Bears and the Ballot Box* that over the last 80 years, Democratic administrations outperformed Republican administrations on 11 of 12 economic indicators—the only indicator on which the Republican administrations outperformed was unemployment rate. And, while President Obama is not included in the rankings because he had not finished his term, if he were evaluated on performance to-date, he would fall in the middle of the pack, according to Deitrick.[79]

In September 2012, Ameriprise Financial published a study of the 11 Democratic and 10 Republican administrations since 1929 and found that Democrats beat Republicans in terms of growth of the stock market (the S&P 500 Index grew on average during each four-year term of Democrats 68.8 percent versus 31.1 percent during each four-year term of Republicans), GDP (4.70 percent versus 1.53 percent) and jobs (59.0 million versus 26.2 million).[80]

And, in another study observed in a 2012 article for *Bloomberg*, quoted in former President Bill Clinton's endorsement speech for the re-election of President Barack Obama at the Democratic National Convention September

5, 2012, over the 52 years since Democrat John F. Kennedy took office in January 1961, the private sector had added over 66 million jobs—nearly two-thirds of which (42 million) came under Democratic administrations, versus about one-third (24 million) under Republican administrations—although Democrats were in the White House during this period only 24 years versus 28 years for Republicans.[81]

In a November 2013 technical paper Alan S. Blinder and Mark W. Watson of the Woodrow Wilson School and the Department of Economics, Princeton University also concluded that the US economy performed better under Democratic administrations than under Republican by various measures.[82] After comparing economic performance under Democratic and Republican presidents since 1947 they concluded that the economy grew on average under Democrats 4.35 percent per year; under Republicans, only 2.54 percent. The economy was in recession for 49 quarters over that period, 41 of which Republicans held the White House; Democrats held the White House during only eight of those 49 quarters.They concluded that 46-62% of the gap in performance is due to three "luck" factors together: oil, productivity and "ICE" (expectations of future conditions). The balance they could not account for. For the purposes of this work, the clear meaning of this conclusion is that the economics community is still having trouble admitting that John Maynard Keynes was right, that use of fiscal policy to counteract inequality and promote economic growth is appropriate. The argument herein is that he was, which would appear to be the best explanation for why Democratic administrations outperform Republican.

Finally, the record since 1980 was summarized by Paul Krugman in a mid-2015 opinion piece—the average percentage rate of growth of the economy while each of the last five presidents was in office (and for President Obama, through that time): Bill Clinton, 3.7; Ronald Reagan, 3.4; Barack Obama, 2.1; George H. W. Bush, 2.0; and George W. Bush, 1.6.[83]

The truth is confirmed by numerous studies: Democrats are better for the economy than Republicans. Of course, anyone familiar with recent political history should not be surprised. Republicans' main constituency is the rich, and the main economic fear of the rich is inflation, for numerous reasons, among them: Inflation erodes the value of previously issued debt instruments like bonds and certificates of deposit; it forces up the interest rates paid on bonds and certificates of deposit, thereby attracting investment money from equity financial instruments like stocks (thus placing downward pressure on stock prices); and inflation complicates planning on the part of business generally. Accordingly, because government deficit spending and rapid economic growth raise the risk of inflation, Republicans have historically at least paid lip service to restraining deficits (except, at least since 1980, when a Republican occupies the presidency) and have favored moderate economic growth. In contrast, as will be seen in Chapter 13, liberalism has long been the philosophy of rapid economic growth, promoted by government spending.

The facts are clear that Democrats have trounced Republicans based on the metric of job growth but, as observed by Paul Krugman, that fact did not stop Senator Rand Paul (R-KY) from spouting the nonsense in early 2015 that the last time our country had created millions of jobs was under President Reagan. Krugman corrected the record: The economy created 22.5 million jobs under Democratic President Bill Clinton after the economy under Republican President Ronald Reagan created 16 million jobs, and if creating "millions of jobs" means increasing the number of jobs by over two million in a year, the economy has done that 13 times since Reagan left office: eight times under Bill Clinton, twice under George W. Bush and three times during the first six years of Barack Obama.[84]

Keynes Was Right and Hayek Wrong: The Coming Collapse of the Trickle-Down Consensus

Daniel Yergin and Joseph Stanislaw, in their outstanding book *The Commanding Heights* (1998) and companion documentary shown on PBS, told the story of the great intellectual debate between John Maynard Keynes, and his argument that it was appropriate for the government to use fiscal and monetary policy to stimulate the economy, versus Friedrich Hayek, and his argument that the government should stay out of the economy and allow the free market to heal economic downturns in its due time. Yergin and Stanislaw concluded their story with the observation—again, in 1998—that Hayek had won and Keynes lost. Roughly two decades before, the West had seen the collapse of the Keynesian Consensus—a collapse that occurred in great part due to two opinions of Keynesians: that there was no way for government to rein in the inflation raging in the late 1960s and 1970s, and that inflation did not matter anyway. In reality, Keynes had concurred, in his book *The General Theory of Employment, Interest and Money* (1936) that it was proper for the central bank of a nation (as in the US, the Federal Reserve) to raise interest rates to combat inflation, and Keynes had previously commented in *The Economic Consequences of the Peace* (1919) on the dangers inflation poses for debauching the currency.[85]

Ironically, similarly, the proponents of trickle-down depart from Hayek in important particulars as well. Hayek, in *The Road to Serfdom*, actually supported a rather expansive social safety net, including government guaranteed health care—arguably, at least, consistent with Obamacare. In that same book he warned of the danger of undermining the middle class and of blindly following *laissez-faire*. (This will be explored later herein.)

With the benefit of greater hindsight, it can now be definitively declared that—although Hayek "won" in the sense that what is called herein the "trickle-down consensus" still reigns—Keynes was ultimately, again, right and the followers of Hayek wrong. Economic growth was more rapid in the roughly three decades following World War II under Keynesianism and prosperity was more broadly shared as the great American middle class was created versus the roughly three decades following 1980 and the advent of Hayek-inspired trickle-down. As will be seen, trickle-down, with its upward redistribution of economic and political power, has resulted in slower economic growth, shrinking prosperity and a declining standard of living, undermining of the political power of the middle class and poor, undermining of the institutions upon which they rely, and decline in their health outcomes. Similarly, as reflected in the six studies reviewed above, Democratic administrations, applying Keynesianism, have historically economically outperformed, based on such measures as economic growth and job creation, Republican administrations applying trickle-down and related conservative economic policies inspired by Hayek and others.

Krugman, in an op-ed in 2015,[86] summarized the nonsense of the trickle-down theory of the Republicans as illustrated over the previous 15 years, observing that Republicans believed during the Bush years that the economy was experiencing healthy growth, there was no housing bubble, and the monetary efforts of the Federal Reserve as well as the fiscal efforts of the federal government to fight the resultant economic crisis—which occurred after implementation of two trickle-down inspired tax cuts that converted budget surpluses into budget deficits—would result in severe inflation. And, of course, they later criticized Obamacare as a job killer. In reality, a housing bubble existed during the Bush years that, when it burst, nearly brought down the entire financial system. Fiscal and monetary stimulation were appropriate to aid recovery, and inflation remains in check still. And, the economy under Obama in 2014 experienced the best job growth in 15 years. Mitt Romney had promised, in May 2012, in an interview with Mark Halperin while campaigning, to get unemployment down to 6 percent and maybe lower by the end of 2016—the unemployment rate under President Obama fell below 6 percent in 2014—two years ahead of Governor Romney's promised deadline.[87]

The facts to rebut and end the trickle-down consensus that has held sway over the US and much of the West over the past three decades are there for all to see. What is lacking is the political movement to secure broad acceptance of these facts.

HOW THE FACTS OF TRICKLE-DOWN'S FAILURE WERE HIDDEN IN ECONOMIC THEORY

The most accurate explanation for growing inequality is given in part of the title of a remarkable book by members of the Sociology Department at the University of California, Berkeley—*Inequality by Design: Cracking the Bell Curve Myth* (1996)[88] —written in response to *The Bell Curve* by Charles Murray and Richard Herrnstein. The main point in *Inequality by Design* is that efforts to reduce inequality must look beyond mere federal programs and address societal values through institutional reforms, for inequality is *not*: (1) Inevitable; (2) Due to differences in intelligence; (3) Necessary to promote economic growth; (4) Due to a decline in worker productivity; (5) Only susceptible to redress with huge federal programs or (6) Reduced by a growing economy. Inequality is intentional.

Guiding all that follows is the idea that people in any society choose their quality of life by the government policies they adopt—simply put, as it will appear in various forms hereafter, prosperity is a choice that we make by the government policies we choose.[89] And, if we define prosperity as a generally good quality of life for all people, we Americans, by promoting government policies pursuant to a trickle-down vision, have been choosing to reject prosperity for most of the past three decades. Of course, also, given that prosperity is a choice, we can also say the opposite is true, as observed by columnist for *The New York Times*, Nicholas Kristof, in his column of the same name: "Inequality is a choice."[90]

A recurring theme herein is that efforts to address inequality have been thwarted by conservative misinformation. In a letter to the editor of *Mother Jones* (January/February 1997), former *Wall Street Journal* columnist and supply-sider Jude Wanniski (see the Introduction) responded to the *Mother Jones* article by Paul Krugman quoted herein. Bear in mind the *facts* on growing inequality as Wanniski explained inequality this way (*and* bear in mind Wanniski was advisor to Republican Jack Kemp's 1996 presidential campaign!):

> The central problem of the last 30 years is that the poor are getting richer much, much faster than the rich are getting richer . . . .Add up the portfolios of the rich and the poor and you will find the poor have become fat and happy, the rich impoverished. This is why we are in the fix we are in. Everyone wants to be poor, because it has so many advantages!

How Terminology Hid the Delusion of Trickle-Down

Conservative economists supported not only trickle-down, but also other concepts that would creep into common usage and hide the reality of the economy—concepts such as "underclass," "wealth effect," "NAIRU" (the

"Non-Accelerating Inflation Rate of Unemployment") and the "natural rate of unemployment." The theory of the underclass would give comfort to the majority of Americans that the suffering of the urban poor was of their own doing—due to lax morals, especially, as encouraged by government-sponsored welfare. The term fell out of favor, but we would do well to remember it today and ask, in light of the fact that the average American family has been "losing ground" (as conservative sociologist Charles Murray titled his book) over the past three decades, is the average American family underclass, too?[91]

Another concept that became popular in the late 1990s with the rise of the stock market, and was perhaps even more nefariously deceptive, is that of the "wealth effect." The term "wealth effect" refers to an increase in consumer spending due to a perceived increase (real or imaginary) in net worth (paper wealth—increase in value of stocks, bonds, IRAs, 401(k)s, homes, etc.) When used in the late 1990s, the term "wealth effect" typically evoked the positive phenomenon of vast numbers of households, flush with their gains from the stock market, cashing in some of their stocks and converting those capital gains to buying consumer goods as a well-deserved reward, thereby fueling consumer spending growth. In reality, the wealth effect refers to the highly irresponsible behavior of substituting ever deeper indebtedness for stagnating wages, which we can now see endangers the long-term prosperity of the nation.

The rosy consumer spending statistics of the late 1990s, it turned out, were due less to consumers cashing in their stock market gains than to the twin emerging changes in consumer behavior: Adoption by vast numbers of Americans of historically low levels of debt aversion and conversion of billions of dollars of home equity into equity-based loans to fund consumer purchases.

The wealth effect, in reality, was simply *the act of people using their home equity—the major component of wealth of the non-rich—as collateral so they could substitute debt for non-existent income and savings, in the process putting their wealth at risk in the event of a decline in home prices.* Amazingly, although this phenomenon had been going on for many years, very few economists had remarked upon the relationship, clearly evidenced by the simultaneous rise in "gross equity extraction rate" (synonymous with "mortgage equity withdrawals" or MEW) and decline in the personal saving rate.[92]

The truth was apparent to anyone who reflected on the facts. Regarding stock ownership, direct and indirect (through 401(k) and IRA and related accounts) in 2012:[93]

1. While almost half of American households owned stocks directly or indirectly (46.9 percent in 2012), less than one-third (31.1 percent) of American households owned more than $10,000 worth.

2. The top 10 percent of income holders owned about 80 percent (80.8 percent) of stocks, while the other 90 percent of America owned slightly less than 20 percent (19.2 percent) of stocks.

Couple these observations regarding concentration of stock ownership with the observation that, even among the top 10 percent of households, most of these families held their stock indirectly, in 401(k) or IRA (or similar) accounts, and held for retirement: Thus, any reaping of stock market gains by these families prior to age 59 ½ will be severely penalized.

Based on similar observations, a report by economists Karl Case, John Quigley and Nobel Prize winner Robert Shiller concluded "[w]e find at best weak evidence of a stock market wealth effect." Further, the authors found results of their research "support the conclusion that changes in house prices should be considered to have a larger and more important impact than changes in stock market prices in influencing household consumption in the U.S. and in other developed countries."[94] Thus, while there was at least the potential that, in the case of a rising stock market, for the very wealthiest, the wealth effect did not simply equate to reduced debt aversion, in the case of rising house prices, the wealth effect is synonymous with reduced aversion to debt combined with reduced savings behavior.

Before leaving the nonsense of the stock market wealth effect, one more observation is appropriate, and it is regarding stock market performance in the twenty-first century. As observed by investment advisor A. Gary Shilling, there have been only five stock market declines of more than 40 percent since 1900—and two happened in the recent space of less than a decade: the 2000–2002 technology-led crash and the 2007–2009 mortgage-driven crash.[95] Thus, even among the minority of American households who own sizeable holdings of stock, those holdings may have been decimated in these two crashes.

About the same time as the wealth effect was in vogue, another misconception—NAIRU—the "non-accelerating inflation rate of unemployment" was popularized. Consensus had come to deem (as it does today) consumer price (wage-price) inflation the ultimate economic evil, and to support growth rates low by historical standards accompanied by moderately high unemployment rates (forget the post-World War II goal of "full employment"!) to combat wage-price inflation.

Although NAIRU fell out of use in the popular media as it had to continually be adjusted downward, while NAIRU was popular the public became conditioned to going behind inflation rates and money supply growth and cheering news of more of their fellow Americans joining unemployment lines. They were conditioned to expect the market to *fall* on what used to be the "good news" of falling unemployment and rising growth. Doubly ironic is the fact that stagflation in the late 1970s disproved the theory of an inverse relationship between the inflation rate and the unemployment rate (the "Phillips Curve," named after the economist A. W. Phillips), yet popular focus during this time returned to unemployment and growth and away from monetary aggregates.[96]

Related to NAIRU was the "natural rate of unemployment." The term implied that in a "mature" market (as though before the country turned 200 years old, it had an "immature" market!), unemployment rates simply could not be expected to ever again be as low as they were in the 1960s and early 1970s (low single digits). The term eventually fell out of favor during the boom in the late 1990s, as it had to be continually revised downward.

How Economic Theory Hid the Delusion of Trickle-Down

Libertarian monetarists—notably, Alan Greenspan among them—denied the ability of bubbles to exist because they believed the free market would never allow assets to be grossly overpriced. Greenspan's monetarist colleague, University of Chicago economist Eugene Fama, in an interview with John Cassidy of *The New Yorker* after the 2008 crisis, observed that he did not even know what a credit bubble is.[97] (Ironically, Fama shared the 2013 Nobel Prize with Robert Shiller, an economist very much a believer in bubbles).

A critical observation is appropriate here. Chairman Greenspan's political ideology was libertarianism, and among his heroes the libertarian Russian émigré and writer Ayn Rand. Greenspan was so devoted to his faith in the free market that he famously opposed Commodities Futures Trading Commission Chairperson Brooksley Born's proposal to prosecute fraud, arguing that it was unnecessary to regulate against fraud because the market itself would punish fraudulent behavior just as it would not allow financiers to set aside insufficient reserves to cover outstanding obligations. In this view, Greenspan and other monetarists (see below) had misconstrued their history. It was not, as they believed, the failure of the Federal Reserve to promptly lower interest rates that triggered the Great Depression but, rather, the failure of the "free market" when the exercise of self-interest was insufficiently regulated.

The libertarian monetarism of the Chicago School fit well over the past three decades with trickle-down-supply-side crony capitalism, neoconservatism and neoliberalism—and clashed with the Keynesians who over that period demanded greater fiscal stimulus (more government spending) to create more demand, and more regulation and higher marginal tax rates to "spread the wealth."

A monetarist philosophy, although accompanied with much less libertarianism, drove Greenspan's successor as Federal Reserve Chairman Ben Bernanke. Bernanke's doctoral dissertation at Princeton attributed the Great Depression to inappropriately tight monetary policy on the part of the Federal Reserve having turned a business cycle contraction into a prolonged depression. In an address at the University of Chicago in 2002 on the occasion of the 90th birthday celebration of Milton Friedman, Chairman Bernanke concluded his remarks by turning to Friedman and Anna Schwartz, co-authors of *A Monetary History of the United States*, which originally promoted this theory, and delivered a tribute: "I would like to say to Milton and Anna: Regarding the Great Depression. You're right, we did it. We're very sorry. But thanks to you, we won't do it again."[98]

Unfortunately, Chairman Bernanke was right, they (central bankers) did do it—but "it" wasn't what Milton Friedman and Anna Schwartz and Ben Bernanke himself thought "it" was. Their critical failure was, in fact, to attempt to fight chronic economic sluggishness solely by keeping interest rates low and opposing regulation and other fiscal measures to help the middle class and poor, with the result that for three and a half decades and counting, revenues from increased productivity have been redistributed upward, creating recurrent debt-fueled bubbles, rising inequality and ongoing demand shortfall. Chairman Bernanke continued to fail to see this well into 2011, admitting that he was unable to explain the failure of the economy to respond to monetary stimulus—as his monetarist theory said it would.[99]

Days after Chairman Bernanke's admission, former Chairman Greenspan observed in an interview, regarding the quantitative easing (buying of bonds by a central bank; a monetary stimulus measure in addition to lower interest rates) by the Bernanke Federal Reserve, that he found no evidence that either the first phase (QE1) or the second phase (QE2) of quantitative easing actually worked to spur economic growth, other than helping with the exchange rate and encouraging export expansion.[100]

Application of expansive monetary policy during an episode of credit overstimulation risks re-inflating bubbles. This "solution," after all, is *further stimulating credit in a setting of already existent credit overstimulation.* Therefore, in addition to stimulative monetary policy, stimulative *fiscal* policy as only the government can provide is appropriate; especially investment in public works and infrastructure, which, as in the case of the Great Depression and the current downturn, will have been neglected because, during the preceding years, trillions of dollars will have been flowing into asset bubbles created due to excessively low interest rates and low labor costs.

The triumph of trickle-down was an overreaction to the stagflation that ended the era of the Keynesian Consensus, and the trickle-down delusion is built on multiple policy delusions. Additional theoretical delusions underpin trickle-down, and those are addressed in Chapter 7, where institutions—such as that of the market—are addressed.

After factual review, perhaps the most important delusional assumption made by trickle-down is that allowing real wages to decline, and addressing the resultant demand shortfall by substituting debt for nonexistent income growth, is benign. Pursuant to this delusion, everyone who supports trickle-down conservative Republican policies—knowingly or unknowingly—has, in effect, been engaged in class warfare in favor of the rich against the middle class and working poor, to the detriment of the American economy and democracy, our institutions, and the health of ourselves and our fellow Americans.

NOTES

1. These are dividends paid after December 31, 2002, by a US corporation and are on stock held for more than 60 days during the 121-day period that begins 60 days before the ex-dividend date, which is the first date following the declaration of a dividend on which the buyer of a stock is not entitled to receive the next dividend payment.

2. Per the Urban-Brookings Tax Policy Center (TPC), Table T13-0020, the average effective tax rate for estates of $5 million to $10 million is 7.7%; $10 million to $20 million 15.8%; and over $20 million 18.8%. This due mainly to deductions afforded to heirs. And, per the TPC, in 2013, only 3,780 estates owed any estate tax at all, and 99.86 % of estates owed none. Only *20* small farms and businesses owed any estate tax at all.

3. Thomas B. Edsall, "Cutting the Poor Out of Welfare," *The New York Times*, June 17, 2014.

4. See also Paul Krugman in "Phony Fear Factor," *The New York Times*, August 9, 2013, and "Republicans Against Reality," *The New York Times*, August 5, 2013.

5. The most prominent commentator to warn against the mistake of austerity has been Paul Krugman—see, for example, "Keynes Was Right," *The New York Times*, December 29, 2011 and "Austerity's Grim Legacy," *The New York Times*, November 6, 2015.

6. Martin Crutsinger, "American Economy Not Healthy Yet, But Healing," *Associated Press*, January 27, 2012. See also, David Leonhardt, "The Role of Austerity," *Economix* blog, *The New York Times*, January 27, 2012, and Motoko Rich, "The Role of Government Spending," *Economix* blog, *The New York Times*, July 29, 2011.

7. Michael Greenstone and Adam Looney, "Should the United States Have 2.2 Million More Jobs?" The Hamilton Project, May 3, 2013.

8. Paul Krugman, "1937," *The Conscience of a Liberal* blog, *The New York Times*, June 3, 2012. The chart, based on data from FRED (the online database of the St.Louis Federal Reserve) also appeared on "This Week with George Stephanopoulos" on June 3, 2012, and he addressed it in his opinion column titled "This Republican Economy" in *The New York Times* June 3, 2012.

9. Mark Thoma, "Per Capita Government Spending by President," Economist's View blog, February 12, 2013. Thoma is a University of Oregon economics professor.

10. Robin Harding, Richard McGregor and Gabriel Muller, "US Public Investment Falls to Lowest Level Since War," *Financial Times*, November 3, 2013. See also, Cardiff Garcia, "The Collapse of US Infrastructure Spending, Charted," FT Alphaville blog site, October 31, 2013. See also Floyd Norris, "Government Shows Growth, After Years of Shrinking," *The New York Times*, November 8, 2014.

11. Paul Krugman, "Ideology and Investment," *The New York Times*, October 27, 2014.

12. And, in 1966, with the Vietnam War raging, 2.6 million people were on active duty; in 2013, that figure was 1.4 million. Floyd Norris, "Bloated Government? Federal Employment at 47-Year Low," Economix blog, *The New York Times*, October 22, 2013.

13. Peak was $325.5 billion; spending dropped $54.5 billion to $271 billion by April 2012; graph: "Total Public Construction Spending (TLPBLCONS)"—FRED –St. Louis Federal Reserve Bank.

14. Graph: "All Employees: Government (USGOVT)"—FRED –St. Louis Federal Reserve Bank. And, Bill McBride, Calculated Risk website, September 7, 2013.

15. Paul Krugman, *End This Depression Now*! (New York, London: W. W. Norton & Company, Inc.; 2012), pp. 214-215.

16. Paul Krugman, in an interview with Joshua Holland, "Paul Krugman: We Could End This Depression Right Now," *AlterNet*, May 22, 2012.

17. Graph: "USGOVT/POP"—FRED –St. Louis Fed.

18. Ben Casselman and Conor Dougherty, "Federal Spending Cutbacks Slow Recovery," *The Wall Street Journal*, July 30, 2012. Obama administration federal spending cuts are recounted in the Prologue to Thomas Byrne Edsall's *The Age of Austerity: How Scarcity Will Remake American Politics* (2012).

19. Joe Weisenthal, "Everything You Know about the Deficit Is Wrong—And Fixing It Will Be Painless," *Business Insider*, December 28, 2012.

20. Senator Marco Rubio (R-FL) was joined by Senator Mitch McConnell (R-KY) in proposing a balanced budget amendment, and they were joined by conservative commentators Joe Scarborough and George Will, all of whom were criticized in an outstanding blog post by Joe Weisenthal of *Business Insider*: "George Will Writes Terribly Ignorant Argument in Favor of Balanced Budget Amendment," *Business Insider*, February 9, 2013.

21. John McCormick and Greg Giroux, "Food Stamp Cut Backed by Republicans with Voters on Rolls," *Bloomberg Business*, August 14, 2013.

22. See the Monthly Statement of the Public Debt of the United States published by the Bureau of the Public Debt in the Treasury Department (dollar amounts in parentheses are in millions)—January 31, 1981 ($847,695) versus January 31, 1989 ($2,448,271); January 31, 2001 ($5,716,071) versus January 31, 2009 ($10,632,080); and January 31, 2009 ($10,632,080) versus October 31, 2015 ($18,152,982); January 1993 ($3,809,334) versus January 31, 2001 ($5,716,071). We can project what President Obama's total will be on January 31, 2017: If we make the fairly conservative assumption that the deficit over the period October 31, 2015 through January 31, 2017 will grow by $600 billion, the debt will have increased in size 1.76 times.

23. See, for example, Thomas Byrne Edsall, *The Age of Austerity: How Scarcity Will Remake American Politics* (2012).

24. See Robert J. Samuelson, "Employers Lack Confidence, Not Skilled Labor," *The Washington Post*, May 5, 2013.

25. Nick Hanauer, "Raise Taxes on Rich to Reward True Job Creators," *Bloomberg Business*, December 7, 2011. Nick Hanauer is a founder of Second Avenue Partners, a venture capital company in Seattle specializing in early state startups and emerging technology. He has helped launch more than 20 companies, including aQuantive Inc.(which became Microsoft Advertising) and Amazon.com, and is the co-author of two books, *The True Patriot and The Gardens of Democracy.* See also Henry Blodget, "Sorry Folks, Rich People Actually Don't 'Create the Jobs'," *Business Insider*, November 29, 2013.

26. Joe Weisenthal, "Chart of the Day: It's Pretty Obvious What's Driving Unemployment," *Business Insider* blog, January 10, 2012.

27. From the *Budget for Fiscal Year 2015, Historical Tables*, Office of Management and Budget; January 2014. "Table 1.2—Summary of Receipts, Outlays, and Surpluses or Deficits (-) as Percentages of GDP; 1930–2019;" *The Budget and Economic Outlook: 2015 to 2025*, the Congressional Budget Office, January 2015; *An Update to the Budget and Economic Outlook: 2015 to 2025*, the Congressional Budget Office, August 2015; and *Monthly Budget Review for September 2015*, the Congressional Budget Office, October 7, 2015, as shown in Table A.1 in the Appendix.

28. Lori Montgomery, "In 2009, Americans Paid Lowest Tax Rates in 30 Years to Federal Government," *The Washington Post*, July 10, 2012.

29. "The U.S. Continues to Be One of the Least Taxed of the Developed Countries," Citizens for Tax Justice, April 8, 2013.

30. Eugene Steuerle, Signe-Mary McKernan, Caroline Ratcliffe and Sisi Zhang, "Lost Generations? Wealth Building Among Young Americans," Urban Institute, March 2013. This report observes that the long-term trend of successive generations acquiring more wealth than their predecessors has broken down under trickle-down, and the age group 29–37 actually *lost* 21 percent in average real net worth from 1983–2010. See also, Suzy Khimm, "How Young People Are Getting Poorer, in One Chart," WONKBLOG, March 15, 2013.

31. Angie Drobnic Holan, in "Grover Norquist Said the Economy Has Grown or Been Damaged by Capital Gains Tax Changes," *Tampa Bay Tribune*, PolitiFact.com, July 19, 2011, rated this claim "False."

32. Carmen DeNavas-Walt and Bernadette D. Proctor, U.S. Census Bureau, Current Population Report, P60-252, *Income and Poverty in the United States: 2014*, U.S. Government Printing Office, Washington, D.C., September 2015. Table A-2, "Selected Measures of Household Income Dispersion: 1967 to 2014" and Table A-4, "Number and Real Median Earnings of Total Workers and Full-Time, Year-Round Workers by Sex and Female-Male Earnings Ratio: 1960 to 2014." Median household income in 2014 was $53,657; in 1997 it was $54,427. For male full-time workers 2014 real median income was $40,638; in 1973 it was $41,634.

33. "Automatic Increases: Wage Statistics for 2014," Social Security Administration, October 23, 2015.

34. Quoting from the Congressional Research Service, "The 2001 and 2003 Bush Tax Cuts and Deficit Reduction," Report R42020 (September 23, 2011). Quoted in Bruce Bartlett, *The Benefit and the Burden: Tax Reform—Why We Need It and What It Will Take* (New York: Simon & Schuster; 2012), p. 221.

35. Thomas L. Hungerford, "Taxes and the Economy: An Economic Analysis of the Top Tax Rates Since 1945," Congressional Research Service, September 14, 2012. See also, David Leonhardt, "Do Tax Cuts Lead to Economic Growth?" *The New York Times*, September 12, 2012, and David Leonhardt, "Tax Cuts and Economic Growth," *Economix Blog*, *The New York Times*, September 12, 2012.

36. Bruce Bartlett, "Are the Bush Tax Cuts the Root of Our Fiscal Problem?" Economix blog at *The New York Times* website, July 26, 2011.

37. Paul Krugman, "Who's Very Important?" *The New York Times*, July 12, 2012; "Policy and the Personal," July 1, 2012; and "The Long Run History of Taxes on the Rich," *The Conscience of a Liberal Blog*, July 15, 2012.

38. Robert Frank, "Millionaires Support Warren Buffett's Tax on the Rich," *The Wealth Report Blog*, *The Wall Street Journal*, October 27, 2011.

39. Robert Frank, "The Rich Are Hoarding Cash—and That's Not Good," *CNBC*, August 8, 2012.

40. "Ronald Reagan's Legacy Clouds Tax Record," *NPR*, February 4, 2011. This is an interview with former Senator Alan Simpson (R-WY). The eleven tax increases are listed by Bruce Bartlett in *The Benefit and the Burden: Tax Reform—Why We Need It and What It Will Take* (New York: Simon & Schuster, 2012), p. 45.

41. Ken Jacobs, Ian Perry, and Jenifer MacGillvary, "The High Public Cost of Low Wages," Research Brief, UC Berkeley Center for Labor Research and Education, April 2015.

42. The Editorial Board, "Picking Up the Tab for Low Wages," *The New York Times*, May 1, 2015.

43. Steven Greenhouse, "The Mystery of the Vanishing Pay Raise," *The New York Times*, November 1, 2015.

44. Jonathan Alter, "Washing Off the Red Ink," *Newsweek*, October 12, 1998.

45. Allison Kopicki, "Poll: Partisan Split Over Tax Policies," The Caucus Blog of *The New York Times*, January 24, 2012.

46. Joel Slemrod, "The Truth About Taxes and Economic Growth," Interview in *Challenge*, vol. 46, no. 1, January/February 2003, pp. 5–14. Slemrod is a tax economist at the University of Michigan, and also found no evidence linking economic growth to capital gains tax cuts.

47. Citations to the Urban-Brookings Tax Policy Center and the Congressional Research Service in Chye-Ching Huang and Chuck Marr, "Raising Today's Low Capital Gains Tax Rates Could Promote Economic Efficiency and Fairness, While Helping Reduce Deficits," Center on Budget and Policy Priorities, September 19, 2012.

48. Tax Policy Center, T11-0114, "Share of Federal Taxes Under Current Law, By Cash Income Percentile, 2011," May 3, 2011.

49. "Who Pays Taxes in America in 2014?" Citizens for Tax Justice, April 7, 2014.

50. Elizabeth Dunn and Michael Norton, "Heavens, Not Havens," *The New York Times*, April 15, 2013. More progressive and happier: Denmark, Finland, Norway, Belgium, New Zealand, the Netherlands and Sweden.

51. According to the Federal Reserve Bank of St. Louis, banks are flush with reserves—they just aren't lending. David Schawel, "Banks Hoard Cash & Securities As Loans Contract," *Economic Musings* blog, July 4, 2011.

52. Chrystia Freeland, "The Rise of the New Global Elite," *The Atlantic*, January/February 2011.

53. See, for example, Edmund L. Andrews, "Greenspan Concedes Error on Regulation," *The New York Times*, October 24, 2008.

54. Jia Lynn Yang, "Does Government Regulation Really Kill Jobs? Economists Say Overall Effect Is Minimal," *The Washington Post*, November 13, 2011.

55. Catherine Dodge and Frank Bass, "Rich-Poor Gap Widens to Most Since 1967 as Income Falls," *Bloomberg Business*, September 12, 2012. See also, Jim Tankersley, "Growth Isn't Enough to Help the Middle Class," *The Washington Post*, February 13, 2013, and Michael A. Fletcher, "Fiscal Trouble Ahead for Most Future Retirees," *The Washington Post*, February 16, 2013.

56. Referenced June 7, 2012; based on distribution of family income—Gini Index.

57. James B. Stewart, "The Myth of the Rich Who Flee from Taxes," *The New York Times*, February 16, 2013.

58. As observed by Andrew Sayer in *Why We Can't Afford the Rich* (2015).

59. "KPMG's Individual Income Tax and Social Security Rate Survey 2012," KPMG International, January 2013.

60. "The Effects of a Minimum-Wage Increase on Employment and Family Income," Congressional Budget Office of the United States, February 2014.

61. "Over 600 Economists Sign Letter in Support of $10.10 Minimum Wage," Economics Policy Institute Press Release, January 27, 2014. According to the "CPI Inflation Calculator" at the Bureau of Labor Statistics website, to have the same buying power as in 1968, when the minimum wage was $1.60, the minimum wage in 2014 would have to be $10.75. Thus, raising the minimum wage to $10.10 would still not raise it to the same level as when it had its highest buying power. See also, Paul Krugman, "Liberals and Wages," *The New York Times*, July 17, 2015.

62. Arindrajit Dube, T. William Lester, and Michael Reich, "Minimum Wage Effects Across State Borders: Estimates Using Contiguous Counties," *The Review of Economics and Statistics*, November 2010, 92(4): 945–964. See also, Annie Lowrey, "Supersize My Wage," *The New York Times Magazine*, December 17, 2013.

63. "The Case for a Higher Minimum Wage," The Editorial Board, *The New York Times*, February 8, 2014. See also, Nelson D. Schwartz, "Low-Income Workers See Biggest Drop in Paychecks," *The New York Times*, September 3, 2015.

64. See Paul Krugman, "The Fiscal Fizzle, *The New York Times*, July 21, 2014.

65. Michael W. L. Elsby, University of Edinburgh; Bart Hobijn, Federal Reserve Bank of San Francisco; and Ayşegül Şahin, Federal Reserve Bank of New York; *The Decline of the U.S. Labor Share*, Prepared for Brookings Panel on Economic Activity, September 19–20, 2013, Brookings Institution, Washington, D.C.

66. Paul Krugman, "Mornings in Blue America," *The New York Times*, March 27, 2015.

67. Reasons unique to the CRA and Fannie and Freddie are derived from blog posts by Dean Baker, "George Will Spreads Some Lies About the Economic Crisis," from the Center for Economic and Policy Research website, July 3, 2011; and Mark Thoma, "Reckless Endanger-

ment of the Truth," *Economist's View* blog, July 4, 2011. Similar observations have been made by NYU economist Nouriel Roubini.

68. Randall S. Kroszner, "The Community Reinvestment Act and the Recent Mortgage Crisis," speech to the Confronting Concentrated Poverty Policy Forum, Board of Governors of the Federal Reserve System, Washington, DC, December 3, 2008. However, the market was also not brought down by buyers at the other end of the spectrum—those upper middle income buyers of "McMansions." Catherine Rampell, "Boom, Bust, Flip," *The New York Times*, October 6, 2013.

69. David Goldstein and Kevin G. Hall, "Private Sector Loans, Not Fannie or Freddie, Triggered Crisis," *McClatchy Newspapers*, October 12, 2008.

70. "Home Price Appreciation Outpaces Wage Growth in 76 Percent of U.S. Markets During Housing Recovery," RealtyTrac, March 25, 2015.

71. This observation is attributable to Deutsche Bank's Torston Sløk. See Myles Udland, "This Chart Tells the Entire Story of the US Housing Recovery," *Business Insider*, March 27, 2015.

72. "Renting Less Affordable Than Ever Before, While Mortgages Remain Affordable, by Historical Standards," press release, PRNewswire, August 13, 2015. Analysis is by Zillow.

73. Peter Gosselin and Jennifer Oldham, "If Economists Were Right, You Would Have a Raise by Now," *Bloomberg Business*, March 15, 2015.

74. "Consumer Expenditures Midyear Update—July 2013 through June 2014 Average," Bureau of Labor Statistics news release April 2, 2015.

75. "Contrary to What You Read in the WSJ, the Shift to Benefits Does Not Explain Sluggish Pay Growth," Beat the Press blog, Center for Economic Progress, November 1, 2015.

76. "Wages Haven't Been This Crucial to U.S. Economy in Half Century," *Bloomberg Business*, March 19, 2015.

77. Michael Kinsley, "Politicians Lie, Numbers Don't," *Slate.com*, September 16, 2008.

78. Richard Carroll, "Democratic Presidents Are Better for the Economy," *Bloomberg Business*, June 25, 2012.

79. Elizabeth Frock, "Democratic Presidents Beat Republicans on 11 of 12 Economic Indicators," *US News & World Report Washington Whispers* online site, August 10, 2012.

80. "Presidential Election 2012," Ameriprise Financial, September 26, 2012.

81. Bob Drummond, "Private Jobs Increase More with Democrats in White House," *Bloomberg Business*, May 8, 2012. Another interesting observation made in the article is relative irrelevance of party regarding government jobs growth: Over that same 52-year period, government agencies added 21,000 jobs per month under Republicans and 22,000 jobs per month under Democrats.

82. Alan S. Blinder and Mark W. Watson, "Presidents and the Economy: A Forensic Investigation," November 2013.

83. Paul Krugman, "Voodoo, Jeb! Style," *The New York Times*, June 19, 2015. Krugman returned to the topic in "Partisan Growth Gaps," *The New York Times*, November 2, 2015.

84. Paul Krugman, "Mornings in Blue America," *The New York Times*, March 27, 2015. Actually, Krugman rounded up the number of jobs created under President Clinton from 22.5 million to 23 million, but the number 22.5 million is used herein for consistency.

85. John Maynard Keynes, *The Economic Consequences of the Peace* (London: Macmillan; 1919; New York: Harcourt; 1920), pp. 235-236.

86. Paul Krugman, "Fraternity of Failure," *The New York Times*, May 15, 2015.

87. Steve Benen, "'Wow, 6 Percent Sounds Pretty Good'," CNBC.com, October 8, 2014.

88. Published by the Princeton University Press in 1996, its authors are Claude S. Fischer, Michael Hout, Martín Sánchez Jankowski, Samuel R. Lucas, Ann Swidler and Kim Voss.

89. See Michael Fairbanks, "Changing the Mind of a Nation: Elements in a Process for Creating Prosperity" in *Culture Matters: How Values Shape Human Progress*, ed. Lawrence E. Harrison and Samuel P. Huntington (New York: Basic Books, 2000), p. 280. The footnote to this quote, Ibid at p. 327 refers to Michael Porter, a Harvard University professor specializing in competitive advantages of businesses, and founder of the Initiative for a Competitive Inner City (ICIC), a group dedicated to expanding inner city business development.

90. Nicholas Kristof, "'Inequality Is a Choice'," *The New York Times*, May 3, 2015. Inspiring Kristof's op-ed was Joseph Stiglitz's 2015 book, *The Great Divide*, chapters of which are entitled "Inequality Is Not Inevitable" and "Inequality Is a Choice." See also Eduardo Porter, "What Debate on Inequality Is Missing," *The New York Times*, May 6, 2015.

91. In a related study, see "The American Middle Class Is Losing Ground," Pew Research Center, December 9, 2015. See also Sam Fleming and Shawn Donovan, "America's Middle-class Meltdown: Core Shrinks to Half of US Homes," *Financial Times*, December 9, 2015.

92. Two economists who did: John Gist and Carlos Figueiredo, "Deeper in Debt: Trends Among Midlife and Older Americans," April 2002, available at the AARP website. Similarly, Stephen S. Roach, former Chairman of Morgan Stanley Asia, in "A Subprime Outlook for the Global Economy," a paper he issued in late 2007, correctly stressed that the Federal Reserve should look not only at "CPI-based inflation" to guide its policy, but also to "the extremes of asset values." Directly to the point: The Federal Reserve should monitor increasing inequality as a warning sign to bubble creation. This phenomenon manifests itself in what is termed herein the "Wealth Effect Scissors" illustrating the debt-for-savings substitution phenomenon of the wealth effect (the crossover year, as shown below, was 1999, and, amazingly, the savings rate went negative in 2005). The term "Household Responsibility Index" refers to an index created herein by subtracting gross equity extraction rate from NIPA (National Income and Products Account) personal saving rate. Households are behaving more responsibly—accumulating more savings than debt—when the index is positive. The table below is derived from Alan Greenspan and James Kennedy, "Sources and Uses of Equity Extracted from Homes," Finance and Economic Discussion Series, Divisions of Research & Statistics and Monetary Affairs, Federal Reserve Board, Washington, D.C., March 2007 (2007–20), Table 24, "Sources and Uses of Equity Extracted from Homes," pp. 24–25, lines 101 and 106. The index went negative in 1999 (the same year in which household incomes peaked) and continued moving more deeply into negative territory as home prices rose toward their peak in early 2006—as shown in Table A.2 in the Appendix; all figures are in *percent of disposable income*.

93. Economic Policy Institute, *The State of Working America 12th Edition*.

94. Karl E. Case, John M. Quigley and Robert J. Shilller, "Comparing Wealth Effects: The Stock Market versus the Housing Market," *Advances in Macroeconomics*, Vol. 5, Issue 1, 2005, Article 1, p. 26, quoted in Alan Greenspan and James Kennedy, "Sources and Uses of Equity Extracted from Homes," Finance and Economics Discussion Series Divisions of Research & Statistics and Monetary Affairs Federal Reserve Board, Washington, D.C., 2007-20, pp. 3–4.

95. A. Gary Shilling, "Will U.S. Avoid Recession in 2012? (Part 1)" *Bloomberg Business*, April 9, 2012.

96. In dissent: University of Texas economist James K. Galbraith in "Test the Limit," *The American Prospect*, September/October 1997.

97. John Cassidy, "After the Blowup: Laissez-faire Economists Do Some Soul-searching—and Finger-pointing," *The New Yorke*r, January 11, 2010; p. 30.

98. Remarks by Governor Ben S. Bernanke at the Conference to Honor Milton Friedman, University of Chicago, Chicago, Illinois, November 8, 2002, Federal Reserve Board website.

99. Agustino Fontevecchia, "Bernanke Admits He's Clueless on Economy's Soft Patch," *Forbes* blog, June 22, 2011.

100. Margo Beller, "Fed's Massive Stimulus Had Little Impact: Greenspan," *CNBC* blog, June 30, 2011.

Chapter Five

Trickle-Down Conservatism Versus the Classical Liberalism It Claims for Inspiration

Friedrich Hayek, although a hero to conservatives, did not consider himself a conservative,[1] and, in the Forward to *The Road to Serfdom* (1944),[2] both criticized conservatism and underestimated its lure:

> Conservatism, though a necessary element in any stable society, is not a social program; in its paternalistic, nationalistic and power-adoring tendencies it is often closer to socialism than true liberalism; and with its traditionalistic, anti-intellectual, and often mystical propensities it will never, except in short periods of disillusionment, appeal to the young and all those others who believe that some changes are desirable if this world is to become a better place.

Trickle-down conservatism thrives on a "winner-take-all" / "might makes right" / "the end justifies the means" attitude promoting outright factual misrepresentations and unexamined plausible assumptions that are attractive to the uninformed, producing winning political campaigns that with each victory further undermine liberal democracy, our economy, our institutions and our health. And, as it continues down its path of societal destruction, trickle-down conservatism disguises itself as defender of classical liberalism. This false façade must be stripped away, and that effort begins below.

LIBERAL DEMOCRACY'S TRICKLE-UP VISION VERSUS THE ILLIBERAL VISION OF TRICKLE-DOWN

Contrasting Visions of Liberalism versus Illiberalism

Alexis de Tocqueville, in *Democracy in America* (1835), described the conflict between liberal and illiberal visions[3]:

> . . . [I]f it seems useful to you to divert the moral and intellectual activity of man toward the necessities of material life, and to use it to produce well-being; if reason appears to you more profitable to men than genius; if your object is not to create heroic virtues, but peaceful habits; if you like to see vices more than crimes, and prefer to find fewer great actions, on the condition of encountering fewer heinous crimes; if, instead of acting within the bosom of a brilliant society, it is enough for you to live in the midst of a prosperous society; if, finally, in your view, the principal object of a government is not to give the entire body of the nation the most strength or the most glory possible, but to provide for each of the individuals that make up the society the most well-being and to avoid the most misery; then equalize conditions and constitute the government of democracy.

There are certain key values that appear in this short quote, and they will appear repeatedly herein as part of the description of a liberal versus illiberal dichotomy. Distinguishing features of this dichotomy are that proponents of the liberal vision seek peace, comfort, prosperity and equality, while proponents of the illiberal vision disdain comfort and do not fear war, for it brings opportunities to confer on the individual heroism and on the nation power and glory. The illiberal vision isn't bothered by the pain imposed by poverty, for in this vision poverty is the cosmic punishment for sloth, weak morals or weak intellect. The illiberal vision doesn't fear the potential excesses of authority when its heroes are in power, for those heroes have glimpsed "the truth," and govern in accordance with it. Illiberalism focuses on human perfection, while, in contrast, liberalism accepts humans as imperfect and does not imagine perfectibility. Illiberalism pursues a preconceived vision of societal perfection, while, in contrast, liberalism envisions liberal democratic governing as a trial and error process toward the greatest freedom and prosperity for the greatest number.

By "equalize conditions," Tocqueville did not mean to impose on society absolute equality of incomes. This was written in the early 1830s, by a gifted young French aristocrat sent to the United States to study the young country's prison system, and he was writing as an admirer of this new nation that was striking in its relative equality (notwithstanding second-class citizenship for women and the enslavement of millions of African Americans, about which he also wrote). From the perspective of one hundred eighty years later, we can say that he was urging the nurture of wealth-spreading public institutions available to all (such as public roads and public schools) and the provision of a baseline quality of life for all. And, it can be observed that he envisioned what will always be a work in progress, evolving and changing as each generation defines that baseline quality of life for itself.

In their insightful and succinct book, *Occidentalism* (2004), authors Ian Buruma and Avishai Margalit sketched a stereotypical image of the liberal West in the eyes of its detractors in the Middle East, drawing a similar dichotomy as Tocqueville. Their title was inspired by Egyptian social thinker Edward Said's *Orientalism*, which addressed the Western stereotypical view of the Middle East. In *Occidentalism*, Buruma and Margalit found that the stereotypical vision of the West promoted by today's Islamist revolutionary jihadist terrorists bears striking resemblance—indeed, borrows heavily from—the illiberal vision promoted by German Romantics prior to World War I. Thus, Buruma and Margalit observed that the story of the "jihadists" is not one of ideas unique to Islam having arisen but, rather, one of bad ideas from the West having contaminated the Islamic world.[4] These jihadists are revolutionaries promoting a radical, primitive version of Islam guiding the application of Sharia law in an illiberal (fascist) totalitarian Islamist state, a concept most successfully promoted currently by ISIS.[5] As they observed, the German Werner Sombart, writing in his 1915 book *Händler und Helden* (*Merchants and Heroes*), criticized the "merchant *Weltanschauung*" of concentrating on material goods and comfort—Sombart's term for the mentality of the bourgeoisie was "*Komfortismus*," a word he created to describe a social system designed with "comfort" as its goal (derived from the German word for it, "Komfort").[6] In an article by Buruma elaborating on the book, he observed that the German Romantic vision sees the West as something like a cancer that undermines humanity and must be destroyed, substituting, as it does, the comfort of the merchant for the opportunity of heroism in war.[7]

Similar critiques of the liberal vision appear in the writings of other German Romantics, and these and similar ideas fueled pre-World War II Japan, Germany under Nazism and Italy under Fascism. The illiberal vision of the German Romantics was also adopted in Russia under Stalin, and later in China under Mao and Cambodia under the Khmer Rouge—as well as in neoconservatism[8]—and in the writings of the originators of political movements that incorporate religion such as Islamist jihadism.[9]

Thus, in the conflict with Islamism, we are experiencing a clash of ideologies—the worldview of classical liberalism from the Enlightenment versus the worldview of illiberalism. Thus, too, we are doomed to fail if we envision we are waging a "War on Terror." As observed in an important 2008 report (*How Terrorist Groups End: Lessons for Countering al Qa'ida*) by the RAND Corporation, there is no battlefield solution to defeating al Qaeda. Al Qaeda and ISIS will be defeated by demonstration—to the very people they are attempting to win over—that liberal democracy will deliver a better way of life. And, this effort is only complicated by the misconception that we are experiencing a "clash of civilizations," leading us to ignore the historical facts that we in the United States have long wrestled ourselves with the value of tolerance, and only in the last half century have we made great strides in achieving that value, and that effort remains ongoing. And, in contrast to the present in the Middle East and North Africa, countries of that region at times over the past century (examples: Lebanon and Iraq), were far more tolerant and pluralistic than they are today. Unfortunately, this ideological battle is being waged at the time that the United States—and the West, generally—due to the broad triumph of trickle-down conservatism—can only offer "free markets and free elections" rather than a fuller explanation of Western liberalism.

We will return to all these topics in greater detail later, but for now it is sufficient to recognize that over-arching all of the conflicts between the West and those movements opposing it is this dichotomy of liberalism versus illiberalism—and that conservatism, under the influence of the trickle-down vision and neoconservatism—increasingly exhibits characteristics similar to those of the illiberal opponents of the West.

That Buruma and Margalit observed similar illiberal strains in neoconservatism should not surprise. The neoconservative mission is to save liberalism from itself by implementing illiberal pre-Enlightenment classical Greek insights, including satisfying imagined cravings for authority and opportunities for glory in military conquest.

To ensure the greatest amount of freedom, modern liberalism draws upon classical liberalism's concept of checks and balances. That concept was carried into the US Constitution, with power divided among the executive, legislative and judicial branches. However, also embodied in liberal democracy is the concept of what is called herein a system of societal checks and balances—the concept introduced earlier that the institutions of liberal democratic *government* are envisioned as combining with capitalism (the institutions of the *market*) and the institutions of *civil society* (voluntary associations) to create the institutional framework for our actions. This institutional framework is molded by and molds our culture and enhances our ability to both defend our individual liberty and leverage our individual efficacy to yield the greatest prosperity and personal power to achieve the greatest personal freedom.

As noted in the Introduction, both Daniel Patrick Moynihan and President Obama observed that culture determines success or failure of a society, and that culture molds and is molded by politics. These observations were echoed in the 2012 book by Daron Acemoglu and James A. Robinson, *Why Nations Fail*, in which it was observed that "while economic institutions are critical for determining whether a country is poor or prosperous, it is politics and political institutions that determine what economic institutions a country has."[10] And, according to Acemoglu and Robinson, the economic institutions that are critical are "inclusive economic institutions"—"those that encourage participation by the great mass of people in economic activities that enable individuals to make the choices they wish."[11] These inclusive economic institutions arise from "political institutions that distribute power broadly in society and subject it to constraints . . . Instead of being vested in a single individual or a narrow group, political power rests with a broad coalition or a plurality of groups."[12]

Cultural values, translated through politics, promoting inclusive political and economic institutions that disperse power, are more critical to our domestic economic success than yet another round of tax cuts for the wealthiest Americans; to our foreign policy success than military strategy alone; and to defending our nation than sacrificing our Constitution and undermining the rule of law in perceived furtherance of our security. In other words, we as a nation can change our politics so that we choose to promote inclusive and power-spreading political and economic institutions, and thereby improve the quality of our lives and those of our fellow Americans—and our fellow inhabitants of this planet. But that requires confronting and rebutting trickle-down conservatism.

Enlightened Self-Interest: Unless We Combat Individualism, We Will Try to Save Everything for Ourselves and, Instead, Lose All

Adam Smith correctly identified the motivating force behind capitalism as self-interest[13]:

> It is not from the benevolence of the butcher, the brewer, or the baker, that we expect our dinner, but from their regard to their own interest. We address ourselves, not to their humanity, but to their self-love, and never talk to them of our own necessities but of their advantages.

While the familiar quote above appears in Smith's *The Wealth of Nations*, reference to an "invisible hand" first appears in *The Theory of Moral Sentiments*, published seventeen years before *The Wealth of Nations*, where he envisioned men being "led by an invisible hand . . . without intending it, without knowing it, [to] advance the interests of society."[14] His later and most famous (and, significantly, only) use of the term "invisible hand" appears in *The Wealth of Nations* in this passage[15]:

> [E]very individual . . . generally, indeed, neither intends to promote the public interest, nor knows how much he is promoting it. . . . [H]e intends only his own security; and by directing that industry in such a manner as its produce may be of the greatest value, he intends only his own gain, and he is in this, as

in many other cases, led by an invisible hand to promote an end which was no part of his intention.

Although Smith identified self-interest as the motivating force behind capitalism, he did not glorify greed and wealth. Rather, he acknowledged the inevitability that individuals will act in their self-interest, and that in doing so they were contributing to the benefit of society—even though they neither intended it nor wanted to do so—and, in concert with government, their actions could be made to benefit society even more greatly (more on this in Chapter 13). And, he condemned the admiration of wealth in *The Theory of Moral Sentiments*[16]:

> This disposition to admire, and almost to worship, the rich and the powerful, and to despise, or, at least, to neglect, persons of poor and mean condition, though necessary both to establish and to maintain the distinction of ranks and the order of society, is, at the same time, the great and most universal cause of the corruption of our moral sentiments. That wealth and greatness are often regarded with the respect and admiration which are due only to wisdom and virtue; and that the contempt, of which vice and folly are the only proper objects, is often most unjustly bestowed upon poverty and weakness, has been the complaint of moralists in all ages.

Thus did Adam Smith well describe the central failing of the moral underpinnings of what would be called herein trickle-down conservatism—a critique in which he was joined by Lord Acton: "There is not a more perilous or immoral habit of mind than the sanctifying of success."[17]

Similarly, Alexis de Tocqueville had no illusions that enlightened self-interest required Americans to *suppress* their self-interest. He titled a chapter in his *Democracy in America* "How the Americans Combat Individualism by the Doctrine of Interest Well Understood" (in the original French, "Comment les Americans combattent l'individualisme par la doctrine de l'intérêt bien entendu").[18] The concept of "interest well understood" or "enlightened self-interest" has been misconstrued by modern conservative thinkers as a mere extension of Tocqueville's marveling at the American propensity for joining in voluntary associations, further supporting the concept of civil society. Tocqueville, however, clarified that he *meant willingness to support government* when he said in that chapter, observing of Americans in contrast to Europeans[19]:

> The Americans, in contrast, take pleasure in explaining almost all the actions of their life with the aid of interest well understood; they show with satisfaction how enlightened love of themselves leads them constantly to help each other and disposes them willingly to sacrifice for the good of the State ["au bien de l'État"] a portion of their time and their wealth. I think that it is in this they often do not do themselves justice, for you sometimes see in the United

States, as elsewhere, citizens give themselves to the disinterested and unconsidered impulses that are natural to man; but the Americans hardly ever admit that they yield to movements of this type; they prefer to honor their philosophy than themselves.

Tocqueville continued, examining the motivation for such feelings, and observed: "The American moralists do not profess that men ought to sacrifice themselves for their fellow creatures *because* it is noble to make such sacrifices, but they boldly aver that such sacrifices are as necessary to him who imposes them upon himself as to him for whose sake they are made." (Emphasis is original.)

Adam Smith expressed a similar sentiment in *The Wealth of Nations*[20]: "Every tax is to the person who pays it a badge, not of slavery, but of liberty. It denotes that he is subject to government, indeed, but that, as he has some property, he cannot himself be the property of a master."

Tocqueville and Smith recognized that there is an element to the functioning of democracy involving *restraint* and *sacrifice* for the common good on the part of those privileged with property. The wonder of a functioning capitalist system is that the rich willingly pay taxes—relinquish some of their own property and freedom—for the benefit of a system providing services that may not be used by themselves, their family, their friends, their neighbors or the companies in which they invest. Yet they recognize it is in their self-interest to do so. It is an investment in the human capital of their fellow citizens, and they recognize they have benefitted from such investments by others before them.

Tocqueville later expounded upon what he termed "interest well understood"—what we today call enlightened self-interest: "The doctrine of interest well understood perhaps prevents some men from rising very far above the ordinary level of humanity; but a great number of others, who fall below, encounter the doctrine and cling to it. Consider a few individuals, it lowers them. Envisage the species, it elevates it." And, he concluded, comparing Americans with his fellow Europeans[21]:

I do not believe, everything considered, that there is more egoism among us [Europeans] than in America; the only difference is that there it is enlightened and here it is not. Each American knows how to sacrifice a portion of his particular interests in order to save the rest. We want to keep everything, and often everything escapes us.

Tocqueville's observation above of nineteenth century Europeans is, again, strikingly similar to a resounding condemnation of the selfishness of eighteenth century British business leaders that appears in Adam Smith's *The Wealth of Nations*—and remains relevant today, in its observations of the effects of globalization and technological change[22]:

> But what all the violence of the feudal institutions could never have effected, the silent and insensible operation of foreign commerce and manufactures gradually brought about. These gradually furnished the great proprietors with something for which they could exchange the whole surplus produce of their lands, and which they could consume themselves without sharing it either with tenants or retainers. All for ourselves, and nothing for other people, seems, in every age of the world, to have been the vile maxim of the masters of mankind.

Thus Smith and Tocqueville observed long ago that it is in the self-interest of those with property to sacrifice some of their property and freedom for the good of all because *trickle-down is a delusion*—the market's benefits to the wealthy and corporations do not trickle-down to everyone else. "Freedom" is often opposed to both equality and prosperity.

The observations of Smith and Tocqueville can be combined into a "yin and yang" of classical liberal theory. Smith, acknowledging the inevitability that humans will act in their self-interest, through the market, proposed that government should channel that self-interest so that it works for the benefit of all. Tocqueville observed that humans, acting from charitable impulses, through government and civil society, by helping others in the long-run help themselves. In fact, this proposition was long before Smith and Tocqueville well summarized by the Jewish scholar Hillel the Elder (c. 110 BCE—c. 10 CE): "If I am not for myself, who is for me? And being for my own self, then what am I? And if not now, when?"

A liberal—trickle-up—vision, thus, calls for balance, and the wisdom on the part of every citizen to help achieve that balance. The economy in any society does not actually run based on the invisible hand alone (the idea that individuals pursuing their own self-interest are guided by an invisible hand to serve the general good). Rather, the invisible hand (of Adam Smith) is balanced by a second invisible hand (of Alexis de Tocqueville), whereby individuals, pursuing their *enlightened* self-interest establish institutions (including the most important—the rule of law) and ethical standards to rein in their self-interest and serve the public good directly, thereby ultimately, indirectly, in the long run, serving their own self-interest.

A similar synthesis can be derived from the messages contained in two monumental books written in 1944, both by men who were born in Vienna, when it was the capital of the Austro-Hungarian Empire. One, mentioned previously, was Friedrich Hayek's *The Road to Serfdom*. Hayek warned that government power should not be allowed to stifle the market, lest totalitarianism result. The other, *The Great Transformation*, was written by social philosopher Karl Polanyi. One of the key insights of Polanyi in *The Great Transformation* was that *a utopian belief in the efficacy of the market* will result in the market having too much authority, leading to its failure and resulting in government and civil society striking back, with the result being fascism.[23] Polanyi stressed that the market economy only works when it is embedded within the political and social structures of society[24] (more on this in Chapter 10).

Ten years later, Republican President Dwight Eisenhower, in a letter he wrote to his brother Edgar on November 8, 1954, expressed concerns similar to Smith, Tocqueville and Polanyi observing the importance of application of a rule of reason, recognizing that the people of America want from the federal government Social Security, unemployment insurance, labor laws and farm programs, and only a few extremists oppose these.[25]

The Interaction of Government Policy, the Market and Civil Society in Theory

In the liberal vision, government policy, the market and civil society all influence, and are influenced by, each other. In his book, *Statecraft As Soulcraft: What Government Does* (1983), the conservative commentator George Will presented a conservative vision of this interrelationship, and how government should influence the market and civil society. Although there will be many points of disagreement with conservatism explored herein, there are important points of agreement with the ideas Will expressed.

Even the seemingly obvious differences in formulation of the goal of statecraft—"soulcraft" in Will's vision—when examined, seem not so great. Use of the term "soul" implies an analysis of an individual's relationship to God. Interestingly, however, Will does not dwell on this relationship but, rather, addresses man's relationship to his fellow man, advocating (long before George W. Bush's "compassionate conservatism") "conservatism with a kindly face"[26] —defending the welfare state, criticizing excessive individualism and libertarianism, and making altruism a mandatory virtue.[27]

Webster's dictionary provides that a synonym for "soul" is "psyche" (the term "psyche" comes from Latin, in turn derived from the Greek word meaning "soul"). A liberal analysis, to complement Will's conservative one, might appropriately have been called "Statecraft as Psychecraft," because, while liberals would question attempting to govern with the intent of managing souls, they would find it appropriate to govern in accordance with inspiring, and enabling, the governed to live fulfilled lives of happiness (in the formulation of the Declaration of Independence: "life, liberty and the pursuit of happiness"). The responsibility for government in this regard was expressly stated in the opinion of the United States Supreme Court in the famous desegregation case of *Brown v. Board of Education* (1954), wherein the Court observed, regarding children in grade and high schools: "To separate them from others of similar age and qualifications solely because of their race generates a feeling of inferiority as to their status in the community that may affect their hearts and minds in a way unlikely ever to be undone."[28]

Will addressed both liberals "and those who call themselves conservatives" when he said: "Politics is more difficult than you think"[29] (a departure from conservative orthodoxy) and "there is more to a social system than can be presumed."[30] Will quoted Justice Felix Frankfurter: "Law is concerned with external behavior and not the inner life of man;" to which he responded: "The purpose of this book is to say why that proposition is radically wrong."[31] On this the present work is in agreement, as well as the following characterization of one role of politics observed by the liberal Daniel Patrick Moynihan and approvingly quoted by Will: "A purpose of politics is to facilitate, as much as is prudent, the existence of worthy passions and the achievement of worthy aims. It is to help persons want what they ought to want."[32]

The Interaction of Government Policy, the Market and Civil Society in History

Basic economic theory says there are three "factors of production": land, labor and capital. (Recently, some economists have added a fourth factor, information, relevant elsewhere herein.) The American political system consists of two major parties, distinguished by their political philosophies and, accordingly, by the constituencies who support them and whose policies they support. The Democratic Party—liberals—envision society as built from the bottom up and promote policies supporting *labor*, and, accordingly, receive disproportionate support from labor groups. The Republican Party—conservatives—envision society as built from the top down, and promote policies supporting *capital* and accordingly, receive disproportionate support from the rich, business and the financial industry.

The past century has seen contests between trickle-down capitalism and liberal capitalism, and those contests can be analyzed as between a liberal capitalist trickle-up vision supporting government policies that favor labor (supported by Democrats) versus a conservative trickle-down vision that favors capital (supported by Republicans): The Gilded Age through the Roaring Twenties and up to Franklin Roosevelt's inauguration in 1933 was dominated by a trickle-down vision and may be called an "Age of Capital" (upset by the Great Depression); the period from 1933 up to Ronald Reagan's win in 1980 was an "Age of Labor" (upset by successive oil crises and resultant stagflation) and from 1980 through the present another "Age of Capital" dominated by a trickle-down vision (currently being upset by the lingering effects of the Great Recession, aggravated by trickle-down policies that converted these lingering effects into a depression).

The first Age of Capital above should be acknowledged as having yielded great inventions: cars, planes, widespread availability of electricity, electric lights, telephones, record players, motion pictures, radios and the beginnings of television—and its excessive faith in the market also gave us the Great Depression. The Age of Labor above gave us great government-assisted discoveries and accomplishments: the creation of the great American middle class (enabling the spread of cars and televisions), the cure for polio, Americans on the moon, and civil and voting rights for all Americans—and its excessive faith in government gave us excessive social spending and inattention to inflation, followed by stagflation. The second Age of Capital commercialized the benefits of the Information Revolution with personal computers, cell phones, and the Internet (with the assistance of the government through DARPA [the Defense Advanced Research Projects Agency])—but its excessive faith in the market repeated the errors that gave us the Great Depression, and gave us successive balance sheet recessions culminating in the Great Recession and ongoing depression.

Complicating the study of all these phenomena together is the fact that no one academic discipline studies this interrelationship of government policy, the market, and civil society. When economists (rightly) admit that the key to economic development is culture, they are also admitting that the key to economics is sociology. The particular field of sociology devoted to sociological insights especially relevant to economics is "economic sociology," or the "sociology of economic life." Much of what appears herein is attributable to the insights of economic sociology, but also political sociology as well. Thus, as observed in the Introduction, perhaps a better description of what appears herein would be "organic sociology."

HOW TRICKLE-DOWN CONSERVATISM UNDERMINES LIBERAL DEMOCRACY

Trickle-Down Conservatism Has Become a Fundamentalist Religious Movement

> Men never do evil so completely and cheerfully as when they do it from religious conviction.—*Blaise Pascal (1623-1662)*[33]

The trickle-down conservatives' use of religion to instill fear in the American people is a method of political demagoguery criticized even by a fellow conservative, commentator Michael Gerson. In a 2015 op-ed he criticized Louisiana Governor Bobby Jindal, who warned that the Muslims are invading the United States to conquer us, colonize us, and install Sharia law, as the governor alleged they have already done in Great Britain.[34] However, Governor Jindal was simply again plowing ground the conservatives have been working ever since 9/11.[35]

Conservatism possesses an inherent weakness—its usefulness as a weapon of religious intolerance—especially evident in the way in which trickle-down conservatism has become an intolerant fundamentalist religion itself, combining intolerant fundamentalist Christianity (conservative Catholicism and fundamentalist evangelical Christianity) and trickle-down economic theory. It thus presents a conflict of visions between its fundamental, illiberal vision with the liberal vision.

And, thus, it is useful to compare the analysis herein of a conflict of visions to that of another analysis of a conflict of visions. Thomas Sowell, libertarian conservative economist and scholar with the Hoover Institution, in his book *A Conflict of Visions: Ideological Origins of Political Struggles* (2002), attributed clashes over equality and other values to two different visions of human nature. One, the "constrained" vision, views man as inherently flawed, limited and dependent on evolved social processes. The other, the "unconstrained" vision, focuses on ends, and argues that man is perfectible. Sowell linked the "constrained" vision with conservatism and the "unconstrained" vision with liberalism. As shown above, however, he had the labels reversed. Neoconservatism, an element of modern movement conservatism and foreign policy ally of trickle-down, strongly embraces a vision of perfectibility.[36] One of neoconservatism's intellectual heroes, Leo Strauss, stressed the "progress toward perfection"[37] on the part of young elites destined to govern, in the vision of the classical Greek philosophers.[38]

Sowell acknowledged the potential of fundamentalist religion's "unconstrained vision" to inspire totalitarianism[39] and was justly concerned that a philosophy that drives its adherents to attempt to achieve human perfection through government control contains within it the potential of totalitarianism, however, so does a philosophy that holds that it, as ordained by God, is always right—as is promoted by trickle-down conservatism and its elements of the Christian fundamentalism of the Religious Right, neoconservatism and trickle-down-supply-side-crony capitalism.

Friedrich Hayek observed in his essay "Why I Am Not a Conservative," regarding classical liberals such as himself, "the liberal is very much aware that we do not know all the answers and that he is not sure that the answers he has are certainly the right ones or even that we can find all the answers."[40] In contrast to the liberal vision, Hayek observed that conservatism holds "if government is in the hands of decent men, it ought not to be too much restricted by rigid rules."[41] He continued: "A conservative movement, by its very nature, is bound to be a defender of established privilege and to lean on the power of government for the protection of privilege. The essence of the liberal position, however, is the denial of all privilege, if privilege is understood in its proper and original meaning of the state granting and protecting rights to some which are not available on equal terms to others."[42]

Hayek's conclusion regarding conservatives is ominously instructive for the analysis that follows: "In the last resort, the conservative position rests on the belief that in any society there are recognizably superior persons whose inherited standards and values and position ought to be protected and who should have a greater influence on public affairs than others."[43] And, of course, conservatives are confident that government is in the hands of "decent men"—"recognizably superior persons"—when it is in conservative Republican hands, guided by the wealthy and business interests, all of whom are entitled to privileges commensurate with their stature.

Hayek in this essay recognized conservatism as an illiberal philosophy. Hayek, however, was, and remains, a hero to American conservatives who shared the conservative vision of a philosophy with an affinity for the classical liberal philosophers such as Adam Smith, Alexis de Tocqueville and John Locke. As will be seen herein, however, Hayek's vision of an illiberal conservatism is more relevant now than it was even in his time, as the trickle-down vision has driven movement conservatism in an extremist, illiberal, direction.

The conservative Andrew Sullivan, in *The Conservative Soul: Fundamentalism, Freedom and the Future of the Right* (2006), criticized the illiberal fundamentalism that has taken control of conservatism and the Republican Party and, echoing Hayek, observed: "The essential claim of the fundamentalist is that he knows the truth."[44]

And yet, as even Sullivan himself has admitted, conservatives like him who oppose this illiberal direction of conservatism are a vanishing breed.[45] As the trickle-down vision has come to dominate conservatism, the reality is that someone like Andrew Sullivan has more in common with liberals than conservatives. Thus, it is not surprising that he endorsed Barack Obama for president in a cover article for *The Atlantic* in December 2007 and endorsed his re-election in January 2012 with an article that appeared on the cover of *Newsweek* under the heading "Why Are Obama's Critics So Dumb?"[46]

Sullivan's observations have been complemented by those of the entrepreneur and venture capitalist Nick Hanauer, who has observed, regarding the obsession of conservatives with the idea that the rich are "job creators," that this concept is only one step away from linking the rich to "The Creator," and, essentially, the deification of capitalists. And, ironically, as Hanauer noted regarding the role of "job creator," capitalism creates the incentive *not* to create jobs but, rather, to attempt to increase productivity without hiring—creating a job is a last resort.[47]

The concept of certainty promoted by the Religious Right, neoconservatism and supply-side-crony capitalism, together with the conservative misconception that fascism is a movement of the left (more on this later), contributed to the self-serving delusions that conservatism is the political philosophy ordained by God, always standing for freedom and democracy, and incapable of repression. These delusions put the nation and the world at risk, especially when complemented by the belief that *America is the nation* ordained by God, whose mission is to spread freedom and democracy, and is incapable of repression—a dangerous misconception fueling conservatism's misconception of "American Exceptionalism."[48]

Conservatism's assertion of certainty granted by the authority of God injects into politics an appeal to a higher authority—one that can be used to justify oppression—political, economic, social, military and judicial. In this manner, it is similar to the Nazis' appeal to both the authority of science and of religion (as Hitler did in *Mein Kampf*) to justify the triumph of one race over others; to the Marxists' appeal to dialectical historical materialism to justify the triumph of one class over another; and the appeal of the modern jihadists to the authority of religion to justify the triumph of one religion over others.

All this is *not* to imply that trickle-down conservatism *equals* Nazism, fascism, Marxism or the jihadist's illiberal Islamist vision. While there will be presented herein conservative and libertarian critiques illustrating similarities between conservatism and fascism, the critique of movement conservatism herein is of its "illiberalism". The point is that Nazism, Marxism, fascism and the fundamentalism of Islamist jihadist revolutionaries all embrace illiberal visions, as does trickle-down conservatism of the Republican Party.

Trickle-Down Conservatism's "Virtual Reality" Undermines Liberal Democracy and the Political Process

Ominously, there are certain beliefs held by conservatives that undercut liberal democracy and the rule of law itself, among them are conservatives' approach to politics as a marketplace and conservatives' certainty that they "know" the answers without the need for facts. The latter shortcoming was addressed extensively in Chapters 1, 3 and 4; the former shortcoming will be elaborated on in detail later herein, where the concept of "rent-seeking," developed by the "Public Choice" theorists James Buchanan and Gordon Tullock, describes a society in which the political system is essentially envisioned as a market itself, easily lending itself to "crony capitalism" described earlier, in which political contributions feed the battle for votes (the currency in politics) and are rewarded with privileges that exempt the donors from competition in the economic market.

Liberal democracy, based as it is on the consent of the governed, only works when the citizens are informed, hence, the importance of respect for knowledge and the rule of law. But a substantial percentage of the voters who call themselves conservative trust neither liberals nor the "mainstream media" to tell the truth, and imagine that liberals "want" socialism accompanied by outlandish benefits from government. Promulgation of untruths pursuant to the conservative trickle-down vision undermines the functioning of liberal democracy, the economy and the rule of law.

Trickle-down's domination of conservatism and, thereby, much of American life in general, has contributed to the devolution of conservatism into political theater that cynically poisons politics and desecrates democracy. This political theater is not the actual practice of politics itself, in which there is debate based on facts, but, instead, the practice of politics by conservative supporters consists of establishing a myth, then loudly demanding the public observe that the other side is being unreasonable in refusing to grant the myth legitimacy, and in failing to join in demanding conservative policies in response to the myth. And the developers and promoters of the myth carry on the charade that they are a grassroots movement of average Americans looking to better their country, whereas, in reality, often they are funded by multibillionaire and multimillionaire businessmen engaging in rent-seeking: looking to maximize their political investments with lower taxes on themselves, less government regulation of their businesses, and less spending on government programs depended upon by the middle class and poor but which impose burdens on their businesses via regulations and taxation.

Driven by the trickle-down delusion, conservatives practice maintenance of a virtual reality in which numerous truths are masked and, viewed as such, it is no wonder that among the heroes of conservatism are entertainers like Glenn Beck and Rush Limbaugh, or politicians like Sarah Palin and Michele Bachmann, known more for their clever slogans than for their deep philosophical insights. Conservatism has devolved into a philosophy that promotes government policymaking based on clever one-liners and compelling misrepresentations of fact that compose a conservative virtual reality for all true believers—compelling misrepresentations that are often spread by Fox News Channel, the conservative commentators like Rush Limbaugh and Mark Levin, websites like Drudge Report and via emails.[49]

Economist Nouriel Roubini linked naïve free market fundamentalist zealotry with naïve foreign policy zealotry of the neoconservatives who believed military overthrow of Iraq followed by one-person-one vote elections would transform the Middle East into liberal democracy.[50] The financier George Soros observed that the source of the ideology of American supremacy is the merger of market fundamentalism with religious fundamentalism.[51] (Note the consistency of these observations, and those following, with Chapter 3.)

In his 2004 book, *The Bubble of American Supremacy: The Costs of Bush's War in Iraq,* Soros, in terms reminiscent of Friedrich Hayek, Andrew Sullivan, Nick Hanauer and Karl Popper (more on him later) criticized the decision to go to war in Iraq as a violation of the deliberative process that is at the core of American democracy—the commitment to Popper's vision of the open society, by which he meant a society dedicated to the proposition that no one has possession of the ultimate truth.[52]

The Fox News Channel Disinformation Machine—How the Republican Propaganda Arm Cynically Disrespects Truth and Undermines Democracy

Glenn Beck, self-described "rodeo clown"[53] and former political commentator for Fox News Channel in a 2010 interview disavowed any responsibility for support of the political process and revealed that what appeared to many deeply faithful conservatives to be passionate promotion of their most deeply held beliefs was but crass manipulation of their emotions in the pursuit of making a buck.[54] Crass manipulation on par with Fox News Channel's continuing claim of "fair and balanced" while owner Rupert Murdoch famously made a $1 million donation to the Republican Governors Association and Fox News Channel President Roger Ailes—who worked with Richard Nixon to fool millions of Americans into believing him to be trustworthy—acts as de facto Republican Party propaganda minister and works ceaselessly to make Fox News Channel into the Republican propaganda machine[55] pursuant to the conservative view of the marketplace of ideas as analogous to the marketplace of goods and services, thereby creating an atmosphere of factual relativity wherein all ideas that appear in print or broadcast media are simply to be weighed and the public is to determine their validity. Thus, too, conservatives—who *profess* belief in absolute truth—are complicit in undermining truth and in spreading the idea that all "truth" is relative. Nowhere, of course, is this more blatant than in the "news" reporting by Fox News Channel, but it also is practiced by Republican politicians with great ease.[56]

Former opinion columnist for *The Washington Post*, William Raspberry, was among the first commentators to raise alarm regarding the disturbing phenomenon of news services intentionally slanting the news in an essay in which he observed that the corrosive effect of Fox News Channel on the news business and democracy worked as long as everyone in the news business is recognized as just promoting their own visions and no one deserves to be taken seriously as reporting the truth—concluding that the effect of acceptance of such an idea would have a huge, destructive effect on democracy.[57]

One powerful example of that destructive effect was illustrated in a study published in October 2003 by the nonpartisan Program on International Policy Attitudes (PIPA), a joint program of the Center on Policy Attitudes and the Center for International and Security Studies at the University of Maryland, and Knowledge Networks.[58] The study found that 60 percent of Americans believed at least one of the following misperceptions: that the US had found clear evidence in Iraq that Saddam Hussein was working closely with al Qaeda; clear evidence of weapons of mass destruction have been found in Iraq; that world public opinion favored the US going to war with Iraq. However, the extent of these misperceptions varied greatly by where Americans got their news: 80 percent of those who relied primarily on Fox

News believed at least one of these untrue things, while only 23 percent who relied primarily on PBS or NPR for their news. In particular, 67 percent of those who relied primarily on Fox News believed the US had found clear evidence that Saddam Hussein was working clearly with al Qaeda, whereas only 16 percent who relied primarily on PBS or NPR did.

A 2010 study, conducted by WorldPublicOpinion.org, a project that is managed by PIPA, found cases where greater exposure to media—especially Fox News Channel—meant greater misinformation on a variety of news subjects,[59] and, as of early 2012, Chris Mooney, author of *The Republican Brain: The Science of Why They Deny Science and Reality* identified at least five additional studies that confirmed this disturbing fact.[60] And, to this list of studies could be added a Fairleigh Dickinson University study released in 2011, the results of which were updated in 2012.[61]

It is an irony of conservative philosophy that its adherents can simultaneously hold two mutually exclusive views on truth. On the one hand, as observed by Friedrich Hayek and George Soros, they believe that there is an ultimate truth that is discoverable by leaders with whom they agree, and those leaders should command in accordance with their perceptions of the truth. On the other hand, these same adherents believe that democracy is, itself, only a marketplace of ideas, such that the "best" ideas will win out, and any behavior, including willful distortion of the truth in the competition that is democracy is acceptable—one need only listen to Fox News Channel to hear the familiar "Some people say . . . " or "A lot of people think . . . " as a cue to prepare for the misrepresentation of truth that will follow.

The Trickle-Down Vision Holds That Governing Is Easy, and Government Simply Needs to Get Out of the Way (Except the Military)

Movement conservatism has always been a reactionary faith, having been originally founded in reaction to the acceptance by Republicans, among them President Eisenhower, of the New Deal social safety net and perceived softness toward communism. And movement conservatism strengthened later in reaction against Sixties liberalism. Accompanying this reactionary faith is belief in the basic incompetence of government—that the best thing government can do is get out of the way (except, inexplicably, the military). Conservatives have learned to not respect the work done by government, and conservatives working in government are expected to either be busily dismantling it or making life better for fellow conservatives and wealthy conservative benefactors. This attitude leads to tangible, unnecessary, increase in suffering, as was evidenced by the late and inadequate federal government response to Hurricane Katrina in 2005.

A related conservative idea is that governing—that being president—is easy, in comparison to running a business. President George W. Bush appeared shocked to find otherwise, as revealed in his April 13, 2004, address to the nation when he used the word "hard" or "hardest" eight times—three different times remarking that forcefully imposing democracy on Iraq was "hard".[62] Later, in his first debate with Senator John Kerry (D-MA) September 30, 2004, President Bush used the word "hard" to describe presidential campaigning and governing—for example, "working hard," "hard choices," "hard work"—22 times. Among them: "In Iraq, no doubt about it, it's tough. It's hard work. It's incredibly hard."[63]

And, in an interview less than two months before the 2008 presidential election, former Hewlett-Packard CEO, economic advisor to the McCain-Palin campaign, conservative Republican (and later failed candidate for governor of California and contender for the 2016 Republican presidential nomination) Carly Fiorina said she believed none of the four major party candidates for president and vice president—not John McCain or Sarah Palin, whom she was advising, nor Barack Obama or Joe Biden—were qualified to be a chief executive officer of a corporation.[64] And, regarding whether Carly Fiorina was, herself, qualified to be CEO of a corporation: She was forced to resign from Hewlett-Packard and Arianna Packard, the granddaughter of HP co-founder David Packard summarized the reasons why, among them that the stock price dropped 50 percent during her tenure only to rise 10 percent when her firing was announced, she laid off 28,000 people and she departed with a $21 million golden parachute she used to finance her 2010 California senatorial campaign.[65] And, five years later, after announcing her presidential candidacy, the judgment of the business community regarding her performance as a CEO had not improved.[66] But her conservative philosophy held that governing a state of 39 million or a nation of 320 million would be easier.

The Conservative Value of Order and Political Weapon of Fear

Conservatives value order, and they are more fearful of disorder than are liberals. Fear of communism unified traditionalists and libertarians when movement conservatism began in the 1950s. Fear of terrorism still unifies today the neoconservatives with the Religious Right and the supply-side-crony capitalists of trickle-down conservatism.

Yet, conservatives overstep their bounds when they convert their concern for order to manipulation and exploitation, for political benefit, of fear on the part of their fellow Americans. The three main components of trickle-down conservatism—the Religious Right, supply-side-crony capitalism of the plutocracy and neoconservatism—coincide with the three main fears that grip a sizeable part of the American electorate: *Cultural insecurity* (fear of expansion of gay rights and continued application of *Roe v. Wade*, as well as fear of being overrun by hordes of non-English-speaking new immigrants—some of them perhaps Muslim), *economic insecurity* (encouraged by constant demands by business for lower taxes and lower wages, failure to deliver which will "require" businesses to lay off employees; coupled with fear of economic competition due to immigration), and *insecurity due to the threat of terrorism* (violent attacks on civilians, again, exacerbated by immigration, especially of Muslims).

That fear of the threat of terrorism was directly confronted by former Senator John Kerry during the 2004 presidential campaign, when he referred to his experience as a prosecutor and the reality that not all crime can be eradicated, but that it can be reduced, and he observed the same applied to terrorism, which can be reduced so that it does not threaten daily life.[67] This led to a flurry of attacks from Republicans alleging that electing John Kerry would let the nation slide back into a "pre-9/11 mindset."[68]

However, John Mueller, who holds the Woody Hayes Chair of National Security Studies at the Mershon Center at Ohio State University argued in an article published just before the 2004 presidential election that what politicians and the media need to provide people is the proper context for assessing the risk that each of us faces of being a victim of terrorism.[69] To the contrary, trickle-down conservatism maintains what Mueller observed Leif Wenar of the University of Sheffield aptly labeled, as he captured in the title of his article, "a false sense of insecurity." Mueller's recommendation as to how to defeat terrorism was to not give in to terrorists by becoming terrified, and to recognize that terrorism is a fact of life to be addressed by military and law enforcement means. That sounds a lot like the wisdom of Senator Kerry, which was so roundly criticized by Republicans in the last days of the 2004 presidential campaign. And, as should be abundantly clear, terrorism does not merit the "existential threat" tag that conservatives so love to use to describe it—*except* to the extent that *conservative* efforts to manipulate American fears of terrorism constitute an existential threat to American liberal democracy.

THE PARALLEL EVOLUTIONS (FOR THE WORSE) OF HAYEK AND CONSERVATISM

Frank Meyer, who collaborated with William F. Buckley, Jr. on the founding of *National Review*, titled a section in his book *In Defense of Freedom: A Conservative Credo* "The Myth of Society."[70] Meyer was attempting to distinguish his conservative vision not only from modern liberalism, but also from "The New Conservatism" derived in great part from the writings of Edmund Burke. Meyer observed of this group that theirs was an organic view of society rather than individualistic[71] and found error in the concept of community as interpreted in the works of the New Conservatives Russell Kirk and Robert Nisbet.[72] Meyer acknowledged the argument of Kirk and Nisbet that the absence of community would make the members of a society atomized and alienated, thus more susceptible to the siren song of a charismatic dictator. Meyer, however, worried that a strong community would reinforce a collective impulse that would render the members of society more susceptible to government imposed collectivism.

The idea that conservatives generally reject the idea of "society" was, erroneously, ascribed to former Prime Minister Margaret Thatcher, with inspiration from Friedrich Hayek. Former Prime Minister Thatcher was greatly impressed by the theories of Hayek. She became such an authority on him that, under the reference to Hayek in *The Concise Oxford Dictionary of Sociology* there appears the statement that for Hayek, as for Prime Minister Thatcher, there was no such thing as society.[73]

This statement is inaccurate. It took as its inspiration a misconstruction of Prime Minister Thatcher's statement in an article titled "AIDS, Education and the Year 2000," in the October 3, 1987 edition of *Woman's Own* magazine wherein, from the context of the quote, the Prime Minister clearly intended to convey the concept that there is no magic bucket of money labeled "society" to which one can plead for help. In such context, the statement is similar to the American view that "there ain't no such thing as a free lunch."

As for Friedrich Hayek, he not only believed that there is such thing as society, but he also, as evidenced by his 1944 work *The Road to Serfdom* and 1960 work *The Constitution of Liberty* held a vision of society very compatible with a modern liberal—and organic—theory of society. In his chapter in *The Constitution of Liberty* entitled "The Creative Powers of a Free Civilization," Hayek made it very clear he believed in society and urged caution in attempting to improve it, addressing both present society and the over-arching broader (in space and time) concept of human civilization[74]:

> [B]efore we can try to remold society intelligently, we must understand its functioning; we must realize that, even when we believe that we understand it, we may be mistaken. What we must learn to understand is that human civilization has a life of its own, that all our efforts to improve things must operate within a working whole which we cannot entirely control, and the operation of whose forces we can hope merely to facilitate and assist so far as we understand them. Our attitude ought to be similar to that of the physician toward a living organism: like him, we have to deal with a self-maintaining whole which is kept going by forces which we cannot replace and which we must therefore use in all we try to achieve. What can be done to improve it must be done by working with these forces rather than against them. In all our endeavor at improvement we must work inside this given whole, aim at piecemeal, rather than total, construction [citation here is to Karl Popper, *Open Society*

> *and Its Enemies* (London, 1945), *passim*], and use at each stage the historical material at hand and improve details step by step rather than attempt to redesign the whole.

Further, Daniel Yergin and Joseph Stanislaw, in their book *The Commanding Heights* (1998), observed that Hayek fought in the Austrian Army during World War I and that his experience there profoundly shaped him. In an interview in the companion video of the PBS series, Hayek reflected on how that previous era of globalization ended, lamenting, "We didn't realize how fragile our civilization was."[75]

Hayek's vision was shaped by having seen the misery and waste created due to government excess in World War I, then, during and after World War II, misery and waste created by both communist and fascist totalitarianism. With this perspective, he warned that the West, with its embrace of Keynesianism and the welfare state, may be heading down a road of creeping totalitarianism itself (a warning in which his rival, John Maynard Keynes, heartily joined in a book jacket recommendation).[76]

Neither Hayek nor his colleague at the University of Chicago, Milton Friedman, would have called themselves proponents of trickle-down, supply-side economics or crony capitalism, although their writings would inspire those who are. As observed previously, Hayek was of the "Austrian School" of economics, while Friedman was a "monetarist." And, even though Hayek is a hero to conservatives, also as observed above, he derided conservatism, and his observations of classical liberalism are useful to modern liberals. As John Cassidy, staff writer on economic issues for *The New Yorker* observed in his essay "The Hayek Century," Hayek was neither conservative nor anti-government in principle, and it was possible to be a follower of Hayek and still believe in active government, as will be demonstrated below.[77]

Hayek observed in *The Road to Serfdom* that, although he opposed centralized planning of the Marxist state, "It is important not to confuse opposition against this kind of planning with a dogmatic laissez faire attitude,"[78] and that "[p]robably nothing has done so much harm to the [classical] liberal cause as the wooden insistence of some liberals on certain rough rules of thumb, above all the principle of laissez faire."[79] Hayek recognized that "a carefully thought-out legal framework is required" in order to successfully use competition as the principle of social organization;[80] further, a functioning capitalist system "depends, above all, on the existence of an appropriate legal system, a legal system designed both to preserve competition and to make it operate as beneficially as possible."[81]

In *The Road to Serfdom* Hayek proposed possible areas for government intervention, guided by the standard that such restrictions "affect all potential producers equally and are not used as an indirect way of controlling prices and quantities"[82]:

> To prohibit the use of certain poisonous substances or to require special precautions in their use, to limit working hours or to require certain sanitary arrangements, is fully compatible with the preservation of competition. The only question here is whether in the particular instance the advantages gained are greater than the social costs which they impose. Nor is the preservation of competition incompatible with an extensive system of social services—so long as the organization of these services is not designed in such a way as to make competition ineffective over wide fields.

Hayek expounded on this list in the context of the two types of security a society might attempt to provide its people[83]:

> These two kinds of security are, first, security against severe physical privation, the certainty of a given minimum of sustenance for all; and, second, the security of a given standard of life, or of the relative position which one person or group enjoys compared with others; or, as we may put it briefly, the security of a minimum income and the security of the particular income a person is thought to deserve.

He continued:

> [T]here can be no doubt that some minimum of food, shelter, and clothing, sufficient to preserve health and the capacity to work, can be assured to everybody . . . .
>
> Nor is there any reason why the state should not assist the individuals in providing for those common hazards of life against which, because of their uncertainty, few individuals can make adequate provision. Where, as in the case of sickness and accident, neither the desire to avoid such calamities nor the efforts to overcome their consequences are as a rule weakened by the provision of assistance—where, in short, we deal with genuinely insurable risks—the case for the state's helping to organize a comprehensive system of social insurance is very strong . . . [and] there is no incompatibility in principle between the state's rendering assistance to the victims of such "acts of God" as earthquakes and floods . . .

It would be disingenuous to quote the above, however, while failing to observe that, regardless, Hayek always opposed federally mandated good faith collective bargaining.[84] Yet, based on the above, liberals can easily find rationale for supporting Hayek's vision—based on the Hayek of 1944 and 1960, who would have been called a socialist by those same conservatives who so admire him today (and, it should be remembered, he was joined in support of a guaranteed minimum income and a universal health care system by Milton Friedman; more on Hayek's support for government institutions appears in Chapter 10).[85]

Hayek in his earlier writings stressed that to a classical liberal, the end *is* the means—i.e., the end is the *process* of governing itself (he was, after all, trained as a lawyer). Yet, he developed a "dogmatic laissez faire attitude" of the sort he had earlier condemned and supported, along with Milton Friedman, an "ends justify the means" approach to implementation of free market reforms with savagery and murder in Chile, as is extensively chronicled by Naomi Klein in *The Shock Doctrine: The Rise of Disaster Capitalism* (2007).[86]

And, trickle-down conservatism forced onto conservatism generally a similar, parallel evolution toward illiberal extremism. From the perspective of the present, we can observe that the implementation of the trickle-down vision in the United States over the past three decades, due to conservatives whose heroes are Hayek and Friedman, has resulted in unnecessary misery here as well. The critique in Chapter 7 will expose the massive failure of the bubble-bust depressionary feedback loop economy that resulted directly from implementation of ideas of conservatives who championed Hayek and Friedman.

Thus, while Frank Meyer argued that society is a myth, other heroes of conservatism, like Hayek, clearly recognized the reality, importance and fragility of society, supported by institutions only government can provide. However, Hayek, Friedman and others would leave an ambiguous legacy due to their actions that undermined that fragile society that they, themselves, had sketched along classical liberal lines.

NOTES

1. See especially his essay "Why I am Not a Conservative" that appears as a Postscript to his book *The Constitution of Liberty* (1960).
2. Hayek, *The Road to Serfdom*, pp. ix-x.
3. From Alexis de Tocqueville's *Democracy in America, De La Démocratie en Amérique*, Bilingual Edition, edited by Eduardo Nolla, translated by James T. Schleifer (Indianapolis, IN: Liberty Fund; 2010), vol. II, part II, Chapter VI, p. 401.
4. Ian Buruma and Avishai Margalit, *Occidentalism: The West in the Eyes of Its Enemies* (New York: Penguin Books; 2004), p. 149. However, as is observed by John Gray in *Black Mass: Apocalyptic Religion and the Death of Utopia* (2007), liberalism can also inspire utopian ideas and must, accordingly, be checked.
5. As to the characterization of jihadists as revolutionaries embracing simultaneously idealism and nihilism, see Lawrence Wright, *The Looming Tower: Al-Qaeda and the Road to 9/11* (New York: Knopf, 2006), p. 187. The similarities between the visions of Islamic fundamentalism and imperialism are explored by the social philosopher Tariq Ali in *The Clash of Fundamentalisms: Crusades, Jihads and Modernity* (2003). The distinctions between the jihadists of al Qaeda and those of ISIS (the Islamic State in Iraq and al Sham; also the Islamic State in Iraq and Syria or the Islamic State in Iraq and the Levant [ISIL]; or simply the Islamic State; known in the Middle East as *Daesh*) are addressed by Graeme Wood in "What ISIS Really Wants," *The Atlantic* , March 2015.
6. Ian Buruma and Avishai Margalit, *Occidentalism: The West in the Eyes of Its Enemies* (New York: Penguin Books; 2004), pp. 52–53.
7. Ian Buruma, "The Origins of Occidentalism," *The Chronicle of Higher Education*, February 6, 2004, Vol. 50, Issue 22, Page B10.

8. Ian Buruma and Avishai Margalit, *Occidentalism: The West in the Eyes of Its Enemies* (New York: Penguin Books; 2004), p. 59.
9. Ibid, p. 72.
10. Daron Acemoglu and James A. Robinson, *Why Nations Fail: The Origins of Power, Prosperity and Poverty* (New York: Crown Business, an imprint of Crown Publishing Group, a Division of Random House, Inc.; 2012), p. 43.
11. Ibid, p. 74.
12. Ibid, p. 80.
13. Adam Smith, *The Wealth of Nations* (New York: The Modern Library, Random House, Inc.; 1937; originally published 1776), p. 14.
14. Adam Smith, *The Theory of Moral Sentiments* (Amherst, New York: Prometheus Books, 2000; originally published in 1759), pp. 264-265. Part IV, Chapter I.
15. Adam Smith, *The Wealth of Nations*, p. 423.
16. Adam Smith, *The Theory of Moral Sentiments* (Amherst, New York: Prometheus Books, 2000; originally published in 1759), p. 84. Section III. Chapter III.
17. Lord Action, *Lectures on Modern History* (1895) Lecture XI, The Puritan Revolution, at Project Gutenberg.
18. From Alexis de Tocqueville's *Democracy in America, De La Démocratie en Amérique*, Bilingual Edition, edited by Eduardo Nolla, translated by James T. Schleifer (Indianapolis, IN: Liberty Fund; 2010), vol. II, Chapter VIII, p. 918.
19. Ibid; pp. 920–921.
20. Adam Smith, *The Wealth of Nations* (New York: The Modern Library, Random House, Inc.; 1937; originally published 1776), p. 808.
21. Ibid; p. 923.
22. Adam Smith, *The Wealth of Nations*, pp. 388 and 389.
23. Karl Polanyi, *The Great Transformation: The Political and Economic Origins of Our Time* (Boston: Beacon Press; 1944, 1957, 2001), p. 237.
24. Karl Polanyi, *The Great Transformation: The Political and Economic Origins of Our Time* (Boston: Beacon Press; 1944, 1957, 2001), p. 57.
25. Document #1147; November 8, 1954, from President Dwight Eisenhower to Edgar Newton Eisenhower , *The Papers of Dwight David Eisenhower, Volume XV—The Presidency: The Middle Way, Part VI: Crises Abroad, Party Problems at Home; September 1954 to December 1954*, Chapter 13: "A new phase of political experience," Johns Hopkins University Press.
26. George Will, *Statecraft As Soulcraft—What Government Does* (New York, NY: Touchstone Books, an imprint of Simon & Schuster; 1983, 1984), p. 130.
27. Ibid, p. 121.
28. *Brown v. Board of Education,* 347 U.S. 483 (1954), 349 U.S. 294 (1955).
29. George Will, *Statecraft As Soulcraft*, p. 12.
30. Ibid, p. 156.
31. Ibid, p. 20. The quote from Justice Frankfurter comes from his opinion in *West Virginia State Board of Education v. Barnette*, George Will, *Statecraft As Soulcraft*, p. 27.319 U.S. 624 (1943) 655.
32. George Will, *Statecraft As Soulcraft*, p. 27.
33. Blaise Pascal (1623-1662), *Pensées*, No. 895.
34. Michael Gerson, "An Invasion of Artificial Outrage," *The Washington Post*, January 29, 2015. The photograph accompanying the essay was of Governor Jindal reading from the Holy Bible during a prayer rally a few days earlier.
35. For reference, see Johann Hari's "Titanic," *The New Republic*, July 1, 2007.
36. The concept of perfectibility in illiberal and conservative thought is also addressed by John Gray in *Black Mass: Apocalyptic Religion and the Death of Utopia* (New York: Farrar, Straus and Giroux; 2007), pp. 26, 35, 38, 41 and 49.
37. Leo Strauss , *Natural Right and History* (Chicago and London: The University of Chicago Press, 1950, 1953, 1965), pp. 134–135.
38. A strikingly similar vision was promoted by Iranian President Mahmoud Ahmadinejad in a speech before the United Nations when he invoked the idea of paving the way for human perfection. See Andrew Sullivan, "When Not Seeing Is Believing," *Time*, October 2, 2006.

39. Thomas Sowell, *A Conflict of Visions: The Ideological Origins of Political Struggles* (New York: Basic Books; 2002), p. 48.

40. The essay appeared as the Postscript to his classic *The Constitution of Liberty*. Friedrich Hayek, *The Constitution of Liberty* (Chicago: The University of Chicago Press; 1960), p. 406. Similar sentiments were expressed by Paul Krugman in "Ideology and Integrity," *The New York Times*, May 1, 2015.

41. Hayek, *The Constitution of Liberty*, p. 401.

42. Friedrich Hayek, *The Road to Serfdom* (Chicago: The University of Chicago Press; 1944, 1976), pp. ix-x. Although Hayek, in *The Road to Serfdom*, characterized fascism and Nazism as movements of the left, he also observed that these doctrines partly owed their success to the justification of privilege, thus he also linked them with conservatism.

43. Hayek, *The Constitution of Liberty*, p. 402.

44. Andrew Sullivan, *The Conservative Soul: Fundamentalism, Freedom and the Future of the Right* (New York: Harper-Collins; 2006), p. 23. He addressed the ideas in the book in an article that appeared before the book was published: Andrew Sullivan, "How Fundamentalism Is Splitting the GOP," *The New Republic*, May 2, 2005. See also Andrew Sullivan, "*Forbes*' Definition of 'Liberal'," *Daily Dish*, January 24, 2009 and Richard Cohen, "A Grand Old Cult," *The Washington Post*, July 4, 2011.

45. See Jennie Rothenberg Gritz's interview with Andrew Sullivan, "Containing Multitudes," November 6, 2007 in *The Atlantic*.

46. Andrew Sullivan, "Goodbye to All That," *The Atlantic*, December 2007. And, Andrew Sullivan, "How Obama's Long Game Will Outsmart His Critics," *Newsweek*, January 16, 2012. See also Andrew Sullivan, "President Obama: The Democrats' Ronald Reagan," *Newsweek*, September 24, 2012.

47. Interview between Nick Hanauer and Lawrence O'Donnell on *The Last Word*, MSNBC, May 17, 2012. Hanauer has been joined by other billionaires concerned about the inequality perpetuated by current policies—see Alan Feuer, "Tycoons to the Barricades," *The New York Times*, July 5, 2015.

48. See Anatol Lieven, "America's Creed Leads to a Clash of Rhetoric and Reality," *Financial Times*, September 6, 2006, p. 15. Lieven is a senior research fellow at the New American Foundation.

49. Paul Farhi, "The E-mail Rumor Mill Is Run by Conservatives," *The Washington Post*, November 17, 2011.

50. Nouriel Roubini, "Who Is to Blame for the Mortgage Carnage and Coming Financial Disaster? Unregulated Free Market Fundamentalism Zealotry," March 19, 2007. Available at the Economonitor website (http://www.economonitor.com/nouriel/2007/03/19/who-is-to-blame-for-the-mortgage-carnage-and-coming-financial-disaster-unregulated-free-market-fundamentalism-zealotry/).

51. See George Soros, "Busted: Why the Markets Can't Fix Themselves," *The New Republic*, September 2, 2002, p. 20 and George Soros, "The U.S. Is in the Hands of a Group of Extremists: Fundamentalism Has Spawned an Ideology of American Supremacy," *The Guardian*, January 26, 2004.

52. George Soros, *The Bubble of American Supremacy: The Costs of Bush's War in Iraq* (New York: Public Affairs, 2004), p. 195. Interestingly, Soros distinguishes between Hayek and Popper (at page 169), implying that Hayek, as the conservatives portrayed him, was the promoter of market fundamentalism as opposed to Popper's promotion of the open society. By contrast, the position taken herein is that Hayek's message, in reality, in contrast to how conservatives interpreted it (until late in his life) is much closer to Popper, whom Hayek admired, as will be observed later in this chapter.

53. See, for example, Brian Stelter and Bill Carter, "Fox News's Mad, Apocalyptic, Tearful, Rising Star," *The New York Times*, March 30, 2009.

54. See Lacey Rose, "Glenn Beck Inc., *Forbes*, April 26, 2010.

55. See, e.g., Gabriel Sherman, "The Elephant in the Greenroom," *New York*, May 30, 2011; and Tim Dickinson, "The Fox News Fear Factory," *Rolling Stone*, June 9, 2011.

56. See, for example, Paul Krugman, "Prostates and Prejudices," *The New York Times*, November 2, 2007—an opinion piece about Rudy Giuliani's loose play with healthcare facts during the campaign for the 2008 Republican presidential nomination.
57. William Raspberry, "Fox's Sandstorm," *The Washington Post*, April 18, 2005.
58. "Misperceptions, the Media and the Iraq War," Program on International Policy Attitudes (PIPA), a joint program of the Center on Policy Attitudes and the Center for International and Security Studies at the University of Maryland and Knowledge Networks, October 2, 2003. Knowledge Networks is a polling, social science, and market research firm based in Menlo Park, California. See also Paul Krugman, "The Murdoch Factor," *The New York Times*, June 29, 2007.
59. Brian Stelter, "Some Viewers Were Misinformed by TV News," *The New York Times* blog, December 17, 2010. The title of the report is "Misinformation and the 2010 Election: A Study of the US Electorate," December 10, 2010.
60. Chris Mooney, "Why Fox Viewers Are Misinformed," *AlterNet*, April 10, 2012.
61. "Study Finds Fox News Viewers Least Informed of All Viewers," *Huffington Post*, May 23, 2012, updated July 23, 2012.
62. George W. Bush White House website, "President Addresses the Nation in Prime Time Press Conference," April 13, 2004.
63. Commission on Presidential Debates, September 30, 2004 Debate Transcript.
64. "McCain Advisor Fiorina: Palin Not Ready to Run a Corporation," CNN.com, September 16, 2008.
65. Andy Barr, "Packard: Fiorina Almost Destroyed HP," Politico.com, March 8, 2010.
66. Matt Krantz, "President Fiorina? How Carly Did at HP," *USA Today*, May 4, 2015. See also Andrew Ross Sorkin, "Fiorina's Record: Not So Sterling," *The New York Times*, August 18, 2015 and Michael Barbaro, "Fiorina's Contradictory Time as the Chief of HP," *The New York Times*, October 27, 2015.
67. John Kerry, quoted by Matt Bai in "Kerry's Undeclared War," *The New York Times Magazine*, October 10, 2004.
68. The term, "pre-9/11 mindset," was used by Republican blogger Matt Margolis in Blogs for Bush October 17, 2004. It was later used in a speech by Vice President Dick Cheney in Clio, Michigan, quoted in an Associated Press story carried by the *Detroit Free Press*, October 20, 2004.
69. John Mueller, "A False Sense of Insecurity," *Regulation*, Fall 2004, pp. 42-46. Mueller holds the Woody Hayes Chair of National Security Studies at the Mershon Center at Ohio State University.
70. Frank S. Meyer, *In Defense of Freedom*, (Chicago: Henry Regnery Company, 1962), p 28.
71. Frank Meyer, *In Defense of Freedom: A Conservative Credo,* p. 4.
72. Ibid, pp. 129-130: Kirk's chapter "The Problem of Social Boredom," in a *Program for Conservatives,* Chicago: Henry Regnery Co., 1954 and Nisbet's chapter, "The Loss of Community," in *The Quest for Community*, New York: Oxford University Press, 1953.
73. *The Concise Oxford Dictionary of Sociology*, Gordon Marshall, ed., (Oxford, New York: Oxford University Press, 1994), p. 210.
74. Friedrich Hayek, *The Constitution of Liberty*, pp. 69–70.
75. Similarly struck by Hayek's lament was Jeffrey E. Garten, Dean of the Yale School of Management who quoted Hayek in his review of the series in "Must-See TV on the Road to Globalism," *BusinessWeek* Online, April 8, 2002. Daniel Yergin later, in the article "What Makes Global Firms Resilient," *Harvard Business Review*, July 2003, also reflected on it.
76. Hayek expressed these fears in *The Road to Serfdom* (1944). As observed earlier, none of the countries of the West became totalitarian, although perhaps due in part to his warning.
77. See John Cassidy, "The Hayek Century," *Hoover Digest* 2000, No. 3. This article was adapted from an article entitled "The Price Prophet" in *The New Yorker*, February 7, 2000.
78. *The Road to Serfdom* (1944), p. 36.
79. Ibid, p. 17.
80. Ibid, p. 36.
81. Ibid, p. 38.

82. Ibid, p. 37.
83. Ibid, pp. 120–122.
84. Hayek impliedly above, however, supported a minimum wage in 1944 in *The Road to Serfdom* and expressly did so in 1973: See *Law, Legislation and Liberty: A New Statement of the Liberal Principles of Justice and Political Economy* . Vol. 2 . (Routledge; 1973), p. 87.
85. Hayek's relative comfort with the Welfare State in lieu of socialism, expressed in *The Constitution of Liberty*, was troubling to his old mentor Ludwig von Mises. See "Liberty and Its Antithesis," *Christian Economics*, August 1, 1960, reprinted in Ludwig von Mises, *Planning for Freedom, and Sixteen Other Essays and Addresses* (1980).
86. As observed by Alan Ebenstein in his biography of Friedrich Hayek, Hayek evolved from a classical liberal to a libertarian in his later work. See: Alan Ebenstein, *Hayek's Journey: The Mind of Friedrich Hayek* (New York: Palgrave Macmillan, 2004), p. 204. Ebenstein's observation was approvingly cited by a noted scholar of Hayek, Bettina Bien Greaves, in her essay, "Hayek the Enigma," *Liberty*, April 2005, p. 47; p. 52. However, given that both Milton Friedman and Friedrich Hayek in their later lives supported implementation of capitalism through violence in Chile, neither, at least at that time, were appropriately called libertarians either.

Chapter Six

Trickle-Down Conservatism Versus Public Opinion

Two broad indicators of American public opinion regarding the trickle-down conservatism of the Republican Party are, first, that concluding with the election of 2012, Democrats have won the popular vote in five of the last six presidential elections and, second, that the last two presidential elections (2008 and 2012) were won by Barack Obama with over 50% of the popular vote—the first president to win back-to-back elections with over 50% of the popular vote in each election since Dwight Eisenhower in the elections of 1952 and 1956.

But mere majorities against them are no impediment to the delusional power-wielding of the trickle-down conservative Republicans. In July and August of 2011 Republicans opposed raising the federal debt ceiling (it had been raised 17 times under President Reagan and 7 times under President George W. Bush), demanding that spending be slashed to address deficit spending, and taxes not be raised. A Gallup Poll, results of which were released during the debate, revealed that *80 percent* of Americans preferred a combination of tax increases and spending cuts.[1]

Bruce Bartlett, former Reagan administration official, observed in an essay published during the debt ceiling crisis that the tax cuts overseen by George W. Bush had slashed federal government revenue with no observable economic benefit, while much greater economic growth was seen under President Clinton, who raised taxes.[2] And, a poll for *The Economist* found that 77 percent of Americans agreed that defaulting on the debt would be serious for the economy—but incoherently two-thirds of Republicans did not want their Representative compromising to get an agreement to raise the ceiling (versus more than two-thirds of Democrats favoring compromise).[3]

In the months leading up to the 2012 election, the extremism from the trickle-down conservatives increased. At a town hall meeting in Palm City, Florida in April, Representative Allen West (R-FL) was asked how many Marxists there are in Congress. He replied with a rough number of the members of the 80-member Congressional Progressive Caucus. That same week, at a National Rifle Association convention, conservative activist and former rock star Ted Nugent promised that he would either be dead or in jail the following year if Barack Obama became president and urged everyone to ride into battle like Braveheart and chop the Democrats' heads off.[4]

Results from a poll taken a few months before the November 2012 election revealed that the conservative spreading of misinformation regarding President Obama's religion had been successful for, while 60 percent of Americans surveyed could successfully identify Governor Romney's faith as Mormon, only 49 percent could properly identify President Obama's faith as Christian, and 17 percent identified it as Muslim—and a greater percentage of Americans were "uncomfortable" with President Obama's faith than with Governor Romney's (19 percent to 13 percent).[5] David Frum, former speechwriter for President George W. Bush, said it best in the title of an article he wrote for *New York* magazine one year before the 2012 election, asking about his party: "When Did the GOP Lose Touch with Reality?"[6]

THE VIEW FROM INSIDE THE BUBBLE: STAY THE TRICKLE-DOWN COURSE

Governor Bobby Jindal of Louisiana, candidate for the 2016 Republican presidential nomination, after the Republicans' loss in 2012 advised his fellow Republicans to continue to show Americans how Republican policies help them achieve the American Dream and issued an essay titled "How Republicans Can Win Future Elections," asserting that to win Republicans must not change their principles—a message he repeated at gatherings of Republicans.[7]

Evidence mounted, however, that Governor Jindal's trickle-down conservative Republican policies were hurting the voters of Louisiana and making it ever more difficult for many of them to achieve that American Dream, even though, in an op-ed in *The New York Times* April 23, 2015,[8] he claimed to have made Louisiana one of the best places for business in America and made a similar claim of success in an interview with host George Stephanopoulos that aired May 31, 2015 on ABC News' *This Week with George Stephanopoulos*.

The facts, though: For all three of the most recent previous years tracked by the Bureau of Economic Analysis (BEA), Louisiana's GDP growth rate trailed the national GDP growth rate: In 2011 Louisiana's GDP growth rate was -2.8 percent—the worst performance of any state and behind the national GDP growth rate of 1.6 percent; in 2012 Louisiana's GDP growth rate was 2.1 percent, placing Louisiana tied for 22nd in the nation for that year and behind the national average of 2.5 percent; and in 2013 Louisiana's GDP growth rate was 1.3 percent, placing Louisiana 34th in the nation and again behind the national average of 1.8 percent.[9] Louisiana also ranked dead last in 2011 on the "Camelot Index," a composite index comparing how the 50 states fare in measures of economic vitality, education, health, crime and governance.[10] Over his first seven years in office, from January 2008 through December 2014, Louisiana added a net of only 1,500 jobs—an increase of less than 0.08 percent—and, obviously, not three times as fast job growth as the nation.[11] The latest unemployment rate for Louisiana when Governor Jindal appeared in his interview with George Stephanopoulos (above) was 6.6 percent—substantially above the national unemployment rate of 5.4 percent and tied for fifth-highest in the nation.[12] According to the Tax Foundation, in 2012 Louisiana was second only to Mississippi in federal aid as a percentage of state revenue. A widely publicized public opinion poll in early 2013 found Governor Jindal's approval rating among Louisiana voters at 38 percent—below that of President Obama at 43 percent. In April 2015, two months before his announced run for the presidency, another poll reflected that his standing among his own constituents *had declined further*, with his approval rating of 32 percent of likely voters in Louisiana—and he was beaten again by President Obama, whose approval rating among likely voters in Louisiana was 42 percent.[13]

Governor Jindal followed a "no taxes" pledge which he declared had to meet Grover Norquist's Americans for Tax Reform approval—essentially ceding Louisiana state budget oversight to Norquist.[14] Louisiana law dedicates state government spending to nearly every category except health care and education, and revenues to the state are shrinking—and Governor Jindal declined the lifeboat offered by Medicaid revenues provided by the Affordable Care Act. Instead, he addressed the resultant revenue shortfall—in one of America's poorest states, with a higher education system already ranked near the bottom in the nation—by slashing state funding for higher education by *80 percent*—from $1.4 billion in FY 2007–2008 to just $284.5 million for the FY commencing July 1, 2013—setting back Louisiana investment in higher education to the lowest level since 1961.[15]

By the beginning of 2015, Louisiana faced a $1.6 billion shortfall—which the governor quickly attributed in interviews to falling oil and gas prices—although, by his own admission, these were responsible for only 25% of the shortfall ($400 million).[16] In response, the president of Louisiana State University—Louisiana's "flagship" institution—announced plans to draw up a bankruptcy plan for the university.[17]

Governor Jindal had launched a PAC in 2013 to promote his views with the name "America Next"—as he was mulling a campaign for the presidency in 2016, it implied a promise that if he were elected president he would apply his policies that failed in Louisiana to America next.[18] He later set up another PAC with the name "American Future Project," followed by yet another super PAC "Believe Again." Meanwhile, back home, in March 2015 an op-ed called for him to resign so that the people of Louisiana could replace him with a governor who would participate in an attempt to address Louisiana's problems.[19] In October 2015, in a poll asking voters to pick the best and worst out of the past 6 governors, Governor Jindal was selected the worst, easily "winning" that ignominious title with 42 percent of the vote.[20]

Similarly, Republican Governor Sam Brownback of Kansas ran for re-election in 2014 on a platform of trickle-down that had yielded such mediocre results even Republicans in the state were voicing opposition to his campaign (although he won a close election).[21]

Activist Gary Bauer, president of the evangelical group American Values concurred that Republicans need change nothing in their agenda[22] and, similarly, rising Republican star Senator Marco Rubio of Florida offered that Republicans simply needed to work harder than ever to get their message out.[23]

Further evidence of Republican Party cluelessness regarding the need to address the unpopularity of trickle-down was illustrated in the ironically-named "Growth & Opportunity Project" report released in early 2013. An editorial by *The New York Times*[24] best captured the report's main weakness—that the Republican Party cannot explain how its trickle-down policies will accomplish its goal of enabling people to need government less.

Regardless, a June 2013 Pew Research Center Poll found that by a 54 percent to 40 percent margin Republicans and Republican-leaning independent voters wanted party leaders to be *more conservative* rather than moderate—in contrast, a December 2012 *Washington-Post*-ABC News Poll found that 53 percent of Americans said the GOP's problem is that it is too conservative (while among Republicans 64 percent thought their party's main problem was leadership and communication).[25]

The Republican Party will not change on its own, as demonstrated by unanimity regarding trickle-down among the large field of 2016 presidential nomination aspirants.[26] The Republican Party will only change when the American people, convinced by the opposition Democrats to vote for *them*, force the Republican Party to change.

It is important to observe that the majority of American voters support the social safety net, even though, paradoxically, substantial percentages of the middle class provide the Republicans the electoral support they need to dismantle the programs upon which those same members of the middle class rely. And, when President George W. Bush, once out of office, lamented that his greatest failure in office was not privatizing Social Security, little was said about how little support there was for this radical proposal and the potentially ruinous effect on the middle class and poor if he had succeeded.[27]

A poll taken by the Pew Research Center for the People & the Press conducted December 7-11, 2011, revealed that 77 percent of the public agreed that power was too concentrated in the hands of a few rich people and large corporations. Not surprisingly, 91 percent of Democrats agreed, but also agreeing were 80 percent of Independents and even 53 percent of Republicans. And, regarding the statement that the "country's economic system unfairly favors the wealthy," 61 percent of the public agreed; 76 percent of Democrats, 61 percent of Independents and 39 percent of Republicans.[28]

Two other polls taken in late 2011 directly addressed the public's attitude toward inequality. A CBS News-*New York Times* poll taken in October of 2011 found, in response to the question of whether people believed income and wealth were fairly distributed in the US or should be more evenly distributed, 66 percent of respondents agreed it should be more evenly distributed. And, Michael I. Norton of Harvard Business School and Dan Ariely of Duke University found in a study they published in January 2011 that when presented a choice of three wealth distribution options—a hypothetical perfectly equal wealth distribution among five quintiles (i.e., each with 20 percent of the nation's wealth), the wealth distribution of the United States, and the wealth distribution of Sweden—92 percent of respondents chose Sweden.[29] Similarly, studies reported in 2015 found that Americans severely misjudged the amount of upward mobility in American society (upward mobility in the US is shockingly low compared to other developed nations, as will be seen later herein).[30]

A Pew Research poll from January 2014 surveyed about 1,500 adult Americans and found 69 percent believed the government should act "to reduce the gap between the rich and everyone else," 54 percent favored "raising taxes on the wealthy and corporations to expand programs for the poor," 73 percent favored raising the minimum wage from $7.25 to $10.10 an hour and 63 percent favored a one year extension of unemployment for those out of work for a long time.[31] Similarly, a Gallup poll of about 1,000 Americans in April 2013 found 52 percent favored the proposition that the government should "redistribute wealth by heavy taxes on the rich.[32] Yet, as observed in Chapter 1, Republicans campaigning for their party's 2016 presidential nomination were opposed to any of these policies supported by a majority of Americans.

The reality is that Americans want social insurance maintained, as was famously recalled by former Senator John Breaux (D-LA) in his quote from a woman who implored of him when she saw him in the New Orleans Airport to not let government get a hold of her Medicare.[33]

And, polls have consistently confirmed large majorities of the American electorate—and even large majorities of Republicans—support maintenance of Social Security, Medicare and Medicaid, as well as increased taxes on the richest Americans. Among those are two respected polls conducted by telephone in April 2011 (a *Washington Post*-ABC News Poll and a McClatchy-Marist Poll), about the time vice presidential candidate and Representative Paul Ryan (R-WI) released "The Path to Prosperity," with its most important proposals to cut taxes further on the rich and cut Medicare (more accurately, to abolish Medicare for those under 55 years of age and replace it with vouchers) and Medicaid (to replace it with block grants to the states). The polls[34] showed the vast majority of Americans opposed both proposals (and revealed surprisingly high Tea Partier support for Medicare and Medicaid), as shown in Table 6.1.

One month after the November 2012 election, results of a McClatchy-Marist Poll conducted December 4 through December 6, 2012 were released, revealing that—among *Republicans*: majorities opposed cutting spending for Medicare (68%-26%), cutting spending for Medicaid (61%-33%) and raising the age to receive Medicare from 65 to 67 (56%-44%).[35]

After the 2012 election, various conservative groups and Republican politicians began to advocate defunding of the Affordable Care Act (Obamacare), although that was opposed by a clear majority (57 percent) of Americans, according to a Kaiser Family Foundation Poll conducted in Au-

Table 6.1. Poll Results: Favorability of Medicare, Medicaid and Raising Taxes on the Rich

Policy Proposal	Percent Opposed
Cut Spending on Medicare *Washington Post*-ABC News Poll	78%
Cut Spending on Medicaid *Washington Post*-ABC News Poll	69%
Cut Medicare and Medicaid McClatchy-Marist Poll	80%
Cut Medicare and Medicaid (Tea Party Supporters only) McClatchy-Marist Poll	70%
	Percent Favoring
Raise Taxes on Americans with annual incomes over $250,000 *Washington Post*-ABC News Poll	72%
Raise Taxes on Americans with annual incomes over $250,000 McClatchy-Marist Poll	64%

gust 2013.[36] Approval of Obamacare continued to steadily grow thereafter, as increasing numbers of Americans found insurance coverage and the number of uninsured continued to fall, although Republicans resolutely ignored these facts.[37]

Other examples of where the Republican Party parts with majority opinion appear in the following pages but, given that President Obama, early in his second administration, put forth a modest proposal to raise the minimum wage from $7.25 per hour to $10.10 per hour, it is worth also observing that 73 percent of Americans supported increasing the minimum wage to $10 per hour in 2012 and indexing it to inflation, resulting in automatic increases without congressional action; 70 percent supported raising it to $10.38 (a previous inflation-adjusted level; in 2013 that would be $10.55 per hour); and 78 percent believed the minimum wage should be high enough so that no family with one full-time worker would fall below the poverty line.[38]

Finally, a comprehensive New York Times/CBS Poll conducted in May 2015 found 57 percent support for government measures to combat inequality and even stronger support for these measures: 68 percent of Americans favored raising taxes on incomes above $1 million, 71 percent favored raising the minimum wage for $10.10 per hour, 80 percent favored requiring employers to offer paid leave to parents of new children and employees caring for sick family members, 85 percent favored requiring employers to offer paid sick leave to employees who are ill, 72 percent favored requiring chain stores and fast-food outlets to provide workers at least 2 weeks' notice of any changes to work schedules or provide them with extra pay and 63 percent viewed trade restrictions as necessary to protect domestic industries.[39]

A CALL FOR A CONSERVATISM THAT IS FACT BASED, NOT FAITH BASED

Nowhere herein is a conservative accused of telling a lie, lying, or being a liar. A lie, by definition, is a knowing misrepresentation of the truth. If the promoter of the misrepresentation does not know the truth, then, by definition, the misrepresentation is not a lie. A few conservative opinion leaders and conservative politicians have created trickle-down conservatism's apparent disrespect for truth and knowledge. In response, far too many of the rest of conservative opinion leaders and conservative politicians have adjusted to accord with this disrespect of truth so they were not rendered irrelevant by the conservative voters who accept this nonsense as truth—conservative voters who imagine the nonsense is truthful because, after all, their heroes promoted it, and they, in turn, promote it.

In so doing, by not demanding of themselves that they test these assertions against the truth, the conservative voters are joining with their leaders in undermining democracy. The damage being inflicted extends beyond the Republican Party—the trickle-down conservatism of the Republican Party is corrosive of American democracy broadly and of the American liberal democratic ideal of rule of, by, and for the people. The most hopeful future is with the remaining conservatives, several of whom appear herein, who question the statements of conservative leaders, test them against the truth, and reject them if they fail, harkening back to a conservatism that predates the current modern trickle-down conservatism, as will be addressed below.

Paul Krugman has been perhaps the most outspoken liberal critic of the aversion to truth exhibited by modern conservatives, especially the House "Freedom Caucus," from his op-ed platform at *The New York Times*.[40] The chapters herein elaborate on the proud cult of ignorance and anti-intellectualism of conservative leaders, marked by their hostility toward the facts and their mystical belief in their ability to create a virtual reality that bends facts to their will (introduced in Chapter 1); their mischaracterization of the classical liberal theory they claim as their inspiration; and their willful neglect of the opinions of the electorate—all of which combine to threaten the future of the nation and the world unless confronted by liberalism, forcing conservatives to engage in *fact based* rather than *faith based* policymaking.[41]

A plea for a conservatism that is fact based is not novel. A similar plea in 2008 came from one of the deans of movement conservatism, the former columnist, Jeffrey Hart, a self-described "Burkean" conservative and "Obamacon" (conservative voter for Obama). Ironically, given Hart's role as a leader of movement conservatism, he gave his vision of conservatism, in an interview the month before the 2008 election, as of the type inspired by Dwight Eisenhower—*conservatism based in fact and analysis*.[42]

Conservatism based in fact and analysis—and compromise—bears scant resemblance to the conservatism of today. Former Florida Governor Jeb Bush addressed that latter concern himself, observing months before the 2012 election that Ronald Reagan himself would have a hard time in the current Republican Party.[43] Former Florida Governor and former Republican Charlie Crist elaborated on those concerns in an op-ed published in the *Tampa Bay Times* in Tampa, the Republican National Convention host city, on the eve of the convention in 2012. He explained he was endorsing Democrat Barack Obama for a second term because of the president's focus on compromise and seeking solutions.[44] He later joined the Democratic Party and ran a losing campaign for governor of Florida in the 2014 election.

Prominent libertarian conservative and Reagan-appointee Judge Richard Posner of the Chicago-based 7th Circuit Court of Appeals observed in an interview that he was becoming less conservative as the Republican Party continued its rightward drift.[45] Ed Rollins, National Campaign Director for the Reagan-Bush 1984 campaign and the 2008 Huckabee campaign, acknowledged in an interview on *Fox & Friends* less than four months before the 2012 election the problem facing his party in attracting women, Latinos and African Americans.[46]

And Bruce Bartlett observed, in an article published in the November/December 2014 issue of *The American Conservative* titled "Obama Is a Republican," other Obamacons beside Jeffrey Hart were Ken Duberstein (Reagan's chief of staff), Charles Fried (Reagan's solicitor general), Ken Adelman (Reagan's director of the Arms Control and Disarmament Agency), Colin Powell (Reagan's national security advisor and secretary of state for George W. Bush) and Scott McClellan (George W. Bush's press secretary).[47]

Again, however, given the extremism of today's conservatism, only liberal Democratic successes will force the Republican Party to abandon its attempts to privatize Social Security, convert Medicare to a voucher system, convert Medicaid to a block grant system turned over to the states, and repeal the Affordable Care Act, and to generally abandon trickle-down to return to fact based policymaking and sensible compromise.

In a 2015 article for *Politico*, Bruce Bartlett acknowledged as much, expressing hope that Donald Trump would win the Republican nomination, fully expecting the result would be a loss for the Republicans on the scale of Barry Goldwater's in 1964, with result being that the party would return, as it did thereafter, to the center-right.[48]

NOTES

1. Jeffrey M. Jones, "On Deficit, Americans Prefer Spending Cuts; Open to Tax Hikes," *Gallup*, July 13, 2011.
2. Bruce Bartlett, "Are the Bush Tax Cuts the Root of Our Fiscal Problem?" *Economix* blog, *The New York Times*, July 26, 2011.
3. YouGov Staff, "77 Percent Agree That Defaulting on the Debt Would Be Serious for the Economy, But There Is a Party Divide," Economist/YouGov, July 8, 2011. The question was, "If you had to choose, would you rather have a congressperson who compromises to get things done or sticks to his or her principles, no matter what?" All respondents preferred compromise 53 percent to 47 percent; Democrats preferred compromise 68 percent to 32 percent; Republicans *rejected* compromise by 66 percent to 34 percent.
4. Eugene Robinson, "Republican Rhetoric Over the Top," *The Washington Post*, April 1, 2012.
5. "Little Voter Discomfort with Romney's Mormon Religion," Pew Forum, July 26, 2012.
6. David Frum, "When Did the GOP Lose Touch with Reality?" *New York*, November 28, 2011.
7. Bobby Jindal, "How Republicans Can Win Future Elections," CNN.com, November 15, 2012. Governor Jindal reiterated that theme two months later at the winter meeting of the Republican National Committee, in his dinner address. John Whitesides, "Bobby Jindal: GOP Principles Are Good, 'But We Might Need to Change Just About Everything Else'," *Huffington Post*, January 24, 2013. He returned again to the message in an address on "The Future of Conservatism" delivered to *National Review* Institute Summit at the Omni Shoreham Hotel in Washington, D.C. on January 27, 2013. Jordan Blum, "Jindal Addresses Conservatives," *The Advocate* (Baton Rouge) January 28, 2013. See also, Paul Krugman, "Makers, Takers, Fakers,"

The New York Times, January 28, 2013, and E. J. Dionne, "Are Republicans Rebranding or Rethinking?" *The Washington Post*, February 6, 2013.

8. Bobby Jindal, "Holding Firm Against Gay Marriage," *The New York Times*, April 23, 2015.

9. These are Bureau of Economic Analysis (BEA) figures, from the BEA website ("Table 1. GDP by State, 2010–2013").

10. The index is issued by Federal Funds Information for States, a non-partisan subscription service created by the National Governors Association and the National Conference of State Legislatures. Jonathan Tilove, "Louisiana Ranks Last on 'Camelot Index,'" *The Times-Picayune*, April 26, 2012.

11. Louisiana Workforce Commission website, "Labor Market Information," and the "Nonfarm Employment" link (http://lwc.laworks.net/sites/LMI/Pages/NonfarmDataSeries.aspx): Annual total nonfarm employment for 2008: 1,937,500 and 2014: 1,939,000.

12. Bureau of Labor Statistics Unemployment Rates for States. For April 2015: Nevada led among states with 7.1 percent, West Virginia was second with 7.0, South Carolina and Alaska were tied for third with 6.7 percent, and Louisiana and Mississippi were tied for fifth with 6.6 percent.

13. Aaron Blake, "Poll: Obama More Popular Than Jindal in Louisiana," *The Washington Post*, April 2, 2013, and Stephanie Grace, referring to a poll conducted by Southern Media and Opinion Research, in "All Signs Point to Yes for Bobby Jindal's Presidential Run and He May Not Have a Plan B," *The Advocate*, May 21, 2015. See also Tyler Bridges, "As He Nears a 2016 Bid, Louisiana's Bobby Jindal Hits Political Bottom," *The Washington Post*, June 6, 2015.

14. See Stephanie Grace, "Bobby Jindal and Grover Norquist Wreck Louisiana," *The Washington Spectator*, June 1, 2015.

15. See Jim Beam, "Governor Won't Sit Down, Talk," *Lake Charles American Press*, May 9, 2013. See also Robert Mann, "How Low Can We Go? Louisiana Higher Education Leaders Decry Deep Budget Cuts," May 10, 2013, citing the monthly research letter *Postsecondary Education OPPORTUNITY*. Investment levels are compared year-to-year based on higher education spending per $1,000 of personal income for each year.

16. Campbell Robertson, "As Jindal's G.O.P. Profile Grows, So Do Louisiana's Budget Woes," *The New York Times*, February 7, 2015. And, see interview on MSNBC's *Morning Joe* February 10, 2015.

17. "Louisiana State to Draft Insolvency Plan as Jindal Cuts Loom," *Bloomberg*, April 23, 2015.

18. See also Dana Milbank, "Bobby Jindal's Unpleasant Record," *The Washington Post*, February 10, 2015.

19. The op-ed, "It's Time for Bobby Jindal to Resign," was written by Robert Mann, an author and former US Senate and gubernatorial staffer and holder of the Manship Chair in Journalism at the Manship School of Mass Communication at Louisiana State University. It appeared in the New Orleans *Times-Picayune* of March 20, 2015. It was cited by Charles M. Blow in "Governor Jindal's Implosion," *The New York Times*, March 23, 2015.

20. Mark Ballard, "In Poll of Louisiana voters, Edwin Edwards Gets Nod as Best Governor, 42 Percent Say Bobby Jindal the Worst" *The Advocate*, Oct. 1, 2015; 10:05 p.m.

21. See especially John B. Judis, "This is What's the Matter with Kansas," *The New Republic*, September 29, 2014. See also, Paul Krugman, "Voodoo, The Next Generation," *The New York Times*, October 6, 2014 and Josh Barro, "Kansas Announces Big Budget Gap; True Gap May Be Even Larger," *The New York Times*, November 13, 2014.

22. John B. Judis, "This is What's the Matter with Kansas," *The New Republic*, September 29, 2014.

23. Peter Wallsten, "Republicans Face Murky Political Future in Increasingly Diverse U.S." *The Washington Post*, November 7, 2012.

24. The Editorial Board, "For the G.O.P., It's Not Just the Message," *The New York Times*, March 20, 2013. See also Sarah Wheaton and Michael D. Shear, "Blunt Report Says G.O.P. Needs to Regroup for '16," *The New York Times*, March 19, 2013. The report was issued March 18, 2013, the day after conclusion of the 2013 Conservative Political Action Conference in

which, although it reflected divisions between Republicans urging change with the times versus those urging ideological purity, no one challenged trickle-down. And see also Jim Rutenberg and Richard W. Stevenson, "G.O.P. Divisions Fester at Conservative Retreat," *The New York Times*, March 16, 2013.

25. Sean Sullivan, "Republicans Want Their Party to Change—Just Not the Way You Think," *The Washington Post*, August 1, 2013.

26. Paul Krugman, "Zombies of 2016," *The New York Times*, April 24, 2015.

27. Becky Schlikerman, "Bush Promotes Book in Chicago," *Chicago Tribune*, October 21, 2010.

28. Reported in "Frustration with Congress Could Hurt Republican Incumbents," *Pew Research Center*, December 15, 2011.

29. Michael I. Norton and Dan Ariely, "Building a Better America—One Wealth Quintile at a Time," *Perspectives on Psychological Science*, January 2011 vol. 6 no. 1 9–12.

30. Michael W. Kraus, Shai Davidai and A. David Nussbaum, "American Dream? Or Mirage?" *The New York Times*, May 3, 2015.

31. "Most See Inequality Growing, but Partisans Differ over Solutions," a Pew Research Center/USA Today Survey, January 23, 2014.

32. Frank Newport, "Majority in U.S. Want Wealth More Evenly Distributed," Gallup, April 17, 2013.

33. Quoted by Dylan Matthews, "Now Don't You Let the Government Get a Hold Of My Medicare," The Treatment Blog, *The New Republic*, August 9, 2009. Original attribution to Haynes Johnson and David Broder, *The System* (1996), p. 558.

34. The policy proposals and results number 1, 2 and 5 come from the *Washington Post*-ABC News Poll conducted of American adults by telephone April 14–17, 2011. The policy proposals and results number 3, 4 and 6 come from the McClatchy-Marist Poll, National Survey, conducted of registered voters by telephone April 18, 2011, Marist College Institute for Public Opinion, Poughkeepsie, NY.

35. McClatchy-Marist Poll National Poll of 1,246 adults; interviews conducted December 4th through 6th, 2012.

36. Chris Cillizza and Sean Sullivan, "People Don't Like Obamacare. They Like Defunding It Even Less," *The Washington Post*, August 28, 2013.

37. See Kathy Frankovic," The Very Slow—But Steady—Growth in Acceptance for Obamacare," YouGov.org, April 24, 2015. This article summarizes the polling results indicating growing approval. See also Paul Krugman, "Nobody Said That," *The New York Times*, April 27, 2015.

38. All from the excellent report by David Callahan and J. Mijin Cha, "Stacked Deck: How the Dominance of Politics by the Affluent & Business Undermines Economic Mobility in America," Dēmos.Org, February 2013. Polling results regarding the minimum wage are, respectively, from Celinda Lake, Daniel Gotoff and Alex Dunn, "Public Support for Raising the Minimum Wage," Lake Research Partners, February 2012; John Zogby, "New Poll by John Zogby Finds 70% Likely Voters Would Support Legislation to Raise Minimum Wage," June 21, 2012; and Benjamin I. Page, Larry Bartels and Jason Seawright, "Democracy and the Policy Preferences of Wealthy Americans," *Perspectives on Politics*, 11:1, pp. 51–73.

39. Noam Scheiber and Dalia Sussman, "Inequality Troubles Americans Across Party Lines, Times/CBS News Poll Finds," *The New York Times*, June 4, 2015.

40. See, for example, Paul Krugman's columns: "Know-Nothing Politics," *The New York Times*, August 8, 2008; "Triumph of the Unthinking," *The New York Times*, May 8, 2015; "Fighting the Derp," *The New York Times*, June 8, 2015; and "They Can't Be Serious," *The New York Times*, August 7, 2015. "Derp" is a term from the cartoon show "South Park," describing the condition where people keep saying the same thing despite being wrong. See also Paul Krugman, "The Crazies and the Con Man," *The New York Times*, October 12, 2015. The "con man" is Paul Ryan, and Krugman criticizes the media for their unwillingness to expose his lack of depth and seriousness.

41. See, for example, Jonathon Gatehouse, "America Dumbs Down," *Maclean's*, May 15, 2014. For a contrast with Asian attitudes, see John W. Traphagan, "Asia's Cult of Intelligence," *The Diplomat*, June 17, 2014.

42. "TDR Exclusive Interview: Obamacon Jeffrey Hart," *The Dartmouth Review*, October 21, 2008.
43. Mark Silva, "Jeb Bush Sees Romney Needing 'Broader' Immigration Ideas," *Bloomberg Business*, June 11, 2012.
44. Charlie Crist, "Former Gov. Charlie Crist: Here's Why I'm Backing Barack Obama," *Tampa Bay Times*, August 26, 2012.
45. Debra Cassens Weiss, "Judge Posner Critic of 'Goofy' Trend in GOP, Says He's Becoming Less Conservative," *American Bar Journal Online*, July 9, 2012.
46. Ed Rollins, long-time Republican political consultant, on *Fox & Friends* with co-host Gretchen Carlson, on the July 10, 2012 show.
47. Bruce Bartlett, "Obama Is a Republican," *The American Conservative*, November/December 2014. Bartlett gave citations to articles supporting his classification of each as an Obamacon.
48. Bruce Bartlett, "The Moderate Republican's Case for Trump: Only Trump Can Make the GOP Sane Again—by Losing in a Landslide to Hillary Clinton," *Politico*, July 27, 2015. See also Thomas Friedman, "My Question for the Republican Presidential Debate," *The New York Times*, August 5, 2015. Friedman laid out a vision of a healthy, balanced, political climate in which the Republicans, as a center-right party, would offer *market*-based solutions in an atmosphere of compromise with the Democrats as a center-left party offering *government*-based solutions.

Chapter Seven

A Narrative of Trickle-Down Failure

The Productivity/Wage Disconnect

President Barack Obama sketched a narrative of the trickle-down failure in a speech delivered December 4, 2013[1]:

> As values of community broke down, and competitive pressure increased, businesses lobbied Washington to weaken unions and the value of the minimum wage. As a trickle-down ideology became more prominent, taxes were slashed for the wealthiest, while investments in things that make us all richer, like schools and infrastructure, were allowed to wither. And for a certain period of time, we could ignore this weakening economic foundation, in part because more families were relying on two earners as women entered the workforce. We took on more debt financed by a juiced-up housing market. But when the music stopped, and the crisis hit, millions of families were stripped of whatever cushion they had left.
>
> And the result is an economy that's become profoundly unequal, and families that are more insecure. I'll just give you a few statistics. Since 1979, when I graduated from high school, our productivity is up by more than 90 percent, but the income of the typical family has increased by less than eight percent. Since 1979, our economy has more than doubled in size, but most of that growth has flowed to a fortunate few.
>
> The top 10 percent no longer takes in one-third of our income—it now takes half. Whereas in the past, the average CEO made about 20 to 30 times the income of the average worker, today's CEO now makes 273 times more. And meanwhile, a family in the top 1 percent has a net worth 288 times higher than the typical family, which is a record for this country.

Devoted as they are to trickle-down economics, conservatives—Republicans—believe that all economic problems are solved by the "free market," an attitude that evolves into the attitude that if what seems to be a problem is *not* solved by the "free market," then it is not really a problem at all. Thus, while liberals—Democrats—deem inequality to be by far the most important problem in the economy, having generally risen over the past three and a half decades, conservatives and Republicans fail to see it as an issue at all, focusing their concern instead on the tangential issues of trade with China and immigration (and never far in the background is the concern about inflation). The context of all that follows, however, is that by far the most important problem in the economy is inequality, and that inequality is caused by wage stagnation, and that wage stagnation is caused by a productivity/wage disconnect.

As observed in the Introduction, the theory behind trickle-down is that if we upwardly redistribute income and wealth by implementing policies that upwardly redistribute revenues attributable to increased productivity (by lowering tax rates on the rich and corporations, reducing regulations designed to cushion the poor and middle class from the harshness of the market and cut spending on the social safety net programs upon which the middle class and poor rely), then the magic of the "free market" will work: rich and corporations will see returns on their investments increased, thus encouraging them to invest more and thereby increase the number of jobs and raise wages.

However, as President Obama observed, all that actually results is that income and wealth are continually upwardly redistributed, creating conditions similar to those that preceded the Great Depression: Upward redistribution of revenues from increased productivity resulted in a productivity/wage disconnect so that only the rich saw their incomes rise, which resulted in a shortfall in demand temporarily compensated for with massive increases in debt, which lasted until demand had been starved to such a degree that prices collapsed, resulting in massive unemployment and default on the debt and foreclosure on the collateral, and extended economic sluggishness—depression—only cured by massive increases in government spending that injected demand back into the economy. The productivity/wage disconnect of then and now will be addressed below, followed by, in greater detail, how it resulted in wage stagnation and rising inequality, followed by why this disconnect exists again today, even after we already learned our lesson in the Great Depression. Spoiler alert: *We, the American people,* created the productivity/wage disconnect politically, encouraged by conservative, Republican, trickle-down nonsense that took hold because we forgot the lesson of the Great Depression.

THE PRODUCTIVITY/WAGE DISCONNECT

Writing about the period just before the Great Depression, the economist John Kenneth Galbraith, in *The Great Crash, 1929*, observed worker productivity rose 43 percent between 1919 and 1929, yet wage growth was stagnant.[2] A huge and growing disconnect between productivity growth and wage growth—of even greater magnitude than that of the Roaring Twenties—has emerged in the economy since 1980, as illustrated by various analyses. And, of course, this disconnect marked a break from the previous generation for whom wages grew in tandem with productivity growth, thus propelling the massive expansion of the great American middle class. Following are several different analyses of disconnect between productivity and wage growth. Although the results vary based on method of calculation, the percentage of the population addressed and the period for which the gap is calculated, the trend is clear that in the roughly three decades following World War II, the revenues attributable to increased productivity were generously shared with workers. Not surprisingly, during the roughly three and a half decades of trickle-down, with its idea that we're all better off if the revenues from increased productivity go to those at the top, there was much less sharing of such revenues with workers.

The Economic Policy Institute calculated that during the 31 years from 1948 to 1979, productivity rose 108.1 percent, and hourly compensation of production/nonsupervisory workers in the private sector rose 93.4 percent. In contrast, for the 34 years from 1979 to 2013, productivity rose 64.9 percent, while hourly compensation of production/nonsupervisory workers in the private sector rose 8.2 percent.[3] Similarly, based on data gathered by *The New York Times*, George Monbiot observed that between 1947 and 1979, productivity rose 119 percent while the income of the bottom fifth of the population *rose by 122 percent*; in contrast, between 1979 and 2009, productivity rose by 80 percent while the income of the bottom fifth *fell by 4 percent.*[4]

Barbara Garson, in *Down the Up Escalator* (2013) observed, from 1971 through 2007 (thus including the recessions of the 1970s and only part of the three decades of trickle-down), productivity rose 99 percent while real hourly wages rose only 4 percent.[5] Yet another study found productivity grew more than 80 percent from 1979 to 2009—and, if median household incomes had kept pace with productivity since 1970, median household incomes would be nearly *$92,000*, rather than less than $50,000.[6]

While workers' productivity has been rising but their incomes have been held stagnant, as during the period before the Great Depression, they have also been deluded, as they were during the period before the Great Depression, into the conviction that they could live like they were rich, *having everything they wanted—by substituting debt for nonexistent income*—thereby condemning the American economy to multi-decadal multi-trillion dollar bubble-bust cycles, wasting and wiping out wealth on a scale not seen since the Great Depression in successive balance sheet recessions—so-called because they are distinguished by depletion of balance sheets (in Japan's balance sheet recession, corporate balance sheets; in the US's balance sheet recession, household balance sheets).[7] And, given that GDP is made up of nearly 70 percent consumption spending, if the vast majority of Americans are producing more but not earning more, these trickle-down policies must be stifling demand and, therefore, stifling economic growth.

A balance sheet recession, thus, differs from a "typical" recession, which is caused by consumer price inflation that encourages creation of excessive inventories in pursuit of illusory demand—so-called "inventory recessions." And while consumer price inflation, accompanied by higher commodity prices and wages is observed in an inventory recession, balance sheet recessions are distinguished by asset price inflation—higher prices for real estate, stocks and bonds—but lower commodity prices and wages.

Household balance sheets in the US are depleted due to trickle-down's upward redistribution of revenues from increasing productivity, which starved wages. Policymakers then attempted to address the resultant demand shortfall by lowering interest rates and instituting financial deregulation, thereby facilitating substitution of debt for nonexistent income. These policies ultimately exhausted the ability of households to raise any more debt and inflated the real estate bubble which, in turn, inflated the financial bubble which, when it burst, pulled down the stock market and the rest of the economy with it. And, based on recent evidence, these balance sheet recessions appear to be occurring with increasing frequency.

Dean Baker, Co-Director of the Center for Economic and Policy Research, in his 2009 book, *Plunder and Blunder: The Rise and Fall of the Bubble Economy*, reinforced the importance of sharing the benefits of increased productivity to economic stability, observing that we did not have trouble with financial bubbles during our period of shared prosperity from 1945 to 1973 and, while he did not claim to have enough evidence to link bubbles with inequality, he did observe that we did not experience bubbles when income was more equally distributed.[8]

While we may not be able to link bubbles directly with inequality, we can link bubbles to the consequences of denying wage increases corresponding to productivity increases, resulting in inflation of upper incomes which, in turn bids up asset values and inflates bubbles, while at the same time falling real compensation for middle and lower incomes results in a demand shortfall compensated for with easy credit and excessive public debt, leading to excessive consumer debt in support of those inflated asset values, with the result that both inflated upper incomes and easy credit support creation of bubbles ultimately destabilizing the entire economy, leading to balance sheet recession and, potentially, depression.

Other contemporary economists are reaching a similar conclusion. As observed in a 2009 article in *The Wall Street Journal*[9] by Steven Gjerstad (visiting research professor at Chapman University) and Vernon L. Smith (professor of economics at Chapman University and winner of the 2002

Nobel Prize in Economics), we may be in the process of discovering that it was excessive mortgage debt in particular and consumer debt generally, especially among the poor and middle class, that caused the Great Depression and is causing our current depression. And, as will be seen herein, that debt was due to chronic failure to share revenues attributable to increased productivity, which caused a demand shortfall which was addressed by providing low interest rates and irresponsibly loosened lending standards that lured these undercompensated families to their financial doom.

In sum, as conservative Republican economic policies suppressed wages and substituted debt for nonexistent wage increases from 1919 to 1929, so conservative Republican trickle-down policies have suppressed wages over the past three and a half decades and substituted debt, with the most extreme effects felt over the past decade and a half. And, as the earlier result was a stock market bubble that burst in 1929, we have seen a series of bubbles over the past three and a half decades (savings & loans, tech, real estate and financial), each of which burst, destroying trillions of dollars in wealth each time and crashing the stock market, culminating in the latest and largest crash in 2008, and, as 2016 dawns, we may be witnessing a bursting bubble in commodities (such as oil, natural gas, copper, gold, silver, etc.), as indicated by the worst 10-year rolling annualized return for commodities since 1938[10] —bursting of a bubble that was fueled by excessive capital expenditures (CAPEX) encouraged by historically low interest rates.

FAILURE TO SHARE THE REVENUES FROM PRODUCTIVITY GROWTH YIELDS MASSIVE GROWTH IN INEQUALITY

Serf City, Here We Come! Vote Republican for Neofeudalism and Get Neofeudalism

A recurring theme herein will be this observation: Although the economy, as measured by Gross Domestic Product (GDP) has been growing over the past three and a half decades (although more slowly than in the period of 1945-1970s), and productivity has been growing, the revenues attributable to that increased productivity have not been shared with the vast majority of workers, leading to stagnating or falling real (inflation-adjusted) incomes, falling real wealth for most American families, stagnant hourly wages, stagnant job growth, stagnant social mobility, and massive increases in income and wealth inequality.[11]

Two stark examples of this last aspect were illustrated in 2013. Jeff Bezos, founder of Amazon, purchased *The Washington Post* for $250 million. It was observed that this amount was *1 percent* of his net worth of $25 billion. For perspective, this is like a family with $50,000 net worth (by at least one measure, roughly the median for American families) buying a $500 refrigerator.

However, one multibillionaire's ability to control the economy pales in comparison to that of numerous multibillionaires and multimillionaires through investment funds created, for example, to take advantage of historically low interest rates and acquire a sizeable portion of the US housing market, with the accompanying impacts of raising home prices around the country and pricing numerous potential homebuyers out of the market—and raising the risk of creation of another housing bubble.

In a graphic illustration of what "neofeudalism" means, a study by Goldman Sachs reported in August 2013 that nearly *60 percent* of all homes sold in the US in 2012 and the first half of 2013—three times the roughly 20 percent average of years 2005, 2006 2007 and 2008—had been purchased entirely with cash, fueling a run-up in home sales and home prices. With home ownership rates declining and real wages falling, the growing all-cash share of sales was attributed in great part to funds making purchases on behalf of wealthy investors, foreign buyers, and wealthy investors buying for themselves.[12]

Another illustration of this neofeudalism appeared in July 2015 as within the same month it was revealed: (1) US wages and benefits grew in the Second Quarter of 2015 at the slowest pace in 33 years,[13] yet (2) US home sales in June 2015 rose to their highest level since February 2007, and the median price for a previously owned home surged up 6.5 percent from the previous year to a record $236,400,[14] with the result that (3) The US home ownership rate fell to 63.4 percent in the Second Quarter of 2015—the lowest reading since *1967*.[15] This raised concerns that a second housing bubble may be developing, although the impact of this bubble bursting was expected to be less catastrophic due to the fact that there had not been a surge in growth of home ownership nor had there been a surge in homeowners entering into home equity lines of credit (HELOCs) and using their homes as collateral for consumer purchases.

Upward Redistribution of Revenues Attributable to Increased Productivity Results in Increase in Share of GDP to Corporate Profits and Decrease in Share of GDP to Wages

The total failure of trickle-down to deliver on its dual promises of job growth and rising wages, and its overwhelming success at delivering to corporations, is captured in the facts that *since recordkeeping began in 1947: corporate profits are at the highest level as a percentage of GDP*—averaging just above 9 percent (while the historical average for corporate profits as a share of GDP is about 7 percent).[16] Not surprisingly, the annualized growth of the S&P 500 under President Obama is the highest among all presidents going back to Herbert Hoover.[17] In contrast, *wages, as a percentage of GDP, are at their lowest level*;[18] and *the civilian labor force participation rate has fallen back to the level it was in mid-1978.*[19]

If corporations were paying their employees that incremental 2 percent of GDP now going to profits but that historically has gone to wages, this would amount to an additional $362 billion paid in wages (assuming GDP of approximately $18.1 trillion).[20] Recall that the Obama administration stimulus package consisted of injection of $787 billion into the economy—$362 billion would be an additional stimulus of nearly half the size of that.

Trickle-Down's *Income* Beneficiaries: The Top 1%

As observed by Thomas Hungerford of the non-partisan Congressional Research Service: "By far, the largest contributor to increasing income inequality . . . was changes in income from capital gains and dividends."[21] In accord, a study for the National Bureau of Economic Research (NBER) by MIT economists Frank Levy and Peter Temin found that the richest 1 percent of tax filers claimed *80 percent* of all tax gains reported in federal income tax returns between 1980 and 2005.[22] The result of this upward redistribution of revenues from increased productivity is that, *including realized capital gains*, the share of income attributable to the top 10 percent of households in 2012 equaled 50.6 percent of national income—the highest level since the IRS income series started in 1917, according to University of California, Berkeley economist Emmanuel Saez (although, due to higher top tax rates, it had fallen back to 48.9 percent in 2013).[23]

Below is a table summarizing results of income data gathered from IRS records (and, as distinguished from Census Bureau data, inclusive of income from capital gains) by Saez and his colleague Thomas Piketty (Paris School of Economics). Some of that data has been analyzed by the Economic Policy Institute, which teased out of it trends in income distribution since 1917 and upward redistribution since 1981. That data is supplemented by Saez's observations of income distribution during the first three years of the recovery from the 2007 recession (2009 through 2012)—bear in mind that income growth after recessions is typically widespread and robust, as shown in Table 7.1.[24]

Notice from the below that the naturally upwardly redistributive tendencies of capitalism are so strong that even taking into account the period of downwardly distributive policies from the beginning of the New Deal in

Table 7.1. Income Inequality—Shares of Real National Income Growth

Period	Bottom 90%	Top 10%	Bottom 99%	Top 1%
1917-1981	69%	31%		
1981-2008	4%	96%		
1997-2008	0%	100%		
2009-2012			5%	95%

1933 through the 1970s, the top 10 percent of incomes were getting 3 times as much income growth than their proportionate share—and as those downwardly distributive policies were weakened they received nearly 10 times their share, or nearly all the income gains. Other observations from the Saez and Piketty data: During the years 1947 through 1985, the concentration of income (including capital gains) in the 1 percent remained relatively flat, never exceeding 13 percent; commencing in 1986 income concentration began rising, ultimately increasing more than *85 percent* to 23.50 percent of all income in 2007—the highest concentration of income since 1928, the eve of the Great Depression (then 23.94 percent). And, although the concentration began falling after 2007, as observed above, it has begun rising again.[25]

Those at the very highest of the income scale did the best, especially during the last three decades, in percentage change in share of national after-tax income, as illustrated by the results of the 2013 CBO study introduced in Chapter 1, as shown in Table 7.2.[26]

With the revenues attributable to increasing productivity being upwardly redistributed, as can be seen from above, the share of after-tax income attributable to the top 10 percent has grown, but nowhere nearly as much as the share attributable to the top 1 percent. And, relative wage stagnation has resulted for the vast majority of Americans. Amazingly, as observed in Chapter 4, the median wage for American workers—that is, the wage level that half of American workers make less than or equal to—was just $28,851.21.[27] Only about 15% of American workers make more than $70,000.

Another trusted measure of income is that of the triennial Federal Reserve Survey of Consumer Finances (SCF).[28] The survey found that the real median income for families headed by someone under 35 years of age in 2013

Table 7.2. Shares of After-Tax Income by Income Group, 1979 and 2010

Income Group	1979	2010	Percentage Increase / Decrease[a]
Lowest Quintile	6.9%	5.4%	-22%
Second Quintile	12.3%	10.3%	-16%
Middle Quintile	16.6%	15.2%	-8%
Fourth Quintile	22.3%	21.4%	-4%
81st – 90th Percentile	14.8%	14.7%	-1%
91st – 95th Percentile	9.4%	9.7%	3%
96th – 99th Percentile	10.6%	11.8%	11%
Top 1 Percent	7.5%	13.2%	76%

a. Percentage change in share of national after-tax income.

had declined by 6% from 1989, even though there were more college graduates in that group in 2013 than in 1989. Conversely, the age group for whom real income had grown the most of the past quarter century was that covering ages 65 to 74.[29]

As the headline read in a 2010 article in *The Wall Street Journal*, the "US economy is increasingly tied to the rich," as indicated by research from Moody's Analytics showing that the top 5 percent of Americans by income account for 37 percent of all consumer outlays—nearly as much as the bottom 80 percent (39.5 percent). The article observed that the US may be becoming a "Plutonomy"—an economy that depends on the spending and investing of the wealthy.[30] The article failed to observe, however: A Plutonomy is doomed to failure because capitalism only works if it works for the workers, providing sufficiently high enough wages that these wages can maintain and grow demand.

Trickle-Down's *Wealth* Beneficiaries: The Top 0.1%

As observed by the Pew Research Center, America's wealth gap between middle-income and upper-income families is the widest on record, and the gap has widened rapidly in recent years.[31] Similarly, New York University economist Edward N. Wolff observed that wealth (net worth) inequality as late as 1983 was close to its 1962 level, although it had reduced sharply from 1969 to 1976 before sharply rising from 1976 to 1983. Total wealth concentration in the top 1 percent was 33.8 percent in 1983; in the next wealthiest 9 percent of households, 34.3 percent; and in the bottom 90 percent of households, 31.9 percent (thus, roughly a 1/3—1/3—1/3 distribution). In 2010, the top 1 percent's share of wealth was 35.4 percent; the next 9 percent of households, 41.3 percent, and the bottom 90 percent, just 23.3 percent; more amazing however, was that the top 20 percent held 88.9 percent of all wealth. Financial (non-home) wealth concentration in the top 1 percent was even greater in 2010 at 42.1 percent, and the top 20 percent held 95.4 percent of all financial wealth. To repeat: In 2010, the top 20 percent of American households held about *89 percent of the total wealth* and *more than 95 percent of the financial wealth* in the country.[32] (In 2014, Philip Vermuelen, a senior economist at the European Central Bank, in a working paper presented evidence of "missed" data on wealthy US households that pushed the share of wealth held by the 1 percent to between 35 percent and 37 percent;[33] similarly, as observed by the Tax Justice Network based on its research, there are massive amounts of wealth in offshore accounts unaccounted for.[34])

A study based on Census Bureau research found that from 2009 to 2011, the top 7 percent of households saw their wealth rise 28 percent, from a mean of $1.7 million to $2.5 million each, while the bottom 93 percent of households saw their wealth fall by a mean of 4 percent, or $6,000 each.[35]

Based on data from the Panel Study of Income Dynamics (PSID), a nationally representative survey collected since 1968, the Russell Sage Foundation issued a report, the findings of which were consistent with those above.[36] That study found that looking at the entire period from 1984 to 2013, the inflation-adjusted net worth for the 95th percentile nearly doubled, the 75th percentile increased by about a third, the median fell by 20 percent, and for the 25th percentile, after starting at a very low level in 1984 fell more than 60 percent by 2013.

The Federal Reserve Survey of Consumer Finances also provides information on wealth (net worth). Among its findings, for the year 2013: The average net worth for the bottom half of American households—62 million American households—was a mere $11,000. In real (inflation-adjusted) terms, that figure was *half* the level of 1989! The top 3 percent of American households held over 54.4 percent of America's wealth. The share of income held by the next 7 percent of American households hovered between 19 and 22 percent over the past 25 years, and in 2013 was 20.9 percent; accordingly, the share of wealth held by the bottom 90 percent fell from 33.2 percent in 1989 to 24.7 percent in 2013. Regarding financial assets (stocks, bonds, mutual funds and private pensions): The wealthiest 5 percent of households owned nearly two-thirds of all such assets; the bottom half of households, just 2 percent.

While the SCF is based on survey results, a study conducted by Emmanuel Saez (the University of California, Berkeley) and Gabriel Zucman (the University of California, Berkeley, and the London School of Economics) was based on projections of wealth derived from comprehensive data on capital income such as dividends, interest, rents and business profits reported on individual income tax returns. The table below is adapted from this analysis and illustrates that wealth is becoming more concentrated even within the top 1 percent.[37] Saez and Zucman found that the bottom 90% of households are poorer today than they were in 1987, and that the next 9% of households were poorer than in 1998—so that the bottom 99% of households had endured a lost decade and a half and was poorer in 2014 than in 1998.[38] The top 0.1%, including 160,000 families with total assets of more than $20 million, saw its share of total wealth rise from 7% in the late 1970s to 22% in 2012 (a level almost as high as in 1929)—versus a 23% share of the *bottom 90%* (down from a peak of 36% in the mid-1980s)—thus, *the top 0.1% of American families own almost as much as the bottom 90%.*[39]

And, working up the wealth scale, the top 0.01% (the top one-hundredth of 1%, consisting of the richest 16,000 families, with wealth of at least $111 million), saw their share of national wealth nearly double since 2002, to 11.2% of the nation's wealth.[40] And, the conclusion of the authors, that the rise of wealth inequality is almost entirely due to the rise of the top 0.1% wealth share, was also similar to that of the Federal Reserve's SCF.

Table 7.3. Shares of Wealth among the Top 1%

Wealth Group	Shares of Wealth among the Top 1%	
	1980	2012
Top 1% - 0.5%	6.9%	7.3%
Top 0.5% - 0.1%	9.4%	12.5%
Top 0.1% - 0.01%	5.4%	10.8%
Top 0.01%	2.6 %	11.2%

Resultant Job Losses Attributable to Trickle-Down

In a paper published by the NBER in August 2012,[41] occupations were divided into (1) "non-routine cognitive," consisting of "managerial, professional and technical workers;" (2) "routine cognitive," consisting of "office and administrative support;" (3) "routine manual," consisting of "blue collar" jobs and (4) "non-routine manual," consisting of "service" jobs. Recovery of jobs was observed in the occupational categories of "non-routine cognitive," "non-routine manual," and "routine" (combining "routine cognitive and "routine manual") over the 25 months following each of three recessions deemed herein inventory recessions (1970, 1975 and 1982) and the three recessions deemed herein balance sheet recessions (1991, 2001 and 2009).

Figure 5 in the NBER report, presenting recoveries in non-routine cognitive, non-routine manual and routine occupations during the 25 months after the *inventory recessions* of 1970, 1975 and 1982 reflected that, after the 1970 recession, within the 25 months following that recession, routine and non-routine cognitive occupations had recovered jobs lost during the recession (only non-routine manual had not recovered). In the 25 months following the 1975 inventory recession, all three occupational categories had recovered; after the 1982 recession, all three occupational categories had recovered robustly.

Figure 6, addressing the 25-month periods following the *balance sheet recessions* of 1991, 2001 and 2009 presented an ominous trend. In the 25 months following the 1991 balance sheet recession, only non-routine cognitive and non-routine manual occupations had recovered the jobs lost during the recession; routine occupations had not. In the 25 months following the 2001 balance sheet recession, only non-routine manual occupations had recovered the jobs lost during the recession; non-routine cognitive and routine occupations had not. And, in the 25 months following the 2009 balance sheet recession, *none of the occupational categories had recovered the jobs lost during the recession* (nor did any of the three even exhibit hopeful trends). Thus, *chronic employment stagnation has been relentlessly working its way up through the economy* in successive balance sheet recessions under trickle-down.

Why Revenues from Productivity Growth Are Not Shared: *We* Demand They Not Be

As observed previously, we, the American voters, have demanded implementation of trickle-down policies—demanded them when we voted for Republicans—and accompanying this demand has been our insistence that the revenues attributable to *our* increased productivity not be shared with us.

From 1945 through the mid-1970s, productivity was growing and income gains were widely shared, creating the great American middle class. By various measures, the increased revenues attributable to increased productivity have been, over the past three decades, and continuing through today, redistributed away from wages and salaries for the 99 percent and instead toward wages and salaries for the 1 percent, stock prices, corporate profits, executive bonuses, dividend payouts, and cash for corporate treasuries.

Nonetheless, various other possible explanations have been offered for this upward redistribution, most prominently globalization and technology, failure of the education system, decline in union membership and the historical trend of returns on capital exceeding overall economic growth—but, while all true, these are inadequate as explanations for the productivity/wage disconnect because what all these explanations have in common is the misperception that these conditions *force* employers to hold down wages and redistribute revenues from increased productivity to themselves and shareholders.

Globalization and Technology

Globalization and the growth of technology are often blamed for the divergence in economic conditions between the rich and everyone else but, while these factors can result in growing inequality, government policy can counteract that trend, as it did in the three decades immediately following World War II. Other developed nations have had to contend with the same global economic climate and technological growth, yet inequality in the US, after starting in the 1970s at an already higher level, rose more rapidly over the past three decades than in any other nation in the OECD, according to a 2010 report by the OECD.[42]

There is a tendency to imagine that the economy has never before faced challenges from technology and globalization on a scale comparable to the present, however, Congress was concerned enough about the impact of technology that it convened a commission named the National Committee on Technology, Automation and Economic Progress to study the phenomenon, and the commission released its report titled "Technology and the American Economy"—*in 1966*. The report observed that the "technological revolution in agriculture" had pushed many African Americans off of farms into cities looking for jobs—"But many arrived just when . . . advancing technology has been reducing the numbers of these semi-skilled and unskilled manufacturing jobs for which they could qualify."[43] Thus, even in the 1960s, the impacts of what we came to call the "Information Age" or "Information Revolution" were being felt, as will be addressed in great detail in Chapter 9.

Joseph Schumpeter famously observed in 1942 (in *Capitalism, Socialism and Democracy*) that the essence of capitalism is "creative destruction," and there are two drivers of that creative destruction—globalization and technology[44]:

> The opening up of new markets, foreign or domestic, and the organizational development from the craft shop and factory to such concerns as U.S. Steel illustrate the same process of industrial mutation—if I may use that biological term—that incessantly revolutionizes [citation omitted] the economic structure *from within*, incessantly destroying the old one, incessantly creating a new one. This process of Creative Destruction is the essential fact about capitalism. It is what capitalism consists in and what every capitalist concern has got to live in. [Italics original.]

What Schumpeter was observing, however, regarding technology, had been in existence since the dawn of the Industrial Revolution. The cotton gin was invented in 1793 and the steamboat was tested as early as 1807, just to list two examples of early technology that would have a massive effect on the economic circumstances of labor. Regarding globalization: In 1295, Marco Polo returned to Venice after having spent 24 years traveling overland from there to China and returning via ship through the South China Sea, the Indian Ocean and the Arabian Gulf. Venetian and Genovese merchants followed over the ensuing centuries, and were followed by merchants from Portugal, Spain, Holland, France, England and Belgium. The British established colonies for trade in North America and in India in the 1600s, and in Africa in the 1700s.

Thus, when Adam Smith was writing *The Wealth of Nations—in 1776—* globalization and technology were very familiar to him. Recall the quote from him in Chapter 5 where he condemned the rich because their actions taken pursuant to shortsighted self-interest, in combination with "the silent and insensible operation of foreign commerce and manufactures gradually brought about" miserable conditions for the workers (more on this in Chapter 13).

The facts of technological change and globalization are not new. What is new is the dedication of average Americans to the idea that government must not intervene in the economy, as it did extensively from the New Deal through the 1970s, to help offset the impacts of technology and globalization, with the result that they have seen their wages become disconnected from their productivity and, consequently, their incomes and wealth shrink in real terms.[45]

Failures of the Education System

Another popular explanation offered for rising inequality is decline in the quality of education. However, this explanation is lacking as well, because GDP is continuing to grow, and productivity continues to grow. If human capital had been in decline for these past three and a half decades, we would have been observing stagnation of productivity over this entire period—but we have not been. What we are observing is productivity growing, but increasing shares of the revenue attributable to that increased productivity are going to the wealthy and corporations—as opposed to being shared with the workers who contributed to that growth in productivity, in contrast to the earlier post-World War II period.

However, the most damning statistic of all regarding the simplistic idea that we can restore growth in wages if only we can get more young people to graduate from high school and college is the observation from a 2012 analysis by the Economic Policy Institute that real wages for recent college graduates and recent high school graduates were lower in real terms in 2011 than in 2000.[46]

Another study, conducted by two former Census Bureau employees on behalf of Sentier Research, focused on the post-recession "recovery" period of June 2009 through June 2013—*during which productivity rose by 7.7 percent*—and found that over that period, among households headed by people with only a high school diploma real median income *declined by 9.3 percent*; among households headed by people with an associate degree, real median income *declined by 8.6 percent*; and among households headed by people with a bachelor's degree or more, real median income *declined by 6.5 percent.*[47] A later study found that over the period 1992 to 2013, the median net worth of African Americans *who finished college* fell nearly 56 percent (adjusted for inflation), while the median net worth of African Americans without college degrees fell only 3.8 percent—while the great fall in net worth for those with a college degree was due in great part to the decline in real estate prices, and the lesser fall for those without college degrees was due in great part to their having less to lose, the fact remains that a college degree is no guarantee of a rising standard of living.[48]

Of course, the circumstances for those without a high school education are even worse. The median wages (in 2013 dollars) of working men age 30 to 45 without a high school diploma in 1990 was $31,000—by 2013 their earnings had plummeted 20 percent to $25,500.[49] Thus, of course we should continue to encourage young people to continue their education, but based on all the above evidence we cannot truthfully tell them that by increasing their productivity through education they can expect to raise their standard of living—because the evidence shows the revenues attributable to their increased productivity will simply be upwardly redistributed.

Decline in Union Membership

As union membership has declined, the middle class's share of aggregate income—the middle class defined as the middle three quintiles (middle 60 percent of total population)—has declined as well. For example, the union membership rate (the percent of wage and salary workers who were members of a union) in 1983 was 20.1 percent, while in 2010 it was 11.9 percent—thus, union membership from 1983 to 2010 declined by *40.8 percent.*[50]

The decline in union membership absolutely is cause, in part, of the decline in the middle class's share of aggregate income, and also the decline in real median income from 1999 through the present. But if union membership promoted the retention of the revenues attributable to increased productivity of union members and other members of the middle class, then union membership would likely not have declined to the degree it has.

Returns on Capital Have Grown Faster than the Growth of the Economy as a Whole

As observed in the table previously, even during the period from 1917 to 1981, the top 10 percent saw a disproportionately large 31 percent share of the growth in real national income, indicating that even in an atmosphere in which government policy has been oriented toward attempting to reduce inequality there is a natural upwardly redistributive tendency of capitalism. This tendency of capitalism to upwardly redistribute income and wealth was explained by Thomas Piketty, in his 2014 book *Capital in the Twenty-First Century*, as due to the fact that returns on capital typically exceed overall economic growth, so that capital grows into an ever-larger share of the economy versus wages in ordinary income. Yet, as also observed herein, profits attributable to corporations have also grown into an ever-larger share of the economy versus wages in ordinary income, but it is unclear how this relates to returns on capital typically exceeding the overall economic growth rate. Instead, it appears that returns on capital typically exceeding overall economic growth is an explanation for rising inequality similar to increasing education, increasing globalization and decreasing union strength—all tend to exacerbate inequality, but, as a society, we have historically had values that led us to favor government policies that ensure revenues attributable to increased productivity are shared—this is the explanation for increasing inequality favored herein, as will be explored below, and, as will also be seen below, it is an explanation in which Piketty himself joined in an article which he co-authored with Emmanuel Saez, which was published about the time his book was published in the US.

Why Revenues from Increased Productivity Are Being Upwardly Redistributed: Values, Norms and Institutions Were Changed by Politics

The most likely reason benefits of productivity increases have not been shared throughout the economy since 1980 as they were before was identified by MIT economists Frank Levy and Peter Temin: "institutions and norms."[51] Paul Krugman, in a 1996 *Mother Jones* article[52] gave a similar reason for rising inequality: "The answer is that values changed—not the middle class values politicians keep talking about, but the kind of values that helped sustain the middle-class society we have lost." He continued, "In short, though America was a society with large disparities between economic classes, it had an egalitarian ethic that limited those disparities. That ethic is gone." He elaborated on this phenomenon in his book, *The Conscience of a Liberal* (2007), in terms that echoed Levy and Temin: "Since the 1970s, norms and institutions in the United States have changed in ways that either encouraged or permitted sharply higher inequality. Where, however, did the norms and institutions come from? The answer appears to be politics."[53] Similarly, Levy and Temin concluded, "Only a reorientation of government policy can restore the general prosperity of the postwar boom, can recreate an equitable distribution of productivity gains where a rising tide lifts all boats."[54] And, fellow Nobel Prize winner Joseph Stiglitz concurred, in a 2014 op-ed in *The New York Times*, observing that we are choosing inequality with our policies and politics that are driving the upward redistribution of revenues attributable to our increased productivity.[55]

This conclusion, that trickle-down policy upwardly redistributes income and wealth, and that only a reorientation of institutions will reverse this upward redistribution, is also supported by a November 2011 NBER paper by Thomas Piketty, Emmanuel Saez and Stefanie Stantcheva (MIT Department of Economics).[56] They tested one aspect of the theory that institutional reform under Reagan in the US and Thatcher in the UK upwardly redistributed incomes—the effect of changes in tax rates on pre-tax incomes—and observed "international evidence shows a strong correlation between top tax rate cuts and increases in top income shares in OECD countries since 1975." In a related observation, they found that the top 0.1 percent of households earn about half of all capital gains.[57] Similarly, *The State of Working America, 12 th Edition*, published in November 2012 concluded that policy changes such as reduced support for unions and minimum wages have undermined incomes.[58]

Finally, as observed above, Thomas Piketty and Emmanuel Saez, in an article they authored published in *Science* magazine in May 2014, agreed that the level of inequality in societies depends on their institutions and policies.[59] Accordingly, Piketty, in *Capital in the Twenty-First Century* (2014), proposed, to counter rising inequality, more progressive taxation—in particular, revival of estate taxes—as one solution, along with a global wealth tax.[60]

Thus, the question of why there has been a growing disconnect between increases in productivity and increases in wages is best answered by reference to *values, norms and institutions that have been molded by and, in turn, mold, our politics*. And, the persistence of trickle-down in the face of overwhelming evidence of its failure is a tribute to the sociological phenomenon of the persistence of bad ideas perpetuated by faith divorced from fact.

Trickle-Down Policies Created the Balance Sheet Recessions and Sluggish Recovery of the Great Depression and Current Trickle-Down Depression

As the Great Depression followed three decades of trickle-down philosophy applied during the Gilded Age and the Roaring Twenties, so the current depressionary feedback loop is holding down wages, employment and demand, reinforced by recurrent balance sheet recessions, amply illustrating that *capitalism, itself*, only works when government intervenes in the economy to ensure benefits from increased productivity flow to all workers.

As noted in the Introduction, Paul Krugman, in his 2012 book, *End This Depression Now!*, made an observation in great part ignored by most Americans: The United States is in a depression. Liberals and Democrats have, perhaps, been leery of agreeing with Krugman for fear of conservatives blaming President Obama for creating the current depression. It is critical, however, to understand what Krugman means by the term "depression"—with reference to the definition of John Maynard Keynes, he said a depression is a situation in which an economy is capable of remaining in "a chronic condition of subnormal activity for a considerable period without any marked tendency either towards recovery or towards complete collapse."[61]

This definition of depression differs from the popular misconception that a depression is a really bad recession—deeper and/or longer lasting than a "typical" recession. However, that is not how Keynes defined depression, or how Krugman defines it. In a depression, an economy can go into a recession, as defined by the NBER, but can come out of that recession and yet remain in stagnant conditions. Krugman has observed that this is what has happened to the US economy, having been in a depression since 2007.

As portrayed by the chart "Percent Job Losses in Post WWII Recessions" appearing at the Calculated Risk finance and economics blog site maintained by former technology executive Bill McBride, after all the post-World War II recessions termed herein inventory recessions (1948, 1953, 1957, 1960, 1969, 1974, 1980 and 1981), recovery in employment was swift—characterized by variations on a "V" curve. In contrast, after the three recessions deemed herein to be balance sheet recessions (1990, 2001 and 2007[62]), employment recovery was more in the shape of a bowl, with employment recovery after the 1990 recession taking 32 months; after the 2001 recession, 47 months; and after the 2007 recession, 76 months (the total number of jobs in the economy in January 2008 peak, 138,365,000, was not eclipsed again until May 2014's jobs number of 138,463,000).[63]

MODELS ILLUSTRATING THE EFFECTS OF TRICKLE-DOWN

The Balloon Economy Model: Illustration of an Economy in an Inflationary Episode versus an Episode of Credit Overstimulation

The term "bubble" is often used to describe the nation's economic conditions since 1980 (from the savings & loan, real estate and junk bond bubble of the late 1980s; to the tech bubble and bond bubble exemplified by the collapse of hedge fund Long Term Capital Management of the late 1990s; to the real estate, finance and stock market bubble in roughly 2005 through 2009), but a better analogy for contrasting what happened in the economy during the inflationary episode in the 1970s and during the recent credit overstimulation episode involves a balloon. (Of course, another way of describing an episode of credit overstimulation is an episode of *debt overstimulation*—poorly compensating for years of falling real wages for the middle class and poor.)

Imagine that you took a deflated hot dog-shaped balloon and drew on it three circles, each right next to the other, and labeled each circle from left to right with what economists call the "factors of production": "labor," "land" and "capital." To help visualize what happened in the economy in the 1970s, pinch off the "capital" circle and begin to inflate the balloon. This represents what the government under liberal Keynesian guidance did, supporting loose (expansionist) monetary policy while placing institutional collars over the flow of funds, favoring labor over capital with rising minimum wage laws, strengthened power for unions, and restrictions on trade. Observe that both wages for labor and the price of land (not only real estate, but also commodities) expand at the expense of return on capital. This illustrates an economy under consumer price inflation.

Now, deflate the balloon and pinch off the "labor" circle and begin to inflate the balloon again. This is essentially what the government under conservative trickle-down-supply-side-crony capitalist policies does, supporting moderately expansionary monetary policy (ever-wary of inflation) and reduced trade barriers while removing institutional collars over the flow of funds, favoring flow of funds to capital while restricting flow to labor as it only slowly raises minimum wage rates and weakens union power. Observe that both return on capital and the price of land expand at the expense of wages for labor, and asset price inflation results (with rising prices for land and for equities).

Inflationary episodes and credit overstimulation bubbles are, thus, but two sides of the same coin of monetary and/or fiscal overstimulation of the economy. Overstimulation of the demand side of the economy leads to consumer price inflation, and a post-inflationary episode of economic decline is an *inventory* recession. Overstimulation of the supply side leads to credit overstimulation, and asset price inflation, and a post-credit overstimulation episode of economic decline is called a *balance sheet* recession because credit overstimulation leads to exhaustion of credit-raising ability.

The Trickle-Down Model of America as a Giant Malevolently Managed Company Store

A more disturbing way of envisioning what has happened over the past three and a half decades under trickle-down economics is to imagine the American economy as a giant, malevolently managed company store, practicing debt peonage by serving the company workers, whose wages are suppressed, and compensating for resultant demand shortfall by expanding credit, leading them further and further into debt:

Middle class and poor Americans have been denied wage gains commensurate with productivity gains—income gains from increased productivity overwhelmingly went to those at the top of the economy (capital) rather than workers (labor). We can see that after real median men's wages peaked in 1973, married couples responded by sending wives into the workforce.[64] Thus, an illusion of household income stability was maintained for many years with the substitution of two incomes for one. Even that ultimately failed, however, as real median *household* incomes peaked in 1999. Couples then responded by, first, working longer hours, and later, by taking multiple jobs.

To maintain their standard of living, Americans stopped saving, then took from their savings, then took from their 401(k)s and IRAs, and then took on record levels of debt secured by their homes in the form of home equity lines of credit (HELOCs). When the incomes of both spouses proved insufficient to sustain their living standards, couples stopped saving. After they consumed their savings, they began tapping their 401(k) retirement accounts to greater degree than in the past—the Federal Reserve found in 2010 9.3 percent of taxpayers with retirement accounts incurred early withdrawal penalties, up from 7.9 percent 2004.[65]

They also began borrowing against the value of their homes (using home equity lines of credit) to finance purchases of consumer goods. This resulted in household debt rising to a record 133 percent of disposable personal income in 2008—a nearly 50 percent increase over the 90 percent level of the previous decade.[66]

As chronicled in an insightful 2005 report from the Federal Reserve Board of San Francisco,[67] rather amazingly, as recently as the 1980s, the personal saving rate for Americans averaged 9.0 percent of personal after-tax income; by the 1990s, it had declined to an average of 5.2 percent; by the 2000-2005 period, it had declined to an average of 1.9 percent—and in 2005, as observed above, dipped *below zero* (i.e., went *negative*, meaning that U.S. consumers were spending more than 100 percent of their after-tax income).

During the period from the mid-1960s through the mid-1980s, household debt (home mortgage plus consumer debt) generally averaged around 50 percent of GDP and around 65 percent of disposable personal income. In 2008, household debt *had doubled* to 100 percent of GDP and about 130 percent of disposable personal income.[68] This increased financialization of the economy was accompanied by high tolerance of fraud, which had a corrosive effect on the continued functioning of the financial industry, a concern raised by Senator Elizabeth Warren (D-MA) and by the economist Simon Johnson.[69]

As families exhausted their ability to take on more debt, and federal tax revenues failed to fund federal spending, federal government debt rose to a percentage of GDP not seen since World War II. Total U.S. credit market (private and public) debt as a percentage of GDP peaked during the Great Depression in 1933 at 260 percent, then remained below 175 percent from 1936 until 1982. It then continually rose (only slowing down its rate of growth during the Clinton years) until it exceeded *375* percent in 2007.[70]

The federal government eagerly fed the debt machine. The Federal Reserve lowered interest rates to near zero. Regulations imposing lending standards were continually reduced or ignored. This orgy of debt led to ever-riskier lending to enable financially unqualified buyers to purchase in a market of rapidly escalating home prices. Simultaneously, children, to finance college, took on more debt, too. If they were unable to find jobs when they graduated, many then returned home to live with their parents. Finally, reversing the trend of elderly parents moving in with their middle-aged children, many parents, as middle-aged children, and their children, began moving in with elderly parents.[71]

Meanwhile, American families are squeezed. Health care costs and education expenses continued to rise faster than did real wages over the past three decades, and unemployment rates and long-term unemployment levels stubbornly remained high. Furthermore, as observed by former columnist for *The New York Times*, Bob Herbert,[72] the burden of unemployment and underemployment continued to fall most heavily on the poor, as illustrated in a study by the Center for Labor Market Studies at Northeastern University in Boston. Researchers there divided American households into ten groups based on annual household income. They then analyzed labor conditions in each of the groups during the fourth quarter of 2009. The highest group, with household incomes of $150,000 or more, had an unemployment rate during that quarter of 3.2 percent. The next highest, with incomes of $100,000 to $149,999, had an unemployment rate of 4 percent. By contrast, the lowest group, with household incomes of $12,499 or less, suffered with an unemployment rate of 30.8 percent. The next lowest group, with incomes of $12,500 to $20,000, had an unemployment rate of 19.1 percent.

And Millennials have been singled out to bear a disproportionate burden of trickle-down's failure. The generation born between the early 1980s and 2000—the Millennials—have suffered disproportionately under trickle-down, especially over the past decade and a half.[73] From 1995 to 2000, inflation-adjusted wages for recent college graduates rose 19.1 percent and for recent high school graduates, 15.4 percent. From 2000-2012, inflation-adjusted wages for recent college graduates *fell 8.5 percent*, and for recent high school graduates, *fell 12.7 percent*.[74] Between 1989 and 2011, the percentage of recent college graduates with employer-provided health care *dropped by nearly half,* from 60.1 percent to 31.1 percent; the percentage of high school graduates with employer-provided health care *dropped by more than two-thirds,* from 23.5 percent to just 7.1 percent.[75] The share of households owing student debt more than doubled between 1989 and 2010, and the average amount of debt per household nearly tripled, to $26,682,[76] while in 2012 state and local spending per college student, adjusted for inflation, hit a 25-year low.[77]

In 1984, the ratio of household wealth of a typical household headed up by someone age 65 or over versus someone under age 35 was 10:1; by 2009, the ratio had increased *by nearly five times*, to 47:1.[78] Not only is there an upward redistribution of incomes and wealth from younger to older Americans, but there is also a disproportionately heavier cost-of-living burden falling on younger Americans as the public sector shrinks versus the market, and it is tougher for younger Americans to find jobs than in the past because older Americans, having seen their incomes stagnate, are clinging to their jobs and working later in life, thereby crowding out younger workers.[79] No wonder, then, that nearly a third—about 32 percent—of America's 18-to 34-years-olds live with their parents (the average vacillated around 27 to 28 percent from 1989 through 2004).[80]

And, while the upper age in the youngest age group in a 2015 three-part study by the Federal Reserve Bank of St. Louis was 40 and, thus, slightly older than Millennials, the study's findings were relevant. The series was titled "The Demographics of Wealth: How Age, Education and Race Separate Thrivers from Strugglers in Today's Economy," and the third essay was titled "Essay No. 3: Age, Birth Year and Wealth." It addressed changes in median wealth of families in three different age groups over the period from 1989 to 2013. Median wealth for a family whose head of household was under 40 dropped by more than 28 percent (from $20,000 to $14,000); median wealth for a family whose head of household was between 41 and 61 fell by 31 percent (from $154,000 to $106,000); and median wealth for a family whose head of household was 62 and older rose 40 percent (from $150,000 to $210,000).[81]

As an aside of hopefulness, Millennials have demonstrated that fewer of their generation than of their parents' are fooled by the trickle-down delusion. As revealed in surveys, most recently in March 2014, more of them are liberal (31 percent) than conservative (29 percent; the remaining 39 percent are moderate).[82]

Regarding this redistribution of wealth from younger to older households, a 2011 Pew Research Center report observed regarding economic trends over the quarter century from 1984 to 2009, median net worth of American householders younger than 35 *fell by 68 percent* (in 2010 dollars, from $11,521 to $3,662), while median net worth for householders 65 and over *rose by 42 percent* (again, in 2010 dollars, from $120,457 to $170,494).[83] The same report observed diverging trends in poverty as well. Admirably, the share of households 65 and older in poverty fell by 2/3 from 33 percent in 1967 to 11 percent in 2010—however, over the same period the share of households younger than 35 in poverty nearly doubled from 12 percent to 22 percent (more on this below).

President Kennedy's quote, "A rising tide lifts all boats," repeated by President Reagan, captured the belief that GDP growth would translate to broadening prosperity. However, we now realize that is not the case. As is illustrated in a 2014 study by the Economic Policy Institute,[84] prior to 1973 (the year of the first of the oil price spikes in the 1970s), economic growth and poverty reduction had moved in tandem. Since then, as we have disconnected productivity growth from wage growth, the poverty rate has remained in the 12 to 15 percent range—higher than it was in the years preceding 1980. A more accurate analogy regarding the economy might be that a top-heavy boat sinks *everyone* on board.[85]

The economic facts regarding the generation of Americans under 35 years of age were well captured in an article by Joel Kotkin that appeared in *Newsweek* just over three months before the 2012 election—its title: "Generation Screwed."[86] In his article, Kotkin observed that, in addition to the loss in net worth experienced by this generation, the unemployment rate for people between the ages of 18 and 29 was 12 percent—half again as high as the national average at that time. Additionally, this group bears student loan debt on average of nearly $27,000 each and credit card and other kinds of debt of $12,700. Finally, the American Bar Association has revealed that among 2011 law school graduates, only 55 percent found a full-time job in the legal field within nine months after graduation, and first-year law school enrollment in 2013 had declined to its lowest level since 1977.[87]

Finally, in a succinct opinion piece in July 2015, Steven Rattner observed that Millennials between 18 and 34 are earning less today (adjusted for inflation) than their same age cohort at any time since 1980, their median net wealth is down 43 percent from the Gen Xers of 1995, and yet they have attended college in record numbers.[88]

AUSTERITY CAUSES SLOW GROWTH, WHICH INCREASES DEFICITS

Shortage of demand, in the past, has been addressed by fiscal stimulus, however, with the triumph of trickle-down, economists, commentators, politicians and others enamored with trickle-down theory obsess with concern about government (local, state and federal) ability to pay off debt rather than trying to help suffering members of the middle class and poor with government spending to spur job growth.

Trickle-down "Austerians" received support from economists Carmen Reinhart (University of Maryland) and Kenneth Rogoff (Harvard) who observed in their 2009 book, *This Time Is Different: Eight Centuries of Financial Folly*,[89] accumulation of excessive government debt inevitably leads to economic misery. A few months after the book was published Reinhart, in a *Forbes* article, characterized a 90 percent ratio of "gross government debt" to GDP as a tipping point beyond which economic growth is impaired,[90] concerns she reiterated in testimony before a bipartisan congressional fiscal commission a few months later.[91] "Gross government debt" was at 90 percent around year-end 2010. Reinhart and Rogoff issued a paper in 2010, "Growth in a Time of Debt," repeating their conclusion—one which other economists had trouble replicating, an effort complicated by their refusal to share their raw data analysis. University of Massachusetts economists Thomas Herndon, Michael Ash and Robert Pollin eventually were given the critical data spreadsheets and found, in results widely reported in 2013, that a spreadsheet coding error skewed the results. They concluded that the average real GDP growth rate for countries carrying a public debt-to-GDP ratio of over 90 percent was not the -0.1 percent as published by Reinhart and Rogoff but actually 2.2 percent. Further, they found no breakpoint beyond which growth falls off rapidly.[92] Their conclusion was supported by an IMF Working Paper published in February 2014.[93]

This finding tends to support numerous economists, among them, Paul Krugman. Krugman expressed concern for the broader problem that we may have causality reversed: stagnant growth may cause higher deficits because of resultant shortfall in revenues, as opposed to the traditional concern that rising deficits result in stagnant growth.[94] (This concern regarding reverse causality was shared by Yale University economist and 2013 Nobel Prize winner Robert Shiller in a 2011 article titled "Debt and Delusion."[95]) For examples, Krugman pointed to how the great decline in GDP immediately after World War II resulted in the debt to GDP ratio growing; that debt rose rapidly in Japan after growth slowed in the 1990s, and that European debt levels rose rapidly after growth slowed there.

Recently, Ireland imposed austerity to fight debt only to see growth slow, imperiling future service of debt, only recently beginning to emerge from this episode, while Iceland, with a debt to GDP ratio of 900 percent, unilaterally cut itself slack with many of its foreign creditors, depreciated its currency, and promoted growth, while it also placed its largest lenders in receivership and forced creditors rather than taxpayers to bear the losses of its banks.

In accord with Krugman and Shiller, Thomas Ferguson, professor of political science at the University of Massachusetts and Robert Johnson, senior fellow and director of the Project on Global Finance at the Roosevelt Institute, concluded in a 2011 study that the risk posed to the debt by austerity causing loss of growth and productivity is much greater than that posed by borrowing at the currently very low cost to spur investment in infrastructure, education and science that would generate gains in growth and productivity.[96] Finally, in accord with Krugman, Shiller, Thomas and Ferguson, Joseph Stiglitz has observed that austerity does not work.[97]

Additionally, to put concerns over debt in perspective, as a percentage of GDP, interest on debt payments since 2002 has been lower than over the previous two decades (1.3 percent of GDP in FY 2014), and through 2024 it is predicted to rise to about 3.0 to 3.3 percent—about the level it was at during the early 1990s.[98] And, as observed earlier, tax revenues as a percentage of GDP had recently been at their lowest levels in 60 years and have only recently risen to 17.5 percent of GDP—during the Clinton administration when the economy was booming tax revenues for three years were above 19 percent of GDP—peaking at 20.0 percent—so there is plenty of room in the economy to raise taxes to offset spending.

Thus, we should not allow trickle-down austerity hysteria to cloud good judgment. The government owes its citizens the obligation to conduct itself so that the functions only it can carry out, and the programs the middle class and working poor count on—among them, Social Security, Medicare, Medicaid, food stamps and continued unemployment compensation benefits—are not compromised. If the federal government holds up its end of the bargain in that regard, then Americans' misplaced faith in the market will be replaced by proper faith in government's ability to both help people directly, improve the quality of their lives indirectly, and to create jobs.

A SUMMARY NARRATIVE OF TRICKLE-DOWN FAILURE

In its brief form, as observed in the Introduction, a summary narrative of trickle-down failure:

> Since 1980, the economy has been growing, and productivity has been growing, but trickle-down values—*that we, the American people promote, pursuant to the Republican Party's conservative ideology*—have rigged the economy to continuously upwardly redistribute those revenues attributable to our increased productivity, yielding a productivity/wage disconnect, resulting in increased concentration of income and wealth at the top, in corporations and among older Americans (beneficiaries of income from Social Security, pensions and investments and continuing income due to delaying retirement), and the lowest percentage of GDP attributable to wages and highest attributable to profits since World War II.
>
> This, in turn, has resulted in slower economic growth, rising inequality, falling social mobility, declining public health, rising political dysfunction and rising economic instability illustrated by recurring bubble-bust episodes and balance sheet recessions, in turn creating low demand, which keeps unemployment high, thereby further depressing wages and demand in a depressionary feedback loop of our own creation. The federal government has countered these conditions with low interest rates and reduced regulation of the extending of credit, but for America to grow it must begin rebuilding its middle class and reversing this upward redistribution by, among other things, spending more to promote job creation, promoting wage increases and returning to more progressive taxation.
>
> But trickle-down has not only distorted our economic thought; it has also distorted our political thought, our sociology and our concept of the rule of law. The result has been that the trickle-down policies promoted by the Republican Party are undermining our economy, democracy, institutions and health.

A more detailed summary narrative follows below:

> From 1945 to 1973, wages grew in tandem with economic growth and productivity growth, due in great part to New Deal, post-World War II and Great Society institutions designed to aid the middle class and poor. These institutions enabled the poor and middle class to increase their productivity and forced the sharing of revenues from increased productivity with them, even though technological change (the Information Revolution) and globalization were, even then, exerting downward pressure on employment and incomes of the middle class and poor.
>
> Under liberals, spending on social insurance grew and interest rates were lowered, and the official policy of "full employment" was pursued, and inequality declined as the rich saw their incomes and wealth grow, but so did

incomes and wealth of the middle class and poor. Over this period, inventory recessions occurred, but recovery was generally rapid, however, consumer price inflation remained a concern.

In 1973, and from 1979 through 1980, two oil price shocks redistributed out of the country to foreign oil producers billions of dollars, much of which would otherwise have gone into wages, and dramatically forced up consumer prices, and this consumer price inflation combined with rising unemployment (creating "stagflation") during recurring inventory recessions. The Carter administration instituted government policy changes to revive the economy—appointing a Federal Reserve Chairman to raise interest rates to fight inflation and deregulating financial, transportation, communications and energy industries.

While higher interest rates were necessary to defeat inflationary expectations in the economy, they prolonged and intensified the recession in the election year of 1980, with the result that the electorate lost patience over the pace of economic recovery, resulting in an overreaction and abandonment of demand-side fiscal stimulation policies for supply-side—trickle-down—policies, and resulting in victory for the Republicans in November of 1980.

The recession continued after the election but, by the early 1980s, GDP growth revived, and productivity resumed growing, yet incomes for the middle class and poor continued their stagnation from the mid-1970s. The combination of the predicted technological change of the Information Revolution and globalization put downward pressure on job creation (initially, although job creation revived) and wages. In the past, these downward pressures had been counteracted by government policies, but, under trickle-down, we would rely upon "free trade," deregulation (e.g., financial deregulation, maintenance of a low minimum wage, weakened support of unions and weak support of equal pay for equal work by women) and tax cuts (skewed to upper incomes) to revive the economy (which resulted in rising deficits and rising government debt).

These government policy changes were accompanied by changes in compensation due solely to changes in values (and not forced by government policy changes): Incomes stagnated as increases in wages and salaries were smaller and came more seldom, and private, traditional defined benefit pensions were phased out in favor of cheaper to administer defined contribution plans such as 401(k)s.

Families initially responded to falling real incomes by sending wives into the workforce, then couples took on multiple jobs, then they depleted family savings, after which they ran up credit card debt, and began tapping their 401(k) retirement accounts (and paying early withdrawal penalties); only after all those efforts failed to enable them to maintain their standard of living, they took on home equity lines of credit secured by the value of their homes—encouraged by irresponsible financial deregulation which, in combination with loose monetary policy (yielding low interest rates), lured millions of American families into substituting irresponsibly high levels of debt for nonexistent income growth.

And, then, these families' homes began to decline in value, signaling that they could take on no more debt, and long-term broad stagnation of demand in the economy was underway.

Thus, although when confronting stagnant wages it is appropriate to attempt to stimulate the economy with low interest rates, those same low interest rates had, and continue to have, a perverse effect of upwardly redistributing income and wealth by forcing investments from safer interest rate denominated savings accounts into equities, thereby inflating the stock market and fattening the salaries of those atop the financial industry and corporations.

The financial deregulation and low interest rates also stimulated widespread fraud in real estate lending and in securitization of mortgages, including issuance of "liar's loans," creation of a derivatives market based on grossly insufficient reserves, the practice of financial alchemy by rating companies converting subprime mortgage loans into AAA-rated investments on behalf of their client investment banks, and issuance by investment banks of mortgage-backed securities to individual clients and then short-selling against them. And, fraud spread outside the real estate industry with the creation of multibillion dollar Ponzi schemes, insider trading, and related illegal and unethical activities that resulted in billions of dollars lost by "investors"—including middle class retirees—unable to sustain such losses.

Perversely, the American people were so fooled by trickle-down theory regarding the importance of finance that there was very little public pressure brought to bear in favor of criminal prosecution of those in the mortgage industry—from CEOs down to those admitting falsifying of loan applications.

The combination of financial deregulation, easy money (low interest rates and low lending standards) for home loans, and tax policy favoring capital over labor created, and continue to create asset price inflation, and, ultimately, bubbles (savings & loan, technology, and real estate which led to a banking crisis—each time accompanied by stock market collapse) which in the past have burst, reflated and will likely burst again in a bubble-bust depressionary feedback loop that every few years destroys trillions of dollars in wealth in balance sheet recessions.

Parallel to these three and a half decades of policy changes in the US, Europe and Japan the consensus that "free trade," deregulation, lower taxes and substitution of market for government institutions—that what is good for those at the top and corporations is good for all—spread across the world via the Washington Consensus and neoliberalism, resulting in global neofeudalism and an all-against-all race to the bottom to cut labor costs.

In sum, government policies over the three and a half decades since 1980 have reinforced a trickle-down vision, changing our values, norms and institutions so that we engaged in individual behavior and implemented government policies intended to reverse and undo New Deal and post-World War II institutions designed to aid the middle class and poor. The result has been that, for most of the past three and a half decades, the economy has been growing and productivity has been growing but because trickle-down values *that we, the American people promote, pursuant to the Republican Party's conservative ideology,* have rigged the economy to continuously upwardly redistribute those revenues attributable to our increased productivity, resulting in increased concentration of income and wealth at the top, in corporations and among older Americans (beneficiaries of income from Social Security, pensions and investments and continuing income due to delaying retirement), and the lowest percentage of GDP attributable to wages and highest attributable to profits

> since World War II. This has caused real incomes to fall for the middle class, poor and young—especially the Millennials and the generations to follow them—and caused a chronic ongoing shortfall in demand, accompanied by the feeling among most Americans that the economy remains in recession—because the economy in fact is in depression, marked by a chronic condition of subnormal activity for a considerable period without any marked tendency either toward recovery or toward complete collapse.
>
> The depression conditions have been exacerbated by the anti-government spending philosophy of trickle-down, cutting the number of government employees and thereby worsening unemployment, and refusing to approve needed infrastructure projects, thereby also worsening unemployment.
>
> Meanwhile, those at the top continue to prosper while many households in the lower 99 percent continue to live paycheck-to-paycheck on falling real wages while their savings and capacity to borrow further have been exhausted, thus, they are increasingly turning to government and, thus, the lower 99 percent are shifting the burden of subsidizing this windfall for the top 1 percent from themselves to future generations.
>
> Trickle-down has resulted in slower economic growth, rising inequality, less social mobility, declining public health, rising political dysfunction and rising economic instability illustrated by recurring bubble-bust episodes and balance sheet recessions, in turn creating low demand, which keeps unemployment high, thereby further depressing wages and demand in a depressionary feedback loop of our own creation. Trickle-down conservatism has also, throughout the West, with the discontent it sewed among the middle class, prompted a political reaction in the form of illiberal right wing populism exemplified most prominently in the US by the Tea Party and, more broadly, by the popularity of Donald Trump's 2016 campaign for the Republican presidential nomination.
>
> The bubble-bust loop created by trickle-down will end only when trickle-down values are ended, and America returns to rebuilding its middle class by government promotion of, among other things, full employment and increased wages to reverse this upward redistribution, along with a more progressive tax system—yet the policies proposed by Republicans continue to promise only to double-down on trickle-down, thereby continuing to starve demand and perpetuate the process described above.

As can be seen from the foregoing, we are not victims of globalization, or technology, or any other forces beyond our power. We are victims of our own failed dogmatic laissez-faire ideology of trickle-down, which we brought upon ourselves and, pursuant to which, we changed our values, norms and institutions and adopted misplaced utopian faith in the market along with the belief that we all do better when the rich do better. It is government policy, combined with our own personal practices, driven by the trickle-down delusion, that has been holding down wages and leading to low demand, and it is low demand that is suppressing job growth, further depressing wages and demand in a depressionary feedback loop. And, thus, trickle-down's values, not a "new normal" of structural employment changes, are causing the current sluggish economic conditions.

Loose monetary policy, although an appropriate stimulant, is nonetheless, itself, a trickle-down tactic, upwardly redistributing incomes as it redistributes from safer interest-sensitive securities to riskier equities—but it was the only option available when Republicans "controlled" both Houses of Congress (with a majority in the House and a filibuster-safe minority in the Senate) and prevented appropriate stimulative fiscal policy. As Federal Reserve Chairman Ben Bernanke himself observed in February 2013, monetary policy cannot carry the entire burden of helping economic recovery—fiscal stimulus is appropriate as well.[99] The basic lesson is clear: *Starve wages—starve demand.* Other lessons follow: Using government policy to upwardly redistribute revenues from increased productivity will result in declining real wages, the effect of which we can temporarily hide by substituting debt, but ultimately we will undermine demand, economic growth and capital growth and democracy itself. In the short-term, of course, declining real wages yield rising business earnings. Over the long-term, however, there is no escaping that real wages must rise for a country to prosper. More broadly, not only must real wages rise, but numerous government protections for the middle class and poor must be strengthened.

And, for all these things to happen, the trickle-down policies of the Republican Party must be confronted and reversed, and in place of them must be substituted appropriate liberal policies such as those proposed in Chapter 14.

NOTES

1. President Barack Obama, "Remarks by the President on Economic Mobility," THEARC, Washington, DC, December 4, 2013.
2. John Kenneth Galbraith, *The Great Crash, 1929* (Boston, New York: A Mariner Book, Houghton Mifflin Company; 1954, 1955, 1961, 1972, 1988, 1997), p. 169.
3. Josh Bivens, Elise Gould, Lawrence Mishel, and Heidi Shierholz, "Raising America's Pay: Why It's Our Central Economic Policy Challenge," Economic Policy Institute, June 4, 2014, Figure A, p. 10.
4. George Monbiot, "The 1% Are the Very Best Destroyers of Wealth the World Has Ever Seen," *The Guardian*, published November 8, 2011. The article also appears, with citations, at www.monbiot.com under the title "The Self-Attribution Fallacy."
5. Barbara Garson, "Do Your Patriotic Duty: Ask for a Raise," *The Los Angeles Times*, May 14, 2013.
6. Monika Bauerlein and Clara Jeffery, "The Speedup," *Mother Jones*, July-August 2011. Although the study upon which these observations were based was not defined, the numbers were consistent with Lawrence Mishel, "The Wedges between Productivity and Median Compensation Growth," Issue Brief #330, Economic Policy Institute, April 26, 2012.
7. Among the economists who have studied balance sheet recessions are Richard Koo, author of *The Holy Grail of Macroeconomics—Lessons from Japan's Great Recession* (2008); Nobel Prize winner Paul Krugman; Cullen Roche, author of the blog *Pragmatic Capitalism* and Stephen S. Roach, a senior fellow at Yale University's Jackson Institute for Global Affairs,

senior lecturer at Yale School of Management, formerly chairman of Morgan Stanley Asia and chief economist at Morgan Stanley and author of *The Next Asia* (2009). See especially his comment, "America's Zombie Consumers," *Room for Debate* blog at *The New York Times*, November 8, 2011, wherein he analogized the state of consumers in the US to the state of "zombie corporations" kept on life-support by Japanese banks in the late 1990s. Evidence in early 2016 indicated the US was entering its own balance sheet recession with corporate balance sheets diminished—at least those of oil and gas exploration and production companies and mining companies.

8. Dean Baker, *Plunder and Blunder: The Rise and Fall of the Bubble Economy* (Sausalito, CA: PoliPoint Press, LLC; 2009), p. 61.

9. Steven Gjerstad and Vernon L. Smith, "From Bubble to Depression?" *The Wall Street Journal*, April 6, 2009. Gjerstad and Smith would expand on their observations in "Monetary Policy, Credit Extension, and Housing Bubbles: 2008 and 1929," *Critical Review* Vol. 21, Numbers 2–3, 2009, pp. 269–300; see especially p. 293.

10. The 10-year rolling annualized return for commodities was -5.1 percent. See "Tyler Durden," "For Commodities, this is the Next Great Depression," Zero Hedge blog, January 7, 2016. The source of the chart cited for support of this observation is that of the CRYTR Index (RJ/CRB Commodity Total Return Index) provided by Bank of America Merrill Lynch Global Investment Strategy, Global Financial Data (GFD).

11. These conditions have combined to create what is well captured in the title of the report on the Findings of the Harvard Business School's 2013–2014 Survey on U.S. Competitiveness: *An Economy Doing Half Its Job*. The report, issued in September 2014, was authored by Michael E. Porter and Jan W. Rivkin, with contributions from Joseph B. Fuller, Allen S. Grossman, Rosabeth Moss Kanter and Kevin W. Sharer.

12. Nick Timiraos, "Report: Half of all Homes Are Being Purchased with Cash," *The Wall Street Journal*, August 15, 2013.

13. Associated Press, "U.S. Paychecks Grow at Record Slow Pace," July 31, 2015.

14. Lucia Mutikani, "U.S. Home Sales Approach Eight-and-a-Half-Year High, Prices Surge," Reuters, July 22, 2015.

15. Kathleen M. Howley, "U.S. Homeownership Rate Falls to the Lowest Level Since the 1960s," *Bloomberg Business*, July 28, 2015.

16. Graph: "Corporate Profits As a Share of GDP (CP/GDP)—FRED –St. Louis Federal Reserve Bank.

17. As of the end of the First Quarter of 2014, it was 17.7 percent, per Floyd Norris, "Corporate Profits Grow and Wages Slide," *The New York Times*, April 5, 2014.

18. Graph: "Compensation of Employees: Wages & Salary Accruals (WASCUR)/Gross Domestic Product, 1 Decimal (GDP)"—FRED –St. Louis Federal Reserve Bank.

19. Graph: "Civilian Labor Force Participation Rate (CIVPART)"—FRED –St. Louis Federal Reserve Bank. It has been argued that Baby Boomers are retiring from the labor force, lowering this figure, however, if employment were growing substantially, younger workers would be entering the economy and taking up the slack—but they are not.

20. National Income and Product Accounts, Gross Domestic Product: Third Quarter 2015 (Second Estimate), Corporate Profits: Third Quarter 2015 (Preliminary Estimate), Bureau of Economic Analysis, November 24, 2015. This observation was first made by Henry Blodget, editor of the blog *Business Insider*, in "The Truth About the Economy: In the 1980s, Greed WAS Good . . . Then We Went Overboard," *Business Insider*, June 26, 2012. See also, Henry Blodget, "Profits Just Hit another All-Time High, Wages Just Hit another All-Time Low," *Business Insider*, April 11, 2013.

21. Thomas L. Hungerford, "Changes in Income Inequality Among U.S. Tax Filers Between 1991 and 2006: The Role of Wages, Capital Income, and Taxes," Congressional Research Service, January 23, 2013.

22. Frank Levy and Peter Temin, "Inequality and Institutions in 20th Century America", NBER Working Paper #W13106, May 2007.

23. "Striking it Richer: The Evolution of Top Incomes in the United States (Updated with 2013 preliminary estimates)," Emmanuel Saez, UC Berkeley, January 25, 2015; see especially Figure 1.

24. See Henry Blodget, "Hey America: Check Out How 90% of Us Have Gotten Shafted Over the Past 30 Years . . ." *Business Insider*, August 22, 2012; and Emmanuel Saez, "Striking it Richer: The Evolution of Top Incomes in the United States (Updated with 2012 preliminary estimates)," September 3, 2013.

25. "Striking it Richer: The Evolution of Top Incomes in the United States (Updated with 2013 preliminary estimates)," Emmanuel Saez, UC Berkeley, January 25, 2015.

26. Adapted from Table 13 of *The Distribution of Household Income and Federal Taxes, 2010*, Congressional Budget Office, December 2013.

27. "Automatic Increases: Wage Statistics for 2014," Social Security Administration, October 23, 2015.

28. Jesse Bricker, Lisa J. Dettling, Alice Henriques, Joanne W. Hsu, Kevin B. Moore, John Sabelhaus, Jeffrey Thompson, and Richard A. Windle of the Federal Reserve Board's Division of Research and Statistics, with assistance from Sebastian Devlin-Foltz and Jacob Krimmel, "Changes in U.S. Family Finances from 2020–2013: Evidence from the Survey of Consumer Finances," Federal Reserve Bulletin September 2014, Vol. 100, No. 4 ("Survey of Consumer Finances 2013").

29. See also Floyd Norris, "Young Households, Even Educated Ones, Lose Ground in Income," *The New York Times*, September 13, 2014.

30. "US Economy Is Increasingly Tied to the Rich," *The Wall Street Journal*, August 5, 2011.

31. Richard Fry and Rakesh Kochhar, "America's Wealth Gap between Middle-Income and Upper-Income Families Is Widest on Record," Pew Research Center, December 17, 2014.

32. Edward N. Wolff, *The Asset Price Meltdown and the Wealth of the Middle Class* (New York University; August 26, 2012), Table 2 and pp. 12–17. This paper is an excellent summary of wealth and income data in prose and table form. An outstanding summary of its wealth and income data, along with other wealth and income data, is found at the website WhoRulesAmerica.net, in the document "Wealth, Income and Power," authored and updated by G. William Domhoff. Domhoff is a sociologist who has been an expert on inequality for many years and is author of *Who Rules America* (1967 and most recently 2009). He is now at the University of California, Santa Cruz.

33. Jeanna Smialek, "Top 1 Percent is Even Richer than Surveys Say, ECB Paper Finds," *Bloomberg*, July 15, 2014. The paper expressly countered the findings of the Federal Reserve's *Survey of Consumer Finances 2010*.

34. Nicholas Shaxson, John Christensen, and Nick Mathiason, "Inequality: You Don't Know the Half of It," Tax Justice Network, July 19, 2012, pp. 6–7. The wealth report cited is by Sylvia Allegretto, co-chair of the Center on Wage and Employment Dynamics of the University of California, Berkeley, which found the top 1% of households owned 33.8% of all the wealth in 1983, while 26 years later, in 2009, the top 1% owned 35.6%, a very small increase.In a separate study, based in part on the results of a study by Credit Suisse Bank, the Tax Justice Network concluded that financial holdings in hidden offshore accounts amount to between $21 trillion (equal to the GDP of the US plus Japan) to $32 trillion (more than twice US GDP). To quote the report: "By their estimates, at least a third of all private financial wealth, and nearly half of all offshore wealth, is now owned by [the] world's richest 91,000 people—just 0.001% of the world's population. The next 51 percent of all wealth is owned by the next 8.4 million, another trivial 0.14% of the world's population." And, the bottom half of the world's population owns roughly as much of the world's wealth—1%—as the bottom half of the US population owns of total US wealth. On the other end of the concentration, the top 10 percent owns 84 percent. James S. Henry, "The Price of Offshore Revisited," Tax Justice Network, July 2012, p. 3.

35. "A Rise for the Wealthy; Declines for the Lower 93%," Pew Research Center, April 23, 2013.

36. Fabian T. Pfeiffer, Sheldon Danziger, and Robert Schoeni, "Wealth Levels, Wealth Inequality, and the Great Recession," Russell Sage Foundation, June 2014. See also Anna Bernasek, "The Typical Household Now Worth a Third Less," *The New York Times*, July 27, 2014.

37. Emmanuel Saez and Gabriel Zucman, "Wealth Inequality in the United States Since 1913: Evidence from Capitalized Income Tax Data," National Bureau of Economic Research Working Paper 20625, October 2014.

38. See also Emmanuel Saez and Gabriel Zucman, "Exploding Wealth Inequality in the US," *VoxEU*, October 28, 2014.

39. This observation was touted by Senator Bernie Sanders (I-VT) in his campaign for the Democratic presidential nomination as in, for example, the first Democratic presidential nomination debate—see Glenn Kessler and Michelle Ye Hee Lee, "Fact Checking the First Democratic Debate," Fact Checker blog, *The Washington Post*, October 13, 2015.

40. See Robert Frank, "Another Widening Gap: The Haves vs. the Have-Mores," *The New York Times*, November 16, 2014.

41. Nir Jaimovich and Henry E. Siu, "The Trend Is the Cycle: Job Polarization and Jobless Recoveries," NBER Working Paper No. 18334, August 2012.

42. *Economic Policy Reforms: Going for Growth*, Part II, Chapter 5 "A Family Affair: Intergenerational Social Mobility across OECD Countries," OECD 2010. The 2010 OECD report updated an earlier OECD report that made similar observations (see *Growing Unequal? Income Distribution in OECD Countries*, OECD 2008).

43. The National Committee on Technology, Automation and Economic Progress, "Technology and the American Economy" (February 1966). This report will be reviewed again in detail in Chapter 9.

44. Joseph A. Schumpeter's use of the term "creative destruction" appears in his chapter entitled "The Process of Creative Destruction," in *Capitalism, Socialism and Democracy* (New York: Harper Colophon, 1942, 1975), the quote comes from pp. 82 and 83.

45. A critique of the view that technology and globalization are responsible for upward redistribution of income and suggestion that the real culprit is rents is presented by Dean Baker of the Center for Economic and Policy Research in "Working Paper: The Upward Redistribution of Income: Are Rents the Story?" CEPR Working Paper, December 2015. The four major areas of rents blamed are patent and copyright protection, the financial sector, pay of CEOs and other top executives, and protectionist measures that boost pay of doctors, lawyers and other professionals. Regardless, for the purposes here, values have changed to support the upward redistribution of revenues attributable to increased productivity and the higher compensation to these individuals.

46. Heidi Shierholz, Natalie Sabadish and Hilary Wething, The Class of 2012: Labor Market for Young Graduates Remains Grim," EPI Briefing Paper #340, the Economic Policy Institute, Washington, DC. See also the Editorial Board, "Where Have All the Raises Gone?" *The New York Times*, March 3, 2014.

47. Robert Pear, "Median Income Rises, But Is Still Below Level at Start of Recession in '07," *The New York Times*, August 22, 2013.

48. Patricia Cohen, "Racial Wealth Gap Persists Despite Degree, Study Says," *The New York Times*, August 17, 2015.

49. This observation is from a study of the Hamilton Project, cited in Neil Irwin, "Why Less Educated Workers Are Losing Ground on Wages," *The New York Times*, April 23, 2015.

50. "Union Members—2011," Economic News Release, Bureau of Labor Statistics, January 27, 2012.

51. Frank Levy and Peter Temin, "Inequality and Institutions in 20th Century America", NBER Working Paper #W13106, May 2007.

52. Paul Krugman, "The Spiral of Inequality," *Mother Jones* November/December 1996.

53. Paul Krugman, *The Conscience of a Liberal* (New York: W. W. Norton; 2007), p. 149.

54. Frank Levy and Peter Temin, "Inequality and Institutions in 20th Century America," NBER Working Paper #W13106, May 2007.

55. Joseph Stiglitz, "Equality Is Not Inevitable," *The New York Times*, June 29, 2014. See also Joseph Stiglitz, "Inequality Is Holding Back the Recovery," Opinionator blog, *The New York Times*, January 20, 2013. Stiglitz would return to addressing inequality in early 2015, in his book *The Great Divide*, followed by another book that released in November 2015, *Rewriting the Rules of the American Economy: An Agenda for Growth and Shared Prosperity*. See also Gillian B. White, "Here's How to Fix Inequality," *The Atlantic*, November 2, 2015.

56. Thomas Piketty, Emmanuel Saez and Stefanie Stantcheva, *Optimal Taxation of Top Labor Incomes: a Tale of Three Elasticities*, NBER Working Paper No. 17616, November 2011.

57. Robert Lenzner, "The Top 0.1% of the Nation Earn Half of All Capital Gains," *Forbes*, November 20, 2011. See also, Laura D'Andrea Tyson, "Tackling Income Inequality," *Economix* blog, *The New York Times*, November 18, 2011.

58. Lawrence Mishel, Josh Bivens, Elise Gould and Heidi Shierholz, T*he State of Working America, 12th Edition*, Economic Policy Institute (Cornell Press: November 2012), Overview, p. 44.

59. Thomas Piketty and Emmanuel Saez, "Inequality in the Long Run," *Science*, May 23, 2014, vol. 344, issue 6186.

60. See Paul Krugman's review of Piketty's book in "Why We're in a New Gilded Age," in *The New York Review of Books*, May 8, 2014. There, Krugman recounted that he was in basic agreement with Piketty's explanation that rising inequality is due to changed social norms manifesting themselves in social and political forces—evidenced by, as observed by Piketty, skyrocketing pay for executives and falling income and inheritance tax rates for the rich. Krugman added the factor of deregulation that accompanied these changed norms. Krugman ended on a hopeful note, as does Piketty, observing the power of the body politic to reverse the upward redistribution. Publishing of Piketty's work prompted a renewal of attention to institution of more progressive taxation—see, e.g., Paul Krugman, "America's Taxation Tradition," *The New York Times*, March 28, 2014, Robert Shiller, "Better Insurance Against Inequality," *The New York Times*, April 12, 2014, and Floyd Norris, "Total Taxes on Wages Are Rising," *The New York Times*, April 12, 2014.

61. Paul Krugman, *End this Depression Now!* (New York: W. W. Norton & Company; 2012), p. x. The quote appears in John Maynard Keynes, *The General Theory of Employment, Interest and Money*, p. 249. Krugman returned in his opinion pieces to the concept of depression—see especially "The Story of Our Time," *The New York Times*, April 29, 2013, wherein he linked austerity to depression.

62. The NBER establishes beginning and ending dates for recessions. The 1990 recession began July 1990 and ended March 1991; the 2001 recession began March 2001 and ended November 2001; and the 2007 recession began December 2007 and ended June 2009.

63. "The Employment Situation—May 2014," BLS, released June 6, 2014; Annalyn Kurtz, "Finally! Job Market Returns to 2008 Peak," *CNN Money*, June 6, 2014; and Nelson D. Schwartz, "217,000 Jobs Added, Nudging Payrolls to Levels Before the Crisis," *The New York Times*, June 7, 2014. Also, the long-term unemployment rate—measuring people out of work for 15 weeks or more—fell below the short-term unemployment rate for the first time in five years, which was good news. Floyd Norris, "A Handful of Indicators Showing Growth on the Jobs Front," *The New York Times*, June 14, 2014.

64. With men's wages stagnating, and the cost of living rising, the rate of entry of married women into the workforce (especially married women with children under age 18), which had been steadily increasing since World War II, accelerated. See Sharon R. Cohany and Emy Sok, "Trends in Labor Force Participation of Married Mothers of Infants," *Monthly Labor Review*, February 2007, Chart 1.

65. Richard Rubin and Margaret Collins, "Early Tap of 401(k) Replaces Homes as American Piggy Bank," *Bloomberg*, May 5, 2014.

66. See Stephen S. Roach, "Dying of Consumption," *The New York Times*, November 28, 2008. Roach was Chairman of Morgan Stanley Asia. He later became senior fellow at Yale University's Jackson Institute for Global Affairs and a senior lecturer at the Yale School of Management.

67. Kevin J. Lansing, "Spendthrift Nation," *FRBSF Economic Letter*, No. 2005–30, November 10, 2005.

68. Figures come from Ned Davis Research, in "Why We Believe We Are in a Secular Bear Market," Comstock Partners, June 17, 2011, and St. Louis Federal Reserve (Table 100*CMDEBT/DPI).

69. Simon Johnson, "No More Cheating: Restoring the Rule of Law in Financial Markets," The Baseline Scenario blog, April 15, 2015.

70. *Flow of Funds Accounts of the United States, Flows and Outstandings, First Quarter 2009*, Board of Governors of the Federal Reserve System, Washington, DC 20551, June 11, 2009, pp. 8 and 9: Total outstanding U.S. debt in first quarter 2009: $52.860 trillion; first quarter 2009 GDP: $14.090 trillion.

71. See Erik Eckholm, "Blue-Collar Jobs Disappear, Taking Families' Way of Life Along," *The New York Times*, January 16, 2008.

72. Bob Herbert, "The Worst of the Pain," *The New Times* (February 9, 2010).

73. Disproportionately feeling the downside of the effects of trickle-down and austerity has contributed to the Millennials being far more liberal than their predecessor generations, as explored in an outstanding article by Peter Beinart in "The Rise of the New New Left," *The Daily Beast*, September 12, 2013.

74. Heidi Shierholz, Natalie Sabadish and Nicholas Finio, "The Class of 2013: Young Graduates Still Face Dim Prospects," Economic Policy Institute, EPI Briefing Paper #60, April 10, 2013, pp. 11–12.

75. Ibid, pp. 13–14.

76. Richard Fry, "A Record One-in-Five Households Now Owe Student Loan Debt," Pew Research Center, September 26, 2012.

77. Andrew Martin and Andrew W. Lehren, "A Generation Hobbled by the Soaring Cost of College," *The New York Times*, May 12, 2012.

78. "Young, Underemployed and Optimistic: Coming of Age, Slowly, in a Tough Economy," Pew Research Center Social & Demographic Trends project, February 9, 2012, p. 6; citation to "The Rising Gap in Economic Well-Being," Pew Research Center Social & Demographic Trends project, November 7, 2011.

79. Floyd Norris, "The Older Cling to Jobs, Crowding Out the Younger," *The New York Times*, May 10, 2014.

80. Torsten Slok, Deutsche Bank Research, reported by Sam Ro, "A Third of America's 18- to 34-Years-olds Live with Their Parents" *Business Insider*, June 2, 2014.

81. The study is available at the St. Louis Federal Reserve website www.st.louisfed.org. See also Robert Frank, "Not So Fast, 1 Percent Whippersnappers," *The New York Times*, November 22, 2015. Robert Frank is CNBC Wealth Editor, author of *Richistan*, and economics professor at Cornell University.

82. "Millennials in Adulthood," Pew Research Center, March 7, 2014.

83. Richard Fry, D'Vera Cohn, Gretchen Livingston and Paul Taylor, "The Rising Age Gap in Economic Well-being," Pew Research Center, November 7, 2011.

84. Josh Bivens, Elise Gould, Lawrence Mishel, and Heidi Shierholz, "Raising America's Pay: Why It's Our Central Economic Policy Challenge," Economic Policy Institute, June 4, 2014, pp. 33–35. See also Neil Irwin, "Growth Has Been Good for Decades. So Why Hasn't Poverty Declined?" and David Leonhardt, "Economic Growth Isn't Leading to Less Poverty," the Upshot blog, *The New York Times*, June 4, 2014.

85. And, in the shipping industry as in the economy, it was government regulation that addressed this problem—refer to the international standards called the "Plimsoll line."

86. Joel Kotkin, "Generation Screwed," *Newsweek*, July 23 and 30, 2012. Kotkin is a contributing editor to the libertarian Manhattan Institute's *City Journal* and is currently serving as a guest lecturer at Singapore's Civil Service College. He is also a distinguished Presidential Fellow at Chapman University and author of numerous books, including *The Next Hundred Million: America in 2050* (2010) and *The City: A Global History* (2006), in both of which he promotes an optimistic vision of growth of American suburbia. He is also author of *The New Geography: How the Digital Revolution Is Reshaping the American Landscape* (2000) and *Tribes: How Race, Religion and Identity Determine Success in the New Global Economy* (1993).

87. Karen Sloan, "ABA: Only 55 Percent of Law Grads Found Full-time Law Jobs," *The National Law Journal*, June 18, 2012. Michael McDonald, "First-Year Law School Enrollment Drops to 36-Year Low," *Bloomberg*, December 18, 2013. Later reports indicated law school enrollment was continuing to drop through 2015.

88. Steven Rattner, "We're Making Life Too Hard for Millennials," *The New York Times*, August 2, 2015.

89. Carmen Reinhart and Kenneth Rogoff, *This Time Is Different: Eight Centuries of Financial Folly* (Princeton, NJ: Princeton University Press, 2009); see especially p. xxv.
90. Daniel Fisher, "The Global Time Bomb," *Forbes*, February 8, 2010.
91. Walter Alarkon, "U.S. Debt Reaches Level at Which Economic Growth Begins to Slow," On the Money, *The Hill*'s Finance and Economy Blog, May 26, 2010.
92. See Brad Plumer, "Is the Evidence for Austerity Based on an Excel Spreadsheet Error?" Wonkblog, *The Washington Post*, April 16, 2013. See also Thomas Herndon, Michael Ash and Robert Pollin, "Does High Public Debt Consistently Stifle Economic Growth?" Mike Konczal, NewDeal2.0 blog, repeated in "Bombshell New Paper Claims that Microsoft Excel Coding Error is Behind the Reinhart-Rogoff Study on Debt," *Business Insider*, April 16, 2013. See also Kevin Drum, "Death by a Thousand Cuts," *Mother Jones*, September/October 2013.
93. Andrea Pescatori, Damiano Sandri, and John Simon, "Debt and Growth: Is There a Magic Threshold?" Research Department, International Monetary Fund, February 2014.
94. Paul Krugman, "Debt and Transfiguration," *The New York Times* blog, March 12, 2010. See also Mark Blyth, "The Austerity Delusion: Why a Bad Idea Won over the West," *Foreign Affairs*, May/June 2013 and *Austerity: The History of a Dangerous Idea* (London: Oxford University Press; 2013). And, see Aditya Chakrabortty, "A Short History of Austerity: It Almost Never Works," *The Guardian*, March 11, 2013.
95. Robert J. Shiller, "Debt and Delusion," July 21, 2011, copyright Project Syndicate.
96. Thomas Ferguson and Robert Johnson, "A World Turned Upside Down? Deficit Fantasies in the Great Recession," *International Journal of Political Economy*, vol. 40, no. 1, Spring 2011, pp. 3–147.
97. Frances Schwartzkopff, "Stiglitz Says Austerity Kills Jobs, Brings Economic Decline," *Bloomberg*, May 13, 2011.
98. Dean Baker, "The Graph You Really Need When Watching the Republican (and Democratic) Conventions," CEPR, August 29, 2012. Also see Danielle Kurtzleben, "National Debt Interest Payments Dwarf Other Government Spending," *U.S. News & World Report*, November 19, 2012. "The Budget and Economic Outlook: 2014 to 2024," CBO, February 2014.
99. Binyamin Appelbaum, "Austerity Kills Government Jobs as Cuts to Budgets Loom," *The New York Times*, February 27, 2013.

Chapter Eight

Trickle-Down's Rule of Law

Power to the Propertied and Powerful

Carved in the stone above the main entrance to the Supreme Court Building are the words, "EQUAL JUSTICE UNDER LAW". As will be seen, the application of the law to all persons equally is one element of the rule of law, a very basic value of all liberal democracies. A related basic value of all liberal democracies is checks and balances—expressed in the Constitution in the separation of the lawmaking powers into Congress in Article I, the law-executing powers into the President in Article II and the power to issue judgments on the law into the courts in Article III. Addressed herein in detail will be a concern oft-voiced in various ways that the courts—especially the Supreme Court—were exceeding their constitutionally allocated authority and, in the words of the administration of President George W. Bush, "legislating from the bench."[1]

The sociologist and social philosopher Herbert Spencer's *Social Statics*, published in 1851, became famous for its promotion of an extreme libertarian free market economic theory, which became the social philosophy of the Gilded Age. In a decision rendered during the Gilded Age, *Lochner v. New York* (1905), the Supreme Court found that the New York legislature, in unanimously enacting the Bakeshop Act in 1895, which limited the number of hours a baker could work each day to ten and each week to 60 had violated the "liberty of contract" implicit in the Due Process Clause of the Fourteenth Amendment. *Lochner* was the most famous of the Court's cases decided pursuant to the doctrine of "Substantive Due Process," in which the Court read into the Due Process Clauses of the 5th and 14th Amendments substantive authority to enforce the freedom of the market of the Gilded Age, enabling the Court to overrule legislation and deny the help of government to the less powerful in the realm of economic regulation. Substantive Due Process was not struck down until the case of *West Coast Hotel v. Parrish* (1937). Justice Oliver Wendell Holmes issued a dissenting opinion in *Lochner*, including the famous quote: "The Fourteenth Amendment does not enact Mr. Herbert Spencer's *Social Statics*." As will be seen herein, we are enduring a period somewhat similar to that earlier one, in which the Court imagines that the Constitution enacts a philosophy of libertarianism, stressing the freedom to use one's wealth freely to obtain political power, and denying the help of government to the less powerful in the realm of politics, thus denying the rule of law and undermining democracy.

As was observed previously in Chapter 5, Friedrich Hayek, in *The Constitution of Liberty* correctly observed: "In the last resort, the conservative position rests on the belief that in any society there are recognizably superior persons whose inherited standards and values and position ought to be protected and who should have a greater influence on public affairs than others."[2] This protection consists of the creation of privilege, and privilege is the opposite of the rule of law.

That said, the Court, in three very important recent decisions that will be discussed herein, has, when faced directly with the opportunity to protect the less powerful, stepped up to the challenge and in the most recent example did so with soaring rhetoric of which a liberal would be proud. Thus, to interpret where the Court is as of 2015, where there is conflict between the freedom of the propertied and powerful and the law's attempts to restrain that power for the benefit of the less powerful, the propertied and powerful win. Where there are attempts by the law to provide more power to the less powerful, without a direct confrontation with the exercise of power by the propertied and powerful, liberalism and democracy triumph and the less powerful win.

Friedrich Hayek, who criticized conservatism and explained why he was not a conservative, was, nonetheless, a great hero to conservatives for, among other reasons, his extensive writings on the nature of the rule of law—and, in those writings, exempting from criticism as violative of the rule of law the most prevalent basis for establishment of privilege throughout history: ownership of property. In the Introduction herein it was observed that libertarianism has lost sight of the historic role of the Left from the time of the French Revolution: the opposition to concentration of power, even when that power is due to wealth. Hayek's observations will be addressed herein, but this oversight will be rectified, as this chapter addresses the perversion of the rule of law by conservatism, especially conservatism driven by the trickle-down delusion, accumulating ever more power in the wealthy.

This chapter addresses the consensus among the three elements of trickle-down conservatism—the plutocratic libertarianism that holds the unfettered market will determine who is superior, in concert with the unfettered (by campaign finance restrictions) electoral process; the neoconservatism shaped by Leo Strauss's "natural right" philosophy;[3] and the traditionalist-Religious Right element of conservatism—that all hold conservatives should govern America because they alone have grasped the truth. This view was criticized by Hayek previously, a criticism in which liberal political scientist Theodore Lowi joined, observing that conservatism's belief that there are people who know the truth and therefore must govern renders it incapable of governing in a democracy.[4]

INTRODUCTION TO THE RULE OF LAW

The Definition of the Rule of Law

For as often as the term is invoked by social scientists, lawyers and political commentators, there is by no means consensus regarding what the term "rule of law" actually means.[5] It does not appear in the Constitution, and the definition of the rule of law has seldom been addressed in US Supreme Court jurisprudence. Yet, the rule of law is of critical importance because it serves as a check on the ability of the propertied and powerful to exert their will over the less powerful.

Given the dearth of Supreme Court jurisprudence regarding the rule of law, it is appropriate to consult the British legal scholar A. V. Dicey, who defined the rule of law in his classic *Introduction to the Study of the Law of the Constitution* (first published in 1885) as consisting of three elements—before each of the three elements, listed below, are short-hand descriptions of them[6]:

1. Due process; no arbitrary exercise of power: "[T]he absolute supremacy or predominance of regular law as opposed to the influence of arbitrary power, and excludes the existence of arbitrariness, of prerogative, or even of wide discretionary authority on the part of the government;"
2. Equal protection of the laws: "[E]quality before the law, or the equal subjection of all classes to the ordinary law of the land administered by the ordinary Law Courts; [and]"
3. Judges decide the law only for the cases before them, applying previous case law: "[Principles are the] result of judicial decisions determining the rights of private persons in particular cases brought before the Courts".

The above definition of the rule of law guides this work. And, from the above, it can be seen that the rule of law does not mean simply the application of the law that on its face applies to a set of facts. If that were the case, then no law would ever be declared unconstitutional. The rule of law, instead, in the context of the Constitution, requires that, if a law conflicts with the Constitution, an effort be made to interpret the law so as to avoid the conflict. If conflict cannot be avoided, then the law must be declared unconstitutional.

Although there is no mention in the Constitution of the rule of law there are, however, requirements to provide for due process (5th and 14th Amendments); restrictions on the arbitrary exercise of power (Articles I, II and III of the Constitution providing authority for the legislative, executive and judicial branches, respectively); and, most importantly for the analysis here, equal protection of the laws (in the 14th Amendment). As envisioned herein, there is no concept of rule of law that exists separately from the implementing provisions of the Constitution.

Internal Conflict in the Definition of Rule of Law

One immediate observation regarding the rule of law's definition is that the common preoccupation of conservatives with judges not "legislating from the bench" is but one aspect of rule of law—one which, as can be seen, has great potential to clash with another aspect of rule of law—that of equality under law.

How is a judge to apply a law which on its face treats citizens unequally based on arbitrary grounds, but which previous judicial opinions have upheld? Should the court side with equality in principle, or side with the tradition of *stare decisis* (literally, in Latin, "to stand for that which is decided," it refers to the doctrine that prior court decisions provide binding precedents)?[7] Does the judge violate the third principle (by ignoring previous case law), and invite charges of ignoring the first (acting arbitrarily and with wide discretion) and overrule prior law in accordance with the second principle above, or does the judge apply the law and satisfy the third and first principles, even though doing so clearly violates the second principle? It should be obvious, then, that even if there is agreement that Dicey's definition of rule of law applies, there will still be disagreement regarding its application.

Not in the Name of "Social Justice"

Before proceeding to critique the conservative undermining of the rule of law, it is important to first address and critique a method of liberal undermining of the rule of law via the concept of "social justice." Friedrich Hayek is the main critic of the concept of social justice, expounding on his views in *The Mirage of Social Justice*, the second volume of his trilogy on *Law, Legislation and Liberty*.[8]

Hayek's dim view of social justice flowed from his great respect for justice itself. Illiberals claim "the end justifies the means." Hayek, educated in Vienna as a lawyer, knew that, in the Western liberal tradition, "the end *is* the means." In other words, justice, under the Western, liberal concept of law, is the full and equal application of the *process* designed to yield the truth—as in a criminal trial, regarding whether the defendant is guilty or not guilty of the charge against him. But, *the truth*, itself, is not the end. Even with all the resources deployed in a criminal trial, often focused on only one person's role in only one crime, we do not claim to reach the truth. Rather, the process yields a verdict, on the charges, of guilty or not guilty.

So aware of the shortcomings of man's ability to arrive at "the truth," in even such a narrow setting, Hayek was loath to extend truth-seeking to the broader arena of setting wages. No one person—no human construction—could possibly have all the information necessary to determine what wage level for a given person satisfies the standard of "social justice." Hayek's caution was appropriate. We cannot justify, for example, a minimum wage on the basis of social justice. Rather, it is justified on the basis of enlightened self-interest, driven by concern that the market will break down if demand is starved, and by concern to prevent class distinctions from arising, which may ultimately lead to revolution. Knowing that value is subjective, we subjectively establish the value of the minimum wage (through trial and error, with reference to experiences in the states) based on what level appears to address these concerns.

THE PRIVILEGE ACCOMPANYING PROPERTY OWNERSHIP

Conservatism and the Themes of Race, Culture and Property in the Late 1950s and 1960s

William F. Buckley, Jr. in *Up from Liberalism* (1959) provided the unifying theme for conservatism: to maintain and enhance the freedom of the individual to freely acquire and dispose of property.[9] (Property unites the three elements of Buckley's conservatism—traditionalism, libertarianism and anti-communism.) Buckley then addressed the civil rights struggle raging in the South, expressing sympathy for white Southerners and, in a footnote, weighed freedom versus property rights and came down on the side of the latter, supporting the Southerners' use of their political power to defend their property.[10]

If we imagine the United States in the 1950s and early 1960s (before such legislation as the Civil Rights Act of 1964, the Voting Rights Act of 1965, Fair Housing Act of 1968 and the Equal Employment Opportunity Act of 1972), we can begin to see the inevitable conflict in the application of the value of "freedom." During the civil rights movement, the right to be served at a luncheon counter, attend a movie, stay at a hotel and compete for a job on an equal footing with whites was framed as an issue of freedom for African Americans.

Conservatives, however, also *correctly* framed this as an impingement on the freedom of the owners of the luncheon counter, movie house, hotel and the establishment placing the want ad to use their property as they saw fit—to associate with, deny service to and hire whomsoever they please.

The right of African Americans to infringe on those freedoms described above became an institution in American society—an example of Americans, as Tocqueville put it, combating individualism by the principle of enlightened self-interest, requiring the property owners to sacrifice. The effect of the civil rights rules is to tear down barriers to exchange, thereby increasing the efficiency of the market and expanding prosperity at the expense of freedom of property.

INSTITUTIONALIZATION OF THE POLITICAL PROCESS AS A "FREE MARKET"—RIGGED IN FAVOR OF THE PROPERTIED

As observed previously, the American people, themselves, have rigged the economic system against themselves and in favor of the rich, demanding their elected politicians enact laws to upwardly redistribute revenues from increased productivity, in the hopes that benefits will ultimately trickle-down to them.

And, also as observed previously, there is a tendency to view politics as a marketplace, in which dollars, spent on speech protected by the First Amendment, convert to votes and influence over political candidates that pays off to the rich individuals making these investments perhaps even more lucratively than engaging in capital investments to increase productivity (more on that below). In the US Supreme Court decision of *Citizens United v. Federal Election Commission* (2010), the Court essentially institutionalized this latter view of the political process, enabling the political system, like the economic system, to be rigged in favor of the rich and powerful.

The French novelist Anatole France famously said, "The law, in its majestic equality, forbids the rich as well as the poor to sleep under bridges, to beg in the streets, and to steal bread."[11] And, in light of *Citizens United* and subsequent rulings, the First Amendment, in its majestic equality, allows rich and poor alike to pool their millions of dollars into tax-free organizations to support their favorite political candidates and issues. *Citizens United*, and its progeny, will be addressed below, but first it is important to review the extensive thought given to the danger of promoting the vision of "politics as marketplace" in recent history.

How the Vision of Politics as Marketplace Undermines the Rule of Law

Crony capitalism, as observed in the Introduction, is a system of institutionalized "rent-seeking" (the term used by "Public Choice School" theorists such as economists James M. Buchanan, Robert D. Tollison, and Gordon Tullock) wherein political influence is used to gain benefits for favored interests that competition in the marketplace would not deliver. Thus, it negates the potential for practice of the rule of law.

Crony capitalism is practiced in much of the developing world because burden-shifting and opportunity-enhancing institutions are either nonexistent or weak. Crony capitalism flourishes under a trickle-down conservative view that "what is good for the wealthy is good for the world." In an idea related to conservatism's concept that governing is easy, conservatism *assumes* the development of the institutions necessary for prosperity and minimizes their importance—assumes that crony capitalists pursuing their self-interest will benefit society—an assumption made early in the Iraq occupation with disastrous and lingering consequences.

In addition to institutionalizing rent-seeking crony capitalism creates "distributional cartels" (the term used by economist Mancur Olson) and operates in a system not unique to conservatives—it also operated in the system created by liberals in the 1960s and 1970s deemed "interest group liberalism" by political scientist Theodore Lowi—all in violation of the rule of law—as will be explored more fully below.

The liberal Theodore Lowi explored what he called "interest-group liberalism" in his 1969 book, *The End of Liberalism: The Second Republic of the United States.*[12] Mancur Olson, in *The Rise and Decline of Nations,* also addressed the functioning of "special-interest groups" attempting to impose "cartelization". Olson described the organizations that attempt to thwart the rule of law for their own benefit as engaging in rent-seeking by forming what he called "distributional coalitions" that used access to government to redistribute income and wealth rather than to produce additional output.[13]

Olson then referred to the book, *Toward a Theory of the Rent-Seeking Society*[14] edited by James M. Buchanan, Robert D. Tollison, and Gordon Tullock. Buchanan would later receive the Nobel Prize in economics for his work applying economic analysis to political decision-making, illustrating the functioning of self-interest in the political realm. This was a continuation of Buchanan and Tullock's pioneering work first published in 1962, *The Calculus of Consent,* wherein they explained their theory that interest groups operate in a system in which organizational costs are incurred in the hopes of extracting "profits" from the political process.[15]

And, in this light, the political process is analogized to the "free market;" votes and influence over lawmakers are to be bought with dollars invested in yielding a return to the investor—"investments" that, if made wisely, will pay off much more lucratively than would investments in capital to enhance competitiveness and increase productivity.

Crony capitalism, thus, is profoundly anti-capitalist. It is, essentially, neo-feudalism, attempting to undo liberalism's distribution of the tax burden and opportunities for advancement in favor of the less advantaged members of society. The sociologist William Julius Wilson described a common element of crony capitalism in *Power, Racism and Privilege: Race Relations in Theoretical and Sociohistorical Perspectives* (1973): "[R]acial stratification is largely a function of dominant-group efforts to control scarce resources either by eliminating or neutralizing subordinate racial members as competitors or by exploiting their labor."[16] Demand for the goods or services one produces is one of those scarce resources. And, history teaches us that *any* differences in people—not only race but also gender, ethnicity, geographic origin, nationality and value of property owned—and now, in the Middle East and North Africa, especially, religion—can be used by one group to distinguish itself from others in order to exploit the labor of the other group and protect itself from competition by that group's members—in order to engage in rent-seeking.

THE *BUSH V. GORE* "SECOND BITE" DOCTRINE ENUNCIATING EQUAL PROTECTION WEIGHTED IN FAVOR OF THE PROPERTIED

Although the rule of law is seldom cited in opinions of the Supreme Court, in the famous case that settled the 2000 presidential election it was referred to in a dissenting opinion. In *Bush v. Gore* (2000), the Supreme Court held that the Florida Supreme Court violated the Equal Protection Clause of the US Constitution in its attempt to ensure that votes cast by African Americans in the 2000 presidential election were counted. The Florida Supreme Court had called for a recount of only those counties using a punch-card system—prevalent in poorer counties and acknowledged as more prone to undercount votes than the more modern optical-scan systems prevalent in wealthier counties—and, accordingly, in the opinion of the Supreme Court, had violated the equal protection rights of those citizens in the wealthier counties.

Justice John Paul Stevens, in a footnote in his dissenting opinion in *Bush v. Gore*, succinctly summarized the facts:

> The percentage of nonvotes in the election in counties using a punch-card system was 3.92%; in contrast, the rate of error under the more modern optical-scan systems was only 1.43% . . . .Put in other terms, for every 10,000 votes cast, punch-card systems result in 250 more nonvotes than optical-scan

systems. A total of 3,718,305 votes were cast under punch-card systems, and 2,353,811 votes were cast under optical-scan systems.

In the body of his opinion, Stevens noted[17]:

> [Title 3 of the US Code] Section 5, like Article II [of the Constitution], assumes the involvement of the state judiciary in interpreting state election laws and resolving election disputes under those laws. Neither §5 nor Article II grants federal judges any special authority to substitute their views for those of the state judiciary on matters of state law . . . .[W]e have never before called into question the substantive standard by which a State determines that a vote has been legally cast.

Justice Stevens ended his dissent with the observation:

> Although we may never know with complete certainty the identity of the winner of this year's Presidential election, the identity of the loser is perfectly clear. It is the Nation's confidence in the judge as an impartial guardian of the rule of law.

The Supreme Court in *Bush v. Gore* engaged in what is called herein a "second bite at the apple" analysis under the Equal Protection Clause in which the majority of the Court, after an assessment of the remedy applied in pursuance of application of equal protection of the law to the aggrieved party, conducted a balancing effort to weigh that remedy against the right to equal protection of the law of another, propertied—privileged—party, to determine whether the remedy violated that privileged party's equal protection rights.

The majority opinion contains the famous statement: "Our consideration is limited to the present circumstances, for the problem of equal protection in election processes generally presents many complexities." More accurately, the application of equal protection requirements as the Court has done in *Bush v. Gore* should be "limited to the present circumstances" because widespread application of its equal protection analysis would risk unraveling *all* equal protection cases ever decided on behalf of plaintiffs, as is understandable if we return to the example of William F. Buckley, Jr. and the conservative perspective above.

As observed above, under modern civil rights legislation and court opinions, there is an impingement on the freedom of the owners of the luncheon counter, movie house, hotel and the establishment placing the want ad. If the Supreme Court looked first to the equal protection rights of plaintiff African Americans in such cases, then weighed their rights against the equal protection rights of the above parties to use their property as they saw fit, associate with whomever they choose, deny service to whomever they please and to hire whomsoever they please, the Court would likely have decided the property owners win—just as the Court in *Bush v. Gore* decided those who own more property win, even though they possessed obvious advantages (in *Bush v. Gore*, a more accurate voting system).

The Equal Protection Clause, and the equal protection element of the rule of law, both require that the party possessing more power—in terms of privilege based on property, wealth, etc.—sacrifice. Conservatives have been right all along: Application of the principle of equal protection actually means that the law grants "more" rights to the less powerful. But it cannot work otherwise, for a "second bite at the equal protection apple" to determine whether the equal protection rights of the privileged have been aggrieved will likely find that they have. Thus, the opinion in *Bush v. Gore* undermines both the Equal Protection Clause and the equal protection component and due process components of the rule of law.

"Our Consideration Is Limited to the Present Circumstances" Except When It Is Not

As will be seen by the following cases, the Court in *Bush v. Gore* enunciated a doctrine of equal protection analysis that rigs the political system in favor of the privileged in parallel to operation of trickle-down economics in the economic system. And, as observed above, the little secret of the Equal Protection Clause is that—functioning as an institution to level the playing field—it really does create a legal privilege on behalf of the party without the privilege of property or other source of privilege.

The clash observed above by William F. Buckley, Jr., between freedom and property rights (and the related right of association), is an old and recurring one—in the past it pitted African Americans against whites in the context of access to public schools, public transportation, public parks, public water fountains, and privately owned accommodations that were open to the white public only (e.g., movie theaters, hotels and restaurants). The US Supreme Court had, for nearly a half decade, decided this clash of freedom versus property in favor of the less privileged party—meaning that the party with valid rights of property and association lost.

With the opinion in *Bush v. Gore*, a new principle was enunciated: Because what is good for those privileged with property is good for everyone, after an equal protection analysis has determined what satisfies equal protection of the laws regarding the less privileged, another equal protection analysis must be applied to determine if equal protection of the laws has been applied to the privileged, ensuring the enjoyment of their privilege—and, if the law has failed to do so, then the law is unconstitutional.

And, as will be seen below, although the Supreme Court under Chief Justice Rehnquist proposed to limit the application of this approach to the circumstances of the case before it, the Supreme Court under Chief Justice

John Roberts, by promoting freedom of speech and religion, has extended the rights of the privileged.

HOW "FREEDOM" BECOMES AN ANTI-DEMOCRATIC BLUDGEON WIELDED ON BEHALF OF THE PROPERTIED

The Supreme Court's decision in *Citizens United v. Federal Election Commission* (2010) has been cited for its extension of the concept, from the previous Supreme Court decision of *Buckley v. Valeo* (1976) that "money is speech," so that limits on political candidates' own personal expenditures are unconstitutional, and the concept that "corporations are people" (they are, under the law, "artificial persons"). However, the most important contribution to the law is the holding of *Citizens United* that the First Amendment allows corporations and unions to spend unlimited amounts of money to influence political campaigns—via what came to be known as "super PACs"—as long as such expenditures are channeled into spending on election campaigns without coordination with the candidate's campaign staff.

The facts that gave rise to *Citizens United* began with the Bipartisan Campaign Reform Act of 2002 (BCRA), popularly called "McCain-Feingold" after Senator John McCain (R-AZ) and Senator Russell Feingold (D-WI), its co-sponsors. Among other things, McCain-Feingold prevented corporations and unions from using their general treasury funds to pay for "electioneering communications" (advertisements on television mentioning a candidate) within 30 days before a primary election or 60 days before a general election.

During the 2004 presidential campaign, Citizens United, a conservative political action group, filed a complaint with the Federal Election Commission (FEC) alleging that commercials on television for Michael Moore's movie, *Fahrenheit 9/11*, a film critical of the Bush administration's response to the attacks of September 11, 2001, constituted electioneering communications that could not be run in the 30-day or 60-day periods of McCain-Feingold. The FEC held against Citizens United.

Citizens United then tried to run television commercials during the 2008 campaign promoting *Hillary: The Movie*, claimed by Citizens United to be a "documentary" critical of Hillary Clinton, to be presented on DirecTV. The United States District Court for the District of Columbia ruled that the commercials violated McCain-Feingold's ban on electioneering communications, and the decision was ultimately taken up by the Supreme Court.

Justice Kennedy, writing for the majority, observed: "If the First Amendment has any force, it prohibits Congress from fining or jailing citizens, or associations of citizens, for simply engaging in free speech." The opinion unleashed millions of dollars to be used in campaigns for the benefit of the fabulously wealthy to influence elections and curry favor from politicians.

To achieve its ends, the Court had to engage in a level of judicial activism rare in the history of the Supreme Court: overruling one previous opinion and partially overruling another. The opinion overruled, *Austin v. Michigan Chamber of Commerce* (1990), had held a Michigan law prohibiting corporations from using treasury money to support or oppose candidates in elections did not violate the First and Fourteenth Amendments. The opinion overruled the part of *McConnell v. Federal Election Commission* (2003) which had upheld McCain-Feingold's restrictions on corporate expenditures defined as "electioneering communications." The Court also upheld the constitutionality of two provisions of McCain-Feingold requiring disclosure of funding sources.

Justice Kennedy, in his majority opinion, observed that, for the purpose of establishing a "compelling government interest" of opposing corruption sufficient to justify government limitations on political speech, independent expenditures do not lead to, or create the appearance of, quid pro quo corruption. "In fact, there is only scant evidence that independent expenditures even ingratiate." And, just in case he was wrong, he added: "The appearance of influence or access, furthermore, will not cause the electorate to lose faith in our democracy." The question begged, then, was what if the Court is wrong about that, too—and "the appearance of corruption" *did* "cause the electorate to lose faith in democracy"?

The confidence of Justice Kennedy in the ethics of *politicians* accepting political donations contrasted with his lack of confidence in *his fellow judges* accepting political donations, expressed in another opinion just two years earlier. There, Justice Kennedy declared in his opinion for the majority in *Caperton v. A. T. Massey Coal Co.* (2008): "We conclude that there is a serious risk of actual bias—based on objective and reasonable perceptions—when a person with a personal stake in a particular case had a significant and disproportionate influence in placing the judge on the case by raising funds or directing the judge's election campaign when the case was pending or imminent." *Caperton* dealt with a West Virginia Supreme Court justice who failed to recuse himself from a case involving a CEO who spent nearly $3 million on independent expenditures in support of the justice's election. Because the independent expenditures constituted the vast majority of spending in the judicial election, Justice Kennedy concluded that the justice should have recused himself.

Thus, according to the Court, politicians are less inclined to succumb to bias due to corporate contributions than are judges—and the Justices provided no explanation for why they thought so poorly of their fellow judges, or, alternatively, thought politicians so noble.

Returning to Justice John Paul Stevens' dissenting opinion in *Citizens United*, Stevens acknowledged the risk of undermining faith in democracy and observed: "A democracy cannot function effectively when its constituent members believe laws are being bought and sold." The majority of the Court, Justice Stevens continued, misunderstood a basic concept in American law since the passage of the Tillman Act in 1907, placing restrictions on campaign spending by corporations[18] —in terms that directly confronted a model of politics that embraces the Public Choice theorists' confluence of the market and politics:

> The marketplace of ideas is not actually a place where items—or laws—are meant to be bought or sold, and when we move from the realm of economics to the realm of corporate electioneering, there may be no "reason to think the market ordering is intrinsically good at all" [citation omitted].
>
> The Court's blinkered and aphoristic approach to the First Amendment may well promote corporate power at the cost of the individual and collective self-expression the Amendment was meant to serve. It will undoubtedly cripple the ability of ordinary citizens, Congress and the States to adopt even limited measures to protect against corporate domination of the electoral process. Americans may be forgiven if they do not feel the Court has advanced the cause of self-government today.

The absurdity of the majority's notion that there *could be* lack of coordination between the super PAC and the candidate was displayed in January 2012 when Republican presidential candidate Governor Mitt Romney went so far as to refer to the pro-Romney super PAC "Restoring Our Future" as his super PAC in an interview on NPR.[19] Not only was there a super PAC openly identified with Romney, but there were also other super PACs openly identified with other candidates as well, and in the campaigning leading up to the 2016 election, candidates engaged in the ruse that they had not yet decided to run so they could help raise funds for their super PACs, which they could not do after they announced their candidacy.

Before leaving the discussion of *Citizens United* and its progeny, it is important to address the concurring opinion in *Citizens United* of Chief Justice John Roberts, in which he was joined by fellow conservative Justice Antonin Scalia. Roberts wrote that he wanted to address "the important principles of judicial restraint and *stare decisis* implicated in this case"—appropriate given that overturning Supreme Court precedent had been repeatedly previously decried by conservatives such as themselves and President Bush as "judicial activism" and "legislating from the bench."[20] The Chief Justice observed that had the Court never abandoned *stare decisis*, "segregation would be legal, minimum wage laws would be unconstitutional, and the Government could wiretap ordinary criminal suspects without first obtaining warrants"—thus equating the removal of the limits on political donations to the level of the most important civil rights opinions issued by the Court.

It should also be observed that *Citizens United* is being used to rebalance *state* election law in favor of the propertied as well. In *Arizona Free Enterprise Club's Freedom Club PAC v. Bennett* (2011), the Arizona Citizens Clean Elections Act created a public financing system to fund the primary and general election campaigns of candidates for state office. Candidates who opted to participate, and who accepted certain campaign restrictions and obligations, were granted an initial outlay of public funds to conduct their campaign. They were also granted additional matching funds if a privately financed candidate's expenditures, combined with the expenditures of independent groups made in support of the privately financed candidate or in opposition to a publicly financed candidate, exceeded the publicly financed candidate's initial state allotment.

Once matching funds were triggered, a publicly financed candidate was to receive roughly one dollar for every dollar raised or spent by the privately financed candidate—including any money of his own that a privately financed candidate spent on his campaign—and for every dollar spent by independent groups that supported the privately financed candidate. When there were multiple publicly financed candidates in a race, each one received matching funds as a result of the spending of privately financed candidates and independent expenditure groups. Matching funds topped out at two times the initial grant to the publicly financed candidate.

Petitioners, past and future Arizona candidates and two independent expenditure groups that spend money to support and oppose Arizona candidates, challenged the constitutionality of the matching funds provision, arguing that it unconstitutionally penalized their speech and burdened their ability to fully exercise their First Amendment rights.

Writing for the majority, Chief Justice Roberts, in a 5–4 opinion, held in violation of the First Amendment government attempts to equalize opportunities for candidates in state electoral contests, observing:

> "Leveling the playing field" can sound like a good thing. But in a democracy, campaigning for office is not a game. It is a critically important form of speech. The First Amendment embodies our choice as a Nation that, when it comes to such speech, the guiding principle is freedom—the "unfettered interchange of ideas"—not whatever the State may view as fair.

In *American Tradition Partnership, Inc. v. Bullock* (2012), in a per curiam (unsigned) 5–4 opinion, the Court held that a 1912 Montana law prohibiting corporate contributions to political parties and candidates violated the First Amendment, citing *Citizens United*. Thus, the Court found the "freedom" accorded to corporations and the right of the propertied to freely use their property through their corporations overrode the interest of states to protect their political process from being bought by corporations and the propertied.

The 501(c)(4) "Social Welfare Organization" Foreign Money Laundry for Federal Election Campaigns

> With all due deference to separation of powers, last week the Supreme Court reversed a century of law that I believe will open the floodgates for special interests—including foreign corporations—to spend without limit in our elections.—*President Barack Obama, in his first State of the Union Address, January 27, 2010, criticizing* Citizens United.
> Not true.—*Justice Samuel Alito, sitting in the audience, mouthing in response.*

There is, unfortunately, compelling evidence that Justice Alito is wrong. For background, among the contribution limits for the 2015-2016 federal elections: For individuals, $2,700 per election to a candidate committee, and for political action committees (PACs), $5,000 multicandidate and $2,700 non-multicandidate.[21] However, corporations organized under Section 527 of the Internal Revenue Code (26 USC Section 527) may, as a result of the *Citizens United* decision, spend unlimited amounts to influence elections as long as the candidates they are supporting do not control or materially participate in their direction, solicit contributions to them or direct disbursements from them (thus satisfying the requirements to be qualifying "independent expenditures").

And, the *Citizens United* decision that independent expenditures by such corporations could not be limited was two months later complemented by the decision in *Speechnow.org v. Fed. Election Comm'n* (D.C. Cir. 2010) in which the Court of Appeals for the DC Circuit held that there could be no limits on contributions made to corporations making only independent expenditures. These two opinions combined created the entity known as the super PAC.

However, although super PACs can solicit and spend unlimited amounts of money—the Koch Brothers famously announced before the 2016 election they planned to raise $889 billion[22] —they must identify their donors. And, per the Foreign Agents Registration Act (FARA), in 22 USC Section 611 and following, and the Federal Election Campaign Act (FECA), 2 USC Section 431 and following, foreign nationals are prohibited from donating to federal campaigns. In order to circumvent this prohibition, some sort of mechanism to launder—hide—the source of contributions was needed, and it was found in the Internal Revenue Code, where among the organizations exempt from federal taxation are those covered by Internal Revenue Code Section 501(c)(4)—so-called "social welfare organizations"—defined as:

> Civic leagues or organizations not organized for profit but operated exclusively for the promotion of social welfare, or local associations of employees, the membership of which is limited to the employees of a designated person or persons in a particular municipality, and the net earnings of which are devoted exclusively to charitable, educational, or recreational purposes.

Making it easier for these organizations to serve as foreign money laundries for federal election campaigns, the word "exclusively" was interpreted by Treas. Reg. section 1.501(c)(4)-1(a)(2)(i) to mean "primarily," and the concept of "educational" has been interpreted to include activities including research and education of the public even if the organization conducts substantial lobbying activities pursuant to a philosophy consistent with a major political party as long as it is not affiliated with that political party, and its research is not directed by, and activities are not funded by, the party. Organizations so qualifying are exempt from disclosure requirements—thus, the result is anonymity for foreign donors to federal election campaigns.

Add to the above the observation of the chairwoman of the Federal Election Commission that the likelihood of election laws being enforced is slim[23] —and it becomes understandable why potential Republican presidential candidates, long before the primary campaign, seek the blessings of multibillionaires in private retreats like those at the Breakers at Palm Beach sponsored by the Club for Growth; Sheldon Adelson's Venetian Casino in Las Vegas; Sea Island, Georgia at a donor conference sponsored by the American Enterprise Institute; and the Ritz-Carleton in Rancho Mirage, California, sponsored by the Koch brothers.[24]

In the 2013-2014 term the Roberts Court, in three cases decided by 5–4 opinions, again used "freedom" as a rationale to strike down laws designed to help protect the middle class and poor and undermined democracy by aiding the propertied and powerful.

The concept that "money is speech" was extended further in *McCutcheon v. Federal Election Commission* (2014), in which the Court struck down the federal aggregate campaign contribution limits, while upholding—at least temporarily—the limit on how much an individual can give to an individual politician's campaign (then, $2600 per election). In his opinion Chief Justice Roberts wrote that only "quid pro quo" agreements in which a political contribution is given in exchange for some official action can be regulated: "Spending large sums of money in connection with elections, but not in connection with an effort to control the exercise of an officeholder's official duties, does not give rise to such quid pro quo corruption."

In *Harris v. Quinn* (2014), the Court held that the plaintiff, non-union home health care providers in Illinois and states with similar programs are only "partial" or "quasi" public employees as opposed to "full-fledged" public employees, so that their First Amendment free speech rights protect them from having to pay a "fair share" assessment of a portion of union dues attributable to union labor representation efforts on their behalf as members of the bargaining unit. Thus, the Court allowed them to be "free riders" and limited the application of the fair share provisions supported by decades of precedent since the Court's opinion in *Abood v. Detroit Board of Education* (1977). Justice Samuel Alito, writing for the majority, observed, "Except perhaps in the rarest of circumstances, no person in this country may be compelled to subsidize speech by a third party that he or she does not wish to support." The Court previously upheld the authority of states to pass "right-to-work" laws exempting private sector employees from having to pay for the benefits of union representation on their behalf as members of a bargaining unit. The *Harris* opinion now calls into question whether a union bargaining on behalf of anyone as member of a public sector bargaining unit may be compelled to pay for the benefits of union representation on their behalf as members of a bargaining unit or if they are free, too, to be free riders.

And, finally, in *Burwell v. Hobby Lobby Stores* (2014), the Court, in another 5–4 decision, held that the owners of a closely held corporation can refuse to provide their female employees no-cost access to certain contraceptives as required by the Affordable Care Act on the grounds that the particular types of contraception violate the owners' religious definition of taking a life, and that thus to provide these contraceptives would violate the owners' freedom of religion under the Religious Freedom Restoration Act of 1993.

And, yet: the Roberts Court Found for the Less Powerful in 2012 and 2015

It was widely anticipated before the Court issued its opinion regarding the Patient Protection and Affordable Care Act (ACA; Obamacare) that the Court would hold unconstitutional at least the individual mandate to purchase health insurance, if not the entirety of the Act. The Affordable Care Act raised the fear, on behalf of the wealthy and corporations, that their taxes will be raised to pay for it, so conservatives—notwithstanding, as observed earlier, that they had originated the idea of the individual mandate—were unified in opposition to it.

In his opinion for the majority in *National Federation of Independent Business v. Sebelius* (2012), Chief Justice John Roberts joined his fellow conservative judicial activists in striking down the provisions of the ACA that required states to either accept an expansion in Medicaid or risk losing existing Medicaid funding. However, he joined the majority on the critical separate issue, holding that the Affordable Care Act's individual mandate to purchase health insurance, enforced by imposition of a penalty paid to the Internal Revenue Service by the individual with that individual's taxes, is a constitutional exercise of the federal government's power to tax (while finding it exceeded Congress' power under the Commerce Clause; Justices Scalia, Alito, Thomas and Kennedy dissented, finding the *entirety* of the Affordable Care Act unconstitutional). In summary, Chief Justice Roberts wrote:

> The Affordable Care Act is constitutional in part and unconstitutional in part. The individual mandate cannot be upheld as an exercise of Congress's power under the Commerce Clause. That Clause authorizes Congress to regulate interstate commerce, not to order individuals to engage in it. In this case, however, it is reasonable to construe what Congress has done as increasing taxes on those who have a certain amount of income, but choose to go without health insurance. Such legislation is within Congress's power to tax.
>
> As for the Medicaid expansion, that portion of the Affordable Care Act violates the Constitution by threatening existing Medicaid funding. Congress has no authority to order the States to regulate according to its instructions. Congress may offer the States grants and require the States to comply with accompanying conditions, but the States must have a genuine choice whether to accept the offer. The States are given no such choice in this case: They must either accept a basic change in the nature of Medicaid, or risk losing all Medicaid funding.

While conservatives criticized Chief Justice Roberts for his opinion upholding the constitutionality of the individual mandate of the Affordable Care Act, claiming that he abandoned his conservative principles, to the contrary, his opinion, first, upheld the conservative principles of judicial restraint and respect for separation of powers; and, second, upheld the individual mandate to purchase private health insurance, which, as observed previously, was a conservative idea in the first place.

Justice Roberts returned to address the Affordable Care Act again in *King v. Burwell* (2015), and again showed judicial restraint. This case turned on the interpretation of six words: "an Exchange established by the State," part of the Affordable Care Act codified in 42 USC §18031. The Affordable Care Act provides that states may establish "Exchanges"—marketplaces allowing people to compare and purchase insurance plans. It also provides that the federal government shall set up a "Federal Exchange," and that a state may elect to not set up its own Exchange and, instead, elect for its residents to use the Federal Exchange. The Affordable Care Act also provides that tax credits are available to subsidize the cost of the health insurance purchased from "an Exchange established by the State." The question before the Court was whether the Affordable Care Act's tax credits are available to residents of states that did not establish their own Exchange and instead relied on the Federal Exchange.

Chief Justice Roberts, writing for the 6–3 majority, observed that, while the plain meaning of the phrase in isolation yielded one interpretation, the phrase had to be interpreted in the broader context of the intent of the Affordable Care Act: "Congress passed the Affordable Care Act to improve health insurance markets, not to destroy them. If at all possible, we must interpret the Act in a way that is consistent with the former, and avoids the latter." Accordingly, the Court found that Congress did not intend to penalize the residents of those states deferring to a Federal Exchange, and, thus, preserved the tax credits assisting an estimated 6.4 million people to afford health insurance in those states, just as in states that had established their own Exchanges.

In the case of *Obergefell v. Hodges* (2015), Justice Anthony Kennedy, philosophically a libertarian conservative, but who also had sided with Chief Justice Roberts in *King v. Burwell*, wrote the opinion for a 5-4 majority that found the Constitution compels the recognition of the right of same-sex marriage—another victory for the less powerful. He closed the opinion with:

> No union is more profound than marriage, for it embodies the highest ideals of love, fidelity, devotion, sacrifice, and family. In forming a marital union, two people become something greater than once they were. As some of the petitioners in these cases demonstrate, marriage embodies a love that may endure even past death. It would misunderstand these men and women to say they disrespect the idea of marriage. Their plea is that they do respect it, respect it so deeply that they seek to find its fulfillment for themselves. Their hope is not to be condemned to live in loneliness, excluded from one of civilization's oldest institutions. They ask for equal dignity in the eyes of the law. The Constitution grants them that right.

And, finally, in the case of *Arizona State Legislature v. Arizona Independent Redistricting Commission* (2015), the Supreme Court was called upon to interpret the "Elections Clause," Article I, Section 4, clause 1 of the Constitution:

> The Times, Places and Manner of holding Elections for Senators and Representatives, shall be prescribed in each State by the Legislature thereof; but the Congress may at any time by Law make or alter such Regulations . . .

In 2000, Arizona voters adopted an initiative, Proposition 106, aimed at "ending the practice of gerrymandering and improving voter and candidate participation in elections." Proposition 106 amended Arizona's Constitution to remove redistricting authority from the Arizona Legislature and vest that authority in an independent commission, the Arizona Independent Redistricting Commission (the Commission). After the 2010 census, as after the 2000 census, the Commission adopted redistricting maps for congressional as well as state legislative districts. The Arizona Legislature challenged the constitutionality of Proposition 106 alleging that the word "Legislature" in the Elections Clause means only the legislature of the state. The Commission argued that the term encompasses all legislative authority conferred by the State Constitution, including popular initiatives. The Supreme Court, in a 5-4 opinion delivered by Justice Ginsburg, held for the Commission, finding that popular initiatives may constitutionally be used by states as a basis for redistricting.

EXTENDING THE RULE OF THE PROPERTIED AND POWERFUL BY OTHER MEANS

Voter Suppression and Gerrymandering

It is not merely the outcome of one election that is at stake, but, rather, the rule of law that underpins our democracy and our entire system of government. Republican efforts at election tampering in battleground states in the presidential elections of 2008[25] and 2012 were well documented—five weeks before the 2012 election, news broke the type of voter fraud the Republicans claimed to be attempting to prevent, as Strategic Allied Consulting, *a contractor for the Republican National Committee,* was accused of committing the fraud.[26]

As documented by the Brennan Center for Justice and New York University School of Law, in the report *Voting Law Changes in 2012*, 16 states passed restrictive voting laws (Florida, Georgia, Illinois, Iowa, Kansas, Mississippi, New Hampshire, Ohio, Pennsylvania, South Carolina, South Dakota, Tennessee, Texas, Virginia, Wisconsin, and West Virginia), and these states accounted for 214 electoral votes, or nearly 79 percent of the total needed to win the presidency, thus these changes held the potential to sway the outcome of the 2012 election.[27]

Republicans, in supporting these measures, have claimed they are attempting ensure that voter fraud (of which there are only a handful of allegations over the last several years in the entire country) is suppressed. And, admittedly, voter ID requirements *fairly enforced* are appropriate. It can easily be imagined that a law requiring mandatory picture identification cards for voters would pass constitutional muster as long as the issuance of such cards was made free and such cards were required to be issued within a few minutes after the voter's picture were taken, as drivers' licenses are (it would be expected that to require a fee to be paid for issuance of a voter identification card would be to institute a requirement of paying to vote—in essence a poll tax—a violation of the 24th Amendment in federal elections and a tax declared unconstitutional by the Supreme Court in the 1966 case of *Harper v. Virginia Board of Elections*).

One Pennsylvania legislator, however, blew Republicans' cover of honest intentions in a Republican State Committee meeting in June 2012. House Republican leader Mike Turzai proudly ticked off the legislative victories of the Republicans since they regained control of both houses and the governor's mansion and proudly proclaimed among them passage of a Voter ID law which would allow Governor Romney to win Pennsylvania, upon which the crowd broke into applause. As of just four months before the election, more than 758,000 registered voters in Pennsylvania did not have photo identification cards required by the law—9.2 percent of the state's 8.2 million voters. In Philadelphia, a Democratic stronghold, 186,830 registered voters—18 percent of the city's total registration—lacked the requisite photo identification.[28]

Turzai's admission was followed the next month by the admission, in a deposition by former Florida Republican Party Chairman Jim Greer, that he had been upset in a December 2009 meeting with party officials because consultants and staff were talking about how to suppress black voting.[29] A study by Massachusetts Institute of Technology Professor Charles Stewart III appeared to indicate nationwide success of this strategy, finding that African Americans waited the longest average time to vote, followed by Hispanics, and whites waited the least time.[30]

The importance of the success of the Republicans' gerrymandering efforts was underscored in the 2012 election which resulted in Democratic candidates receiving 1.4 million more votes for the House of Representatives, yet Republicans won control of the House by a 234 to 201 margin. Associate professor of molecular biology and neuroscience at Princeton University Sam Wang, author of the Princeton Election Consortium website, observed in an op-ed that using the statistical tools that he has used in his field of neuroscience and that have enabled him to accurately predict electoral outcomes, he has found strong evidence that the Republicans' actions are the cause of this aberration.[31]

However, the biggest blow to free elections in the US was dealt by conservatives on the Supreme Court, who were again able to overcome their "reluctance" to "legislating from the bench" when they encountered the Voting Rights Act of 1965, which had, in 2006, been renewed for 25 years by a 390–33 vote in the House of Representatives and a 98–0 vote in the Senate, and signed into law by conservative Republican President George W. Bush. The Court, in an opinion written by Chief Justice Roberts, in *Shelby County v. Holder* (2013), held that Section 4 of the Voting Rights Act was unconstitutional. Section 4 contained the formula that determined whether certain states, counties and municipalities had to run their voting laws through "preclearance" procedures with the Department of Justice. The coverage turned on whether a jurisdiction had a voting test in the 1960s or 1970s, and had low voter turnout at that time.

The Court's opinion cited numerous changes since that time, among them increased voter participation rates and increased political office holding by African Americans—but Congress was privy to this information as well and was, as observed in a fiery dissent by Justice Ruth Bader Ginsburg, charged with "enforcing" each of the Civil War Amendments "by appropriate legislation." Ironically, Justice Roberts' opinion observed, "Indeed, the Tenth Amendment reserves to the States all powers not specifically granted to the Federal Government, including 'the power to regulate elections'"—an observation equally applicable to the 2000 case of *Bush v. Gore*—yet the opinion presented no explanation of why this principle applied in one case but not the other.

Days after the opinion was issued, the title of an article in *The New York Times* duly reported the expected result: "After Ruling, States Rush to Enact Voting Laws."[32] The article recounted the response of Texas officials within hours of the ruling, vowing to begin enforcing strict voter identification laws along the lines of those above, designed to restrict African American and Latino voting. Mississippi and Alabama followed, and expectations were that the holdup in the North Carolina legislature of similar proposals would be overcome, as indeed it was.

The Texas voter identification laws were challenged and found unconstitutional by a federal District Court in Texas, but that opinion was vacated and stayed by the Fifth Circuit Court of Appeals in an opinion upheld by the Supreme Court in *Veasey v. Perry* (2014). That opinion was harshly criticized by Justice Ruth Bader Ginsburg, who observed: "Between 2002 and 2011, there were only two in-person voter fraud cases prosecuted to conviction in Texas." Yet, the District Court found that the law may prevent more than 600,000 registered Texas voters—about 4.5% of all registered voters—from voting in person for lack of sufficient identification. In reality, of course, the Texas law was not a well-intentioned effort to get at a serious problem of voter fraud but, instead, as observed by the District Court in its opinion, operated as an unconstitutional poll tax.

Violation of the Rule of Law by Vindictive Abuse of Public Office to Punish Political Enemies

The Nixon administration famously maintained a secret "enemies list" and prided itself on "dirty tricks" it played on its enemies. A dirty trick by the Bush administration might have put at risk the life of an American intelligence agent—and may have put at risk the lives of her informants. Prior to the invasion of Iraq, former Ambassador Joseph Wilson had been sent to Niger to investigate rumors that Saddam Hussein was attempting to acquire "yellow cake"—uranium ore—for use in nuclear weapons. Upon his return, Wilson wrote a report questioning the allegations. After the president referred in a speech to evidence that the US had indicating that Saddam Hussein had been attempting to acquire yellow cake uranium in Niger, Wilson wrote an op-ed piece in *The New York Times* expressing skepticism about the president's claims that Iraq was shopping for enriched uranium in Africa. Later, Wilson's wife, Valerie Plame, was identified as a CIA analyst in a syndicated newspaper column by conservative Robert Novak.[33] An investigation into the leak of Plame's identity resulted in charges against I. Lewis "Scooter" Libby, the former chief of staff to Vice President Dick Cheney. Libby was convicted in March 2007 of perjury and obstruction of justice. He was sentenced to two-and-a-half years in prison and fined $250,000. President Bush then commuted his sentence.

Brazen Partisanship, Corruption and Deception Undermining the Rule of Law

As observed earlier, an important source for insight into the administration of President George W. Bush is the 2008 book by his former press secretary, Scott McClellan, *What Happened*. A recurring theme in that book is that the White House of George W. Bush suffered from a "permanent campaign" mentality that infected policy decisions with politics and led to a "propaganda" effort to sell the nation on going to war in Iraq. *Time* reporters Michael Duffy and Dan Goodgame, in their 1992 book on the White House of George H. W. Bush, had similarly marveled at the single-minded focus on re-election that drove its domestic policy.[34]

And, too, as observed earlier, it is brazen partisanship when your party's leader in the Senate declares it his mission to make the president, who happens to be a member of the other party, a one-termer, and your party's former leader in the House defines bipartisanship as "date rape."

The Rule of Law and the K Street Project: "To the Victor Goes the Spoils"

The K Street Project was named after the street in Washington, DC on which many lobbyist offices are located. Launched in 1995 by Grover Norquist (Americans for Tax Reform) and then-House majority whip Tom DeLay (R-TX), it was an influence-peddling rent-delivery machine for those sharing a trickle-down "what's good for the wealthy is good for the world" attitude. Other individuals associated with the project were Karl Rove, Dick Cheney, Newt Gingrich, former House Majority Leader Dick Armey (R-TX) and convicted felon Jack Abramoff. The principle behind the K Street Project was expressed best by Armey, in a widely quoted gloat: "There's an old adage. To the victor goes the spoils." And, they certainly did—when the Democrats wrote the 1995 budget, the average Democratic district got $35 million more than the average Republican District; with the Republicans writing the 2001 budget, the average Republican district got *$612 million* more than the average Democratic District.[35]

From its beginning, the goals of the K Street Project were to pressure Washington lobbying firms to hire Republicans as lobbyists, to reward such lobbyists with access to Republican lawmakers, and to pressure the lobbyists for campaign contributions. It represents the institutionalization of crony capitalist influence-peddling, which was formerly disdained as at least unethical, if not illegal, with "pay to play" guaranteed access to Republican lawmakers, ever-decreasing taxes on the wealthiest Americans, and special government benefits for favored businesses.

The Rule of Law and the Politicization of US Attorney Appointments

As observed above, the rule of law includes the requirement that power not be wielded arbitrarily—Article II, Section 3 of the Constitution provides the President "shall take care that the laws be faithfully executed . . . " The Justice Department, of which the Attorney General's office is part, is an executive branch office and, thus, bound by this requirement of the Constitution.

In March 2007, numerous news organizations began to focus on the firings of US Attorneys by the office of Attorney General Alberto Gonzales . The dismissed United States Attorneys had been appointed by President George W. Bush and confirmed by the Senate . Under the law the president has discretion to dismiss US Attorneys without cause, but allegations were raised that the firings were due to their failure to demonstrate that they were "loyal Bushies" in the terminology of a widely circulated email authored by Chief of Staff to the Attorney General, D. Kyle Sampson.[36]

The apparent triggers to concerns regarding loyalty generally consisted of either not vigorously enough prosecuting allegations of Democratic wrongdoing or prosecuting too vigorously allegations of Republican wrongdoing. The administration and its supporters responded that the attorneys were dismissed for poor job performance, although several had been commended for their excellence.

THE RULE OF LAW IN THE "WAR ON TERROR"

It is no exaggeration to say that the "War on Terror" imperils the rule of law as no other phenomenon in the history of the United States of America has. Even during the Civil War, when President Lincoln famously suspended the writ of habeas corpus, this act was recognized as creating a constitutional crisis. However, even though the Civil War lasted several years, it was expected by combatants that the war would eventually end, as one side surrendered, pressed for terms of peace, and a peace treaty was signed. This is the way World War I and World War II ended as well. The Cold War came to an end with the fall of the Soviet Union, the tearing down of the Berlin Wall, and other objective evidence of cessation of hostilities. How will the "War on Terror" end?

Denying Applicability of International Law to the United States and Endorsement of Torture

Conservatives at the time leading up to and after commencement of the Iraq invasion denied the existence of international law.[37] To the credit of the Bush administration, however, Alberto Gonzales (then counsel to the president) wrote an op-ed in *The New York Times* acknowledging that the administration did recognize international law, but that its interpretation of international law led it to deny application of prisoner of war status to al Qaeda terrorists and their collaborators in Afghanistan, the Taliban. Al Qaeda terrorists, claimed the administration, were not prisoners of war under the treaty known as the Third Geneva Convention because that treaty applies to States, and al Qaeda is not a State. The Taliban, while covered by the treaty, did not qualify as prisoners of war because, under the terms of the treaty, combatants must distinguish themselves from the civilian population, which the Taliban did not do.[38]

The administration's position lost in the U.S. Supreme Court, in the case of *Hamdan v. Rumsfeld* (2006), which held that Guantánamo detainees are subject both the provisions of the Universal Code of Military Justice and the Geneva Conventions. Thus, the narrow, critical distinction drawn by Gonzales was refuted by the Court.

Prior to that opinion, in *Hamdi v. Rumsfeld* (2004), Justice Sandra Day O'Connor, writing for the Court, held that "although Congress authorized the detention of combatants in the narrow circumstances alleged here, due process demands that a citizen held in the United States as an enemy combatant be given a meaningful opportunity to contest the factual basis for that detention before a neutral decisionmaker."

However, despite this progress, the clearly erroneous, more general proposition that the United States, because of its superiority (in neoconservative theory), is released from having to abide by the treaties it has signed, had already been released into the public and poisoned discourse, spreading the idea that the US is immune from international standards regarding prisoners' rights regarding due process and freedom from torture.

The National Defense Authorization Act—Better Is Expected of Democratic Administrations

Regrettably, it is wrong to imply that the record of the United States regarding the defense of the rule of law against infringements on behalf of the "War on Terror" improved remarkably after President Obama took office. As the Obama administration ended 2015, Guantánamo was still open, and the National Defense Authorization Act (NDAA), signed by President Obama, was still on the books. The NDAA's Section 1021 "Homeland Battlefield" provisions authorize military detention for people deemed to have "substantially supported" al Qaeda, the Taliban, or "associated forces."

In May 2012, US District Judge Katherine Forrest of Manhattan issued a temporary injunction blocking enforcement of the indefinite detention powers of the NDAA, and in September issued a permanent injunction in the case of *Hedges et al v. Obama et al*, in the Southern District of New York, brought by the former war correspondent for *The New York Times* and Pulitzer Prize winner Chris Hedges.[39] However, on July 17, 2013, the Second Circuit Court of Appeals overturned the district court's permanent injunction based on the rationale that the plaintiffs lacked legal standing to challenge NDAA's indefinite detention powers. When the Supreme Court declined to hear the case on April 28, 2014, the Second Circuit's decision was made the final word on the matter, and the indefinite detention powers of the NDAA remain the law.

NOTES

1. As will be seen later herein, the term "legislating from the bench" is used by conservatives to criticize liberal Supreme Court opinions striking down laws for unconstitutionality, while conservatives are silent regarding use of the term regarding *conservative* Supreme Court opinions striking down laws for unconstitutionality.
2. Friedrich Hayek, *The Constitution of Liberty*, p. 402. Repeated from Chapter 5.
3. Leo Strauss, *Natural Right and History* (Chicago and London: The University of Chicago Press, 1950, 1953, 1965), pp. 134–135.
4. Theodore J. Lowi, *The End of the Republican Era* (Norman, OK: The University of Oklahoma Press, 1996), p. 259.
5. Richard Bellamy, professor of Political Science at University College London, edited *The Rule of Law and the Separation of Powers* (London: Ashgate Publishing Company; 2005) which contains several law review articles addressing the question in its first part titled "Defining the Rule of Law." One of the articles addresses the question in detail, but makes no mention of Dicey's formulation: Jeremy Waldron, "Is the Rule of Law an Essentially Contested Concept (in Florida)?" 21 *Law and Philosophy*, pp. 137–164.
6. A. V. Dicey, *Introduction to the Study of the Law of the Constitution* (8th edition, 1915; reprinted by Liberty Fund, Indianapolis, 1982), pp. 120 and 115.
7. Parenthetically, it should be noted that even though the Supreme Court does not resolve rule of law cases often, a similar conflict is the disagreement regarding the approach of the Supreme Court to decisions: Should the Supreme Court be "strict constructionist" (looking to history to guide interpretation), or is the Constitution a "living document" (changing in meaning with the times)?
8. Friedrich Hayek, *The Mirage of Social Justice* (Chicago and London: The University of Chicago Press, 1976).
9. William F. Buckley, Jr., *Up from Liberalism* (New York; Bantam Books, 1959, 1968), p. 175.
10. Ibid, footnote, pp. 112–113.

11. Anatole France, (1844–1924), *The Red Lilly* (1894), chapter 7. France's real name was Jacques Anatole François Thibault. He was born in Paris, France, and was a successful novelist and ally of Emile Zola (author of *J'Accuse*) in the Dreyfus Affair.

12. Theodore Lowi, *The End of Liberalism: The Second Republic of the United States* (New York, W.W. Norton & Co., Inc., 1969, 1979).

13. Mancur Olson, *The Rise and Decline of Nations* (New Haven: Yale University, 1982), p. 44.

14. James M. Buchanan, Robert D. Tollison, and Gordon Tullock, editors, *Toward a Theory of the Rent-Seeking Society* (College Station, TX: Texas A&M University Press, 1980).

15. James M. Buchanan and Gordon Tullock, *The Calculus of Consent* (Ann Arbor, MI: The University of Michigan Press, 1962, 1965), p. 286.

16. William Julius Wilson, *Power, Racism and Privilege: Race Relations in Theoretical and Sociohistorical Perspectives* (New York: The Free Press; 1973), pp. 189, 190.

17. Below is 3 USC 5 in its entirety: "If any State shall have provided, by laws enacted prior to the day fixed for the appointment of the electors, for its final determination of any controversy or contest concerning the appointment of all or any of the electors of such State, by judicial or other methods or procedures, and such determination shall have been made at least six days before the time fixed for the meeting of the electors, such determination made pursuant to such law so existing on said day, and made at least six days prior to said time of meeting of the electors, shall be conclusive, and shall govern in the counting of the electoral votes as provided in the Constitution, and as hereinafter regulated, so far as the ascertainment of the electors appointed by such State is concerned."

And, Article II of the Constitution provides, in pertinent part: "Each state shall appoint, in such manner as the Legislature thereof may direct, a number of electors, equal to the whole number of Senators and Representatives to which the State may be entitled in the Congress: but no Senator or Representative, or person holding an office of trust or profit under the United States, shall be appointed an elector."

18. *Citizens United* did not find unconstitutional the Tillman Act of 1907 because the Tillman Act bans *direct* corporate donations to campaigns.

19. Interview with Mitt Romney, *Morning Edition, NPR* January 20, 2012. For a profile of a creator of the Restore Our Future super PAC, see Jane Mayer, "Attack Dog," *The New Yorker*, February 13, 2012.

20. For a critique of the opinion, see E. J. Dionne Jr., "The *Citizens United* Catastrophe," *The Washington Post*, February 5, 2012. See also the George W. Bush White House website, which, in 2015 (it was still being maintained), revealed "about 461 results found" for the term "legislating from the bench"—the term was used by President George W. Bush in speeches commending Chief Justice John Roberts' nomination to the Supreme Court and Justice Samuel Alito's Senate confirmation to the Supreme Court, and in numerous radio addresses and speeches to conservative groups, as well as by others in the Bush administration, including Vice President Cheney, Attorney General Gonzales, and White House Press Secretaries Ari Fleischer and Scott McClellan.

21. For a summary of contribution limits, see the document "Contribution Limits for 2015–2016 Federal Elections" at the Federal Election Commission (FEC) website. For a PAC to be classified as a multicandidate committee, it must have been registered with the FEC for 6 months, received contributions from more than 50 people, and contributed to at least five candidates.

22. Nicholas Confessore, "Koch Brothers' Budget of $889 Million for 2016 Is on Par With Both Parties' Spending," *The New York Times*, January 27, 2015.

23. Eric Lichtblau, "F.E.C. Can't Curb 2016 Election Abuse, Commission Chief Says," *The New York Times*, May 2, 2015.

24. The Editors, "The Invisible Primary," *The Nation*, May 11, 2015. See also, Dana Milbank, "For the GOP, 'One Man, One Vote' Becomes 'One Billionaire, One Ballot'," *The Washington Post*, April 27, 2015.

25. Bob Herbert, "The Real Scandal," *The New York Times*, October 21, 2008.

26. Allied was run by Nathan Sproul, a former head of the Arizona Christian Coalition and for three years executive director of the Arizona Republican Party. He claimed that as a result

of voter fraud allegations against him in 2004 he was asked by the RNC to change the name of his firm. Joseph Tanfani, Melanie Mason and Matea Gold, "RNC Cuts Ties with Voter-Driven Firm Accused of Fraud," *The Los Angeles Times*, September 28, 2012 and Jerry Markon and T. W. Farnam, "Businessman Who Cut Ties with GOP at Center of Voter Fraud Probe in Florida," *The Washington Post*, October 2, 2012.

27. See also Alex Slater, "Voter ID Laws: The Republican Ruse to Disenfranchise 5 Million Americans," *The Guardian*, August 10, 2012.

28. Angela Couloumbis, "A Top Republican's Remark about Voter ID Brings Him Under Political Fire," *The Philadelphia Inquirer*, June 28, 2012, and Bob Warner, "Voter ID Law May Affect More Pennsylvanians than Previously Estimated," *The Philadelphia Inquirer*, July 5, 2012. And President Obama carried Pennsylvania.

29. Alex Seitz-Wald, "Fla. Republican: We Wanted to Suppress Black Votes," *Salon.com*, July 27, 2012.

30. Charles Stewart III and Stephen Ansolabehere, "Waiting in Line to Vote in 2012," July 28, 2013.

31. Sam Wang, "The Great Gerrymander of 2012," *The New York Times,* February 3, 2013. See also Paul Krugman, "The Crazy Party," *The New York Times*, September 20, 2013.

32. Michael Cooper, "After Ruling, States Rush to Enact Voting Laws," *The New York Times*, July 6, 2013.

33. Robert Novak, "Mission to Niger," *The Washington Post*, July 14, 2003.

34. Michael Duffy and Daniel Goodgame, *Marching in Place* (New York: Simon & Schuster, 1992) p. 68.

35. David Pace, "Billions in Federal Spending Shifted to GOP Districts after 1994 House Takeover," *Associated Press*, August 5, 2002.

36. See Sheryl Gay Stolberg, "On a Very Hot Seat with Little Cover and Less Support," *The New York Times*, April 20, 2007.

37. Among conservatives voicing this opinion were Ann Coulter on CNN with Wolf Blitzer December 12, 2003 and Tom Barrett, in "What International Law?" *Conservative Truth.org*, November 17, 2002.

38. Alberto R. Gonzales, "The Rule of Law and the Rules of War," *The New York Times*, May 15, 2004.

39. Basil Katz, "U.S. Judges' Rule Protects Reporters, Activists in Their Middle East Work," *Reuters*, September 12, 2012.

III

Trickle-Up:
The Way the World *Really* Works

Chapter Nine

The Information Revolution, Globalization and Trickle-Down Versus the Poor and Middle Class

Human beings cannot be treated merely as commodities or tools. If an apple spoils before it is sold, it is thrown away; if a screwdriver has served its usefulness, it goes back into the toolbox until needed again. Humans can neither be thrown away nor put back into storage. When one of us loses a job, it affects not only the one who is now unemployed but also that person's entire family, that family's finances presently and long into the future, and perhaps the mental and physical health of that individual and potentially that of other family members as well. This is a failure in fact of trickle-down, hidden in economic theory that blithely ignores such concerns. Perhaps it was motivation over these sociological concerns that prompted Friedrich Hayek to observe, in *The Road to Serfdom* (1944), "Probably nothing has done so much harm to the [classical] liberal cause as the wooden insistence of some liberals on certain rough rules of thumb, above all the principle of laissez faire."[1]

Charles Horton Cooley was an American sociologist whose insights regarding "the self" will be addressed in detail. One of his famous pronouncements was, "Each man must have his 'I,' it is more necessary to him than bread; and if he does not find scope for it within the existing institutions he will be likely to make trouble."[2]

Cooley recognized the necessity of a good sense of well-being, and that how an individual forms the image of self is socially determined, as the individual sees himself as he imagines he is seen. And, how an individual—especially a male, given the historical expectation to be the breadwinner—

sees himself is determined in great part by whether he has a job, with a good, and growing, income.

Recall Reverend Dr. Martin Luther King Jr.'s stirring "I Have a Dream" speech was delivered in 1963 at the "March on Washington for Jobs and Freedom." Five years later, imbued with appreciation of the critical, spiritual importance to a sense of self of having a job, a then-young Reverend Jesse Jackson, seizing on the dispiritedness of his flock at Resurrection City during the Poor People's Campaign in Washington gave hope to them with these words, which they repeated:

> I am
> Somebody.
> I am
> God's child.
> I may not have a job, but I am somebody.[3]

As will be seen herein, it began to be recognized beginning in the 1950s, and increasingly in the 1960s and 1970s, that the Information Revolution and globalization would increase productivity, thus creating the needed rationale for increased wages—yet, at the same time, enabling more work to be done by fewer workers and by workers in other countries, thus, although many new jobs would be created, many millions of jobs would be lost in agriculture and heavy manufacturing, and unemployment rates in these areas would rise, thereby ultimately putting *downward* pressure on wages, especially of unskilled workers, resulting in massive material and spiritual pressure on the middle class and poor and resultant negative social change.

This negative social change—brought on by poor economic circumstances—began with the working poor, spreading through their ranks, and then began moving up through the middle class. Because the poor have always been the "canary in the coal mine," whose declining conditions provide warnings of economic and social disaster that has the potential to work its way next into the lower middle class, then the middle class, and on up through the economy generally, this chapter and the one following addressing institutions refer to the effects on the poor first, and then the middle class.

And, into this setting of downward pressure on wages (hidden at the time by consumer price inflation, which was pushing up nominal wages), we, the American voters, imposed the policies recommended by trickle-down economics: upwardly redistributing the revenues attributable to the increased productivity that resulted from the Information Revolution and globalization and increasing the downward pressure on the wages of the poor and middle class. Liberals would remind the public of the economic context for the social dysfunction observed especially in America's inner cities in the 1960s and thereafter, but the various conservative explanations for this dysfunction would capture public attention. These explanations, among them the lure of welfare for those with moral inferiority, intellectual inferiority and decline in values due to the supposed failure of elites to pass on their values to their fellow citizens will be explored below and rejected in favor of a liberal explanation that focuses on how declining economic circumstances change behavior, lowering the labor force participation rate for men, resulting in postponement or abandonment of marriage due to fewer good prospects for husbands, social isolation (essentially, loss of connectedness) and further socioeconomic decline.

THE IMPORTANCE OF A JOB TO SOCIAL STATUS AND SELF-ESTEEM

Sociologists Peter L. Berger and Thomas Luckmann in their seminal work *The Social Construction of Reality: A Treatise in the Sociology of Knowledge* (1966) provided three broad insights useful here: (1) Much of what is called "knowledge" is socially defined;[4] (2) The concept of the "self" is socially defined (addressed below); and (3) The concept of "reality" is socially defined.[5]

The Looking-Glass Self

Berger and Luckmann described the "self" in terms that borrowed heavily from the "symbolic-interactionist" school of sociology. They referenced George Herbert Meade—but another symbolic-interactionist, Charles Horton Cooley, quoted earlier, is preferred herein for his introduction to the concept of the self. Cooley used the term "social self" (borrowed from William James's *The Principles of Psychology* [1890]), which he defined as "simply any idea, or system of ideas, drawn from the communicative life, that the mind cherishes as its own."[6] Cooley then defined "the looking-glass self" in poetry:

> Each to each a looking-glass.
> Reflects the other that doth pass.

He elaborated: "As we see our face, figure, and dress in the glass, and are interested in them because they are ours, and pleased or otherwise with them according as they do or do not answer to what we should like them to be; so in imagination we perceive in another's mind some thought of our appearance, manners, aims, deeds, character, friends and so on, and are variously affected by it."[7] In short, the definition of the "looking-glass self" is that we all see ourselves as we imagine others see us.

Berger and Luckmann built on the theories of James, Cooley and Meade in describing how a child's image of self develops, similarly based on the response of others toward the child.[8] Thus, objective factors that shape self-image—factors such as a "good job," how one is viewed by those with whom one comes in contact, how one's group is viewed by the larger society, the attractiveness of one's neighborhood—are critical to development of self-image.

A recurring theme herein is that economic circumstances influence self-esteem and culture, and, thereby, influence social, economic and political conditions. Perhaps no more succinct statement of the importance of a job comes from the management theorist Peter Drucker, who observed in *The New Society: The Anatomy of Industrial Order* (1950)[9]:

> [S]ocial effectiveness, citizenship, indeed even self-respect depend on access to a job. Without a job man in industrial society cannot possibly be socially effective. He is deprived of citizenship, of social standing, of the respect of his fellow men, if not of his family and, finally of self-respect. No amount of economic relief can possibly offset the social destruction of chronic unemployment in an industrial society.

Similarly, the Harvard sociologist Daniel Bell noted, in his 1996 "Afterward" to the re-release of his 1976 work, *The Cultural Contradictions of Capitalism*, Aristotle had written in *Politics* two thousand years ago that a successful democracy needs its citizens with self-esteem and, Bell reasoned, if self-esteem is necessary for democracy and a job is necessary for self-esteem, then full employment policy must be the basic characteristic of the good society, and not provision of basic welfare.[10] Two years later, Congress passed and President Carter signed into law the Full Employment and Balanced Growth Act—popularly, the Humphrey-Hawkins Full Employment Act—which asserted "the responsibility of the Federal Government to use all practicable programs and policies to promote full employment . . . ."[11] Ironically, as observed by Michael Porter, Harvard Business School professor, we are relearning the lesson today that economic development cannot be separated from social progress.[12]

Parenthetically, it is important to note that conservative economic theory views all long-term unemployment as voluntary. Conservatives observe that an unemployed person has numerous options: he can recognize that his labor is not worth what he is charging for it (that is why, in conservative theory, he lost his job in the first place). Recognizing this, he can take a lesser-paying full-time job, or a part-time job. He can go back to school in order to raise his skill level to the level of income he believes he deserves. He can "vote with his feet": move to another city, state, or country in search of work. Or, he can dip into his savings, or secure a loan from family, friends, a bank and/or a venture capital source and start up a business for himself.

Liberals, in contrast, recognize the reality that people sometimes involuntarily lose their jobs, and the loss of a job is a staggering blow economically (a cessation of income), socially (a blow to self-esteem) and emotionally (potentially undermining relationships with one's spouse, one's children, other relatives and friends) and even, perhaps, physically (as health is undermined either due to lack of health care or emotional stress).

Further, the effect of job loss or of any blow to self-esteem is even more devastating to someone whose self-esteem is already under attack due to reduced social status, as were African Americans in the late 1950s and early 1960s, the period addressed by Charles Silberman, in *Crisis in Black and White* (1964), wherein he observed the self-hatred of African American men in the inner cities that were beginning to empty out.[13] In an application of the "looking-glass self" addressed above, Silberman described the observation of psychiatrists Abram Kardiner and Lionel Ovesey[14] who noted that self-esteem is suffering because of the unpleasant image reflected back from the behavior of others toward them.[15] Similarly, Ralph Ellison, in his 1947 classic, described feeling as though he were, as he described it in the title of his work, *The Invisible Man,* doubting his very existence.[16] James Baldwin described feeling like "nobody knows my name" (in his book of the same title published in 1961). In his classic "Letter from a Birmingham Jail," Dr. Martin Luther King, Jr., described "forever fighting a degenerating sense of nobodiness." W.E.B. DuBois described it as "a sense of never being heard."[17]

Looking outwardly for definition, one who has suffered social and economic humiliation perceives condemnation and turns it inward. Thus, one can see that the roots of self-hatred identified by Ellison, Baldwin, King and DuBois are *social*: One is only an invisible man if *no one else* can see you. If you feel like nobody knows your name, you ascribe to everyone else an uncaring attitude towards your welfare, undermining your self-esteem. One fights a degenerating sense of nobodiness only in a social context, if you are treated as nobody. And, finally, you are only never heard if *no one else* can hear you. Looking outwardly for validation—that someone sees you, hears you, knows your name, knows you are somebody—and perceiving nothing in response from society—one perceives condemnation and turns it inward.

An attitude emerges that amounts to a "dropping out" of dominant society. A counterculture begins to emerge among similarly-situated individuals, as in the case of "prison chic" fashion and "gansta rap" music.

However, a job is critical to the self-esteem not only of African Americans, or the poor or the middle class. Having a job is critical to the self-esteem of everyone, as illustrated in a study published by the NBER which found a relationship between having a job and life expectancy.[18] Phillip B. Levine, an economics professor at Wellesley College and two Wellesley colleagues and report co-authors Courtney C. Coile and Robin McKnight concluded that life expectancy of Baby Boomers ages 57 to 61 who lose their jobs and their health insurance may be decreased as much as three years. However, the life expectancy of those younger (ages 55 to 56) and older (ages 62 to 65) who lose their jobs appears to be unaffected. Presumably, for that older group, life expectancy is not affected because the safety net provided by Social Security and Medicare cushions the impact.

THE NEGATIVE EFFECTS OF THE INFORMATION REVOLUTION AND GLOBALIZATION COMPOUNDED BY TRICKLE-DOWN

The Historical Context of Slavery, Jim Crow, the Great Depression, World War II—and the Eve of the Information Revolution

The Great Depression hit African Americas harder economically than it did whites. However, the Great Depression was followed by hopeful economic conditions during and after World War II and the Korean War, especially in the cities of the North, Midwest and West to which African Americans moved from the rural South in search of opportunity. These economic conditions were accompanied by hopeful social conditions, among them the integration of the military, accompanied by expectations of grant of full citizenship by a nation grateful for their service; expanded opportunities for African Americans in federal employment; the 1954 school desegregation case of *Brown v. Board of Education*; and the desegregation of Little Rock, Arkansas schools.

Drawing on the writings of E. Franklin Frazier, some commentators, notably Lawrence Harrison, in *Who Prospers? How Cultural Values Shape Economic and Political Success* (1992), have advanced the argument that the "underclass" is an outgrowth of bad values created by slavery. The fact is, however, that black male labor force participation rates *exceeded* those for white males in the 1950s and the rates were almost identical in 1960. Why, suddenly, after almost 100 years, did slavery exert its influence and drive down black male labor force participation rates from 1960 to 1980, or raise illegitimacy rates and crime rates during that period? The theory cannot provide an answer and, accordingly, fails, except as providing, in combination with the Great Depression, a context for how vastly worse conditions were for African Americans just before World War II. Additionally, both slavery and the Great Depression reinforced the agrarian nature of African American employment and the associated molding of values by an agrarian society. In this regard, one thinks of the concepts of work as being by the sweat of the brow rather than the seat of the pants, and consisting of physical labor.

Recall, as observed by Joseph Schumpeter in Chapter 4, the essence of capitalism is "creative destruction," and that the two drivers of that creative destruction are technology and globalization. It should be no surprise, as will be seen below, that numerous writers foresaw that the Information Revolution and globalization would drive economic growth but simultaneously suppress middle class and working poor income and job growth, hitting hardest African Americans. This impact would manifest itself in an anomalous display of social indicators that would be addressed in what would become among the most famous government reports ever published.

"Moynihan's Scissors"

The 1957-1958 and 1960-1961 recessions were devastating, and resulted in lingering stagnancy in the economy until the 1961 tax cuts (wherein the Kennedy administration reduced marginal income tax rates). As observed by Fred Siegel in his 1997 book *The Future Once Happened Here*, as late as 1957, welfare rolls were growing, but they did not explode in growth until the 1960s, when they were accompanied by growth in crime and illegitimacy rates.[19] Welfare rules had been loosened, but something more was happening.

In *Miles to Go*, Daniel Patrick Moynihan elaborated on the subject of his research when he was Assistant Secretary of Labor for Policy Planning and Research. In 1963 he had begun an effort to develop correlations between economic data (then termed "manpower" data) and indicators of social dysfunction. The results of his research were published in 1965, in a document titled "The Negro Family: The Case for National Action." The report came to be referred to simply as *The Moynihan Report*.

There was, when it was issued, and continues to be, much confusion regarding what the report actually says. Moynihan's key observation was that the number of Aid to Families with Dependent Children (AFDC; "welfare") cases being opened had for many years risen and fallen in tandem with the unemployment rate, yet, after several years of unemployment rates *falling*, the number of AFDC cases being opened continued to rise (in 1960, 1963 and 1964[20]). UCLA sociologist James Q. Wilson would call this split "Moynihan's scissors." Two separate lines of explanation, broadly divided into conservative and liberal, developed to explain this phenomenon. They will be addressed below, as will three separate definitions of "culture of poverty" that arose and guided this debate.

The preferred liberal explanation for the explosion in welfare payments recognizes that this growth in welfare occurred among a population that had only recently experienced much hopefulness in terms of economic improvement in the late 1940s and 1950s, only to have that hope dashed by massive social and economic change in the late 1950s and early 1960s. There was a *massive loss of good-paying jobs that were based on physical labor*—jobs especially well-suited to the African American male recent migrants to the

Northern, Midwestern and Western industrialized cities from the agrarian societies of the South (as such jobs had been well-suited to the many Irish, Italian and Eastern European immigrants from agrarian societies who preceded them, as observed by economist Thomas Sowell[21]).

In a 1965 article in the journal *Daedalus*, titled "Employment, Income, and the Ordeal of the Negro Family," Daniel Patrick Moynihan addressed this phenomenon emphatically: "The underemployment of the Negro father has led to the break-up of the Negro family." This underemployment and unemployment fed feelings of low self-worth, hopelessness and failure that, in turn, changed behaviors that would have supported the poor moving into, and the middle class staying in or even moving up out of, the middle class.

The Inception of the Information Revolution

Jeremy Rifkin, in *The End of Work: The Decline of the Global Labor Force and Dawn of the Post-Market Era* (1995), chronicled a number of studies that long ago raised concerns regarding the effect of post-World War II technological and managerial change on society in general, and African Americans in particular (because they held the most vulnerable jobs), thus foretelling the devastating effects of what we would come to call the Information Revolution and globalization that prominently manifested itself in the late 1950s and 1960s, and in what we would later call the underclass. These studies all reflected on the effect of "cybernation" on unskilled workers in general, and African Americans in particular, because they represented a disproportionate share of the unskilled workforce. African American workers were predicted to be, and became, the first victims of the post-World War II Information Revolution and globalization, the changes wrought by which directly created "underemployment"—stagnant or declining real wages—and rising inequality of incomes and wealth.

Rifkin begins the story with Norbert Wiener, the father of cybernetics (the theoretical study of information flow in a system). Wiener, himself, invented the term, deriving it from the Greek word *kybernan*, meaning to steer or govern. In *The Human Use of Human Beings* (1950), Wiener equated the "automatic machine" to slave labor, and he warned of its potential to create widespread unemployment.

In 1964 a group that called itself the "Ad Hoc Committee on the Triple Revolution" ("Cybernation, Weaponry and Human Rights") issued a report which recognized that African Americans were hardest hit by cybernation.[22] That same year, in his essay "The Problems of the Negro Movement," Tom Kahn[23] (more on him below) similarly observed, "For the vast majority of Negroes . . . an economic crisis is in the offing . . . .*It is as if racism, having put the Negro in his economic 'place,' stepped aside to watch technology destroy that place.*"[24] (Italics original.)

In 1966, the prominent African American auto worker and political activist James Boggs addressed these concerns in an article titled "The Negro in Cybernation."[25] Sidney Wilhelm, in his 1970 book ominously titled *Who Needs the Negro?* echoed this sentiment.[26]

As observed previously, pressed by this effort, Congress convened The National Committee on Technology, Automation and Economic Progress to study the report, and that commission released its own report in 1966, titled "Technology and the American Economy." The report observed, regarding what would come to be called the Information Revolution[27]:

> The technological revolution in agriculture has compounded the difficulties of a large section of our Negro population. Pushed out of rural areas, many have migrated to cities in search of livelihood. But they have arrived just when deficient economic growth rates have increased the competition for available jobs and when advancing technology has been reducing the numbers of the semi-skilled and unskilled manufacturing jobs for which they could qualify.

And, looking into the future[28]:

> Unless Negroes, and to a lesser degree, youth, are able to penetrate growing occupations and industries at a more rapid rate than in the past, their high unemployment rates will continue or even rise . . . .The needs of our society provide ample opportunities to fulfill the promise of the Employment Act of 1946: "a job for all those able, willing, and seeking to work." We recommend a program of public service employment, providing, in effect, that the Government be an employer of last resort, providing work for the "hardcore-unemployed" in useful community enterprises.

The post-World War II technological and managerial changes in not only the American economy but the world economy as well ushered in a structural shift from an industrial to an information-based society. Different writers have given different names to this phase of development, but each has either warned of the effect this revolution would have on African Americans, or chronicled the effect as it happened. Ralf Dahrendorf addressed it in *Class and Class Conflict in an Industrial Society* (1959). Zbigniew Brzezinski called it the "technetronic era" in *Between Two Ages: America's Role in the Technetronic Era* (1971).[29] Daniel Bell called this era "post-industrial society," the "knowledge society"[30] and, presciently, a "service class society"[31] in *The Coming of Post-Industrial Society* (1973).[32] And Peter Drucker, in *Post-Capitalist Society* (1993) called it "post-capitalist society." Jeremy Rifkin dubbed it both "post-market society" and also "the third industrial revolution" (the first was based on steam power, the second on oil and electricity, and the third began immediately after World War II) in *The End of Work.* Other writers who have also linked urban decline with global economic change are Mickey Kaus in *The End of Equality* and Newt Gingrich's favorite futurist, Alvin Toffler, in *The Third Wave*. This era has also widely been called "The Information Age."

Bell, in *The Coming of Post-Industrial Society,* traced his first use of the term "post-industrial society" to 1959.[33] By the term, he was referring to a "social framework" (this concept and that of "institutions" will be addressed in detail in the following chapter).[34]

He presciently observed (again—*in 1973*), that the post-industrial society is based on services and, thus, knowledge, and that reality itself had transformed from being the natural world of the preindustrial age to the technical world of the industrial age to the social world of the modern age.[35] The sociologist Bell foresaw a society in which, using the same terms as the sociologists Berger and Luckmann, the social world became reified. However, explicit in Berger and Luckmann's analysis was the concept that the individual could escape from this socially-created world—it was created by humans and was not actually "real." In Bell's analysis, this socially-created world *is* the real world. As for what the implications would be for those at the margin—economically and socially, such as the new migrants to the industrialized cities of the Northeast, Midwest and West, from the agrarian South—the African Americans—Bell quoted a prescient essay he had written in 1962 ("The Post-Industrial Society") in which he observed that education would provide the opportunity for advancement and, because educational opportunity was so color-based, class society three decades on would become color-based.[36]

The management theorist Peter Drucker, coincidentally writing thirty-one years later, confirmed Bell's prediction, observing that the shrinkage of manual jobs in the mass production industries had most greatly affected African Americans, and that the traditional factors of production—land, labor and capital—had become secondary to knowledge, the most important resource in what he called the "Knowledge Society."[37]

"Culture of Poverty": Liberal and Conservative Definitions, and How the Liberal Concept of Culture of Poverty Is Extended by the Concept of "Social Isolation"

Given the importance of sense of self to an individual, and the importance of a job to one's sense of self, it would appear important, for the benefit of society, that institutions in the market, government and civil society promote and reinforce a positive sense of self and, if they fail to do so, societal dysfunction will result. The term "culture of poverty" became a popular term for that dysfunction, and it will be explored herein.

According to Herbert Gans in *The War Against the Poor* (1996) the originator of the term "culture of poverty" was Oscar Lewis, who first used it in his *Five Families: Mexican Case Studies in the Culture of Poverty* (1959) to refer to culturally transmitted dysfunctional values arising apart from influence of economic circumstances.[38]

Gans observed that when Michael Harrington (addressed below) used "culture of poverty" to describe a culture that developed in response to restricted social and economic opportunity, Lewis was not pleased that he had redefined the term as such and continued to use it himself with reference solely in his more restricted original sense.[39] William Julius Wilson provided his own critique of the term "culture of poverty" as well, however, that critique was directed at the conservative culture of poverty theory originated by Lewis, and expanded upon by other conservatives such as Charles Murray and Myron Magnet, for whom the term meant a culture distinguished by capitulation to the lure of welfare and/or weak intellect.

The critical difference between the conservative culture of poverty concept (of Lewis, Murray and Magnet) and the liberal concept of culture of poverty (of Michael Harrington and his associate Tom Kahn), extended by William Julius Wilson's concept of "social isolation" (more on it below) is that the liberal vision acknowledges *economic circumstances and social status can affect self-esteem*—at one extreme enhancing it; at the other crushing it—*and, in doing so, economic circumstances can mold and influence culture (values) but also, even if they do not influence culture, they can influence behavior*. Thus, the liberal concept of culture of poverty begins with economic circumstances, and ends not only with cultural response but also with behavior in response to limited economic circumstances even if culture remains committed to "middle class" values. In contrast, the conservative culture of poverty concept ignores economic circumstances except only as an end result which does not interact with the theory's other elements. And, thus, the conservative culture of poverty concept begins with cultural, moral or intellectual deficiencies of those in poverty. As an aside, the focus herein will be on how poor economic circumstances can negatively affect behavior, however, evidence is growing that positive economic circumstances—wealth—can shape people's opinions as well, making them support policies more attuned to trickle-down conservatism.[40] Below, the liberal concept of culture of poverty will be addressed, followed by the conservative.

Before proceeding however, a cautionary note, elaborating on the above: As William Julius Wilson observed, and as will be borne out by research conducted by the sociologist and hero to conservatives Charles Murray in his 2012 book *Coming Apart: The State of White America, 1960-2010*, what *appears* to be cultural change may in fact be a change in behavior in response to economic circumstances that occurs even though culture has not truly changed—as in the concept from the 1960s and 1970s of "trying to get over"—if one can only get a handle on the bills and save a little then one might be able to act on those aspirations like getting a college education, getting married, buying a house, etc. This concept is tragic for policymakers and Americans of means to behold because it captures the idea that there are those of our fellow Americans who still believe in the American Dream but believe that, because of limited economic opportunity and circumstances, the dream is not for them.

Harrington and Kahn: Basis for the Liberal Concept of Culture of Poverty

Michael Harrington's *The Other America* (1962) helped inspire President Lyndon Johnson's War on Poverty, and perhaps because of present-day criticisms of that movement as "simply throwing money at social problems" there is a tendency to misconstrue and forget the prescience of both that work and Kahn's. Harrington opened his book by contrasting the world he was addressing with the world described in a previous book in the 1950s on the "familiar America": John Kenneth Galbraith's *The Affluent Society* (1958).

In his first chapter, titled "The Invisible Land," Harrington described his book as dealing with the "other America" of poverty, hidden from the rest of us.[41] Among the reasons these other Americans were hidden was (in this observation he preceded Edward C. Banfield's 1970 book, *The Unheavenly City*) the impact of government housing programs after World War II that warehoused people in already existent slums.[42]

Harrington wove in this chapter a theory linking social psychology to sociology to economics, which combined into a self-reinforcing vicious cycle, leading him to focus on the aspects of this new poverty that crush aspirations[43] and result in immunity from progress.[44] He acknowledged that the vicious circle of the culture of poverty[45] created its own language, psychology and worldview.[46]

Harrington acknowledged the impact of economic events in enforcing these detrimental attitudes, observing the devastating effects inflicted by the recessions of 1957-1958 and 1960-1961: Median family income for African Americans rose from 51 percent of white family income in 1947 to 57 percent in 1952, and then declined back to the 1947 level by 1959.[47]

In his chapter titled "The Twisted Spirit," Harrington described in detail a "personality of poverty," exhibited by the "other Americans," shaped by the culture of poverty. This personality was marked by, among other undesirable traits, hopelessness, depression and passivity broken by outbursts of violence.[48] To address the culture of poverty, Harrington urged destruction of the pessimism and fatalism that accompany it.[49]

Harrington was not only an early exponent of "culture of poverty," but he preceded Francis Fukuyama's observations on the importance of "trust" and preceded William Julius Wilson's observations regarding behavior deemed "socially pathological" as being a natural response to slum life and in use of the term "social isolation".[50]

Returning to Tom Kahn's 1964 essay, "Problems of the Negro Movement,"[51] Kahn observed that the civil rights movement had "entered a critical period"[52] —an "historic turning point . . . Toward which portion of the Negro community will they orient their policies and programs?"[53] Echoing his mentor Harrington, he observed that the same technological revolution creating two Americas—the affluent society and the other America, was also dividing the black community among the black bourgeoisie and technocrats, on the one side, and the majority of blacks on the other.

In a discussion reminiscent of that of William Julius Wilson regarding affirmative action much later: "Preferential treatment . . . benefits most those Negroes who need it least."[54] Nonetheless, as did Wilson, Kahn saw a role for affirmative action that addressed not racial but *class* differences: "Preferential treatment, yes—but as A. Philip Randolph declares, preferential treatment for all the unemployed, the poor, the sick, the aged, disadvantaged youth—for the other America."[55]

Kahn viewed the challenge as being to rescue African Americans from "isolation" linked to the "very nature of class unemployment," which "tends to induce passivity, not revolt."[56] And Kahn echoed Harrington's observations regarding the economic situation, but spelled it out in detail with a critical observation: "The Negro's *relative* income gains were actually registered between 1940 and 1954, when Negro family median income jumped from 37 percent to 56 per cent of the white figure." The obvious reason for this gain: ". . . World War II (not the New Deal, after eight years of which 24 per cent of the Negro work force was still unemployed against 13 per cent of the white). War production created a shortage not only of skilled workers but of semiskilled and unskilled workers . . . in the relatively prosperous postwar years the unemployment rate among Negroes was only about 60 per cent higher than the white rate. *Since 1954 it has been 250-350 per cent higher.*"[57] (Emphasis original.)

Kahn observed that the result was "what Professor Charles Killingsworth of Michigan State University has called the 'invisible army of the unemployed'—'people forced out of the labor market some time ago who are willing and able to work, but have become too discouraged to search for jobs' and are therefore not counted as part of the labor force by the government."[58]

Kahn cautioned about the effect the "technological revolution" and "the impact of cybernation" would have on the long-term employment prospects of African Americans, theorizing that it would create an "underclass,"[59] and he observed regarding the then-recently proposed solution of "bussing": "The fact is that bussing and related devices may be well-intentioned, but they are makeshift, stopgap measures which raise more questions than they answer. Among them: *what judgment should be rendered of a society that would rather dislocate its children than reorganize its cities?*"[60] (Emphasis original.)

He observed, ominously: "The trend toward de facto segregation of Negroes in declining job categories can only reinforce the association between Negro and failure. The view that Negroes are racially inferior yields to a vaguer, but no less malevolent, conception of most Negroes as socially or morally incompetent to realize their potential."[61] (To social or moral incompetence can be added the allusion to intellectual incompetence on the part of Charles Murray and Richard Herrnstein in their 1994 book *The Bell Curve*, a critique of which, presented by Thomas Sowell, will be addressed below.) Finally, Kahn made the following observation about what would later be termed "white flight," and, disdaining the simple explanation of white racism: "What whites are fleeing is city life itself, which has become increasingly intolerable—overcrowded, underserviced, dreary, and filthy."[62]

Wilson Extends the Liberal Concept of Culture of Poverty to Apply to Behaviors—Absent Cultural Change—Adapted in Response to Economic Circumstances

The theory of social isolation put forth by William Julius Wilson in *The Truly Disadvantaged: The Inner City, The Underclass, and Public Policy* (1987) extends the "culture of poverty" theory of Harrington and Kahn by observing that depressed economic circumstances, *even if they do not negatively influence culture and cultural aspirations*, nonetheless negatively influence social, economic, and political *behavior* (a lesson that will be revisited in addressing, below, the working class whites that are the subjects of Charles Murray in his book *Coming Apart*). As Wilson said in *The Truly Disadvantaged*: "[I]f underclass blacks have limited aspirations or fail to plan for the future, it is not ultimately the product of different cultural norms but the consequence of restricted opportunities, a bleak future, and feelings of resignation from bitter personal experience. Accordingly, behavior described as socially pathological and associated with the ghetto underclass should be analyzed not as cultural aberration but as a symptom of class and racial inequality."[63]

Wilson continued, regarding the effects on behavior wrought by depressed economic and social circumstances:

> If I had to use one term to capture the difference in the experiences of low-income families who live in inner-city areas from the experiences of those who live in other areas in the central city today, that term would be *concentration effects*. The social transformation of the inner city has resulted in a disproportionate concentration of the most disadvantaged segments of the urban black population, creating a social milieu significantly different from the environ-

ment that existed in these communities several decades ago. [Emphasis original.][64]

He concluded: "The net result is that the degree of social isolation—defined in this context as the lack of contact or of sustained interaction with individuals and institutions that represent mainstream society—in these highly concentrated poverty areas has become far greater than we had previously assumed."[65]

Wilson returned to his concern about "the absence of a strong institutional resource base"[66] in inner city neighborhoods in *When Work Disappears: The World of the New Urban Poor* (1996), attributing the behaviors of the underclass to economic stagnation and limited opportunity resulting therefrom. The importance of a "strong institutional resource base," to which Wilson alluded, will be explored in detail in the following chapter.

Returning to his theory of social isolation in *The Truly Disadvantaged*, Wilson observed that, while racism still exists in America (again, writing in 1987), it is an insufficient explanation for economic class divisions because racial characteristics are shared across those class divisions. Wilson proposed, instead, as an explanation, historical racial bias, in combination with underemployment and unemployment, and other factors that reinforced social isolation. Examples of such other factors addressed by Wilson and others: (1) The GI Bill, which subsidized mortgages only for *new* construction, which occurred predominantly in the suburbs; (2) Interstate highways, funded in great part by the federal government, which facilitated the movement of whites to those new suburbs built with government support, and also often ran through and destroyed African American neighborhoods; (3) Redlining (banks, with the cooperation of the federal government, literally drawing "red lines" around neighborhoods in which one or more African American families lived, and putting them off-limits for federally-supported loans); (4) Blockbusting (in which unscrupulous speculators spread fear of African American families moving into a neighborhood so as to force real estate prices down); (5) Discrimination toward African Americans when they attempted to borrow for home improvement loans, so their ability to refurbish their homes was impeded; (6) "Urban renewal," which destroyed many neighborhoods and institutions in inner-city African American neighborhoods and substituted for less-dense housing patterns dense concentrations of poor families warehoused in high-rise rent-subsidized slums; (7) Urban decline, meaning the decline in services, cleanliness, and quality of life and the rise in crime as the tax base declined with more affluent citizens fleeing, (8) Integration, followed by forced busing to achieve racial mixing, served to encourage movement of whites and prosperous African Americans out of the inner city; (9) Race riots experienced by many American cities in the 1960s[67] and (10) Loosening of qualification requirements of AFDC (welfare).

This emphasis, by Wilson, on the breakdown of social (cultural), economic and political institutions distinguishes his theory from the "mismatch" theory, which emphasizes the mismatch between the skills required for pre-Information Age jobs versus those required for the jobs of the Information Age, during which the economy of many cities began to recover and prosper. Social isolation theory accepts those aspects of mismatch theory supported by the evidence. The number of manufacturing jobs declined. As manufacturing jobs left, poverty became concentrated and increased, and this trend continued even after the influx of high skill-requiring jobs reduced the overall unemployment rate. Well-paying low skill jobs left the cities and were replaced by high paying high skill jobs for which inner city residents' qualifications do not match. Further complicating the lives of inner city unskilled workers is the difficulty of getting to jobs in the suburbs commensurate with their skills due to poor public transportation systems. Additionally, competition for those low-skills jobs in the inner city intensified with the arrival of new immigrants. Those new immigrants began arriving long after the deindustrialization in Chicago, Detroit, and other large urban areas that began in the mid-1950s. Thus, these new immigrants had not been given an opportunity to build a stake in the old industries—fortunately for them—limiting the destabilizing effect of deindustrialization on social institutions on which these new immigrants rely.

To all the above factors observed by the mismatch theory, the theory of social isolation adds that the result of all these impacts has been downward pressure on male labor force participation rates, resulting in reduction in attractive potential husbands, leading to greater social isolation and fewer marriages per population (plus other indicators of institutional decline, such as declining attendance at religious services)—captured in the term Wilson and his colleagues created: the "male marriageable pool index." Accompanying these changes has been increased concentration of unemployment and underemployment, and with these changing culture and changing behaviors. As will be seen below, Wilson's explanation for the various indicators of societal institutional decline, also observed by conservative sociologist Charles Murray in *Coming Apart*, is superior to Murray's explanation of the same phenomenon.

The explanatory value of Wilson's concept of the male marriageable pool index is supported by an outstanding 2008 essay by Bob Herbert in *The New York Times*.[68] The first observation of note there is that illegitimacy has been rising since the 1960s among *all* women in the US. Herbert observed that a study by the Center for Labor Market Studies at Northeastern University in Boston revealed that in 2006, for the first time in US history, *a majority of all births to women under age 30* (50.4 percent) were out of wedlock; by comparison, in 1960, just 6 percent of all births to women under 30 were. For insight regarding causality, Herbert quoted Andrew Sum, director of the

Center for Labor Market Studies, who observed that the marriage rates of all native-born young males and young black males (22-32 years old) in the US are strongly correlated with their annual earnings. Sum concluded, in terms reminiscent of Wilson, that the decline over the past 30 years in real earnings of these young men without college degrees was tied to the rise in out-of-wedlock births. And, as observed by Isabel Sawhill of the Brookings Institution, although college-educated adults are still marrying and planning families, the remaining two-thirds of young adults are not.[69]

Support for William Julius Wilson's idea that economic circumstances that influence behavior are responsible for declining marriage rates rather than changing values is also supported by the observations of Andrew J. Cherlin, Johns Hopkins University sociologist, in *Labor's Love Lost: The Rise and Fall of the Working-Class Family in America* (2014), which found that the gap in marriage rates among professional, technical, and managerial occupations versus craftsmen and artisans and versus service workers has been widest over history when income inequality was highest. And, he found current patterns in marriage rates paralleled those of the Gilded Age—as does income inequality, as observed earlier.[70] (As an aside, a study on African American fathers revealed they do not suffer a pathology of neglect—in contrast, by several standards, they are more attentive to their families than are white fathers.[71])

And, the explanatory value of the concept of social isolation has received support from later research conducted for the Annie E. Casey Foundation addressing the effects of "concentrated poverty"—defined as those census tracts with poverty rates of 30 percent or higher.[72] As the KIDS COUNT report observed, even when family incomes are held constant, families living in areas of concentrated poverty will struggle to meet basic needs and the children are more likely to experience severe stress and incur behavioral and emotional problems.[73] Additionally, the explanatory value of the concept of social isolation has been supported by data that show when children of poor families move out of areas of concentrated poverty, their odds of escaping poverty are greatly increased.[74]

WHY THE CONSERVATIVE CULTURE OF POVERTY THEORY FAILS

The liberal culture of poverty theory posits that declining economic circumstances can undermine a person's sense of economic wellbeing, which in turn risks undermining their sense of self-worth and causing them to lose faith in the ability of institutions to help them, sending them spiraling further downward in socioeconomic wellbeing and ever more deeply withdrawing from the very societal institutions that can help them. They may still believe in morality—and in institutions such as the job market, marriage, college, church—but tend to lose faith in the relevancy of these institutions to them. Declining economic circumstances, thus, can change a culture, instilling into it a sense of defeatism, and, even if these declining economic circumstances do not change culture, they can change behavior of individuals when they no longer believe the institutions of society are relevant to them.

In contrast, the conservative culture of poverty explanation starts with an explanation of inferiority: either moral (indicated by susceptibility to the lure of welfare, rejection of the institution of marriage and turning to a life of crime) or intellectual. The moral inferiority explanation posits that the lure of easy money from welfare created a collapse in values of, especially, inner city African Americans (the "underclass"), creating a culture of dependency on welfare, accompanied by rising illegitimacy and rising crime rates. The leading proponent of this theory, conservative sociologist Charles Murray, has written three books that promote variations on this theoretical theme. Combined, their message is that those in poverty are there due to their own fault, either because of bad morals (laziness and failure to wait for marriage to have children) or weak intellect. Any possible link between declining economic circumstances and their declining socioeconomic situation is ignored.

In his first influential book *Losing Ground: American Social Policy, 1950-1980* (1984), Murray concluded that the perverse incentives of welfare and the changes in risks associated with crime and the changes in the educational environment reinforced each other, radically altering the incentives presented to the inner-city African Americans in the underclass.[75] While this explanation did allow Murray to blame liberalism for the problems of the underclass—liberal welfare policies, liberal tolerance toward crime and liberal educational reforms—it did not explain why the underclass failed so miserably while other groups in the population did not.

Myron Magnet, a conservative journalist, in *The Dream and the Nightmare: The Sixties Legacy to the Underclass* (1993; sponsored by the Scaife Foundation) attempted to answer why the underclass was so lured by welfare. To Magnet, they possessed weak morals, as also evidenced by their allegedly rapidly rising illegitimacy rates—and these weak morals were due to embrace of the perverse liberal values of the 1960s (which he originated, ironically, with the liberal writers of the 1950s who borrowed such values from black ghetto culture).

Returning to Charles Murray, *The Bell Curve: Intelligence and Class Structure in American Life* (1994), which he wrote with Richard Herrnstein, offered a different explanation for *why* the members of the underclass were uniquely attracted to welfare: not because of bad morals borrowed from liberals but because of their intellectual inferiority.

As an aside, in *America in Black and White: One Nation, Indivisible* (1997), Harvard historian Stephan Thernstrom and his wife Abigail Thernstrom, a senior fellow at the conservative Manhattan Institute with Charles Murray, admitted that they, too, had no explanation for the negative changes they observed among African American families but were confident they could rule out economics.[76]

Murray changed his focus to poor whites, in *Coming Apart: The State of White America, 1960-2010* (2012). Here he observed that society is dividing into classes based on bourgeois values, with a fabulously rich small percentage of households in the upper class, dedicated to bourgeois values, valiantly posed against the growing horde of poor working class whites, who have lost their industriousness, honesty, religion and respect for marriage.

In *Coming Apart*, Murray's most recent explanation for social decline is similar to that of Magnet: it's the fault of the upper class—although rather than blaming elite embrace of ghetto values, Murray blamed the elites for embracing the bourgeois values of industriousness, honesty, religion and respect for marriage but failing to defend and promote those values to poor working class whites and everyone else. Murray's explanation for this failure is the popular conservative idea of the triumph of liberal cultural relativism. He links this failure with the disintegration of civilizations identified by historian Arnold J. Toynbee in *A Study of History*, observing that the current upper class has lost confidence in its morals and, while its members continue to practice these morals themselves, to the detriment of the rest of society they no longer urge them on everyone else.[77]

The consistency throughout Murray's, Magnet's and the Thernstroms' works is the blindness to the effect a downturn in economic circumstances can have on its victims, imposing a sense of defeatism and behavior that results in abandonment of institutions. This blindness leads them to look elsewhere for explanations for cultural changes: government policy changes, failure on the part of elites to spread their values that lead to success and low IQ scores. By addressing below the errors in their analyses we are led back to the importance of downturn in economic circumstances.

Flaws in Murray's, Magnet's and the Thernstroms' Analyses

There was no rise in illegitimacy rates unique to nonwhites. A major flaw in Murray's and Magnet's analyses is that there was no rapidly rising illegitimacy rate peculiar to nonwhites.[78] Data in *The Moynihan Report* revealed that the ratio of illegitimacy rates for nonwhites versus whites over the period 1940 to 1963 began at greater than 8:1, peaked in 1953 at a ratio of more than 11:1, and during the ten years after that white illegitimacy rates grew faster than those for nonwhites so that the ratio in 1963 was below 8:1.[79] Thus, nonwhite illegitimacy rates were several times higher than white rates going back almost to the origin of AFDC (it began in 1935 as a program to feed widows and orphans), but white illegitimacy rates grew faster than Murray's alleged illegitimacy rate explosion among nonwhites. In fact, not only were illegitimacy rates not growing at a uniquely high pace for nonwhites at the time of Murray's book but, as observed by Bob Herbert in his outstanding essay in *The New York Times* in 2008 cited above, illegitimacy has been rising since the 1960s among *all* women.

And, not only were illegitimacy rates for African Americans rising more slowly than for whites, but, it may be added, that "Moynihan's scissors"—the observation of AFDC case openings continuing to rise in the face of falling unemployment rates—appeared first in 1960, 1963 and 1964, *before* the arrival of "Sixties values" condemned by Magnet (the "Summer of Love" was not until 1967).

The rate of increase in opening of AFDC cases among the underclass rose in tandem with a rise in the nonwhite male labor force nonparticipation rate. In 1986 William Julius Wilson and Kathryn Neckerman published an analysis which showed that the crossover of Moynihan's scissors disappears when the number of AFDC cases is charted against the nonwhite male labor force nonparticipation rate. Labor force participation rates remained fairly stable from 1954 to 1981, except for a deep setback from 1954 to 1964 (although for African American females in age groups 18-19 and 20-24 it *edged upward*). For females, both African American and white, over the period 1954 to 1981, there was a general *upward* trend in labor force participation rates, and for white males, there was general stability. In contrast, there was a *downward trend* for all age groups among African American males after starting off at a higher rate than for white males in the 18-19 and 20-24 age groups.[80]

These facts call into question two popular explanations for the decline of the inner city: The liberal explanation of racism in employment hiring practices; and the conservative explanation of welfare's destruction of work ethic among African Americans. The explanation of racism in hiring practices fails when it is observed that the labor force participation rates of African American females, after declining from 1954 to 1964 for all age groups, generally rose for all age groups afterward—thus, they were hardly being shut out of the labor market. Similarly, if welfare were so destructive of work ethic, why did it not destroy the work ethic of African American females, who were its primary beneficiaries?

Similarly, conservative analyses leave out the important observation that labor force participation rates for *all* American men, even in the prime working ages of 25 to 54 years, have been going down for the past 50 years, as was observed in a Labor Department report issued in 2006: "A significant development in the labor force over the past 50 years has been the steady decline in labor force participation among men aged 25 to 54 years. After peaking at 97.4 percent in the mid-1950s [1955, to be precise], the participation rates for these men has fallen steadily, reaching a low of 90.5 percent in 2005."[81]

The same Labor Department report also confirms the common sense assumption that, in the face of economic downturn, the younger workers feel the impact most acutely—a chart[82] there shows that, for the economic downturn period of March 2001 through March 2006, labor force participation rates for them dropped nearly 6 percent, far more than for older groups (it actually rose more than 4 percent for men and women 55 years and older). Finally, the report also showed a continuing decline in labor force participation rates from 2000 to 2005 for African American youths—for the age group 16-19 years, labor force participation rates declined 6.8 percent; for the age group 20 to 24 years, labor force participation rates declined 1.7 percent.[83] Thus, in defiance of the popularly promoted expectation of a labor force participation rate increase among young African Americans as a dividend to the Welfare Reform Act of 1996, no such dividend was evident by 2005. And, in defiance of expectations of massive retirements of Baby Boomers, while the overall labor force participation rate in February 2014 was a 36-year low of 63 percent, the participation rate for men and women 65 years old and older was 18.9 percent, near a 52-year high.

As an aside, conservatives leapt on the decline of the labor force participation rate during President Obama's first term as indicative of undermining of the work ethic by a permissive Democratic administration—but a review of the labor force participation rate from 1993 to the present reveals that the labor force participation rate rose under the Democratic administration of President Clinton, then declined under the Republican administration of President George W. Bush, and only continued to decline under President Obama.[84] Conservatives have offered no explanation of how President Bush, under whose administration this decline started, undermined the will to work.

A more satisfactory explanation for the decline in the labor force participation rate is the observation that, contrary to conservative dogma, not all unemployment is voluntary, and *economic circumstances, themselves, influence behavior, values and institutions* regardless of the population's race—be they the inner city underclass African American populations addressed by Murray, Magnet and the Thernstroms earlier or the white working class population addressed later by Murray.

Another indicator of social decline that was observed by Murray, also addressed in the Moynihan Report, was declining church attendance. Researchers W. Bradford Wilcox of the University of Virginia, Jeremy E. Uecker, University of North Carolina at Chapel Hill and Andrew Cherlin and Matthew Messel, Johns Hopkins University in a study published in 2012 of data from the General Social Survey (GSS) and the National Survey of Family Growth (NSFG) found that over the last four decades, monthly (or more frequent) participation in religious services declined the most among whites without college degrees, suggesting a link between declining economic circumstances and declining church attendance among working class whites.[85]

Similarly, a study released in 2013 titled "Intimate Inequalities: Love and Work in a Post-Industrial Landscape," chronicled the results of work in which sociologists in the US interviewed and surveyed more than 300 working and middle class people aged between 18 and 70 regarding how their employment status affected their relationships. Sarah Corse, a sociology professor at the University of Virginia and leader of the study, reported two important conclusions, both supportive of what is said here and disturbing: The first, that insecure work undermines people's lives outside of work and, second, that marriage is becoming a social institution for the middle class but not the working poor.[86] The study made no mention of its subjects expressing regret that the new upper class had let them down by not passing on its values to them.

Genetically based intergroup differences in IQ scores are also inadequate explanation for socioeconomic performance. In his essay "Ethnicity and IQ,"[87] conservative economist Thomas Sowell presented three examples of evidence against a genetic basis for intergroup differences in IQ: (1) Ethnic groups have raised their IQ scores over time; (2) "Generation-norming" obscures the fact that African Americans today correctly answer the same numbers of questions as past generations of whites; and (3) Among African Americans and other ethnic groups many more females than males score highly, thus strongly suggesting the influence of environmental factors.

More than anyone else, Sowell has developed a vast collection of evidence across history and across various ethnic groups and nationalities illustrative of the fact the economic circumstances themselves shape cultures (although he personally embraces a conservative culture of poverty vision). This evidence complements the social isolation theory of William Julius Wilson and his colleagues, illustrating, globally, cultural adaptation to economic circumstances. Sowell has amply illustrated the relative advantage certain ethnic groups that came from urban environments (such as the Jews, Chinese and Indians) had over ethnic groups that came from agrarian societies (such as the African Americans, Irish, southern Italians and Scotch-Irish) in modern, urban, and now information-based economies. Especially relevant to the African American experience are Sowell's accounts of the strikingly similar path trod by the Irish, who also came from the bottom rungs of agrarian society, and, in the cities, moved into physical labor jobs in heavy industry and also into government, accompanied by big city machine politics. Both ethnic groups were penalized by a historical lack of value placed on education, due to their shared histories of being at the bottom of agrarian economies and, for both groups, actively being discouraged, by their masters, from bettering themselves with education. And, both ethnic groups pursued advancement through the political sector, with the African American dominance of big city politics in the United States following a similar path trod by the Irish roughly a half century before.[88]

An alleged collapse of moral values among working class whites is not supported by the facts. William Julius Wilson, in a review of Murray's book, *Coming Apart*, observed that Murray's argument fails when confronted with the National Vital Statistics System, which shows a sharp drop in teenage pregnancies among all racial and ethnic groups since 1991, and the Justice Department's Uniform Crime Reports, which show a sharp drop in violent crimes among all racial and ethnic groups during the same period. Wilson also noted that research indicated a rapid increase over the past 20 years in children expecting to earn four-year college degrees and this increase was greatest among children whose parents did not have college degrees.[89] Far more explanatory of the cultural breakdown among working class whites is the same explanation as that offered by Wilson for the experience of inner city African Americans commencing with the 1960s: the decline in economic opportunity.[90]

Conclusion: The values are still there, but negative economic circumstances have instilled a sense of defeatism and despair in many members of the working class regarding their ability to access the societal institutions of marriage, religion and the market to work for them. From the above there is evidence that there has not been a collapse of moral values among working-class whites nor, for that matter, has there been a collapse of moral values among inner city African Americans (previously dubbed the "underclass"). In these populations there is still a desire to avoid teenage pregnancy, a desire to get a college education and a desire to get married, and crime rates are continuing their long decline (absent some recent exceptions). What does appear to be happening, however, is that although those moral values are still in place, growing numbers of Americans despair of acting on those values and availing themselves of the institutions of society—institutions such as the job market, marriage, college education and religion.

Murray and conservatives like him—still embracing the conservative culture of poverty theory that ignores the influence of economic circumstances and social status upon culture—continue to ignore that during the latter thirty-five of the fifty years addressed in *Coming Apart*, trickle-down has been suppressing wages and upwardly redistributing revenues attributable to increased productivity, so that increased effort by those not in the upper class fails to bring them a commensurate increase in reward.

June Carbone of the University of Minnesota Law School and Naomi Cahn, of George Washington University Law School applied the insights of Moynihan and Wilson and observed that in the top 20 percent of income earners, 80 percent are married; in the bottom 20 percent of income earners, less than 20 percent are married. Their explanation for the phenomenon is in the subtitle of their 2014 book: *Marriage Markets: How Inequality Is Remaking the American Family*. They observed—as Murray observed—that, marriage is increasingly being viewed as something that only the upper middle class and rich can afford although, unlike Murray, they recognize that among both men and women generally marriage is still seen as desirable. Thus, the values are still there, favoring marriage, but negative economic circumstances have instilled a sense of defeatism and despair of ability on the part of working class of their ability to access the societal institution of marriage to help them.

As an aside, Murray's blindness to the point that work is failing to deliver to the working class the income that they need to access this most basic and important of our societal institutions is all the more fascinating in that Murray reveals himself to share the illiberal ideas regarding work critiqued by Adam Smith and Alexis de Tocqueville previously and shared with the various illiberals critiqued earlier herein. In *Coming Apart*, Murray critiques Europe's "short weeks and frequent vacations"[91] and observes that for Europeans the "idea of work as self-actualization has faded." For the Europeans, "The purpose of life is to while away the time between birth and death as pleasantly as possible, and the purpose of government is to make it as easy as possible to while away the time as pleasantly as possible—the European Syndrome." Actually, Tocqueville might have called much the same liberal vision "the American Syndrome" in 1835 when he penned a similar—but admiring—description of America, quoted earlier. And, perhaps the European experience of living through the alternative illiberal visions of the "purpose of life" expressed in Fascism, Falangism and Nazism—recall "*Arbeit Macht Frei*"—"work makes (one) free"—the sign over the gates of Nazi concentration camps—has led Europeans to choose a liberal route to happiness.

Charles Horton Cooley was right: Humans must have a good sense of self, or they will inflict damage on society and themselves and never avail themselves of the formula for happiness. And social isolation resulting from downward pressure on wages and job loss is a major impediment to the creation of a good sense of self.

We should reflect on Friedrich Hayek's lament, observed earlier: "We didn't realize how fragile our civilization was." Today, still, we do not realize how fragile *the self* in each of us is. We should reflect, too, on the prescience of numerous social commentators who observed that the Information Revolution and globalization would put downward pressure on wages and job creation—and we should reflect on our responsibility for inflicting further damage on our fellow Americans and perhaps even ourselves and future generations by compounding the negative effects of the Information Revolution and globalization with trickle-down policies. Trickle-down reinforced the downward pressure on wages and job creation and upwardly redistributed the revenues resulting from the enhanced productivity delivered by the Information Revolution and globalization. The results, again: Real median wages for males peaked in 1973; real median family incomes peaked in 1999; the percentage of Americans in the work force in 2014 was back to where it was in 1978, and inequality of incomes of the 1 percent hovered at levels not seen since 1928 and for the top 10 percent exceeded 50 percent of total income—its highest level since records began to be collected in 1917. And these self-inflicted assaults on the economic well-being of our fellow Americans resulted in social wounds and wounds to individual mental and physical health as well—again, as predicted.

Critically—and this will be addressed again in detail in Chapter 11, in the discussion of the observations of studies regarding the effects on us humans of inequality—we humans do not do well with having our dreams about our economic futures crushed, and those economic impacts change our social behavior, perhaps change our values, and may change our families. As was predicted by numerous social scientists, the Information Revolution imposed wrenching changes on the inner-city African Americans who in it lost their jobs in the industrialized cities of the North and Midwest. And, as a result, as observed by Harrington, Kahn and Wilson and his colleagues, they incurred changes to their behavior, perhaps changes to their values, and perhaps also their families; the whites who were addressed by Charles Murray in *Coming Apart* did also. The poor were the canary in the coal mine, their social pathologies providing a warning to social scientists regarding future impacts on working poor and lower middle class whites also lacking college educations, but, instead of taking it as a warning, they were viewed as somehow uniquely flawed. But they were not; they were very much like their similarly situated white brothers and sisters in the United States and Russian brothers and sisters after the fall of the Soviet Union, both populations of whom saw their mortality rates climb when sudden changes in economic circumstances suddenly upset their dreams of comfortable futures, as will be addressed in Chapter 11.

Finally, before leaving the lesson that changes in economic circumstances change behavior, the examples given thus far have addressed downward changes in economic circumstances—but we know that upward improvements in economic circumstances change behavior, and that fact was illustrated by a study published in December 2015 by the NBER, by researchers Viktar Fedaseyeu of Bocconi University, Erik Gilje of the University of Pennsylvania and Philip E. Strahan of Boston College.[92] The researchers found that after hydraulic fracturing of formerly uneconomic oil and gas reserves spurred the energy booms that began in 2003, support for conservative interests rose, and Republican political candidates gained votes, leading to a near doubling in the probability of a change in incumbency, at the expense of Democrats. US House members' voting records from boom districts changed as well, becoming more conservative not just on economic issues but also on issues unrelated to energy policy.[93]

We must stop these counterproductive policies that upwardly redistribute economic and political power and, instead, begin rebuilding *incomes* and *wealth* and the *institutions* that in a liberal democracy both defend an individual against the oppression that leads to feelings of powerlessness, and help an individual leverage his or her power to increase that power and self-esteem—increase one's ability to influence one's human environment and productivity. Understanding those institutions and how they work is the subject of the next chapter; the imperative of equality will be addressed in the chapter after that.

NOTES

1. Friedrich Hayek, *The Road to Serfdom* (1944), p. 17. See also Ralph Nader, *Unstoppable: The Emerging Left-Right Alliance to Dismantle the Corporate State* (New York: Nation Books, a Member of the Perseus Books Group; 2014), Chapter 2, especially pp. 27–28; there appears therein a critique of modern conservatism's mischaracterization of Smith, Hayek, Wilhelm Röpke and other heroes of conservatism similar to that herein.
2. Charles Horton Cooley, in *Human Nature and the Social Order*, ch. 6 (1902).
3. For background, see Kathy Lohr, "Poor People's Campaign: A Dream Unfulfilled," *Morning Edition, NPR*, June 19, 2008.
4. Peter L. Berger and Thomas Luckmann, *The Social Construction of Reality* (New York: Anchor Books; 1967), p. 1.
5. Ibid, p. 89.
6. Charles Horton Cooley, *Human Nature and the Social Order* (New York: Scribner's, 1902), p. 179.
7. Ibid, p. 185.
8. Peter L. Berger and Thomas Luckmann, *The Social Construction of Reality* (1967), pp. 132–133.
9. Peter Drucker, *The New Society: The Anatomy of Industrial Order* (New York: Harper, 1950, 1993), p. 199.
10. Daniel Bell, *The Cultural Contradictions of Capitalism* (New York: Basic Books, 1976, 1996), p. 336.
11. The Act established that by 1983 unemployment rates should be not more than 3 percent for persons aged 20 and over, and not more than 4 percent for persons aged 16 and over. It amended the Employment Act of 1946, which encouraged the federal government to "promote maximum employment, production, and purchasing power."
12. Nicholas Kristof, "Enjoying the Low Life?" *The New York Times*, April 9, 2015.
13. Charles E. Silberman, *Crisis in Black and White* (New York: Vintage Books; 1964), pp. 70–71.
14. Abram Kardiner and Lionel Ovesey, *The Mark of Oppression* (Cleveland, Ohio: World Publishing Co., 1962).
15. Charles E. Silberman, *Crisis in Black and White* (New York: Vintage Books: 1964), p. 109.
16. Ralph Ellison, *The Invisible Man* (New York: Vintage Books, 1947, 1972), p. 1.
17. W.E.B. DuBois, *Dusk of Dawn* (New York: Harcourt Brace & Co.; 1940), pp. 130–131. Quoted in Silberman, p. 109.
18. Courtney C. Coile, Phillip B. Levine and Robin McKnight, "Recessions, Older Workers, and Longevity: How Long Are Recessions Good for Your Health?" NBER Working Paper No. 18361, September 2012. See also Catherine Rampell, "In Hard Economy for All Ages, Older

Isn't Better . . . It's Brutal," *The New York Times*, February 3, 2013; and Göran Therborn, *The Killing Fields of Inequality* (Cambridge, UK and Malden, MA: Polity Press; 2013), pp 10–11. Therborn is Professor Emeritus of Sociology at the University of Cambridge.

19. Fred Siegel, *The Future Once Happened Here: New York, D.C., L.A. and the Future of America's Big Cities* (San Francisco, Encounter Books: 1997), pp. 55–56.

20. The findings were revealed in Table 22, "Cases Opened under AFDC (Excluding Unemployed Parent Segment)".

21. See especially, Thomas Sowell's *Ethnic America: A History* (1981); *The Economics and Politics of Race* (1983); *Civil Rights: Rhetoric or Reality* (1984); *Race and Culture: A World View* (1994) and *Black Rednecks and White Liberals* (2005).

22. Members: Robert Theobald, Donald Michael, Gunnar Myrdal, Linus Pauling, A. J. Muste, Michael Harrington, Bayard Rustin, Irving Howe, W. H. Ferry, Robert Heilbroner, and Tom Hayden and Todd Gitlin of SDS. This report is discussed in greater detail in Daniel Bell's *The Coming of Post-Industrial Society*, pp. xxi and 462. Bell credited Donald Michael with invention of the term "cybernation;" defined as "the combination of the computer and the automated self-regulating machine."

23. A. Philip Randolph was the Director of the 1963 March on Washington, Bayard Rustin was deputy, and Rustin's chief assistant was Tom Kahn. Kahn served as Executive Secretary of the League for Industrial Democracy and authored *Unfinished Revolution* (1960) and *The Economics of Equality* (1964) as well as numerous essays, including "The Problems of the Negro Movement," (1964). Kahn was also influenced by, and a close ally of Michael Harrington.

24. Tom Kahn, "Problems of the Negro Movement," *Dissent*, Vol. 11, January 1964, No. 1, pp. 108–138.

25. James Boggs, "The Negro in Cybernation," in *The Evolving Society; The Proceedings Of The First Annual Conference On The Cybercultural Revolution—Cybernetics and Automation*, 1966. He returned to that theme in *Education To Govern*, originally published as a pamphlet by the All-African People Union in April 1971.

26. Sidney Wilhelm, *Who Needs the Negro?* See also Clarence Lusane, Persisting Disparities: Globalization and the Economic Status of African Americans , 2 *Howard Law Journal* 431–450, 436–439, 450 (Spring 1999).

27. The National Commission on Technology, Automation, and Economic Progress, "Technology and the American Economy" (Volume 1, February 1966), p. xii.

28. The National Commission on Technology, Automation, and Economic Progress, "Technology and the American Economy" (Volume 1, February 1966), p. 110.

29. Zbigniew Brzezinski, *Between Two Ages: America's Role in the Technetronic Era (*New York: Viking Press, 1971; reprinted in 1982 by Greenwood Press). Brzezinski explained that he favored "technetronic" over "post-industrial" because it conveyed more directly the character of the principal impulses driving the change: technology and electronics. (See page 9.) The two ages we were between were the age of the industrial society and the age of the technetronic society.

30. Daniel Bell, *The Coming of Post-Industrial Society* (New York: Basic Books; 1973, 1976), p. 212.

31. Ibid, page 55, footnote 14.

32. Bell noted at least a dozen books that at the time he wrote his preface to the 1999 reissuance of the book addressed the themes of the post-industrial society (and had the term in their titles). Ibid, pp. xx and xxi. While some other names for this phenomenon are listed herein, Bell lists even more in a sweeping, and rather humorous, treatment of the phenomenon in footnotes on pages 54 and 55.

33. Daniel Bell, *The Coming of Post-Industrial Society* (New York: Basic Books; 1973, 1976), p. 36.

34. Ibid, pp. 8 and 9.

35. Ibid, p. 127.

36. Ibid, p. 145.

37. Peter F. Drucker, "The Rise of the Knowledge Society," *The Wilson Quarterly* Vol. XVII, No. 2, (Spring 1993), pp. 52–69.

38. Oscar Lewis, The Culture of Poverty," in Daniel P. Moynihan, ed., *On Understanding Poverty* (New York: Basic Books, 1968), pp. 187–200, see especially p. 188. See also Herbert Gans, *War Against the Poor: The Underclass and Antipoverty Policy* (New York: Basic Books; 1996), p. 24.

39. Gans, p. 26, citing Susan Rigdon, *The Culture Façade: Art, Science and Politics in the Work of Oscar Lewis* (Urbana: University of Illinois Press, 188), p. 90.

40. Noam Scheiber, "2016 Hopefuls and Wealthy Are Aligned on Inequality," *The New York Times*, March 30, 2015.

41. Michael Harrington, *The Other America*, First published by The Macmillan Company, 1962, reprinted, Baltimore, MD: Penguin Books, 1972, p. 3.

42. Ibid, p. 5.

43. Ibid, p. 11.

44. Ibid, p. 13.

45. Ibid, p. 16.

46. Ibid, p. 18.

47. Ibid, p. 77.

48. Ibid, p. 129 and 141.

49. Ibid, pp. 176 and 177.

50. Ibid, p. 141.

51. Tom Kahn, "Problems of the Negro Movement," *Dissent*, Vol. 11, January 1964, No. 1, pp. 108-138.

52. Ibid.

53. Ibid.

54. Ibid.

55. Ibid.

56. Ibid.

57. Ibid.

58. Ibid.

59. Kahn here used a term coined by the Swedish economist Gunnar Myrdal two years previously. Myrdal had used the term "under-class" in his *Challenge to Affluence*, published in 1963. See Chapter 2, "The Invention of the Underclass Label," in Herbert J. Gans, *The War Against the Poor: The Underclass and Antipoverty Policy* (New York: Basic Books, 1995).

60. Tom Kahn, "Problems of the Negro Movement," *Dissent*, Vol. 11, January 1964, No. 1, pp. 108–138.

61. Ibid.

62. Ibid.

63. *The Truly Disadvantaged: The Inner City, The Underclass, and Public Policy* (Chicago: University of Chicago Press, 1987; 1990), p. 14.

64. Ibid, p. 58.

65. Ibid, p. 24.

66. Ibid, p. 18.

67. In the following years, the listed major American cities experienced race riots: In 1964: Philadelphia and New York City (Harlem); 1965: Los Angeles (Watts); 1966: Cleveland, OH; 1967: Detroit, Milwaukee and Newark; 1968: Baltimore, Chicago, Louisville and Washington, DC.

68. Bob Herbert, "Dubious Milestone," *The New York Times*, June 21, 2008. See also the outstanding collection of articles by Natalie Angier under the heading "The Changing American Family," *The New York Times*, November 26, 2013.

69. Isabel Sawhill, "Beyond Marriage," *The New York Times*, September 14, 2014.

70. See Andrew J. Cherlin, "The Real Reason Richer People Marry," *The New York Times*, December 7, 2014.

71. Charles M. Blow, "Black Dads Are Doing Best of All," *The New York Times*, June 8, 2015.

72. KIDS COUNT Data Snapshots on High-Poverty Communities, Annie E. Casey Foundation, February 2012.

73. Citation to M. A. Turner and D. R. Kaye, "How Does Family Well-Being Vary Among Different Types of Neighborhoods?" The Urban Institute, Washington, DC (2006).
74. David Leonhardt, Amanda Cox and Claire Cain Miller, "An Atlas of Upward Mobility Shows Paths Out of Poverty," *The New York Times*, May 4, 2015.
75. See Charles Murray, *Losing Ground: American Social Policy, 1950-1980* (New York: Basic Books, Inc.: 1984), pp. 167–168.
76. Stephan Thernstrom and Abigail Thernstrom, *America in Black and White: One Nation, Indivisible* (New York: Simon & Schuster, 1997), p. 255.
77. Charles Murray, *Coming Apart: The State of White America, 1960–2010* (New York: Crown Forum, an imprint of the Crown Publishing Group, a division of Random House, Inc.; 2012), p. 289. Discussion of Toynbee begins on page 286.
78. This observation was made by Robert Reich in *The Work of Nations* (1991), Daniel Patrick Moynihan, in his book *Miles to Go* (1996) and Michael Lind, in *Up from Conservatism: Why the Right Is Wrong for America* (1996).
79. Source: "The Negro Family: The Case for National Action," Office of Planning and Research, United States Department of Labor (March 1965). Adapted from Table 3, "Estimated Number of Illegitimate Births and Ratio of Illegitimate Births to All Live Births by Color, 1940-63," p. 59, as shown in Figure A.3 in the Appendix.
80. As shown in Figure A.4 in the Appendix. Source: *Employment and Training Report of the President 1981* Table A-30.
81. Abraham Mosisa and Steven Hipple, "Trends in Labor Force Participation in the United States," *Monthly Labor Review*, October 2006, p. 47.
82. Ibid, p. 39, Chart 3.
83. Ibid, p. 40, Table 3.
84. Graph: "Labor Force Participation Rate" (USALFPRNA)—FRED –St. Louis Federal Reserve Bank.
85. W. Bradford Wilcox of the University of Virginia, Jeremy E. Uecker, University of North Carolina at Chapel Hill and Andrew Cherlin and Matthew Messel, Johns Hopkins University, "No Money, No Honey, No Church: The Deinstitutionalization of Religious Life Among the White Working Class." Published in the journal *Research in the Sociology of Work*, volume 23 (2012).
86. Sam Marsden, "Job Insecurity Leaves Marriage the Preserve of Middle-Class Couples—Study," *The Telegraph*, August 13, 2013.
87. Thomas Sowell, "Ethnicity and IQ, "*The American Spectator*, February 1995.
88. See especially Thomas Sowell, *The Economics and Politics of Race: An International Perspective* (New York: William Morrow; 1983), p. 132.
89. William Julius Wilson, "The Great Disparity," *The Nation*, July 10, 2012; published in the July 30/August 6, 2012 issue. See also the report by Stephanie J. Ventura, M. A., Sally C. Curtin, M. A., Joyce Abma, Ph.D., Division of Vital Statistics, and Stanley K. Henshaw, Ph.D., The Guttmacher Institute, "Estimated Pregnancy Rates and Rates of Pregnancy Outcomes for the United States, 1990–2008," vol. 60, no. 7., National Vital Statistics Reports, June 20, 2012. The study regarding educational aspirations was by Brian A. Jacob and Tamara Wilder Linkow, "Educational Expectations and Attainment," in *Whither Opportunity*, ed. Greg Duncan and Richard Murnane (New York: Russell Sage, 2011).
90. In accord is Paul Krugman, in "That Old Time Whistle," T*he New York Times*, March 17, 2014.
91. Charles Murray, *Coming Apart: The State of White America*, 1960–2010 (New York: Crown Forum, an imprint of the Crown Publishing Group, a division of Random House, Inc.; 2012), p. 284. All the quotes from *Coming Apart* following are found on the same page.
92. Viktar Fedaseyeu, Erik Gilje and Philip E. Strahan, "Voter Preferences and Political Change: Evidence from Shale Booms," NBER Working Paper No. 21789, December 2015. See also Bob Ryan, "The American Shale Boom Did Wonders for Republicans," *Business Insider*, December 16, 2015.
93. In this regard, see also Paul Krugman, "Privilege, Pathology and Power," *The New York Times*, January 1, 2016.

Chapter Ten

How Liberal Institutions Work for the Poor and Middle Class

As observed in Chapters 5 and 9, Karl Polanyi was the most prominent social theorist to warn against giving the market too much power over society. He also stressed the critical importance of liberal cultural institutions which were being undermined indirectly by the Information Revolution and globalization before they began to be indirectly, and directly, undermined by trickle-down.[1] Similarly applicable to us today is Polanyi's warning that fascism results from destruction of liberal democratic institutions as the market overwhelms society—an appropriate warning in today's age of trickle-down and the urge to convert everything to commodities that can be bought and sold and a profit made off of the exchange.[2] What Polanyi's warning meant was that excessive reliance upon the market leads the middle class to a turn to right wing populism, embracing illiberalism—rejection of liberal democracy and liberal values (among them, checks and balances, respect for knowledge, tolerance, equality, peace and the rule of law), abandoning hope in the ability of government to help them, and embracing capitalism and sympathetic conservative elites (but rejecting liberal elites). With this perspective, it can be seen Polanyi was describing a phenomenon similar to the Tea Party, and its rejection of government, including government programs to help the middle class; also immigration, civil rights, same sex marriage, etc. And, this turn toward right wing populism is occurring in other developed countries as well.

Jose Ortega y Gasset famously observed in *The Revolt of the Masses* that the politically powerful majority must share political power with the politically powerless minorities;[3] in doing so he was expressing a recurring theme in liberalism—that *through government* the powerful—be they powerful politically (in number) or economically (in wealth)—must share with the powerless. This theme, as observed previously, was expressed by Adam Smith in

The Wealth of Nations and Alexis de Tocqueville in *Democracy in America*. As Ortega y Gasset observed, it is no surprise that humanity should be so eager to get rid of liberal democracy because indulging in selfishness is so alluring. And, it is ironic that Ortega y Gasset's warning of an illiberal "revolt of the masses" was taken to heart by conservatives, yet these same conservatives remain oblivious to the danger posed by their own ideology, inspiring an illiberal "revolt of the elites," encouraged to exploit their superior economic power and ability to undermine our economy, democracy, institutions and health.

All of the above reflects a fundamental theme throughout this work, but especially in this chapter, of the inevitability of conflict. Somewhat counterintuitively, although liberalism stresses the concept of connectedness, it does not envision a world of harmonious coexistence. Rather, it envisions a world in which the exercise of freedom by individuals inevitably brings them into conflict. What harmony does result in society is due to the work of the institutions of the market, civil society and government, resolving those conflicts. One of the most important examples of conflict is that between the employer and the employee—the employee's wages are the employer's costs, but also the employee's costs are the revenues of employers. Institutions help employers and employees negotiate their way through their conflict so that the system functions best for all. (Not only do employers and employees conflict over compensation, but employees need government-sponsored institutions such as safety-net programs and student loans for their children, while paying for these institutions raises taxes the employer pays and, potentially, creates federal budget deficits, which may raise interest rates the employer pays to borrow money for expansion of his business.[4])

In their book *Why Nations Fail* (2012) introduced in Chapter 5, Daron Acemoglu and James A. Robinson observed the interrelationship of "inclusive" and "extractive" economic and political institutions[5] and contrasted the "virtuous circle" created by inclusive institutions versus the "vicious circle" resulting from extractive institutions.[6]

They observed the crucial elements in the creation of inclusive institutions—while they do not name them, among these would be those liberal institutions such as those observed herein—checks and balances, respect for knowledge, tolerance, equality, peace and the rule of law—spread knowledge and pluralism (the phenomenon of different groups working together, which does not happen absent the value of tolerance, stressed herein).

However, Acemoglu and Robinson omitted a concept critical to understanding the function of institutions: that those with the power to create the extractive economic and political institutions they condemn must exercise restraint and sacrifice to refrain from doing so and, for the good of society, act against their own apparent self-interest and, motivated by enlightened self-interest, support inclusive economic and political institutions. Included in this concept of restraint and sacrifice is the foregoing of the use of the extractive political institution of war and, instead, embracing the liberal value of peace.

This is in great part what liberal institutions do: They act as *restraint* on the powerful, both restricting their exercise of power and enabling the less powerful to leverage their own power to confront the powerful. And, it is this apparent *sacrifice* on the part of the powerful, acting out of *enlightened* self-interest—willingly foregoing the use of their power to crush liberal institutions—that enables these institutions to exist and flourish, and their success is critical to national economic and political success—to the success of *all.* Below is more detail on those dual functions of institutions.

INSTITUTIONS BOTH CONSTRAIN AND LEVERAGE

Douglass North, Nobel Prize winning economist and leading figure in the movement called the "New Institutional Economics"[7] (which concentrates on transaction costs and property rights[8]) defined institutions as human "constraints" on social, political and economic conduct.[9] However, North's definition, while extremely helpful, covers only the aspect of institutions wherein they act as a *constraint* on human behavior—there is also the positive capability of institutions to reduce transaction costs and provide for more efficient use of property rights (thereby enhancing productivity). Thus, another aspect of institutions is that they act as a positive *leverage* of human behavior, raising the productivity—the efficacy—of an individual actor dramatically—in the market, in government, and in civil society.

It is critical to observe that North's definition of institutions, subject to the addition above, thus characterizing institutions as constraining power used against one and leveraging one's own power, precisely dovetails with the concept of a system of societal checks and balances discussed earlier. Just as with checks and balances purely in the government realm (between legislative, executive and judicial branches), there is a system of checks and balances between government (the political realm), the market (the economic realm) and civil society (the social realm)—institutions that intervene on behalf of individuals, defending them against the power exerted over them by other individuals, and allowing them to leverage their own power, be it economic, political or social (in the setting of the family and voluntary institutions).

The importance of institutions in liberal democracy in protecting against the abuse of individuals by other individuals can hardly be overstated. As Hayek observed about Adam Smith, in terms similar to what Alexis de Tocqueville said about democratic institutions in the Introduction[10]:

> [T]he main point about which there can be little doubt is that Smith's chief concern was not so much with what man might occasionally achieve when he was at his best but that he should have as little opportunity as possible to do harm when he was at his worst . . . .It is a social system which does not depend for its functioning on our finding good men for running it, or on all men becoming better than they now are, but which makes use of men in all their given variety and complexity, sometimes good and sometimes bad, sometimes intelligent and more often, stupid.

THE CONSTANCY OF CONNECTEDNESS—AND CONFLICT

The important role of institutions in leveraging both one's efficacy and one's defense against power exerted by others is revealed when we turn to the effect of imposing an illiberal "winner take all" or "might makes right" vision on society—whether the source of that might is economic, political, military, or perceived intellectual or moral superiority. An ironic distinction between conservatism and liberalism is that conservatism focuses not on how people are connected but, rather, how they are separated by their differences in culture, values, intelligence, talent, race, etc.—yet conservatism envisions that all these differences will be harmonized by the magic of the market and one-person-one-vote democracy (the fallacy of this vision is illustrated by the years of conflict unleashed and still raging in Iraq and more recently having spread from Iraq to Syria). Liberalism, which, as observed in the Introduction in contrast, sees people as connected and as basically similar the world over, envisions that all these people interact in a setting of social, political and economic conflict—as will be seen, the sociologist Peter Berger described the conditions as "chaos"—yet, because of the functioning of institutions that help people negotiate their way through this conflict, societies can provide a good quality of life for their citizens. Analysis of concepts important to understanding the functioning of institutions follows below.

Connectedness, Organic Theory, Hayek and Obama

In contrast to the conservative vision driven by the trickle-down delusion, a liberal vision of societal development is an organic theory of development. An organic theory treats society as though it were an organism (as also imagined by Friedrich Hayek, in Chapter 5, and in strikingly similar terms by Barack Obama below). As in this work, it addresses political, economic and social ideas and institutions all together. Key here is that all the institutions of civil society, government and the market are connected.

A liberal vision of development that derives its insights from an organic vision of society is the vision sketched by Senator Barack Obama in the Democratic primary presidential debate at Howard University (June 28,

2007), wherein he addressed the problems of the African American community[11]:

> And I also think there's a broader issue, though, here, and this is going to be true on all the issues we talk about—the problems of poverty, lack of health care, these are—lack of educational opportunity—are all interconnected. And to some degree, the African American community is weakened. It has a disease to its immune system. When we are impoverished, when people don't have jobs, they are more likely to be afflicted not just with AIDS but with substance abuse problems, with guns in the streets. And so it is important for us to look at the whole body here and make absolutely certain that we are providing the kinds of economic development opportunities and jobs that will create healthier communities; that we've got universal health care that ensures that people can get regular treatments. Those are the kinds of strategies that over the long term are going to make a difference in our communities.

This idea of connectedness, observed in the Introduction as central to a liberal vision of development, was expressed by Senator Obama as well in a June 4, 2007 interview on CNN.[12] In response to the question of what kind of moral and political imagination would he bring to finding some real solutions as president, he answered—in terms evocative of the Reverends John Donne and Dr. Martin Luther King, and President Theodore Roosevelt (all quoted in the Introduction)—that his starting point is that he is his brother's keeper and his sister's keeper and has a stake in the lives of his fellow citizens, and we are all in this together. This connectedness, however, also results in the constancy of class conflict due to the anarchy of production in a capitalist system, as seen below.

Class Conflict and the Anarchy of Production—and the Need for Government Institutions to Protect the Middle Class and Poor from Exploitation by the Rich and Powerful

Class conflict is not a new concern—it has been with us since this country's beginning and is inevitable. Contrary to the misinformation promoted by conservatives, the concept of class struggle did not begin with Karl Marx. It was addressed in James Madison's *The Federalist No. 10,* published in 1787; and Thomas Jefferson and Andrew Jackson each addressed class conflict while serving as president (from 1801-1809 and 1829-1837, respectively). In contrast, Karl Marx was not even born until 1819; *The Communist Manifesto* was not published until 1848; Volume I of *Das Kapital* was not published until 1867.

As observed by the historian Arthur Schlesinger, Jr. in *The Vital Center* (1949), classes have been around from the beginning of the country, so much so that James Madison addressed them in the *Federalist No. 10*, which provided in part[13]:

> [T]he most common and durable source of factions has been the various and unequal distribution of property . . . .The regulation of these various and interfering interests forms the principal task of modern legislation, and involves the spirit of party and faction in the necessary and ordinary operations of the government.

Schlesinger observed that the Founding Fathers disagreed not over the reality of class conflict but over its origin: whether, as Alexander Hamilton and John Adams claimed, it was the inevitable result of natural differences in the talents of men, or, as Thomas Jefferson and Andrew Jackson claimed, it was the result of unnatural tyrannies, imposed by fraud and maintained by force—such as when the rich and powerful bend the laws in their favor. It is this latter formulation of class conflict that motivated American liberalism from the time of Jefferson and Jackson through Franklin Roosevelt and, thus, as Schlesinger observed, Roosevelt's government intervention on behalf of the less powerful is not a European import, nor is it Marxist, because it does not extend that class conflict to the Marxist solution of a proletariat revolution and dictatorship.

Giving rise to class conflict is the concept identified as the "anarchy of production"—which, like the concept of class, is by no means unique to Marxists or Marxist-Leninists. The Austrian economist and free market champion Ludwig von Mises approvingly referenced the concepts of "anarchic production" or "anarchy of production" in four different places in his magnum opus *Human Action* (originally published in 1949).[14]

The anarchy of production leads to the propensity for markets to overproduce. Adam Smith acknowledged this propensity in *The Wealth of Nations*, criticizing the predisposition of merchants to conspire to prevent competition from forcing prices down. Despite the many shortcomings of the system they proposed as an antidote to the failings of capitalism, the Marxists Nikolai Bukharin and Yevgeni Preobrazhensky provided, in the concept of the anarchy of production, a valuable critique of that system, linking anarchy of production with class conflict.[15]

Facts support the recognition that the interests of capitalists and workers are not smoothly harmonized by the market, and, thus, the need exists for governmental institutions to intervene on behalf of the workers. This need for government institutions to intervene on behalf of workers has again become especially acute with the emerging of the Information Revolution and its accompanying creation of a society in which knowledge workers are dominant, creating class conflict between them and those in manual or service work, as observed by the management theorist Peter Drucker.[16] A similar failure of the market that must be addressed by governmental institutions is the tragedy of the commons, presented below.

HOW INSTITUTIONS HELP US PREVENT SELF-INTEREST FROM DESTROYING HUMANITY

As observed previously, over the past three decades it has become an accepted delusion that the exercise of freedom and self-interest through the free market is not to be meddled with, and conservatives have come to link, consciously or unconsciously, wealth with godliness, and unregulated markets and unregulated elections with harmony as intended by God. However, as observed by Adam Smith, Alexis de Tocqueville, Friedrich Hayek, and Karl Polanyi, there are times in which we should use institutions to save ourselves and society from victimization by excessive individualism, self-interest, freedom and the free market, and to those we turn below.

The Tragedy of the Commons

The tragedy of the commons is an instructive model for illustrating decision-making in the context of an environment in which resources are limited—be they natural resources or human capital. Applied to such an environment, strategies indicated by game theory,[17] especially the concepts of "zero-sum games" (in which the players' fortunes are inversely related, and one's gain is another's loss, thus resolution requires winners and losers) and "non-zero-sum games" (with "win-win" resolutions), and the importance of trust (as indicated by the game the "prisoners' dilemma"[18]) illustrate the value of a collaborative versus competitive mindset.

William Forster Lloyd introduced the parable of the "Tragedy of the Commons" in his 1833 book on population.[19] Lloyd observed that when pastureland (the "commons") is available to all, cattle-owners have a short-term interest in increasing the size of their herds. But, unchecked, the size of the herds on the commons will soon exceed its carrying capacity. The commons will be doomed by overgrazing, and everyone will lose. The argument was used by Lloyd to dispute Adam Smith's idea of the "invisible hand" popularly mischaracterized by conservatives and liberals alike as Smith's urging for a market without any government intervention—what Adam Smith actually said, in the tradition of enlightened self-interest, will be addressed in Chapter 13.

The ecologist Garrett Hardin, in a 1968 article in *Science* magazine[20] revived the tragedy of the commons theory and applied it in the context of the environment. In his tragedy of the commons the reader is again asked to imagine a pasture open to all, with grazing animals on a common ground. The conclusion, as described in the *Encyclopedia of Environmental Science*, is that individual rational behavior, acting merely to maximize personal gain, without restraint, results in long-range damage to the environment and to the well-being of all the actors.[21]

Another area in which the tragedy of the commons has long been observed, and institutions have addressed it, is in the exploration for and production of oil and natural gas. Long ago the Texas Railroad Commission, the Texas state agency that regulates oil and gas production, recognized that allowing the unrestricted drilling of wells for oil and gas production would have numerous negative consequences. Unregulated drilling and unregulated production resulted in premature loss of reservoir pressure, resulting in waste—leaving behind—of oil and gas resources. Additionally, the race to deliver oil and gas to the market resulted in falling oil and gas prices. Accordingly, the Railroad Commission began to study reservoir performance and issued rules regarding spacing of drilling of wells and proration orders setting "allowables" for production of oil and gas. Oil and gas conservation agencies in other producing states followed suit, and the Texas Railroad Commission coordinated with these other states' agencies through the Interstate Oil Compact Commission (IOCC) to maintain higher oil prices. When the Organization of the Petroleum Exporting Countries (OPEC) was formed, the member nations used the Texas Railroad Commission's practices of restricting production to support prices as a model.[22]

Economists have observed that the tragedy of the commons manifests itself in two ways. It either grants benefits without costs, or exacts costs without benefits. Those benefits without costs are called "positive externalities," while the costs without benefits are called "negative externalities." Examples of positive externalities can be seen in the political arena, where an entire population can benefit from a fair-minded political candidate who wins, although only a small group of citizens (typically) will have worked in and funded that politician's campaign. Another example is in the activities of unions, which may secure benefits for all workers, although not all workers are members of the union and, in "right-to-work" states, are not required to pay union dues even though they benefit from the work of the union (they are "free-riders"). Negative externalities are most pointedly observed in the context of energy choices with the negative externalities of the necessity of military involvement in the Middle East to keep oil and gas flowing and the impact on the environment in terms of increased emissions of air pollutants and greenhouse gases—these costs are borne by all, but the profits from such operations go only to the oil and gas producers.

Important to understanding the applicability of the concept of the tragedy of the commons as applied to economic development is the realization that investment in the economy comes not just from the private sector, but also from the public sector, and we are all better off with public institutions that are subsidized disproportionately by the rich but are open to all—rich, middle class and poor alike. Failure to recognize this leads to a diminution of "non-commodified public spheres"[23] —institutions such as public schools, libraries, museums and noncommercial public broadcasting stations disappear, while public lands and the electromagnetic spectrum are sold off to the highest bidder—this leads to a waste of human capital and productivity, and a vacuum for democratic citizenship.[24]

To further appreciate the necessity of institutions, it is important to properly characterize the market as a process and the actors in it as they really are rather than as neoclassical economics assumes them to be—as addressed below.

Neoclassical Economic Theory's Misunderstanding of the Institution of the Market and How That Has Supported Trickle-Down

Chapter 4 addressed how economic theory hid the facts regarding the failures of trickle-down. This section and those following will return to how economic theory has supported the delusion of trickle-down.

Friedrich Hayek viewed economics as "a coordination problem," a view he shared with fellow Austrian economist Ludwig von Mises, who, in *Human Action*, identified the market as a "process."[25] Hayek observed that the market's real function is to spread information,[26] an observation in which he was joined by fellow Austrian economist Israel M. Kirzner,[27] and both critiqued modern neoclassical economic theory as envisioning a model of the economy in which the actors in the economy are atomistic individual "rational economic agents" possessing "perfect knowledge" and operating in a system of "perfect competition" in which supply, demand and price tend toward coinciding with each other at "equilibrium" in a market operating independent of society rather than its institutions being socially embedded along with those of government and civil society. (The Austrians are joined by other economists in their critique of neoclassical economics, and all are joined under the heading "heterodox economics.") For that matter, the accompanying misconception that economics itself operates outside of the other social sciences is also condemned, for economics itself is embedded among, and cannot be understood separate from, the other social sciences.

The Austrians recognized that the neoclassical model of the economy, treating knowledge as given to all in a setting of equilibrium, eliminates the role of the entrepreneur. In fact, the entrepreneur gathers and acts on data that is *not given* to all and the actions of the entrepreneur are constantly creating *disequilibrium*—adding to the chaos rather than creating harmony—as observed by Schumpeter, the entrepreneur is constantly engaging in "creative destruction." To which it can be added that under trickle-down conservatism—as well as under Austrian economics (a major shortcoming of it)—there is no room for the operation of the institutions necessary to help the market avoid chaos and depressions, institutions which trickle-down and the

Austrians envision as unnecessary because both suffer under the delusion that markets are self-correcting.

An even more basic theoretical misconception underlying trickle-down economics is that there is such an objectively definable thing *as* a "free market." There is no such thing as a "free market," except as an imaginary ideal. A popular bumper sticker during the collapse of the Keynesian Consensus was "TANSTAAFL—There Ain't No Such Thing as a Free Lunch." Perhaps after the collapse of the trickle-down consensus we will see bumper stickers displaying other eternal truths: "TANSTAAFM—There Ain't No Such Thing as a Free Market" and "TANSTAFT—There Ain't No Such Thing as Free Trade."

Trickle-down not only renewed Americans' faith in the myth that there is such a thing as the "free market;" but also that the "free market" is self-correcting toward "equilibrium;" that the "free market" always properly values assets (the "Efficient Market Hypothesis" or "EMH"); that individuals always act rationally in attempting to maximize their own economic self-interest ("Rational Expectation Hypothesis"); that they do so based on "perfect knowledge" and in a setting of "perfect competition;" that the market itself is "perfect" and incapable of failure (unless, the theory goes, liberals are too loose with monetary policy); that inequality is benign; that economists may ignore inequality and focus exclusively on fighting inflation; that the market is always the most appropriate determinant of compensation, in accordance with productivity—or, more recently, perhaps even divorced from productivity; and that unemployment is always voluntary—and always due to the failure of greedy workers to lower their wage demands to accord with what the market decrees is their appropriate wage level.

And, as observed previously, trickle-down theory got support from monetarists who believed that the only policy necessary to pull an economy out of depression was lower interest rates, thereby increasing the money supply. It should now be abundantly clear that Keynes was right in 1936 when he urged abandonment of supply-side policies of his day in favor of stimulating demand not just with stimulative monetary policy but also with stimulative fiscal policies.

Oddly, in the widely acclaimed 2014 work of economist Thomas Piketty, *Capital in the Twenty-first Century*, there are two references to the idea that growing inequality is not due to market imperfection[28] —which illustrates the point that there is disagreement over the most basic questions of the *function of a market*. A market exists to provide general prosperity—to provide for the general welfare; the material well-being of all the members of society. A market is functioning imperfectly if it is operating so as to continually increase concentration of income and wealth at the top, thereby continually increasing inequality and thereby continually sowing the seeds of its own doom (through sluggish growth, economic instability and, ultimately, political instability) and with it the society in which it operates. It is no slight to the wonders of the market to admit that misguided government policies can rig the market so that revenues attributable to increased productivity are continually upwardly redistributed and, in so doing, government can force the market to fail in its mission to provide general prosperity.

Similarly, there is misunderstanding of the *function of the corporation.* Milton Friedman, in an essay published in *The New York Times Magazine* in 1970, originated the idea that corporations exist only to make money for their shareholders.[29] This idea should have been immediately questioned for, if that were the case, shareholders would stand first in line in the liquidation of a corporation under bankruptcy law—instead, they rank at the very bottom, primed by every other creditor. In an outstanding critique of the shareholder value theory,[30] the management theorist Steve Denning observed that Peter Drucker, in his 1974 classic *Management: Tasks, Responsibilities, Practices,* posited that the corporation exists to serve the customer, without whom the corporation would disappear. Thus, Friedman provided a supply-side—trickle-down—explanation for the existence of the corporation, while Drucker corrected this error with a demand-focused explanation.

In sum, neoclassical economists have treated the market as something that operates in perfect harmony, at best self-correcting or, at worst, occasionally needing slight correction by simply appropriately, depending on circumstances, raising or lowering interest rates through monetary policy (and no, or only minimal, government intervention otherwise), and the main instrument for the operation of the market, the corporation, need not focus on anything other than keeping its shareholders, who are disproportionately represented among the rich, happy—because, under trickle-down theory, we all do better if the rich do better.

Trickle-Down's Failure to Acknowledge the Market's "Embeddedness"—That the Market is Embedded in Society

Another major failure of some neoclassical theory and certainly of trickle-down is such a critical flaw that it will be addressed in detail herein. A critical concept herein, from the statements of Karl Polanyi previously, is that the institutions of the market only exist in the context of the other sources of institutions of society—the market is "embedded" in society amongst the institutions of government and of civil society—and is subject to the influences of government and civil society.[31]

To otherwise envision the market, as loosed from these controls, imperils not only the economic wellbeing of the people—but also the very existence of American liberal democracy. Polanyi illustrated this risk with one of the most important concepts in *The Great Transformation,* that of "the commodity fiction," which is the principle that no arrangement may exist that interferes with the functioning of the market. He observed the negative effects upon humans of organizing society in accordance with the market and this commodity fiction.[32]

Building on Polanyi's observations, Mark Granovetter (Stanford sociologist) and Richard Swedberg (Cornell sociologist) observed that economic action is a form of social action and economic institutions are a form of social institutions[33] and, as such, economic action is embedded in social networks.[34]

In contrast, as observed herein, trickle-down has, for the past three and a half decades, promoted the concept of the market as unmoored from the rest of society, with disastrous results.

The Market Needs Government Institutions

Friedrich Hayek recognized that "a carefully thought-out legal framework is required" in order to successfully use competition as "the principle of social organization."[35] Continuing, he observed that a functioning capitalist system "depends, above all, on the existence of an appropriate legal system, a legal system designed both to preserve competition and to make it operate as beneficially as possible."[36] And from a section titled "The Needed Institutions" economist Mancur Olson, in *Power and Prosperity* elaborated on Hayek's ideas, that legal institutions and a stable political order are necessary to reap the benefits of the free market.[37]

INSTITUTIONS AS MEDIATING STRUCTURES AND HOW CONSERVATISM UNDERMINES THEM

To elaborate on a point made previously, institutions work as follows: The *social* institutions of *civil society* alternatively impose upon the freedom of / defend individuals from the *legal* institutions of *government* that alternatively impose upon the freedom of / defend individuals from the *financial* institutions of *the market* that alternatively impose upon the freedom of / defend individuals from, in turn, the institutions of civil society and government. To tinker too much with the balance is to risk upsetting the whole system.

Peter Berger, in an essay in *National Review* magazine in 1977, warned conservatives against utopianism, but his lesson is a good one for liberals as well[38]:

> Unlike the enthusiasts for revolution and radical change, the conservative ought to be prudent about upsetting the fragile structures that protect men's lives from the terrors of chaos. His ought to be a prudence born of knowledgeable skepticism regarding all utopian promises, and born especially of a care to avoid the senseless suffering that most attempts to realize such promises have

> produced historically. The great radicalisms of the modern era have all claimed to love mankind; the conservative ought to cultivate affection for individual men in their concrete and irreplaceable particularity.

And, long before the term was popularized by President George W. Bush, he concluded: "Such a conservatism of compassion is rooted in a long tradition of moral wisdom of both classical and biblical inspiration."[39]

Berger later, in a paper for the American Enterprise Institute, teamed up with Richard John Neuhaus, and they observed that while modern liberalism was rightly sensitive to the potential for business to undermine necessary liberal institutions, it was blind to the potential for government to do the same; in contrast, conservatism was appropriately sensitive to the potential for government to undermine necessary liberal institutions, but it was blind to the analogous potential of business.[40]

ILLIBERAL DEMOCRACY AND TOTALITARIANISM

The concept of illiberalism is more varied than might be initially imagined. The illiberal vision that might first come to mind is that of communism—a totalitarianism that rejects both democracy and capitalism. However, totalitarianism can also come in the form of fascism. As in the Fascism of Italy and the Nazism of Germany, the new Il Dulce or Führer will have arisen via one-person-one-vote democracy and preside over a totalitarian system combined with crony capitalism. However, a third version of illiberalism is exhibited in the conservative illiberal vision, and it is identified by Fareed Zakaria as "illiberal democracy" in his 2003 book, *The Future of Freedom: Illiberal Democracy at Home and Abroad*. This is democracy deemed synonymous with one-person-one vote elections—coupled with crony capitalism and rejecting liberal values (such as those herein of checks and balances, respect for knowledge, tolerance, equality, peace and the rule of law). This conservatism champions freedom, but it is a freedom without restraint, for it envisions ultimate truth as the arbiter of justice, determining winners and losers. It champions winners in a winner-take-all, might-makes-right vision. It praises knowledge, but demands the teaching of religion in science classes and suppresses scientific inquiry. It talks of general prosperity, but it skews benefits to the wealthy, unconcerned about inequality. It praises tolerance, but ignores its own intolerance. It talks of peace, but praises war for its opportunities for national pride and heroism. And, it praises the rule of law, but excuses its adherents from the application of it.

The potential for illiberal democracy to morph into totalitarian democracy was addressed in the classic study of the ideology of the French Revolution, *The Origins of Totalitarian Democracy* (1970), by J. L. Talmon. Talmon observed that the Enlightenment in the 1700s created not only liberal democracy but also illiberal, totalitarian democracy (which he also called "political Messianism"[41]). Liberalism and illiberalism were differentiated from each other by the assumption in liberalism that politics is the result of trial and error, conducted by innately flawed participants, and that politics is but part of overall society—one could say "embedded" in society, as Polanyi did regarding the market. On the other hand, the illiberal totalitarian democratic school assumes that perfectibility of human endeavor is achievable—that ultimate truth is knowable—and that pursuit of that truth must occur in a system in which the political is all. It should be observed that, regarding Talmon's observations, he had in mind a totalitarianism of the Left,[42] although he observed that where results are concerned the distinction between totalitarianisms of the Left and Right may make little difference.[43]

Thus, as Neuhaus and Berger alleged, the Enlightenment is responsible not only for the rise of liberal democracy but also for the rise of totalitarian—illiberal—democracy. Nonetheless, the allegation that liberal democracy *leads to* fascism, as made by Leo Strauss[44] and Friedrich Hayek[45] is rebutted by recent history. What leads to totalitarian democracy is the *denial* of liberalism—the assumption that the views of one party represent the ultimate truth in politics—represent God's will. This was precisely the way Hitler, Mussolini and Franco attempted to deny liberalism, and is precisely the way in which conservatives attempt to deny liberalism, as was observed by Karl Popper, Friedrich Hayek (in his critiques of conservatism) and, in the present day, George Soros. And, as values of individualism and short-term self-interest leave no room for liberal values, laying the groundwork for the destruction of all liberal institutions as a precursor to fascism, as observed by Polanyi, the values of the fundamentalist free market and fundamentalist religion combine to provide conservatism its illusion of ultimate truth today.

This is the gaping hole in the vision of the conservatives (and the neoconservatives): Their philosophy attempts to avoid going down the road to one imagined version of authoritarianism by imposing their own real version of authoritarianism, based on trickle-down's upwardly redistributionist of economic and political power and crude one-person-one vote majority-rule illiberal democracy to the exclusion of liberal institutions. Those liberal institutions include *public* institutions like Obamacare, Social Security, Medicare, Medicaid, unemployment insurance, public transportation and public education—especially public universities. And, as alleged above in this chapter, conservatives' blindness to the effect of economic circumstances upon behavior leads them to support low-wage policies that undermine the very institutions they hold dear: marriage and religion. Thus, as stated in the title of this work, conservative policies—Republican policies—undermine institutions relied upon by the poor and middle class.

Liberalism's insistence upon institutions will be contrasted further with illiberalism's undermining of them below; what follows after that is an analysis of the values and attitudes that maximize the functioning of institutions.

"COERCIVE DEMOCRACY" OR THE "SHOCK DOCTRINE": TRICKLE-DOWN'S IGNORANCE OF THE IMPORTANCE OF INSTITUTIONS APPLIED ABROAD WITH MISSIONARY ZEAL

Among the insights provided by former Bush press secretary Scott McClellan in his 2008 book, *What Happened: Inside the Bush White House and Washington's Culture of Deception*, was the observation that driving President Bush in Iraq was a belief that the US through application of military force—"coercive democracy"—could convert the Iraqi dictatorship (and then the rest of the Middle East) into liberal democracies.[46]

This vision of "coercive democracy" is synonymous with the "shock doctrine" described by Naomi Klein, who examined the Bush administration's efforts in Iraq in an outstanding article that appeared in the September 2004 issue of *Harper's* magazine.[47] (She later expanded on her observations and applied them globally in her 2008 book mentioned above, *Shock Doctrine: The Rise of Disaster Capitalism*.) Klein's criticism of the Bush administration was *not* for the absence of a plan but, rather, for the extraordinary violence underlying its ideology. The plan, consisting of economic "shock therapy" of the sort roundly criticized by Nobel laureate Joseph Stiglitz (in *Globalization and Its Discontents*) previously for hobbling the former Soviet Union's transition to capitalism, consisted of implementing Washington Consensus reforms (privatization, deregulation, lower marginal tax rates) so rapidly that the people were too stunned to react. As devastating as Stiglitz had found those reforms in his study, Klein quoted Stiglitz as finding in Iraq an even more extreme version of what he had found in the former Soviet Union.[48]

As Klein observed, the widely reported inaction of U.S. troops in the face of widespread looting and domestic violence during the war was consistent with the neoconservative shock therapy—no application of the conservatives' vaunted "broken windows" strategy of crime prevention in Iraq! However, as she observed, in the case of Iraq, the shock elicited an effect that was the opposite of what was intended,[49] jolting the Iraqis into violent reaction, including the blowback of religious fundamentalism,[50] rendering the nation of Iraq *not* a capitalist paradise but, rather, a dystopia in which one risks a horrible death just going to a business meeting.[51] As she concluded, it must have been a shock to the neoconservatives that their faith in greed to accomplish good proved such a failure.

The foreign policy allies of the trickle-down-supply-side-crony capitalists, the neoconservatives, could claim among their ranks in the early days of their philosophy sociologists keenly aware of the crucial importance of liberal institutions that "combat individualism" and of the distinction between a liberal democracy and an illiberal democracy based solely on a crude one-person-one vote system in a "free market" capitalist setting. The trickle-down-supply-side-crony capitalists and their modern neoconservative allies, in contrast, imposed illiberal crude one-person-one vote democracy by brute force, with the naïve expectation of liberal institutions springing forth from where they have never before existed, propelled by the magic of self-interest—of greed—and one-person-one vote democracy. Of course, if they actually understood liberalism and took to heart Thomas Hobbes' famous critique of anarchy (creating lives "solitary, poor, nasty, brutish and short"), they would have recognized that it was precisely the inability of self-interest—greed—to serve as an organizing force that doomed their mission.

MAXIMIZING INSTITUTIONAL FUNCTIONING

Social Capital, Civil Society and Equality

The sociologist Francis Fukuyama's definition of "social capital" emphasized that the efficacy of the set of informal norms and values that constitute social capital is enhanced by trust.[52] He traced the first use of the term "social capital" to Lyda Judson Hanifen in 1916 to describe rural school community centers. Jane Jacobs also used it in her classic work *The Death and Life of Great American Cities*. The economist Glenn Loury, as well as the sociologist Ivan Light, used the term "social capital" in the 1970s to analyze the problem of inner-city economic development, making parallel observations regarding lack of social capital as those made by William Julius Wilson regarding social isolation. In the 1980s, the term social capital was popularized by the sociologist James Coleman and the political scientist Robert Putnam, whose work will be addressed below. Fukuyama emphasized that the success of social capital was based on what he called "the radius of trust"[53] —the extent to which trust extends among society's members.

In understanding the concept of social capital, it is helpful to put it in the context of other types of capital—economic and political. Economic capital—typically simply referred to as capital, refers to money, or money in combination with commercial paper (legal instruments that represent money, varying based on degree of liquidity—how quickly they can be converted to cash). Capital, then, refers to how much money is available for putting into action, be it for spending, or lending. Political capital, a term famously used by President George W. Bush after his 2004 reelection when he boasted of how much he had and how he planned to use it, is a synonym for political power—the ability to accomplish things in the political arena, as in the ability to call in favors and deliver votes on pieces of legislation. Social capital, similarly, refers to the ability to get things done, but in the sphere of voluntary associations, through "social networks" and employing "norms of reciprocity."

Alexis de Tocqueville observed, "There is nothing, in my opinion, that merits our attention more than the intellectual and moral associations of America . . . .In democratic countries the science of association is the mother science; the progress of all the others depends on the progress of the former."[54]

Importantly, for the purpose of illustrating the liberal value of equality, Tocqueville concluded: "Thus the most democratic country on earth is, out of all, the one where men today have most perfected the art of pursuing in common the object of their common desires and have applied this new science to the greatest number of things. Does this result from an accident, or could it be that in fact a necessary connection exists between associations and equality?"[55] Tocqueville then answered his own question: "Among the laws that govern human societies there is one that seems more definitive and clearer than all the others. For men to remain civilized or to become so, the art of associating must become developed and be perfected in the same proportion as equality of conditions grows."[56]

Perhaps the most famous inquiry into social capital was Harvard political scientist Robert Putnam's *Bowling Alone: The Collapse and Revival of American Community* (2000). Interestingly, Putnam did not make the claim in the book that he did in an earlier article,[57] that a high incidence of social capital was linked to economic growth. The idea that it might be had already been questioned, before the book was published, by Stephen Knack and Philip Keefer, then of the World Bank, in a study that appeared in 1997 in the prestigious journal *The Quarterly Journal of Economics*.[58] In their article, Knack and Keefer addressed, among other matters, the conflict between the theory of Putnam that associational activity aided growth and that of the economist Mancur Olson that values (such as trust and civic cooperation) were more important to economic growth, and that associational activity can restrict growth, arguments Olson made in *The Rise and Decline of Nations* (1982). They concluded that trust and civic cooperation are associated with stronger economic performance although associational activity is not (contrary to Putnam's 1993 findings across Italian regions). Parenthetically, it should be observed that the latter part of the third conclusion above, that trust and norms of civic cooperation are greater in countries less polarized along lines of class or ethnicity, is confirmed in another article which appeared directly in front of Knack's and Keefer's. The article, by then World Bank economists William Easterly and Ross Levine, found, as did Mancur Olson and in an interesting parallel with the sociologist Francis Fukuyama, that interest group polarization led to rent-seeking behavior which, in turn, reduced economic growth. They also found that trust—the value Fukuyama addressed in detail—was greater in countries with strong property regimes and less class or ethnic polarization.[59]

Spontaneous Sociability

Francis Fukuyama, in *Trust: The Social Virtues and the Creation of Prosperity* (1995), elaborated on another institution necessary to growth. He contrasted "traditional sociability"—ability to associate in established social group[60] —with "spontaneous sociability"—which he defined as the ability to cross from existing social groups into new associations and cooperate in them.[61]

Traditional sociability, according to Fukuyama, can foster what was referred to by Mancur Olson as "distributional cartels"[62] and thereby be an obstacle to growth. Spontaneous sociability, by contrast, the ability to bring together new groups, can be helpful from an economic development standpoint if it is used to build wealth-creating economic organizations.[63]

Fukuyama cited Spain as an example of a society in which traditional sociability is a hindrance to economic development, as it is a victim of "excessive individualism" and a narrow "radius of trust."[64] Parenthetically, Fukuyama observed that a group formed of spontaneous sociability, based on shared values rather than contract, falls under what the sociologist Emil Durkheim characterized as "organic solidarity."[65]

It is important to pause here, and give credit to the concept that Fukuyama coined. While there is no guarantee that increased associational activity—increased social capital—will increase economic activity, it would appear that the prevalence of spontaneous sociability, directed toward economic activity, would. The term is key to understanding the emphasis placed herein on the liberal value of *tolerance*—oddly, as critical as the concept is to economic success and success of liberal democracy, Fukuyama did not elaborate on it further.[66]

Synthesizing the works above, together with that of Acemoglu and Robinson, we can conclude that there can be "good" social capital that promotes economic growth and "bad" social capital that suppresses it. Bad social capital can be observed where ample social capital exists in a society in the form of a willingness of members to form organizations; however, such organizations are formed along family, ethnic or class lines and exclude those outside of the family, ethnic or class group. They are, to use Mancur Olson's term, "distributional cartels," like Acemoglu and Robinson's "extractive" political and economic institutions, and in contrast with their "inclusive" ones.

As Olson observed in *The Rise and Decline of Nations*, these distributional cartels, which are also formed in stable democratic societies by interest groups, use their political influence to create barriers to entry and other rigidities in the economy to preserve their position (thus, engaging in crony capitalism or rent-seeking). Absent shocks from the outside (e.g., due to war as in Germany and Japan), revolutions or market-opening trade agreements, the economies in such societies tend to stagnate.

Clusters

The importance of Fukuyama's concept of spontaneous sociability—and of tolerance—becomes ever clearer in the context of clusters of similar complementing businesses, operating in an environment in which competition is allowed to flourish. Insights regarding clusters are provided in the work of Harvard Business School professor Michael Porter, which stresses that clusters enhance productivity.[67] Clusters represent, in the economic realm, the collaboration in voluntary associations (as in the civil realm) for the benefit of all members. And, as Porter observed, the greatest innovation arises when clusters overlap each other—assuming there is the receptivity to sharing of information embodied in Fukuyama's concept of spontaneous sociability.

The Necessity of Sacrifice by the Powerful to Create Institutions to Build from the Bottom Up

The tendency of the institutions of the market to reward selfishness with wealth and establish a hierarchy that must be combated by other institutions from civil society (e.g., charity and union organizing) and government (e.g., regulation, tax policy and social insurance) was foreseen by Adam Smith and Alexis de Tocqueville.

Fukuyama's observation above that societies must overcome excessive individualism echoes Tocqueville's similar observation in the Introduction, that the powerful in society must sacrifice some of their power, creating wealth-spreading institutions (such as public education, public health care, public works and a social safety net) for the benefit of the less powerful, and ultimately, for the benefit of all. Thus we see the recognition that, *contra* conservatism, "freedom" and "individualism" are not enough, nor is it enough for the rich to do better—we only do better if we all do better.

This was Tocqueville's great insight regarding why his concept of "self-interest rightly understood," or "enlightened self-interest" took hold in America but not his native Europe—as quoted in Chapter 5 previously, he believed that Americans knew to sacrifice a portion of their interests to the good of all, while his fellow Europeans tried to save everything for themselves and ended up losing it.

Dani Rodrik of Harvard University's John F. Kennedy School of Government, in an article in the *European Economic Review* titled "The 'Paradoxes' of the Successful State," similarly concluded that the provision by government of social insurance for the benefit of the disadvantaged members of society was a necessary institution for the state to provide to benefit the market and enhance economic growth.[68]

Similarly, Lawrence Harrison of Harvard University, observed in *Underdevelopment Is a State of Mind: The Latin American Case*: "My own belief is that the society that is most successful at helping its people—all its people—realize their creative potential is the society that will progress the fastest."[69] Continuing, attempting to explain the failure of Latin American economies to economically develop[70]:

> In my view, the principal explanation is the failure of most Latin American countries, and most especially Argentina, to develop political systems that adequately reflect and further the interests of the poor . . . . Viable democracies, in turn, reflect the value and attitude systems that attach importance to questions of equity and progress for the entire society.

Harrison's conclusion is strikingly similar to the conclusion of the Peruvian economist, Hernando de Soto, in the latter's book *The Mystery of Capital: Why Capitalism Triumphs in the West and Fails Everywhere Else* (2000). Again, an element of the theory that follows is the concept, from Tocqueville, of self-interest rightly understood. Everyone in a society, especially those of means, willingly must give a share of their income—their property—to support institutions that create opportunities for others than themselves and their family, friends, neighbors and fellow tribesmen—opportunities for people they do not even know nor will ever know.

In his book de Soto asked why it is that capitalism thrives only in the West (he did not address Asia) and he answered his question: the inability of the rest of the world to produce capital.[71] In other words, de Soto's answer to the mystery of why Latin America has failed to develop as rapidly as its neighbors to the north is precisely one of the favorite subjects of the New Institutional Economists introduced at the beginning of this chapter: failure to develop the institution of an efficient (low transaction cost) private property regime.

What de Soto criticized is the view that the culture of the poor dooms them to economic failure. The cultural deficiencies examined in the present work, however, are those *not* only of the poor but, *more importantly*, those of people of means. Indeed, de Soto himself hinted, at the end of his book, that it is a defect in the *prevailing* culture that is at fault—the disinterest of the elites in changing the status quo.[72] This conclusion was given weight in the observations of John Gravois, staff reporter at the *Chronicle of Higher Education* and a contributing editor at *Sixbillion.org*, in a January 28, 2005 posting on *slate.msn.com* titled "The De Soto Delusion." Gravois recounted that implementation of de Soto's approach had, in fact, led to poorer groups in those areas where it was tried either falling prey to eviction or selling out based on the assumption that they will find somewhere else to settle, thus, capital is not being accumulated. He had the opportunity to challenge de Soto personally and ask him how to avoid the squatters falling prey to abuse by the wealthy. De Soto responded that the wealthy should know it is in their best interests to integrate the poor into the economy.

Indeed, they *should*—but the problem is that they do not, or, if they do, they are nonetheless able to ignore it. Thus, while de Soto's observations are important as part of the argument to the wealthy that it is in their best interests to have the productive power of the poor brought into the economy, *it is convincing the wealthy of that fact* that is the real key—as Harrison observes, echoing the insight of Alexis de Tocqueville and Adam Smith.

Most certainly this observation could be extended to Latin America of today, as well as the trickle-down conservatism permeating the United States presently. And, it is not too extreme to say that Tocqueville, Smith and Harrison were echoing a theme in Western culture that can be traced back to Jesus of Nazareth—quoting from the book of *Mark*, chapter 8 verses 34-36:

> And he called to him the multitude with his disciples, and said to them, "If any man would come after me, let him deny himself and take up the cross and follow me. For whoever would save his life will lose it; and whoever loses his life for my sake and the gospel's will save it. For what does it profit a man to gain the whole world and forfeit his life?

Thus, freedom, democracy and capitalism are necessary but insufficient conditions for attaining the most prosperous society—they must be combined with liberal institutions that downwardly diffuse and share political power, income and wealth, fostering respect for checks and balances, knowledge, tolerance, equality, peace and rule of law.

These liberal institutions will *constrain* the abuse of power by the powerful—be they powerful socially, economically or politically. And, these liberal institutions will enable the members of society to *leverage* their power in the social, economic or political spheres. And, it is in the enlightened self-interest of the elites to forfeit some of their freedom and property, and combat their individualism by working against their immediate self-interest to support these liberal institutions.

NOTES

1. Karl Polanyi, *The Great Transformation: The Political and Economic Origins of Our Time* (Boston: Beacon Press; 1944, 1957, 2001), p. 76.
2. Ibid, p. 237.

3. Jose Ortega y Gasset, *The Revolt of the Masses* (London, 1932), p. 83, quoted in Friedrich Hayek, *Law, Legislation and Liberty*, vol. 2, *The Mirage of Social Justice* (Chicago and London: The University of Chicago Press, 1976), p. 133.

4. See Paul Krugman, "Why Inequality Matters," *The New York Times*, December 16, 2013.

5. Daron Acemoglu and James A. Robinson, *Why Nations Fail: The Origins of Power, Prosperity and Poverty* (New York: Crown Business, an imprint of Crown Publishing Group, a Division of Random House, Inc.; 2012), pp. 429–430.

6. Ibid, p. 309.

7. The insights of the New Institutional Economics are very similar to those of "economic sociology," the term used by Neil J. Smelser and Richard Swedberg, editors, in *The Handbook of Economic Sociology* (Princeton, NJ: Princeton University Press, 1994). *The Sociology of Economic Life*, edited by Mark Granovetter and Richard Swedberg (1992), uses the term "the sociology of economic life" for the same sociologically based study of institutions and economic phenomena.

8. See, e.g., Douglass C. North, "Understanding Economic Change," in *Transforming Post-Communist Political Economies*, Joan M. Nelson, Charles Tilly and Lee Walker, eds. (Washington, D.C.: National Academy Press; 1997), pp. 13–18.

9. Douglass North, "Institutions," *Journal of Economic Perspectives* 5: 97–112 (1991); p. 97. Quoted in Oliver E. Williamson, "Transaction Cost Economics and Organization Theory," Chapter 4 (pp. 77–107) of Neil J. Smelser and Richard Swedberg, eds., *The Handbook of Economic Sociology* (Princeton, NJ: Princeton University Press; 1994), p. 79.

10. Friedrich A. Hayek, *Individualism and Economic Order* (Chicago: University of Chicago Press; 1948), pp. 11–12.

11. Transcript of the Third Presidential Primary Debate, June 28, 2007 at the C-SPAN website.

12. "Special Edition: Sojourners Presidential Forum," *The Situation Room*, CNN.com, June 4, 2007.

13. See Arthur M. Schlesinger, Jr., *The Vital Center* (1949, re-published in 1998 by Transaction Publishers, New Brunswick, New Jersey), pp. 171–175. Madison defined a "faction" as "a number of citizens, whether amounting to a majority or minority of the whole, who are united and actuated by some common impulse of passion, or of interest, adverse to the rights of other citizens or to the permanent and aggregate interests of the community." *Federalist No. 10*.

14. Ludwig von Mises, *Human Action: A Treatise on Economics*, 4th Revised Edition (Little Rock, AR: Fox & Wilkes, a division of Laissez Faire Books: 1996), pp. 239, 257, 582 and 692.

15. Nikolai Bukharin and Yevgeni Preobrazhensky, *The ABC of Communism* (Ann Arbor: The University of Michigan Press, 1966; originally published in England in 1922), pages 45–46 (Section 13 "Fundamental Contradictions of the Capitalist System").

16. Peter Drucker, "The Age of Social Transformation," *The Atlantic Monthly*, November 1994.

17. Founded by John von Neumann and Oskar Morgenstern and publicized in their book, *Theory of Games and Economic Behavior*, published in 1944 by Princeton University Press.

18. The game the "prisoners' dilemma" assumes that two men have been arrested for a crime they both committed. Each, apart from and unbeknownst to the other, is offered a deal by the police. If one agrees to testify against the other, and the other refuses to cooperate, the one testifying goes free and the one who refused to talk serves ten years. However, if both agree to testify, both serve two years. If both refuse to testify, both serve six months. The game, thus, illustrates the concept of trust—albeit among criminals, but the lessons apply nonetheless. Each knows that he gets the best outcome if he testifies and his accomplice does not, however, under that scenario there is a clear winner and loser. If both trust each other to refuse to testify, both then reap the second-best outcome for each: six months in prison—a tie. To work, trust must overcome the temptation to sell out your accomplice and also the fear that you are exposed to the worst possible outcome if your accomplice remains silent.

19. W. F. Lloyd, *Two Lectures on the Checks to Population* (Oxford Univ. Press, Oxford, England, 1833), reprinted (in part) in *Population, Evolution, and Birth Control*, G. Hardin, Ed. (Freeman, San Francisco, 1964). The term is also sometimes referred to as "tyranny of the commons," which comes from the satirist Jonathan Swift who, in 1701, referred to the constitution of Athens as a "Dommitio Plebis, or Tyranny of the Commons." Jonathan Swift, *A Discourse of the Contests and Dissensions between Nobles and Commons in Athens and Rome, with the Consequences They Had Upon Both States* (London: John Nutt; 1701).

20. Garrett Hardin, "The Tragedy of the Commons," *Science*, v. 162, pp. 1243–1248, 1968.

21. R. De Young, (1991) "Tragedy of the Commons," in D. E. Alexander and R.W. Fairbridge (Editors), *Encyclopedia of Environmental Science*, Hingham, MA: Kluwer Academic Publishers.

22. Melissa C. Lott, "World's First Oil Cartel—Deep in the Heart of Texas," *Scientific American*, January 10, 2012.

23. Henry Giroux, "Neoliberalism and the Demise of Democracy: Resurrecting Hope in Dark Times," *Dissident Voice*, August 7, 2004.

24. Ibid. See also Henry Giroux, *Proto-Fascism in America: Neoliberalism and the Demise of Democracy* (2004).

25. Ludwig von Mises, *Human Action: A Treatise on Economics*, 4th Revised Edition (Little Rock, AR: Fox & Wilkes, a division of Laissez-Faire Books: 1996), p. 257.

26. Friedrich A. Hayek, "The Use of Knowledge in Society", reprinted from the *American Economic Review*, XXXV, No. 4 (September 1945), pp. 519-530, in *Individualism and Economic Order* (South Bend: Gateway Editions, Ltd., by arrangement with The University of Chicago Press, 1977), p. 86.

27. Israel M. Kirzner, *Competition and Entrepreneurship* (Chicago and London: The University of Chicago Press, Phoenix Edition, 1978), p. 214.

28. Thomas Piketty, in *Capital in the Twenty-first Century* (Cambridge, MA; Belknap Press, an imprint of Harvard University Press, 2014), pp. 27 and 424.

29. Milton Friedman, "The Social Responsibility of Business Is to Increase Its Profits," *The New York Times Magazine*, September 13, 1970.

30. Steve Denning, "The Origin of the World's Dumbest Idea," *Forbes*, June 23, 2013.

31. As introduced in Chapter 5; again, see Karl Polanyi, *The Great Transformation: The Political and Economic Origins of Our Time* (Boston: Beacon Press; 1944, 1957, 2001), p. 57.

32. Ibid, pp. 76–77.

33. See the discussion of "economic sociology," as presented in *The Sociology of Economic Life*, edited by Mark Granovetter and Richard Swedberg (Boulder, San Francisco and Oxford: Westview Press, 1992), p. 6. See also: Neil J. Smelser and Richard Swedberg, editors, in *The Handbook of Economic Sociology* (Princeton, NJ: Princeton University Press, 1994).

34. The concept of "embeddedness" is key to Granovetter's theory. In this regard, see the discussion on how social norms are "embedded in scripts" in Cristina Bicchieri, *The Grammar of Society: The Nature and Dynamics of Social Norms* (Cambridge University Press; 2005). See also *The Sociology of Economic Life*, edited by Mark Granovetter and Richard Swedberg (Boulder, San Francisco and Oxford: Westview Press, 1992), p. 9.

35. Friedrich A. Hayek, *The Road to Serfdom* (Chicago: The University of Chicago Press, 1944, 1976), p. 36.

36. *The Road to Serfdom*, p. 38.

37. Mancur Olson, *Power and Prosperity: Outgrowing Communist and Capitalist Dictatorships* (New York: Basic Books, 2000), p. 185.

38. Peter L. Berger, "Intellectual Conservatism: Two Paradoxes," *National Review*, May 12, 1972, pp. 507–510. ©2015 *National Review*. Used with permission. Reproduced in Peter L. Berger, "Intellectual Conservatism: Two Paradoxes," *Facing Up to Modernity*, (New York: Basic Books, Inc., 1977), p. 116.

39. Ibid.

40. Richard John Neuhaus and Peter Berger, "To Empower People: The Role of Mediating Structures in Public Policy," (Washington, DC: American Enterprise Institute, 1976; reprinted in Michael Novak, editor, *To Empower People: From State to Civil Society, Second Edition* (Washington, DC: AEI Press, 1996), p. 162.

41. J. L. Talmon, *The Origins of Totalitarian* Democracy (New York: W. W. Norton & Company Inc., 1970), pp. 1–2.
42. Ibid, pp. 6–7.
43. Ibid, p. 7.
44. Leo Strauss, in his book *Natural Right and History* (1950), found the origination of fascism in the loss of purpose—nihilism—he associated with excessive modern liberalism.
45. Friedrich Hayek, in *The Road to Serfdom* (1944), found the potential for fascism to originate in the growth of government that accompanied modern liberalism.
46. Scott McClellan, *What Happened: Inside the Bush White House and Washington's Culture of Deception* (New York: Public Affairs, 2008), pp. 138–139.
47. Naomi Klein, "Baghdad Year Zero: Pillaging Iraq in Pursuit of a Neocon Utopia," *Harper's* September 2004, p. 44. The reference to "Year Zero" is a reference to the French Revolution, in which the revolutionaries even remade the calendar, commencing with Year Zero of the Revolution. Recall that the French Revolution ushered in the mass use of the guillotine and the Reign of Terror led by Robespierre and the Montagnards, and one gets a sense of the scale of terror the US unleashed in Iraq.
48. Ibid, p. 44.
49. Ibid, p. 49.
50. Ibid, p. 51.
51. Ibid, p. 53.
52. Francis Fukuyama, "Social Capital," in *Culture Matters: How Values Shape Human Progress*, ed. Lawrence E. Harrison and Samuel P. Huntington (New York: Basic Books, 2000), p. 98. Elsewhere Fukuyama defines social capital more briefly—emphasizing trust (p. 26), or citing James Coleman for the idea of cooperation, with a footnote to James S. Coleman, "Social Capital in the Creation of Human Capital, *American Journal of Sociology 94*, (1988): S95-S120. For other detailed analyses of social capital, see Robert D. Putnam, "The Prosperous Community: Social Capital and Public Life," *The American Prospect* 13 (1993): 35–42; and Putnam, "Bowling Alone," *Journal of Democracy* 6 (1995): 65–78.
53. Francis Fukuyama, "Social Capital," in *Culture Matters: How Values Shape Human Progress*, ed. Lawrence E. Harrison and Samuel P. Huntington (New York: Basic Books, 2000), p. 99.
54. From Alexis de Tocqueville's *Democracy in America, De La Démocratie en Amérique*, Bilingual Edition, edited by Eduardo Nolla, translated by James T. Schleifer (Indianapolis, IN: Liberty Fund; 2010), vol. III, part 2, Chapter V, p. 902.
55. Ibid; p. 897.
56. Ibid; p. 902.
57. Robert Putnam (with Robert Leonardi and Raffaella Y. Nanetti), *Making Democracy Work* (Princeton, N.J.: Princeton University Press, 1993).
58. Stephen Knack and Philip Keefer, "Does Social Capital Have an Economic Payoff? A Cross-Country Investigation," vol. CXII, Issue 4, November 1997, *The Quarterly Journal of Economics*, pp. 1251–1288, p. 1252.
59. William Easterly and Ross Levine, "Africa's Growth Tragedy: Policies and Ethnic Divisions," vol. CXII, Issue 4, November 1997, *The Quarterly Journal of Economics*, pp. 1203–1250, p. 1241.
60. Francis Fukuyama, *Trust: The Social Virtues and the Creation of Prosperity* (New York: Free Press Paperback, a Division of Simon and Schuster Inc., 1995, 1996), p. 159.
61. Ibid, p. 27.
62. Mancur Olson, *The Rise and Decline of Nations: Economic Growth, Stagflation, and Social Rigidities* (New Haven: Yale University Press, 1982).
63. Francis Fukuyama, *Trust: The Social Virtues and the Creation of Prosperity* (New York: Free Press Paperback, a Division of Simon and Schuster Inc., 1995, 1996), p. 159. Fukuyama's assessment of the relationship between social capital and economic development is mixed, as social capital is championed as critical to prosperity on pp. 27, 33 and 355, but on p. 321 its link to economic performance is questioned. Regardless, the importance of spontaneous sociability to economic performance should be clear.

64. Ibid, p. 56. The reference inside the quote is from Lawrence E. Harrison in *Who Prospers?* (New York: Basic Books, 1992), p. 55. Harrison was a senior associate at Harvard University's Academy for International and Area Studies; currently he is Senior Research Fellow and Adjunct Lecturer at the Fletcher School at Tufts University.

65. Ibid, p. 27, citing Emil Durkheim, *The Division of Labor in Society* (New York: Macmillan 1933), pp. 181–182.

66. Fellow sociologist Lawrence Harrison approvingly referred to the concept as "spontaneous association" in *The Central Liberal Truth: How Politics Can Change a Culture and Save It from Itself* (Oxford University Press: Oxford and New York, 2008), at p. 50.

67. Michael Porter, "Attitudes, Values, Beliefs and the Microeconomics of Prosperity" in *Culture Matters: How Values Shape Human Progress*, Lawrence E. Harrison and Samuel P. Huntington, editors (New York: Basic Books; 2000), p. 19. See also, Michael Porter, *On Competition* (1998).

68. Dani Rodrik, "The 'Paradoxes' of the Successful State," *European Economic Review* 41 (1997), pp. 411–442; p. 440.

69. Lawrence E. Harrison, *Underdevelopment Is a State of Mind: The Latin American Case* (Lanham, MD: Madison Books, co-published by arrangement with The Center for International Affairs, Harvard University; 1985), p 2.

70. Ibid, p. 115.

71. Hernando de Soto, *The Mystery of Capital: Why Capitalism Triumphs in the West and Fails Everywhere Else*, (New York: Basic Books, 2000), pp. 5–7.

72. De Soto, pp. 211–212.

Chapter Eleven

The Liberal Value of Equality—and Why Government Policies Must Support a Strong Middle Class

The liberal commitment to equality is *not* a commitment to absolute equality of income and/or wealth but, rather, a commitment to support of income- and wealth-spreading institutions so that, as a general trend, inequality is decreasing in degree and general prosperity is spreading. Such reduction in inequality, as will be shown by numerous studies following, actually supports economic growth long-term. A commitment to equality also means a commitment to provide equality of opportunity—including broad access (regardless of gender, religion, ethnicity or sexual orientation) to education; equal protection against crime; equal protection against—and treatment of—illness and injury. Related to all these is equal application of the law—application of the rule of law—and preservation of liberal democracy.[1]

INEQUALITY UNDERMINES OUR ECONOMY, DEMOCRACY, INSTITUTIONS AND HEALTH

In contrast to the appropriate concern on the part of liberalism toward inequality, inequality does not especially concern conservatism. Time has exposed the Republican campaign themes of "compassionate conservatism" (of the 2000 campaign) and the "ownership society" (of 2004) as woefully inadequate to remedy growing inequality, and soon they were abandoned by their trickle-down conservative Republican proponents anyway.

Liberals oppose inequality for various reasons, among them that inequality:

1. Offends our sense of morality;
2. Offends our sense of social justice; and/or
3. Violates enlightened self-interest, a concept the validity of which we believe in based on:

a. A theoretical basis from Smith, Tocqueville, Hayek, and Polanyi;
b. Keynesian economic theory of demand management (from *The General Theory of Employment, Interest and Money*); and
c. Investment in human and social capital inuring to everyone's benefit, as described in University of Chicago economist Gary Becker's groundbreaking book *Human Capital* and Robert Dahl's and Charles E. Lindblom's book *Politics, Economics and Welfare*. An example of this spirit is a quote from Benjamin Franklin, in *Poor Richard's Almanack*, which is cited by Becker (and borne out by his research): "An investment in knowledge pays the best interest." This investment, hopefully, insulates society against the undermining of social and political institutions which can be maintained only by a strong middle class. Sufficiently undermined, liberal democracy itself crumbles into illiberalism—as Polanyi observed, this most likely means illiberalism of the right.

4. Empirical evidence proving inequality[2]:

a. Impedes economic growth;
b. Impedes social mobility;
c. Reduces political participation;
d. Creates economic and socio-political instability; and
e. Shortens life spans and impairs health.

This work does not advance a moral argument for equality, leaving that to theologians and moral philosophers, although examples will be given to illustrate the universality of basic religious and moral lessons regarding man's obligations towards fellow man, lending support to the secular enlightened self-interest argument. Also, this work expressly rebuts the social justice argument as being contrary to rule of law. Under the rule of law, justice is a process. We know justice is served when due process is accorded, and due process is defined as the legal process under the Constitution. We may say "justice was done" to refer to an end that we believe is "just," but, again, presupposed is some process applied before we arrived to this end. Social justice is an end in itself, and no process for determining it has been satisfactorily proposed.

The argument advanced here is trial and error application of enlightened self-interest—and it is argued that trickle-down conservatism has discarded this concept *necessary* to the survival of capitalism. Substantial evidence indicates that capitalism is the best system for ensuring prosperity, that prosperity is best ensured by enhancing productivity, and that it is in the best interest of society that revenues attributable to increased productivity be shared with the workers who, after all, contributed to this increased productivity.

Equality in History

Tocqueville continued, in the Introduction to *Democracy in America*: "Among the new objects that attracted my attention during my stay in the United States, nothing struck me more vividly than the equality of conditions. I discovered without difficulty the prodigious influence that this primary fact exercises on the march of society; it gives a certain direction to public mind, a certain turn to the laws; to those governing, new maxims, and particular habits to the governed."[3]

The historian Gordon S. Wood, in his essay "Thomas Jefferson, Equality and the Creation of a Civil Society," echoed Tocqueville's observation that ordinary Americans embraced social equality to a greater degree than other peoples, and credited Thomas Jefferson and the American Revolution with creating this attitude. Wood concluded, in observations reminiscent not only of the insights of Jefferson but also Tocqueville and Francis Fukuyama, regarding the voluntary organizations of civil society[4]:

> And all the while equality was what made this civil society work. It became the central force of the culture and the source of modern associational life. Americans became the ultimate contract-making people, held together not by traditional tribal blood or hierarchical dependency but by the modern trust that came from treating everyone, even strangers, as equal individuals. This modern trust among equal individuals may not run deep, may not compare to the tribal ties for which men may die, and may not create the kind of romantic communities that some of us yearn for; but it is enough for a functioning, prosperous, democratic civil society. And it is the kind of trust that depends on a belief in the equality for which Jefferson has been the supreme spokesman.

INEQUALITY UNDERMINES ECONOMIC GROWTH, SOCIAL MOBILITY AND ECONOMIC AND SOCIO-POLITICAL STABILITY

We're *Not* No. 1!

Historically a misconception has existed that inequality must be tolerated to achieve growth. As observed by Nancy Birdsall, David Ross and Richard

Sabot[5] this misconception came from two sources. The first, from Nicholas Kaldor,[6] was based on the assumption that because a high level of savings is required for growth, then there must be concentration of income in the hands of the rich to create these savings. The second, from Simon Kuznets,[7] was that inequality would naturally arise as productivity increased. They concluded, after a review of East Asia, that there is no need to tolerate high levels of income inequality to get rapid economic growth.

Michael Lipton (professor of economics at the University of Sussex), referring to the results of two 1994 studies and one 1995 study, went further, concluding that inequality actually inhibits economic growth, and that poverty reduction may promote economic growth.[8]

In "How the Pie Is Sliced, America's Growing Concentration of Wealth," *The American Prospect*, Summer 1995, New York University Professor of Economics Edward N. Wolff examined the relationship of equality and economic growth over the past half century and concurred, finding that equality and growth appeared to be complementary.

The conclusion that inequality impedes growth was typical of studies prior to 1996. Beginning around that time, through about 2009, there emerged studies indicating high inequality in wealth and human capital development impeded growth, but evidence conflicted regarding inequality of income. Studies after 2009 however, such as those following, clarified that income inequality does impede long-term economic growth (although its effect on short-term economic growth may range from negative to imperceptible to positive).[9]

More recently, a study Andrew Berg and Jonathan D. Ostry of the IMF, released in September 2011 found that, when comparing the experiences of numerous national economies, greater inequality correlated with less sustained economic growth—in fact, more equal income distribution was a greater influence on sustained economic growth than trade openness, strong political institutions, high foreign direct investment, exchange rate competitiveness and low external debt.[10] Berg and Ostry were joined by Charalambos G. Tsangarides in a February 2014 IMF Discussion Note that reinforced these earlier findings, and also failed to find much support for the idea that fiscal redistribution hinders economic growth.[11] Researchers at the IMF continued to address the subject of inequality's effect on growth and concluded, in a June 2015 IMF Discussion Note that their research suggested increased income for the rich does not trickle-down benefits to the middle class and poor. To the contrary, increasing the income share for the poor and middle class matters much more for economic growth and stability than increasing income share of the rich, and this is due, as is observed herein, to interrelated aspects of economics, sociology and politics.[12]

Similarly, a study by *Standard & Poor's*, issued in August 2014, found that income inequality is dampening growth, and observed that not only were

Standard & Poor's economists reducing their estimates of future growth because of continuing inequality, but in doing so they were joining the Federal Reserve, the International Monetary Fund, and the Congressional Budget Office. The report concluded that the challenge going forward to improve growth is to pull more Americans out of poverty and boost the purchasing power of the middle class.[13] Note: The conclusion was not, as has been assumed under trickle-down, that if we just get the economy growing again, everyone's income will rise. That assumption is now turned on its head: If we are to achieve sustained economic growth, we must raise the incomes of everyone, especially the poor and middle class, and grow their buying power.[14]

Similarly, the OECD released a report at year-end 2014 in which that organization found that inequality of income holds back economic growth and also found, as did the IMF study, little evidence that redistribution hinders growth.[15] Also in 2014, the World Bank's International Comparison Program determined that, based on that body's calculation of "purchasing-power parities," China surpassed the Unites States as the world's top economic power.[16]

Finally, according to another report by the OECD, although growth in the US over the past 40 years was faster than in France or Australia, it was slower than Austria, Germany and the Netherlands.[17] Based on changes in median disposable income from 2000 to 2010, Australia, Sweden, Canada, Great Britain, Mexico, France, Italy and Germany have all seen larger increases in real median disposable income than has the US—in which real median disposable income over that period *fell by 4 percent*.[18] And Great Britain, which had also aggressively implemented trickle-down, according to a Social Mobility and Poverty Commission Report faces the prospect in the decade 2010-2020 of seeing a rise in absolute poverty (defined as household income below 60% of median earnings) from 2.6 million to 3.5 million.[19]

In 2015 a new formulation of the problem emerged, best framed by Harvard Business School international economic growth expert Michael Porter, as a recognition that we cannot separate economic development from social progress. The occasion for Porter's comments was the release of the Social Progress Index for 2015. Porter helped devise the Social Progress Index, and this latest version of it ranked the US 30th in life expectancy, 55th in women surviving child birth, 32nd in preventing early marriage, 38th in the equality of the education system, 49th in high school enrollment rates and 87th in cell phone usage.[20] As for the measure of maternal deaths in childbirth, a 2014 study placed the US in the even worse position of 60th in the world—also concluding that the US is one of only eight countries in the world to see a *rise* in maternal mortality over the past decade, and that a woman giving birth in the US is more likely to die than a woman giving birth in China.[21]

Returning to 2015, the investment bank Morgan Stanley released a report similarly concluding that persistent inequality impedes, over the long run, economic growth, mobility and support for institutions.[22] The report listed the United States as, among developed nations, regarding level of inequality, behind only the economically-challenged "PIGS" nations of Portugal, Italy, Greece and Spain.

Thus, a consensus among economists is emerging that not only is the United States enduring persistently high levels of inequality—among the very highest in the developed world—but that this persistently high inequality is undermining economic growth, social and economic mobility, democracy, institutions and health.

Waking Up from the American Dream: The Facts Regarding Income and Mobility in the US versus Other OECD Countries

Somewhat similar to Kuznet's and Kaldor's misconceptions that inequality must be tolerated as a trade-off for greater growth is the misconception that inequality must be tolerated as a trade-off for greater income and income mobility.

In 2014, it was reported that the US middle class is no longer the richest in the world in terms of median per capita income after taxes—that honor now belongs to Canada.[23] Additionally, as pointed out by Nicholas Kristof,[24] arguably the discrepancy is even greater than reported because Canadians receive essentially free health care while Americans pay for theirs in after-tax dollars. Kristof also observed that Canadians and Europeans on average work fewer hours, live longer and have higher economic mobility than do Americans. The stress the American middle class feels under trickle-down is measurable, as 59 percent of the respondents to the Allstate/*National Journal* Heartland Monitor Poll in 2013 expressed concern about falling out of their economic class in the next few years. Respondents were twice as likely to say they have less opportunity to get ahead than did their parents' generation, and just 21 percent thought it "very realistic" they could pay for their children's college education.[25] However, at least our middle class is *second* in the world—the poorest 10 percent of Americans rank *18th* among the 34 OECD countries.[26]

Studies have shown mobility is down in the US, and we have been falling behind Europe. The Pew Charitable Trust in 2007 released a series of studies, including one on mobility, produced by the Economic Mobility Project (a joint effort of conservative and liberal think tanks: the American Enterprise Institute, the Heritage Foundation, the Brookings Institution and the Urban Institute). That study found, consistent with the observations above, that real median income for men has remained essentially flat for the past three decades, and most of the financial gains made by households over that period are due to the entry of wives into the workforce. Regarding mobility from the lowest quintile (lowest 20 percent of households) to the highest quintile (highest 20 percent of households): Only six percent of children born to parents of the lowest quintile moved up to the highest quintile. Even more sadly, 42 percent of children born in the lowest quintile stayed in the lowest quintile. And, similarly, about four in ten children born in the top quintile stay in the top quintile. The study also noted that other developed nations had greater mobility than the US.[27]

Similarly, in their paper, "Europe vs. The United States: Is There a Trade-Off Between Mobility and Inequality?," economists Mercedes Sastre and Luis Ayala similarly observed that the United States is more unequal than the UK, Italy, Germany, Spain and France but also added that it is only in the middle of the pack among other developed nations in terms of mobility.[28]

In yet another study, the economist Gary Solon observed that lower mobility tends to correlate with greater inequality, and factors that increase inequality, such as rising returns to human capital or declining progressivity in public human investment (such as public investment in education and healthcare) correspond to declining intergenerational mobility.[29] Solon's conclusion was later confirmed by Miles Corak, Professor of Economics at the University of Ottawa, in a broader analysis.[30]

And a 2010 report of the Organization for Economic Cooperation and Development (OECD) concluded income mobility in the United States is now exceeded by numerous other countries, including Denmark, Australia, Norway, Finland, Canada, Sweden, Germany, Spain and France (although the US is barely ahead of Italy and the UK). As the report observed, "intergenerational social mobility tends to be lower in more unequal societies."[31] Thus, as a result, over the last 12 years, the US has gone from having the highest share of employed 25- to 34-year-olds among the world's biggest economies to having among the lowest—trailing Canada, Germany, Japan, Great Britain, France, Australia, Russia and Sweden.[32]

The concept that inequality, marked by extreme income concentration at the top, lowers intergenerational social mobility was dubbed "the Great Gatsby Curve" by former chair of President Obama's Council of Economic Advisors, Alan Krueger. Conservatives championed a National Bureau of Economic Research Study by Raj Chetty, Nathanial Hendren, Patrick Kline, Emmanuel Saez and Nicholas Turner released in January 2014 that contradicted the theory of the Great Gatsby Curve, finding that extreme concentration of income at the top of the economy did not correlate with decline in intergenerational mobility[33] (although the study concurred with others that intergenerational mobility in the United States is not only significantly lower than in most other developed countries, but that it has been so for a long time, preceding the recent rapid rise in inequality).

Critically, however, a second paper, by Raj Chetty, Nathanial Hendren, Patrick Kline and Emmanuel Saez also released in January 2014 found that although there was little support for the Great Gatsby Curve, inequality in terms of income stagnation among middle class and poor *is* strongly negatively associated with social mobility[34]:

> We conclude that there is a robust negative correlation between inequality within the current generation of adults and mobility across generations. However, intergenerational mobility is primarily correlated with "middle-class" inequality and not the extreme upper tail inequality of the form that has increased dramatically in recent decades. Interestingly, this pattern parallels the results we obtained for segregation above: segregation of affluence is not significantly correlated with intergenerational mobility, while segregation of poverty (the separation of the poor from the middle class) is strongly negative [*sic*] associated with mobility.

The studies together confirm the observation of James Carville quoted in the Introduction: The problem is not that the rich are getting richer. The problem is that everyone else is standing still or getting poorer.

Inequality Correlates with Increased Economic Instability

In the years leading up to the Great Depression, income and wealth were becoming more and more concentrated (as has been happening again over the past three decades). Marriner Eccles, a successful banker in the Roaring Twenties, went on to serve in the administration of Franklin Roosevelt, and ultimately became Chairman of the Federal Reserve from 1935-1948. In his book, *Beckoning Frontiers: Public and Personal Recollections* (1951), Eccles remarked upon the effect of ever-greater wealth concentration, in terms consistent with those herein, that ever greater concentration of income and wealth creates ever greater demand for borrowing, until credit eventually runs out, crashing the entire system—thus, it is in the interests of all to get more income to lower-income groups, to yield greater economic stability. Similarly, in his book *Inequality and Instability* (2012), University of Texas economist James K. Galbraith linked inequality with the creation of bubbles, which create instability.

As observed earlier, consistent with the concern of Eccles, our policies have aided the substitution of *debt* for *income.* Rather than pay people more, and regulate the amount of debt they can incur, we have gradually reduced restrictions on debt to enable people to buy on credit, which they needed to do because their wages were falling in real value. As a result, we built a house of cards out of debt secured by home values.

Symptomatic of that increasing reliance on debt in lieu of income is the observation regarding reasons for bankruptcy filings. As Elizabeth Warren and Amelia Warren Tyagi reveal in *The Two-Income Trap: Why Middle-Class Mothers and Fathers Are Going Broke* (2003), 87 percent of bankruptcy filings are due to one of three reasons: job loss, medical problem, or divorce or separation. The remaining 13 percent are due to bad investment, being a crime victim, credit card overspending, natural disaster, other explanation or no explanation.[35] The facts show, thus, bankruptcy is most often due not to personal failings but, instead, to circumstances that could befall any of us due to no fault of our own,

It appears that the "lost decade" to which President Obama referred in his initial State of the Union Address—the years 1999 through 2008— with its tech bubble and crash, followed by real estate bubble and crash, followed by financial crisis, was so volatile in great part due to inequality. And this volatility was manifested in four of the worst fifteen years in S&P 500 history.[36]

Inequality Correlates with Reduced Political Participation and Increased Socio-Political Instability

As Daron Acemoglu and his colleague James Robinson observed in *Why Nations Fail*, increasing concentration of income and wealth at the top tends to lead to increasing concentration of political power at the top, and those with that economic and political power then tend to use it to change the laws in their favor, ever further concentrating economic and political power.[37] Additional evidence indicates that increasing concentration of income and wealth at the top also correlates with generally reduced political participation and increased political instability, hindering democracy; as observed by Robert Dahl and Charles E. Lindblom in *Politics, Economics and Welfare,* "Inequality obstructs the achievement of democracy."[38] And, as observed by Alberto Alesina and Roberto Perotti in a 1996 study, income inequality leads to socio-political instability, thereby reducing investment and growth.[39] Similarly, Ethan B. Kapstein, in *Sharing the Wealth: Workers and the World Economy* cited Dahl and Lindblom regarding the links between income inequality and both political instability[40] and economic underperformance.[41]

In *Voice and Equality: Civic Voluntarism in American Politics* (1995), Sidney Verba (Harvard University), Kay Lehman Schlozman (Boston College) and Henry E. Brady (University of California, Berkeley) extensively documented the correlation between inequality in income and education with that of level of political participation.[42] And, as observed by Alec MacGillis in an op-ed in *The New York Times* in late 2015, the support from poor white areas for Republican politicians who want to slash the safety net may best be explained by the combined effect of older voters who believe their government benefits have been earned through hard work voting to cut spending on other social programs in the hope of preserving theirs, while the voters they condemn for being on government benefits—their neighbors[43] —turn inward the condemnation and simply withdraw from society, including withdrawing from political participation and voting.[44]

As a corollary to the evidence that inequality produces political instability, it has also been found, not surprisingly, that excessive political instability tends to result in reduced economic growth. Michael Devereux and Jean-Francois Wen (of the University of British Columbia and Wilfrid Laurier University, respectively) concluded in their paper, "Political Instability, Capital Taxation and Growth," that political instability reduces average growth rates while simultaneously tending to increase the size of government.[45]

Finally, business leaders promoting immigration law overhaul and spending on infrastructure have found themselves opposed by a Republican Party dominated by an ultraconservative plutocracy. A comparison regarding political donations over the three and a half decades of trickle-down reveals a startling fact: In 1980, the top 0.01 percent of donors contributed less than 10 percent of all campaign contributions—by 2012, this group, consisting of only 16,068 families with annual incomes above $10,250,000—were contributing *more than four times as much in percentage of all campaign contributions*: 44 percent.[46]

EQUALITY IS A MATTER OF LIFE AND DEATH BECAUSE INEQUALITY IMPAIRS HEALTH AND SHORTENS LIFE SPANS

As observed in the Introduction, trickle-down kills—literally. Evidence presented above shows that trickle-down increases inequality, which undermines growth, mobility and social, economic and political stability. The evidence presented below indicates that inequality also worsens health outcomes—to paraphrase Tocqueville from Chapter 5: If you want to live longer, equalize conditions.

Dahl and Lindblom, in *Politics, Economics and Welfare* (1953, 2000), cited earlier, observed: "Chronic illness is three times as prevalent among the poor as among the well-to-do, and disability destroys three times as many work days for the very low income groups as for those at upper income levels."[47]

A study conducted in the 1990s led by epidemiologist George A. Kaplan, formerly of the California Health Services Department and later at the University of Michigan, found a strong correlation between mortality rates and degree of income inequality among the 50 states.[48] Statistics also indicated that the states with the highest rates of inequality also have among the nation's lowest standardized test scores, highest high school dropout rates, highest obesity rates and highest crime rates.

Noreena Hertz, in her book *The Silent Takeover: Global Capitalism and the Death of Democracy* (2001), a few years later observed that it is not national wealth but, rather, egalitarian wealth distribution that results in better overall health, including lower mortality rates, lower murder rates and lower violent crime rates, citing research by, among others, Richard Wilkinson, addressed below.[49]

Over the past decade, inequality's negative effect on health has been indicated by numerous studies. The differences that inequality exacts on health have led to the observation that there is a "social gradient in health" that affects everyone, such that differences in longevity can be primarily traced to socioeconomic status. These are the observations of Michael Marmot, professor of epidemiology and public health, University College London and author of *The Status Syndrome* (2004). Marmot was interviewed by journalist Paul Solman on the PBS show "Newshour," February 23, 2007.[50] Marmot there observed that there is a gap in longevity among actors who win the Academy Award versus those who do not and extended the lesson to the US generally, based on 30 years of research confirmed by others that economic inequality results in shorter life spans. Marmot elaborated on why he believed this is so, attributing causation to lack of control over one's life and lack of autonomy—powerlessness—plus lack of social engagement.

Marmot joined with other researchers in a study comparing health of middle-aged Americans with their counterparts in the UK, who spend much less on healthcare. The results, reported in 2006 in the *Journal of the American Medical Association*[51] revealed that white middle-aged Americans are not as healthy as their English counterparts across all socioeconomic status groups, and, although in both countries lower income and education levels are associated with poor health, even the healthiest Americans (those with highest income and education levels) had rates of diabetes and heart disease similar to the least healthy (those with lowest income and education levels) in England.[52]

The correlation between social status and health was also observed by Christopher von Rueden, assistant professor in the Jepsen School of Leadership Studies at the University of Richmond, whose work was reported in the journal *Evolution, Medicine and Public Health.* Von Rueden and his colleagues measured the social status of men in four villages of the Tsimane, a small, pre-industrial politically egalitarian society of forager-horticulturists in Amazonian Bolivia. They found that Tsimane men with less political influence had higher levels of the stress hormone cortisol and experienced higher levels of respiratory illness (the most common form of sickness and death in their society).[53]

And, by no means are the effects of low self-esteem limited to adults. In a study presented at the annual meeting of the American Association for the Advancement of Science in Boston in February of 2008, neuroscientists revealed that many children growing up in poor families experience elevated levels of stress hormones, thus impairing their language development and memory.[54] The damage to the brain is most harmful between the ages of six months to three years. According to Jack Shonkoff, director of Harvard University's center on the developing child, excessive levels of these hormones both disrupt the formation of the synapses between cells in the developing brain and the supply of blood to the brain, disrupting the brain architecture. Thus, researchers at the University of Oregon concluded that, contrary to the unfocused Head Start program that has shown relatively modest results, training of *parents* to improve communication skills and to control their children's bad behavior, thereby reducing family stress, may better prepare poor children for school.[55] Shonkoff concluded, however, the only way to actually remove the impact of poverty on young brains would be to eliminate poverty itself.

More recently, Richard Wilkinson, a professor of medical epidemiology at Nottingham University, and Kate Pickett, a lecturer in epidemiology at York University again confirmed that inequality has numerous negative social and health consequences throughout society. In their book, *The Spirit Level: Why More Equal Societies Almost Always Do Better* (2009), they compared the level of health and social problems against the level of income inequality in 20 of the world's richest nations, and in each of the 50 states of the United States.

What they found led the authors to reject the idea that more equal societies have fewer social pathologies because they have fewer poor people. Rather, they countered that in unequal societies it is greater inequality itself that harms the vast majority of the population.[56] The phenomena they observe are for entire populations: more unequal societies display five times the rates of mental illness, five times the imprisonment rates, six times the rates of clinical obesity,[57] and many times higher murder rates. Lives are shorter, pregnancy rates are higher, illegal drug usage and alcohol abuse are more common, math and literacy scores are lower, dropout rates are higher and less is spent on education and welfare in more unequal states; and teenage birth rates are higher in more unequal countries and states. And, as babies born to teenage mothers grow up, they tend to cut short their educations, engage in more juvenile crime, and become teenage parents themselves.

And, inequality in incomes in the US tends to correlate with unequal health outcomes among states and counties.[58] Even counties in adjacent states display massively different life expectancies correlating to income. As observed by *The New York Times*' Annie Lowrey, in Fairfax County, Virginia, with median household income of over $109,000, men have an average life expectancy of 82 years and women, 85, on par with Sweden. A mere 350 miles away in adjacent West Virginia, in McDowell County, with median household income of under $23,000, men have an average life expectancy of 64 years and women, 73, on par with Iraq.[59]

Similarly, it has been found that people living in counties with the highest levels of inequality suffer from shorter life spans. These findings were made across counties of the nation by researchers in the County Health Rankings and Road Map Project, a collaboration of the University of Wisconsin Population Health Institute and the Robert Wood Johnson Foundation.[60] The South generally, which displays high inequality, displays lower healthy life expectancy (HLE) than elsewhere in the nation.[61] In fact, the thirteen worst states for life expectancy are all in the South and all voted for Mitt Romney in 2012, while the eight best states for life expectancy all voted for President Obama.[62] The poorer health outcomes for these Southern and Red States are observed even though the Red States are subsidized by the Blue States. As was observed by New Jersey Governor and candidate for the 2016 Republican presidential nomination Chris Christie in response to criticism of his attitude about federal spending by fellow candidate Senator Rand Paul (R-KY): New Jersey is a donor state, getting less than a dollar back from every dollar it sends Washington, while Kentucky gets a premium back on every dollar it sends Washington.[63]

A 2013 article in *The Washington Post* reviewed three studies that all confirmed not only is there a gap between upper and lower income groups regarding longevity but also that during the past several decades that gap has grown wider.[64] One study, from the University of Washington, observed that in St. Johns County, Florida, women are expected to live nearly 83 years, four years longer than two decades ago; men more than 78 years, six years longer than two decades ago. In poorer neighboring Putnam County, where incomes and home values are about half that of St. Johns, women are expected to live to just over 78 years, less than a year longer than two decades ago; men to just over 71 years, a year and a half longer than two decades ago. The second study, a Social Security study, found that over the past three decades the life expectancy of male workers retiring at 65 had risen six years in the top half of the income distribution but only 1.3 years in bottom half. And the third study, by the Congressional Budget Office, found that in 1980 life expectancy at birth was 2.8 years longer for the highest socioeconomic group in the study versus the lowest, but by 2000 that gap had grown to 4.5 years.

A 2008 study by economists Betsey Stevenson and Justin Wolfers found a clear relationship between income and happiness.[65] The rising inequality caused by trickle-down economics was squarely blamed, in a study titled "Trickle-Down Consumption" by the University of Chicago's Marianne Bertrand and Adair Morse, for Americans saving less, going into bankruptcy more often, and demanding government policies to make it easier to become more deeply indebted so as to keep up with the rich—the authors concluded:

"Middle income households would have saved between 2.6 percent and 3.2 percent more by the mid-2000s had incomes at the top grown at the same rate as median income."[66] And, aggravating the fact that real median per capita income has stagnated since 2000 is the fact that, although many consumer goods have become less expensive or better quality (think consumer electronics and cars), the prices of three of the biggest middle class expenditures—housing, health care and education—have far outpaced the rate of inflation.[67]

Similar conclusions regarding how middle income families are harmed by the upward redistribution of income and wealth by trickle-down were made by Cornell University economist Robert H. Frank in *The Darwin Economy* (2011), in which he used the term "expenditure cascades" to describe the same changing of frame of reference that accompanied the race to keep up with rapidly rising peers.[68] Worse, the suicide rate has risen sharply—by 28 percent—among Americans ages 35 to 64 from 1999 to 2010, as reported by the Center for Disease Control (CDC) "Morbidity and Mortality Report" published in 2013.[69]

Similarly negative impacts on health were attributed globally to inequality in *The Body Economic: Why Austerity Kills* (2013), by David Stuckler of Oxford University and Sanjay Basu of Stanford—among the negative impacts observed: rising suicide rates in Greece, falling life spans in especially economically hard hit counties in the US, and falling life spans accompanied by rising alcohol death reports in countries that embraced economic Shock Therapy, such as Kazakhstan, Latvia, Lithuania and especially Russia.

And, as observed in the Introduction, a study found that over a quarter century—from 1992 through 2006—the life spans for average American women in numerous counties had declined.[70] The results of the study were referred to by Hillary Clinton in her address to the fourth annual Women in the World Summit in 2013, wherein she observed "women lead shorter lives in America than in any other major industrialized country." She continued[71]:

> Think about it for a minute. We are the richest and most powerful country in the world. Yet many American women today are living shorter lives than their mothers, especially those with the least education. That is a historic reversal that rivals the decline in life expectancy for Russian men after the disintegration of the Soviet Union.

The particular group that has been hit hardest in America, white women who have not graduated from high school, now can expect to die five years earlier than their mothers' generation (falling from a lifespan expectancy of almost 79 to just over 73).[72] Not surprisingly, this group has also seen over this period a decline in socioeconomic status and, as observed in an insightful

2013 article by Monica Potts in *The American Prospect*, an increase in a sense of desperation.[73]

Additionally, residents of distressed urban areas have been found to suffer disease related to early aging and excess mortality, based on a study of residents of Detroit in which venous blood was drawn and measured for telomere length, an indicator of stress-mediated biological aging, and these findings were linked to respondents' community survey responses.[74]

For how health outcomes in the US compare with the rest of the OECD, based on the Global Burden of Diseases, Injuries, and Risk Factors Study 2010 (GBD 2010), the health of the US population has improved only gradually and has fallen in standing compared with 34 OECD countries between 1990 and 2010 by every measure including death rates, life expectancy, diminished function and quality of life.[75]

In 2015, two additional studies, one from Corey M. Abramson, Assistant Professor of Sociology at the University of Arizona titled *The End Game: How Inequality Shapes Our Final Years* and the other from the National Academy of Sciences titled *The Growing Gap in Life Expectancy by Income: Implications for Federal Programs and Policy Responses*, long-touted longevity gains are going mainly to men and women atop the income ladder and, as found by previous studies, lower income women are actually experiencing declining life expectancies—with the result that high earners are also getting greater federal benefits in terms of Social Security, Medicare and Medicaid.[76]

Conversely, the mortality rate for white non-Hispanic men and women between the ages of 45 and 54 increased by about a half a percent per year between 1999 and 2013; from 1978 to 1998 the mortality rates for this group were dropping an average of 2 percent per year, as observed by Angus Deaton, 2015 Nobel Prize winner in economics in 2015, and his wife Anne Case, both economics professors at Princeton University.[77] Driving this increase in mortality rates is an increase among white non-Hispanics with less than a high school degree or a high school degree only; so great was this increase that it overcame a decrease by those with some college, no bachelor's degree, and with a bachelor's degree or more. Rising death rates is a phenomenon that distinguishes white non-Hispanics with less than a high school degree or less than a college degree from any other age group, or racial or ethnic group in America and distinguishes them from their counterparts in other developed countries (members of the OECD such as France, Germany, Great Britain, Canada, Australia and Sweden)—and identifies them with, as observed above by Hillary Clinton regarding another study, Russian men, who similarly experienced rising mortality rates after the collapse of the Soviet Union. Rates of suicide, alcohol and drug poisoning, and chronic liver diseases and cirrhosis are on the rise for this group, and a cause appears to be, as the authors of the study observe, the dawning realization by this group that they will not be better off than their parents were.

Although neither the study itself nor the articles from *The New York Times*[78] and *The Washington Post*[79] addressing its findings link the desperation driving these rising mortality rates with the desperation driving the campaigns of Trump, Carson, Fiorina and Cruz, they should. More than three decades of income stagnation—marked by declining real incomes more recently—along with the gradual disappearance of defined benefit pension plans are leading middle-aged white non-Hispanic Americans with no more education than a high school degree to realize their 60s and 70s will not be as bright and secure as their parents', and leading them to the populist anti-Washington campaigns of the three candidates who have never held elective office and the remaining candidate most widely disliked among his peers for being impossible to work with.

We Should Tell the Truth: Wealth Is Not Due to Merit Alone

Admittedly, no research is presented here to support the idea that we could improve mental health not only by reducing inequality but also by telling the truth—that wealth is due in great part to luck, unrelated to merit. However, the idea that merit[80] alone is responsible for determining fortunes has been questioned by numerous commenters, heroes to liberals and conservatives (among the latter, below, Mancur Olson and Friedrich Hayek). The influence of luck in success undercuts both the faith of the right that the market fairly distributes rewards and the idealism of the left that by balancing opportunity (in e.g., education and standardized tests), closer equality of outcomes can be achieved.

The classic iconoclastic work from the left is *Inequality: A Reassessment of the Effect of Family and Schooling in America* (1972), written by Harvard University's Christopher Jencks, Malcolm Wiener Professor of Social Policy at Harvard University, and his associates, who concluded in their study that economic success is due in great part to luck.[81] The solution they proposed is a balance of underwriting downside risk through social insurance and spreading the burden of paying for government.[82] In a section entitled "Many Fortunes Are Due to Luck," Mancur Olson, an economist who was a hero to conservatives, came to strikingly similar conclusions in his 2000 book, *Power and Prosperity: Outgrowing Communist and Capitalist Dictatorships*.[83]

Similarly, Alan Krueger, former chairman of the Council of Economic Advisers, also observed that, in a study he conducted of identical twins with the same level of education, earnings differed by as much as 25 percent in half the sample and 50 percent in a quarter, leading him to conclude that luck is an important determinant of economic success.[84]

A fitting close to this section is this quote from Friedrich Hayek, echoing Smith, Jencks, Olson and Krueger[85]:

> It is probably a misfortune that…popular writers…have defended free enterprise on the ground that it regularly rewards the deserving….It is therefore a real dilemma to what extent we ought to encourage in the young the belief that when they really try they will succeed, or should rather emphasize that inevitably some unworthy will succeed and some worthy fail.

The Hoped-for Convergence in Incomes Is a Mirage

Finally, time alone will not cure inequality—the long hoped-for convergence of incomes within countries and across countries is proving to be mythical as observed by Nancy Birdsall in a 1998 essay.[86] Globally, the gap between rich and poor is widening.

THE NECESSITY OF A STRONG MIDDLE CLASS—IN THEORY AND IN EVIDENCE

No Bourgeoisie, No Democracy, and No Liberalism, No Bourgeoisie—the Convergence of Polanyi and Hayek, and Hayek's Tragic Failure

The recognition of the importance of the middle class goes all the way back to Aristotle, who observed in 306 B.C.[87]:

> Thus it is manifest that the best political community is formed by citizens of the middle class, and that those states are likely to be well-administered, in which the middle class is large, and stronger if possible than both the other classes, or at any rate than either singly; for the addition of the middle class turns the scale, and prevents either of the extremes from being dominant. Great then is the good fortune of a state in which the citizens have a moderate and sufficient property; for where some possess much, and others nothing, there may arise an extreme democracy, or pure oligarchy; or a tyranny may grow out of either extreme….[W]here the middle class is large, there are least likely to be factions and dissensions.

Similarly, Friedrich Hayek observed in *The Road to Serfdom*, "It should never be forgotten that the one decisive factor in the rise of totalitarianism on the Continent, which is yet absent in England and America, is the existence of a large recently dispossessed middle class."[88] And, regarding "the conquest of unemployment": "There can be no doubt that this must be the goal of our greatest endeavor; even so, it does not mean…it must be accomplished 'at any price.'"[89] Hayek also observed that it was "[t]he resentment of the lower middle class, from which fascism and National Socialism [Nazism] recruited so large a proportion of their supporters…"[90] Continuing: "Above all, [the totalitarians] were successful because they offered a theory, or *Weltanschauung*, which seemed to justify the privileges they promised to their supporters."[91]

Thus we observe a convergence between Polanyi, in the last chapter, and Hayek in *The Road to Serfdom*. Both Polanyi and Hayek warned that a dispossessed middle class would turn resentful and look to right wing populism—to fascism—as a cure. Both also observed this represents a rejection of liberal democracy. What Hayek did not see, however, is that his own, personal turn from liberal democracy toward libertarianism would provide support for the theory of trickle-down that would undermine the middle class not only in the US but also in the UK and other developed countries of the world, thus providing precisely the environment of middle class resentment that would give rise to the right wing populism and, potentially, fascism, against which he had warned in 1944.

Thus, as observed by sociologist Barrington Moore, in the famous quote from *The Social Origins of Dictatorship and Democracy: Lord and Peasant in the Making of the Modern World* (1966), throughout Western history "a vigorous and independent class of town dwellers has been an indispensable element in the growth of parliamentary democracy. No bourgeois, no democracy."[92] And, without liberal democracy, there is no bourgeoisie.

And, a Corollary: No Liberal Democracy and No Bourgeoisie—Not Much Economy

Although one of the heroes herein is Friedrich Hayek, an equally important hero is his friend and intellectual rival, John Maynard Keynes. Keynes was right (in, for example, his 1936 book, *The General Theory of Employment, Interest and Money*), and Hayek and others wrong about what drives an economy: demand; not supply. Hayek recognized, as the above quotes show, the political importance of a strong, growing and happy middle class, but it was Keynes who recognized the necessity of a strong, growing and happy middle class for the growth of demand which, in turn, drives a strong and growing economy that promotes a strong, growing and happy middle class.

Building on Keynes, for capitalism to flourish institutions are needed to mitigate the income-, wealth- and power-concentrating effects of capitalism and democracy—to "spread the wealth" in the words of then-Senator Obama, uttered during his 2008 campaign to Samuel J. "Joe the Plumber" Wurzelbacher. "Spreading of the wealth" is a permanent fixture of any economy, and what the president was proposing was sharing the wealth downward, in opposition to the practice over the past three and a half decades of concentrating the wealth—redistributing revenues from increased productivity—

upward from the middle class and poor disproportionately to the richest 1 percent.

Thus, it can be said that capitalism requires a cultural contradiction to flourish: a balancing of immediate self-interest and enlightened self-interest.[93] Mistakenly believing the keys to growth around the world are stabilization of inflation and removal of governmental barriers to the exchange process, thereby freeing *self-interest* to do its work, we have ignored the insight of enlightened self-interest: that we need to also establish the government institutions necessary to enhance the ability of such self-interest to work for the public good.

Self-interest, without the balance provided by enlightened self-interest, leads to a host of dysfunctional conditions, including destruction of demand as wealth and income are redistributed upward from the middle class and poor to the rich, inequality, intolerance, collusion in restraint of trade, corruption and, ultimately, destruction of the middle class, the economy, liberal democracy, our institutions and the health of ourselves and our fellow citizens.

The Evidence Regarding the Need for a Strong Middle Class

The theory behind why we need a strong middle class is supported by observations based on fact. The development economist William Easterly, in a summary of what in great part constitutes his life's work, concluded[94]:

> One way to summarize the conditions favorable for growth is that progrowth policies are more likely when the two most common forms of social polarization, class conflict and ethnic tensions, are absent. Let's call a situation of a high share of income for the middle class and a high degree of ethnic harmony a middle-class consensus. Societies with a middle-class consensus are more likely to have good economic policies, good institutions, and high economic growth. Examples of countries with a middle-class consensus and high growth are Korea, Japan, and Portugal. Countries plagued by both race and class include Bolivia, Guatemala, and Zambia—all with low economic growth.

Note that Easterly's conclusion is similar to the observations of Friedrich Hayek and Karl Polanyi. And Easterly's conclusion is also echoed in the United Nations Conference on Trade and Development, *Trade and Development Report, 1997*. There it is persuasively argued that more equal distribution of income in developing countries can enhance growth. The causal relationship between greater inequality and reduced incentives for growth is explored, and the report concludes that the absence or weakening of a solid middle class can contribute to weakening of the economy and social and political stability, resulting in a vicious cycle downward, thus the report recommends appropriate redistribution policies.[95] And, as found in a study by the Equality of Opportunity Project, a smaller middle class correlates with lower rates of upward mobility.[96]

CONCLUSION: INEQUALITY CAUSES INEQUALITY AND OTHER PROBLEMS, REQUIRING GOVERNMENT SOLUTIONS

Thus, regarding inequality, we can conclude, as did Nancy Birdsall in a 1998 article in *Foreign Policy*, inequality leads to inequality.[97] Or, as more broadly stated by Barbara Ehrenreich in *Fear of Falling*, echoing Michael Harrington's and William Julius Wilson's observations quoted herein previously: "The point is that it is *poverty* that causes the poor to live differently from the middle class, not welfare or other forms of liberal intervention."[98] (Italics original.)

Poverty causes poverty, and inequality causes inequality, and inequality undermines growth, mobility, social, economic and political stability, institutions and health. Carefully crafted, moderate government policies must be used, again, as from the New Deal period through the 1970s, to downwardly distribute the revenues attributable to increased productivity—must be used to overcome the upward redistribution of income and wealth under the trickle-down delusion.

Revitalizing public institutions, re-instituting increased progressivity into tax rates, and attempting to reverse three and a half decades of upward redistribution of income and wealth may seem radical in light of the rightward shift of the political spectrum over the past three and a half decades, but historically Americans have recognized these measures as good mainstream policies invoked to break the cycle of the very real evil of inequality. The case should not be that difficult to make, but it will require a serious attempt, addressing the facts of those past three and a half decades, as is done here.

NOTES

1. Application of similar observations to the Arab world is provided in the "Arab Human Development Report 2002," published by the United Nations Development Programme (UNDP). A summary of its findings are provided in the article "Self-Doomed to Failure," *The Economist*, July 4, 2002. The component of building a knowledge society versus ignorance was addressed specifically by the UNDP the following year, in the "Arab Human Development Report 2003."

2. The evidence presented herein will attempt to illustrate the efficiency-enhancing effects associated with a more egalitarian economy. This concept comes from Samuel Bowles and Herbert Gintis' *Recasting Egalitarianism* (Verso Books; 1998). Bowles is Professor of Economics at the University of Siena and Director of the Economics Program at the Santa Fe Institute. Gintis is a member of the External Faculty of the Santa Fe Institute. Both are Emeritus Professors of Economics at the University of Massachusetts. Bowles and Gintis argued that market failures linked to breakdowns in accountability contribute to inefficiency. A somewhat similar observation is made herein regarding the failure of the market to account for externalities in the context of the tragedy of the commons.

3. From Alexis de Tocqueville's *Democracy in America, De La Démocratie en Amérique*, Bilingual Edition, edited by Eduardo Nolla, translated by James T. Schleifer (Indianapolis, IN: Liberty Fund; 2010), vol. I, Introduction, p. 4.

4. Gordon S. Wood, "Thomas Jefferson, Equality, and the Creation of a Civil Society," 64 *Fordham L. Rev.* 2133 (1996).

5. Nancy Birdsall, David Ross and Richard Sabot, "Inequality and Growth Reconsidered: Lessons from East Asia", *The World Bank Economic Review* (Volume 9, No. 3: 477–508; September 1995). Nancy Birdsall was formerly executive vice-president of the Inter-American Development Bank and is currently President of the Center for Global Development, David Ross is with the Department of Economics, Bryn Mawr College and Richard Sabot is with the Center for Development Economics, Williams College and the Policy Research Department at the World Bank.

6. Citation is to Nicholas Kaldor, "Capital Accumulation and Economic Growth" in Nicholas Kaldor, ed., *Further Essays on Economic Growth* (1978).

7. Citation to Simon Kuznets, "Economic Growth and Income Inequality", *American Economic Review*, March, 45: 1–28; 1955.

8. Michael Lipton, "Comment on 'Research on Poverty and Development Twenty Years after *Redistribution with Growth*,' by Pranab Bardhan." In Michael Bruno and Boris Pleskovic, eds., *Annual World Bank Conference on Development Economics 1995*, pp. 73–80. Washington, D.C.: World Bank.

9. See Heather Boushey and Carter C. Price, "How Are Economic Inequality and Growth Connected? A Review of Recent Research," Washington Center for Economic Growth, October 2014.

10. Andrew G. Berg and Jonathan D. Ostry, "Equality and Efficiency," *Finance & Development*, September 2011. See also Steven Pearlstein, "The False Choice between Equality and Efficiency," *The Washington Post*, March 24, 2012. Presumably, this is the study referred to by President Obama in his Osawatomie speech.

11. Andrew G. Berg, Jonathan D. Ostry and Charalambos G. Tsangarides, "Redistribution, Inequality, and Growth," International Monetary Fund Research Department, February 2014, p. 26. See also Phillip Inman, "IMF Study Finds Inequality Is Damaging to Economic Growth," *The Guardian*, February 26, 2014.

12. Era Dabla-Norris, Kalpana Kochhar, Frantisek Ricka, Nujin Suphaphiphat, and Evridiki Tsounta, "Causes and Consequences of Income Inequality: A Global Perspective," International Monetary Fund Discussion Note, June 2015, p. 4.

13. Joseph Maguire, "How Increasing Income Inequality Is Dampening U.S. Economic Growth, and Possible Ways to Change the Tide," *Standard & Poor's*, August 5, 2014.

14. In accord, see Joseph Stiglitz, "Inequality Is Holding Back the Recovery," Opinionator blog, *The New York Times*, January 20, 2013.

15. Cingano, F. (2014), "Trends in Income Inequality and its Impact on Economic Growth," OECD Social, Employment and Migration Working Papers, No. 163, OECD Publishing. See also OECD (2014), "Focus on Inequality and Growth—December 2014" and also Larry Elliott, "Revealed: How the Wealth Gap Holds Back Economic Growth," *The Guardian*, December 9, 2014.

16. Joseph Stiglitz, "The Chinese Century," *Vanity Fair*, January 2015.

17. Eduardo Porter, "Blessings of Low Taxes Remain Unproved," *The New York Times*, March 13, 2013.

18. Eduardo Porter, "Inequality in America: The Data Is Sobering," *The New York Times*, August 1, 2013.

19. Patrick Wintour, "Britain Faces Future Divided by Rich and Poor, Poverty Commission Warns," *The Guardian*, October 20, 2014.

20. Nicholas Kristof, "Enjoying the Low Life?" *The New York Times*, April 9, 2015.

21. See Carol Morello, "Maternal Deaths in Childbirth Rise in the U.S.," *The Washington Post*, May 2, 2014. The study cited in the article is from the Institute for Health Metrics at the University of Washington and was published in the weekly medical journal *The Lancet*. See also the Every Mother Counts 2014 Impact Report.

22. See "Sustainable Economics: Mind the Inequality Gap," Morgan Stanley, November 24, 2015. See also Kasia Klimasinka, "The U.S. Is the Most Unequal Developed Economy Outside Southern Europe," *Bloomberg*, November 24, 2015.

23. David Leonhardt and Kevin Quealy, "The American Middle Class Is No Longer the World's Richest," *The New York Times*, April 23, 2014.

24. Nicholas Kristof, "It's Now the Canadian Dream," *The New York Times*, May 15, 2014.

25. Ronald Brownstein, "Meet the New Middle Class: Who They Are, What They Want, and What They Fear," *The Atlantic*, April 2013.

26. *United States: Tackling High Inequalities; Creating Opportunities for All*, OECD, June 2014.

27. See Eugene Robinson, "Tattered Dream: Who'll Tackle the Issue of Upward Mobility?," *The Washington Post*, November 23, 2007.

28. Mercedes Sastre and Luis Ayala, (November 2002) "Europe vs. The United States: Is There a Trade-Off Between Mobility and Inequality?", *Working Papers of the Institute for Social and Economic Research*, paper 2002–26. Colchester: University of Essex.

29. Gary Solon, "A Model of Intergenerational Mobility Variation Over Time and Place" (2004). In Miles Corak (editor). *Generational Income Mobility in North America and Europe*. Cambridge University Press (2004).

30. Corak, Miles (April 1, 2004). "Do Poor Children Become Poor Adults? Lessons for Public Policy from a Cross Country Comparison of Generational Earnings Mobility." Paper prepared for presentation at the *Colloque Devenir Des Enfants de Familles Défavorisées en France*. The paper is a summary and extension of an introductory chapter by the author in *Generational Income Mobility in North America and Europe*, published in 2004 by Cambridge University Press. See also Michael Greenstone, Adam Looney, Jeremy Patashnik and Muxin Yu, "Thirteen Economic Facts about Social Mobility and the Role of Education," The Hamilton Project, June 2013 and Fareed Zakaria, "Social Immobility Erodes the American Dream," *The Washington Post*, August 14, 2013.

31. *Economic Policy Reforms: Going for Growth*, Part II, Chapter 5 "A Family Affair: Intergenerational Social Mobility across OECD Countries," OECD 2010. See also, Fareed Zakaria, "The Downward Path of Upward Mobility," *The Washington Post*, November 9, 2011; Jason De Parle, "Harder for Americans to Rise from Lower Rungs," *The New York Times*, January 5, 2012, E. J. Dionne Jr., "A Challenge to Conservatives," *The Washington Post*, July 15, 2012 and Joseph Stiglitz, "Equal Opportunity, Our National Myth," *The New York Times*, February 17, 2013. The 2010 OECD report updated an earlier OECD report that made similar observations (see *Growing Unequal? Income Distribution in OECD Countries*, OECD 2008).

32. David Leonhardt, "The Idled Young Americans," *The New York Times*, May 5, 2013.

33. Raj Chetty, Nathanial Hendren, Patrick Kline, Emmanuel Saez and Nicholas Turner, "Is the United States Still a Land of Opportunity? Recent Trends in Intergenerational Mobility," National Bureau of Economic Research, NBER Working Paper 19844, January 2014. Chetty is a professor of economics at Harvard as is Nathanial Hendren; Saez and Kline are at the University of California, Berkeley; and Turner is with the Office of Tax Analysis, at the Treasury Department. See also, Scott Winship and Donald Schneider, "The Collapse of the Great Gatsby Curve," The Manhattan Institute, February 3, 2014; David Leonhardt, "Upward Mobility Has Not Declined, Study Says," *The New York Times*, January 23, 2014; and "Mobility, Measured: America Is No Less Socially Mobile than It Was a Generation Ago," *The Economist*, February 1, 2014.

34. Raj Chetty, Nathanial Hendren, Patrick Kline and Emmanuel Saez, "Where Is the Land of Opportunity? The Geography of Intergenerational Mobility in the United States," National Bureau of Economic Research, January 2014, p. 39.

35. Elizabeth Warren and Amelia Warren Tyagi, *The Two-Income Trap: Why Middle-Class Mothers and Fathers Are Going Broke* (Cambridge, MA: Basic Books, 2003), p. 81. Source for the figures is the 2001 Consumer Bankruptcy Report. Warren, who was a bankruptcy law professor at Harvard University is now a US Senator from Massachusetts; Tyagi, her daughter, was a McKinsey consultant.

36. Four of the fifteen worst years for the stock returns in the S&P 500: 2000 (-10.139%), 2001 (-13.043%), 2002 (-23.366%) and 2008 (-38.486%); see Barry Ritholtz, "2011: How

Volatile a Year?" posted January 1, 2012, in Markets, Technical Analysis, in The Big Picture blog.

37. That those who have now so concentrated their power will use it to rewrite the rules in their favor and against the middle class was the fear expressed regarding the future of the United States by Daron Acemoglu, MIT economist and co-author of *Why Nations Fail*, in an interview with Pat Garofalo, "MIT Economist: Income Inequality in the US Is Crushing the Middle Class' Political Power," *ThinkProgress*, March 23, 2012 at 5:55 p.m.

38. Robert Dahl and Charles E. Lindblom, *Politics, Economics and Welfare* (Second Printing: New Brunswick, NJ., Transaction Publishers, 2000; original printing Chicago: University of Chicago, 1953, 2000), p. 140.

39. Alberto Alesina and Roberto Perotti, "Income Distribution, Political Instability, and Investment" *European Economic Review* 40 (1996) pp. 1203–1228, p. 1225.

40. Ethan B. Kapstein, *Sharing the Wealth: Workers and the World Economy* (New York: W. W. Norton & Company, Inc., 1999), pp. 34–37. Kapstein is Arizona Centennial Professor of International Affairs at Arizona State University and Senior Director for Research at the McCain Institute for International Leadership in Washington DC, a think-tank associated with Arizona State University.

41. Ibid, pp. 112–117.

42. In this regard, refer also to the classic 1970 work by economist Albert O. Hirschman, *Exit, Voice and Loyalty: Responses to Declines in Firms, Organizations and States*.

43. The condemnation of one's own neighbors deemed unworthy of government help was, of course, the basis of the 2009 rant of CNBC commentator Rick Santelli that launched the Tea Party movement (recounted in the Introduction).

44. Alec MacGillis, "Who Turned My Blue State Red?" *The New York Times*, November 22, 2015. The state mainly addressed in the article is Kentucky—the same state addressed by Matt Taibbi in "The Truth About the Tea Party," *Rolling Stone*, October 14, 2010, cited in Chapter 1. Alec MacGillis is a political reporter for ProPublica and the author of *The Cynic: The Political Education of Mitch McConnell*. MacGillis previously wrote about politics for *The Washington Post* and *The New Republic*.

45. Michael Devereux and Jean-Francois Wen, "Political Instability, Capital Taxation and Growth," *European Economic Review* 42 (1998) pp. 135–1651; p. 1649.

46. And from these 16,068 families the number of donors included in the 0.01 percent share of voting age population was 24,092 in 2012. Adam Bonica, Nolan McCarty, Keith T. Poole and Howard Rosenthal, "Why Hasn't Democracy Slowed Rising Inequality?" *Journal of Economic Perspectives*, vol. 27 no. 3, Summer 2013 pp. 103–124. Economic information comes from Thomas Piketty and Emmanuel Saez, published later: Emmanuel Saez, "Striking It Richer: The Evolution of Top Incomes in the United States (Updated with 2012 preliminary estimates) September 3, 2013.

47. Robert Dahl and Charles E. Lindblom, *Politics, Economics and Welfare* (Second Printing: New Brunswick, NJ., Transaction Publishers, 2000; original printing Chicago: University of Chicago, 1953), p. 141. Citation to J. Frederick Dewhurst and Associates, America's Needs and Resources, *The Twentieth Century Fund*, New York, 1947, pp. 310–311.

48. Gene Koretz, "The Unhealthy U.S. Income Gap," *Business Week*, November 10, 1997.

49. Noreena Hertz, *The Silent Takeover: Global Capitalism and the Death of Democracy* (London: Arrow Books, The Random House Group Limited; 2001, 2002), p. 64. Among the works she cited were Richard G. Wilkinson's *Unhealthy Societies: The Afflictions of Inequality* (London, 1996), Richard G. Wilkinson, "Income, Inequality and Social Cohesion," *American Journal of Public Health*, September 1997; and McDonough et al. "Income Dynamics and Adult Mortality in the United States 1972 through 1989," *American Journal of Public Health*, September 1997.

50. Michael Marmot, professor of epidemiology and public health, University College London and author of *The Status Syndrome* (2004). interviewed by journalist Paul Solman on the PBS show "Newshour," February 23, 2007.

51. James Banks, PhD; Michael Marmot, MD; Zoë Oldfield, MSc; James P. Smith, PhD; "Disease and Disadvantage in the United States and in England," *The Journal of the American Medical Association*, Vo. 295 No. 17, May 3, 2006, pp. 2037–2045.

52. See also Moises Velasquez-Manoff, "Status and Stress," *The New York Times*, July 28, 2013.

53. Christopher von Rueden, "How Social Status Affects Your Health," *The New York Times*, December 14, 2014.

54. Clive Cookson, "Poverty Mars Formation of Infant Brains," *Financial Times*, February 16, 2008. All quotes herein come from this article. See also Paul Krugman, "Poverty Is Poison," *The New York Times*, February 18, 2008.

55. See "Parental Intervention Boosts Education of Kids at High Risk of Failure," Public and Media Relations at the University of Oregon, February 15, 2008.

56. Richard Wilkinson and Kate Pickett, *The Spirit Level: Why More Equal Societies Almost Always Do Better* (London: Allen Lane: An Imprint of Penguin Books; 2009), p. 181.

57. In this regard, also see Steve Crabtree, "Obesity Linked to Long-Term Unemployment in U.S.," Gallup, June 18, 2014.

58. See *The State of US Health: Innovations, Insights, and Recommendations from the Global Burden of Disease Study* (Seattle, WA: Institute for Health Metrics and Evaluation; 2013).

59. Median household incomes were obtained from the Census Bureau; life expectancies from Annie Lowrey, "Income Gap, Meet the Longevity Gap," *The New York Times*, March 16, 2014.

60. Margot Sanger-Katz, "Income Inequality: It's Also Bad for Your Health," The Upshot blog, *The New York Times*, March 30. 2015.

61. See "State-Specific Healthy Life Expectancy at Age of 65 Years—United States, 2007–2009," *Morbidity and Mortality Weekly Report*, Centers for Disease Control and Prevention, Vol. 62, No. 28, July 19, 2013.

62. Worst, in order: Mississippi, West Virginia, Kentucky, Alabama, Tennessee, Oklahoma, Louisiana, Arkansas, Georgia, North Carolina, Texas, South Carolina and Missouri. Best, in order: Hawaii, Connecticut, Minnesota, Florida, Colorado, Vermont, New Hampshire and Washington. This observation was made by Steve Ramirez in "Deadly Conservative Ideology Strangling Red States," Corporate Justice Blog, August 7, 2013.

63. Governor Christie made this statement July 30, 2013, and he correctly quoted the conclusion of the Tax Foundation for the period 1981 through 2005, that New Jersey received 61 cents for each dollar it sent Washington while Kentucky got back $1.51. See "Chris Christie Claims Kentucky Gets More Than Twice Back in Federal Funding from Washington Than New Jersey," PolitiFact.com., August 4, 2013. It appears that the subsidies more recently have increased for, as revealed in article in *The Economist*, over the period 1990-2009, for every dollar New Jersey sent to the federal government it got 57 cents back, while for every dollar Kentucky sent to the federal government, it got $1.63 back. See "America's Fiscal Union: The Red and the Black," *The Economist* online, August 1, 2013.

64. Michael A. Fletcher, "Research Ties Economic Inequality to Gap in Life Expectancy," *The Washington Post*, March 10, 2013.

65. Betsey Stevenson and Justin Wolfers, "Economic Growth and Subjective Well-Being: Reassessing the Easterlin Paradox," *Brookings Papers on Economic Activity*, Spring 2008.

66. Marianne Bertrand and Adair Morse, "Trickle-Down Consumption," University of Chicago Booth School of Business, University of California at Berkeley, Haas School of Business, NBER and CEPR, March 5, 2013. See also Brad Plumer, "'Trickle-Down Consumption': How Rising Inequality Can Leave Everyone Worse Off," WONKBLOG, March 27, 2013.

67. See Patricia Cohen, "Middle Class, or So They Think," *The New York Times*, April 11, 2015.

68. Robert H. Frank, "Does Inequality Matter? How 'Expenditure Cascades' are Squeezing the American Middle Class," Salon.com, December 5, 2011.

69. Tara Parker-Pope, "Suicide Rates Rise Sharply in U.S.," *The New York Times*, May 3, 2013. See also "New CDC Report Finds Stunning Suicide Increases Among Middle-Aged Americans," *PBS Newshour*, May 3, 2013.

70. David A. Kindig and Erika R. Cheng, "Even As Mortality Fell in Most US Counties, Female Mortality Nonetheless Rose in 42.8 Percent of Counties from 1992 to 2006," *Health Affairs*, Vol. 32, Issue 3, March 2013. The researchers examined trends in male and female

mortality rates from 1992–96 to 2002–06 in 3,140 US counties. They found that female mortality rates increased in 42.8 percent of counties, and male mortality rates increased in 3.4 percent. Medical care variables, such as proportions of primary care providers, were not associated with lower rates.

71. See "Hillary Clinton at Women in the World Summit," C-SPAN, April 5, 2013. See also "Hillary Clinton: Helping Women Isn't Just a 'Nice' Thing to Do," *The Daily Beast*, April 5, 2013.

72. S. Jay Olshansky, Toni Antonucci, Lisa Berkman, Robert H. Binstock, Axel Boersch-Supan, John T. Cacioppo, Bruce A. Carnes, Laura L. Carstensen, Linda P. Fried, Dana P. Goldman, James Jackson, Martin Kohli, John Rother, Yuhui Zheng and John Rowe, "Differences In Life Expectancy Due To Race And Educational Differences Are Widening, And Many May Not Catch Up," *Health Affairs*, August 2012.

73. Monica Potts, "The Life and Death of Crystal Wilson," *The American Prospect*, July/August 2013.

74. Arline T. Geronimus (Stanford University and University of Michigan), Jay A. Pearson (Duke University), Erin Linnenbringer (University of Michigan and Washington University, St. Louis), Amy J. Schulz (University of Michigan), Angela G, Reyes (Detroit Hispanic Development Corporation), Elissa S. Epel (University of California, San Francisco), Jue Lin (University of California, San Francisco), and Elizabeth H. Blackburn (University of California, San Francisco), "Race-Ethnicity, Poverty, Urban Stressors, and Telomere Length in a Detroit Community-Based Sample," *Journal of Health and Social Behavior*, American Sociological Association, April 30, 2015.

75. The Global Burden of Diseases, Injuries, and Risk Factors Study 2010 (GBD 2010) published in *The Lancet* (2012 Dec 13; 380) as well as in the *Journal of the American Medical Association* (2013 July). See Harvey V. Fineberg, MD, PhD, "Editorial," *Journal of the American Medical Association* (2013 July).

76. See also Paula Span, "Income Inequality Ages Badly," *The New York Times*, October 13, 2015.

77. Case, Anne, and Angus Deaton. 2015. "Rising Morbidity and Mortality in Midlife Among White Non-Hispanic Americans in the 21st Century." Proceedings of the National Academy of Sciences. The study was published November 2, 2015. See also Editorial Board, "Death Among Middle-Aged Whites, *The New York Times*, November 5, 2015; Ross Douthat, "The Dying of the Whites," *The New York Times*, November 8, 2015; and Paul Krugman, "Despair, American Style," *The New York Times*, November 9, 2015. See also Andrew J. Cherlin, "Why Are White Death Rates Rising?" *The New York Times*, February 22, 2016.

78. Gina Kolata, "Rise in Deaths for U.S. Whites in Middle Age," *The New York Times*, November 3, 2015. See also Laura Beil, "Small Towns Face Rising Suicide Rates," The *New York Times*, November 3, 2015. And, a study published in 2015 revealed drug overdose death rates increased in 26 states and Washington, D.C., and overdoses continue to outpace car crashes as the leading cause of injury-related deaths. See Mary Bowerman and Tyler Pager, "Report: Drug Overdose Death Rates Increase in 26 States," *USA Today*, June 18, 2015.

79. Lenny Bernstein and Joel Achenbach, "A Group of Middle-Aged Whites in the U.S. Is Dying at a Startling Rate," *The Washington Post*, November 2, 2015.

80. Elsewhere even the measurement of merit itself is questioned. For example, Carnegie Mellon professors Patrick D. Larkey and Jonathan P. Caulkins, in their 1992 paper "All Above Average and Other Intended Consequences of Performance Appraisal Systems," concluded that 100 years of dealing with performance review systems revealed they were inherently unable to produce objective results. And, a 1997 paper that appeared in *Nature*, by Christine Wenneras and Agnes Wold, "Nepotism and Gender Bias in Peer-Review," concluded women seeking research grants needed to be 2.5 times more productive than men to receive the same competent score.

81. Christopher Jencks, Marshall Smith, Henry Acland, Mary Jo Bane, David Cohen, Herbert Gintis, Barbara Heyns and Stephen Michelson, *Inequality: A Reassessment of the Effect of Family and Schooling in America* (New York: Basic Books, Inc., 1972), p. 265.

82. Ibid, pp. 8–9.

83. Mancur Olson, *Power and Prosperity: Outgrowing Communist and Capitalist Dictatorships* New York: Basic Books, 2000): p. 189.
84. See E. J. Dionne Jr., "Great Gatsby Economics Are No Party for the Middle Class," *The Washington Post*, June 16, 2013.
85. Friedrich A. Hayek, *Law, Legislation and Liberty, Volume 2: The Mirage of Social Justice* (Chicago: The University of Chicago Press; 1974), p. 74.
86. Nancy Birdsall, "Life Is Unfair: Inequality in the World", *Foreign Policy* (Summer 1998), pp. 76-93.
87. *Aristotle's Politics*, translated by Benjamin Jowett, New York: The Modern Library, Random House, Inc. (1945) Book IV, Chapter 11, pp. 191–192.
88. Hayek, *The Road to Serfdom*, p. 209.
89. Ibid, p. 206.
90. Ibid, p. 117.
91. Ibid, p. 118.
92. Barrington Moore, *The Social Origins of Dictatorship and Democracy: Lord and Peasant in the Making of the Modern World* (Boston: Beacon Press, 1966), p. 418.
93. This cultural contradiction is to be distinguished from what Harvard sociologist Daniel Bell had in mind in his book *The Cultural Contradictions of Capitalism.* There, the cultural contradiction that Bell found "striking" was the clash between the social structure required to achieve economic efficiency and self-indulgent culture. Daniel Bell, *The Cultural Contradictions of Capitalism* (New York: Basic Books, 1976, 1996), page 37. As Bell was writing this in the 1970s, this concern was reflecting revulsion to the 1960s cultural changes (wrought, in part, by the market itself through advertising).
94. William Easterly, *The Elusive Quest for Growth: Economists' Adventures and Misadventures in the Tropics* (Cambridge, MA: MIT Press, 2001), p. 279.
95. United Nations Conference on Trade and Development, *Trade and Development Report, 1997*, p. 152.
96. Paul Krugman, "Stranded by Sprawl," *The New York Times*, July 29, 2013. See also Raj Chetty, Nathanial Hendren, Patrick Kline, Emmanuel Saez and Nicholas Turner, "Is the United States Still a Land of Opportunity? Recent Trends in Intergenerational Mobility," National Bureau of Economic Research, NBER Working Paper 19844, January 2014; and Raj Chetty, Nathanial Hendren, Patrick Kline and Emmanuel Saez, "Where Is the Land of Opportunity? The Geography of Intergenerational Mobility in the United States," January 2014.
97. Nancy Birdsall, "Life Is Unfair: Inequality in the World", *Foreign Policy* (Summer 1998), p. 80.
98. Barbara Ehrenreich, *Fear of Falling: The Inner Life of the Middle Class* (New York: HarperCollins Publishers, 1989), pp. 21–22.

Chapter Twelve

The Liberal Values of Checks and Balances, Knowledge, Tolerance, Peace and the Rule of Law

This chapter will illustrate the degree to which the liberal values in addition to equality (addressed previously)—checks and balances, respect for knowledge, tolerance, peace and the rule of law—all intertwine with and reinforce each other. And, as is observed by Ian Buruma and Avishai Margalit, *Occidentalism* (2004),[1] building upon Adam Smith, Alexis de Tocqueville and the observations of the importance of the middle class (from Aristotle, Bell, Moore, Hayek and others), a liberal democracy measures its success not by its imagined progress toward human perfection and triumph of its military and its most talented citizens, but by the degree of comfort and happiness it delivers to all its citizens, which it does through practice of liberal values—and, as Buruma and Margalit observe, that is why liberalism is a threat to illiberalism.

THE SYSTEM OF SOCIETAL CHECKS AND BALANCES

The Forgotten Lesson of Classical Liberalism: Freedom, but Subject to Checks and Balances

> Whilst all authority in it will be derived from and dependent on the society, the society itself will be broken into so many parts, interests, and classes of citizens, that the rights of individuals, or of the minority, will be in little danger from interested combinations of the majority.—*James Madison,* Federalist *No. 51*

In the Introduction, the concept of a system of "societal checks and balances" was introduced. While a governmental system of checks and balances means separation of powers, i.e., division of government among three branches—executive, legislative and judicial—derived from the writings of James Madison and others, the concept of a system of societal checks and balances envisions the application of checks and balances on the most macro scale, to the functioning of society based on a blend of the institutions of civil society, the market and government. It also means the orderly relinquishment of power in accordance with the rule of law, and when the governed demand it, in accordance with the law.

To understand the gravity of the present debate it is necessary to understand its context. Former Secretary of State Hillary Rodham Clinton, in a 1998 article in *New Perspectives Quarterly*, described society as like a three-legged stool, the legs of which are the market, government and civil society (consisting of the family and all the voluntary organizations in society, including religious institutions, private educational institutions and other associations).[2] And, as with a stool, if imbalance occurs—if the institutions of government, the market, or civil society obtain too much power—the nation, like a stool, can topple.

This also is the lesson of a synthesis of the messages contained in two monumental books addressed previously, published in 1944, both of which were written by authors born in the Austro-Hungarian Empire. One, *The Great Transformation*, was written by social philosopher, Karl Polanyi. The other was *The Road to Serfdom*, written by Austrian economist Friedrich Hayek.

One of the key insights of Polanyi in *The Great Transformation* was that *a utopian belief in the efficacy of the market* will result in the market having too much authority, leading to its failure and resulting in government and civil society striking back. For support for his thesis, he cited the effects of the Great Depression and the occurrence of fascism.[3]

The 2001 re-issuance of Polanyi's classic contains a foreword by Joseph Stiglitz, Nobel Prize winner in economics, and an introduction by Fred Block, professor of sociology at the University of California, Davis. Both point out the continuing relevance of this work, however, both failed to acknowledge another of the key insights of Polanyi: That Christianity *itself*, through what the Utopian Robert Owen called the "individualization" of man as separate from society[4] aided proponents of the market in undermining government support of civil society, thereby undermining, first, government, then civil society, then all of society itself—of course, this observation has renewed relevance with the merging of Christian fundamentalists and business interests under the banners of conservatism and the Republican Party addressed in Chapter 3. Liberals carry forward Polanyi's concern today, believing that conservatism undermines society and prosperity by placing excessive emphasis on the individual at the expense of community, and on freedom at the expense of the liberal values necessary to maintain society.

In a significant parallel to Polanyi's fear of utopianism, in *The Road to Serfdom* Hayek warned that *a utopian belief in the efficacy of government to run a planned economy* will lead to failure and will tend to lead to excessive government dominance of the market, then of civil society, too. Hayek recognized that no one person can have all the information necessary to direct an economy efficiently, and, as a corollary, no one claiming to have such information should be trusted with that responsibility. Thus, too, a synthesis of the observations of Polanyi and Hayek yields what is the key to the liberal vision presented herein: a recognition that a *balance* must be struck among the institutions that compose civil society, the market and government.

The belief that, at all times and in all places, the prescription for economic growth is to cut taxes and regulation, privatize, and institute "free" trade and "free" elections (without the institutions of liberal democracy) has severely hampered the developing economies of the world. Four books that will be explored herein address the negative results of the application of modern conservatism to the developing world. Fareed Zakaria's *The Future of Freedom: Illiberal Democracy at Home and Abroad* (2003) examines how the West's application of the simplistic definition of democracy criticized herein—simply, elections with one person-one vote majority rule not accompanied by liberal values—has resulted in the illiberal democracy in which government arbitrarily exercises power. His lesson is that illiberal democracy has often, the world over, led to tyranny of the majority.

Joseph E. Stiglitz, in *Globalization and Its Discontents* (2002) presents a lesson that is the parallel to that of Zakaria, but applied to capitalism. Crude capitalism has often, the world over, led to tyranny of the wealthy—economic power, for the good of society, must be balanced by liberal values that serve as a check on that wealth to preserve the power of the poor. The Washington Consensus, the name given to rediscovered crude capitalism applied to developing nations—calling for privatization, deregulation, lower marginal tax rates and reduced government spending—all too often has resulted in reduced growth and increased corruption in the countries around the world that have had it forced upon them. Similarly, Noreena Hertz's *The Silent Takeover: Global Capitalism and the Death of Democracy* (2002) examined how the Washington Consensus leads to a shift in power to corporations, undermining freedom and democracy around the world.

Amy Chua, in *World on Fire: How Exporting Free Market Democracy Breeds Ethnic Hatred and Global Instability* (2002) combines these themes, examining how it is that introduction of the free market and democracy foments ethnic rage. In societies marked by a "market dominant minority," she observes that the majority, once democracy is implemented, tends to vote in measures that first rescind rule of law for the minority, and second abolish the democracy that gave the group in power its power. Her work, published before the US invasion of Iraq, has proved ominously prescient when applied to the aftermath of the Iraq War—more on Iraq below.

The Resource Curse: The Observation That Natural Resource Endowment in Ethnically Divided Countries, Absent Liberal Values and Institutions, Leads to Political Instability and Low Economic Growth—Compounded in Iraq after Our Invasion by Shock Therapy Blowback

Numerous commentators have observed that the legendary curse of King Midas, who wished for and got the power that turned everything he touched into gold, and ended up miserable, has a modern-day variant: the "resource curse." In his 2003 book, *The Future of Freedom: Illiberal Democracy at Home and Abroad*, *Newsweek International* Editor Fareed Zakaria, citing a study by Harvard economists Jeffrey D. Sachs and Andrew M. Warner that found "a statistically, inverse, and robust association between natural resource intensity and growth over the past twenty years,"[5] warned that the prospects for democracy were bleak in countries well-endowed with the *curse* of "natural endowments" (such as oil and gas and mineral deposits, agricultural resources, and good natural ports) but lacking a middle class, wealth-redistributing institutions and a history of the rule of law.[6] In an in-depth article on Iraq in *Foreign Affairs* the following year, Nancy Birdsall and Arvind Subramanian (a Division Chief at the International Monetary Fund) elaborated on the phenomenon, finding that oil riches tend to impede the development of the institutions necessary for functioning liberal democracy and a market-based economy.[7] Similar observations about the ability of presence of oil resources to impede rather than promote growth were made by former London School of Economics professor of international relations Fred Halliday in his 2005 book, *The Middle East in International Relations*.[8]

The main way that natural endowments impede the development of institutions and values is that they yield large rents—(that term observed earlier addressed by Buchanan and Tullock, meaning economic reward in excess of the effort expended politically) creating the temptation for governments or oligarchies to control and exploit them.[9] Comfortably established with these rents, the elite see no reason to establish institutions necessary to promote growth—institutions that would also serve to promote spreading of income and wealth.

Their proposed cure for Iraq's curse, after reviewing several options, was to have the international community—ideally the UN—supervise the distribution of at least half of the oil revenues directly to the Iraqi people, with the balance retained by the government.[10] One option not examined was institution of a change in the property regime so that rights to minerals and hydrocarbons are vested with the owner of the surface of the land, as is generally the case in the United States. This would not only have the advantage of spreading wealth via direct distribution and likely enhancing production, but would also require Iraqi citizens to cooperate with each other in creating and operating the different functions (landmen and lawyers to prepare leases and contracts to pool capital to fund drilling and production; geologists, geophysicists and reservoir engineers to find and map prospects; drilling engineers to drill the wells; and facility and structural engineers to design the equipment, structures and pipelines used in production and transportation).

As observed above, the same year that Zakaria's book was published, Yale University Law School Professor Amy Chua's book, *World on Fire*, added to our understanding by illustrating how ethnic divisions undermine democracy's prospects (lessons also eloquently stated by Robert Kaplan in his 2000 book *The Coming Anarchy—Shattering the Dreams of the Post-Cold War*).

And, in observations in a 2006 article echoing Birdsall and Subramanian, University of Chicago political science professor Carles Boix provided a plausible explanation for why it is that economies "blessed" by immense natural resources of fertile land, minerals and oil have such a difficult time developing into democracies: The vast amounts of money ruling elites extract from these resources discourage them from creating institutions and empowering their populations when, even though that would increase growth, it also may upset their own power.[11] And, as observed by Fareed Zakaria, the West is far from free of blame for, in exchange for oil, it has allowed many of the countries that produce it to live by their own rules, imposing despotism on their people and resisting modernizing reform.[12]

Iraq presented an especially difficult environment for the blossoming of liberal democracy (complicated by the actions of the neoconservatives as observed by Naomi Klein in Chapter 10) because it combined its vast oil wealth with ethnic diversity: its Kurdish North, Sunni Muslim Center and Shiite South and East (along with other smaller ethnic groups, including Yazidis and Christians). Thus, Iraq fit an all-too-familiar pattern: It was another nation hobbled by the combination of an abundance of oil and ethnic diversity, held together by a brutal dictator in the absence of the institutions necessary for liberal democracy to survive—and into that setting we disbanded the institutions that did exist (the military and the Ba'ath party organization, which was composed of prominent members of the Sunni minority, and former Ba'athists in the military were later found to have joined ISIS), with the hopelessly naïve expectation that liberal democratic institutions would miraculously generate themselves with none having existed there before. As the neoconservatives had joined with fellow conservative Republicans in wildly misgauging the efficacy of a trickle-down model applied domestically, they massively miscalculated the efficacy of a trickle-down model applied to Iraq—as they had also horribly miscalculated previously in the former Soviet Union.

As for the appropriate cure for such a nation, World Bank economists David Dollar and Aart Kraay concluded that better rule of law—better enforcement of property rights—raises per capita income and income of the poor, while democracy—better developed political rights—has no strong effect on either per capita income or income of the poor (though the authors found that democracy provided non-material benefits).[13] And into this legal setting of Dollar and Kraay should be added the "middle class consensus" of William Easterly from the previous chapter. In order, then, the tasks, as Zakaria especially addresses, are to create stability, build the economy (all the while encouraging tolerance), build the wealth-spreading institutions, *and only then* institute democracy. It is a common sense lesson applicable to both nation-building and domestic policy: We cannot constantly cut taxes and regulations. Some degree of regulation is needed in order to keep society functioning, and taxation is necessary to keep funding government.

RESPECT FOR KNOWLEDGE

Although this work criticizes conservatism for its disrespect for knowledge, facts and truth, conservative media has stood up for truth on one prominent occasion, and that should be acknowledged. On election night November 6, 2012, Fox News Channel had called Ohio and the election for President Obama. Karl Rove, sitting with Megyn Kelly, Fox News Commentator, challenged the Fox numbers specialists, alleging there were still votes to count in Ohio that could swing that state to the Republicans. Megyn Kelly asked if this were something he came up with to feel better or was it real. When he insisted it was real, Kelly got up from her chair, walked over to where the number specialists were, and got confident assurances from them that the election could be called, demonstrating a healthy respect—even in the halls of Fox News Channel—for knowledge, unbiased analysis and the facts.[14] Such instances of members of the media challenging political commentators and politicians are far too rare, however.

The Undermining of Democracy in Conduct of Domestic Policy by Disregarding Knowledge—Truth—and Promoting Ignorance

It was ironic that, during the 2016 presidential campaign, much was made by political commentators of the relatively high level of lack of trustworthiness poll respondents gave to Hillary Clinton, while, due to modern conservatism's disregard of the value of knowledge—of truth—none of the Republican presidential candidates merited being called trustworthy. Trustworthiness is just not a trickle-down conservative Republican value.

Conservatism gave America, in the words of conservative George Wallace, a distrust of "pointy-headed intellectuals," and a distrust of knowledge. This legacy was built on by President George W. Bush, who led so many Americans to discover a new word—"incurious"[15] —as he headed a conservative administration that provided numerous examples of disrespect for knowledge. Reporter Ron Suskind, in an article in the January 2003 issue of *Esquire* cited previously,[16] revealed the frustration of an unnamed senior White House official who complained that all policy came from the political calculations of Karl Rove. Another former administration staffer who did give his name—John DiIulio, University of Pennsylvania professor, author, and domestic affairs expert who formerly headed the White House Office of Faith-Based and Community Initiatives—expressed similar frustrations and famously dubbed it the "reign of the Mayberry Machiavellis".

The conservative vision is the dangerous vision of politics as a marketplace in which votes are analogous to dollars, confirmed in the words of President Bush himself in 2004 when he claimed after his close re-election to have earned political capital that he planned to use. In this vision of politics, words are tools in advertising campaigns, used in marketing pitches of the four-year ad campaign of a presidency.

Rush Limbaugh, who emerged in the early days of the first Obama administration as the leading conservative spokesman, expressed this vision in his address at the Conservative Political Action Conference February 28, 2009, famously reiterating his desire that President Obama fail and offering an explanation of the conservative philosophy that inaccurately placed in the Preamble to the Constitution reference to "inalienable rights" and listed four of them—adding "freedom"—to the three "unalienable rights" of "Life, Liberty and the pursuit of Happiness" referred to in the Declaration of Independence.[17] Conservative love and reverence of our founding documents apparently does not extend to knowing what they say.

Common Core is a federal government effort to detail what kindergarten through grade 12 students should know in the English language arts and mathematics at the end of each grade. Not surprisingly, it had the support of conservatives initially when it began in the 1990s to set these national standards, given the importance of education to conservatives, then as evidenced by conservative support for the works of educator E. D. Hirsch, Jr.[18] and conservative hero William J. Bennett.[19] By 2014, however, conservatives who had initially supported the Common Core began reversing themselves—among them, Governor Bobby Jindal (R-LA), who initially supported Common Core but announced he was opposing it soon after an open letter to him was posted on the Tea Party of Louisiana website.[20] The letter's text was in bold lettering and emphasis was provided with underlining and red and blue text. The letter quoted John Birch Society favorite W. Cleon Skousen's *The*

Naked Communist (1958)[21] and warned that Common Core was part of the socialists' plans to use public schools for federal indoctrination camps.

Finally, throughout President Obama's presidency, conservatives criticized him for illegitimately holding his office. A prominent line of attack, addressed earlier, was the erroneous claim that he was born in Kenya (which, again, even if true, would not necessarily have disqualified him because, due to his mother indisputably having been American, rendered him an American citizen at birth and thus a court would be expected to have found him a "natural born citizen" and competent to run for president). Another line of attack was that he lacked government experience before he became president. The facts, however, are that he had been in government 11 years before his election as president (he served from 1997 through 2004 in the Illinois legislature and 2004 up to his inauguration in January 2009 in the United States Senate). In contrast, one of conservatives' most revered presidents, Ronald Reagan, served only eight years in government before he became president (January 1967 to January 1975 as Governor of California) and George W. Bush served only five years in government (January 1995 through December 2000 as Governor of Texas) before he became president. Additionally, three of the leaders for much of the 2016 Republican presidential candidate race—Donald Trump, Ben Carson, and Carly Fiorina—had no government experience at all. As observed repeatedly herein: To modern, trickle-down conservatism, facts do not matter.

Ignorance of Science

As observed by Andrew C. Revkin, in *The New York Times* in October 2004, scientists over the previous nearly four years of the Bush administration had been criticizing the anti-science attitude of the administration,[22] a criticism that was joined in the following month in a post-2004 election op-ed by former conservative and colleague of William F. Buckley, Jr., Garry Wills, raising concern for the future of America's heritage.[23] Journalist Chris Mooney expanded on these observations in his books *The Republican War on Science* (2005) and *The Republican Brain* (2012). Jonathan Amos, in "US Scientists Reject Interference," BBC News, December 14, 2006 observed that a statement protesting political interference in the scientific process and demanding a restoration of scientific integrity to government policymaking was signed by 10,000 researchers, including 52 Nobel laureates.

Former Surgeon General Richard H. Carmona testified in 2007 before a Congressional panel that top officials in the Bush administration prevented him from speaking about stem cells, emergency contraception, sex education, or prison, mental and global health issues; delayed for years an important study on second-hand smoke; ordered him to mention President Bush three times on every page of his speeches and discouraged him from attending the Special Olympics because of the association of the Kennedy family with the event.[24]

Republicans reiterated their hostility toward knowledge and the reckless disregard for the damage this does to democracy when the National Republican Congressional Committee (NRCC) launched fake news sites to attack Democratic candidates in the months before the 2014 midterm elections, a measure the audacity of which was well captured by Dana Milbank of *The Washington Post* in his op-ed addressing the stunt: "Republicans Embrace Their Phoniness."[25] But phoniness of Republicans in the domestic policy realm would be eclipsed by their phoniness in foreign policy, especially as demonstrated in their propaganda campaign to sell the Iraq invasion.

The Undermining of Democracy in the Propaganda Campaign to Sell the Iraq Invasion

> That's a very volatile part of the world, and if you take down the central government of Iraq, you could very easily end up seeing pieces of Iraq fly off: part of it, the Syrians would like to have to the west, part of it—eastern Iraq—the Iranians would like to claim, they fought over it for eight years. In the north you've got the Kurds, and if the Kurds spin loose and join with the Kurds in Turkey, then you threaten the territorial integrity of Turkey. It's a quagmire if you go that far and try to take over Iraq.—*Secretary of Defense Dick Cheney, April 15, 1994*[26]

> Simply stated, there is no doubt that Saddam Hussein now has weapons of mass destruction.—*Vice President Dick Cheney, August 26, 2002*[27]

> Extremists in the region would have to rethink their strategy of jihad.—*Vice President Dick Cheney, addressing the effect of a pre-emptive strike by the US in Iraq, August 26, 2002*[28]

Former President George W. Bush, in interviews after the release of his book *41: A Portrait of My Father by George W. Bush* (2014), was asked why it was that he felt it necessary to eradicate Saddam Hussein although his father, as president during the Persian Gulf War, after getting the Iraqi Army out of Kuwait, did not pursue Saddam to Baghdad. His answer was that the concerns expressed soon after the Persian Gulf War regarding the potential ungovernability of Iraq after deposing of Saddam Hussein were immediately overridden by the attacks of September 11, 2001, based on the concern that Saddam would put his weapons in the hands of terrorists.[29] Even at that time, however, it was widely recognized that Saddam Hussein, although a Sunni as are the al Qaeda militants, presided over a secular dictatorship which effectively kept al Qaeda out of Iraq (until the United States toppled it) and, thus, it would have been highly doubtful there was a relationship between Saddam

Hussein and al Qaeda (and none was ever proven). Similarly, post-Persian Gulf War sanctions required Saddam to destroy his weapons of mass destruction (WMD), and early indications on the ground by UN inspectors confirmed that he had complied. Finally, of course, in the period from September 11, 2001 up to March of 2003, as a nation we indulged in the delusion of many Bush administration advisors that we would be greeted as liberators, which also proved horribly wrong.[30]

In 2005 the militants were not in the last throes of the insurgency—our military presence continued in Iraq, battling militants, for another six years until withdrawal in December 2011, then had to re-engage in 2014 to confront ISIS, which was a spinoff of al Qaeda in Iraq and supported by former Ba'athists—Sunnis who had been elites in the military of Saddam Hussein. Of course, too, simply stated, there was plenty of doubt about the extent of Saddam's involvement in weapons of mass destruction because UN inspectors continued to report finding no evidence of them.

The contrast between the cautionary prescience Secretary of Defense Cheney displayed in 1994 and the recklessness with which Vice President Cheney urged invasion of Iraq appears to some as duplicity.[31] No attempt will be made here to explain the contradiction between the two opinions, however, what is clear from the facts is that President Bush and Vice President Cheney created the war at their own option, and in the face of repeated reports by the Director-General of the International Atomic Energy Administration (IAEA) Mohamed ElBaradei regarding the findings of UN weapons inspectors that had commenced November 27, 2002, confirming that Iraq had complied with its obligations dating to 1991 and the end of the Persian Gulf War: no evidence was found of revival of a nuclear weapons program, nor of any attempt by Iraq to import uranium since 1990 nor of any attempt to import aluminum tubes for centrifuge enrichment—findings summarized in a July 3, 2003 UN press release.[32]

The Slam Dunk Case to Fool the American Public into Going to War in Iraq

As recounted by members of the Bush administration, a propaganda campaign was launched to market the invasion of Iraq to the American people, misleading them into believing that an unbiased assessment of evidence conducted by the administration, based on evidence only they saw, confirmed, by a preponderance of the evidence, an Iraq-al Qaeda connection and the existence of WMD. The American people only found out after the fact that a preponderance of evidence was never the test. Rather, in the famous standard of Vice President Cheney, the actual test was that if there was even a "one percent chance" Iraq had WMD, then America should attack.[33]

Simultaneously, the threat of imminent deployment of WMD by Iraq was pressed, as evidenced by Secretary of State Condoleezza Rice's ominous warning that the "smoking gun" everyone was looking for might turn out to be a "mushroom cloud." To support the fear of nuclear attack, the theory of an Iraqi attempt to acquire nuclear weaponry was promoted. Reporting showed the administration promoted weak evidence that supported its claims and withheld from the public strong evidence that would undermine it.[34]

In his chapter titled "Selling the War," Scott McClellan elaborated on the propaganda efforts, corroborating claims from other members of the administration that "what happened" was that the administration focused on molding the propaganda to market the invasion of Iraq at the expense of determining the truth on the ground and publicizing it.[35]

While McClellan's book provided a rich insider's account of the propaganda campaign for war, it is not the only source for insight regarding this propaganda campaign. White House Chief of Staff Andrew Card, who previously worked in the automobile industry, famously, in trivializing terms referring to his experience in marketing cars, explained in September 2002 that from a marketing perspective the administration knew better than to try to sell a war in August.[36]

In his 2004 book, *Plan of Attack*, Bob Woodward recounted an exchange that became famous—that between President Bush and CIA Director George Tenet, December 21, 2002—one month after McClellan had determined the president was sold on war and less than three months before the invasion of Iraq. On that day, in a meeting among Tenet, his top deputy John McLaughlin, President Bush and Vice President Cheney regarding the proof that the Iraqis possessed weapons of mass destruction, Tenet famously called it a slam dunk case. Less famous however, but very telling regarding what Tenet meant, was President Bush's question that elicited Tenet's response. The president, after expressing concern that the evidence of WMD presented would not convince the public and asking if what he had seen was all they had was what prompted the "slam dunk" response.[37]

As famous as Tenet's "slam dunk" response became, the above exchange remained ambiguous. Did Tenet understand the president to be complaining that, after all the buildup regarding evidence of WMD, the evidence presented did not convince *him* of the presence of WMD, or that the evidence was weak support to the marketing effort the president planned to make to the American people to convince *them* of the existence of WMD and the need to wage war on Iraq?

Tenet would later get the opportunity to clarify that he understood the president to be asking the latter question, in a CBS News *60 Minutes* interview with Scott Pelley that aired in 2007.[38] In response to Pelley's question of what did he mean by "slam dunk," Tenet responded that he meant he thought they could put together a better case for public consumption—because that was what the meeting was about. Tenet's deputy, John McLaughlin, supported this version of the conversation, recalling it was a PR meeting.[39]

Further support for the assertion that the decision had already been made to invade Iraq prior to that meeting is found in the "Downing Street Memo"—a leaked briefing paper prepared July 21, 2002 in advance of a meeting with Prime Minister Tony Blair, summarizing a meeting between Sir Richard Dearlove, head of the British Secret Intelligence Service MI6 and Bush administration officials. The memo concluded that among the Bush administration military action in Iraq was inevitable and intelligence and facts were being fixed around invasion.[40]

A critical element of fixing the intelligence and facts around the policy of invasion was chronicled by reporter Seymour Hersh in his outstanding investigative article "The Stovepipe" (*The New Yorker*, October 27, 2003). The administration established at least three separate agencies, one within the Office of the Vice President, one in the Defense Department and one in the Pentagon, each with the specific purpose of gathering intelligence data favorable to the administration's argument that Iraq had weapons of mass destruction, and avoided the "vetting" process.[41]

So successful was the propaganda campaign that, although as observed above, many Americans were convinced otherwise, no convincing evidence ever appeared of:

1. A connection between Iraq or Saddam Hussein personally and al Qaeda or Osama bin Laden;
2. Existence, in Iraq, of large hidden stockpiles of, or an ongoing program to reconstitute, weapons of mass destruction (chemical, biological or nuclear) after they were destroyed following the Persian Gulf War; or
3. Aggression against the US by Iraq (other than firing on, unsuccessfully, US and Coalition Forces enforcing the UN Security Council's no-fly zone over Iraq).

Defense Secretary Donald Rumsfeld would later deny any part in the propaganda promotion. However, Robin Wright, Middle East expert for *The Washington Post* exposed the existence of memos (which Rumsfeld called "snowflakes") Rumsfeld sent to staff urging them to keep rallying support for war in Iraq.[42] Karl Rove in November 2007 also attempted to re-write history, promoting the delusion that it was Congress that had pushed the administration to issue the resolution allowing the authority to attack Iraq, against the opposition of the administration![43] By 2014 an influential NBC News/Wall Street Journal/Annenberg poll showed the vast majority Americans—71 percent—believed the War in Iraq "wasn't worth it".[44]

The Surge Was a Failure—Disrespect for Truth and Resultant Undermining of Democracy in the 2016 Presidential Campaign

> A successful strategy for Iraq goes beyond military operations. Ordinary Iraqi citizens must see that military operations are accompanied by visible improvements in their neighborhoods and communities. So America will hold the Iraqi government to the benchmarks it has announced.
>
> To establish its authority, the Iraqi government plans to take responsibility for security in all of Iraq's provinces by November. To give every Iraqi citizen a stake in the country's economy, Iraq will pass legislation to share oil revenues among all Iraqis. To show that it is committed to delivering a better life, the Iraqi government will spend $10 billion of its own money on reconstruction and infrastructure projects that will create new jobs. To empower local leaders, Iraqis plan to hold provincial elections later this year. And to allow more Iraqis to re-enter their nation's political life, the government will reform de-Baathification laws, and establish a fair process for considering amendments to Iraq's constitution.—*President George W. Bush, in "The President's Address to the Nation," January 10, 2007, explaining plans for the "surge" to take place later that year in Iraq, defining it as military effort that will be accompanied by political benchmarks to consolidate and hold the gains made in that military effort.*

Senator Lindsey Graham (R-SC), in an interview conducted days after he announced he was seeking the 2016 Republican nomination for president, repeatedly claimed the "surge" in Iraq, launched in 2007, "worked".[45] In reality, as the quote above by President Bush illustrates, because war is but the use of violence to achieve political ends, a strategy that yields military victory—as the surge did—but does not result in political victory so that the ground won can be held and governed is, ultimately, a failure. We know the surge failed because President Bush listed a series of political "benchmarks" by which success could be measured—and they were not all achieved. And, the allegation by Senator Graham and other Republican candidates and conservative commentators that President Obama, by withdrawing forces in December 2011—thus honoring the Status of Forces Agreement signed by President Bush December 14, 2008[46] providing that US combat forces would withdraw from Iraqi cities by June 30, 2009, and all US combat forces would be completely out of Iraq by December 31, 2011—sacrificed the gains of the surge and led to the emergence of the Islamic State—is, like so much else related to the Bush administration and the Iraq War, not supported by the facts.[47]

Additionally, for perspective, three years—the time negotiated by President Bush to stand up the Iraqi military (in his phrasing, "as Iraqis stand up, Americans will stand down"[48]) and honored by President Obama—is longer than it took the US, along with its allies, to defeat Hitler (the US landed in French North Africa in Operation Torch November 8, 1942 and Germany surrendered May 7, 1945). Finally, from late 2010 through 2011, President Obama's administration did try to negotiate a second Status of Forces Agreement, delaying US exit, but that effort was rebuffed by the Iraqi leadership unwilling to agree to legal immunity for US troops.

The Iraq War Was a Mistake, and Potential 2016 Republican Presidential Candidates Showed They Will Distort the Truth in Exchange for Power

With the Iraq War, the neoconservative-trickle-down-supply-side-crony capitalist vision had struck a major blow to American democracy. To intentionally mislead the American people into going to war—to make a case for going to war to support an affirmative decision that was already made in the absence of clear and convincing evidence—is an egregious violation of the trust of the American people and of the rule of law. And, policy statements from the Romney-Ryan campaign in 2012, combined with the presence of neoconservative advisors from the administration of President George W. Bush in both the Romney 2012 and Jeb Bush 2016 campaigns promised a continuation of foreign policy guided by neoconservatives oblivious to the truth if the Republicans take back the White House in 2016, including agitation for an attack on Iran—a nation, like Germany, of *80 million people*—even though in 2007 a National Intelligence Estimate was released that concluded Iran had ceased its nuclear weapons program in 2003.[49]

In May 2015, after he had announced he was running for president in 2016 and then remembered that by doing so he was rendering himself unable to meet directly with the super PAC organized on his behalf to raise unlimited amounts of money to support his campaign (Right to Rise), and he quickly retracted his announcement,[50] Jeb Bush was asked by Megyn Kelly of Fox News (Monday, May 11, 2015) whether knowing what he knows now would he have authorized the invasion of Iraq. That interview was the first of five attempts over several days to answer the question (as recounted by Chuck Todd on NBC News' *Meet the Press* May 17, 2015), to which Bush finally responded that he would not have invaded Iraq. To their credit, Senators Ted Cruz (R-TX) and Rand Paul (R-TX), also presidential candidates, clearly stated that knowing what we know now, the Iraq War was a mistake. Less clear about his opinion was Senator Marco Rubio (R-FL), also a candidate for president.

The 1994 warning of then-Defense Secretary Cheney that Iraq would prove a "quagmire" was prescient, as much of Iraq fell victim first to al Qaeda in Iraq and then to ISIS. And the rise of ISIS came to be widely acknowledged as aided by the Bush administration's neoconservative-inspired removal of the dictatorial military hand that held together Kurds, Shia and Sunnis in an albeit uneasy alliance, combined with the "de-

Ba'athification" of the Iraqi military and society that followed, leaving a military vacuum in the north of Iraq, into which ISIS moved and established itself. And, yet, conservative Republicans in advance of the 2016 presidential election clamored for a return to Iraq and invasion of Syria to halt ISIS and even an attack on Iran—begging for one "quagmire" after another.[51]

It should be patently obvious that, if knowledge and its transmission to the greatest extent throughout society are so important to success of a society, important values for a society's members to hold are those of respect for knowledge, curiosity about the world, a commitment to education and a commitment to testing ideas with evidence and reason. Ironically, trickle-down conservatism, while professing a commitment to ultimate truth, suffers from a conflict in its contributing elements that leads it to promote ignorance, incuriosity and distortion of the truth—whatever truth is politically unpalatable to it. In the process, it undermines democracy, while liberal respect for knowledge, as it has since the dawn of the Enlightenment, supports it.

TOLERANCE

> Love your neighbor as yourself.—*Jesus of Nazareth, Matthew 27:39.*

> You have heard that it was said, "Love your neighbor and hate your enemy." But I tell you, love your enemies and pray for those who persecute you.—*Jesus of Nazareth, Matthew 5:43–44.*

> Judge not, lest ye be judged.—*Jesus of Nazareth, Matthew 7:1 and Luke 6:37.*

> The Senators and Representatives before mentioned, and the members of the several state legislatures, and all executive and judicial officers, both of the United States and of the several states, shall be bound by oath or affirmation, to support this Constitution; but no religious test shall ever be required as a qualification to any office or public trust under the United States.—*US Constitution, Article VI*

Conservatives have long recognized the potential difficulty of assimilation of ethnic groups in America, although they opposed the tolerance that liberals urged to promote that assimilation. After the first publication of the groundbreaking book by neoconservatives (at the time) Nathan Glazer and Daniel P. Moynihan titled *Beyond the Melting Pot: The Negroes, Puerto Ricans, Jews, Italians, and Irish of New York City* (1963, 1970), a young Kevin Phillips had written *The Emerging Republican Majority* (1969), wherein cultural differences among voters were analyzed for their trending growing affinity for the Republican Party—especially revealing was the observation that the formerly "Solid South"—solidly Democratic—was evolving, due in great part to the Democratic Party's support for the Civil Rights Movement, toward a solidly Republican direction.[52] Soon thereafter, Michael Novak, an American of Slovak descent (who would go on to become an influential Catholic and conservative commentator) analyzed the experiences of the Poles, Italians, Greeks and Slovaks in America and predicted that they would not "melt" into the prevailing WASP (White Anglo-Saxon Protestant) culture in *The Rise of the Unmeltable Ethnics* (1972).

As observed previously, absent liberal values, corruption tends to accompany ethnic diversity, as do inequality, class distinction and low economic growth—to quote William Easterly: "The worst case for good policymaking and political freedom is to have both high inequality and high ethnic diversity."[53] And as was seen in the previous chapter regarding inequality, intolerance also has been found to have the effect of shortening life spans.[54] Actually, perhaps the *worst* case for good policymaking and political freedom is to have high inequality, high ethnic diversity, *and* rich natural resources. Of course, to *prevent* ethnic diversity would be anti-democratic and anti-capitalist, thus, the failing is not the fact of ethnic diversity but of intolerance and inequality.

Intolerance Is Illiberal, Whether Religious or Ethnic

William Julius Wilson, in his 1973 book, *Power, Racism, and Privilege: Race Relations in Theoretical and Sociohistorical Perspectives* elaborated on the distinction he drew between ethnocentricism and racism, observing that ethnocentrism involves group distinction while racism involves exploitation.[55] Racism is a philosophy based on stealing at least part of the value of one person's labor, with such theft justified by the "inferior" race of that person. It is an example of rent-seeking (and, thus, directly violates the rule of law). The problem of ethnicity and international politics was addressed by Daniel Patrick Moynihan in his outstanding book *Pandaemonium: Ethnicity in International Politics* (1993). He predicted therein that although fellow sociologist Francis Fukuyama had proclaimed, upon the death of Soviet communism, the "end of history" and the triumph of liberal democracy, ethnicity would yet persist.[56] Indeed, with the benefit of two decades passed since his book was published, we can see the re-emergence of ethnicity driving a not-yet-dead totalitarianism in the form of radical Islamism. And, within that movement, we can see the prescience of Moynihan in addressing ethnicity as a world problem. Additionally, we can appreciate the prescience of Moynihan regarding not only how ethnicity would come to motivate dissension, but how it would, in the context of principles of the United Nations, drive the movement toward self-determination.[57]

Moynihan recounted how in the 1950s he and his colleague, Nathan Glazer, began the research that culminated in the book mentioned above, *Beyond the Melting Pot: The Negroes, Puerto Ricans, Jews, Italians, and Irish of*

New York City (1963), wherein they observed that "melting pot" did not, in fact, happen.[58] Moynihan's insights into ethnicity gave him a somewhat unique perspective on the Soviet Union. He proudly observed that, in the 1970s he predicted that, due to ethnic strife, the Soviet Union would collapse before the end of the 1980s—this later merited a "you were right, I was wrong" letter from Henry Kissinger.[59]

Regarding the Middle East, Moynihan recounted that *Jews* were a plurality in Baghdad in 1921, when, pursuant to the Sykes-Picot Agreement entered into between Britain and France in 1916 in anticipation of Germany losing the war the British carved out Iraq from predominantly *Christian* Assyria in the North and Muslim Babylonia in the South, and within Islamic Iraq were divisions among the Kurds, Shiites and Sunnis[60] and noted how little had changed when the British returned to the region in the Persian Gulf War[61] (and, it could be added, when the British returned again in 2003 with American troops).

Finally, absent the liberal value of tolerance, and absent dictators to force diverse ethnic groups within their borders to live together, a vacuum is created that in several of the countries of the Middle East and North Africa (witness Iraq, Syria, Libya and Yemen) has resulted in anarchic, apocalyptic religious war zones.

The Conservative—Illiberal—Values of Intolerance, and Tolerance of Intolerance Regarding Religion, Race and Sexual Orientation

Returning to America, a recurring conservative theme is that there is a "cultural war" in America, in which their values—the "right" values—are under attack because there are some people (liberals) who do not share them. Republican former presidential candidate and current conservative commentator Pat Buchanan, in his speech at the 1992 Republican National Convention in Houston, declared, speaking of George H. W. Bush, that he was involved a religious war and culture war crucial to the future of the country.[62] But, as former conservative Garry Wills observed, the liberals were not actually godless but, rather, just had the "wrong" version of God and religion.[63]

Photographs of David Duke in a Nazi uniform taken while he was a student at Louisiana State University, and dressed in his outfit as Imperial Wizard of the Ku Klux Klan, circulated prior to the 1991 Louisiana gubernatorial runoff against the Democrat Edwin Edwards. Duke's history and views, however, were insufficient to deter a majority of Republicans and majority of whites from voting for him.

David Duke's history was in the news again in late 2014, when a blogger (Lamar White, at Louisiana politics blog CenLamar), broke the news about the appearance of Congressman Steve Scalise (R-LA) at a white supremacist convention in May 2002, when the congressman was a state legislator. The sponsor of the convention, European-American Unity and Rights Organization (EURO), founded by David Duke and a then-neighbor of Congressman Scalise and known associate of David Duke (Kenny Knight), had invited him to speak.

Fellow Louisiana Congressman Cedric Richmond (D-LA), an African American, came to Congressman Scalise's defense, clarifying that Congressman Scalise did not share the beliefs of that organization, and expressing hope that his fellow congressman can use the lessons from this episode for good.[64] And, columnist Jarvis DeBerry of *The Times Picayune* provided a good example of such an opportunity, quoting Knight from an interview in *The Washington Post* wherein Knight observed that Congressman Scalise had agreed to speak to the organization even though he knew who Knight was.[65] That, as DeBerry observed, was the real issue—not an allegation that Congressman Scalise was himself racially intolerant but, rather, that he was wrong to have tolerated racial intolerance in 2002. And, this lesson would also explain that 1991 election result: A majority of Louisiana's Republicans should not be assumed to have been in 1991 racially intolerant themselves but, rather, they embraced a conservative value of tolerance toward racial intolerance. An emphatic rejection of tolerance toward racial intolerance would help the nation, and it would especially help the Republican Party.

"Ethnic Conflict": Using a Convenient Method of Dividing Combatants to Extract Rents in a Power Struggle

One interpretation of the attacks of September 11, 2001 is that they were examples of collateral damage wreaked upon the West—collateral damage resulting from a war in Islam between the fundamentalists and moderates.[66] Another way of reading the attacks, however, is to recognize that throughout history and throughout much of the world, differences in religion, race, ethnicity, geography, etc. have always been used as a convenient method of dividing combatants in a struggle to extract rents—and violence in general, and revolution and war in particular, are just the most extreme ways of extracting rents. Thus, under the heading of tolerance, we see the necessity of not only tolerance, but all the other liberal values of checks and balances, equality, peace and the rule of law—and respect for knowledge, lest society slip back into intolerance due to the teaching of illiberalism, thereby undermining peaceful coexistence.

At the time that William Julius Wilson wrote *Power, Racism and Privilege*, there was a debate regarding whether ethnic conflict, consisting of, e.g., Jim Crow America and apartheid South Africa, simply arose due to a desire for people to exist with their own race and culture ("cultural pluralism") or whether there was an overarching economic component to these conflicts, involving economic exploitation of labor based on a convenient method of dividing the population, such as race, religion or ethnicity, as Wilson alleged.

Similarly, the *Harvard International Review* in 2007 contained a special section as part of its series "Reversing the Trend," titled "Toward Coexistence: Making Sense of Ethnic Conflict."[67] In a series of five articles, all the authors questioned the idea that purely ethnic factors motivate ethnic conflicts. Charles King, Chairman of the Faculty at the School of Foreign Service at Georgetown University, in his contribution "Scots to Chechens: How 'Ethnic' is Ethnic Conflict?"[68] questioned the very concept of "ethnic conflict'"—observing that, during the 1960s, when there actually was a much greater incidence of "ethnic conflict" after the collapse of colonialism than in the 1990s after the end of the Cold War, many of the postcolonial wars in Africa at that time might have been labelled "ethnic conflicts."[69]

What we now know from our study of them is that "ethnic conflicts" are, in reality, battles to control resources over which an identifiable group wants to extract rents, and liberal values are necessary to defeat these impulses and enable peaceful coexistence.

The Potential to Overcome, via Institutionalized Tolerance, the Temptation to Violate Rule of Law

In his May 2000 research paper for the World Bank, "Can Institutions Resolve Ethnic Conflict?,"[70] William Easterly surveyed the literature regarding the effects of heterogeneity (ethnolinguistic, racial, religious and ethnic) on a variety of characteristics and found that a high level of ethnic diversity results in:

1. Reduced income and growth, explaining Africa's poor growth;[71]
2. Less spending on public goods in ethnically diverse cities and counties in the U.S.;[72]
3. Lower public support for higher education in states with more religious-ethnic heterogeneity;[73]
4. Lower high school graduation rates in states with higher religious-ethnic diversity;[74]
5. Lower primary school funding in more ethnically diverse districts in Kenya;[75]
6. Poor quality of government services;[76]
7. Greater political instability, which, in turn, leads to higher government consumption;[77]
8. Bloated government payrolls;[78]
9. More adverse reaction to external terms of trade shocks;[79]
10. Diversion of foreign aid proceeds into corruption;[80]
11. Lower trust;[81]

12. Lower participation in social clubs;[82] and
13. Hampered early stages of nation-building and growth.[83]

A study by World Bank economists Philip Keefer and Stephen Knack similarly concluded that "social polarization" in the form of income inequality, land inequality and ethnic tensions reduces the security of property rights and contract rights and, accordingly, reduces economic growth.[84]

PEACE AND NONVIOLENT RESISTANCE

As observed previously, there has long been, and remains, a clash of the classical liberal democratic vision, stressing peace, versus the illiberal vision, which embraces the Orwellian concept of perpetual war for peace and elevates the romantic ideal of war for its opportunities for individual heroism and national greatness through empire-building.

Joshua S. Goldstein, professor emeritus of international relations at American University and author of *Winning the War on War: The Decline of Armed Conflict Worldwide,* combined with Steve Pinker, a psychology professor at Harvard University and author of *The Better Angels of Our Nature: Why Violence Has Declined*, in their 2011 essay, "War Really Is Going Out of Style,"[85] to trace the decline of the annual rate of battle deaths worldwide per 100,000 population from almost 300 during World War II, to almost 30 during the Korean War, to low teens during the Vietnam War, to single digits in the late 1970s and 1980s, to fewer than one in the 21st century. Among the reasons for decline of war—both conflicts that involve at least 1,000 battle deaths a year (their definition of "war") and those conflicts involving fewer than that—are that war no longer pays in the sense of territory gained, the international community has moved aggressively to prevent war, and there is a growing repugnance in the world toward institutionalized violence. Further warning against future engagement in war came from former Defense Secretary Robert Gates in 2011 when he reflected on the uncertainty of ultimate outcome after military engagement with a large American land army in places like Iraq and Afghanistan.[86]

Similarly, Erica Chenoweth, Assistant Professor of Government at Wesleyan University and director of Wesleyan's Program on Terrorism and Insurgency Research, based on the results of her study of 323 nonviolent and violent insurgency campaigns from 1900-2006, concluded that the success rate for nonviolent campaigns was much greater than for violent campaigns, and the advantage in favor of nonviolent campaigns has held since 1960, and has been strongest since 2000.[87] Additionally, she found the probability of being a democracy five years after the conflict has ended is 4 percent after violent campaigns versus 41 percent after nonviolent; and the probability of experiencing a civil war with ten years of the end of the conflict is 43 percent after violent campaigns versus 28 percent after nonviolent campaigns. And, the presence of a radical flank in nonviolent campaigns was found to suppress campaign membership. The conservative commentator George Will summarized the too-seldom acknowledged admirable record of the nations of the world, observing that the risk of dying from state-sponsored violence is lower now than at any time since the 1920s.[88]

Thus, the lessons of nonviolent resistance taught by Mahatma Gandhi, Martin Luther King, Jr. and Nelson Mandela are not only consistent with classical liberal theory but also have increasing relevance for today.

RULE OF LAW

The discussion of the definition of the rule of law and differences between liberal and conservative understandings of it, addressed previously, will not be repeated herein. Instead, this section will concentrate on the observable impacts that disregard of the rule of law has on those societies that fail to operate in accordance with it. First, however, the notion held by some libertarians that the necessity of the law can be ignored, it should be observed, was addressed by James Madison in *Federalist* No. 51: "If men were angels, no government would be necessary." Presumably, libertarians would not care to argue the other side.

Disregard of the Rule of Law: Linking Corruption with Political Instability and Low Economic Growth

International Monetary Fund economist Vito Tanzi listed particular government activities that provide opportunities for corruption: regulations, licensing and permitting, taxation, government spending decisions, providing goods and services at below market rates, bureaucracy, other discretionary decisions (e.g., zoning, privatization, government investment), and he listed negative effects of corruption gleaned from previous studies[89]:

1. Reducing investment, and, consequently, rate of growth;[90]
2. Reducing expenditures for education and health because such expenditures are less easily manipulated by public officials to extract bribes;[91]
3. Increasing public investment because public investment projects can be easily manipulated by public officials to extract bribes;[92]
4. Reducing operation and maintenance expenditures because such expenditures are less easily manipulated by public officials to extract bribes;[93]
5. Reducing productivity of public investment and of a country's infrastructure;[94]

6. Reducing tax revenue because corruption results in uneven tax administration and levy of tax customs, thereby reducing ability of government to make needed expenditures;[95] and

7. Reducing foreign direct investment because corruption has the same effect as a tax and operates like a tax.[96]

Tanzi concluded his paper with four recommendations for reducing corruption. Observing that the fight against corruption cannot succeed without reform of the state, he recommended official commitment by leadership to address it, reduction in regulations and increase in transparency, raising public sector wages and prosecuting corruption, and addressing financing of political parties (presumably through public financing).

The Incompatibility of the Rule of Law and Illiberal Islamism

Because the rule of law compels the separation of church and state, numerous commentators from the West[97] have observed that the Middle East and North Africa would benefit from a version of the Peace of Westphalia that ended the Thirty Years' War that raged in Europe from 1616 to 1648. The Peace of Westphalia finally established the law of the state as superior to the law of religion. The Thirty Years War consisted of numerous conflicts that revolved around, ultimately, religious-based conflict between Catholic and Protestant.

The Middle East and North Africa are currently the location of numerous conflicts that revolve around religion. History provides, in the Peace of Westphalia, the model for how the West resolved its religious conflicts: ensuring that government is always superior to religion. This, combined with the Western liberal value of tolerance—so that government is superior to ethnicity—has served the West well (notwithstanding that the West could do better).

In an outstanding essay, Muhamad Mugraby, former lecturer in legal philosophy, civil liberties and private international law at the Lebanese University Law School, and a lawyer practicing in Beirut, addressed impediments to the operation of the rule of law in the Middle East and elsewhere—impediments due to the failure of these nations to ever establish the supremacy of the rule of law of the state to the rule of religious law.[98] Mugraby observed at the outset that the Universal Declaration of Human Rights decrees in the Preamble that human rights shall be protected by the rule of law[99] and, in Article 7 provides for equal protection of the law.[100]

However, he observed that the rule of law and liberal democracy have never been fully recognized in an area from Morocco to Bangladesh.[101] In this area, religion is sovereign over the state.[102] This conflict over sovereignty leads to two results, both of which are impediments to development:

1. There is no sense of or accountability to the nation[103] and
2. Because the rights of citizens are based on status as determined by religion, "Equality under the law or equal protection of the law is impossible."[104]

Mugraby next presented numerous examples of these two phenomena in nations of the region; below is an illustrative partial list:

1. In one nation (unnamed), a fellow legal practitioner was looking for the legal authority for the concept that in an intestate succession (one in which the deceased died without a will) the daughter receives one-half the inheritance of a son, and he found no authority other than a verse in the Koran.
2. In Lebanon, "internal law recognizes nineteen self-administered, independent religious communities, with the power to apply their own personal and family law and to run their own courts outside the framework of the national judiciary."[105]
3. Islamic law of inheritance is applied throughout the region, but Islamic Sunni rules apply only to Sunnis, Islamic Shiite rules to Shiites, and Jews are subject to their own inheritance laws. Additionally, family law, including matters of marriage, divorce, and child custody, is mostly religious law, thus making "[m]arriages outside the faith a risky adventure that could end in disaster."[106]
4. Similarly, even in "secular India," there are "at least a dozen federal statutes that apply to marriage and divorce . . . apply[ing] separately to Muslims, Hindus, Christians, Jews, Parsi, Kazis, foreigners and others. The Hindu Marriage Act is a codification that also applies to Buddhists but not to Muslims, Christians, or Jews, where religious law continues to be recognized."[107]

Concluded Mugraby, separation of church and state will make possible rule of law and equal protection of the laws, enabling peaceful coexistence—critically, too, he concluded that "the achievements of the West should not be recognized as Christian in character, but universal in nature."[108]

Mugraby's observations also hold a lesson regarding the concept of dhimmitude—the application of a separate set of laws to non-Muslims in Muslim-majority countries. Dhimmitude, and the systems cited by Mugraby, render application, to these lands, of the rule of law impossible because rule of law is accorded to the *individual*—whereas, under Islamic law, it is accorded to the individual as a member of a certain *class*. Thus, as in the West, so in Islamic countries, the law of the state must be supreme to religious edict, and the law must apply equally to everyone.

The Rule of Law and Women

Another problem for the application of rule of law to the lands addressed by Mugraby, one which for its immensity can only be touched on here, is the law's treatment of women. Such was expressly recognized in the United Nations Development Programme *Arab Human Development Report 2002* and elaborated upon in the United Nations Development Programme *Arab Human Development Report 2005: Towards the Rise of Women in the Arab World*. And, included in the concept of equal treatment of women is equal access to education, which is not only a stimulant of economic growth but also an effective anti-terrorism policy.[109] The rule of law, of necessity, requires equality under law for women.

CONCLUSION: LIBERAL VALUES ARE NECESSARY COMPLEMENTS TO CAPITALISM AND DEMOCRACY

Even a society with both capitalism and democracy will not succeed at providing prosperity without the addition of institutions to support the liberal values of checks and balances versus winner-take-all, commitment to knowledge versus ignorance, equality versus inequality, tolerance versus intolerance, the rule of law versus corruption and peace versus war. Of course, underlying all these values is the value of humility—to reiterate the lesson of Friedrich Hayek, "the liberal is very much aware that we do not know all the answers and that he is not sure that the answers he has are certainly the right ones or even that we can find all the answers."[110] And this idea, itself, is a reiteration of the concept from the Book of *Isaiah*, 55:8: "'For my thoughts are not your thoughts, neither are your ways my ways,' declares the LORD."

Conservatism, especially conservatism dominated by a trickle-down vision, displays blindness to all of these liberal values and concepts.

NOTES

1. Ian Buruma and Avishai Margalit, *Occidentalism: The West in the Eyes of Its Enemies* (New York: Penguin Books; 2004), p. 72.
2. Hillary Rodham Clinton, "Civil Society: The Space that Matters Most," *New Perspectives Quarterly* vol. 15 no. 2 (Spring 1998), pp. 12–14. The remarks here were adapted from a talk she gave at the Annual Meeting of the World Economic Forum at Davos, Switzerland February 2, 1998. She developed in detail a similar vision of society in her widely-misunderstood book *It Takes a Village*.
3. Karl Polanyi, *The Great Transformation: The Political and Economic Origins of Our Time*, Boston: Beacon Press (1944, 1957, 2001), p. 140.
4. Karl Polanyi, *The Great Transformation: The Political and Economic Origins of Our Time*, Boston: Beacon Press (1944, 1957, 2001), p. 133.
5. Jeffrey D. Sachs and Andrew M. Warner, Natural Resource Abundance and Economic Growth," NBER Working Paper 5398, December 1993, p. 21.

6. Fareed Zakaria, *The Future of Freedom: Illiberal Democracy at Home and Abroad* (New York, London: W. W. Norton and Company, 2003), p. 74.
7. Nancy Birdsall and Arvind Subramanian, "Saving Iraq from Its Oil," *Foreign Affairs* July/August 2004, p. 77.
8. Fred Halliday, *The Middle East in International Relations* (Cambridge, UK: Cambridge University Press, 2005), pp. 276–277.
9. Nancy Birdsall and Arvind Subramanian, "Saving Iraq from Its Oil," *Foreign Affairs* July/August 2004, p. 81.
10. Ibid, pp. 88–89.
11. Carles Boix, "The Roots of Democracy," *Policy Review* February and March 2006, No. 135, p. 20.
12. Fareed Zakaria, "Rogue Offspring," *Newsweek*, December 18, 2006.
13. David Dollar and Aart Kraay, "Property Rights, Political Rights, and the Development of Poor Countries in the Post-colonial Period," Development Research Group, World Bank, October 2000.
14. Noreen Malone, "Megyn Kelly Can Save Fox News," *The New Republic*, November 9, 2012.
15. See Eugene Robinson, "President on Another Planet," *The Washington Post*, August 22, 2006. "Incurious" was also often applied to Donald Trump in the 2016 presidential race.
16. Ron Suskind, "Why Are These Men Laughing?," *Esquire*, January 2003, p. 98.
17. From the FoxNews.com website, "Transcript of Rush Limbaugh's Address at CPAC," March 1, 2009. The Preamble to Constitution provides: "We the People of the United States, in Order to form a more perfect Union, establish Justice, insure domestic Tranquility, provide for the common defence, promote the general Welfare, and secure the Blessings of Liberty to ourselves and our Posterity, do ordain and establish this Constitution for the United States of America."
18. For example: *Cultural Literacy: What Every American Needs to Know* (1987), *The Dictionary of Cultural Literacy* (1988), *The New Dictionary of Cultural Literacy: What Every American Needs to Know* (2002) and *The Knowledge Deficit: Closing the Shocking Education Gap for American Children* (2006) and especially *The Making of Americans: Democracy and Our Schools* (2009).
19. For example: *The Book of Virtues: A Treasury of Great Moral Stories* (1993) and *The Educated Child: A Parent's Guide from Preschool through the Eighth Grade* (1999).
20. The letter was dated June 15, 2014, and authored by Bob Reid, spokesman for and member of the Board of Directors, TEA Party of Louisiana, LLC, teapartyoflouisiana.net.
21. See especially Sean Wilentz, "Confounding Fathers: The Tea Party's Cold War Roots," *The New Yorker*, October 18, 2010.
22. Andrew C. Revkin, "Bush vs. the Laureates: How Science Became a Partisan Issue," *The New York Times* Tuesday, October 19, 2004.
23. Garry Wills, "The Day the Enlightenment Went Out," *The New York Times*, November 4, 2004.
24. Gardiner Harris, "Surgeon General Sees 4-Year Term as Compromised," *The New York Times*, July 11, 2007.
25. Dana Milbank, "Republicans Embrace Their Phoniness," *The Washington Post*, August 13, 2014. For details, see Shane Goldmacher, "NRCC Launches Fake News Sites to Attack Democratic Candidates," *The National Journal*, August 12, 2014.
26. Former Vice President Dick Cheney, in an interview with C-Span, April 15, 1994.
27. Former Vice President Dick Cheney, to the Veterans of Foreign Wars Convention, Nashville, TN, August 26, 2002, quoted in Linda D. Kozaryn, "Cheney Says Grave Threats Require Pre-Emptive Action," American Foreign Press Service, US Department of Defense, August 26, 2002.
28. Ibid.
29. See, for example, *CBS News Face the Nation*, November 9, 2014, interview between Bob Schieffer and former President George W. Bush.
30. This glib explanation that 9/11 changed everything fits with the message critical of the Iraq War delivered by Michael Moore in his movie, *Fahrenheit 9/11*, the title of which took

inspiration from science fiction writer Ray Bradbury's book *Fahrenheit 451*. In the future society in which *Fahrenheit 451* is set, facts provided by the in-depth analysis of books is no longer relevant, as in the society of September 11, 2001, when heat of the moment rendered in-depth analysis of facts no longer relevant. The title of Bradbury's book referred to the temperature at which paper burns (actually around 450° C; around 840° F), as the citizens in his story begin to burn books as useless.

31. Among them, Andrew Bacevich, in his interview with Bill Moyers on *Moyers & Company*, June 20,2014, and see Andrew Bacevich, "The Duplicity of the Ideologues," *Commonweal*, June 4, 2014.

32. "United Nations Weapons Inspectors Report to Security Council on Progress in Disarmament of Iraq," Press Release SC/7682, July 3, 2003.

33. Ron Suskind, *The One Percent Doctrine* (New York: Simon & Schuster; 2006), see especially pp. 62 and 149–150.

34. Barton Gellman and Walter Pincus, "Depiction of Threat Outgrew Supporting Evidence," *The Washington Post*, August 10, 2003; A1.

35. See especially Scott McClellan, *What Happened: Inside the Bush White House and Washington's Culture of Deception* (New York: Public Affairs, 2008), pp. 131, 132 and 135.

36. Elizabeth Bumiller, "Traces of Terror: The Strategy; Bush Aides Set Strategy to Sell Policy on Iraq," *The New York Times*, September 7, 2002.

37. Bob Woodward, *Plan of Attack* (New York: Simon & Schuster; 2004), p. 249.

38. "George Tenet: At the Center of the Storm," CBS News *60 Minutes* interview with Scott Pelley, April 29, 2007.

39. Ron Suskind, *The One Percent Doctrine* (New York: Simon & Schuster; 2006), p. 188.

40. See Walter Pincus, "Memo: U.S. Lacked Full Postwar Iraq Plan," *The Washington Post*, June 12, 2005 and Jefferson Morley, "The Downing Street Memo Story Won't Die," washingtonpost.com., June 7, 2005.

41. See also Robert Dreyfuss and Jason Vest, "The Lie Factory," *Mother Jones*, January/February 2004.

42. Robin Wright, "From the Desk of Donald Rumsfeld," *The Washington Post*, November 1, 2007.

43. In November 2007 Karl Rove told interviewer Charlie Rose that Congress had pushed the administration into the war in Iraq, against the opposition of the administration. That assertion was contradicted by the White House chief of staff at the time, Andrew Card, in an interview with Joe Scarborough on MSNBC's "Morning Joe" on November 30, 2007. The assertion is also contradicted by several press briefings on the subject in September 2002 (all available at the White House website). See, for example, "President Bush Discusses Iraq with Reporters," September 13, 2002, wherein President Bush concludes a press conference with: "My answer to Congress is, they need to debate this issue and consult with us, and get the issue done as quickly as possible." That was followed by more statements of urgency in "President Discusses Iraq, Domestic Agenda with Congressional Leaders," (September 18, 2002); "President Bush to Send Iraq Resolution to Congress Today" (September 19, 2002) and, finally, "President Urges Congress to Pass Iraq Resolution Promptly" (September 24, 2002).

44. Carrie Dan, "Not Worth It: Huge Majority Regret Iraq War, Exclusive Poll Shows," NBCNews.com., June 24, 2014.

45. The interview was with Joe Scarborough on MSNBC's *Morning Joe*, June 4, 2015.

46. See George W. Bush White House Archives, "President Bush and Iraq Prime Minister Maliki Sign the Strategic Framework Agreement and Security Agreement," December 14, 2008. President Obama would later attempt to negotiate a second status of forces agreement with Iraqi President Jalal Talibani, but that agreement was never finalized due to failure of Iraq to agree to legal immunity for any American troops.

47. See, for example, the opinion piece by Alex Kingsbury, senior associate producer for WBUR's "Radio Boston," who reported from Iraq for *US News and World Report* in 2007 and 2008: "Why the 2007 Surge in Iraq Actually Failed," *The Boston Globe*, November 17, 2014. See also Peter Beinart, "The Surge Fallacy," *The Atlantic*, September 2015. Beinart argues that Republicans, having misunderstood the Iraq War, are taking a dangerously hawkish turn on foreign policy in 2016 election campaigning.

48. President's Radio Address from Crawford, Texas, The White House of George W. Bush, August 13, 2005.

49. Maureen Dowd, "Neocons Slither Back," *The New York Times*, September 16, 2012. Peter Baker and Robin Wright, "A Blow to Bush's Tehran Policy," *The Washington Post*, December 4, 2007.

50. Benjy Sarlin, "Oops: Jeb Bush Accidentally Says He's 'Running for President,'" MSNBC.com, May 13, 2015. See also Nicholas Confessore and Eric Lichtblau, "'16 Campaigns, Official or Not, Are Remade by 'Super PACs'," *The New York Times*, May 18, 2015.

51. See Jon Basil Utley, "The New Lie About Iraq," *The American Conservative*, May 19, 2015, and Ahmed Alimay, "Calm Down. ISIS Isn't Winning." *The New York Times*, May 22, 2015.

52. See Kevin Phillips, *The Emerging Republican Majority* (Princeton and Oxford: The James Madison Library in American Politics, Princeton University Press; 1969, 1970 and 2015). In this later paperback edition appears a new preface by the author and a General Editor's Introduction by Princeton University historian Sean Wilentz. See especially Map 47 therein and the accompanying discussion, pp. 554–556.

53. William Easterly, *The Elusive Quest for Growth: Economists' Adventures and Misadventures in the Tropics* (Cambridge, Massachusetts: MIT Press; 2002), p. 275. See also Chapter 10 and William Easterly and Ross Levine, "Africa's Growth Tragedy: Policies and Ethnic Divisions," *Quarterly Journal of Economics*, Vol. CXII, Issue 4, November 1997, 1203–1250, p. 1241.

54. See Christopher Ingraham, "The Most Racist Places in America, According to Google," Wonkblog, *The Washington Post*, April 28, 2015.

55. William Julius Wilson, *Power, Racism, and Privilege: Race Relations in Theoretical and Sociohistorical Perspectives,* (The Free Press, A Division of Macmillan Publishing Co., Inc., New York, 1973), page 31.

56. Daniel Patrick Moynihan, *Pandaemonium: Ethnicity in International Politics* (Oxford: Oxford University Press, 1993), p. 53. As Daniel Patrick Moynihan predicted that ethnic diversity would doom the former Soviet Union, the potential for ethnic strife to doom the jihadist movement exists, too. The enmity that drives the civil war raging in the Middle East was addressed in an insightful article, "Why They Hate Each Other: Behind the Sunni-Shi'ite Divide," by Bobby Ghosh, *Time,* March 5, 2007 (pp. 28–40).

57. Ibid, p. 62. Moynihan devoted an entire chapter to "self-determination of peoples."

58. Daniel Patrick Moynihan, *Pandaemonium: Ethnicity in International Politics* (Oxford: Oxford University Press, 1993), p. 22. See also page 32.

59. The event is recounted in Daniel Patrick Moynihan's *Pandaemonium: Ethnicity in International Politics* (Oxford: Oxford University Press, 1993).

60. Daniel Patrick Moynihan's *Pandaemonium: Ethnicity in International Politics* (Oxford: Oxford University Press, 1993), p. 129.

61. Daniel Patrick Moynihan's *Pandaemonium: Ethnicity in International Politics* (Oxford: Oxford University Press, 1993), p. 131. See similar observations in Fareed Zakaria, "We Are Not Losing the War Against Radical Islam," *Newsweek*, July 2, 2007.

62. Quoted in Theodore J. Lowi, *The End of the Republican Era* (Norman, OK and London: University of Oklahoma Press, 1995, 1996) p. 211. Citing Patrick Buchanan, "The Election Is About Who We Are—Taking Back Our Country," delivered at the Republican National Convention, Houston, Texas, 17 August 1992, reprinted in *Vital Speeches of the Day,* 15 September 1992, pp. 712–715.

63. See Robert H. Nelson, *Economics as Religion: From Samuelson to Chicago and Beyond*, University Park, PA: The Pennsylvania State University Press, 2001, footnote, p. 264. Citing Garry Wills, "The Born-Again Republicans," *New York Review of Books*, September 24, 1992, p. 14. See also Garry Wills, *Under God: Religion and American Politics* (New York: Simon and Schuster, 1990).

64. Jonathan Martin and Jackie Calmes, "Republicans Try to Fix Damage Scalise's 2002 Speech Could Do in 2016," *The New York Times*, December 31, 2014.

65. Jarvis DeBerry, "Steve Scalise Should Have Had Sense Not to Speak to Group of White Nationalists," *The Times-Picayune*, December 31, 2014.

66. This was the interpretation of religious scholar Reza Aslan in *No god but God: The Origins, Evolution, and Future of Islam* (2005). See Max Rodenbeck, "'No god but God': The War Within Islam," *The New York Times*, May 29, 2005.
67. "Toward Coexistence: Making Sense of Ethnic Conflict," *Harvard International Review*, Winter 2007, vol. XXXVIII, No, 4.
68. Charles King, "Scots to Chechens: How 'Ethnic' is Ethnic Conflict?" *Harvard International Review*, Winter 2007, vol. XXXVIII, No, 4., pp. 68–72.
69. Ibid, p. 69.
70. William Easterly, "Can Institutions Resolve Ethnic Conflict?" World Bank Working Paper No. 2482 (November 2000).
71. William Easterly and Ross Levine, "Africa's Growth Tragedy: Policies and Ethnic Divisions, November 1997, *Quarterly Journal of Economics*. CXII (4), p. 1203–1250.
72. Alberto Alesina, Reza Baqir, and William Easterly, "Public Goods and Ethnic Divisions," *Quarterly Journal of Economics*, November 1995.
73. Claudia Goldin and Lawrence Katz, "The Shaping of Higher Education: The Formative Years in the United States 1890 to 1940," *Journal of Economic Perspectives*, Winter 1999, Volume 13, No. 1, pp. 37–62.
74. Goldin and Lawrence Katz, "Why the United States Led in Education: Lessons from Secondary School Expansion, 1910 to 1940," NBER Working Paper 6144, August 1997.
75. Ted Miguel, "Ethnic Diversity and School Funding in Kenya, Mimeo, Harvard University, November 1999.
76. Paulo Mauro, "Corruption and Growth," *Quarterly Journal of Economics*, CX (1995), pp. 681–712; Rafael La Porta, Florencio Lopez-de-Silanes, Andrei Shleifer and Robert Vishny, "The Quality of Government," National Bureau of Economic Research Working Paper Series 6727, September 1998.
77. Mauro, 1995, Ibid; Anthony Annett, "Ethnic and Religious Division, Political Instability and Government Consumption," IMF Mimeo, March 1999.
78. Alberto Alesina, Reza Baqir, and William Easterly, "Redistributive Government Employment," *Journal of Urban Economics*, 1999.
79. Dani Rodrik, "Where Did All the Growth Go? External Shocks, Social Conflict and Growth Collapses," *Journal of Economic Growth*, Volume 4, Issue 4, December 1999, pp. 385–412.
80. Jakob Svensson, "Foreign Aid and Rent-seeking," World Bank, Development Economics Research Group, Policy Research Working Paper 1880 (1998).
81. Alberto Alesina and Eliana La Ferrara, "The Determinants of Trust," NBER Working Paper No. W7621 (March 2000); Paul Zak and Stephen Knack, "Trust and Government," World Bank mimeo, 1999.
82. Alberto Alesina and Eliana La Ferrara, "Participation in Heterogeneous Communities," NBER Working Paper 7155, June 1999.
83. Irma Adelman and Cynthia Taft Morris, *Society, Politics and Economic Development: A Quantitative Approach* (Baltimore: Johns Hopkins Press, 1967).
84. Philip Keefer and Stephen Knack, "Polarization, Politics and Property Rights: Links between Inequality and Growth," *Public Choice*, World Bank Policy Research Working Paper 2418 (August 2000).
85. Joshua S. Goldstein and Steven Pinker, "War Really Is Going Out of Style," *The New York Times*, December 17, 2011.
86. Thom Shanker, "Warning Against Wars Like Iraq and Afghanistan," *The New York Times*, February 25, 2011, published February 26, 2011.
87. Erica Chenoweth, "The Myth of the Radical Insurgent," presented at the International Studies Association Annual Meeting, San Diego, CA, April 1–4, 2012.
88. George Will on ABC News' *This Week with George Stephanopoulos*, September 16, 2012.
89. Vito Tanzi, "Corruption Around the World: Causes, Consequences, Scope and Cures," May 1998, International Monetary Fund Fiscal Affairs Department, p. 29.
90. Paolo Mauro, "Corruption and Growth," *The Quarterly Journal of Economics*, vol. CX, issue 3, August 1995, pp. 691–712.

91. Paolo Mauro, "The Effects of Corruption on Growth, Investment and Government Expenditure: A Cross-Country Analysis," in Kimberly Ann Elliott, editor, *Corruption in the Global Economy* (Washington: Institute for International Economics, 1997).
92. Vito Tanzi and Hamid Davoodi, "Corruption, Public Investment, and Growth," IMF Working Paper 97/139 (Washington: International Monetary Fund, 1997).
93. Tanzi and Davoodi, Ibid.
94. Tanzi and Davoodi, Ibid.
95. Tanzi and Davoodi, Ibid.
96. Shang-Jin Wei, "How Taxing Is Corruption on International Investors?" (*Working Paper 6030*, NBER, May 1997).
97. For example, see David Brooks, "After the Fall," *The New York Times*, December 10, 2006. His observations were prescient—see Emma Sky, "'Iraq Is Finished'," *The Atlantic*, April 8, 2015. See also, David Brooks, "No War Is an Island," *The New York Times*, July 29, 2014. Other examples: Andrew Sullivan, "The Thirty Years' War Brewing in the Middle East," *The Sunday Times*, December 17, 2006 and Richard Haass, "The New Thirty Years' War," *Project Syndicate*, July 21, 2014. This continued a theme that Haass struck both in an interview on *Meet the Press* (December 10, 2006) and in a December 10, 2006 article for *Time* magazine ("Avoiding Iraq Syndrome"), wherein he presciently foresaw the future of Iraq as dystopian due to continuing religious conflict.
98. Muhamad Mugraby, "Some Impediments to the Rule of Law in the Middle East and Beyond," 26 *Fordham Int'l L. J.* 771, March 2003.
99. Ibid, p. 771.
100. Ibid, pp. 771 and 772.
101. Ibid, 772, 773.
102. Ibid, p. 775, quoting Bernard Lewis, *What Went Wrong* (2003), p. 113.
103. Ibid, p. 781.
104. Ibid, p. 777.
105. Ibid, p. 775.
106. Ibid, pp. 777–778.
107. Ibid, p. 780.
108. Ibid, p. 784.
109. Nicholas Kristof, "Smart Girls vs. Bombs," *The New York Times*, April 12, 2015.
110. The essay from which this quote appeared, "Why I am Not a Conservative," appeared as the Postscript to his classic *The Constitution of Liberty.* Friedrich Hayek, *The Constitution of Liberty* (Chicago: The University of Chicago Press; 1960), p. 406. Again, similar sentiments were expressed by Paul Krugman in "Ideology and Integrity," *The New York Times*, May 1, 2015.

Chapter Thirteen

Trickle-Up

A Bottom-Up, Post-Bubble Economic Growth Model Based on Growing the Middle Class

THE TRICKLE-UP—LIBERAL—VISION: TO HELP THE MIDDLE CLASS AND POOR, HELP THE MIDDLE CLASS AND POOR

In contrast to the conservative trickle-down vision, which posits that to help the middle class and poor you must help the rich, the liberal trickle-up vision[1] provides that *to help the middle class and poor, help the middle class and poor*. And, the trickle-up message to businesses is: *If you want a future for your business, give a present to your workers—share with them the revenues attributable to increased productivity.* This is not a new idea—an especially good statement of it was expressed by the mid-19th century American social philosopher Orestes A. Brownson[2]:

> The men of wealth, the business men, manufacturers and merchants, bankers and brokers, are the men who exert the worst influence on government in every country, for always they strive to use it as an instrument of advancing their own private interests. They act on the beautiful maxim, "Let government take care of the rich, and the rich will take care of the poor," instead of the far safer maxim, "Let government take care of the weak, the strong can take care of themselves."

The late 19th century social philosopher William Jennings Bryan, former Representative (D-NE), in his famous "Cross of Gold" Speech, July 9, 1896, at the Democratic National Convention in Chicago expressed similar sentiments:

> There are two ideas of government. There are those who believe that if you just legislate to make the well-to-do prosperous, that their prosperity will leak through on those below. The Democratic idea has been that if you legislate to make the masses prosperous their prosperity will find its way up and through every class that rests upon it.

And in the 20th century, former Senator John Breaux (D-LA) put similar observations in the context of the American political party system[3]:

> The Democratic party best represents the ideas and goals of middle-class working people: people who need the help and assistance of government. The Republicans believe in a trickle-down formula, where the very wealthy do well. I don't think that works. If working-class people do well and succeed, they buy goods and services. So I think a "trickle-up" theory works better than trickle-down. I grew up as a traditional Democrat, and I've felt more comfortable about that as I've been exposed to the philosophy of the Republican party.

As observed in Chapter 2, on the campaign trail in early 2008 then-Senator Obama framed the problem for the next president as figuring out how to create bottom-up economic growth in lieu of trickle-down growth of the Republicans. After his election, as President Obama he addressed the Economic Recovery Advisory Board in November 2009 and charged them with developing a "post-bubble growth model, one that is sustainable."[4]

To implement this trickle-up vision, a good guide was given by Harvard sociologist William Julius Wilson in *The Truly Disadvantaged*—who deemed such an approach as one with an (albeit admirable) "hidden agenda": "*[T]he hidden agenda for liberal policymakers is to improve the life chances of truly disadvantaged groups such as the ghetto underclass by emphasizing programs to which the more advantaged groups of all races and class backgrounds can positively relate* [italics original]."[5]

Inspired by his vision of a bottom-up, post bubble growth model—President Obama pushed for and signed the Affordable Care Act, pushed through the auto industry bailout, pushed through a stimulus bill that cut taxes for 95 percent of Americans and provided funding for needed infrastructure improvements, cut in half the loan rates on federal student loans so as to make a college education more affordable, secured authorization for the federal government to negotiate directly with drug companies to lower prescription drug costs under the Medicare health insurance program for senior citizens and the disabled, pushed through the Dodd-Frank financial regulations providing for a consumer financial protection agency and extending needed resolution authority over financial entities, ended the war in Iraq on President Bush's timetable, eliminated Osama bin Laden and other al Qaeda leaders, and began withdrawal from Iraq and Afghanistan.

PRELIMINARY THOUGHTS ON LIBERALISM AND TRICKLE-UP

What Liberalism and Trickle-Up Are *Not*

Before proceeding, it is appropriate to distinguish the liberalism urged herein from what it is *not*. It is not liberalism catering to its special interest bases, or liberalism opposed to economic growth, or liberalism shackled with socialist and welfare-statist leanings—as liberalism was 75 years ago, and as will be confronted below.

Prominent liberals at the time of the Great Depression had an affinity for socialism—for a system in which ownership of the means of production was vested not in private hands but in the state. The liberal philosopher John Dewey in his 1935 classic, *Liberalism and Social Action* declared that liberalism must go forward and socialize the means of production.[6] A similar affinity for socialism was expressed by Stuart Chase in his 1932 book, *A New Deal*, which famously ends with the rhetorical question of why should the Russians have all the fun remaking the world.[7] This was no aberration. Earlier in his book Chase observed that the potential changes necessary to control the economy must include collectivism and may require temporary dictatorship.[8] Regardless, Franklin Roosevelt closed his nominating speech before the 1932 Democratic National Convention in Chicago promising a "new deal," and the term came to be used to describe his program for getting the country out of the Great Depression.[9] He would go on to appoint Chase Secretary of the Treasury.

There are numerous other examples of socialism and communism having been supported by American liberals in the twentieth century. Eugene V. Debs was a Socialist Party of America candidate for President of the United States in five elections, and he received the support of many liberals in campaigns. Sidney Hook in his youth was a supporter of Debs, and, after graduating with his Ph.D. from Columbia University, where he studied under John Dewey, he became an enthusiastic Marxist and supporter of the Soviet Union, and in 1932 supported for president Communist Party candidate William Z. Foster. Hook broke with communism and in 1947 authored in the *Partisan Review* an essay titled "The Future of Socialism," wherein he warned against 1948 Progressive Party presidential candidate Henry Wallace, who had condemned Truman's firm stand against the Soviet Union.[10] The Alger Hiss case revealed that the Soviet Union had the support of at least some successful liberals in America, and Whittaker Chambers' autobiography (*Witness*) detailing his role in exposing Hiss was criticized in many liberal circles.

And, as observed in the Introduction, the inexactitude in terminology used by Vermont Senator and 2016 candidate for the Democratic presidential nomination, Bernie Sanders, is rejected. By calling himself a socialist, or even a democratic socialist or social democrat—all meaning, more properly, a supporter of the Nordic Model of capitalism with a strong social safety net supported by progressive taxation—Senator Sanders and those liberals who engage in similar inexactitude in terminology give ammunition to Republicans who claim the dream of the Democratic Party is to destroy capitalism and socialize the means of production using *The Communist Manifesto* as a guide.

Liberalism: The Philosophy of Economic Growth

Daniel Bell in his classic *The Cultural Contradictions of Capitalism*, (originally published in 1976; re-issued in 1996) observed that American liberalism's economic philosophy was dependent on economic growth,[11] and liberalism's answer to poverty was that growth would provide jobs and raise the incomes of the poor,[12] and the increasing tax receipts from growth would finance public services and a generous social safety net.[13] In the same paragraph, Bell delivered an early critique of the anti-growth attitude of the New Left (what he called "the new politics") which he recounted as promoting "zero economic growth" in contrast to the pro-growth policies of Keynesianism and macroeconomic planning and as attacking affluence as a worthy goal because it spoils the environment and leads to overcrowding in cities.[14] The Keynesian revolution was adopted by liberals and not only were earlier liberals pro-growth—they favored higher growth rates than did their overly cautious conservative contemporaries in the late 1940s and 1950s, the latter being more concerned about price stability—among those liberals in that era who demanded greater economic growth from the steel industry than did their timid conservative peers were Walter Reuther, Leon Keyserling, and others who urged the government to set target growth figures.[15] The imperative of growth became so ingrained that its origin as a liberal innovation was forgotten.[16]

For Bell, indeed for liberals generally,[17] programs providing for full employment, minimum wages, education and healthcare are essential for a functioning society because they support the dignity of a person and his or her self-esteem. By doing so, they thereby enable the equal political participation of citizens. That equal participation is the basis upon which a self-governing society depends.

All Honest Work Is Honorable

Liberals have also on occasion expressed the attitude that certain occupations in themselves are denigrating. In his chapter entitled "Why, Among the Americans, All Honest Professions Are Considered Honorable," Tocqueville observed[18]:

> American servants do not believe themselves degraded because they work; for around them everyone works. They do not feel debased for the idea that they receive a salary; for the President of the United States also works for a salary. He is paid to command, just as they are paid to serve.
>
> In the United States, professions are more or less difficult, more or less lucrative; but they are never noble or base. Every honest profession is honorable.

The Reverend Dr. Martin Luther King, Jr. similarly often championed honorable work, regardless of the status of the profession.[19] Harvard anthropologist Katherine Newman picked up this theme and addressed it in book form in *No Shame in My Game* (2000).[20] Liberalism demands the admiration of all honest work, inspired by Tocqueville, King and Newman.

But, Must We Call Ourselves "Liberals"?

The term "liberal" has been used herein consciously, as opposed to the term "progressive," which many liberals prefer. Progressivism began as a pragmatic approach to bettering people's lives by using government to alleviate Gilded Age abuses of big business: low pay, long hours, unsafe working conditions, use of child labor, and lack of job security for workers; a cozy crony capitalist relationship between business and government; and massive inequality.

Progressivism arose as a repudiation of classical liberalism, which, at that time (as perhaps is the case again), was interpreted as standing for free markets and the use of the Constitution to strike down most attempts at government regulation. The inspiration for modern progressivism comes from the early progressives: William Jennings Bryan, Theodore Roosevelt, William Howard Taft, Woodrow Wilson and Robert LaFollette.

Although Progressives would later lead Franklin Roosevelt's reforms, prominent Progressives also allied with radicals and other proponents of socialism (such as Dewey and Chase, above) or near-fascism (such as Louisiana Governor Huey Long). Progressivism today is less an ideology than a return to a pragmatic attitude towards governing that looks for ways to use government to improve quality of life generally, but blends liberalism's concerns for individual rights.

Liberalism, by contrast, is an ideology. This work takes inspiration from the classical liberal heroes: Adam Smith, Alexis de Tocqueville, Thomas Jefferson, James Madison and others, as well as their later interpreters like Friedrich Hayek (especially in his earlier writings) and those who expanded on their ideas of society and economy such as Karl Polanyi and John Maynard Keynes. However, it dissents from the interpretation of classical liberalism that gave rise to the Progressives' revolt against it, taking a broader, more accurate, reading of classical liberalism's lessons as lessons for implementation of enlightened self-interest.

In their recommended policy prescriptions, though, modern progressives and liberals are so similar that the terms are appropriately used interchangeably. Nonetheless, key to understanding the present work is the truism that if you don't define your convictions, your opponents will define them for you—and you won't like it. Because liberals have been for the past quarter century (or more) running from the label "liberal" due to the success of conservatives in making liberal a term of derision (equating it with socialist, anti-American, mentally deranged, etc.), the term liberal has become a void into which conservatives can pour all sorts of nonsense. And, a liberal—not a progressive—is the ideological counterpart to a conservative.

Conservatism, in its extreme modern form of trickle-down conservatism, has abandoned the classical liberalism which conservatives claimed for their intellectual heritage. Simultaneously, modern liberals have abandoned their affinity for socialism and "welfare-statism" and are ready to pick up and defend the mantle of classical liberalism. Modern liberalism, at least in its American form, can now lay claim to being the modern heir to classical liberalism in a way unlike ever before.

It is past time to resurrect the proud term "liberal," and to recognize that, because trickle-down conservatism has forced conservatism to abandon classical liberalism, it is *only* modern liberals who defend that faith—especially the aspect of that faith embodied in the quote from Friedrich Hayek in Chapter 5: "The liberal is very much aware that we do not know all the answers and that he is not sure that the answers he has are certainly the right ones or even that we can find all the answers."[21]

At its most basic level, the policy prescription of this book is a commitment to checks and balances, respect for knowledge, tolerance, equality, peace and rule of law domestically and internationally. Liberalism seeks a high quality of life—a sense of dignity and self-worth—for everyone. It is, in that word so popularly used in distinguishing liberalism from conservatism, a "nuanced" approach to development—encouraging, by enhancement of the income- and wealth-spreading institutions that underlie the free market and democracy, growth in productivity, sharing of the revenues attributable to that increased productivity, and enhancement in quality of life from the bottom up.

Not Occupy Wall Street But Occupy Washington

Before proceeding to a trickle-up narrative, it is worthwhile to reflect on the disappointing progress made by the Occupy Wall Street Movement. Occupy Wall Street began as an effort by the Vancouver, Canada based anti-consumerist and pro-environmental Adbusters Media Foundation with one simple demand: "[W]e demand that Barack Obama ordain a Presidential Commission tasked with ending the influence money has over our representatives in Washington." Their statement continued: "Beginning from one simple demand—a presidential commission to separate money from politics—we start setting the agenda for a new America."[22]

The attractiveness of focusing on Wall Street is, obviously, that it is a physical place that is also a symbol of capital, capitalism and consumerism, and it is also the source of millions of dollars injected into politics. And, as a place, it provided a template for other "Occupy" rallies around America and the world (Occupy Oakland, Occupy Washington, Occupy New Orleans, etc.)

The Occupy Movement stalled, however, divided among idealistic anarchists versus other members of the movement wanting to make concrete demands and pursue tangible change.[23] Yet, even those who pursued tangible change were hobbled because the movement's founding demand was incoherent and the forum for its cause was private property that, although it was set aside for public use, was neither public land nor logistically attractive for the long-term.

The demand—a presidential commission to separate money from politics—collides with several realities. One, political, is that Occupy Wall Street's demand to get money out of politics would require that a law to accomplish this end start in Congress—where Republicans held a majority in the House and a sufficient number of seats in the Senate to maintain a filibuster. The second reality, legal, is that the Supreme Court would have likely struck down any attempt to remove money from politics as violating the First Amendment's freedom of speech as interpreted by *Citizens United* and its progeny. Thus, Occupy Wall Street's demand was aimed at the executive branch, while the action it demanded could only be delivered by the legislative branch, which would prove futile because it would be declared unconstitutional by the judicial branch.

At least two other problems arise from the original forum for its cause—Wall Street. Wall Street does not make federal campaign laws; Washington does. And, while Wall Street is the seat of capital, where many people in the financial industry work, when people who did not work in New York's Financial District arrived at Zuccotti Park (the site in which the Occupy Wall Street participants camped), they were physically on land owned by Brookfield Office Properties (the park was named after John Zuccotti, who had been the US Chairman of Brookfield Properties), in the land of capital. The park, although privately owned, is open to the public under agreement with the city, but it did not have sanitation facilities on-site and when sanitation began to become a concern, Brookfield Properties and the New York Police Department successfully challenged in court the right of the protestors to maintain tents, generators and other structures.

What should be clear by now—and will be emphasized in the pages that follow—is that we, the American people, don't need to narrow our cause to getting excessive money out of politics, and we don't need to take our argument to Wall Street. The appropriate cause is to improve quality of life for all Americans and the setting for such an effort is not Wall Street but, rather, Washington, DC and demanding that the politicians elected to represent us in the White House, the Senate and the House of Representatives do their jobs *and work for us*.

TRICKLE-UP THEORY FROM SMITH, TOCQUEVILLE AND OTHERS

The attitude of Scottish Enlightenment philosopher and father of capitalism, Adam Smith, toward self-interest was not to glorify it, but, rather, to simply recognize its inevitability—and, along with its inevitability, its tendency to work for the benefit of all, which could be enhanced with appropriate government institutions.[24]

A distillation of Adam Smith's observations, as they apply today: The exchange process (what he called "the propensity to truck, barter and exchange"), functioning based on appeals to the self-interest of people, leads them, as if by an invisible hand, to serve the public good. It also, however, leads to the division of labor, which, in turn, leads to class divisions, which are unwarranted—being only the outgrowth of the division of labor necessary for society to prosper. Smith did *not*, as did Ayn Rand and others after him, glorify self-interest. To the contrary, he observed that businessmen driven by "mean rapacity" and "monopolizing spirit"[25] were led "on many occasions" to "deceive and even to oppress the public."[26] The same self-interest that leads people to serve society as if by an invisible hand leads those of the upper class to collude, attempting to manipulate the market in order to further enhance their wealth. To counteract this, government should fight inequality, ensure the poor a living wage, impose the rule of law and progressive taxation, and promote high growth, and a high wage economy—all of which, it should be observed, are consistent with the observations of Alexis de Tocqueville, whose *Democracy in America* followed 59 years later, and the New Deal, the Great Society, and Democratic liberalism.

Below are supporting quotes from Smith's *The Wealth of Nations* and *The Theory of Moral Sentiments* regarding each key topic included in this summary:

The Exchange Process and the Division of Labor

> The greatest improvement in the productive powers of labour, and the greater part of the skill, dexterity, and judgment with which it is any where directed, or applied, seems to have been the effects of the division of labour.[27]

> This division of labour, from which so many advantages are derived, is not originally the effect of any human wisdom, which foresees and intends that general opulence to which it gives occasion. It is the necessary, though very slow and gradual, consequence of a certain propensity in human nature which has in view no such extensive utility; the propensity to truck, barter, and exchange one thing for another.[28]

We Are Motivated by More Than Mean Self-Interest

It is ironic that conservatives cite Adam Smith for the source of the idea that all humans are motivated exclusively by their own self-interest—Smith famously did say:

> It is not from the benevolence of the butcher, the brewer, or the baker, that we expect our dinner, but from their regard to their own interest. We address ourselves, not to their humanity, but to their self-love, and never talk to them of our own necessities but of their advantages.[29]

However, before those lines appeared in *The Wealth of Nations*, the following appeared in *The Theory of Moral Sentiments*:

> How selfish soever man may be supposed, there are evidently some principles in his nature, which interest him in the fortune of others, and render their happiness necessary to him, though he derives nothing from it, except the pleasure of seeing it. Of this kind is pity or compassion, the emotion which we feel for the misery of others, when we either see it, or are made to conceive it in a very lively manner. That we often derive sorrow from the sorrow of others, is a matter of fact too obvious to require any instances to prove it; for this sentiment, like all the other original passions of human nature, is by no means confined to the virtuous and humane, though they perhaps may feel it with the most exquisite sensibility. The greatest ruffian, the most hardened violator of the laws of society, is not altogether without it.[30]

Adam Smith's recognition that man is not motivated by the feelings of his own self-interest alone, but also for compassion for others, and concern for and desire to ameliorate their suffering, though he derives no tangible benefit from it, will be emphasized throughout in the quotes that follow.

The Invisible Hand

As observed in Chapter 5, Adam Smith's reference to an "invisible hand" first appears in *The Theory of Moral Sentiments*, where he envisioned men being "led by an invisible hand . . . without intending it, without knowing it, [to] advance the interests of society."[31] His later and most famous—and, significantly, only—use of the term in *The Wealth of Nations* appeared in this passage:

> [E]very individual . . . generally, indeed, neither intends to promote the public interest, nor knows how much he is promoting it. . . . [H]e intends only his own security; and by directing that industry in such a manner as its produce may be of the greatest value, he intends only his own gain, and he is in this, as in many other cases, led by an invisible hand to promote an end which was no part of his intention.[32]

Class Distinction, Its Origins and Its Lack of Basis

Adam Smith, as observed in Chapter 5, condemned the admiration of wealth in *The Theory of Moral Sentiments*. In *The Wealth of Nations* he returned to this theme, observing that we assume our ultimate status in capitalism as verification of our distinguishing merit when, in fact, we are not so different from each other[33]:

> The difference of natural talents in different men is, in reality, much less than we are aware of; and the very different genius which appears to distinguish men of different professions, when grown up to maturity, is not upon many occasions so much the cause, as the effect of the division of labour. [Citation omitted.] The difference between the most dissimilar characters, between a philosopher and a common street porter, for example, seems to arise not so much from nature, as from habit, custom and education. When they came into the world, and for the first six or eight years of their existence, they were, perhaps, [citation omitted] very much alike, and neither their parents nor play-fellows could perceive any remarkable difference. About that age, or soon after, they come to be employed in very different occupations. The difference of talents comes to be taken notice of, and widens by degrees, till at last the vanity of the philosopher is willing to acknowledge scarce any resemblance . . . .By nature a philosopher is not in genius and disposition half so different from a street porter, as a mastiff is from a greyhound, or a greyhound from a spaniel, or this last from a shepherd's dog.

Why What's Good for Business and the Wealthy Is Not Necessarily Good for All

Adam Smith importantly rejected the underlying false principle of trickle-down—that what is good for the business and the wealthy is good for all—

and he warned against the danger of collusion by businessmen to rig the market in their favor.

> People of the same trade seldom meet together, even for merriment and diversion, but the conversation ends in a conspiracy against the public, or in some contrivance to raise prices. It is impossible indeed to prevent such meetings, by any law which either could be executed, or would be consistent with liberty and justice. But though the law cannot hinder people of the same trade from sometimes assembling together, it ought to do nothing to facilitate such assemblies; much less to render them necessary.[34]

> To widen the market and to narrow the competition, is always the interest of the dealers . . . .The proposal of any new law or regulation of commerce which comes from this order, ought always to be listened to with great precaution, and ought never to be adopted till after having been long and carefully examined, not only with the most scrupulous, but with the most suspicious attention. It comes from an order of men, whose interest is never exactly the same with that of the public, who have generally an interest to deceive and even to oppress the public, and who accordingly have, upon many occasions, both deceived and oppressed it.[35]

Beware of Capture of Democracy by Business

He also warned about the danger of collusion by businessmen to secure political power for themselves.

> [T]he monopoly which our manufacturers have obtained . . . has so much increased the number of some particular tribes of them, that, like an overgrown standing army, they have become formidable to the government, and upon many occasions intimidate the legislature. The member of Parliament who supports every proposal for strengthening this monopoly, is sure to acquire not only the reputation of understanding trade, but great popularity and influence with an order of men whose numbers and wealth render them of great importance. If he opposes them, on the contrary, and still more if he has authority enough to be able to thwart them, neither the most acknowledged probity, nor the highest rank, nor the greatest public services, can protect him from the most infamous abuse and detraction, from personal insults, nor sometimes from real danger, arising from the insolent outrage of furious and disappointed monopolists.[36]

Globalization's Benefits to the Wealthy Do Not Trickle Down (More Critiques of Self-Interest)

Smith also expressed concern that resonates today regarding the prevalence of trickle-down, and the degree to which we all take it as the "natural state of things"—so that we worry, erroneously, about collusion on the part of labor but not capital—when businessmen are always and everywhere conspiring to prevent the increase of wages:

> We rarely hear, it has been said, of the combinations of masters, though frequently of those of workmen. But whoever imagines, upon this account, that masters rarely combine, is as ignorant of the world as of the subject. Masters are always and every where in a sort of tacit, but constant and uniform combination, not to raise the wages of labour above their actual rate. To violate this combination is every where a most unpopular action, and a sort of reproach to a master among his neighbors and equals. We seldom, indeed, hear of this combination, because it is the usual, and one may say, the natural state of things which nobody ever hears of.[37]

> But what all the violence of the feudal institutions could never have effected, the silent and insensible operation of foreign commerce and manufactures gradually brought about. These gradually furnished the great proprietors with something for which they could exchange the whole surplus produce of their lands, and which they could consume themselves without sharing it either with tenants or retainers. All for ourselves, and nothing for other people, seems, in every age of the world, to have been the vile maxim of the masters of mankind.[38]

The last sentence above, also appearing in Chapter 5 herein, as observed there bears a striking similarity to Tocqueville's lament regarding the shortsightedness of his European contemporaries regarding the effects of globalization and technology.

High Profits Indicate a Country on the Road to Ruin

Conservatives would be shocked to see how Adam Smith would respond to the current situation observed in the Introduction and Chapter 4, in which the economy has been experiencing the lowest percentage of GDP attributable to wages and highest attributable to profits since World War II:

> But the rate of profit does not, like rent and wages, rise with the prosperity, and fall with the declension of the society. On the contrary, it is naturally low in rich, and high in poor countries, and it is always highest in the countries which are going fastest to ruin.[39]

Thus, record high profits as a percentage of GDP, as seen in the US today, would have been condemned by Smith as an indicator of national weakness.

Smith not only distrusted the wealthy and their attempts to use government to restrain competition, but also recognized that corporations, themselves, were designed to restrain competition, as revealed below.

Corporations Designed to Restrain Competition

> It is to prevent this reduction of price, and consequently wages and profit, by restraining that free competition which would most certainly occasion it, that all corporations, and the greater part of corporation laws, have been established.[40]

Smith not only distrusted corporations, but also distrusted those who would run them, as shown below:

> The directors of such companies, however, being the managers rather of other people's money than of their own, it cannot well be expected, that they should watch over it with the same anxious vigilance with which the partners in a private copartnery frequently watch over their own . . . .Negligence and profusion, therefore, must always prevail, more or less, in the management of the affairs of such a company.[41]

The Necessity of Government Support of Education and Other Public Institutions

Smith supported public education:

> The man whose whole life is spent in performing a few simple operations, of which the effects too are, perhaps, always the same, or very nearly the same, has no occasion to exert his understanding, or to exercise his invention in finding out expedients for removing difficulties which never occur . . . .His dexterity at his own particular trade seems, in this manner, to be acquired at the expence of his intellectual, social, and martial virtues. But in every improved and civilized society this is the state into which the labouring poor, that is, the great body of the people, must necessarily fall, unless government takes pains to prevent it.[42]

> For a very small expence the public can facilitate, can encourage, and can even impose upon almost the whole body of the people, the necessity of acquiring those most essential parts of education.[43]

For a Living Wage and Sharing in Revenues Attributable to Their Own Labor

And, he supported a living wage and the sharing of revenues attributable to the increased productivity of an enterprise with the workers:

> Is this improvement in the circumstances of the lower ranks of the people to be regarded as an advantage or as an inconveniency to the society? [Citation omitted.] The answer seems at first sight abundantly plain. Servants, labourers and workmen of different kinds, make up the far greater part of every great political society. But what improves the circumstances of the greater part can

never be regarded as an inconveniency to the whole. No society can surely be flourishing and happy, of which the far greater part of the members are poor and miserable. It is but equity, besides, that they who feed, cloath and lodge the whole body of the people, should have such a share of the produce of their own labour as to be themselves tolerably well fed, cloathed and lodged.[44]

Promotion of Growth and High Wages

Adam Smith continued, in terms that should make conservatives and liberals alike realize that, contrary to what so many of us have been taught, he was laying the liberal groundwork for which John Maynard Keynes' *The General Theory of Employment, Interest and Money* (1936) was merely complementary:

The liberal reward of labour, therefore, as it is the necessary effect, so it is the natural symptom of increasing national wealth.[45]

It deserves to be remarked, perhaps, that it is in the progressive state, while the society is advancing to the further acquisition, rather than when it has acquired its full complement of riches, that the condition of the labouring poor, of the great body of the people, seems to be the happiest and the most comfortable. It is hard in the stationary, and miserable in the declining state. The progressive state is in reality the cheerful and the hearty state to all the different orders of the society. The stationary is dull; the declining melancholy.

The liberal reward of labor, as it encourages the propagation, so it increases the industry of the common people. The wages of labour are the encouragement of industry, which, like every other human quality, improves in proportion to the encouragement it receives. A plentiful subsistence increases the bodily strength of the labourer, and the comfortable hope of bettering his condition, and of ending his days perhaps in ease and plenty, animates him to exert that strength to the utmost. Where wages are high, accordingly, we shall always find the workmen more active, diligent, and expeditious, than when they are low . . . .[46]

A Living Wage Should Ensure Ability to Purchase the Necessaries of Life

And, Adam Smith did not define the appropriate wage by merely what would provide a mean existence but, rather, what provides a standard of living commensurate with the nation and time in which the worker lives:

By necessaries I understand, not only the commodities which are indispensably necessary for the support of life, but whatever the custom of the country renders it indecent for creditable people, even of the lowest order, to be without.[47]

From the above, then, we see that Smith understood that he answered *An Inquiry into the Nature and Causes of the Wealth of Nations* with the observation that the wealth of a nation is the wealth of all the people of the nation, not just the wealth of those at the top.

Support of the Government with Progressive Taxation to Provide the Necessaries of Life

Smith, in a footnote, approvingly cited *Sketches of the History of Man* (1774), by Henry Home, Lord Kames, where the author gave "six general rules" as to taxation, among them: "'To remedy' inequality of riches 'as much as possible, by relieving the poor and burdening the rich'."[48] And, for the rich to contribute in respective proportion to the revenue which they enjoy under the protection of the state necessitates progressive tax rates:

> The necessaries of life occasion the great expense of the poor . . . The luxuries and vanities of life occasion the principal expense of the rich; and a magnificent house embellishes and sets off to the best advantage all the other luxuries and vanities which they possess . . . It is not very unreasonable that the rich should contribute to the public expense, not only in proportion to their revenue, but something more than in that proportion.[49]

> The subjects of every state ought to contribute towards the support of the government, as nearly as possible, in proportion to their respective abilities; that is, in proportion to the revenue which they respectively enjoy under the protection of the state. The expence of government to the individuals of a great nation, is like the expence of management to the joint tenants of a great estate, who are all obliged to contribute in proportion to their respective interests in the estate.[50]

The Wealthy Derive Benefits from the Civil Government Their Taxes Support

And, regarding those taxes that the wealthy must pay to support the Good Society of Adam Smith, Smith would give no sympathy to the conservatives who moan about high taxes but, instead, remind them of the benefits they derive from them:

> It is only under the shelter of the magistrate that the owner of that valuable property, which is acquired by the labour of many years, or perhaps of many successive generations, can sleep a single night in security.[51]

Taxes Signify Liberty, Not Slavery

And, Smith would remind them of their station:

> Every tax, however, is to the person who pays it a badge, not of slavery, but of liberty. It denotes that he is subject to government, indeed, but that, as he has some property, he cannot himself be the property of a master.[52]

Similarly, in modern times, as observed by Francis Fukuyama, it is a sign of a healthy modern democracy to be able to extract taxes from the elites, as opposed to their being able to shield themselves from paying taxes and to shift the burden of public spending onto everyone else.[53]

In ignoble contrast, House Speaker John Boehner (R-OH) characterized the dispute with Democrats over the Sequester in 2013 as over how much money to steal from the American people to fund more government.[54]

A TRICKLE-UP NARRATIVE

What follows is a trickle-up narrative—in opposition to the trickle-down narrative previously described. It is a narrative of capitalism in which we all participate—and we have a responsibility to demand that capitalism work for all of us because history shows when it does not work for all of us, it has only been a matter of time before it works for only the very few.

Ironically, this narrative is a narrative of the *achievable*—in fact, of what had been achieved before, and can be achieved again, if we stop taking as acceptable the demonstrable nonsense of trickle-down.

As observed in the quotes that begin this chapter, the American Dream is based on the idea that if the middle class and poor do well, then their success will trickle-up benefits to the rich. Much of the point of this book is to illustrate that, certainly from the time of Franklin Roosevelt's inauguration in 1933 up through the 1970s, this was the vision for America. Below is an attempt to create the narrative of this vision—a trickle-up narrative—describing this system that was in place for just over four decades and built the great American middle class:

> During the Gilded Age and the Roaring Twenties, the economy grew and productivity grew, yet the benefits of that productivity, pursuant to a trickle-down philosophy, were being upwardly redistributed. To compensate for what would have been a shortfall in demand, credit was loosened and indebtedness encouraged—but, eventually, citizens exhausted their savings and their ability to borrow, and, living on stagnant and then falling real wages, demand began to decline and a balance sheet recession resulted, evolving into the Great Depression.
>
> Beginning with the inauguration of Franklin Roosevelt in 1933, in the depths of the Great Depression, the federal government launched massive public works projects that put millions to work. Also launched were social insurance programs that began to form the social safety net, including Social Security. Federally mandated collective bargaining supported unions which, in

turn, campaigned to improve working standards and wages. Child labor laws were passed and enforced. A federally mandated minimum wage was established, which gradually rose; progressive income tax rates shifted the burden of support for government onto those who could bear it most easily (to pay off the federal debt incurred during the Great Depression and World War II, the highest marginal federal income tax rate was raised to 91 percent); and business—especially the financial industry— was subjected to regulation protecting the middle class and poor.

The massive increase in public spending accelerated with the onset of World War II, but at the end of the war fear again arose that the Great Depression would resume. The GI Bill was enacted, subsidizing education and mortgages to facilitate purchase of housing for millions. More public works projects were launched, most prominently the construction of the Interstate highway system. And, to serve the new families that had access to subsidized mortgages, the home building industry boomed and with it the construction of public schools and public playgrounds, public roads and public transportation systems, and public water and public sanitation systems. To provide the higher education opportunities to accommodate those returning GIs and, later, their children, lavish state funding of state-supported colleges and universities resulted in tuition that was reasonable or even free. Social Security was supplemented by Medicare, Medicaid, Aid to Families with Dependent Children and Food Stamps (today, the Supplemental Nutrition Assistance Program or SNAP).

Manufacturing—making things—was a major source of employment, while the financial industry—making money by lending money and insurance—was a much smaller share of the economy.

Under liberals, spending on the social safety net grew and interest rates were lowered, and the official policy of "full employment" was pursued, so that when unemployment rose, needed infrastructure programs were undertaken, and government employment grew, and inequality declined as the rich saw their incomes and wealth grow, but less rapidly than did incomes and wealth of the middle class and poor. Over this period, inventory recessions occurred, but recovery was generally rapid, however, consumer price inflation remained a concern.

Thus, from 1945 to 1973, wages grew in tandem with economic growth and productivity growth, due in great part to New Deal and post-World War II institutions designed to aid the middle class and poor—which received a boost during the 1960s under former FDR protégé Lyndon Johnson. These institutions enabled the poor and middle class to increase their productivity and forced the sharing of revenues of increased productivity with them, even though technological change (the Information Revolution) and globalization were, even then, exerting downward pressure on employment and incomes of the middle class and poor (downward pressure hidden by consumer price inflation also artificially inflating wages).

In 1973, and from 1979 through 1980, two oil price shocks dramatically forced up consumer prices, and this inflation combined with rising unemployment (stagflation), creating stubborn inventory recessions. The Carter administration instituted government policy changes to revive the economy—appointing a Federal Reserve Chairman to raise interest rates to fight inflation and deregulating financial, transportation, communication and energy industries.

While higher interest rates, implemented in 1980, were necessary to defeat inflationary expectations in the economy, they prolonged and intensified the ongoing recession, with the result that the electorate lost patience over the pace of economic recovery, resulting in an overreaction and abandonment of demand-side policy for supply-side—resulting in victory for the Republicans in 1980 followed by more deregulation and tax cuts to revive the economy (yielding rising federal deficits and rising government debt).

By the early 1980s, GDP growth revived, and productivity resumed growing, yet incomes for the middle class and poor continued their stagnation from the mid-1970s, to the point that, with real GDP and productivity rising, in 2016 real (inflation-adjusted) median family incomes were nonetheless lower than in 1997, and real median earnings for male full-time workers were lower than in 1973.

Government policies over the three and a half decades since 1980 have reinforced a trickle-down vision, changing our values, norms and institutions so that we engaged in individual behavior and implemented government policies intended to reverse and undo New Deal and post-World War II institutions designed to aid the middle class and poor. The result has been that, for most of the past three decades, revenues from increased productivity have been redistributed upwards, redistributing income and wealth upwards—especially to the top 1 percent of households, corporations and older Americans—and causing real incomes to fall for the middle class and poor.

Since his inauguration, President Obama has acted pursuant to his promise to return America to a trickle-up agenda: He pushed for and signed the Affordable Care Act, pushed through the auto industry bailout, pushed through a stimulus bill that cut taxes for 95 percent of Americans and provided funding for needed infrastructure improvements, cut in half the loan rates on federal student loans so as to make a college education more affordable, secured authorization for the federal government to negotiate directly with drug companies to lower prescription drug costs under the Medicare health insurance program for senior citizens and the disabled and pushed through the Dodd-Frank financial regulations providing for a consumer financial protection agency and extending needed resolution authority over financial entities.

The additional policies that must be undertaken to undo trickle-down's upward redistribution of income and wealth, and raise wages, stimulate mobility and economic growth, and make life more comfortable for the middle class and poor, as befitting the richest nation on Earth, will be addressed in the chapter following.

NOTES

1. See Paul Krugman, "Inequality Is a Drag," *The New York Times*, August 8, 2014.
2. Orestes A. Brownson, *The American Republic: Its Constitution, Tendencies, and Destiny* (New York: P. O'Shea; 1866), p. 383.

3. From an interview conducted with Senator John Breaux (D-LA), July 25, 1990, quoted in Nicol C. Rae's *Southern Democrats* (Oxford, New York: Oxford University Press, 1994) p. 104–105. By permission of Oxford University Press, USA.

4. President Barack Obama, "Remarks by the President during the Meeting of the President's Economic Recovery Advisory Board, November 02, 2009, the Roosevelt Room, the White House.

5. William Julius Wilson, *The Truly Disadvantaged: The Inner City, The Underclass, and Public Policy* (Chicago: University of Chicago Press, 1987; 1990), p. 163. See also a very similar formulation by Barack Obama, *The Audacity of Hope* (New York: Three Rivers Press, an imprint of Crown Publishing Group division of Random House, Inc.; 2006), p. 247.

6. John Dewey, *Liberalism and Social Action*, Capricorn Books, G. P. Putnam's Sons: New York, 1935, 1963; pp. 88–91.

7. Stuart Chase, *A New Deal* (New York: The Macmillan Company, 1932), p. 252.

8. Ibid, p. 173.

9. To be precise, the term "new deal" was inserted, uncapitalized, at the end of his speech by presidential speechwriter Judge Samuel Rosenman. Actual inspiration for the term is debated, although it is known that the current issue of *The New Republic* on the newsstands at the time of the speech, July 2, 1932, contained an article by Stuart Chase titled "A New Deal for America." See Robert Schlesinger, *White House Ghosts: Presidents and Their Speechwriters* (New York: Random House; 2008), pp. 6–9.

10. The essay is quoted in the editorial "Totalitarian Liberalism" *Time*, February 17, 1947.

11. Daniel Bell, *The Cultural Contradictions of Capitalism* (New York: Basic Books, 1976; 1996), p. 79.

12. Ibid, p. 80.

13. Ibid. Here Bell referenced John Kenneth Galbraith's *The Affluent Society*.

14. Ibid, p. 80. See also p. 202. John Maynard Keynes, in *The General Theory of Employment, Interest, and Money* (1936) famously criticized economic society (p. 372) for failing to provide full employment and arbitrarily distributing income and wealth. Keynes proposed in *The General Theory* the principles of modern fiscal and monetary policy which helped create the booming economy of 1947–1973. This same observation regarding liberalism's position at the forefront of efforts to grow the economy rapidly was made by Alan Wolfe, professor of sociology at Boston University, in *America's Impasse: The Rise and Fall of the Politics of Growth* (1981).

15. Daniel Bell, *The Cultural Contradictions of Capitalism* (New York: Basic Books; 1976, 1996), p. 79.

16. Ibid, p. 79.

17. The pro-growth attitude of liberalism in the 1950s was also remarked upon by Barbara Ehrenreich in *Fear of Falling: The Inner Life of the Middle Class*, New York: HarperCollins Publishers, 1989), pp. 21–22, citing Alan Wolfe, *America's Impasse: The Rise and Fall of the Politics of Growth* (New York: Pantheon Books, 1981), p. 28.

18. From Alexis de Tocqueville's *Democracy in America, De La Démocratie en Amérique*, Bilingual Edition, edited by Eduardo Nolla, translated by James T. Schleifer (Indianapolis, IN: Liberty Fund; 2010), vol. II, part II, Chapter 18, pp. 970–971.

19. See, for example, Dr. Martin Luther King, Jr.'s address before the First Annual Institute on Non-Violence and Social Change, held in Montgomery, Alabama in December 1956, reprinted in *I Have a Dream: Writings and Speeches that Changed the World/Martin Luther King, Jr.*: foreword by Coretta Scott King; edited by James Melvin Washington (New York: HarperCollins Publishers, 1992), p. 20.

20. Katherine S. Newman, *No Shame in My Game: The Working Poor in the Inner City* (New York: Vintage 2000).

21. Friedrich Hayek, *The Constitution of Liberty* (Chicago: The University of Chicago Press; 1960), p. 406.

22. 13 July 2011, in the *Adbusters* blog.

23. For more information on Occupy Wall Street, see Mark Binelli, "The Battle for the Soul of Occupy Wall Street," *Rolling Stone*, June 7, 2012.

24. Credit for inspiring a critical re-examination of the relevance of Smith's theory to modern liberalism goes to Michael Lind, who undertook a similar exercise in *The Next American Nation: The New Nationalism and the Fourth American Revolution* (New York: The Free Press, 1995); see especially pp. 335 and 336.
25. Adam Smith, *The Wealth of Nations* (New York: The Modern Library, Random House, Inc.; 1937; originally published 1776), p. 460.
26. Ibid, p. 250.
27. Ibid, p. 3.
28. Ibid, p. 13.
29. Ibid, p. 14.
30. Adam Smith, *The Theory of Moral Sentiments* (Amherst, New York: Prometheus Books, 2000; originally published in 1759), p. 2. Section 1: "Of the Sense of Propriety," Chapter 1: "Of Sympathy".
31. Adam Smith, *The Theory of Moral Sentiments* (Amherst, New York: Prometheus Books, 2000; originally published in 1759), pp. 264-265. Part IV, Chapter I.
32. Adam Smith, *The Wealth of Nations*, p. 423.
33. Ibid, pp. 15 and 16.
34. Ibid, p. 128.
35. Ibid, p. 250.
36. Ibid, p. 438.
37. Ibid, pp. 66 and 67.
38. Ibid, pp. 388 and 389.
39. Ibid, pp. 249 and 250.
40. Ibid, p. 123.
41. Ibid, p. 700. For a general critique of corporations from a modern perspective, see especially David C. Korten, *When Corporations Rule the World* (Kumarian Press Inc., San Francisco: 1995, 1996, 2001).
42. *The Wealth of Nations*, pp. 734 and 735.
43. Ibid, p. 737.
44. Ibid, pp. 78 and 79.
45. Ibid, p. 73.
46. Ibid, p. 81.
47. Ibid, p. 821.
48. In volume I, pages 747 and following of *Sketches of the History of Man*, cited by Smith in *The Wealth of Nations* at page 779.
49. Ibid, pp. 793 and 794.
50. Ibid, p. 777.
51. Ibid, p. 670.
52. Ibid, p, 808.
53. Francis Fukuyama, "Left Out," *American Interest*, January–February 2011.
54. Ashley Parker, "Boehner Halts Talks on Cuts, and House G.O.P. Cheers," *The New York Times*, March 1, 2013.

Chapter Fourteen

Liberal Reclaiming of the American Dream

> We are determined to make every American citizen the subject of his country's interest and concern; and we will never regard any faithful law-abiding group within our borders as superfluous. The test of our progress is not whether we add more to the abundance of those who have much; it is whether we provide enough for those who have too little.
> —President Franklin Delano Roosevelt, Second Inaugural Speech, January 20, 1937.

> If a free society cannot help the many who are poor, it cannot save the few who are rich.
> —President John F. Kennedy, Inaugural Speech, January 20, 1961.

This work began, in the Introduction, with an Inaugural Address quote that set the tone for the ensuing three and a half decades and counting. This final chapter begins with two Inaugural Address quotes, each of which set the tone for their respective periods, and which are good guides for us to use to recalibrate ourselves as we go forward, having realized that we have been fooled in our own period, and we are eager to correct our mistakes.

A preliminary step in this recalibration is to decide, if we believe the US economy is too unequal, then how do we appropriately measure equality? It is certainly not *actual* income or wealth equality, so what is it? In the context of incomes and wealth, it is the utilitarian test met when incomes and wealth are roughly converging, much more in keeping with the income distribution of the 1945-1973 era. Again, this is not a measure based at all in rights, or fairness, or social justice but, rather, a measure based in what is good for *all* the American people (especially the middle class); a judgment we are now better qualified to make not only due to improved measurement capability but also due to our much better understanding of the negatives associated with inequality. Accordingly, the following proposed policy measures are designed to distribute back to the non-rich a share of the revenues attributable to their own increased productivity. We fully expect that resulting from this will be not only rising wages and a reinstitution of some degree of convergence of incomes but also increased economic growth, increased job growth, increased social mobility, strengthened democracy, strengthened institutions and better health outcomes for ourselves and our fellow Americans.

The concept of the "looking glass nation" is proposed to describe the introspection that must accompany an attitude of humility: to see the actions of the United States as people elsewhere see them—in the domestic policy realm this concept forces all of us Americans to face the uncomfortable truth that even though we are the richest nation on Earth, by many measures we are horribly failing our fellow citizens, forcing them to live lives much meaner than necessary. Such self-examination supports numerous domestic policy recommendations below.

Certain basic truths guide the following recommendations: There is no escaping that we must return tax revenues from the recent levels below 16 percent of GDP to the historical 20 percent range to avoid further undermining the social insurance safety net relied upon by our less fortunate fellow Americans. And, there is no escaping that we must reconnect productivity and compensation.[1] Only if we raise real wages can we attain sustained economic growth. And, we will know that we are beginning to again connect wages to productivity when we see that the rich are not continually getting richer and the middle class and poor are enduring stagnant wages or, even worse, getting poorer and poorer. To free up our businesses, proposed herein are lower taxes and relieving them of the burden of supporting our bloated health care system that does not even cover all our citizens—other developed nations are able to not so burden their businesses and cover all their citizens; we Americans can too.

DOMESTIC POLICY RECOMMENDATIONS

To Raise Wages[2]

The first priority is to raise wages. Among the possible fiscal policies to accomplish this would be to unfreeze federal pay. Additionally, the minimum wage should be raised for "tipped employees" from the current $2.13 it has been at since 1991 and the minimum wage for regular employees should be raised from the current $7.25 per hour, to $12.00 per hour. The minimum wage has the effect of raising other wages as well, thus lifting needed demand in the economy.

Another appropriate policy would be to make unpaid internships illegal, and subject internships to the minimum wage laws.[3]

Additionally, we should provide a "social contract" provision in the corporate tax regulations requiring that the total annual compensation of the highest paid executive of a corporation availing itself of the flat corporate tax rate provided below must not be paid at ratio to the median compensation level of that corporation higher than 100 to 1 (the ratio of CEO-to-worker in 2014 was 303-to-1[4]).

Regarding Tax Policy[5]

Raise the Earned Income Tax Credit (EITC). This tool for addressing inequality was first proposed by the conservative hero and Nobel Prize winning economist Milton Friedman in *Capitalism and Freedom* (1962), where he proposed "a negative income tax" that would "set a floor below which no man's net income (defined now to include the subsidy) could fall."[6] President Nixon championed the idea, working with Senator Daniel Patrick Moynihan (D-NY), and it was signed into law by President Ford in the Tax Reduction Act of 1975, and renewed by President Reagan in the Tax Reform Act of 1986. Additionally, raising the EITC has the effect of helping the lowest-paid workers without raising the risk of increasing unemployment by raising costs for employers. Another appropriate policy to help families is to raise the child care tax credit.

And, an important establishment of principle is made by removing the tax code's penalty against workers by removing the distinction between "ordinary income" and "capital gains," "interest" and "dividend income." President Reagan famously cut the highest marginal income tax rate from 70 percent to 50 percent; and again to 28 percent—but that 28 percent level applied to both ordinary income and capital gains. Multibillionaire financier Warren Buffet famously observed the unfairness in the fact that his secretary's effective tax rate was higher than his. We are overdue for eliminating this egregious tax penalty on working Americans.

To respond to the reality of extremely high incomes, institute a new 50 percent bracket for household incomes over $1 million a year. The previously mentioned comprehensive New York Times/CBS Poll conducted in May 2015 found 68 percent of Americans favored raising taxes on incomes above $1 million[7] and 50 percent was the highest marginal tax rate approved in 1982 under President Reagan.

Regarding the payroll deduction: Remove the cap on the payroll tax deduction, thereby ensuring the future funding of Social Security. Two-thirds of Americans over the age of 65 depend on an average Social Security benefit of $15,168.36 for at least half of their income. As this is written in 2015, earned income in excess of $118,500 is entirely exempt from the 6.2%

payroll tax that funds Social Security (employers match with 6.2%). Only about 5% of working Americans make more than $118,500 and are thus subject to this regressive exemption, elimination of which would help eliminate concerns over funding of Social Security according to the Congressional Budget Office, and raising taxes on wealthier Americans to pay for Social Security is broadly favored.[8] Additionally, affluent citizens tend to live longer than the rest of the population, so it can be expected their benefits will cost more, thus, it is appropriate that they not be advantaged with a cap on their contributions.

Regarding Medicare: Revise the funding of Medicare so that it is funded by a flat 1.45 percent tax regardless of income, and raise Medicare deductibles for the highest-earning retirees. As this is written in 2015, Medicare is funded by a flat 1.45% tax on the first $200,000 of earnings for a single person and $250,000 for a married couple (matched by a 1.45% tax paid by the employer), after which it rises (per the Additional Medicare Tax of the Affordable Care Act) by only 0.9 percent on all incomes above the $200,000 and $250,000 levels. Again, because affluent citizens tend to live longer than the rest of the population, it can be expected their benefits will cost more, thus, it is appropriate that they not be advantaged with low contribution levels.[9]

Return the estate tax to the Clinton-era tax levels whereby the first $1 million in the estate is exempt and rates on excess of $1 million start at 18 percent, and rise to 55 percent for portions of estates over $3 million. The American Taxpayer Relief Act of 2012 set the basic exclusion amount for estates at $5,000,000 indexed for inflation so that, for estates of any decedent dying during calendar year 2015, the basic exclusion amount was $5,430,000—for reference the 2013 basic exclusion amount of $5,250,000 excluded *99.86 percent* of all estates and all but 20 small businesses and farm estates nationwide that year.[10]

Returning to the tax policy addressed earlier, for corporations that elect to abide by a requirement that no officer, employee or consultant receives compensation from that corporation in excess of 100 times the median income of any employee of the corporation: provide for a corporate income tax reduced to a 12.5% flat tax rate—matching Ireland, the lowest rate in the OECD. Remove the tax incentives for corporations to move domestic manufacturing jobs overseas. Incentivize repatriation and creation of jobs at home by American corporations, thereby recognizing that corporations are simply more adept at avoiding paying income taxes than any politicians will ever be at designing ways to force them to share in the funding of government.

Reduce Military Spending

Cutting military spending to just more than twice as much as any other nation on Earth should be sufficient; *we don't need to spend, as we do now, more than the next 7 nations combined.*[11]

Regarding Health Care and Public Safety

With more stable funding in place, recognize the fact that health care is an example of market failure, and expand Medicare to all Americans, resulting in a single payer system, with the mandate to bring down health care costs and take the load off American businesses. And cap Medicare growth starting with the first year after implementation of its expansion to GDP growth plus 1 percentage point. The health care system in the US is horribly inefficient and wasteful when compared with the rest of the world. Not only does the US have the highest health care spending in the world—equivalent to 17.9 percent of its GDP in 2012—government spending in the US "free market" health care system on a per-person basis is behind only Luxembourg, Monaco and Norway—and, as observed previously, for all this expense, heath care outcomes in the US are worse than those in the rest of the developed world.[12] Finally, universal health care must, to work most efficiently, be accompanied by a shift toward healthy communities—supported by changes in laws, changes in zoning, and changes in the mindset of the average American.[13]

Allow the free market to operate for drugs and other medicines, beginning with the decriminalization and taxation of marijuana and removal of the ban on import of medicines (and make them subject to FDA approval, in the same way that imported food is regulated).

Provide federal government backing for loans for the expansion of medical schools subject to commitments by those schools to expand the rolls of graduates by established percentages. An already existent doctor shortage is almost certain to worsen with an aging population and the implementation of the Affordable Care Act expanding health care coverage for millions of Americans.[14]

Regarding Job Creation

Pass a Subsidence and Relative Sea Level Rise Response Act (SARSLRRA) creating a National Office of Coastal Restoration to begin to rank coastal restoration projects nationwide, secure funding for them, and provide staffing and funding to build up the nation's infrastructure to combat the coastal land loss resulting from tidal rise and subsidence which, as revealed by Hurricanes Sandy, Katrina and others, is worsened with every hurricane that hits our shores. These public works projects would be funded by the revenues generated by a carbon tax—thus linking the doctrine of the sovereign's obligation to defend property with the doctrine of public trust.

Pass the American Jobs Act to supply needed funding to other public works and infrastructure enhancement programs, supported by a 6.6-cent increase in the gasoline tax (raising the gasoline tax to 25 cents per gallon, at a time that gasoline prices are low, from its current level of 18.4 cents per gallon, where it has been since 1993).

Reform patent and copyright law to promote creativity and democracy rather than suppress it. An important starting place is reform of copyright law, defining, in statute, what constitutes "fair use" that may not be burdened by a fee when appropriately invoked. A recommended definition for a fair use standard comes from the fair use guidelines of the University of Chicago Press: A qualifying use must comply with all of the following requirements: When quoting from a book or periodical, the author of a new work may quote no more than 300 consecutive words and no more than a total of 5,000 words from that book or periodical; in addition, the quoted words must not constitute more than 5 percent of the Source Work or more than 5 percent of the new work. Amazingly, the term "fair use," despite its wide use, is simply disregarded by most periodicals and many book publishers. For the good of the free flow of information necessary for democracy, this situation cannot be allowed to stand.

The DREAM Act

Renew the push for the signing of the DREAM (Development, Relief and Education for Alien Minors) Act.

The Postal Accountability and Enhancement Act

Repeal the Postal Accountability and Enhancement Act of 2006 (PAEA) requiring the Postal Service to fund future health care benefits to retirees for the next 75 years over a ten-year span.[15]

Education

Provide a tax deduction for higher education expenses. States were spending 28 percent less per student nationwide in 2013 than five years before, and these cuts have continued and will impede the ability of young people to support themselves economically and impede economic growth.[16] Pass the measure proposed by Senator Elizabeth Warren (D-MA) to cap student loan rates at the rate charged banks for lending of reserves. Pass the measure proposed by President Obama to make community college tuition free.

Energy Policy

Accelerate the "all of the above" energy strategy combining six elements: Safe development of natural gas; approval of export of oil and fast track approval of proposed projects for export of natural gas and liquefied natural gas; opening of new areas in federal waters for oil and gas exploration and production; increase of use of energy from renewable sources such as wind, solar and hydropower; higher fuel efficiency standards and more rapid development of natural gas fuel cell technology. "The natural gas boom has led to cleaner power and greater energy independence. That's why my administration will keep cutting red tape and speeding us new oil and gas permits." These are the words of President Obama in his February 12, 2013, State of the Union Address, meriting an endorsement by the editorial board of *The Washington Post*. Due in great part to these efforts, natural gas, which emits 45% less carbon dioxide per btu created than even the cleanest coal, is now generating more electricity than any other fuel.[17] Liberals should correct the Republican narrative that Democratic administrations, such as the Obama administration, have been impeding Republican efforts to open up offshore oil and gas exploration and production. In reality, it has long been Republican administrations that supported moratoria on lease sales that would have opened up new areas for offshore oil and gas exploration and production, while the Obama administration led the way in offering to expand access.[18] Additionally, for efficiency, the Bureau of Ocean Energy Management and Bureau of Safety and Environmental Enforcement should be merged.

Financial Reform

Use the Consumer Finance Protection Bureau to force restructuring of consumer and home loans in conjunction with the restructuring of student loans. Restructure Fannie Mae and Freddie Mac to counteract their tendency to artificially prop up home prices. Apply the standards of the Kanjorski Amendment to Dodd-Frank, allowing federal regulators to preemptively break up large financial institutions that pose a "grave risk" to financial or economic stability—thus ending the perception that any financial firm is "too big to fail."

On a parallel legislative track, Glass-Steagall should be reinstated to separate capital in banks from capital in investment firms (and to separate insurance underwriting from banking) because "too big to fail" is "too big to exist." Create a public, transparent market for trading of credit default swaps. To restore transparency, eliminate off-balance sheet financing and restore mark to market accounting. Bar rating agencies from providing services to the financial institutions they rate. Reinstate the tighter rules on stock buybacks that were in place before they were loosened in 1982. The concern about the degree to which stock buybacks distort the economy and fuel inequality has been raised by both *The Economist*[19] and the entrepreneur Nick Hanauer.[20] Prosecute to the full extent of the law the executives responsible for the practice of fraud in the financial industry, starting with those in the mortgage industry.

PULSE: People United for Labor's Support and Enhancement

A recommendation for the domestic agenda that is not a government policy recommendation: Unions currently suffer from having to draw their support from members alone—a shrinking base—however, there are potentially many Americans who are not union members but who, nonetheless, are thankful for the benefits provided to them by unions over the course of history, and who would be pleased to support union efforts in the political arena.

A recommendation here is that unions—perhaps through the AFL-CIO—join with an organization like Americans for Democratic Action (ADA) to jointly form an organization to leverage the goodwill toward unions felt by many Americans who are not union members—perhaps through an organization with the name "PULSE"—standing for "People United for Labor's Support and Enhancement." PULSE would collect donations and represent the interests of tens of millions of working people, union members *and* non-union members, before Congress.

Liberal Political Action Conference (LPAC): The Return of Liberal Ideological Warfare versus Conservatism

Another recommendation for the domestic agenda that is not a government policy recommendation: Creation of a Liberal Political Action Conference (LPAC) modeled on the Conservative Political Action Conference (CPAC). ADA could sponsor LPAC as part of its biennial meetings.

As observed previously, there is no "class war" in America for the simple reason that one of the supposed combatant sides in this imaginary war—workers—have voluntarily given in, won over by the trickle-down ideology that all government policy should be directed to those atop the economy because what is good for the rich is good for everyone.

There are, however, as observed in the Preface, the beginnings of ideological warfare waged by liberals against trickle-down. In the preceding pages, we have seen quotes from President Obama, former President Bill Clinton, and Nobel Prize winners Paul Krugman and Joseph Stiglitz criticizing trickle-down economics. And, as observed in the Preface, they have been joined in their critiques of trickle-down by two figures who will be prominent in politics in 2016 and beyond: former Secretary of State and candidate for the

2016 Democratic presidential nomination, Hillary Clinton,[21] and Senator Elizabeth Warren (D-MA).[22]

It should be observed of both Hillary Clinton and Elizabeth Warren that earlier in their lives they supported the Republican Party. Hillary Clinton was a Young Republican and "Goldwater Girl" in high school in 1964, and expressed, in her book *Living History* (2003), admiration for the individualism of Barry Goldwater and his support of individual rights, and cherished her visit with him and his wife at their home in 1996.[23] Elizabeth Warren was a Republican because she, as she recounted, believed the party best supported the free market.[24] She delivered, in her speech to the 2015 AFL-CIO National Summit on Raising Wages, the most thorough critique of trickle-down of anyone.[25]

That former Republicans would drive the liberal takedown of trickle-down makes sense, for they are most intimately familiar with it and, accordingly, most familiar with its claims and shortcomings. In confronting and defeating trickle-down, they will be recalibrating the Democratic Party slightly leftward, appropriately, as a previous group of Democrats had recalibrated the Democratic Party slightly rightward. The rise of that previous group of Democrats, who formed the now disbanded Democratic Leadership Council (DLC), is documented by the DLC's founder, Al From, in his book *The New Democrats and the Return to Power* (2013). As was observed by a former President of the DLC Bill Clinton, in the foreword to the book, the founders of the DLC were young Democrats who were inspired by the Civil Rights Movement. Although their think tank was called the Progressive Policy Institute (PPI), the "New Democrats" as they called themselves shunned ideology and the "liberal" label. The changes they supported—moving the party toward the center—they supported because they wanted to *preserve* the Civil Rights Movement and the social safety net, and they believed that to do so it was necessary to also promote economic growth and prosperity.

Thus, we see a parallel and contrast to the present era in the runup to the 2016 election. A new group of Democrats, many of them who may have previously identified themselves as libertarians philosophically, and many of them former Republicans, because they know that it is necessary to protect and defend the social safety net, return to more progressive taxation and impose other liberal measures to raise wages generally to stimulate demand in order to promote economic growth and prosperity, will recognize that to succeed they will need to directly confront and defeat trickle-down economics by embracing ideology and the liberal label. And, in doing so, they will be acting consistent with the trickle-up vision and emphasis on balance of the classical liberal domestic policy vision of Smith and Tocqueville.

But first: These warriors on behalf of the 99% will need our help. We are long overdue for a March on Washington for Wages to Match Productivity. We must get the attention of lawmakers and our fellow Americans immediately. And the chant will be:

> Hey, Hey, ho, ho;
> Trickle-down has got to go!

"IF YOU WANT TO LIVE LIKE A REPUBLICAN, YOU HAVE TO VOTE DEMOCRAT!"

Lessons Learned: We Have Been Here Before, and the Answer Is the Same Now as Then

Trickle-down economics has created a depression, similar, although, thanks to federal government economic intervention on behalf of the less fortunate, not as severe as the Great Depression, and the problem now is the same as the US experienced in the 1930s. Trickle-down economics is a delusion. It has never worked; it does not work now, and it never will. All it does and will ever do is upwardly redistribute economic and political power.

We know that trickle-down has undermined the economy because we know that from just after World War II through the 1970s, government intervened in the economy to attempt to ensure that the revenues attributable to increased productivity were distributed among everyone in the economy who contributed to this increased productivity, thus providing a check on the growth of income and wealth inequality. However, since 1980, the economy has been growing, and productivity has been growing, but trickle-down values—that we, the American people promote—have rigged the economy to continuously upwardly redistribute those revenues attributable to our increased productivity, resulting in increased concentration of income and wealth at the top, in corporations and among older Americans (beneficiaries of income from Social Security, pensions and investments and continuing income due to delaying retirement), and the lowest percentage of GDP attributable to wages and highest attributable to profits since World War II. But trickle-down has not only distorted our economic thought; it has also distorted our political thought, our sociology and our concept of the rule of law. The result has been that the trickle-down policies promoted by the Republican Party are undermining our economy, our democracy, our institutions and our health.

Trickle-down not only contradicts the facts; it also contradicts the theories it claims for support and public opinion. Trickle-down attained its power over the economy because supporters of trickle-down—supply-side—economic theory distorted economic theory generally, ignoring the actual statements of their ideological heroes, misinterpreting and all but wiping out the contribution of John Maynard Keynes and his followers, and ignoring the facts that contradicted their theories. The result has been massively increased inequality, impeded economic growth, impeded job growth, impeded economic and social mobility, reduced political participation, increased economic and socio-political instability and shorter life spans and otherwise undermined health.

A Sampling of the Economic Facts Addressed Herein That Have Been Ignored by the Republicans

If you want the economy to grow and the number of jobs to grow, vote Democrat. Democratic administrations have historically performed better than Republican administrations by nearly every economic measure, as revealed by numerous studies (six have been cited herein). Economic growth since 1980 was greatest under Clinton, then Reagan, then Obama (thus far), then George H. W. Bush, then George W. Bush. Job growth: As with economic growth, the greatest growth in jobs since 1980 came under Clinton, followed by Reagan, Obama, George H. W. Bush and George W. Bush. Through December 2015, the private sector, under President Obama, had 69 straight months of private sector job growth, the longest streak on record, and more workers were hired in 2014 than in any year since 1999. Federal deficits and federal debt: Every Republican administration since Reagan took office in 1981 has run a deficit. The debt nearly tripled under Reagan and nearly doubled under George W. Bush. In contrast, under President Clinton, the federal budget ran in surplus for four years. Under President Obama, after sharing with President Bush a high deficit in the fiscal year they shared (October 2008 through September 2009) due to tax cuts, wars in Afghanistan and Iraq and as federal spending increased to address the Great Recession, the deficit has declined every year as a percentage of GDP. Federal employment: Federal employment under President Obama has fallen to its lowest level in 47 years. The number of public sector employees generally has declined under President Obama—by comparison, public sector employment increased under every other president since 1980. Health care: The Affordable Care Act is not a government takeover of healthcare—it implements a requirement to purchase private insurance subject to a tax penalty—a system that was proposed by the conservative Heritage Foundation, endorsed by hero to conservatives economist Milton Friedman, and implemented by 2012 Republican presidential candidate Mitt Romney when he was Governor of Massachusetts. And because of the Affordable Care Act, millions of Americans who previously did not have health insurance now do.

If we cut government spending—impose austerity and balance the federal budget with cuts in spending—we also will cut GDP and jobs. To aid GDP growth, we need to increase spending on infrastructure.

We are not in an age of scarcity, and we do not have to cut spending.

Lack of demand is the main suppressant of economic growth, not budget deficits and uncertainty over regulatory and tax policy.

Cutting taxes, especially upper bracket income taxes and capital gains taxes, to encourage investment, because those in the top brackets are the "job creators," will not make the economy grow faster, and benefits will not trickle-down to everyone else in the form of more jobs and rising incomes, and revenues to the government will not grow.

A low-wage policy is crony capitalism in practice, with private profits being underwritten by public spending.

We will not destroy the incentive to invest if we modestly raise tax rates on capital gains, dividends and interest.

We do not need to simplify the tax code with a flat tax—we already essentially have one when we account for all taxes paid.

We do not need, in order to promote economic growth and job growth, to cut the regulations designed to cushion the middle class and poor from the harshness of the market and to protect the environment.

The US is among the most unequal nations not only in the developed world but in the entire world.

If we modestly raise taxes, there will not be a mass exodus of the rich to where taxes are lower.

There is no economic consensus regarding job loss attributable to a minimum wage hike, but there is consensus that a higher minimum wage will raise wages for millions of workers.

American families cannot forever substitute debt for falling real income.

The American government cannot go broke as it helps the middle class and poor.

"Free trade" is not the answer to raise Americans' incomes and add jobs.

By reporting "per capita" income, "per capita" wealth, "real wages per worker" and "real hourly wage rate" trickle-down's acolytes mislead by use of aggregates.

Obamacare—based on a conservative idea—has not cost the economy jobs.

The housing bubble that led to the financial crisis was not due to the Community Reinvestment Act and irresponsible borrowing by minorities but, rather, by irresponsible actions of the financial community.

Housing prices over the past two years nationwide have outpaced wage growth by a 13:1 ratio and have outpaced wage growth in 76 percent of US housing markets.

If trickle-down economics were right, you would have a raise by now.

And, of course, if trickle-down economics were right, inequality would not have grown like it has over the past three and a half decades.

Ignoring the Facts, the Republican Party Continues to be Driven by Faith in Trickle-Down

Regardless of all the above, the Republican Party will continue to push for privatization of Social Security, conversion of Medicare to a voucher program, conversion of Medicaid to a block grant program to be implemented individually by each state, abolition of Obamacare and opposition to implementation of a single-payer system in its place, and ever-greater restrictions on unemployment compensation, disability benefits, support to offset higher education costs, and support for public institutions generally, driven by its trickle-down delusion based in faith that what's good for the rich is good for all, and the corollary that that the market is always better than government.

Trickle-down has spread like a cancer through government and the social sciences, moving from economics to political thought. There it misrepresented classical liberalism as simply standing for the principle of "freedom." It ignored that the application of such a simplistic notion concentrates ever-greater power in those atop society. Thereby it distorted classical liberalism into a philosophy defending privilege and power and allied with conservatism (the Right); the exact opposite of its historical role in fact of promoter of downwardly diffused economic and political power and defender of the less powerful, as represented by modern liberalism (the Left).

Trickle-down has also infected sociology, undermining the public—government—institutions upon which the poor and middle class rely. Trickle-down indirectly undermines these institutions by demanding we ignore the obvious effect on culture and behavior wrought by economic circumstances, even when the evidence of such effect is plainly presented by the facts as revealed by research. The effect of this imposed willful ignorance is to leave us wondering why the poor and middle class are abandoning the very institutions such as marriage and religion civil society provides them for support—when the obvious answer is the debilitating effect that declining economic circumstances have on self-esteem, leading those who have suffered from declining economic circumstances to withdraw from society. Simultaneously, trickle-down has directly undermined these government institutions by waging a policy war against them, simultaneously attempting to cut the spending necessary to maintain them and to privatize them.

And, trickle-down has distorted our concept of the rule of law, indirectly undermining our democracy. When the Supreme Court has encountered conflicts between the propertied and privileged versus the less powerful, the Court has used both the Equal Protection Clause and the First Amendment's freedoms as bludgeons on behalf of the propertied and powerful to find on their behalf. Trickle-down has also driven its adherents to directly undermine the rule of law and democracy by gerrymandering and attempting to deny their opponents the right to vote.

And, trickle-down drives its adherents to ignore the overwhelming popular support for higher taxes on the 1%, a higher minimum wage, Obamacare (to either leave it alone or strengthen it), Social Security, Medicare and Medicaid.

If You Want to Restore the American Dream for *All* Americans, You Have to Vote Democrat!

The above rephrasing of the title of this subchapter, words made famous by President Harry Truman, was never more accurate than today. In his famous speech on the steps of the Lincoln Memorial, Dr. Martin Luther King, Jr. famously invoked that dream, as did Barack Obama, in his speech before the 2004 Democratic National Convention. However, as Joseph Stiglitz has observed, we risk making the American Dream a myth.[26] Stiglitz's observation was supported by Elizabeth Warren in her first policy speech since being elevated to Strategic Policy Adviser to the Senate Democratic Policy and Communications Committee, wherein she issued a warning: the game is rigged, making it more difficult for average Americans to achieve the American Dream, but we have the power to change that politically.[27]

The position here, however, is *not* that the American Dream is a myth, or that it is dead. The American Dream—not the dream supported by anecdotes of heroic and gifted individuals who triumphed against the odds but, rather, the American Dream that average people, through perseverance, can achieve a comfortable quality of life for themselves and their families—that dream—is now deemed unachievable by most Americans.[28] Their pessimism seems justified, looking at the statistics: According to an analysis by *USA Today*, in 2014 living the American Dream would cost the average family of four about $130,000 per year—more than all but about one in eight households earned that year according to the Census Bureau.[29]

The Problem Is Inequality. And the Solution Is Government

Americans living in areas hit by natural disasters such as Hurricanes Katrina and Sandy know that, contrary to the quote from President Reagan's Inaugural Address that began the Introduction, sometimes government *is* the solution. Regarding the problem of inequality, caused as it is by government policies that upwardly redistribute economic and political power, undermining our economy, democracy, institutions and health—government *is* the solution. To get the government policies necessary to address this inequality means overcoming the delusion of trickle-down economics—a political ideology that united the Holy Rollers (the fundamental Christians) with the high rollers (the rich)—masquerading as an actual, but utopian, economic ideology, justifiable only by resort to faith and not facts.

The American Dream for the Americans described above—average Americans—is, statistically speaking, slipping away as these Americans see their incomes and wealth shrinking in real terms, *which is why we can't wait to begin to implement government policies to make the American Dream real again for all Americans*. We can't wait because our economy is in a depressionary feedback loop; our democracy is being undermined as millions are withdrawing from participation in the political process, despairing of their voices ever being heard; our institutions are failing because of neglect or outright attack; and the health of millions of our fellow Americans is still declining notwithstanding the bold improvements wrought by the Affordable Care Act. We can't wait because the simplistic call by conservatives and Republicans for "freedom" is not enough—it must be supplemented by the call by liberals and Democrats to apply the truth of connectedness—that we are all keepers of each other. We can't wait—2016 is the year that the effort to confront and defeat trickle-down and replace it with liberal values and liberal policies must commence at a level of intensity commensurate with that of the Civil Rights Movement. This movement, however, will not be a movement for civil rights, or even poor people—it is a movement of the 99%.

As can be seen from the foregoing, we have the power to revive the American Dream for all if we but use it. But for liberals to revive the American Dream we will have to ideologically confront and defeat trickle-down conservatism with a coherent critique and provide a well-articulated, unifying liberal vision to replace it.

In August of 2013, the fiftieth anniversary of the March on Washington for Jobs and Freedom, many Americans reflected upon what "dream deeply rooted in the American Dream" *they* had for America. The dream herein is for Americans to recognize that to defeat the trickle-down delusion and its accompanying depression it is necessary for us to come to our senses and reject trickle-down, and implement in its place the trickle-down depression's liberal cure: the liberal policies that helped create the great American middle class after World War II, based on the liberal vision that if we spread the American Dream to all, we'll all do better because *we'll all* do better.

The liberal understanding of the American Dream is that *ordinary* people are able to achieve a good quality of life if they are willing to work hard. It is these ordinary people we celebrate on Labor Day every year. The Republicans are wrong. They call the rich, many of whom benefit from government aid "job creators;" they call those middle class and poor who benefit from government aid "losers"—but we know that we are, all of us, worthy and entitled to partake in the American Dream. And we know we live in the nation exceptionally blessed and entrusted to carry forward liberalism and the American Dream *for all Americans*—a dream that must be saved from the delusional Republicans who misconstrue and undermine it.

We—you—have a choice. You can choose to be part of the problem, putting the American Dream further out of reach for more and more of your fellow Americans by voting Republican—or, you can be part of the solution and:

> *VOTE DEMOCRAT TO RESTORE THE AMERICAN DREAM FOR ALL AMERICANS!*

NOTES

1. For an especially succinct promotion of this view, see William Galston, "Closing the Productivity and Pay Gap," *The Wall Street Journal*, published February 19, 2014. Galston holds the Ezra K. Zilkha Chair in Governance Studies and is a senior fellow at the Brookings Institution. He was formerly the Saul Stern professor and Dean of the School of Public Policy at the University of Maryland See also Harold Meyerson, "Share the Dividends of Increased Productivity," *The Washington Post*, February 20, 2014.

2. The difficulty of addressing poverty with government benefits in the absence of high wages is addressed in "Taxing Hard-Up Americans at 95%", *The Economist*, September 7, 2013.

3. See Ross Perlin, *Intern Nation: How to Earn Nothing and Learn Little in the New Economy* (2011).

4. For reference, the Economic Policy Institute, in a study of the compensation of the chief executives of the 350 publicly owned US firms with the largest revenues, found that the CEO-to-worker compensation ratio in 2014 was 303-to-1; lower than the peak of 376-to-1 in 2000, but *more than 15 times higher* than the ratio in 1965 of 20-to-1. Lawrence Mishel and Alyssa Davis, "Top CEOs Make 300 Times More Than Typical Workers," EPI Policy Issue Brief #399, June 21, 2015.

5. Tax reform is more broadly addressed by Joseph Stiglitz in his White Paper entitled "Reforming Taxation to Promote Growth and Equity," Roosevelt Institute, May 28, 2014.

6. Milton Friedman, *Capitalism and Freedom* (Chicago: University of Chicago Press; 1962), pp. 191–192. See also Rose and Milton Friedman, *Free to Choose* (Chicago: University of Chicago Press; 1979), pp. 120–123.

7. Noam Scheiber and Dalia Sussman, "Inequality Troubles Americans Across Party Lines, Times/CBS News Poll Finds," *The New York Times*, June 4, 2015.

8. Thomas B. Edsall, "The War on Entitlements," the Opinionator blog, *The New York Times*, March 6, 2013.

9. Thomas B. Edsall, "The War on Entitlements," the Opinionator blog, *The New York Times*, March 6, 2013.

10. *Revenue Procedure 2013–35* Internal Revenue Service. Chye-Ching Huang and Nathaniel Frentz, "Myths and Realities About the Estate Tax," Center for Budget and Policy Priorities, Revised August 29, 2013. See also Dana Milbank, "Republicans Push for a Permanent Aristocracy," *The Washington Post*, April 15, 2015. And, as observed by Paul Krugman, Theodore Roosevelt, appropriately, in his famous New Nationalism speech in 1910, urged inheritance taxes as a curb on large fortunes. Paul Krugman, "America's Taxation Tradition," *The New York Times*, March 28, 2014.

11. Based on 2014 defense expenditures, compiled by the Stockholm International Peace Research Institute, SIPRI Military Expenditure Database, April 2015, from the website of the Peter G. Peterson Foundation.

12. Based on World Health Organization statistics. "Healthcare Spending Around the World, Country by Country," *The Guardian Datablog*, June 30, 2012.

13. The best guide for what is envisioned here is the visionary book by Thomas Farley (former New York City Health Commissioner) and Deborah A. Cohen (senior natural scientist, RAND Corporation), *Prescription for a Healthy Nation: A New Approach to Improving Our Lives by Fixing Our Everyday World* (Boston: Beacon Press; 2005).

14. Annie Lowrey and Robert Pear, "Doctor Shortage Likely to Worsen with Health Law," *The New York Times*, July 28, 2012.

15. See "Nader: Postal Crisis 'Manufactured'," Common Dreams.Org, September 23, 2011, and Ron Nixon, "Trying to Stem Losses, Post Office Seeks to End Saturday Letter Delivery," *The New York Times*, February 7, 2013.

16. Phil Oliff, Vincent Palacios, Ingrid Johnson and Michael Leachman, "Recent Deep State Higher Education Cuts May Harm Students and the Economy for Years to Come," Center on Budget and Policy Priorities," March 19, 2013.

17. Editorial Board, "A Natural Gas Strategy Democrats Should Heed," *The Washington Post*, February 14, 2013. Per EIA for December 2015: Natural gas, 34%; coal, 28%; nuclear, 21%; hydroelectric, 7%; renewables, 9% (including 0.5%, solar); other, 1%.

18. President George H. W. Bush issued Executive OCS Leasing Moratorium of 1990 on sales outside the Central Gulf of Mexico and Western Gulf of Mexico overlapping a pre-existing Congressional Moratorium through 2000. That was extended by President Clinton. President George W. Bush signaled his trepidation over the controversy by issuing a proposal to lift the OCS Leasing Moratorium on areas other than the Central Gulf of Mexico and Western Gulf of Mexico January 16, 2009—so that the document was published in the Wednesday, January 21, 2009 Federal Register—*the day after President Obama's inauguration*. President Obama became the first president since President Reagan to propose a Mid Atlantic Sale, among other Gulf of Mexico Sales, and this proposal was published in the *April 2, 2010* Federal Register—only 18 days before the Deepwater Horizon blowout on BP's Macondo Prospect, resulting in 11 workers killed, 16 others injured and the worst oil spill in US history. The Obama administration imposed a one year leasing moratorium, which it lifted with the Western Gulf of Mexico Sale in late 2011 and the Central Gulf of Mexico Sale in early 2012, and issued a Draft Programmatic Environmental Impact Statement for geological and geophysical exploration on the Atlantic Outer Continental Shelf in June 2012. The administration proposed an Atlantic Sale for 2021, but withdrew it in the face of protest from coastal communities.

19. "The Repurchase Revolution" *The Economist*, September 13, 2014.

20. Nick Hanauer, "Stock Buybacks Are Killing the American Economy," *The Atlantic*, February 2015.

21. Angie Drobnic Holan and Nai Issa, "In Context: Hillary Clinton and Don't Let Anybody Tell You That Corporations Create Jobs," *Politifact.com*, *Tampa Bay Times*, October 30, 2014. Addressed is a speech Hillary Clinton delivered on behalf of Massachusetts gubernatorial candidate Martha Coakley at a rally for her in Boston, October 24, 2014.

22. Ryan Grim, "Elizabeth Warren Simplifies Thomas Piketty: 'Trickle-Down Doesn't Work. Never Did,'" *Huffington Post*, April 25, 2014.

23. Hillary Rodham Clinton, *Living History* (New York: Simon & Schuster; 2003), p. 21.

24. George Packer, *The Unwinding: An Inner History of the New America* (New York: Farrar, Straus, and Giroux; 2013), p. 346.

25. See at Senator Elizabeth Warren's website the text of her speech, titled "Senator Warren's Remarks at AFL-CIO National Summit on Raising Wages," January 7, 2015.

26. See Joseph Stiglitz, in an interview conducted by Alexander Jung and Thomas Schultz, published in "The American Dream Has Become a Myth," *Spiegel Online,* October 2, 2012. See also Joseph E. Stiglitz, "The Myth of America's Golden Age," *Politico Magazine*, July/August 2014.

27. Lucy McCalmont, "Warren: American Dream Is Slipping Away," *Politico*, November 19, 2014. She returned to these themes—see Patrick Caldwell, "Elizabeth Warren Tells Stephen Colbert 'the Game Is Rigged'," *Mother Jones*, September 24, 2015 12:26 PM EDT.

28. The American Dream was deemed unachievable by 59 percent of all Americans surveyed in CNNMoney's American Dream Poll conducted by ORC International May 29 to June 1, 2014; 63 percent of young adults age 18 to 34. Tami Luthby, "The American Dream Is Out of Reach," CNNMoney, June 4, 2014.

29. Howard R. Gold, Special to *USA Today*, July 4, 2014.

Appendix

Table A.1. Selected Years' Deficits/Surpluses as a Percentage of GDP

Presidency	FY	Revenues	Expenditures	Deficit (-)/ Surplus
Reagan	1982	18.6	22.5	-3.9
Reagan	1983	17.0	22.8	-5.9
---	---	---	---	---
Bush I/Clinton	1993	17.0	20.7	-3.8
Clinton	1994	17.5	20.3	-2.8
Clinton	1995	17.8	20.0	-2.2
Clinton	1996	18.2	19.6	-1.3
Clinton	1997	18.6	18.9	-0.3
Clinton	1998	19.2	18.5	0.8
Clinton	1999	19.2	17.9	1.3
Clinton	2000	20.0	17.6	2.3
Clinton/Bush II	2001	18.8	17.6	1.2
Bush II	2002	17.0	18.5	-1.5
Bush II	2003	15.7	19.1	-3.3
Bush II	2004	15.6	19.0	-3.4
Bush II	2005	16.7	19.2	-2.5
Bush II	2006	17.6	19.4	-1.8
Bush II	2007	17.9	19.0	-1.1
Bush II	2008	17.1	20.2	-3.1
Bush II/Obama	2009	14.6	24.4	-9.8
Obama	2010	14.6	23.4	-8.7
Obama	2011	15.0	23.4	-8.5
Obama	2012	15.3	22.1	-6.8
Obama	2013	16.8	20.9	-4.1
Obama	2014	17.6	20.4	-2.8
Obama	2015	18.2	20.7	-2.5

Table A.2. The "Wealth Effect Scissors"

Year	Gross Equity Extraction Rate[a]	NIPA Personal Savings Rate[b]	"Household Responsibility Index"
1991	1.66	7.26	5.60
1992	1.42	7.70	6.28
1993	1.21	5.78	4.57
1994	1.24	4.84	3.60
1995	1.53	4.64	3.11
1996	1.87	4.02	2.15
1997	2.06	3.65	1.59
1998	3.34	4.33	0.99
1999	3.63	2.37	-1.26
2000	3.19	2.34	-0.85
2001	4.24	1.77	-2.47
2002	6.34	2.36	-3.98
2003	6.21	2.14	-4.07
2004	8.69	2.01	-6.68
2005	8.23	-0.39	-8.62

Notes: a. "Gross equity extraction" from existing homes: "the discretionary initiatives of homeowners to convert equity in their homes into cash by borrowing in the residential mortgage market." It is synonymous with "mortgage equity withdrawal," abbreviated "MEW." (Ibid, pp. 1 and 3.) b. The National Income and Product Accounts (NIPA) definition of the personal saving rate portrays personal saving as a percentage of disposable income. (Ibid, p. 10.)

Table A.3. Illegitimacy Rates* and Ratio of Nonwhite to White Illegitimacy Rates

Year	White	Nonwhite	Ratio Nonwhite to White
1963	30.7	235.9	7.68
1962	27.5	229.9	8.36
1961	25.3	223.4	8.83
1960	22.9	215.8	9.42
1959	22.1	218.0	9.86
1958	20.9	212.3	10.16
1957	19.6	206.7	10.55
1956	19.0	204.0	10.74
1955	18.6	202.4	10.88
1954	18.2	198.5	10.91
1953	16.9	191.1	11.31
1952	16.3	183.4	11.25
1951	16.3	182.8	11.21
1950	17.5	179.6	10.26
1949	17.3	167.5	9.68
1948	17.8	164.7	9.25
1947	18.5	168.0	9.08
1946	21.1	170.1	8.06
1945	23.6	179.3	7.60
1944	20.2	163.4	8.09
1943	16.5	162.8	9.87
1942	16.9	169.2	10.01
1941	19.0	174.5	9.18
1940	19.5	168.3	8.63

Source: "The Negro Family: The Case for National Action," Office of Planning and Research, United States Department of Labor (March 1965). Adapted from Table 3, "Estimated Number of Illegitimate Births and Ratio of Illegitimate Births to All Live Births by Color, 1940-63," p. 59.

Table A.4. Labor Force Participation Rates (Percent)

	1954	1964	1974	1981
White Males				
16-17	47.1	43.5	53.3	53.6
18-19	70.4	66.6	73.6	74.1
20-24	86.4	85.7	86.5	87.1
White Females				
16-17	29.3	28.5	43.3	46.1
18-19	52.1	49.6	60.4	64.2
20-24	44.4	48.8	63.8	71.5
Black Males				
16-17	46.7	37.3	34.6	31.9
18-19	78.4	67.2	62.4	56.3
20-24	91.1	89.4	82.1	78.9
Black Females				
16-17	24.5	19.5	24.2	24.7
18-19	37.7	46.5	44.6	44.1
20-24	49.6	53.6	58.2	60.1

Index

www.ingramcontent.com/pod-product-compliance
Ingram Content Group UK Ltd.
Pitfield, Milton Keynes, MK11 3LW, UK
UKHW041143300926
15471UKWH00011B/109

9 780761 866978